"In this seminal work on global Christianity, Graham Joseph Hill weaves together essential elements for understanding God's missional movement in our day. A book of this breadth and depth will serve Christians in the West as well as Majority World Christians for ages to come. The paradigm shifts offered in world Christianity make this a must-read for the whole church as we learn to be the whole body of Christ in this global and hyper-local world."

—Lisa Rodriguez-Watson
National director, Missio Alliance

"In a breathtaking tour de force of scholarship, Graham Joseph Hill offers in his book a panoramic view of the major paradigm shifts in the study of contemporary Christianity as a world religion. I strongly recommend this volume for undergraduate and graduate courses on missiology and ecclesiology and for general readers who want to understand what is happening to Christianity today."

—Peter C. Phan
Chair of Catholic social thought, Georgetown University

"It is long past time those of us from the West learned how to learn from our global colleagues. Graham Joseph Hill leads us across a large and varied terrain of glocalized Christian holistic reflection and action, helping us see not simply how to listen but to learn and grow from the insights, actions, and priorities of the Majority World church. Western Christians absolutely need this book."

—Scott Moreau
Professor emeritus of intercultural studies, Wheaton College

"Graham Joseph Hill went to and from the ends of the earth—crossing theological traditions, cultures, and even oceans and continents—to bear witness to the gospel through the many perspectives of world Christianity at the beginning of the twenty-first century. *World Christianity* unfolds the many tribes, languages, peoples, and nations that anticipate the coming reign of God, while providing a theoretical and methodological frame for comprehension and analysis."

—Amos Yong
Professor of theology and mission, Fuller Seminary

"How can we become more global without losing our connection to the local? How can we become more global by learning a narrative that embraces our local story into the global church's story? I recommend heartily the new book by Graham Joseph Hill called *World Christianity: An Introduction*. This truly is an important book, and its impact will take years to absorb—generations. Absorbing it, however, can be revolutionary as it draws us into a worldwide movement of God."

—Scot McKnight
Professor of New Testament and award-winning author

"Global theologian Graham Joseph Hill has made listening to Majority World Christians a cornerstone of his life, work, scholarship, and ministry. *World Christianity: An Introduction* presents an invaluable picture of the myriad expressions of world Christianity that are still dominated by Western voices. Hill helps inaugurate a new chapter in our global understanding that describes a diverse but united faith for all peoples with humility, diversity, and equity as essential features of an international community."

—Todd M. Johnson
Distinguished professor of mission and global Christianity,
Gordon-Conwell Theological Seminary

"*World Christianity* is a splendid introduction to the newly expanding and changing contours of Christian faith. Despite the often-coercive effects of Western colonial mission, Christianity has been practiced around the world in a myriad of ways that are now emerging with unprecedented energy. Graham Joseph Hill manifests an important tilt: turning away from gazing solely upon the traditional Western navel of theology and turning toward the creative faith of Christians scattered across the globe."

—Peter Walker
Principal, United Theological College

"This book is an exercise of a white male theologian in trying to make sense of 'world Christianity': Thought-provoking, challenging, and urging for more theological conversations in worldwide relationality and for a more conscious theological praxis. The book compels theological educators to dwell on questions such as: What does it mean to learn together? It is an invitation to head towards writing a textbook in *World Christianity* with colleagues from East and West and North and South."

—Dorottya Nagy
Professor of theology and migration, Protestantse Theologische Universiteit

World Christianity

World Christianity

An Introduction

GRAHAM JOSEPH HILL

Foreword by Scot McKnight

CASCADE *Books* • Eugene, Oregon

WORLD CHRSITIANITY
An Introduction

Copyright © 2024 Graham Joseph Hill. All rights reserved. Except for brief quotations in critical publications or reviews, no part of this book may be reproduced in any manner without prior written permission from the publisher. Write: Permissions, Wipf and Stock Publishers, 199 W. 8th Ave., Suite 3, Eugene, OR 97401.

Cascade Books
An Imprint of Wipf and Stock Publishers
199 W. 8th Ave., Suite 3
Eugene, OR 97401

www.wipfandstock.com

PAPERBACK ISBN: 979-8-3852-0130-3
HARDCOVER ISBN: 979-8-3852-0131-0
EBOOK ISBN: 979-8-3852-0132-7

Cataloguing-in-Publication data:

Names: Hill, Graham Joseph, author.
Title: World Christianity : an introduction / Graham Joseph Hill.
Description: Eugene, OR: Cascade Books, 2024. | Includes bibliographical references.
Identifiers: ISBN 979-8-3852-0130-3 (print). | ISBN 979-8-3852-0131-0 (print). | ISBN 979-8-3852-0132-7 (epub).
Subjects: LSCH: Christianity. | Church history. | Globalization—Religious aspects—Christianity.
Classification: BV600.3 H541 2024 (print). | BV600.3 (epub).

VERSION NUMBER 100324

Unless otherwise noted, Scripture quotations taken from The Holy Bible, New International Version® NIV® copyright © 1973, 1978, 1984, 2011 by Biblica, Inc. Used with permission. All rights reserved worldwide.

For my wife, Shyn

Contents

List of Tables | ix
Foreword by Scot McKnight | xi

1. Introduction: The Vitality of World Christianity | 1

SEVEN PARADIGM SHIFTS SHAPING WORLD CHRISTIANITY
Part 1: *Paradigm Shifts in World Christianity* | *17*
  2. World Christianity Methodology | 19
  3. Polycentricity | 39
  4. Polyvocality | 58
  5. Interculturality | 74
  6. Integrality | 111
  7. Pentecostality | 131
  8. Glocality | 142

THIRTEEN EXPRESSIONS OF THOSE PARADIGM SHIFTS
Part 2: *Renewing Our Mission* | *165*
  9. Contextualizing Mission | 167
  10. Liberating People | 187
  11. Showing Hospitality | 209
  12. Embracing the Spirit | 227
  13. Caring for Creation | 256
  14. Living Ethically | 278
  15. Transforming Neighborhoods | 306

Part 3: *Revitalizing Our Churches* | *319*
  16. Inculturating Faith | 321
  17. Devouring Scripture | 354

CONTENTS

18. Renewing Education | 377
19. Practicing Servantship | 413
20. Recovering Community | 435
21. Developing Spirituality and Discipleship | 453
22. Conclusion: World Christianity: A Cause for Renewal, Celebration, and Joy | 481
23. A Closing Prayer | 489

APPENDIX 1
Who Are These Majority World and Indigenous Theologians and Practitioners? | 491

Appendix 2
World Christianity Links at GrahamJosephHill.com | 492

Appendix 3
The Global Church Project Video Series | 494

Appendix 4
Other Books and Resources by Graham Joseph Hill | 496

Bibliography | 499

List of Tables

TABLE 1.1. Changing distribution of Christian believers: 1900 to 2050 (number of Christians in millions) | 3

TABLE 1.2. Percentage of the world's Christian in each continent: 1900 to 2100 (rough percentages) | 3

TABLE 1.3. *Holisticostal* Theology, Church, and Mission: Seven Paradigm Shifts and Thirteen Expressions | 9

TABLE 2.1. Eighteen Qualities and Features of World Christianity Methodology | 28

TABLE 2.2. Methodological Hallmarks of a Theology of World Christianity | 36

TABLE 3.1. Fifteen Qualities of Polycentricity | 55

TABLE 4.1. Fifteen Qualities of Polyvocality | 71

TABLE 5.1. Ten Features and Themes of Intercultural Theology | 105

TABLE 5.2. Fifteen Qualities of Interculturality | 107

TABLE 6.1. Fifteen Qualities of Integrality | 128

TABLE 7.1. Fifteen Qualities of Pentecostality | 136

TABLE 8.1. Fifteen Qualities of Glocality | 154

TABLE 22.1. Western-centric Worldview Versus a Holisticostal Worldview | 483

Foreword

Scot McKnight

When you and I think of the "face" of the church today, who do we see? Who do we think God sees? Besides the obvious—God sees each of us (that's nice, and that's right, and now let's move on to the answer to the question)—I'd like to suggest that God sees the face of the church from a global perspective. This means the church's face is morphing from a European-North American face to an African-Latin American-Asian one. God sees the church for what it is, while we see the church through our own lens.

For those who are willingly shifting to a more global perspective on the church, there is also a change in what mission means. No one is more alert to the global and theological shape of missions today than Graham Joseph Hill, an Australian theologian who made his mark with an informed and distinguished book called *Salt, Light, and a City: Introducing Missional Ecclesiology*.

Strikingly, the first-century church—by divine design—was not locked into a culture the way we can be today. The apostle Paul's vision, which he called at times the "mystery," was to expand God's old people, Israel, not by abandoning Israel or by imposing on Israel but by *adding to Israel God's new people who were gentiles*. The apostle Paul's heartbeat was a missiology of new creation in which Paul would have to learn to express the gospel in new contexts, see what God created in new contexts, and keep *all these people in one fellowship*. His vision, if you know anything about the Roman Empire, was breathtakingly radical and seen as foolhardy by more than one people group, including the apostle Paul's fellow citizens.

Graham Joseph Hill, if I may put my way of framing this book, asks us to return to the New Testament era so we can learn how to be the church of divine intent. He wants to change our conversations from monolithic and monocultural to multicultural exchanges. Gone will be the paternalism of previous generations, and a whole new conversation will arise where the "Majority World" churches will contribute to the Euro-shaped cultures. We are only salty and full of light when we let Paul's "mystery" of including gentiles and Jews at the one table become the fertile ground in which we plant the gospel and learn from one another.

What Graham Joseph Hill has done, however, is offered a challenge, not least in taking what has become a famous line about American elitism from the days of our founding fathers—a "city set on a hill"—and turning it into a multicultural, global ecclesiology and mission: the city set on a hill, he proposes, is the global church in its mission.

How can this happen? In typical missiology, missions, and missional classes, we ask one another to read and discuss the standard Eurocentric theologians of brilliance—but Graham Joseph Hill discusses in this book theologians many of us never assign or even read. We enter Paul's "mystery" when we become a fellowship of "differents" by listening to our brothers and sisters in their lived theology worldwide. Before you turn the page to begin this remarkable book, skip to appendix 1 and tally up the percentage of these global theologians you recognize and read. My guess is that you will, like me, be embarrassed enough to start reading this book seriously—in a listening mode.

Rev. Canon Dr. Scot McKnight
Professor of New Testament and award-winning author

1.

Introduction
The Vitality of World Christianity

THIS BOOK PROVIDES AN accessible introduction to the discipline, methodology, and field of world Christianity. I aim to introduce you to the *seven paradigm shifts* in world Christianity and their *thirteen expressions*: renewing our mission and revitalizing our churches.

Picture a mighty river. It was once thought to flow mainly through the lands of the Western world, nourishing the civilizations that claimed heritage to Jerusalem, Athens, and Rome. But, the riverbanks have burst. The waters have found new courses, surging with life-giving force through the continents of Africa, Asia, and Latin America. The currents of Christianity are re-charting their path, and this book serves as both a cartography and a guide for the conscientious traveler seeking to understand these transformative waters.

What you have before you is not merely an introduction but an invitation—no, a clarion call—to awaken to the dawn of a new epoch in global Christianity. We will examine paradigmatic shifts, each like a tributary contributing to reshaping our understanding of the faith. As we explore, key questions will serve as our compass.

- How is Christianity's center of gravity moving from Western countries to the Majority World?
- What are the core practices and methodologies of world Christianity as a discipline?
- What significant paradigm shifts are reshaping world Christianity?

- How are these paradigm shifts manifesting in Majority World ecclesiology and missiology?
- What do Majority World, Indigenous, and First Nations Christians teach Western Christians about worship, fellowship, discipleship, ministry, mission, and theology, and how to practice the Great Commandment (Matt 22:37–40) and the Great Commission (Matt 28:19–20)?
- How can Christianity reject Western-centric, colonial, monolithic, paternalistic, and monocultural perspectives and instead pursue humble, mutual, global-local, and intercultural exchanges?

Majority World and Indigenous churches are redefining twenty-first-century Christianity. Western churches must decide how they'll respond. Stephen Bevans puts it well:

> We are now living in a "world church" where most Christians are [from the Majority World]. David Barrett's statistical studies have basically confirmed this shift, and Philip Jenkins has predicted that by 2025 fully two-thirds of Christians will live in Africa, Latin America, and Asia . . . Scholars are fairly unanimous in acknowledging the accuracy of the facts. The "average Christian" today is female, black, and lives in a Brazilian *favela* or an African village.[1]

Some statistics illustrate this shift in twenty-first-century global Christianity. The Pew Research Center's report *Global Christianity* analyzes the size and distribution of the world's Christian population. The report maps the changes over the last century (1910 to 2010). It concludes: "A century ago, the Global North (commonly defined as North America, Europe, Australia, Japan, and New Zealand) contained more than four times as many Christians as the Global South (the rest of the world). Today, the Pew Forum study finds, more than 1.3 billion Christians live in the Global South [61% of all Christians live in Asia, Africa, and Latin America], compared with about 860 million in the Global North (39%)."[2] The Center for the Study of Global Christianity says, "By 2050 we anticipate that 77 percent of all Christians will live in the Global South."[3] That is an astounding shift in only one hundred years.[4]

---

1. Bevans et al., "Missiology after Bosch," 69.
2. Pew, *Global Christianity*.
3. Zurlo et al., "World Christianity and Mission 2020."
4. See Barrett et al., *World Christian Encyclopedia*, 12–15.

INTRODUCTION

Using the World Christian Database, Philip Jenkins offers Table 1.1, "Changing distribution of Christian believers."

Table 1.1. Changing distribution of Christian believers: 1900 to 2050 (number of Christians in millions)

	1900	1970	2010	2050
Africa	10	143	493	1,031
Asia	22	96	352	601
North America	79	211	286	333
Latin America	62	270	544	655
Europe	381	492	588	530
Oceania	5	18	28	38
Total	558	1,230	2,291	3,188

Source: Jenkins, *Next Christendom*, 3.

Christianity in North America, Europe, and Oceania grew from 465 million in 1900 to 902 million in 2010.[5] This number is likely to *shrink* to 901 million by 2050. Christianity in Africa, Asia, and Latin America grew from 94 million in 1900 to 1.389 billion in 2010. This number is likely to *grow* to 2.287 billion by 2050. The Center for the Study of Global Christianity at Gordon Conwell Seminary puts the changes this way:

Table 1.2. Percentage of the world's Christian in each continent: 1900 to 2100 (rough percentages)

	1900	1950	2000	2050	2100
Africa	2%	5%	18%	36%	50%
Asia	4%	5%	13%	18%	18%
North America	14%	18%	12%	9%	8%
Latin America	11%	18%	25%	20%	14%
Europe	67%	52%	30%	15%	8%
Oceania	2%	2%	2%	2%	2%

Source: Zurlo, "Who Owns Global Christianity."

Let's take China, for example. Professor Fenggang Yang of Purdue University makes a meaningful prediction. If current growth rates continue, China will have more Christians within one generation than any other nation. In 1949, Protestant churches in China had one million members. In 2010, that number was 58 million (compared with 40 million in Brazil and 36 million in South Africa). By 2025, there are likely to be 160 million Christians in China. By 2030, it will likely be 247 million (outnumbering

---

5. Oceania includes Australia, Micronesian, Melanesian, and Polynesian countries.

Christians in Mexico, Brazil, and the United States). In an interview with *The Telegraph*, Fenggang Yang says, "Mao thought he could eliminate religion. He thought he had accomplished this. It's ironic—they didn't. They failed completely."[6]

Philip Jenkins concludes:

> We are currently living through one of the transforming moments in the history of religion worldwide. Over the last five centuries, the story of Christianity has been inextricably bound up with that of Europe and European-derived civilizations overseas, above all in North America. Until recently, most Christians have lived in white nations . . . Over the last century, however, the center of gravity in the Christian world has shifted inexorably away from Europe, southward, to Africa and Latin America, and eastward, toward Asia. Today, the largest Christian communities on the planet are to be found in those regions.[7]

What does all this mean for the mission, theology, worship, and church communities worldwide? What does it mean particularly for the Western church? In the fifth chapter of Matthew's Gospel, in verses thirteen to sixteen, Jesus deploys images of ineffable beauty and striking profundity, likening his church to salt, light, and a city on a hill. In a world often marred by decay, darkness, and isolation, Jesus envisages his followers as preservative agents, illuminators of truth, and a communal nexus of vibrant life. "Let your light shine before people," he declares, "that they may see your good deeds and praise your Father in heaven." The church's missional thrust, at its very core, gravitates towards a purpose grander than itself: the worship and glorification of the Triune God.[8]

What a vision of the church—this "other city"—constructed not from bricks and mortar but from the living stones of every tribe, tongue, and nation.[9] Indeed, God's dream for God's ecclesia is that it should sculpt its social realities and raison d'être around the interplay of diversity and unity, plurality and oneness. Within this polyphonic harmony, Western voices find their place alongside those of Indigenous wisdom and Majority World vibrancy to form a "city on a hill," a celestial Jerusalem on earthly pilgrimage.

---

6. Phillips, "China on Course to Become 'World's Most Christian Nation' Within 15 Years." See: Yang and Tamney, *Confucianism and Spiritual Traditions in Modern China and Beyond*; Yang and Lang, *Social Scientific Studies of Religion in China*; Yang, *Religion in China*.

7. Jenkins, *Next Christendom*, 1.

8. Driver, *Images of the Church in Mission*, 170–81; Hill, *Salt, Light, and a City*, xiii.

9. Harvey, *Another City*, 23–25.

INTRODUCTION

Those of us who are dwellers in Western lands must wake from the slumber of our Eurocentric and Americentric illusions. A new narrative, global and missional, beckons to us from the wise communities of the Majority World and the Indigenous cultures, who might teach us the vital essence of being what one might call a 'holisticostal' community. These communities—often born in the crucible of persecution, alienation, and marginalization—have not merely survived but flourished. They've burgeoned in numbers and depth, embodying the Pauline mystery of strength in weakness.

When I speak of Majority World Christians, I am summoning into your mind those communities stretching across Africa, Asia, the Caribbean, Eastern Europe, Latin America, the Middle East, and Oceania.[10] Why do I choose the term "Majority World"? Because it reflects the demographic reality: these lands are where the majority of the world's populace resides and where the majority of Christ's body is manifest. I avoid terms like "Non-Western" or "Third World" for they are laden with the undertones of Western-centricity, of an implicit hierarchy. At the Lausanne Forum for World Evangelization, convened in Pattaya, Thailand, in 2004, this term was universally adopted, a choice lauded by scholars like Timothy C. Tennent for its precision and equity.[11]

Indigenous and First Nations peoples are "those ethnic groups that were Indigenous to a territory before being incorporated into a national state, and who are politically and culturally separate from the majority ethnic identity of the state that they are a part of."[12] Think of the Indigenous Australians, the Native Americans, and myriad other communities. They stand as witnesses to the ancient rhythms of land and life, echoing in their lived experiences the narrative of God's particular care for the marginalized and dispossessed.

So, as we step forward into the daunting but exhilarating terrain of global Christianity, may we do so with humility and fervor, ever mindful that we are, each of us, but single notes in the grand symphony of God's redemptive plan. This symphony finds its most sublime expression when all its diverse notes resound in harmonious praise to the Father, the Son, and the Holy Spirit.

This book has two aims. The first aim is to introduce readers to personalities, themes, and methodologies in world Christianity. The second aim is to

---

10. I don't deal with diasporas in this book mainly because there are so many worthy contributors in that group, and I don't have the space to treat them well.

11. Tennent, *Theology in the Context of World Christianity*, xx.

12. Sanders, "Indigenous Peoples: Issues of Definition," 4.

help Christians understand and respond to seven paradigm shifts revolutionizing world Christianity and its theologies and practices, especially in church and mission (missiology and ecclesiology).

To achieve these aims, Western Christians must converse with Majority World, diaspora, and Indigenous Christians, and Christians from all over the globe must listen and learn from each other. Listening to others helps us grow in our understanding and practice of mission, church, and theology. We've marginalized or ignored Majority World, diaspora, and Indigenous voices for far too long. We must truly become a humble, attentive, worldwide church. This book's aim shapes its structure, as summarized below.

The structure of this book is simple. Part one presents a methodology for studying world Christianity and examines *seven paradigm shifts* shaping world Christianity. Parts two and three outline the *thirteen missiological and ecclesiology expressions* of those paradigm shifts. Part two considers what Majority World Christianity teaches us about renewing our missions and engagement with the world. Part three contemplates what Majority World Christianity teaches us about Christian community, discipleship, and church revitalization.

Part 1. Paradigm Shifts in World Christianity

Seven integrated paradigm shifts are revolutionizing world Christianity, including theologies and practices of church and mission—world Christianity methodologies, polycentricity, polyvocality, interculturality, integrality, pentecostality, and glocality. These seven approaches are combined and interdependent. As a shorthand, I call this *holisticostal*. Holisticostal missions and movements are reshaping the church and the world.

In part one, I show that holisticostal mission, theology, and ministry is an approach that integrates the empowering and diversifying work of the Holy Spirit, holistic transformation, intercultural engagement, and the inclusion of diverse voices and centers of authority.

Part one presents a methodology for the discipline of world Christianity and proposes that seven paradigm shifts are transforming world Christianity and its theologies and practices. Part one shows how Western conversations are impoverished and insufficient when isolated from Indigenous and Majority World Christians. We need local-global exchanges that reshape our conversations (glocalization).

INTRODUCTION

Why "Holisticostal"?

I've recently developed a word designed to capture the complex, multi-layered nature of mission, theology, and ministry in our time. That word is *holisticostal*, a neologism cradled within which lie the facets of world Christianity methodologies, polycentricity, polyvocality, interculturality, integrality, pentecostality, and glocality—each a gem in its own right, yet astonishingly radiant when brought together in unity and diversity. This isn't a mere academic artifact; it's a living, breathing vision of what the church can be when the winds of the Spirit blow freely through its corridors.

Let's begin with *world Christianity methodology*. The emergence of a methodology and discipline of "world Christianity" is timely and vitally significant in our increasingly interconnected global context. As global issues intensify—including migration and diaspora, the refugee crisis, the rise of global megacities, and climate change—they bring diverse communities into closer contact and underscore the need for a shared, global perspective on Christianity. World Christianity, as a field and methodology, acknowledges and embraces the global diversity and interconnectedness of Christian faith and practice, promoting a richer and more comprehensive understanding of Christianity in its many cultural contexts worldwide. It moves beyond a Western-centric view of Christianity to explore how people worldwide understand and practice their faith, highlighting the local particularities and global connections that define Christianity today. This global perspective is essential for addressing contemporary challenges, promoting intercultural dialogue, and fostering a more inclusive and equitable global Christian community.

Now let's turn to *polycentricity* and *polyvocality*. Picture a council of prophets, each speaking from distinct points on a compass, yet all tuned to the voice of the one true God. Here, the idea is simple yet profound: multiple centers of authority and a choir of voices—diverse yet harmonious—guide the church's mission and ministry. It rejects the monolithic in favor of a spiritual ecosystem rich in texture and tone.

Interculturality is the next chapter in this unfolding story. Visualize a grand feast to which all nations and tribes are invited. The beauty here is not mere tolerance but a jubilant celebration of each other's uniqueness. An intercultural missional mindset bridges canyons of misunderstanding, forging unity from the raw materials of diversity. The apostle Paul, himself a cosmopolitan Jew, would likely have found this resonant with his expansive vision.

Integrality brings us into the sacramental realm, where matter and spirit, body and soul, are reconciled. This is an echo of Jesus's ministry, touching lepers even as he touched hearts, feeding bodies and souls. The integral approach resists the temptation to spiritual escapism and instead embraces the call to earthly service, realizing that the kingdom of God has come near.

The *pentecostal* element—let's call it *pentecostality*—is a crown jewel. Recall the rush of a mighty wind, the tongues of fire, and the cacophony of languages on that ancient Pentecost. The Spirit's arrival was an event and an inauguration—a setting forth of the church's ongoing nature as a body bursting with dynamic diversity. The Spirit animates the church not as a monolithic institution but as a complex, vivid network of gifts, vocations, and cultures.

Finally, we turn to *glocality*. Glocalization holds paramount significance in reshaping global Christianity, promoting a faith expression that is both universally resonant and locally relevant. As global Christianity intersects with myriad cultures and contexts, glocalization enables the faith to be authentically expressed in diverse local cultures while maintaining its global essence. This balance fosters a more inclusive, contextual, and empathetic Christian community worldwide, nurturing unity while honoring diversity. The emphasis on local contexts and global connections, inherent in glocalization, encourages mutual learning, respect, and collaboration among Christians worldwide, contributing to the growth, resilience, and vibrancy of global Christianity.

So, what is *holisticostal*? It's a theological concept that displays new patterns of interconnectedness, each one revealing the radiant beauty of God's intentions for his people. It is the call to mission infused by the Spirit, centered in Christ, grounded in the Scriptures, and embracing the polyphony of global voices in a dynamic conversation.

Jesus said, "You are the salt of the earth." Salt is holisticostal—it preserves, flavors, enriches, and purifies. Salt loses its essence if it becomes insular if it disconnects from the wider world for which it was intended. The moment we yield to a monochromatic vision of the church—Eurocentric, Americentric, or otherwise—we risk losing our "saltiness," the essence of our call and vocation.

Thus, we arrive at a crucial juncture. Our world is yearning for a church that is both global and local, rooted yet diverse, complex but unified. It longs for exchanges characterized by mutuality, respect, partnership, and symbiosis. Such an exchange keeps the church "salty," keeps it vital. In this, we find not merely a strategy but a deep resonance with the core of the gospel message.

So, let us step boldly into this holisticostal vision, bearing in mind that we might embody this calling by grace, through faith, and in the power of

INTRODUCTION

the Spirit. Only then can we truly be, both globally and locally, the salt of the earth—rich in flavor, varied in form, yet unified in purpose.

Table 1.3. *Holisticostal* Theology, Church, and Mission:
Seven Paradigm Shifts and Thirteen Expressions

Seven Holisticostal Paradigm Shifts
1. World Christianity Methodology
2. Polycentricity
3. Polyvocality
4. Interculturality
5. Integrality
6. Pentecostality
7. Glocality
Thirteen Expressions of these Shifts
1. Contextualizing Mission
2. Liberating People
3. Showing Hospitality
4. Embracing the Spirit
5. Caring for Creation
6. Living Ethically
7. Transforming Neighborhoods
8. Inculturating Faith
9. Devouring Scripture
10. Renewing Education
11. Practicing Servantship
12. Recovering Community
13. Developing Spirituality and Discipleship

Part 2. Renewing Our Mission

"You are the light of the world. A city on a hill cannot be hidden. Neither do people light a lamp and put it under a bowl. Instead, they put it on its stand, giving everyone in the house light. In the same way, let your light shine before others, that they may see your good deeds and glorify your Father in heaven." Globally and locally, you are the light of the world. Be light.

Light illuminates, reveals, and dispels darkness. The church is light when doing good deeds—healing, liberating, and redemptive. It's light when its being, faith, and deeds glorify the Father. The church is light when it participates in God's redemptive mission in the world as a holisticostal community.

To do this, we must renew our mission. Having outlined the seven paradigm shifts in world Christianity, *part two explores their seven expressions in areas relating to Christian mission (missiology).* Part two explores how Indigenous and Majority World Christians teach us to renew our mission. We renew our mission through contextualization, liberation, hospitality, Spirit-empowerment, creation-care, ethics, and the transformation of neighborhoods. Our mission is transformed by world Christianity methodology, polycentricity, polyvocality, interculturality, integrality, pentecostality, and glocality advances.

Part 3. Revitalizing Our Churches

"You are a city set on a hill. A city on a hill cannot be hidden." Globally and locally, you are a city set on a hill. Be a city set on a hill.

This means that we are an alternative and counter-cultural movement. We have a distinct culture, politics, and social existence. We are a people gathered from every tribe, language, people, and nation. We are *in* the world but not *of* the world. We are *in* the world but *distinct from* the world. We are *within* the world and *for the sake of* the world.

To be this alternative city or culture, we must renew our mission, community, ethics, and worship. We need to pursue the *revitalization of our churches* so that they *are* distinct. By distinct, I mean an alternative city (*altera civitas*).

We are a "city on a hill" that witnesses Jesus Christ and his eternal kingdom while we are a holisticostal church. Having outlined the seven tectonic shifts in world Christianity, *part three explores their six expressions in areas relating to Christian community (ecclesiology).* In part three, I demonstrate how Indigenous and Majority World Christians teach us to revitalize churches. We revitalize churches by inculturating faith, devouring Scripture, renewing education, practicing *servantship* (servant leadership), recovering the community, and developing spirituality and discipleship. Practical theology is revolutionized by world Christianity methodology, polycentricity, polyvocality, interculturality, integrality, pentecostality, and glocality innovations. In the final chapter, I challenge the reader to adopt a world Christianity narrative shaped around holisticostal commitments.

INTRODUCTION

Embracing the Holisticostal Vitality of World Christianity and God's Kingdom

There's an ever-widening conversation about God's mission and the church's participation therein. These are matters too grand to be confined to one or two cultural perspectives, too complex to be elucidated merely by the voices that have, historically, been the loudest. The kingdom of God is polyphonic, a celestial symphony of diverse instruments and harmonies. In the tension of this cosmic music, I have previously offered my contributions, dialoguing with eminent theologians from European and American traditions in two extensive volumes: *Salt, Light, and a City*.

Yet, I have come to see, more starkly than ever, that the conversation has far too long been dominated by a narrow chorus—predominantly white, predominantly male, predominantly Western. Of course, this is not a new observation, but its urgency cannot be overstated. Though I fit within this demographic profile, I recognize that this melodious chorus is inadequate to convey the full scale and grandeur of God's intentions for the world. The kingdom's composition needs other notes, timbres, and melodies; this current work seeks to usher them in.

We are responsible for listening intently to the Majority World, Indigenous voices, and the underrepresented but rich perspectives from Africa, Asia, Latin America, the Caribbean, and beyond. The theological acumen and missional vitality emanating from these corners of God's vineyard are not merely enriching but fundamentally necessary for a full-bodied understanding of ecclesiology and mission. To do otherwise—to persist in the lopsidedness of the current Western-dominated discourse—is to risk a sort of theological malnourishment. The church in the West must realize it can be both teacher and student, speaking but listening, lest it find itself in the ironic position of being a herald that has lost its ability to hear.

Why, you might ask, is this shift urgent? It is nothing short of fidelity to the Spirit, who, like a divine conductor, is bringing voices from the margins to the center stage. A Spirit-led mission, a Spirit-breathed theology, must inevitably reflect the 'holisticostal'—a term I have coined in this book—the vitality of a world Christianity methodology, polycentricity, polyvocality, interculturality, integrality, pentecostality, and glocality kingdom of God. We would do well to listen, for these voices are not asking for permission to join the conversation; they are already profoundly engrossed in their own dialogues, pulsating with a missional verve that many Western congregations yearn for.

So, come then, take this sojourn with me. You will encounter in these pages a spectrum of voices that challenge, provoke, and inspire. They will dare us to reimagine church and mission in ways that reflect the kingdom's full, magnificent diversity. They will prod us into forms of worship and community life deeply rooted in the global reality of God's redemptive work. They will help us understand afresh what it means to be 'salt, light, and a city' in a world yearning for the taste, sight, and structure of God's reign.

Through it all, the Spirit beckons us toward a richer, more complex understanding of God's kingdom and the church's role in it—an understanding as holisticostal as the kingdom itself. What lies ahead is an invitation not just to learn but to be transformed, to become the sort of church that genuinely mirrors the multifaceted magnificence of God's ongoing mission. So let us venture forth, listening and learning, as we seek to be ever more faithfully the community of salt, light, and a city that God has called us to be.

An Invitation

In my musings as a theologian, I am ever-aware of the glasses through which I view the world—that of a white male, shaped and molded by a very particular cultural, linguistic, and theological milieu. This understanding profoundly humbles me. The sprawling panorama of world Christianity cannot be fully encompassed by any singular vantage point, mine especially. As such, I extend a heartfelt invitation to my colleagues and fellow scholars from the Majority World, Indigenous communities, and First Nations peoples to critically engage with the contents of this book. I hope that through dialogue, critique, and contribution, the pages of this text become a springboard toward a richer and more diverse exploration of our faith. The global Christian community contains innumerable expressions, each unique and essential. It is a longing of my heart to see theologians and practitioners from the myriad cultures, continents, and traditions of our world come forward, hand in hand, to craft a holistic and inclusive textbook on world Christianity. The book you hold is but a stepping stone—a nascent attempt to encapsulate the vastness of our shared faith. Let it also be an invitation, beckoning a forthcoming era where a symphony of voices from every corner of our globe collaboratively pens a more comprehensive and intercultural narrative of world Christianity.

INTRODUCTION

Study Questions

1. What does the growth of the Majority World churches mean for the mission and theology and worship and communities of the church worldwide?
2. What does this shift in world Christianity mean for Western churches and theology?
3. Why do we assimilate a Eurocentric and Americentric view of the world? How do we change this?
4. How would you define polycentric mission?
5. "New voices are rising. These include women, minorities, the poor, Indigenous groups, and Majority World leaders." What's one practical way you can listen and learn from these voices?
6. Who is an Indigenous or First Nations theologian from your country that you could learn from and which of their books will you purchase and study?

SEVEN PARADIGM SHIFTS
SHAPING WORLD CHRISTIANITY

PART 1

Paradigm Shifts in World Christianity

Over recent decades, world Christianity has undergone profound transformations, prompting theologians and religious practitioners to rethink intercultural and practical theology. Seven notable paradigm shifts stand at the forefront of these changes, offering new perspectives and guiding the global Christian community toward a more inclusive, dynamic, and holistic understanding of faith.

In the tidal waves of change washing over global Christianity, we are witnessing a tectonic shift, indeed, seven shifts realigning the very topography of faith. These seven paradigm shifts are beckoning signposts to an expansive theological exploration and ecclesial practice backdrop. They are markers on the kingdom road map, guiding us towards a more nuanced, integrated, and radically incarnational faith.

Firstly, we discover *world Christianity methodology*, which transforms Christian theology and practice. Secondly, we find *polycentricity*, a concept that disrupts our conventional Eurocentric or Western-centric understandings, instead drawing us to acknowledge the pulsating vitality of Christian expressions in Africa, Asia, and Latin America. These aren't mere satellites of Western Christianity but robust centers reshaping the very conversation of global discipleship. Then there's *polyvocality*, a paradigm that invites a choral richness, enjoining us to hear the symphony of faith articulations from varied traditions and contexts without letting one voice drown out the rest.

Interculturality, the fourth shift, is an antidote to the parochialisms and ethnocentrisms that have often marred the church's witness. It's not merely about "tolerating" diversity but celebrating and learning from the plethora of cultural articulations of the gospel. The fourth paradigm, *integrality*, summons us to a holistic vision of the gospel that refuses to truncate human existence into "spiritual" and "secular" compartments. It views the mission of God as interwoven with social justice, ecological stewardship, and economic righteousness.

Fifthly, we arrive at *pentecostality*. Here, the Holy Spirit emerges not as a footnote but as the dynamic center, empowering the church to live into its polycentric, polyvocal, intercultural, and integral calling. This Spirit broods over the chaos of our fragmented narratives and brings forth a new creation, community, and way of being "church." Finally, *glocality* puts the local and global into a dynamic, transformative conversation.

Together, these shifts are redefining the contours of world Christianity and revolutionizing how theologians and practitioners approach church and mission (ecclesiology and missiology). My term for these seven integrated shifts is *holisticostal* mission, ministry, and theology.

I've coined a term for these seven paradigm shifts, which don't operate in isolation but converge in a dynamic interplay: *holisticostal*. It is a mission, a ministry, and a theology that arises from the crucible where these seven elements meld, reshaping not merely categories but our understanding of what it means to follow Jesus in a complex and pluralistic world.

In part one, I outline world Christianity as a discipline and methodology and consider the seven holisticostal shifts. I examine glocalization, which challenges us to see "the local in the global and the global in the local"—the local and global are integrated and interdependent.

In this opening section, I aim to sketch the academic and ecclesial frameworks that can sustain a meaningful dialogue about these seven holisticostal paradigms. This involves delving into what I would call a "glocalized" theology—seeing "the local in the global and the global in the local." Far from being mutually exclusive, these spheres are deeply entangled, each serving as a lens through which to understand the other better and together providing a more complex, colorful, and ultimately more faithful picture of the expansive project we call world Christianity.

2.

World Christianity Methodology

The First Paradigm Shift

As we commence this expedition through the grand narrative of global Christianity, we must pause and consider the cartography of scholarly terrain. The disciplines of practical theology, intercultural theology, and world Christianity are not isolated islands in an academic archipelago but interlocking landforms in a rich and complex continent. Viewing them as wholly independent would be as misleading as reductionist.

Let me be clear: while there exists a certain distinctiveness within each of these disciplines and methodologies—each with its contours, its particular landmarks—it is precisely in their overlap, their rich interplay, that some of the most profound insights are to be found. In this volume, I respectfully salute this triad of interwoven disciplines as I map out the methodological course for our journey through world Christianity.

So, there will be instances in these pages where you will find me laboring in the vineyards of practical theology, meandering through the rich fields of intercultural theology, or setting sail on the expansive waters of world Christianity. Often, you will find me engaging in a harmonious blend of all three. These are not rivalrous undertakings. Far from it, they are harmonious endeavors, each enriching and informing the other in a divine choreography of interdisciplinarity.

It is true, perhaps much to the academic purist's discomfort, that the terms "intercultural theology" and "world Christianity" sometimes find themselves used in a manner that suggests interchangeability. While subtleties may be lost in this linguistic flexibility, my abiding allegiance is to the methodologies and radiant vistas of world Christianity. This discipline not only stands with its unique bearing but also graciously borrows from the other two, enriching itself while preserving its unique timbre and methods.

Thus, as we examine this elaborate maze, I invite you to keep your eyes open to the interlocking disciplines that inform our quest. The richness of our journey depends not on a simplistic division of these disciplines but on a deep appreciation for how they mutually illuminate and invigorate one another.

Practical or Applied Theology

To adequately consider practical theology, one must first come to terms with its multifaceted identity, a project undertaken with vigor by scholars in the field. Helen Cameron et al. provide one such vista: "Practical theology is a discipline committed to making whole and dynamic the truthfulness of Christian thought and action, through the bringing together aspects of faith which, in truth, can never be separated from one another. Practical theology seeks explicit and varied ways to enable the Christian practitioner to articulate faith—to speak of God, in practice."[1] John Swinton and Harriet Mowatt also weigh in, writing, "Practical Theology is critical, theological reflection on the practices of the Church as they interact with the practices of the world, to ensure and enable faithful participation in God's redemptive practices in, to and for the world."[2]

As we might expect in such a rich field of inquiry, various seminal figures have provided contours and landmarks. Thinkers like Dale Andrews, Don Browning, Elaine Graham, Thomas Groome, Gerben Heitink, and Richard Osmer have contributed significantly, among many others, and the choir of their voices echoes in academic halls and parish pews alike.[3]

Practical theology finds itself wonderfully and challengingly poised at the crossroads of grand theological ideas and the gritty particularities of lived faith. It aims to be neither a remote ivory tower nor a retreat into the comfort of unexamined devotion. In this energetic tension, practical

---

1. Cameron et al., *Talking about God in Practice*, 20–21.

2. Swinton and Mowatt, *Practical Theology and Qualitative Research*, 6.

3. Andrews, *Practical Theology for Black Churches*; Browning, *Fundamental Practical Theology*; Browning, *Practical Theology*; Browning et al., *Education of the Practical Theologian*; Graham, *Transforming Practice*; Groome, *Sharing Faith*; Heitink, *Practical Theology*; Osmer, *Practical Theology*.

theology claims its unique character, tirelessly working to make sense of faith within the labyrinth of human existence.

At the epicenter of this quest lies the notion of reflective practice. Far from standing on the sidelines as a detached observer, practical theology plunges into the depths of real-world religious phenomena. It holds the actions and beliefs of faith communities up to the light, scrutinizing and refining them in an ongoing cycle of theological examination.

The versatility of practical theology is evident in its willingness to seek wisdom from neighboring disciplines like sociology, psychology, and education, among others. This isn't an eclectic shopping spree but a deeply considered methodological choice. It acknowledges that understanding religious practices and beliefs necessitates a comprehensive grasp of the human condition in various dimensions.

When you get to the crux of the matter, the term "praxis" seems to distill the essence of practical theology. It denotes a concern for marrying theory with practice, aiming to understand religious actions and enrich their meaning and effectiveness.

Perhaps Richard Osmer's articulation of the "four tasks" best captures the discipline's methodological sophistication. There's an initial mapping of the terrain by describing a religious practice or situation, then an interpretative phase that considers its significance in wider historical and cultural contexts. This groundwork is followed by forming a normative response, often rooted in classical theological traditions. The whole endeavor then culminates in constructing actionable strategies in sync with theological and practical wisdom.

Following in the footsteps of scholars like Don S. Browning, the discipline works to yoke theological concepts to the lived experiences of individuals and communities. It seeks not only to hover above the sphere of human experience with high-flown theological ideas but to incarnate these ideas in the daily challenges and opportunities of human living.

The pastoral heartbeat of practical theology is palpable. Informed by its insights, pastors and counselors approach their tasks with a new depth, and its influence can be felt in the methodologies of ministries spanning a wide array of community and individual concerns.

True to its nature, practical theology employs empirical methods to provide solid ground for its reflections. It does not shy away from the rigor of interviews, surveys, and direct observations, ensuring that its assessments are not castles in the sky but are deeply rooted in the lived experiences of communities of faith.

Yet, practical theology is not satisfied with being a mere chronicler. It picks up the lens of critique, evaluating practices against established theological norms, hoping to generate richer, more robust, and theologically congruent ways of practicing faith.

The discipline, acutely aware of its social and cultural milieu, gives due weight to contextual factors. Recognizing that faith is practiced in particular spaces shaped by history, culture, and a host of other influences, it pays close attention to these shaping forces as it conducts its theological analysis.

Lastly, practical theology is, at its core, a conversation—a multi-voiced dialogue within religious traditions, between theological experts and ordinary believers, and even between faith communities and the wider societies in which they exist. These dialogues bring new perspectives into view, enriching the discipline and allowing for constructive growth and understanding.

Practical theology emerges as a lively nexus of thought and action, dynamically engaged with the Word and the world. Its incorporation of real-world phenomena, interdisciplinary wisdom, and commitment to the transformative power of reflective religious practice make it a vital, pulsating part of the theological constellation today.

Intercultural Theology

The rich nature of human experience calls for a theological imagination capable of grasping its complexity. Here enters intercultural theology, to which Henning Wrogemann offers a precise introduction: "From a cultural-semiotic perspective, [intercultural hermeneutics] is the attempt to decode other, foreign cultures using the medium of their conceptions and terminology, i.e., to identify that meaning, those referential connections, and that relevance that things have for people from the culture in question."[4]

The guild of scholars who map this complex field is noteworthy and varied, featuring names like Walter Hollenweger, Maria Pilar Aquini, and Maria Jose Rosado-Nunes.[5] Each adds unique contours to a sprawling theological scene that increasingly demands attention in our globalized, multicultural epoch.

Intercultural theology, as a discipline, positions itself as a theological cartographer of the crossroads where cultures and religious traditions meet,

---

4. Wrogemann, *Intercultural Theology*, 1:154–55.

5. Hollenweger, "Intercultural Theology"; Hollenweger and Jongeneel, *Pentecost, Mission, and Ecumenism*; Aquini and Rosado-Nunes, *Feminist Intercultural Theology*; Bernhardt, "Interkulturelle Theologie"; Cartledge and Cheetham, *Intercultural Theology*; Flett, "Method in Mission Studies"; Gruber, *Intercultural Theology*; Küster, "Intercultural Theology is a Must"; Schreiter, "Changing Contexts of Intercultural Theology"; Wrogemann, *Intercultural Theology* (three volumes).

converse and even clash. In a world swept up in the tides of globalization, the discipline offers a lighthouse illuminating the multifaceted interactions that characterize contemporary spiritual and secular cultures and interactions.

At its core, intercultural theology thrives on dialogue. This is not a sign of indecisiveness but an acknowledgment that no single religious or cultural narrative can claim to possess the complete lexicon in which the Divine has chosen to speak. Through the mutuality of discourse, the lexicons of diverse traditions can enrich, clarify, and deepen our collective understanding of divine mysteries.

The dialogical principle, however, is anchored in the recognition that theology is always conducted within particular frameworks—each constituted by specific socio-cultural and historical realities. Therefore, the vocation of intercultural theology lies in its acute sensitivity to context. It seeks to interpret the gospel's eternal melodies in ever-changing cultural keys.

The discipline is not merely content with a seat at the table. It challenges the architectural designs of the table itself, particularly when these have been drafted according to Western blueprints. It carries the democratic impulse into the theological sphere, diversifying the voices that shape our conceptions of the Divine and thereby widening the spectrum of theological discourse.

For intercultural theology, the "faith once delivered to the saints" is lived out in the myriad marketplaces, temples, and homes that dot the global context. By attentively listening to the daily rhythms of faith as they resound in diverse cultural auditoriums, the discipline gains valuable insights into the multitude of ways spirituality is conceived and practiced.

Justice, that great biblical theme, pulsates at the heart of intercultural theology. In kinship with other contextual theologies like feminist and liberation theology, it engages in a vigorous critique of entrenched power dynamics and systemic injustices, seeking to articulate a spiritually enriching and socially transformative faith.

Today's world is not a monolith but a mosaic—elaborate patterns of cultural overlap and intermixture shape each piece. Intercultural theology celebrates this hybridity, even as it engages in postcolonial self-examination, interrogating the imperial shadows that still haunt theological and missiological conversations.

The discipline employs a kaleidoscopic lens, synthesizing insights from academic theology, practical theology, and religious studies. This multifaceted perspective enriches its analytical depth and counters the reductive tendencies that often beset theological endeavors.

Intercultural theology brings the "other" from the margin to the center, offering a platform for voices often relegated to the periphery. It aspires to enlarge our theological canvases by incorporating the hues and textures from genuinely engaging those outside our immediate cultural or religious circles. It invites us to transcend parochialism, broadening our theological imagination's horizons.

Henning Wrogemann's definition of intercultural hermeneutics, placed at the outset, serves as a thematic overture, encapsulating the grand symphony of intercultural theology. It calls us to the noble task of decoding our global neighbors' spiritual and cultural lexicons, not as an academic exercise but as a pathway to mutual enrichment and understanding.

So, intercultural theology stands as a sentinel at the frontiers of religious thought, inviting us toward a future marked by deeper dialogue, greater inclusivity, and a richer, more harmonious melody of global faith expression.

World Christianity

Peter Phan says *world Christianity* studies "the historical, sociological, cultural and theological *diversity* and *multiplicity* of Christianity."[6] In my conversation with Lamin Sanneh at Yale University on April 20, 2015, he made the following insightful observation: "We in the West are a confident and articulate people, and theology has served us well as a vehicle of our aspirations, desires, and goals. There is no shortage of theological books on all sorts of imaginable subjects, with how-to-do manuals instructing us about effective ministry, how to fix our emotions, how to affirm our individual identity and promote our choices and preferences, how to change society through political action, how to raise funds and build bigger churches, about investing in strategic coalitions, etc. All this language leaves us little time or space to listen to God with the chance that God may have something, and even something else, to say to us, especially if that something else challenges what we want to hear. Regarding the cultural captivity of the gospel in the West, the renewal of world Christianity may have lessons to teach us all."[7]

Some influential scholars in the discipline of world Christianity include Andrew Walls, Dorottya Nagy, Lamin Sanneh, Martha Frederiks, Klaus Koschorke, Brian Stanley, and Peter C. Phan.[8] There are, of course, many others.

---

6. Phan, "World Christianity," 175 (emphasis in original).

7. Hill and Sanneh, "Conversation With Lamin Sanneh."

8. Walls, *Missionary Movement in Christian History*; Walls, *Cross-Cultural Process in Christian History*; Sanneh, *Whose Religion is Christianity?* Sanneh, *Translating the Message*; Sanneh, *Disciples of All Nations*; Koschorke, *History of Christianity in Asia*,

In his article "Method in Mission Studies: Comparing World Christianity and Intercultural Theology," John G. Flett argues that the two approaches to mission studies, world Christianity and intercultural theology, are complementary rather than contradictory.[9] Flett says that world Christianity outlines the worldwide spread and development of Christianity, including related historical and sociological factors. He then proposes that intercultural theology examines how Christian faith and culture engage.

Flett then argues that world Christianity is primarily concerned with mission's historical and sociological dimensions. In contrast, intercultural theology primarily concerns mission's theological and missiological dimensions. He argues that world Christianity is more descriptive, while intercultural theology is more normative.

However, Flett argues that these two approaches are not mutually exclusive; they are complementary and enrich our theology and practice of mission. Flett then discusses the implications of his argument for the methodology of mission studies. He argues that mission studies should be descriptive and normative and use world Christianity and intercultural theology. He also argues that mission studies should be contextual, considering the specific needs and contexts of the studied people. Flett's article provides a helpful overview of the two approaches to mission studies and their implications for methodology. His argument that the two approaches are complementary rather than contradictory is valuable to mission studies.

For Flett, world Christianity and intercultural theology are both necessary for a comprehensive understanding of mission. World Christianity is primarily concerned with mission's historical and sociological dimensions, while intercultural theology is primarily concerned with mission's theological and missiological dimensions. World Christianity is more descriptive, while intercultural theology is more normative. Mission studies should be descriptive and normative and use both world Christianity and intercultural theology. Mission studies should be contextual, considering the people's specific needs and contexts. Flett's article is a valuable resource for anyone interested in mission studies. It provides a clear and concise overview of the two main approaches to mission studies and argues persuasively that the two approaches are complementary rather than contradictory.

While I value Flett's scholarship and advocacy for world Christianity, intercultural theology, and mission studies, I bring a different perspective

---

Africa, and Latin America, 1450–1990; Stanley, *Christianity in the Twentieth Century*; Phan, *Christianity with an Asian Face*; Phan, *In Our Own Tongues*; Phan, "Doing Theology in World Christianity"; Fredericks, "World Christianity"; Nagy, "Recalling the Term 'World Christianity.'"

9. Flett, "Method in Mission Studies."

on some similarities and differences between world Christianity and intercultural theology. Flett rightly highlights the historical and sociological emphasis of world Christianity as a discipline. However, in my opinion, he overstates the descriptive nature of world Christianity. It's not the case that intercultural theology is normative and critical while world Christianity is descriptive.

Seeing world Christianity as diverse yet unified by Christ presents a vision that challenges our existing paradigms and invites us to venture into uncharted territories of theological exploration. This discourse is not simply about categorizing diverse expressions of the Christian faith globally. Instead, it offers a critical framework for understanding Christianity as a dynamic and complex reality situated within a matrix of power relations, cultural interactions, and historical influences.

To this end, scholars of world Christianity examine topics of considerable import, such as the multifaceted nature of religious dialogue—encompassing not merely interfaith but also intercultural, ecumenical, and socio-political conversations. With an analytical finesse, they dissect the contextual elements that shape Christian expressions, scrutinize the colonial shadows cast upon the faith, and offer a more nuanced understanding of the power dynamics at play.

Not to be lumped together simplistically with intercultural theology, world Christianity sets its gaze on a broader horizon. It focuses on themes like power dynamics, colonization, diversity, marginalization, and shared humanity. It is not merely descriptive but analytical and critical, challenging the hegemony of dominant cultures and elevating the voices of those often relegated to the periphery.

If one might venture to encapsulate the essence of world Christianity, it would be that of a critical, analytical, and theologically informed discipline. This lens can sharpen our understanding of the faith's multifaceted expressions, enabling us to avoid cultural imperialism and champion a pluralistic ethos in our ecclesial practices. It serves as a cartography of global Christian experiences that enriches our faith and deepens our grasp of mission, worship, and theology. While it remains an emerging field, the potential for transformational insights cannot be underestimated.

It would be remiss not to acknowledge world Christianity's paradigm-shifting impact. No longer confined to a Eurocentric or Western-centric vantage point, it affirms the global nature of Christian faith, especially acknowledging the growing Christian presence outside the West.

What we have here is not a fleeting flirtation with diverse Christian expressions but a profound archaeological project. It unearths the rich Christian traditions of Africa, Asia, Latin America, the Middle East, the

Caribbean, Oceania, and Indigenous cultures, underscoring their historical rootedness.

Similarly, contextual theologies find their home within this discipline. Theological articulation, it contends, is always entwined with cultural, social, and historical contexts. In this crucible of diversity, open dialogue flourishes—dialogue that celebrates the polycentric and decentralized nature of theological authority and acknowledges that wisdom can emanate from any corner of the global Christian community.

Methodologically, world Christianity adopts an interdisciplinary stance. It draws from history, anthropology, cultural studies, and sociology to offer a kaleidoscopic view of Christianity's global incarnations. It also engages in postcolonial critique, taking stock of the complex legacies of Christian missions and colonialism.

This academic endeavor also highlights the ecumenical milieu, examining the confluence of multiple ecclesial expressions and denominations. It explores the complicated relationships between Christianity and other religious traditions, acknowledging the realities of religious pluralism.

Rather than an undue preoccupation with formal doctrines, world Christianity orients itself towards the quotidian experiences of ordinary believers, existing within a myriad of sociopolitical realities. It critically examines how Christianity has operated both as an instrument of empire and a voice of resistance, thereby illuminating the complexity of its historical and contemporary manifestations.

In its majestic scope, world Christianity extols the virtues of diversity within unity, challenging us to rethink our inherited norms and doctrines, particularly those tinged with colonial hues. At its core, it aspires to a vision of shared humanity, celebrating each culture's unique contributions to the Christian story while affirming our shared human journey.

Finally, we see a set of holisticostal commitments in world Christianity that bring together the world Christianity methodology, polycentricity, polyvocality, interculturality, integrality, pentecostality, and glocality dimensions of the faith. These nuances, dear reader, are worth further exploration in subsequent discourses. For now, let us be content to stand on the shores of this vast intellectual ocean, contemplating the immeasurable depths that await our discovery.

PART 1: PARADIGM SHIFTS IN WORLD CHRISTIANITY

Table 2.1. Eighteen Qualities and Features of World Christianity Methodology

1. Global Perspective: Prioritizes a sweeping understanding that captures the diverse expressions and cultures of Christianity worldwide.
2. Historical Depth: Dives deep into history to contextualize the emergence and evolution of global Christian movements and traditions.
3. Contextual Theologies: Recognizes theologies arise out of specific cultural, historical, and regional experiences.
4. Intercultural Dialogue: Champions dialogues that bridge cultural gaps, encouraging shared understandings and learnings.
5. Interdisciplinary Approaches: Draws from various academic disciplines to comprehensively understand global Christianity.
6. Collaborative Learnings and Partnerships: Emphasizes learning and growing in collaboration with varied Christian traditions and communities.
7. Attention to Migration and Diaspora: Directs attention to the significant influence of migration patterns on society and Christian expressions and beliefs.
8. Postcolonial Critique: Takes an evaluative approach to understanding and critiquing remnants of colonialism in Christian narratives.
9. Ecumenical Sensitivity: Holds an unwavering appreciation for Christ's diverse but united body, promoting unity amid diversity (and diversity amid unity).
10. Inculturated Leadership: Recognizes and uplifts leadership that emerges directly from grassroots Christian communities.
11. Religious and Secular Pluralism: Engages with the myriad of religious and secular beliefs that coexist with Christianity on the local and global stage.
12. Lived religion: Honors the everyday lived experiences and expressions of faith by Christians locally and globally.
13. Examining Power Dynamics and Hierarchies: Takes a discerning look at power structures, promoting a more egalitarian understanding of Christian theology and institutions.
14. Diversity and Multiplicity: Revels in the diversity of traditions, practices, and beliefs within world Christianity.
15. Critical Consciousness: Promotes a conscious engagement that is introspective and responsive to global Christian dynamics.
16. Shared Humanity: Holds dearly the commonalities that unite humanity, emphasizing shared experiences and values.
17. Flexibility and Adaptability: Highlights the need for adaptability in methodologies, understanding that contexts and realities are ever-changing.
18. Comprehensive Commitments: Embraces a "holisticostal" approach, incorporating elements like world Christianity methodologies, polycentricity, polyvocality, interculturality, integrality, pentecostality, and glocality, to get a fuller picture of the global Christian panorama.

Methodological Hallmarks of a Theology of World Christianity

This book on world Christianity fits into my broader theological project and method. I call this theological enterprise *Methodological Hallmarks of a Theology of World Christianity*.[10]

Now, to explain this theological method and why I call it *Methodological Hallmarks of a Theology of World Christianity*. This is an applied and intercultural theology. Its purpose is to serve, equip, enrich, and reflect the worldwide Body of Christ and enhance theology, *communio*, and mission. It is constructed through a *glocal*, attentive conversation, which honors the voices and contributions of all cultures, but especially those that have been silenced, ignored, and marginalized. This theology prioritizes intercultural, glocal, missiological, and applied theological themes.

Below are the ten *Methodological Hallmarks of a Theology of World Christianity*. These ten methodological hallmarks shape my theological enterprise and everything I do in this book.

Here, I describe these ten methodological hallmarks in shorthand. They are a work in progress. I will explain them in more detail in a future work.

1. *Communio* is the essential and unifying theological motif.

The center of this theological vision and method is the eternal community of the triune God and the community he constitutes. This is not some abstract notion of community. This is not a "communiology," it is a theology.

Communio is the foundation, means, and telos of creation. The triune God exists in eternal *communio* and invites his church into that love. *Communio* is essential to our individual and corporate being, purpose, and future. The triune God calls us into communion with the divine nature, his future glory, fellow Christians, the gospel, and his sufferings, consolations, and hope. We share this vital fellowship with the Trinity and God's people. A common possession unites Christians. This possession is the divine life and grace offered us in the life, death, resurrection, and hope of Jesus Christ.

Communio ensures that this is a trinitarian theological vision and method. *Communio* tells us that the triune God is the essence, source, aim,

---

10. I've given these methodological hallmarks a different name in my series *Salt, Light, and a City*, but "Methodological Hallmarks of a Theology of World Christianity" is my preferred title.

and direction of human desire and life. We desire union with God and with others.

The church is a trinitarian, global-local, missional, diverse, transformed, sanctified, and historical-eschatological community. The triune God calls it into *communio* with Godself and each other, shaping us into the new humanity in Jesus Christ. This communion makes us attentive to and passionate about world Christianity methodology, polycentricity, polyvocality, interculturality, integrality, pentecostality, and glocality.

So, *communio* is the essential and unifying motif in *Methodological Hallmarks of a Theology of World Christianity*. This theological imagination is shaped for and by the new humanity in Jesus Christ. This community comes from every nation, culture, ethnic group, and language.

2. The gospel is the climax of the defining narrative.

A narrative defines my theological method. This is the triune God's story, especially the story of Jesus Christ. The gospel is the climax of this defining narrative.

First Corinthians 15:3–4 tells us that the gospel is "of first importance." What is the gospel? "Christ died for our sins in accordance with the Scriptures, he was buried, and he was raised on the third day in accordance with the Scriptures." How does this gospel shape our lives, communities, and theology? "For Christ's love compels us because we are convinced that one died for all, and therefore all died. He died for all, that those who live should no longer live for themselves but for him who died for them and was raised again" (2 Cor 5:14–15).

Methodological Hallmarks of a Theology of World Christianity attends to the entire, defining biblical narrative (creation to eschaton). In one sense, this whole narrative is the story of Jesus and the gospel. But, in another sense, the gospel is the climax of that story, as revealed in the person and work of Jesus Christ.

The entire defining biblical story describes our being. It frames our identity. It determines our purpose. It gives us our mission. It reveals our hope. This story shapes my theology's vision—a vision of God (the *visio Dei*). This biblical narrative must frame, infuse, and shape all theology. This includes our Christology, pneumatology, eco-theology, missiology, ecclesiology, soteriology, and eschatology.

The gospel story extends from creation to the end of history and the consummation of God's kingdom. *Methodological Hallmarks of a Theology of World Christianity* acknowledges the centrality of biblical witness and narrative. At the same time, it honors the climax of that story, in the person and work of Jesus Christ. So, the gospel calls us to attend to personal salvation and the restoration of all things in Christ. The gospel is an invitation to join the story of the triune God, of biblical Israel, of the Jewish Jesus, and of God's reign. A narrative defines *Methodological Hallmarks of a Theology of World Christianity*, and the gospel is the climax of that story.

3. Mission is the "mother," wellspring, and driving force.

Mission is the impetus, power, energy, motivation, fountain, and "mother" of my theological method. As Martin Kähler says, "Mission is the mother of theology."[11] For the early church, theology grew out of mission, and mission was enriched by theology. David Bosch says the church theologized out of (and as a result of) its missionary encounter with the world. So, we must theologize in mission. We need a missional theology and a theological mission.

Communio leads to the mission of God, the gospel story, and us joining in that mission and story. The missional God (*missio Dei*) has a missional church. The church does not have its own mission. God has a mission, and the church joins that mission.

Since *communio* includes restoring all things in fellowship with the triune God, our mission must be integral and holistic. We join the messianic mission of the Son, in the power of the Spirit, to the glory of the Father. Such an integral mission dismantles all polarities and oppositional binaries. We tear down false divides, such as evangelism–justice, sacred–secular, proclamation–action, practical–theological, Word–Spirit, and more. *Communio* leads to an integral mission incorporating proclamation, justice, healing, creation care, politics, signs and wonders, reconciliation, and human flourishing.

Methodological Hallmarks of a Theology of World Christianity privileges and accentuates mission. Missional theology permeates, penetrates, and shapes *Methodological Hallmarks of a Theology of World Christianity*.

4. Transformation and renewal are the goals.

The church needs transformed and renewed theology, practices, and spirituality. Transformation and renewal are the goals of *Methodological Hallmarks of a Theology of World Christianity*. So, my theology seeks orthodoxy

---

11. Bosch, *Transforming Mission*, 15–16.

(renewed beliefs), orthopraxis (transformed practices), and orthokardia (renovated hearts). All three need to be dynamic, transforming, life-giving, and integrated. All three are about personal and corporate transformation.

Methodological Hallmarks of a Theology of World Christianity refuses imposed and abstract beliefs. It rejects practices that are pragmatic and culturally reduced. It denies spiritualities that are consumeristic and gnostic. Instead, it integrates orthodoxy, orthopraxis, and orthokardia in multiple ways and at many levels. This requires us to shatter false polarities and divisions, seeking integration. If transformation and renewal are the goals, theology must take on specific features for the discipline and methodology of world Christianity. It must strive to be integrated, integral, holistic, interdependent, missional, disciplined, renovating, revitalizing, prayerful, desirous, loving, gracious, hope-filled, and communal.

5. Attentiveness is the principle mode through which theology is constructed.

Theology is continually unfolding in response to the ongoing revelation of divine truth. God continues to reveal himself and his ways to us by many means, persons, cultures, and traditions. (I am not discounting the unique place of Scripture in this revelation). So, theology is *in via*, *en route*, partial, unfolding, and "on the road."

Methodological Hallmarks of a Theology of World Christianity is a work of discernment and the Spirit. It involves hermeneutical awareness and cultural intelligence. It requires attentiveness to the interpretations, lives, cultures, traditions, and views of others. It is about discerning God's divine presence in community and conversation. It comprises prayer, contemplation, study, embodiment, and more.

Methodological Hallmarks of a Theology of World Christianity demands attentiveness to (and conversations with) the church and world. We listen to what God is saying through his church by listening to traditions, interpretations, cultures, ecumenical dialogue, World Christianity, global and local theologies, and "the least of these." We notice what God says by listening to philosophy, science, religions, cultures, worldviews, and more. God is not in all these things at all times. But he is often trying to speak to us in those places. Attentiveness is the principle mode through which we construct theology. Hence, my passion for building theology in conversation with Euro-American, Majority World, Indigenous, First Nations, and diaspora voices.

6. The church is the primary social location.

God calls his church to be a distinct people with a distinct ethic, a distinct story, a distinct peace, a distinct community, a distinct diversity, and a distinct witness. The church is a distinct gathered and sent people. *Methodological Hallmarks of a Theology of World Christianity* sees the church as the primary social location for theology. We theologize as we gather. We theologize as we disperse (in schools, institutions, workplaces, families, and more). We theologize as we join God in his mission in the world.

The *ekklesia* is a gathered and dispersed embodiment of social, missional, and kingdom ethics. We construct theology as a distinct and alternative *polis*. We need academic theology done in institutions. However, the church is the primary social location of *Methodological Hallmarks of a Theology of World Christianity*.

Today, more than ever, we need ecclesial theology. This involves training pastor-theologians, but it is much more than that. We need whole faith communities doing theology together for the good of the church, its *communio*, its theology, and its mission. Ecclesial theology forms as the church gathers and disperses. Ecclesial theology is formed, embodied, and written in the church's service. We must train, support, and release the whole believing community to do ecclesial theology together. Ecclesial theology is undertaken and embodied for fellowship, maturity, discipleship, ministry, witness, ethics, and mission. The church is the primary social location for theology—especially the local church.

7. Culture is the conversation partner.[12]

Culture is theology's counterpoint, mirror, conversation partner, protagonist, foil, enricher, and more. *Methodological Hallmarks of a Theology of World Christianity* is socially and culturally engaged and located. But it is not socially and culturally reduced.[13] *Methodological Hallmarks of a Theology of World Christianity* explores where society, culture, and theology have enriched, shaped, and shackled each other. Sometimes, all these things happen at once. This theology dialogues with a wide range of disciplines. This is a two-way conversation. These disciplines include ethics, politics, philosophy, cultural studies, sociology, social theories, postcolonialism, gender and racial studies, cultural intelligence, aesthetics, creative arts, ecology, health,

---

12. Here I mirror some of Sarah Coakley's language but provide my own emphases. Coakley, *God, Sexuality, and the Self*, 88–92.

13. See point 5 of Coakley's théologie totale. Coakley, *Sexuality, and the Self*, 90.

education, business and leadership studies, history, and more. This theology is interdisciplinary.

8. Eschatology is the orientation.

Christianity is an eschatological faith—it is a religion of hope. *Methodological Hallmarks of a Theology of World Christianity* is eschatologically oriented. It is captivated by a vision of the rule and reign and kingdom and hope of God. This vision frames all our present efforts and theologizing.

The church is a prophetic voice and a sign of hope. God compels the church to work toward the final reconciliation and restoration of all things. The eschatological kingdom shapes our theology, social ethics, mission, community, reconciliation, and justice. It forms our desire for the new humanity in Christ and our efforts toward peace and reconciliation. We need to root our theology in practices of compassion, forgiveness, grace, and love as a response to eschatological hope.[14] We need to relinquish self-centeredness and champion generosity, compassion, and forgiveness. We do this to show the inaugurated, but not yet consummated, kingdom of God.

The kingdom and reign of God is not the church. But, the kingdom is not entirely distinct from the church. The kingdom needs a church, and the church needs the kingdom. The church is part of God's kingdom and essential to God's kingdom, but not the total of it. The kingdom is present wherever God rules. God rules in the church, the lives of individuals, nations, and cultures, and wherever God's word takes root and grows. It is a now-but-not-yet kingdom to use the terms of an *inaugurated eschatology*.

Hans Küng calls the church *the eschatological community of salvation*. The eschatological life, message, death, resurrection, and reign of Jesus Christ ushered in the kingdom.[15] As *the eschatological community of salvation*, the church is *an anticipatory sign* of God's final and already present reign. God's eschatological reign shapes all dimensions of the church's nature, structures, and mission. This, of course, includes its theology. As a servant of God and his eschatological reign, the church directs its whole being toward the kingdom and messianic mission of Jesus Christ.[16] Eschatology orients *Methodological Hallmarks of a Theology of World Christianity*. It mediates faith and helps integrate our thoughts, hopes, compassion, justice, prophetic voices, reconciliation, peace, creation care, and so on.

---

14. Volf, "Against a Pretentious Church," 284.
15. Küng, *Church*, 81.
16. Küng, *Church*, 96–103.

9. Scripture is the "norming norm."

As Stanley Grenz and John Franke say, Scripture is theology's "norming norm."[17] It plumbs, measures, illuminates, adjudicates, enlivens, inspires, norms, and more. The Scriptures are the authoritative word of God, inspired by the Holy Spirit. They have absolute and final authority in all aspects of corporate and individual faith, ethics, conduct, witness, and theology.

Methodological Hallmarks of a Theology of World Christianity embraces biblical authority and does not shy away from it. As I say elsewhere in this book, I'm struck by a trend as I serve among churches in Australia, North America, Europe, and the United Kingdom. Western Christians seem to have a declining passion for memorizing, contemplating, interpreting, and applying Scripture. I find this deeply concerning. When I serve in Asia, Africa, and Latin America, I see the opposite. People are passionate about Scripture. They devour, honor, and memorize it. They interpret it contextually while maintaining a conservative bias. They apply it creatively and bravely. This is instructive for those of us in the West. We need a revival in our enthusiasm for Scripture. This is not so that we "fall in love" with Scripture. Instead, we devour Scripture to know, adore, follow, and magnify our Lord Jesus Christ.

We need to combine faith in God, confidence in Scripture, and contextual forms of interpretation. *Methodological Hallmarks of a Theology of World Christianity* makes some assertions about Scripture. I unpack these in more detail in the chapter of *GlobalChurch* I just mentioned. The Bible must be devoured to know, love, serve, and glorify Christ. Scripture must be interpreted glocally (globally and locally). The Bible is to be believed and obeyed and identified with and applied. (Here, I tend toward critical realism.) Scripture needs to be contextualized. It can be interpreted by ordinary believers in communities. It confronts and transforms cultures, principalities, and powers. The oppressed, marginalized, weak, and despised understand the Bible. It is critical in pluralist settings. Scripture must be interpreted in communities. It needs to be read and applied with spiritual expectation. The Bible is a theological text and must be read and interpreted theologically. The Christian Scriptures are Christianity's and theology's "norming norm."

---

17. Grenz and Franke, *Beyond Foundationalism*, 57.

10. Love is the integrative power.

God is love. But love is rarely at the center of theology. *Methodological Hallmarks of a Theology of World Christianity* acknowledges that love is the integrative power that unites faith, hope, community, mission, and all the rest. Humans desire union with God and others—a loving, intimate, transforming *communio*. The nature of love is most clearly expressed on the Cross of Christ. So, *Methodological Hallmarks of a Theology of World Christianity* is cruciform. Love is the integrative power in discipleship, fellowship, mission, and theology because *communio* is creation's foundation, means, and telos. Love is central to theology because God is love and showed us what love is—Christ died for us.

These are the methodological hallmarks of *Methodological Hallmarks of a Theology of World Christianity*. They are formative for my research and writing on world Christianity, including the book you hold.

Table 2.2. Methodological Hallmarks of a Theology of World Christianity

1. *Communio* is the essential and unifying theological motif.
2. The gospel is the climax of the defining narrative.
3. Mission is the "mother," wellspring, and driving force.
4. Transformation and renewal are the goals.
5. Attentiveness is the principle mode through which theology is constructed.
6. The church is the primary social location.
7. Culture is the conversation partner.
8. Eschatology is the orientation.
9. Scripture is the "norming norm."
10. Love is the integrative power.

World Christianity Methodology: Concluding Reflections

World Christianity emerges not as a mere footnote in the theological narrative but as a radiant, pulsating arena that insists we recalibrate our hermeneutical lenses. In doing so, it challenges us to reconsider not only the spatial geography of our faith but also its temporal horizons, allowing for a kind of historical depth that includes the magnificent traditions of Africa, Asia, and Latin America and well beyond the familiar contours of Western Christendom. Far from being a discipline that accentuates diversity for its own sake, world Christianity demands that we see the Christian story as deeply implicated in the socio-political realities, past and present, of cultures around the globe.

Here's my proposal: "World Christianity as a discipline and methodology seeks to provide a holistic, nuanced, intercultural, polycentric, and globally aware understanding of Christianity." Allow this statement to echo in your ears momentarily, as it encapsulates the ethos that sustains this monumental shift in perspective. In that ethos, one detects an outright rejection of monolithic narratives and a yearning to welcome the complexity of Christian faith as it interweaves through varying cultures and historical epochs.

At the heart of world Christianity lies an interpretive model that is inherently global. The days are long past when Christianity could be regarded as a predominantly Western phenomenon, for the truth is that most Christians today reside outside of the West. This is no minor detail; it forms a foundational pillar upon which the discipline rests, undergirding its commitment to a robust historical narrative that gives voice to traditions often marginalized in other frameworks.

The insistence on contextual theologies is a critical counterpoint to any temptation toward doctrinal or interpretive uniformity. Theology here is not a static entity but a dynamic discourse that emerges from a multiplicity of socio-cultural frameworks. Central to this endeavor is a commitment to "intercultural dialogue," aimed not simply at informational exchange but at fostering a climate of mutual respect and deepened understanding among the global Christian community.

The methodological richness of World Christianity is staggering. Drawing from diverse academic disciplines like anthropology, history, and sociology, it's holistic in its scope and interdisciplinary approach. Such a comprehensive vision allows it to present a more authentic portrayal of Christianity, which places everyday believers from many backgrounds at center stage.

One mustn't overlook the discipline's deliberate engagement with power dynamics, examining the oft-complicated relationship between Christianity and various imperial, colonial, and state entities. Such scrutiny enriches our understanding and gives voice to the marginalized, thereby illuminating otherwise obscured theological insights and perspectives.

World Christianity provides multifaceted insights into Christianity's global mosaic. The discipline doesn't shy away from the complexities introduced by contemporary phenomena like migration and diaspora. It discerns their influential role in shaping the global contours of Christian faith and practice. This is accompanied by a deeply ingrained sense of ecumenical sensitivity and an earnest exploration of religious pluralism, crafted into a narrative that, while cognizant of diversity, underscores our shared human experience.

In the following chapters, I engage in a vivid exploration of how this remarkable field of study is animated by a range of paradigm shifts: world Christianity methodologies, polycentricity, polyvocality, interculturality, integrality, pentecostality, and glocality. Each serves as a lens through which we might better understand the terrain and the very texture of World Christianity. We shall find that these paradigms, along with other commitments such as emphasis on dialogue, lived religion, and critical consciousness, forge a World Christianity that is not just a field of study but a living community.

So, let us venture into this intellectual journey, aware that we are exploring a living, breathing entity that both illuminates and challenges, that both enriches our vision and convicts our conscience, a discipline that indeed transforms world Christianity.

Study Questions

1. How do we "listening and learning from those beyond one's cultural or religious group"?
2. What's one core feature of intercultural theology?
3. How would you define "world Christianity"?
4. Which of the "eighteen features of the discipline and methodology of world Christianity" do you want to examine further and why?
5. How might world Christianity help us understand and address "the cultural captivity of the gospel in the West"?
6. Why must we challenge Americentric, Eurocentric, and Western-centric approaches to Christian faith and theology? What are one or two ways we can amplify and learn from Majority World, Indigenous, and First Nations forms of faith and theology?

3.

Polycentricity

The Second Paradigm Shift

"Mission is from everywhere to everywhere, and from everyone to everywhere." Contemplate the profundity that undergirds this simple pronouncement. It hints at a seismic shift in how we conceive of Christian mission and theology, encompassed in polycentricity. The era has indeed elapsed when we could casually, if not arrogantly, construe mission as a venture from the "Christian West to the rest." The scope is far broader now; the paradigm has been inexorably altered. We stand in the middle of a divine drama where the proclamation of the Christian message is neither confined nor confined by geographic or cultural boundaries. The gospel is transcultural, an open invitation for participation to all nations, tribes, and tongues.

God's mission, you see, is not a project sequestered to a single clerical institution or a privileged group of theologians. It's as if we're attending a celestial symphony in which diverse individuals, communities, and churches bring unique instruments and timbres to create an elaborate, harmonious composition. Each contributes according to their gifts, their histories, their soulful inclinations—each a note in the melodious chorus that is the kingdom of God.

As we contemplate the genesis of this polycentric approach—a subject fertile for scholarly exploration—we should ask: Where did this transformative concept originate? Who are the trailblazers, the intellectual architects who've sown seeds of such fertile ground? Importantly, how can we, standing on their scholarly shoulders, incarnate this polycentric vision in the embodied practice of mission?

The term *polycentric* eschews a monolithic or hierarchical focus, instead inviting us to imagine multiple centers of influence, mission, and authority. In a world that often attempts to impose a uniformity of thought and practice, this polycentric lens provides fresh air, suggesting a devolution of power to enable an amalgam of voices in decision-making processes. It's a concept with its tendrils in multiple spheres—governance, economics, urban design, or even environmental stewardship. Yet its most striking feature is its flexibility and its valorization of localized solutions. Rather than insisting on a rigid, one-size-fits-all strategy, polycentricity recognizes that each community and culture has its own set of problems that require unique solutions crafted with local hands and hearts.

In this diversified setting, authority becomes decentralized yet profoundly collaborative. Various centers, autonomous yet interdependent, contribute to the unfolding story of God's mission, each adapting to its specific context while serving the collective purpose. In this way, polycentricity serves as both an antidote to the centralizing tendencies of yesteryear and an invitation to a richer, fuller, more dynamic engagement with the world God loves.

Polycentricity in Nature and Humanity

Polycentricity is a term brimming with latent potential, which, like an uncut gem, only reveals its many facets as we turn it this way and that in the light of inquiry. It is a principle that dances through both the animate and inanimate world, natural and constructed environments alike. Yet, it is not just a sterile concept but a living, breathing reality that pulses through ecosystems, biological organisms, human institutions, and even our digital age. It beckons us to consider a world not under the heavy hand of a single monolithic authority but alive with multiple centers of influence, each humming in its sphere yet contributing to a more magnificent symphony.

Consider the majesty of the natural world. Ecosystems are marvelously polycentric. Within these verdant habitats, myriad species coexist, each manifesting its unique role into the community's life. Unlike earthly monarchies, no one species can be said to hold the scepter of dominion; instead, the ecosystem thrives on a harmonious balance, a living liturgy of interdependence and mutual respect, a dance choreographed by the Creator's hand.

POLYCENTRICITY

Now, let your mind wander to the grand architecture of the human brain. Various cerebral neighborhoods—some handling the majestic art of sensory perception, others orchestrating the precise movement of limbs, others channeling the torrents of emotion—converse in a cacophony of electrical signals. This is not an isolated solo but a harmonious ensemble; through the labyrinthine pathways of synapses, these different regions collaborate in an act of cerebral polyphony, culminating in the complex phenomenon we call consciousness.

Then, as if your gaze shifted from the cosmic heavens to the tiniest mote dancing in a sunbeam, consider the cellular level—the genetic networks that infuse our being. No single gene is the composer of this symphony. Instead, each one adds its unique note to the musical score that defines the organism. Here, too, the beauty of polycentricity unfolds, a principle that underpins the grand narrative of life.

This principle reappears in our creations as if echoing the Creator's artistry. The Internet—a sprawling globe-encompassing network of machines—is a witness to human-engineered polycentricity. There is no solitary gatekeeper or monolithic control tower; its resilience and robustness derive from a multitude of autonomous yet interconnected nodes.

Reflect upon our modern metropolises: cities as effervescent hubs of human activity, each a polycentric microcosm. Commercial districts, cultural hotspots, and residential havens coalesce to form the complex puzzle of a city. They are vivid manifestations of a polycentric vision, each a realm unto itself but together composing the greater whole.

In governance as well, particularly those vast empires of environmental care, layers of jurisdiction interlock like pieces of a complex mosaic. Local, regional, national, global—each tier imparts its unique gifts, its specific gravitas, to the ever-evolving conversation of governance.

As we glide through the digital seas of the twenty-first century, even currencies and organizations don the garb of polycentricity. Whether cryptocurrencies enable direct transactions without a governing intermediary or Decentralized Autonomous Organizations pioneering new forms of collective decision-making, polycentricity infuses new life into old structures. It's a fluid dance of power, always in motion, yet beautifully harmonious.

From the breathtaking complexity of living ecosystems to the silicon veins of the Internet, from the bustling streets of modern cities to the transformative world of digital currencies, polycentricity permeates our reality. Each instance, whether carved by the hand of God or modeled by human ingenuity, demonstrates the enduring appeal and effectiveness of a system where multiple centers collaborate in a delicate balance of unity and diversity. In this, we discover a principle and a guiding philosophy. This vision speaks to us of the interconnectedness of all things and beckons us toward a future full of yet more wondrous diversity and harmony.

Biblical and Theological Foundations for Polycentric Mission and Ministry

Scriptural exegesis offers a rich wellspring of theological thought, reaching into the very marrow of our faith. Far more than a mere academic exercise, it uncloaks God's dream for his world, a dream braided not in monotones but in glorious polyphony. When we allow this text, this living word, to breathe into our ecclesial models and frameworks, we stumble upon something quite transformative: the notion of polycentricity.

The biblical narrative emphasizes a multitude of centers rather than a centralized authority, each resonating with the divine melody. Yes, we are beckoned towards a framework where multiple nuclei of authority, wisdom, and inspiration emanate from a single locus and the splendid diversity of God's global church. This is a dance, not a march; a symphony, not a solo. The text is replete with paradigms that challenge us and prompt us to wrestle with our fondness for neat and tidy centers of control.

Let us journey from Genesis to Revelation, that grand corridor of God's unfolding drama. Genesis 12:3 offers the ancient witness to God's universal project, wherein God covenants with Abraham to be a conduit of blessing for all families of the earth. This isn't a provincial God tied to one culture or ethnicity. Instead, it's a declaration of a God who anticipates a rich, polycentric mosaic, each tile gleaming with its own hue yet contributing to a more fabulous masterpiece.

Our Savior's words in Matt 28:19-20, the Great Commission, echo this sentiment. Jesus does not say, "Go and make disciples of your own kind." Oh no, he calls for disciples "of all nations." It's a clarion call for a polycentric mission, where the gospel takes root in manifold cultures, enriching the very soil it touches.

Then comes the narrative of Acts—a true watershed in the early church. Recall Acts 10:34-35, where Peter, the rock on which the church would be built, awakens to a stunning realization. He declares that God has room for the gentile and that there are no second-class citizens in God's kingdom. His vision shatters the illusion of a centralized faith tethered to a single cultural or ethnic identity.

Ephesians, that celestial symphony penned by Paul, reminds us in Eph 4:4-6 that, amidst our colorful diversity, we share "one Lord, one faith, one baptism." This is not uniformity but unity in diversity—a polycentric church where the Spirit of God dwells as comfortably in a cathedral as in a storefront sanctuary.

Again, in Paul's first letter to the Corinthians, we read in 1 Cor 12:4–6 about a diversity of gifts but the same Spirit. It is as though each gift, each service, and each form of leadership constitutes a center of influence and power, all harmonized by the same divine conductor.

Finally, the apocalyptic vision in Rev 7:9 shows us a panorama where a multitude from every tribe, language, people, and nation gathers before the throne. This eschatological hope anchors our polycentric dream—a people displaying all of humanity's rich heritage.

What does all this mean for the church today? The biblical roots of polycentricity reveal the grandeur of God's cosmic plan, which rejects monopolies of ecclesial power and invites us into a collaborative, multifaceted mission. It calls us to engage various cultural realities, recognize diverse expressions of the Christian faith, and respect manifold centers of ecclesial authority and wisdom.

We find ourselves, therefore, not at the end of our theological inquiry but at the beginning of a transformative journey. The scriptural exegesis has laid before us the building blocks of a polycentric theology. It is a robust theology that contains the diversity of spiritual gifts, the universality of God's call, and the pluriform expressions of ecclesial life.

In this manner, polycentricity emerges as a divine stratagem that honors diversity while engendering unity. In doing so, it propels the church into a future where the gospel, so deeply rooted in the biblical narrative, finds its expression in every tongue, tribe, and nation, drawing us all into the ever-expanding circle of God's grace.

Polycentric Approaches Are Reshaping All Fields

Polycentricity is a term replete with echoes of ancient philosophy yet pregnant with contemporary relevance. It's as though the corridors of time have found themselves spiraling around this one idea, whose Greek etymology—"multiple centers"—informs numerous disciplines. But what is this framework that tantalizingly opens our imaginations, inviting us to gaze through its prism at a world that is more like a living organism than a mechanical contraption?

Allow me to invite you on a journey spanning the spheres of governance, business, and Christian mission and ministry. At its core, polycentricity asserts a grand departure from the straitjacket of centralization, hailing instead a constellation of autonomous yet interwoven decision-making centers. It's an orchestration where each instrument plays its part, each contributing to a symphony grander than the sum of its melodies.

Within the amphitheaters of political science and governance, polycentricity is not so much a concept as an unfolding reality. It represents the complex architecture of federal systems, wherein authority cascades across multiple layers of governance. This isn't chaos; it's harmony. It allows the local choir to sing its unique song, even while it contributes to the national orchestra. In this milieu, decisions are not dictated from a monolithic center but emerge in consonance with local communities' genuine needs and voices.

This ancient principle takes on new flesh in modern enterprises' boardrooms and hallways. Gone are the days when a singular CEO or managerial board monopolized decision-making. Now, the symphony of leadership resounds through every department and every team. Each unit, acting with its mandate yet aligned with the greater corporate mission, exemplifies polycentricity in action.

The law—that web of human affairs—has its rendezvous with polycentricity. Legal theorist Lon Fuller introduced us to polycentric legal problems, those complex puzzles with overlapping issues and interests that defy the linear logic of traditional litigation.[1] Each legal challenge is a node in an interconnected network, demanding a more organic, relational approach to justice and resolution.

Let us not forget economists Elinor and Vincent Ostrom, who dared to apply this radical principle to the commons—to our shared resources.[2] They whispered the audacious belief that polycentric systems could yield more sustainable stewardship than centralized or privatized models. It's as though the land, the water, and the air themselves breathe more freely under the aegis of this decentralized governance.

Politicians, urban planners, and scholars like Walter Christaller and August Lösch extend this notion to cityscapes, painting a picture of not one centralized hub but multiple thriving centers.[3] These, in turn, contribute to a city's resilience and sustainability, capturing the interplay of social and economic forces that make up our contemporary metropolises.

Finally, the polycentric lens rests on the church—the Body of Christ. Here, it finds its richest and most profound resonance. It's as though Paul's words in 1 Corinthians 12 materialize before our eyes, bringing unity in

---

1. Fuller, "Forms and Limits of Adjudication."

2. Ostrom, "Polycentric Systems for Coping with Collective Action and Global Environmental Change."; Ostrom, "Polycentricity (Part 1)."

3. Christaller, *Central Places in Southern Germany*; Lösch, *Economics of Location*.

diversity. The Christian mission isn't a monologue; it's a dialogue, a multilogue. In this sacred arena, polycentricity celebrates unique vocations and ministries, each acting in concert to manifest the kingdom of God on Earth.

So, what are we to make of this panoramic view of polycentricity? Across diverse disciplines, it serves as a lens through which we can fathom the complexity and relationality of modern systems. It beckons us to ponder new possibilities for governance, leadership, stewardship of resources, and the church's mission in a fractured world. Far from an academic term, polycentricity is an invitation to participate in a grander narrative that honors both the individual and the collective in a dance of beautiful, orchestrated freedom.

Polycentric Approaches to Christian Ministry: The Influence of Newbigin, Taylor, and Roxburgh

Let's examine theological discourse, where the tones of polycentricity permeate the leaves and branches of Christian ministry and leadership. Like wayfarers on an ancient pilgrimage, we encounter trailblazers who've ventured before us: Lesslie Newbigin, John V. Taylor, and Alan Roxburgh, a triad of scholars whose insights illuminate our understanding like stars in the night sky.

Lesslie Newbigin, that redoubtable British missionary and theologian, invites us to reimagine the geometry of Christian mission. He suggests that the compass of the church doesn't pivot around a singular Western axis. Instead, it should radiate outward from myriad centers, each locale contributing its unique voice to the divine chorus. In his view, the church's mission is not directed from a single center but involves a global partnership where each local church contributes to the broader mission. Newbigin's vision shatters the monochrome Western-centered paradigms and invites us into the diversity and multiplicity of local expressions of faith, thereby renewing the very essence of Christian ministry.[4]

Then comes John V. Taylor, another voice singing in the British theological choir. His tome, *The Go-Between God*, is like a river running through the heart of Christian leadership, carving new pathways as it flows. Taylor ushers us into the subversive reality of the Holy Spirit, who anoints not just the few but the many. Taylor speaks about the Holy Spirit enabling every Christian to participate in the mission of God, a divine symphony where

---

4. Newbigin, *Open Secret*; Taylor, *Go-Between God*; Roxburgh, *Missionary Congregation, Leadership, and Liminality*.

every instrument has its role, displacing hierarchical models in favor of a polycentric ensemble.

But the conversation does not end there; it crosses the Atlantic, landing on the fertile ground of Alan Roxburgh, a Canadian pastor and consultant. Roxburgh envisions the church as a celestial constellation, a web of stars, each shining its own light. Roxburgh views the church as a polycentric network where various ministries can exist autonomously yet interdependently, each bringing its unique contribution to its mission. It's as if the Body of Christ has finally recognized that each limb and organ has a part to play in the divine drama unfolding in our midst.

These theological cartographers draw us a map of prodigious possibilities. A polycentric approach to Christian ministry and leadership celebrates diversity not as a problem to be solved but as a God-given asset. The kaleidoscopic expressions of faith and culture enhance the church's global witness and foster a profound sense of mutual enrichment. It reflects that grand biblical vision, portrayed so vividly in 1 Corinthians 12, where each member of the body, endowed with unique spiritual gifts, is indispensable to the whole.

However, as we meander through these theological terrains, we must tread carefully. The diverse panorama that polycentricity offers us is not without its perils. Unity and doctrinal integrity, those fundamentals of the Christian faith, must not be lost amid the variegated hues of our diverse global community of faith. As we apply this approach, our journey requires enthusiasm, discernment, exploration, and a commitment to the foundational doctrines that anchor our faith.

Thus, we find ourselves in the expansive terrain of polycentricity, a domain of not simply decentralization but glorious interdependence. It's a territory marked by the footprints of great thinkers, yet welcoming to all who would join in this most sacred of adventures—the church's continuing mission to reflect the manifold wisdom of God to a fragmented world.

Polycentric Approaches to Christian Mission: The Influence of Escobar, Franklin, Handley, Newbigin, Roxburgh, Sanneh, Walls, and Yeh

As we meander through the sacred corridors of theology and mission, we find ourselves standing at the threshold of an emerging vista: Polycentric Christian Missiology—a field ripe for exploration, illuminated by the lanterns of profound thinkers. Just as pioneers like Andrew Walls, Lamin Sanneh, and Lesslie Newbigin laid the foundational stones for a Majority World

POLYCENTRICITY

theology and mission, new navigators guide us through the multiple centers of Christian understanding and propagation.

Take Samuel Escobar, the brilliant theologian from Latin America. His work has been like the wind that fills the sails of a global Christian mission. Samuel Escobar is a renowned Latin American theologian who showed how "Christian mission is truly global, with missionaries from all places going to all peoples." In the grand narrative of God's story, every tongue, tribe, and nation contributes to the divine discourse.[5]

Kirk Franklin, too, has given us new lenses through which to view this mosaic. With meticulous care, he's penned studies such as "A Case Study: A Journey of Leading in Polycentric Theory and Practice in Mission" and co-authored with Nelus Niemandt "Polycentrism in the Missio Dei."[6] His work is a clarion call for polycentric leadership within the global mission— a call for voices from every nook and cranny of the earth to contribute to the theological dialogue.

Here, we must not overlook the enduring legacy of Lesslie Newbigin. Though his language doesn't explicitly name it as polycentric, the spirit of his work undoubtedly dances to the same tune. Lesslie Newbigin's work focuses on contextualizing the gospel, considering culture and community in missiology. His wisdom shows us that the gospel's full richness shines through the prism of multiple cultural facets.[7]

Alan Roxburgh continues in the same vein, where the mission is not just a solitary voice but a choir, each singer bringing their pitch, timbre, and tone.[8] Alan Roxburgh's writings emphasize missional theology and leadership, including polycentric approaches. He suggests that each culture and community contributes a vital verse to the grand hymn of God's mission on earth.

Drawing from the well of history, Lamin Sanneh, that extraordinary scholar of world Christianity, emphasizes the translatability of the Christian faith.[9] Sanneh argued for the importance of vernacular translations in Christian missions, reminding us that the gospel is a treasure not to be hoarded but shared generously across languages and cultures.

Then there is Andrew Walls, a colossus straddling the domains of history and missiology. He points to the southern skies, telling us to behold

---

5. Escobar, *New Global Mission*. Quotation from the book's description.

6. Franklin, "Case Study"; Franklin and Niemandt, "Polycentrism in the Missio Dei."

7. Newbigin, *Open Secret*.

8. Roxburgh, *Missionary Congregation, Leadership, and Liminality*.

9. Sanneh. *Whose Religion is Christianity?*

the new constellations in Christendom. Walls has emphasized the shift of Christianity's center to the Global South. His work recalibrates our compass, teaching us to value the voices rising from Africa, Latin America, and parts of Asia as equal contributors to the divine dialogue.[10]

Allen Yeh and Joseph Handley have further enriched the material.[11] With historical scrutiny, Yeh analyzes events that have shaped our polycentric understanding. Handley takes a pioneering step into leadership theory, grounding the polycentric ethos in a domain where it had been sorely lacking.

We are witnessing a Copernican revolution in Christian missiology. A polycentric approach beckons us to leave behind the shackles of a unidirectional, Eurocentric model, recognizing the panorama of global Christianity. It's an approach that takes seriously the diverse tongues of Pentecost and the many-colored wisdom of God, bringing them into a glorious narrative that tells an old story in endlessly new ways. It's as if the church has suddenly realized that it is not a solo but a symphony—a global, polyphonic, multi-voiced composition, singing the praises of the One who calls us all to join in divine transformative and transcultural work.

The Munich School of World Christianity and Klaus Koschorke's Contributions to Polycentric Missiology

The Munich School, guided by the ever-insightful Klaus Koschorke, stands as a poignant reminder that the Spirit blows where it wills and not merely where we have charted its path.[12] In what can only be described as an advent of epistemological humility, the Munich School gracefully retires the tired Eurocentric paradigms that once dominated the thinking about Christian mission. The consequence? A global theological and missiological culture is now fertile for the growth of a "polycentric" perspective—a perspective that displays the Christian diversity across the globe, showing its magnificent colors not as anomalies but as integral shades in the design.

In this regard, Klaus Koschorke is nothing short of a modern-day cartographer of Christian thought. With every paper and book, he doesn't just critique the Eurocentric outlook; he presents us with a theological atlas that is deeply pluralistic. Koschorke, a man with his feet planted firmly in the German intellectual tradition and eyes cast broadly toward the globe, calls

---

10. Walls, *Missionary Movement in Christian History*.
11. Yeh, *Polycentric Missiology*; Handley, *Polycentric Mission Leadership*.
12. Hermann and Burlacioiu, "Introduction," 4–27.

upon us to recognize that the Western expressions of Christianity are but local dialects in a much larger conversation.[13]

What the Munich School proffers, under Koschorke's astute watch, is nothing less than a recalibration of our spiritual compasses. The School insists that the manifold richness of the Christian tradition must not be understood as product of the "West for the rest" but rather as a worldwide and living religion constituted by diverse global and local communities. The global-local Christian community is the body of Christ in its glorious plurality—a plurality that, far from being a threat, serves as the church's very lifeblood.

Koschorke's stellar contributions to polycentric mission theology touch the essence of the faith's "intercultural translatability," as he says. His work portends not just a Christianity open to different cultural readings but one that actively anticipates them. As Koschorke masterfully shows, Christianity is not an artifact to be encased in Western museums but a living narrative being penned by hands as diverse as the humanity it claims to redeem.

Thus, this Munich School—a lighthouse on the rocky shores of academic discourse—casts its beam across the vast sea of Christian understanding. It alerts us to submerged rocks of hubris and cultural myopia while signaling towards the open waters of a Christianity that is as vast, diverse, and beautifully complex as the world it seeks to serve. In advancing the polycentric approach, the School, in its wisdom and humility, encourages us to appreciate the rich diversity of global Christianity—each element a story, each variation a confession, each design a prayer. It invites us to contribute actively to this divine expression.

Respecting the Centers

Polycentric missions shine with kaleidoscopic beauty—where every shade and hue is part of a glorious painting, a picture more significant than the sum of its elements! But there lies the rub: the temptation to frame some portraits as finer, more significant than others. Yes, North America looms large with its industrial and cultural strength; Africa, with its rich diversity of tradition and wisdom, too often looms small. But the haunting echo of Scripture—"The first shall be last and the last first"—calls us to reassess such hierarchies.

---

13. Koschorke, et al., *History of Christianity in Asia, Africa, and Latin America, 1450–1990*.

PART 1: PARADIGM SHIFTS IN WORLD CHRISTIANITY

Enter Jay Matenga, a voice in the wilderness, who addresses this issue in his aptly titled work "Centring the Local."[14] Matenga invites us into a kind of Pauline vision—think of Corinthians, where every member, regardless of its apparent grandeur or insignificance, contributes indispensably to the body. The lynchpin of such a polycentric mission? Inclusive collaboration. What does this look like in practice? A round, not rectangular table, where no head denotes importance, and every voice—be it from Nairobi or New York—adds a verse to the great symphony of Christian mission.

But let's not mistake this for a mere procedural nicety. The real marrow of this approach is the radical act of recognizing local expertise. Each 'center,' steeped in its own culture, history, and wisdom, brings a unique flavor to the ecclesial feast. To truly value this means more than passive nodding during global Skype meetings; it demands we carve spaces—real, tangible platforms—where local wisdom doesn't just contribute but leads.

However, as Matenga and others would caution us, even the most well-intentioned collaboration can be undone if equitable decision-making is not at its heart. Even in the church, power has a magnetic quality, drawing more and more to itself unless intentionally distributed. Thus, a genuinely polycentric approach is not just multipolar but seeks to make every pole a magnet, drawing ideas, strategies, and contributions toward itself. In this endeavor, the Pauline spirit reigns supreme: every member, regardless of its strength or volume, must be heard—nay must be felt—to create a body that walks in unison towards its divine calling.

Yet we must also address, with the wisdom of serpents and the innocence of doves, the tangled webs of power imbalances. Power is often the currency of the world but a thorny issue in the kingdom. The polycentric model demands vigilance, an ever-watchful eye on how power circulates, settles, and, unfortunately, can ossify. Suppose the polycentric mission is to move from theory to praxis. In that case, it must champion transparency, accountability, and, most importantly, the Jesus-modeled kenosis—the self-emptying that lays down power for the sake of others.

Let us not see polycentrism as a mere strategy but as a theology that reflects a Triune God who exists in an eternal, collaborative relationship. Let us strive for a polycentric praxis that accommodates and celebrates every voice, realizing that in this divine choir, the African rhythm is just as essential as the American melody and the Asian harmony as crucial as the European counterpoint. In so doing, may we sketch on earth the glorious, polycentric, and yet harmonious portrait of heaven.

---

14. See Matenga, "Centring the Local."

POLYCENTRICITY

A Summary of Polycentric Christian Leadership and Ministry

Imagine the ancient mosaic art form: tiles of diverse shapes, colors, and textures come together to form a narrative more grand, more glorious than the sum of its disparate parts. Now picture the Christian community as such a mosaic, a new humanity narrating the grand story of God's love and redemptive plan for the world. This is the essence of polycentric Christian leadership and ministry—a paradigm-shifting vision with the transformative power to reconfigure our understanding of ecclesial structures and roles.

The central genius of the polycentric model lies in its daring decentralization. Picture a solar system with not one but several suns, around which planets rotate and revolve. Gone are the days when the Western, often colonial, vision of Christianity serves as the solitary sun, monopolizing the spiritual heavens. Instead, leadership positions and authoritative voices emerge from diverse geographical and cultural terrains, each contributing its unique gravitational pull to hold the heavenly body in balance. Here, the radiance of African spirituality illuminates alongside the intellectual traditions of European theologies, and the mystic wisdom of the Eastern churches dances in rhythm with the dynamic ministries emerging from Latin America.

At the very heartbeat of this model is mutual learning—an ecclesiastical symposium where the teaching is not a monologue but a dialogue, indeed a polylogue. Ideas and interpretations aren't merely parachuted from an all-knowing center but are developed through interactions with various Christian traditions worldwide. This allows for contextualizing the gospel, acknowledging that the word must become flesh differently in different cultural milieus.

Yet this model is not an anarchy; it is a choreography. It shatters traditional hierarchies not to create a void but to fill the space with a symphony of voices singing in harmony but not unison. Therefore, every 'center' is an indispensable voice in a choir, an essential hue in a mural, and a crucial flavor in a divine recipe. Equity and equality aren't buzzwords in this paradigm; they are the building blocks upon which this celestial city is constructed.

Perhaps the most remarkable feature of this model is its adaptability. The polycentric approach offers an antidote in an era desperately seeking one-size-fits-all answers. It champions adaptive over technical change, heralding the wisdom of context-specific solutions. This is not a model with a set "operating manual"; it writes its script as it listens, deeply and attentively, to the cries and whispers, the hosannas and lamentations emanating from every corner of the global Christian community.

The polycentric vision isn't just an alternative model of governance. It is an eschatological foretaste of the kingdom, a glimmering snapshot of a future where every tribe, tongue, and nation brings unique gifts to the New Jerusalem. This is a unity not of suppression but of celebration—a unity that doesn't silence the diverse melodies but harmonizes them into a new, heavenly song. Let us adopt and adapt this polycentric model as a living witness to a God who is as gloriously diverse as God is profoundly one.

A Summary of Polycentric Christian Missions, Missiologies, and Theologies

Ponder a symphony, resounding not from a single instrument but a full orchestra, each contributing a unique timbre, texture, and tone, merging into a harmonious grandeur that transcends any solitary melody. This is the sweeping vision of polycentric Christian missiologies and theologies: a grand orchestration of faith perspectives that tell a richer, more nuanced story of the Creator and God's creation. It's a narrative that dares to envision Christian thought as a global phenomenon and the product of human diversity—cultural, linguistic, and societal.

The linchpin of this expansive vision is cultural contextualization, an acknowledgment that the gospel, like an eternally resonant symphony, can be played in different keys without losing its fundamental tune. This is not the watered-down syncretism some might fear; instead, it affirms the divine genius that made the gospel so inherently translatable. It confirms that the "Word became flesh" not merely in a specific time and place but can incarnate anew across myriad cultures and epochs.

Emerging from the Majority World are fresh winds of the Spirit, revivifying the faith in ways that demand global attention. For too long, the Christian imagination has been somewhat captive to the Northern or Western hemisphere. Now, Africa, Asia, and Latin America are rising not as mere spectators but as active players on the world stage of Christian mission and theology. Lamin Sanneh, a guiding light in this dialogue, advocates for a Christianity unshackled from the limits of culture or language. Sanneh calls for a faith that can be translated without being domesticated, challenging and enriching us all.

In this celebration of global voices, vernacular theologies—the grassroots reflections on God's activity in specific contexts—are welcomed to the banquet of Christian discourse as honored guests. They arrive bearing gifts:

their unique wisdom, drawn from lived experiences that enrich the global understanding of faith. This approach reveres native intelligence as divinely inspired, not merely as folklore to be collected but as vital voices in the choir of Christian thought.

This all-embracing framework turns its back on unilateral monologues. It embraces instead the concept of a divine dialogue—a Holy Conversation—conducted not within the echo chamber of a single tradition but among a multiplicity of perspectives. Collaboration, then, is not an optional extra but the very pulse of this model. Theologies and missions rise not from the singular vision of an isolated center but from the interplay of a community caught up in the divine dance of the Trinity itself.

The polycentric model reminds us that neither theology nor mission lives in splendid isolation. They are embedded within broader canvases—social, economic, environmental—thus compelling us to read Scripture and live out faith in dialogue with the more significant issues of justice, poverty, and creation care.

In essence, the polycentric paradigm suggests not merely a method but a profound ecclesial maturity. It dares to dream of a church as wide as the world, as diverse as humanity, and yet as one as the God in whose image we are made. This isn't merely missiology or theology; it is doxology—a paean of praise to the God who loved the world in all its glorious diversity.

Practical Ways We Can Apply Polycentric Approaches to Ministries, Missions, and Theologies

Christianity is a fascinating mosaic, a faith born in the Middle East, nurtured in the Mediterranean world, and now flourishing in every nook and cranny of God's good earth. It is as though the Spirit of God, like some divine artist, has been carefully placing tiles of diverse colors, shapes, and textures into this ever-expanding work of art. When we step back to behold it, what do we see? Not a monochrome, but a magnificent polyphony of cultures, languages, and experiences—a polycentric vision of what the Body of Christ can, and indeed must, be.

But this vision isn't a mere celebration of diversity for its own sake, as crucial as that is. No, it beckons us toward a grander theological vision: the coming together of all things in heaven and on earth under the lordship of Christ. The church is called to be a sign and foretaste of that coming unity. To that end, the principles of polycentricity not only enrich us but also instruct us, reminding us that no single culture, no single ecclesial tradition, has a monopoly on the manifold wisdom of God.

PART 1: PARADIGM SHIFTS IN WORLD CHRISTIANITY

In the grand theater of ministry and missions, polycentricity advocates for a global partnership of equals, transcending the old, tired boundaries of culture and geography. Visualize an environment in which a church leader in Nigeria and a missionary in Indonesia learn from each other with the humility and eagerness of fellow disciples at the feet of Jesus. Consider the mutual edification that comes when local churches engage in cultural exchange programs, becoming living epistles written not with ink but with the Spirit, testifying to God's boundless creativity and infinite love (2 Cor 3:3).

Leadership in this divine orchestra is not the domain of one instrument or section alone. A polycentric approach calls for leaders who reflect the rich heterogeneity of God's global family. It requires that we don't merely translate our theology into other languages but let the global church's languages translate us, broadening our horizons and deepening our insights.

As for the rich field of theological reflection, being polycentric is recognizing that the Spirit has been speaking through the ages across continents and cultures. Indigenous theologies, First Nations spirituality, and theological perspectives from Asia, Africa, and Latin America aren't footnotes to Western theology but represent unique, Holy Spirit-inspired understandings of God and God's kingdom and mission. To ignore them is to impoverish our collective theological enterprise.

What, then, are the intentional steps we must take? The list is as comprehensive as it is compelling: from engaging in language and cultural studies to fostering an atmosphere of mutual respect and learning through exchange programs; from advancing diverse leadership to undertaking research collaborations that cross-pollinate theological thought; from celebrating and praying for the global church to acknowledging and rectifying past historical errors in mission.

These actions, far from optional add-ons, are essential practices for a church committed to reflecting the polycentric character of God's kingdom. When we uphold these principles, what emerges is a robust, dynamic form of Christianity—one as variegated and yet as harmonious as the hues of a stained-glass window illuminated by the singular light of Christ. We, the global church, bear collective witness to this light—to this all-encompassing, radiant vision of God's kingdom. In doing so, we become a living, breathing foretaste of the glory that is to come when every tribe, tongue, and nation gather around the throne, not in a monotone of praise, but in a harmonious, multicolored, and polycentric doxology to the One who sits on the throne and to the Lamb, forever and ever.

Table 3.1. Fifteen Qualities of Polycentricity

1. Global Scope: Mission is from everywhere to everywhere; the Christian faith is global and cross-cultural.
2. Collaborative Endeavor: Involves a network of diverse individuals, churches, and communities, each contributing their unique gifts and perspectives.
3. Decentralization: Authority and decision-making are decentralized, encouraging diverse and independent perspectives across multiple centers of influence.
4. Flexibility and Adaptability: A polycentric approach allows theologies, ministries, and missions to be flexible and adaptable, adjusting to local contexts, needs, and challenges.
5. Localized Solutions: Tailor-made solutions for problems are encouraged, recognizing that one-size-fits-all strategies aren't universally effective or appropriate.
6. Inclusive Collaboration: Active participation from all relevant centers is prioritized, ensuring diverse voices are heard and respected through open dialogue and regular communication channels.
7. Recognition of Local Expertise: Each center brings unique knowledge, skills, and experiences. Local actors are acknowledged and valued for their contributions.
8. Equitable Decision-making: Decision-making processes are designed to be fair and inclusive, ensuring that power is distributed among all stakeholders and that the impact on all centers is considered.
9. Addressing Power Imbalances: Actively mitigates power dynamics between different centers by fostering transparent and accountable governance mechanisms.
10. Cultural Contextualization: The gospel is adapted to fit different cultures, languages, and societies while maintaining its core message.
11. Majority World and First Nations Influence: Acknowledges the growing contribution and leadership in Christian missions, theologies, and ministries from Africa, Asia, Latin America, diaspora, Caribbean, Oceanian, Eastern European, Middle Eastern, Indigenous peoples, and First Nations.
12. Mutual Interchange: There is an emphasis on mutual exchange and learning among the different centers of Christianity, fostering a global conversation and partnership.
13. Vernacular Theologies: Theologies and interpretations of the gospel from various cultural and societal contexts are acknowledged and valued.
14. Holistic / Integral Approach: Takes a comprehensive view of mission and ministry, considering the social, economic, cultural, and environmental contexts in which it occurs.
15. Regeneration and Renewal: Fosters a fresh understanding of the gospel through the lens of diverse cultures and contexts, bringing new life, creative approaches, and a more profound commitment to unity in the body of Christ.

PART 1: PARADIGM SHIFTS IN WORLD CHRISTIANITY

Polycentricity: Concluding Reflections

Polycentricity is a term that might sound academic and obscure, but it is nothing less than the map by which we investigate the glorious and infinitely varied environment of God's kingdom on earth. For far too long, Christianity has, unwittingly perhaps, imbibed the colonial mindset, viewing the faith through the narrow lens of Western-centric ideas and structures. But if we look closely, very closely, at the story of God's redemptive purpose, we'll find that it is anything but parochial. It is polycentric, bursting forth in a multitude of directions, like the tongues of fire at Pentecost, reaching into the far-flung corners of the world and the hidden recesses of the human heart.

Consider for a moment the extraordinary narrative of the Christian mission. A polycentric vision shifts the axis from the centralized headquarters, often associated with Western paradigms, to a more decentralized engagement with local contexts. Rather than seeing mission as something that goes out from a central hub, as if from a command center, we find ourselves invited to see multiple centers of God's dynamic activity. In this vision, the local pastor in rural Africa and the underground church leader in Asia are not merely recipients of Western missionary strategy; they are, in fact, colaborers, theologians, and mission strategists in their own right.

Oh, the mutual enrichment that follows! When we begin to glimpse the kingdom through the eyes of brothers and sisters from different cultures and contexts, it's like listening to a choir where each section brings its own timbre and pitch to a grand and glorious harmony. Polycentric principles thus result in a much richer, more authentic composition of theological reflection and praxis. The whole Body becomes nimbler and more attuned to the complex and variegated world in which we witness the risen Christ.

But this is not just a matter of strategy or effectiveness, as important as these may be. At its heart, polycentricity is deeply and profoundly theological. It is rooted in the Trinitarian nature of a God who is at once unity and diversity. By embracing a polycentric approach, we come closer to reflecting the very nature of the God we worship, a God whose image is borne by people from every tribe, tongue, and nation.

Let's not underestimate the regenerative energy this polycentric perspective injects into the sinews and muscles of the Body of Christ worldwide. When diverse communities engage in mutual listening and learning, the act becomes a means of grace. Our varied perspectives and insights, far from threats to our unity, can stimulate spiritual vitality, open up new avenues for the proclamation of the gospel, and pave the way for creative expressions of worship and service that would have been unimaginable in a monolithic structure.

So, let us welcome this grand vision with open arms and willing spirits. In so doing, we participate in a reality simultaneously as wide as the world and as particular as everyone within it. We glimpse a foretaste of that great day when the symphony of God's redeemed people will rise in a crescendo of praise to the One who has made us all one, even while marvelously making us each wonderfully, splendidly, uniquely different. Thus, the polycentric model isn't just an option for an increasingly global church; it is the heartbeat of a faith that is catholic and diverse, universal and particular, one and many. Amen, come Lord Jesus.

Study Questions

1. How would you define polycentricity in a simple sentence?

2. "Mission is from everywhere to everywhere, and from everyone to everywhere." What's one practical way this polycentricity changes how Christians engage in mission?

3. What biblical or theological foundation for polycentric mission and ministry stands out most and why?

4. Which of the "fifteen qualities of polycentricity" are most difficult to implement and why? What are the solutions to those challenges?

5. "Polycentric principles lead to a more authentic, inclusive, and effective practice of ministry, leadership, mission, and theological reflection." Explain why this may be the case.

6. How do we actively confront and mitigate power imbalances between different centers to genuinely prioritize and amplify Majority World, Indigenous, and historically marginalized perspectives and contributions?

4.

Polyvocality

The Third Paradigm Shift

THE RESONANCE OF POLYVOCALITY—a harmony, not a cacophony that captures the wondrous multiplicity of the Divine calling across variegated lands and cultures! Picture a grand choir assembled from every corner of the earth; each voice distinct yet contributing to a melodious hymn that glorifies the Creator. In the Western mind, we are often held captive by the monologue, the singular voice, as though truth itself would splinter if more than one voice were to resound. Yet, consider the richer, more textured song that emerges when we dare to move beyond our insular podiums.

In their twin volumes, my books *Salt, Light, and a City* are not merely academic exercises or theological exposés; they are an invitation to participate in this grand choir of divine activity. The first volume lays the groundwork, a concerto of sorts, where Western theologians—each a virtuoso in their theological tradition—set forth their scores.[1] Here, the ecclesiological discourse takes place within the comforting bounds of familiar tunes: Coakley to Zizioulas, Moltmann to LaCugna, and so forth. It is like listening to a familiar hymn, each verse carefully inscribed within the canons of Western Christianity.

However, the crescendo is reached in the second volume.[2] Here, a new score is presented, not written in the familiar notations of Western

---

1. Hill, *Salt, Light, and a City* (vol. 1).
2. Hill, *Salt, Light, and a City* (vol. 2).

seminaries or theologies but in the polyrhythmic, polyphonic languages of the Majority World. These are voices often relegated to the margins, but in this new theological symphony, they come to the center, enriching our collective understanding of God's mission. They compel us to reconsider what we thought we knew, inviting us into an ecclesiological dance that is not only polycentric but dazzlingly polyvocal.

Integrating these voices into a harmonious whole doesn't dilute the faith but amplifies it. Just as a diamond reflects the light most brilliantly when viewed from multiple angles, the church also shines most resplendently when it embodies the full diversity of its global communion. Therefore, the current and future ecclesial dialogues should be polycentric, embracing interculturality, integrality, and pentecostality. This new ecclesial reality—vivid and inclusive—demonstrates the adaptability and universality of the Christian message. In so doing, it bears witness to the encompassing grandeur of the God we serve—a God for whom every voice matters, whose image is reflected in the manifold diversity of God's creation.

To partake in this movement is not simply to broaden our intellectual horizons or to make cosmetic alterations to our traditional ways of doing things. It is to partake in the in-breaking kingdom of God, a kingdom as wide and as varied as the world it has come to redeem. We are thus beckoned to set aside our parochial instincts, not out of a sense of begrudging obligation, but because we recognize that in the many voices and perspectives of global Christianity, we find a more complete, more beautiful song of praise to our Creator. Indeed, mission and ministry in our day must not merely pay lip service to these ideals but embody them as we endeavor to form a church that looks—and sounds—more like the kingdom for which it longs.

Polyvocality in Nature and Humanity

In the garden of creation, a symphony is already in full swing: a polyphonic concerto enriched by countless voices, each a singular melody contributing to the grand hymn that fills the air. You see, the narrative of polyvocality begins not in our human endeavors but in the divine artisanship of the Creator. As we take our seats in this celestial concert hall, we see the polyvocality principle incarnated in the nature of creation and human creativity.

Let us first turn our gaze to the natural world, an ecosystem where the Creator's voice sang life into being. Here, polyvocality thrives unbidden. A forest is not merely a collection of trees but a choir of flora and fauna, fungi and bacteria, each with a role and a voice. Conceive for a moment the delicate balance, the complex relationships, each entity speaking and listening in a conversation of life and sustenance. Unsurprisingly, the discourse on climate change and environmental preservation has moved toward a polyvocal ethos. We are learning, gradually but meaningfully, to incorporate Indigenous wisdom, such as the water preservation techniques of Native Americans or the fire management insights of the Aboriginal and Torres Strait Islander communities. Once relegated to the margins, such voices emerge as crucial contributors, offering a wider, richer perspective on how to be stewards of God's Earth.

Shift your attention to human endeavor. Consider literature. In the polyphony of narrative, authors like William Faulkner, in works like *As I Lay Dying*, paint a story that resonates with the multitudes of human experience.[3] Fifteen characters, fifteen voices, each wrestling with the same story but from distinct vantage points. It is as though Faulkner knew that the truth is often polyvocal, residing not in a single voice but emerging through the interplay of many.

In the sprawling digital agora of our time, platforms like Twitter (now X), Facebook, and Reddit have become the epitome of human-constructed polyvocality. Here, each voice, tweet, or post adds to the cacophony—or symphony, depending on your perspective. However dissonant the dialogue may seem at times, the sheer diversity of voices enriches the conversation, allowing us to glimpse the breadth and depth of collective human thought.

The same can be said of academia. Consider the burgeoning field of urban development studies, a confluence of sociology, architecture, economics, and environmental science. Here, each discipline is a voice in a scholarly choir, their harmonized outputs far more illuminating than any could be in isolation.

What of the cities themselves, those fascinating clusters of human life? We hear the polyphony of urban development in their winding streets and towering skyscrapers. Planners and architects lay down the score, but the performance is communal—business owners, residents, and tourists each add their verse to the ongoing song. Each urban space, therefore, becomes a unique composition, its character shaped by the voices that contribute to its ever-changing narrative.

In both the natural and human-made worlds, polyvocality emerges as a profound metaphor for the rich diversity of life. It serves as a clarion call to listen intently to the multitude of voices surrounding us, reminding us that truth is often most vividly and faithfully represented when articulated from a multiplicity of perspectives. If the Creator has infused such diversity

3. Faulkner, *As I Lay Dying*.

into creation and humanity's nature, then it behooves us to learn the art of listening—to nature, each other, and the One who made us all.

Biblical and Theological Foundations for Polyvocal Mission and Ministry

In the symphony of God's creation, every voice holds an invaluable note, harmonizing with the beautiful diversity of what we collectively call the church. A single melody, as melodic as it might be, can never capture the full orchestration of the Divine. The concept of polyvocality, therefore, is not merely an extraneous layer of theological reflection. It serves as a critical cornerstone, a celestial cornerstone, you might say, embedded deep within the bedrock of Holy Scripture.

The Bible begins with the splendid account of God's creation in Genesis, where we find that humanity was molded "in the image of God; male and female God created them" (Gen 1:27). We are thus reminded that in the Divine Imagination, each person holds irreplaceable worth. As reflections of this Divine Image, each one of us contributes unique, vital timbres and hues to the varicolored canvas of the church.

Let us journey next to the bustling streets of Jerusalem during Pentecost, as recounted in Acts 2. The Holy Spirit, rushing like a mighty wind, imbues the disciples with the miraculous ability to speak in languages not their own. At this foundational moment for the church, God's Spirit eradicates language barriers, endorsing a divine polyvocality that allows the Good News to be heralded in a chorus of human tongues. This was the language of the kingdom—diverse yet harmonious.

We find further accentuation of this theme in Paul's rich epistolary writings. He describes the church as a body, a wondrous organism comprising many unique and indispensable parts (1 Cor 12:12–27). Paul recognizes that the church is a composite of many voices, not a monologue. The apostle even lists the gifts bestowed by the Holy Spirit, each crucial for the vitality and full functioning of this divine body (1 Cor 12:4–11; Rom 12:6–8).

Paul's letter to the Ephesians carries this theme forward. The apostle speaks of the reconciliation wrought by Christ, who broke down the dividing wall of hostility (Eph 2:14). Thus, the gospel is no tribal deity, no parochial narrative. It's a universal claim—extending its open arms to embrace the richness of every culture, the distinctiveness of every voice.

Galatians 3:28 may well be seen as the crescendo of this Pauline symphony: "There is neither Jew nor gentile, neither slave nor free, nor is there male and female, for you are all one in Christ Jesus." Each voice, each person, irrespective of social categorization, holds a revered space in the kingdom's choir.

We mustn't overlook Paul's bold assertion in Col 1:20, speaking of redemption and reconciliation that stretches its arms wide enough to include all things, whether on earth or in heaven. The scope is cosmic and universal. This amplifies our imperative to include the many and varied expressions of faith in our understanding of the gospel.

We discover, therefore, that the scriptural narrative, from Genesis to Revelation, is a polyphonic symphony replete with various timbres and tones. By embracing this divine polyvocality, we offer the world a richer, more profound articulation of the gospel that captures the unfathomable richness of God's revelation. Such a polyvocal approach fosters not only a pluralism of expression but also a depth of understanding, enabling us to better reflect the multifaceted wisdom of the Divine in our collective mission and ministry.

Polyvocality is Reshaping Many Fields and Disciplines

In the complex labyrinth of human experience and endeavor, with its myriad corridors of thought, culture, and action, a new refrain is being heard: the refrain of polyvocality. This term stands not merely as an esoteric concept confined to the ivory towers of academia but as a compelling narrative resonating through the multiple spheres of human interaction, from the intricacies of theology to the exactitudes of science, the complexities of governance, and the dynamics of the marketplace.

One may consider polyvocality as a counter-narrative to the hegemony of a monolithic voice, which seeks to silence all others in its quest for unquestioned authority. Instead, polyvocality insists upon a kind of democratic concerto in which each instrument or voice—though distinct and often disparate—contributes to forming a richer, more beautiful melody.

Within the ambit of Christian ministry, the embrace of polyvocality presents an opportunity and an imperative. The global Christian community is a splendid mosaic made up of countless colors, textures, and patterns. To truncate this divine design into monochrome would be to rob it of its God-intended beauty and intricacy. Thus, a polyvocal approach becomes essential in allowing the church to communicate the depth and breadth of its ancient yet ever-new message to many cultures.

In the domain of humanities, the significance of polyvocality becomes even more conspicuous. The once-prevailing narrative, emanating from a limited cultural or social viewpoint, now must make room for a chorus of

POLYVOCALITY

voices that have long been marginalized or silenced. Literary critics such as Mikhail Bakhtin have championed the notion of "heteroglossia," recognizing the symphony of perspectives that can coexist within a single text.[4]

The anthropological field, too, is experiencing a methodological reformation. Gone are the days when one voice could authoritatively speak for an entire culture or community. Scholars like Clifford Geertz and James Clifford have insisted on including multiple perspectives, elevating anthropology from a mere descriptive practice to an interpretive, polyvocal discipline.[5]

Science, the often-assumed bastion of objectivity, is also being nudged into recognizing the merit of polyvocality. Interdisciplinary approaches, which involve harmonizing varying scientific disciplines, yield a more comprehensive understanding of phenomena as complex as climate change or global health issues. The universe, it seems, is far too labyrinthine to be understood from any single vantage point.

Musicology has long practiced polyvocality, albeit in a different key. A musical composition, after all, gains its depth and beauty not from a single voice but from the interplay of multiple harmonies and melodies. So, it is in governance and politics where participatory systems are becoming more receptive to the polyvocal contributions of their constituents.

Similarly, in business and commerce, successful enterprises have begun to realize that the crowd's wisdom often exceeds the insight of the solitary genius. Today's competitive advantage belongs to those organizations that can effectively synthesize multiple viewpoints into a cohesive strategy.

Across these diverse fields, we observe a common denominator: an acknowledgment of the insurmountable complexities of human life that require a symphony rather than a solo performance. In essence, the thematic unity amid the diversity of disciplines that polyvocality brings is akin to the beautiful tension of an orchestra—a multitude of instruments, each valuable, contributing to the grandeur of the symphony.

In this era of unparalleled global interconnectedness, this symphonic polyvocality will allow us to ponder the manifold complexities we face. As we grapple with the daunting challenges and exciting opportunities that lie ahead, let us attune our ears to this ever-expanding chorus. For in the fullness of its harmonies and the richness of its tones, we may find a more comprehensive understanding of our complex world and a more fruitful and compassionate way of engaging with it.

---

4. Bakhtin, "Discourse in the Novel."
5. Geertz, *Interpretation of Cultures*; Clifford, *Writing Culture*.

PART 1: PARADIGM SHIFTS IN WORLD CHRISTIANITY

Does Everyone Contribute to Everything?

The beauty of polyvocality—a concept often misunderstood yet pregnant with transformative possibilities. To some, the term conjures an image of cacophonous chatter, a disordered disarray of everyone speaking at once about everything. Yet that is to miss the mark rather dramatically. Polyvocality is not about unbridled verbosity but the harmonious concert of human voices, each offering nuanced, often neglected notes to the grand symphony of intellectual and practical discourse.

Let us dispel the myth that polyvocality advocates for a cacophonous assembly where everyone chimes in on every subject. The beauty of an orchestra is not that every instrument plays every note but that each contributes where it is most fitting and effective, bringing forth its unique timbre to add depth and richness to the whole composition. So, it is with polyvocality.

The term "Many Voices, Valued Perspectives" encapsulates the true spirit of this concept. It recognizes the inherent limitations and unique strengths that each of us brings to the communal table. Every gardener knows that not all plants require the same amount of water, sunlight, or soil nutrients. Likewise, not every voice will have the same relevance or expertise across all subjects. Still, each has its place in the ecology of discussion, and each can flourish when tended to appropriately.

This is not a call to silent deference; far from it. Instead, it's a clarion call for deliberate and thoughtful inclusivity that seeks out voices that are often sidelined, bringing them into the heart of the discussion where their insights are most needed. This practice creates a rich collage of thought, pieced together not only for the beauty of its many colors but also for its overall strength and integrity.

When we speak of polyvocality in this way, we invoke not just a method but a vision of human interaction that reflects the exquisite design evident throughout creation. For those of us inclined toward faith, this can be seen as a reflection of the divine image in which we are all made, which is endlessly diverse yet perfectly unified. For those of more secular persuasions, it is a vital principle for understanding the complexities of our pluralistic, interconnected world.

So, let us espouse the "Many Voices, Valued Perspectives" idea as an eloquent and practical maxim. Let us ensure that this is not a mere slogan but a lived reality affecting our corporate bodies, whether in governance, business, academia, or faith communities. For it is in the mingling of many voices, each valued for its unique contributions, that we find the most symphonic, the most poetic, and indeed, the most truthful expressions of our shared humanity.

POLYVOCALITY

Shaping Polyvocal Churches, Ministries, Theologies, and Missions

The majesty of God's kingdom—a realm so saturated with diversity that to behold it is to glimpse the face of the Infinite One whose image we all bear. Like an artisan whose every stroke of the brush or chisel adds a unique hue or contour to a grand masterpiece, so has the Creator imbued humanity with an array of features, talents, and stories that collectively bear witness to Divine artistry. In that, we find the imperative not merely to tolerate diversity but to cherish it as essential for reflecting the true glory of the God we worship.

Consider the manifold dimensions that make up this rich harmony of divine and human interaction, not as separate notes but as chords in a grand symphony. The church of Christ must be as expansive as the sky and as varied as the stars. We are called to be an orchestra where every culture and race adds its distinctive sound, challenging our petty parochialisms and inviting us into a grander, more inclusive narrative that reflects a God who, in God's very being, is a community of love.

Generational diversity offers another breathtaking layer to this divine composition. The elders' wisdom and the youth's vitality should not be ships passing in the night but elements integrated closely together, strengthening the dynamism of the faith community. How impoverished our understanding of God would be if it were solely viewed through the lens of the old or the young. Each generation brings melodies and harmonies to the ongoing song of faith, helping the church remain grounded yet ever-growing.

Let us not forget those among us whose physical or cognitive abilities differ from the majority. Their voices, steeped in resilience and profound wisdom, sing of God's grace in poignant verses that many of us can scarcely comprehend. They bear witness to a God whose love knows no boundaries, whose image is reflected not in strength but vulnerability and interdependence.

The linguistic range and variance of our faith communities, too, should be as variegated as the tongues of Pentecost, for each language captures nuances of the divine that others may overlook. Each tongue sings God's praise in tones and semitones unheard in other idioms, and in this multilingual chorus, we discern more fully the God who speaks every language fluently.

Our understanding of what constitutes a family or a committed relationship, too, must be nuanced and broad, allowing us to recognize the Spirit's work in places and relationships we might not have expected. Singleness and marriage, celibacy and parenthood, each have their timbre and pitch, contributing to the richness of the communal hymn of life and love.

Our faith community must ring out with voices from every corner of the socio-economic spectrum, reminding us that in God's kingdom, the world's values are turned on their heads: the first are last, and the last are first. This varied voice cacophony is a powerful counter-melody to the world's anthems of power and privilege.

While our faith centers unequivocally on Christ, the interreligious dialogue can add tones of grace, peace, and understanding in a world so profoundly scarred by religious strife. We gain nothing by drowning out the voices of others; indeed, we find our voice enriched when we learn to sing not just in monologue but in dialogue with our global neighbors.

Last but never least, the Spirit has endowed spiritual gifts upon each one of us, gifts as varied and numerous as the stars, yet each contributing to the constellation that is the body of Christ. This recognition invites a dynamic, living faith, not a static or monolithic one. It bespeaks a God who delights in diversity, speaks through prophets and poets, caregivers and question-askers, in a Spirit-infused cacophony that somehow, mysteriously, coheres into the divine harmony of the kingdom of God.

In this sumptuous diversity, we find not just an ecclesial ideal but a divine command that mirrors the manifold richness of the God whose image we bear. Suppose we aspire to reverberate with the harmonies of heaven. In that case, we must attune ourselves to the diverse and manifold voices that make up God's earthly choir, for it is in this polyphony of voices that the symphony of God's kingdom is most vividly and compellingly played.

Polyvocal Approaches to Christian Ministry and Leadership

In the grand story of Christian history, we witness a sublime and transformative shift: the flowering of polyvocality within the garden of ministry and leadership. This is not a sudden transplantation of an alien species into the ecclesiastical soil; instead, it's a long-neglected native bloom that is finally being cultivated with care. The roots go deep into our Christian heritage, emerging through the apostle Paul's articulation of the church as a body—varied, multi-functional, yet essentially one (1 Cor 12:12–27)—and extending to the modern awakening to Christianity as a global phenomenon, intrinsically multi-tonal.

Imagine a council of Christian leaders as a choir of disparate yet harmonious voices. Once, perhaps, a monolithic cantor may have directed the hymn, but now, it's increasingly understood that such a symphonic expression of faith requires more than a single melody. We are drawn, therefore, to the orchestration of this heavenly music through polyvocality. This approach disperses the scepter of authority and allows for intermingling a wide array of timbres and tunes.

What, one might ask, is the fruit of this polyvocal approach? First and foremost, it celebrates the multifaceted wonder of the global body of Christ. In such an orchestra, the kora from West Africa dialogues with the sitar from India, each offering unique scales and sonorities contributing to the fuller apprehension of divine revelation. In the resonance of these diverse voices, all find a home; all sense the affirming nod of a faith that places immeasurable value upon their contributions.

Secondly, when the church's leadership opens its arms to welcome the various songs of its constituency, it positions itself to minister to the world in a key that is much more in tune with the varied harmonies of human needs and aspirations. It listens to the unique rhythms and melodies of different cultures and social strata and then improvises its lines in a way that can be heard and understood.

Thirdly, and most compellingly, a polyvocal lens grants us a kaleidoscopic view of theology. Through this multi-angled prism, we see facets of God, Scripture, and Christian praxis that we had never glimpsed before. Here, we enter into a divine dialogue, with each voice adding depth and hue to our understanding of the ineffable.

But what does this look like in the everyday, rough and tumble of communal life? In a polyvocal community, decision-making becomes a choir practice where each voice warms up, vocalizes, and eventually harmonizes. The result is a robust and profoundly resonant chord that echoes far beyond the four walls of the church.

The importance of individual narrative is emphasized, of personal odysseys that contribute invaluable verses to the song of collective faith. The storytelling elder and the questioning youth, the conservative and the liberal—all offer rhythms and riffs that contribute to the ongoing melody of the community's lived experience.

Conflicts, when they arise, are treated not as disruptive noise but as discordant notes that challenge the community to find a new, reconciling chord. Polyvocality provides the sheet music for this challenging yet rewarding task, a guide for harmonizing diverse perspectives into a richer, more complex composition.

From an architectural standpoint, a polyvocal community resembles less a medieval cathedral with its soaring spires and centralized altar and more a circle of pilgrims, each contributing to the liturgy. Far from being a top-down pronouncement, leadership is dispersed, echoing the New Testament model of multiple apostles, prophets, teachers, and guides. Such decentralization imbues the community with an agile adaptability, able to pivot and respond to new challenges with diverse solutions.

So, we see that polyvocality is not merely a methodology but a pilgrimage—a journey of continuous learning and spiritual exploration marked by milestones of mutual discovery. In an ever-changing world, this adaptability and constant collective learning is not a luxury but a necessity.

Thus, as we espouse polyvocality, we find it is far from a concession to modernity or a dilution of the faith. Instead, it is a robust affirmation of Christianity's most ancient and sacred truths, expressed now in a language as diverse as the world it seeks to serve, as multi-voiced as the God we worship. It offers a vision for a church that is not just a congregation but a conversation, not just a body, but a body that sings. In that singing—in that holy cacophony of voices—we might hear the echo of the voice of God.

Polyvocal Approaches to Christian Mission and Intercultural Service

The age-old tale of the church, traditionally considered a unified voice proclaiming the gospel, finds itself at an intriguing crossroads—cued in by the mellifluous tones of what we might call "polyvocality." It is as though the body of Christ, that ancient yet ever-new metaphor has discovered that its hands, feet, eyes, and ears each possess not merely different functions but different timbres, harmonies, and even languages. How might this polyvocal community resound with the gospel in a world splintered by dissonance yet deeply hungering for a new song?

The term "polyvocal" might seem like a modern introduction to Christian discourse. Still, it stands in line with the Pauline vision, where the body is not one part but many—each part honored and indispensable. The apostle Paul reminds us in his first letter to the Corinthians that unity in diversity reflects the nature of the triune God we serve. Now, in our global context—a tumultuous medley of cultures, languages, and life stories—this Pauline vision is revitalized in the concept of polyvocality within the mission and intercultural work of the church.

First, let us consider how a polyvocal Christian mission helps us honor the multifaceted image of God in humanity. Each voice, whether melodious or gruff, contributes a unique timbre to the choir of Christian witness. A church that listens as keenly as it speaks will soon find that the contributions of each member are not mere window dressings but essential hues in the stained glass that let the light shine through in varicolored patterns, each one telling a different part of the old, old story.

In the sphere of intercultural work, polyvocality acts as a bridge over waters troubled by misunderstanding and prejudice. Different cultures offer different windows onto the same cosmic truth; when we respect and engage with those perspectives, we can see a three-dimensional view of God's kingdom. Rather than offering a monologue, the Christian mission turns into a dialogue, perhaps even a multilogue, where voices once marginalized contribute to a fuller, richer understanding of the gospel message.

Polyvocality is not a mere add-on; it's essential to the mission's effectiveness. Contemplate a symphony where each orchestra section pays heed to the others; the resulting music is more than the sum of its parts. In a polyvocal approach, strategies emerge not from a single conductor but from a community of musicians. Each voice, then, becomes an active participant in the unfolding drama of redemption, making the mission agile and deeply resonant with the lived experiences of the community.

What of unity? The temptation may be to think that polyvocality encourages a form of relativism or disunity—quite the contrary. Just as a choir blends different voices into a harmonious whole, so too can a polyvocal approach foster unity amidst diversity. This unity echoes the prayer of Jesus himself—that all may be one, even as Christ and the Father are one. Polyvocality, in honoring each voice, reflects the kingdom where every tribe, tongue, and nation contributes its verse to the eternal song of the Lamb.

In an age of clamor and dissonance, polyvocality offers a model of Christian mission as a harmonious composition of many voices. It does not simply make room for multiple perspectives; it celebrates them, bringing them together in a glorious concerto that displays the manifold wisdom of God to the principalities and powers in the heavenly realms. So let the church be genuinely the church—many voices, many rooms, but one House, one symphony—each contributing its part, until all, join in the final chorus where "every knee shall bow and every tongue confess that Jesus Christ is Lord, to the glory of God the Father" (Phil 2:10–11).

Practical Ways We Can Apply Polyvocal Approaches to Ministries, Missions, and Theologies

Imagine the fascinating intricacy of a kaleidoscope—each colored piece is an essential element contributing to the grandeur of the whole. The Christian community, spread across continents, cultures, and traditions, offers us nothing less. It is a panorama of God's redemptive story, a symphonic tale told in many tongues through many lives, each contributing to the harmonious chorus that sings of Christ's redeeming love.

How, then, do we do justice to this vast plurality? How can the individual pieces of glass in this kaleidoscope, these myriad voices, not merely exist alongside each other but interact, learn, enrich the whole, and reflect a brighter, clearer image of Christ? This is where polyvocality becomes instrumental, not as a superficial nod to diversity but as a necessary, indeed crucial, theological and practical stance.

In ministries and missions, the "polyvocal" approach makes space for a richer dialogue—nay, a symphony—where each orchestra section takes turns leading the melody. In concrete terms, this could mean fostering community dialogues that aren't merely perfunctory but deliberately curated to ensure a representative mix of voices. Leadership teams—those groups often tasked with setting the agenda and tone of ministry—must mirror the complexity and breadth of the communities they seek to serve. By doing this, we construct platforms where every voice is valued, promoting a fuller sense of unity and collective ownership.

Picture the pulpit not as a monologue station but as a dialogue hub, where sermons are more than single-stream articulations of faith, but conversational forums enriched by diverse theological perspectives, themes, and cultures. Even more, envision small group settings where believers from various walks of life explore Scripture together, each lens contributing to a fuller picture of the divine narrative.

The canvas gets even broader when we turn our eyes to mission fields. Here, polyvocality means more than the integration of local styles of worship or architecture. It means an active, intentional engagement with local communities to discover what the gospel looks like in their cultural milieu. Partnerships with local churches and organizations are not optional add-ons but foundational for a mission that doesn't just speak but listens, learns, and loves.

The polyvocal approach manifests in a willingness to transcend boundaries in the scholarly avenues of theology and missiology. Imagine scholarly dialogues enriched by voices from the favelas of Brazil, the bustling streets of Lagos, and the serene monasteries of Eastern Orthodoxy. Each context offers new windows to glimpse facets of God's self-revelation. These exchanges allow the global church to examine the richness of its diversity, thereby forming a more complete theological picture.

In a world clamoring for the gospel, the tasks ahead may seem daunting: drafting inclusive policies, forming interdisciplinary collaborations, and establishing global networks. But consider these not as hurdles but as valuable elements, contributing to the broader realization of God's kingdom on Earth.

POLYVOCALITY

So, let the church rise to the symphony of polyvocality, each voice cherished and critical. For in this harmony, we don't merely hear the sounds of unity in diversity; we hear the very heartbeat of God, communicating through God's people, drawing all things unto Godself in a cosmic crescendo of redemption and love. As each voice finds its place in this heavenly melody, we discover the beauty of a faith that is ever ancient, ever new, and as multifaceted as the One who is its Beginning and End.

Table 4.1. Fifteen Qualities of Polyvocality

1. Diverse Voices: Incorporating and recognizing a range of voices and perspectives from different backgrounds, cultures, and experiences.
2. Cultural Sensitivity: Acknowledging and respecting the diverse cultural contexts of the communities being served fosters mutual understanding.
3. Inclusive Decision-Making: Involving diverse individuals in the planning and implementation phases ensures that multiple viewpoints are considered.
4. Acknowledgment of Context: Valuing local communities' unique circumstances and perspectives ensures relevant and meaningful engagement.
5. Active Listening: Prioritizing a culture where all voices are genuinely heard and respected rather than passively acknowledged.
6. Equitable Participation: Creating structures that ensure every person has a fair opportunity to contribute to discussions and decisions.
7. Empowerment: Enabling local communities to own and participate in the mission rather than imposing external solutions.
8. Continuous Learning: Fostering an environment where diverse voices and experiences contribute to all participants' collective growth and understanding.
9. Unity in Diversity: Demonstrating how different voices can collaborate towards a shared goal, reflecting the diverse yet unified body of Christ.
10. Conflict Resolution: Encouraging open dialogue among diverse voices to resolve misunderstandings and conflicts fosters a climate of peace.
11. Flexible Implementation: Allowing adaptability in strategies based on the diverse needs and voices of the communities served.
12. A Platform for Marginalized Voices: Providing specific opportunities for marginalized groups to express their perspectives and have their voices amplified.
13. Interfaith, Intercultural, Ecumenical Dialogue: Dialogue and learning across cultures, religions, and traditions.
14. Training and Education: Educating members about the importance of diversity and inclusion enriches the organization's culture and approach to polyvocality.
15. Theological Richness: Encouraging a deeper and more nuanced understanding of Scripture and theological concepts by inviting diverse interpretations, broadening the collective knowledge base.

Polyvocality: Concluding Reflections

The twenty-first century is a time in which the world, its cultures, languages, and even its challenges are a click away. We are akin to those ancient sailors who, with wide eyes and audacious hearts, discovered new lands and new people. Today's explorers, however, chart a sea of digital information and a land of social complexities. The question that looms large for us—those of us sailing in the waters of Christian ministry, mission, and theology—is how to adapt our age-old navigational skills to this brave new world.

The time for monovocality—a single voice calling out in a chamber that echoes only its timbre—is past. Indeed, one might argue it was a distorted period, for the Body of Christ, that glorious yet diverse community, is intrinsically polyvocal. Like a choir that combines the rustic baritone, the soaring soprano, the robust alto, and the harmonious tenor, the church must affirm each voice's unique quality while creating a celestial harmony.

In ministry and leadership, this means breaking free from a monocentric orbit. The gravitational force must not rest on a single point—usually the pulpit—but should instead be a dynamic interplay among the many. To be polyvocal is to acknowledge and affirm that every voice has a sanctified resonance. This is not mere inclusivity for its own sake, but a means of sacred assembly designed to foster a potent sense of belonging and nourish the spiritual growth that thrives in rich soil and under the care of many hands.

Shift now your gaze to the arena of Christian mission and intercultural work. Here, too, the melody should be a polyphonic composition. It is all too easy to project onto others a mirror of our understanding, but what is needed is a kaleidoscope that refracts light in manifold directions. Listening—authentic listening—to the diverse voices of the communities we engage with can transform our mission strategies from neo-colonial impositions to life-affirming acts of service, lovingly calibrated to the timbre and tempo of each locale.

What of theology and missiology? These aren't merely academic disciplines, but rich schools of thought nurtured through collective insight. Visualize a roundtable where Augustine converses with Luther, Aquinas listens to Barth, and voices from the Global South, the East, and the margins join all. Such a polyvocal orchestra could create a theological symphony of dazzling timbre and harmony, infinitely richer for its diversity.

But let's not be naive: incorporating multiple voices is a demanding endeavor, requiring far more than a mere opening of doors. It requires an internal reconstruction of our hearts and minds. It involves the humility of stepping back, the courage to invite others forward, and the wisdom to know when to speak and when to listen. True polyvocality is not a matter of ticking boxes but a significant, soul-searching commitment to the full spectrum of God's rainbow-hued family.

As you think about the early Christian communities, you find a microcosm of what we envision here. Those first gatherings were far from monolithic; they were, indeed, the seedbeds of a rich, polyvocal faith—a cacophony of fishermen, tax collectors, Roman citizens, and renegade Pharisees, all transformed by a shared story, a shared meal, a shared mission.

For those of us marching to Zion in this interconnected age, polyvocality isn't merely an option; it's an imperative echoing from the essence of the triune God who created, redeemed, and sustains us. It is as necessary as the compass for the sailor, as the North Star for the lost. It is the melody that, if sung in harmony, will enable us to consider and respond to the complexities of a world yearning to hear the song of God's love anew. In this divine music, every voice—yes, every voice—is indispensable.

Study Questions

1. Polyvocality means "many voices and perspectives contributing, valued, and heard." What difference does this make to Christian worship, theology, and mission?
2. How would you define polyvocality in a simple sentence?
3. How does Pentecost lead to polyvocal approaches to church and mission?
4. "Polyvocality can be a powerful tool for fostering unity within diversity. Encouraging dialogue and collaboration among diverse voices can help build bridges of understanding and cooperation within the global Christian community." Do you agree with this statement? Why or why not?
5. Would you add anything to the "fifteen qualities of polyvocality," and what would that be? Or would you modify the wording of any of the qualities in any way?
6. Why is it important to listen to historically silenced voices and ensure their contributions are valued?

5.

Interculturality

The Fourth Paradigm Shift

To speak of intercultural theology is to invite ourselves into a vast, richly decorated room adorned with artistic works from every corner of the globe. In this room, echoes of ancient prayers resound in multiple languages, hymns in myriad musical styles rise like incense, and the collective wisdom of centuries fills the air. Intercultural theology is not a new venture but a rediscovery of the grand diversity inherent in the pursuit of the Divine.

"Unity in diversity" is the underlying motif in this complex composition. Picture a musical score where each line represents a different culture. Far from being a cacophony, this is a symphony of intertwined narratives, each one singing out its unique theological insights, rituals, and practices. The phrase "unity in diversity" captures this opulent, polyphonic discourse. Here, the Western canon doesn't drown out other voices but learns to sing harmoniously, creating a richer, more textured chorus.

Christian ministry is the hand that lifts the conductor's baton, channeling this theological harmony into concrete action. Here, the ethereal becomes tangible, the transcendent immanent. As hands wash feet and bread is broken, the grand concepts of intercultural theology become daily acts of love and kindness, stretched across the chasms of language, ethnicity, and history. In doing so, we do not merely disseminate ideas but incarnate God's love in ways that speak eloquently to every cultural context.

The globalizing cadence of our age amplifies the urgency of this endeavor. Cultures no longer reside in isolated rooms but intermingle in a complex dance of influence and adaptation. Misunderstandings can easily occur on this crowded dance floor, but so too can new forms of beauty, enriching our collective understanding of the Divine. Intercultural theology serves as the choreographer, leading us through the steps that honor each culture's unique rhythm and grace, even as we move in unison.

What we are describing, then, is nothing less than a divine symphony, a heavenly chorale sung by a multicultural choir. Each voice, each culture, and each tradition brings its distinctive timbre and pitch, and the resulting harmony is richer for this very diversity. We are not creating a plain, single-colored picture, but a vibrant and detailed mosaic where each piece adds to a larger, more intricate image. Far from diluting our faith, this intercultural dialogue deepens it, enriching our palette of spiritual wisdom. We begin to see God not as a local deity confined to our limited understandings but as the God of all nations, peoples, and languages—a God whose love knows no borders, whose grace recognizes no outgroup.

In a world that too often celebrates division, intercultural theology is an act of holy resistance. It rejects the narrative of "us versus them" and instead invites us into a grander story—one where we are coauthors and collaborators, crafting a narrative of unity in diversity. Here, the particularities of culture and tradition aren't obstacles but gateways to a deeper understanding of God and, in turn, a more profound love for our neighbor. Thus, each of us, in our language and tradition, with our unique gifts, contributes to this ongoing act of Divine worship, adding our voices to God's magnificent, intercultural symphony.

Biblical and Theological Foundations for Intercultural Mission and Ministry

Consider the magnificent narrative arc of Scripture, from the initial brushstrokes of Creation to the cosmic denouement in Revelation, and discover therein the striking themes of intercultural mission and ministry. To fail to discern these themes would be akin to admiring a grand cathedral while ignoring its foundational stones. These elements form the foundation of God's grand design, articulating his boundless affection and radical inclusivity for all humanity across the spectrum of cultures and epochs.

Genesis, the grand overture to God's cosmic symphony, commences with a motif that resounds throughout the ensuing movements: every human being, in all their cultural and ethnic variegation, is an image-bearer of

God—the imago Dei. The theological cornerstone thus laid allows no room for cultural discrimination; rather, it beholds in every face, every lifestyle, every cultural nuance, a facet of God's dazzling creativity.

But Genesis isn't content merely to establish a principle. As the narrative unfolds like the opening of ancient scrolls, the offspring of the primeval family burgeon into diverse peoples, tribes, and tongues (Gen 10). Far from a tragic episode, The Tower of Babel catalyzes God's grand plan to diversify and then gloriously reunify humanity in a magnificent act of new creation.

Old Testament texts offer yet more hues to this emerging picture. Consider Abraham, called to be a blessing to "all families of the earth" (Gen 12:3), or Jonah, reluctantly learning that God's mercy extends even to the Assyrians of Nineveh. The implication is unambiguous: the God of Israel is also the God of the nations.

In the New Testament, Jesus emerges as a Jewish messiah and the World's True Lord. Observe him as he strides across cultural, societal, and religious boundaries, treating Samaritans and Roman centurions with the same regard as his Jewish brethren. In each crossing, Jesus offers not just tolerance but full-bodied engagement, a redemptive love that transfigures social norms. Consider his conversation with the Samaritan woman at the well. This exchange serves not just as cultural critique but as revelatory dialogue, offering living water that quenches the deepest thirsts of humanity.

The book of Acts demonstrates the early church as a microcosm of this expansive, border-defying love. From the cacophonous beauty of Pentecost, where Parthians, Medes, and Elamites hear the wonders of God in their tongues, to the Jerusalem Council, where cultural sensitivity wins the day, we glimpse a community that is not merely multi-ethnic but gloriously intercultural.

Paul, that indefatigable apostle, takes up this theme like a skilled composer introducing a recapitulation. "There is neither Jew nor Greek," he asserts, "for you are all one in Christ Jesus" (Gal 3:28). This isn't merely an erasure of cultural identities but their fulfillment, the many becoming one without losing their many-ness.

The culmination of this divine symphony, of course, finds its finale in the book of Revelation. Here, John's apocalyptic eye glimpses a throng comprised of every tribe, tongue, and nation, praising God in a multitude of languages and styles. The eschatological confirmation is that God's love, grace, and redemption are as vast as the earth and as diverse as its people.

To speak of intercultural theology and ministry is to engage with the very heartbeat of the biblical narrative. This is not a side issue, a theological eccentricity, or a cultural fad. It is central, essential—indeed, indispensable—to fulfilling the church's mandate in an ever-shrinking world.

Understanding God through the rich prism of global cultures enriches our shared spirituality, deepens our corporate wisdom, and broadens the reach of God's inexhaustible grace. Far from diluting the faith, intercultural mission enhances it, seasoning it with spices from every conceivable cultural kitchen and thus preparing a banquet at which all may feast and find it good.

Intercultural Approaches are Reshaping all Fields

Intercultural thought and practice have introduced seismic shifts into the very heart of human disciplines. Once fragmented and ignored, it is as though a grand, beautiful mosaic is finally coming together to reveal an incredible design that is greater than the sum of its parts. From the descriptive texts of anthropology to the penetrating scrutiny of psychology, from the poetic narratives of literature to the ethical canons of economics and sociology, and yes—reaching even the lofty towers of theology and ministry—the intercultural discourse is sweeping through like a gust of fresh wind, reinvigorating, illuminating, harmonizing.

In anthropology, luminaries like Clifford Geertz and Franz Boas have reoriented our gaze.[1] No longer can we, with colonial hubris, judge the diversity and expressions of human cultures through the narrow lenses of our societal norms. Their advocacy for cultural relativism has sounded like a clarion call, urging us to approach different cultures with the humility of learners, not the arrogance of judges.

Sociology, that keen observer of human interaction, has also felt the stirring of this wind. Scholars like Stuart Hall examine the nuances of cultural identity and hybridity, providing a grammar to articulate the rich complexity that emerges when cultures intersect, converse, and blend.[2] Amartya Sen, that meticulous economist, invites us to reconsider our economic development paradigms, to approach them not as universal mandates but as culturally inflected human activities, each with its validity and vitality.[3]

In literature, wordsmiths like Chimamanda Ngozi Adichie create stories not shackled to a single cultural setting but dance freely across boundaries, defying neat categorizations.[4] Such narratives beckon us to uphold a broader understanding of human experience that strikes a chord with the diversity of a global world.

1. Geertz, *Interpretation of Cultures*; Boas, *Race, Language, and Culture*.
2. Hall, *Representation*.
3. Sen, *Development as Freedom*.
4. Adichie, *Half of a Yellow Sun*.

Psychology has not been left untouched. Consider Urie Bronfenbrenner's ecological systems theory, which resounds like a hymn to the cultural ecosystems shaping human souls.[5] Think, too, of Geert Hofstede, who challenges us to account for cultural dimensions when scrutinizing human behavior, lest we impose monolithic standards upon the world's kaleidoscopic diversity.[6]

Let us not forget theology, that ancient discipline, pondering God and humanity. Liberation theologians like Gustavo Gutierrez and feminist voices like Rosemary Radford Ruether have burst onto the stage, calling for a re-examination of theological discourses shaped predominantly by Western minds.[7] Their works serve as prophetic reminders that God's image is reflected not in a single culture but in the multiplicity of global human experiences.

Similarly, in missiology and ministry, thinkers like Lesslie Newbigin and Andrew Walls counsel us to cultivate a gospel expression that is both transcultural and contextual, advocating not for a bland uniformity but for a rich assortment of Christian witness.[8] Emmanuel Katongole's theology of diverse cultural expressions further enriches our models of ministry, leading us toward the promise of a genuinely intercultural fellowship.[9]

Indeed, these shifts are not merely academic curiosities; they bear the weight of urgent necessity. For we find ourselves in a world where the barriers between "us" and "them" are crumbling, and in their place, God is fashioning a human family ever more interconnected and interdependent. In such a world, the intercultural approach doesn't just enrich our intellectual and spiritual endeavors; it becomes the sine qua non for human flourishing, mutual understanding, and the unity our fractured world desperately needs. This, I submit, is a movement of the Spirit, sweeping us into an era of global empathy, broadened understanding, and deepened love. So let us ride this wind, for it carries the fragrance of the kingdom.

---

5. Bronfenbrenner, *Ecology of Human Development*.

6. Hofstede, *Cultures and Organizations*.

7. Gutierrez, *Theology of Liberation*; Ruether, *Sexism and God-Talk*.

8. Newbigin, *Gospel in a Pluralist Society*; Walls, *Missionary Movement in Christian History*.

9. Katongole, *Sacrifice of Africa*.

Fields and Disciplines that Have Shaped Intercultural Theory, Theology, and Missiology

We stand at the nexus of intersecting disciplines, each contributing its distinct hue and pattern to our understanding of the human story. At this riveting crossroads of intercultural theory and theology, a profound dialogue unfolds, illuminating the cavernous depths and scintillating surfaces of cultural interaction with a brilliance akin to the dawning sun illuminating a multi-faceted diamond.

Just behold how cultural anthropology, with guiding stars like Clifford Geertz and Margaret Mead, plunges like a deep-sea diver into the oceanic richness of human cultures.[10] With each return to the surface, they offer us pearls of wisdom about cultural relativism and human behavior, invaluable gems that set the stage for the dramatic play of intercultural dialogue.

Turn your eyes to cross-cultural psychology, where scholars like Harry Triandis and Shalom Schwartz operate as keen cartographers, meticulously mapping out the psychological backdrops carved and molded by cultural forces.[11] They give us the contours and elevations, the mountains and valleys of the human mind as influenced by its cultural climate, contributing thereby a vital topographical layer to our exploration.

Nor should we overlook social psychology, where luminaries like Muzafer Sherif and Gordon Allport unfold the drama of social interaction as though they were master playwrights.[12] They bring us face-to-face with the realities of group dynamics and prejudice, adding tension, conflict, and resolution to the narrative of intercultural encounters.

The discipline of sociolinguistics, championed by the likes of Dell Hymes and Deborah Tannen, unfurls before us like a great scroll, where each line and letter tells the story of how we speak, how we communicate, how we understand and misunderstand each other across the boundaries of culture and community.[13]

This parade of disciplines marches forward with intercultural communication specialists like Edward T. Hall and Richard Wiseman, who serve as our skilled interpreters, parsing out the enigmas of verbal and nonverbal signals, the subtleties and complexities of dialogues that crisscross geographical and psychological terrains.[14]

---

10. Geertz, *Interpretation of Cultures*; Mead, *Coming of Age in Samoa*.
11. Triandis, *Culture and Social Behavior*; Schwartz, *Cultural Values*.
12. Sherif, *Robbers Cave Experiment*; Allport, *Nature of Prejudice*.
13. Hymes, *Foundations in Sociolinguistics*; Tannen, *You Just Don't Understand*.
14. Hall, *Silent Language*; Wiseman, *Intercultural Communication*.

PART 1: PARADIGM SHIFTS IN WORLD CHRISTIANITY

Let us also tip our hats to scholars of discourse analysis, figures like Judith Butler and Norman Fairclough, who remind us that language is not just a tool but a living and evolving reality in which power dynamics and identities are constructed, deconstructed, and reconstructed.[15] They challenge us, with prophetic urgency, to consider how our words not only reflect but create our world.

Among these noble disciplines, let us not forget postcolonial theory and studies, with Homi Bhabha and Gayatri Chakravorty Spivak acting as its heralds.[16] They peer into the painful but illuminating interstice between colonizer and colonized, pulling from it insights that demand a reconstruction of history, an acknowledgment of the lingering imbalances of power, and a call for authentic voices to be heard.

Intersectionality, as articulated by Kimberlé Crenshaw, adds yet another brushstroke to our canvas, exposing the intertwined lines and shapes of gender, race, and class that together form the complex identity of individuals and communities in our pluralistic world.[17]

Now to the domain of intercultural theology—where the sky meets the earth, the human meets the divine! There, figures like Kwok Pui-Lan and James H. Cone invite us into an expansive theological environment, asking us to consider how each culture might cast its light upon the eternal, adding nuance and depth to our understanding of God, justice, and liberation.[18]

Within this expansive chorus, other voices join in. From missiology, cultural studies, globalization studies, migration and diaspora studies, feminist and womanist theologies, to Indigenous studies—each field, each scholar, each insight becomes a note in a harmonious yet complex melody, contributing to a symphony of understanding that is at once rich, deep, and infinitely varied.

What we are witnessing is nothing short of a profound renaissance in intercultural theory and theology—a breathtaking expansion that welcomes the contributions of disciplines as varied as the stars in the night sky, yet each shining its light on the great mystery of human existence. This is an urgent task, for as our world shrinks through technology and grows through diversity, understanding the layered complexity of intercultural interactions is no longer a luxury but an imperative.

---

15. Butler, *Gender Trouble*; Fairclough, *Language and Power*.

16. Bhabha, *Location of Culture*; Spivak, *In Other Worlds*.

17. Crenshaw, *On Intersectionality*.

18. Kwok, *Postcolonial Imagination and Feminist Theology*; Cone, *Black Theology of Liberation*.

INTERCULTURALITY

As we stand at the crossroad, beholding the insights offered by myriad disciplines, we must, as stewards of the gospel and God's wisdom revealed in Christ, exercise both discernment and caution. The enticements of theories like intersectionality, discourse analysis, sociolinguistics, and the like offer potent lenses, often revealing blind spots in our comprehension, illuminating the places where tradition or oversight have cast shadows. Yet, it is imperative that we not be swept away uncritically by the currents of their underlying premises. Some of these theories, while keenly insightful, are rooted in frameworks that are distinctly humanistic and occasionally atheistic in orientation. Their premises, if unchecked, can lead us astray from the anchor of divine truth. They are, after all, human constructs, and like all human endeavors, they are susceptible to the frailties and biases of their progenitors.

In our laudable pursuit of deeper understanding, we must never lose sight of a foundational tenet of biblical interpretation: that its locus is not primarily in the multifaceted reading communities of today but in the original intent of the inspired authors. The vast array of disciplines and methodologies described herein are not ends in themselves but rather heuristic tools instrumental in guiding us ever closer to the heart of the sacred text. While these tools help us bridge the chasm between our contemporary milieu and the ancient world of the Scriptures, we must always resist the temptation to mold the text to fit our contemporary agendas, worldviews, or cultural sensibilities. Instead, we must allow the text, in its divine wisdom, to mold us.

In this breathtaking dance between text and interpretation, between ancient intent and contemporary insight, we tread the delicate balance of fidelity and exploration. While we deeply value the rich contributions of each discipline and the insights they bestow, our ultimate allegiance is to Jesus Christ, and our commitment must be to a faithful interpretation of sacred narratives and texts according to the original intent of their authors. Thus, let us engage these tools with humility and discernment, ever seeking the true heart of the message, ever aspiring to discern the presence of the Divine amidst the chorus of human voices. Only then can we genuinely aspire to glimpse the expansive kingdom that beckons, a realm where every voice, every insight, and every soul finds its true resonance within the eternal symphony of God.

The Deficiency of Monocultural Approaches to Theology, Literature, Biblical Interpretation, Ministry, and Missions

We find ourselves at a significant juncture in the road where the old maps won't do anymore, where the compass needles of yesterday's theologies and methodologies waver uncertainly. We are led to reconsider and re-examine the well-trodden paths of monocultural approaches that have been worn into our collective academic and spiritual cultures and traditions. What a constellation of scholarly endeavors brings to our attention is not just a critique but a clarion call—a call for a new cartography in the lands of theology, literature, biblical interpretation, ministry, and missions.

Paul F. Knitter jolts us from our religious parochialism with his work, *The Myth of Religious Superiority*.[19] He beckons us to consider, perhaps uncomfortably, that the God who called Abram out of Ur has always been a God of manifold revelations, always communicating his name in languages that transcend our theological lexicons. Knitter's argument for an intercultural theology is like a prophet's voice in the wilderness, saying that we must treasure the particularities of all religious contexts to find the universal.

Turn we must to Neil Ten Kortenaar's compelling study, *Postcolonial Literature and the Impact of Literacy*.[20] The insufficiencies of a Eurocentric literary hermeneutic stand revealed as ancient scrolls unfolded to the light of day. He makes a passionate plea for a lens ground and polished in the workshops of intercultural dialogue. This lens allows us to see the myriad shades and colors of the text, which our old monocles rendered only in black and white.

Now comes R. S. Sugirtharajah, wielding his *Postcolonial Criticism and Biblical Interpretation* as a plow that breaks the hardened soil of biblical exegesis.[21] How can we understand the texts of our faith, born in the cultural intersections of the ancient world, if we do not decolonize our hermeneutics? He calls for a biblical interpretation incorporating many cultural expressions, each contributing its narrative to the grand story of God's interactions with humanity.

Emmanuel Y. Lartey's work, *In Living Color*, turns the spotlight onto the stage of pastoral care, revealing the discordant notes struck when cultural sensitivity is lacking.[22] He pleads for an approach that isn't colorblind but rather color-rich, that sees each person as a work of art painted in the

---

19. Knitter, *Myth of Religious Superiority*.
20. Ten Kortenaar, *Postcolonial Literature and the Impact of Literacy*.
21. Sugirtharajah, *Postcolonial Criticism and Biblical Interpretation*.
22. Lartey, *In Living Color*.

palette of their cultural, historical, and personal experiences. Such an approach, he argues, is not just pastoral; it is deeply incarnational.

Then we have Andrew Walls, a historian who serves as a kind of physician diagnosing the ailments of our missionary endeavors. In *The Missionary Movement in Christian History*, he invites us to reimagine missions as a two-way street, a dialogue where every culture is not just a recipient of, but a contributor to, the Christian story.[23]

What these voices collectively shout from the rooftops is the grand imperative to welcome and champion the intercultural as the very essence of our human and divine engagements. No longer can we afford the luxury of monochrome visions in a polychromatic world. The richness of humanity's experience of the divine, the infinite shades of meaning in our stories, the multiple textures of our collective journey towards wholeness—they all cry out for an approach that values the distinct yet interconnected cultures, wisdom, and perspectives of what we call human civilization.

So, let us heed these scholarly trumpets as they announce the dawn of a new day in our various disciplines. Let us lay down the monocles of our monocultural pasts and pick up the kaleidoscopes of an intercultural future, where each shifting pattern, informed by diverse perspectives, reveals anew the manifold wisdom of God. As we lean into this grand narrative, we move closer to a kingdom vision, a symphony of redeemed cultures singing in harmonious diversity. Indeed, the God who made the many one at Babel and Pentecost calls us to a similar oneness today—a oneness not of uniformity but of harmonious, intercultural unity.

Shifting from Monocultural (and Merely Contextual and Inculturation) Approaches to Intercultural Ones

The ground we tread upon—this rich soil of Christian theology, missiology, missions, and ministry—has for too long been cultivated with the tools of a limited toolbox. Those tools—monocultural, contextual, inculturation approaches—are by no means unworthy; indeed, they have their merit. But they have sketched a one-dimensional view of a stunningly multi-dimensional cosmos of divine and human interaction.

The monocultural vista, often with the best intentions, functions like a garden tilled and sown by one pair of hands, from one tradition, and in one style. The fruit of that garden may be sweet, but it is often just one kind of fruit, bereft of the rich variety that the wider earth can offer. Then we have the contextual and inculturation models, like gardeners who, realizing

23. Walls, *Missionary Movement in Christian History*.

the limitations of monoculture, have decided to add new plants to their plots—but always on their terms, transplanting them in ways conditioned by a single, dominant perspective.

But then we come to the burgeoning promise of intercultural approaches—those glorious meeting places where divine gifts distributed across the breadth of humanity can be gathered and shared, like a potluck feast where every dish is both a revelation and a treasure. Intercultural theology is not the elevation of one choir to sing the hymns of heaven but a heavenly chorus where each voice, imbued with the unique timbre of its cultural richness, adds to the harmonious praise of the God who is both One and All.

Think about it; God's image, the *imago Dei*, is refracted in the multitude of cultural lenses human civilization has produced. Each lens can provide a unique focus on the God who remains ineffably beyond all our categories yet imminently involved in each cultural narrative. It is not merely an exercise in academic breadth but a sacred calling to listen to the manifold ways God's voice has reverberated across the spectrum of human experience.

When we turn our eyes to missiology and missions, the embrace of interculturality marks nothing less than a Copernican revolution. Gone are the days when the "Christian West" could consider itself the unmoving center of the universe, around which all other cultures must orbit. No, the celestial dance is far more elaborate and far more beautiful, with each culture not merely receiving but also contributing to the understanding and living out of the gospel of Jesus Christ. Thus, the missions field transforms into a fertile ground for reciprocal engagement, a banquet of heavenly food where all are guests and hosts.

If theology and missions are the words and sentences of God's love letter to the world, Christian ministry is the penmanship, the tangible script, the living expression. Intercultural ministry listens before it speaks; it learns before it teaches. It regards everyone as made in the image of God, etched in the hues of culture, history, and personal journey.

So, let us not be mere spectators but active participants in this grand transformation. The clarion call is sounded; the urgency is palpable. In a world humming with the melodies of manifold cultures, the transition to intercultural approaches is not a luxury but a necessity, not a trend but an imperative. As we heed this call, we may find that the multi-dimensional environment we cultivate will yield a more equitable and inclusive church and a foretaste of the kingdom where every tongue, tribe, and nation will find its home. In this intercultural vision lies the promise and potential for a more robust, vivacious, and expansive expression of the Christian faith for today and future generations.

Shifting from Merely Missional Approaches to Intercultural Ones

Missional theology is a phrase that has stirred the hearts of the faithful, reminding us that the church is not a static entity but a dynamic movement participating in the *missio Dei*, God's grand and glorious mission for the world. There is something enthralling about it, isn't there? Like the mysterious allure of a siren's song, it calls us out of our comfortable havens of liturgy and doctrine into the choppy waters of God's broader work in the world. Yet, might we not require more than a single compass if we are to traverse these waters with wisdom?

Intercultural theology is an indispensable partner to missional theology; the two rivers converge to form a greater flow. The intercultural approach does not simply invite us to admire the vast and diverse ocean of Christian theologies; it invites us to be co-creators in God's grand design, to hold streams from different parts of the world and find the unique lakes, rivers, and oceans that emerge when they meet.

The biblical narrative itself, far from a monocultural tale, tells of a God whose mission stretches from the patriarchal tents of the desert to the multicultural turmoil of the early church in Acts, from the poetry of Hebrew prophets to the cosmic vision of a multiethnic, multilingual choir in the book of Revelation. The God of the Bible is a God who speaks many languages, embraces many cultures, and has chosen, astonishingly, to use this diversity as a central platform for divine revelation.

But let us not deceive ourselves into thinking that adopting an intercultural approach somehow diminishes our commitment to missional theology. Quite the contrary, it heightens, enriches, and vivifies it. A genuinely missional church is not a cultural imperialist, exporting a pre-packaged gospel to other lands. Instead, it is a humble learner, an attentive listener, eager to hear the word of God spoken afresh in the tongues of brothers and sisters from around the globe. It acknowledges, with humble joy, that the *missio Dei* is not about God endorsing our mission but about us joining God's mission, which, astonishingly, has been unfolding through diverse cultures long before we arrived on the scene.

Indeed, to embrace intercultural theology is to accept an invitation to a table where the menu offers dishes not of our own making, where the conversation carries accents not our own, and where the storytelling includes plots and characters we haven't encountered. It's precisely in this unfamiliar territory that we may find our theological imaginations expanded, our missional strategies refined, and our hearts warmed to the fire of God's multifaceted love for the world.

In a world as complex as ours—where borders may be lines on a map but are also often lines in human hearts—an intercultural approach to missional theology isn't merely an excellent idea. It is an urgent necessity. It is a divine mandate. It is a window into the manifold wisdom of God. As we look through this window, may we see, perhaps for the first time, the grandeur of a God who is both infinitely beyond us and intimately among us—in every tribe, every tongue, every nation. For in that grandeur lies our mission, and in that intimacy lies our hope.

Shifting from Merely White, Western, Mostly-Male, Euro-and-Ameri-Centric, and Academic Approaches to Intercultural Ones

The stories of church history are often read as though composed on parchment in monochrome ink, most of its pages penned by white, Western, primarily male hands. This is not without its virtues, for those hands have written brilliant exegeses, founded great institutions, and borne witness to Christ in far-flung lands. Yet, if we have eyes to see and ears to hear, the Spirit is stirring a palette of colors into the inkpot, adding contrast and brilliance to what was often a singular, though profound, tone. The question at the heart of this moment is not whether the old ink was adequate—indeed, it has etched indelible marks—but whether we are prepared to welcome the symphony of colors and sounds beckoning us into a richer, more complete composition.

The biblical text itself has always danced to a rhythm of diversification. From Abraham's call to be a blessing to the nations to the psalmist's cry that all peoples clap their hands and shout to God with cries of joy, the story of God has been one of centrifugal force, forever spiraling outwards. In the early church, no sooner had the ink dried on the narrative of a Jewish messiah than it had to be amended to include Cornelius, a Roman centurion, and an Ethiopian eunuch. The text practically shivers with the tension of including the "other."

Embracing an intercultural approach is not so much an innovation as a reclamation, a return to the biblical affirmation that all humans are bearers of the *imago Dei*. Each culture, each voice, and each marginalized person brings a unique and indispensable hue to our understanding of God's character. The wisdom of Western academic theology is not so much replaced as it is illuminated and complemented by the perspectives of our African, Asian, Latin American, and Pacific sisters and brothers; by the voices of Indigenous peoples; by the stories of women; and by the oral traditions that are their kind of theological treatise.

Think not that this is merely an act of courtesy, as though we simply make room on our benches and pews for these voices. No, this shift to an intercultural dialogue is transformative; it reorients us, destabilizes us in the best of ways, pulling us into a theological narrative larger and more profound than our solitary streams could fathom. It's not a mere alteration of seating arrangements at the table of discourse; it's an expansion of the menu, with new dishes and flavors enriching the feast.

Imagine a kind of ministry and mission that doesn't just echo in cathedrals and seminaries but also in bustling marketplaces, in rural farmlands, on social media platforms, in homes, and in hearts where "official theology" has seldom tread. Envision a church less concerned with policing its borders than celebrating its center, Christ himself, known more fully as we know each other.

My friends, as we stand on the cusp of an age marked by astounding global connection and perplexing dissonance, the call to intercultural theology, missiology, ministry, and missions is neither optional nor peripheral. It is central. It is urgent. To be Christian in the twenty-first century is to recognize that our theology can no longer afford to be less than as global as the gospel, as wide as the love of Christ, and as deep as God's riches, wisdom, and knowledge. It is a grand invitation to enter a more expansive narrative that celebrates the body of Christ in all its magnificent, diverse splendor. Let us, then, pen this new chapter together, each with our unique ink, all with a common hope.

Shifting from Inculturation and Contextualization to Interculturality

Much like the world it seeks to engage, the panorama of missiology and theology is not static but dynamically evolving. We stand, I believe, on the cusp of a shift as profound as it is timely, moving away from paradigms of inculturation and contextualization towards the expansive horizon of interculturality. It is a shift in strategy and imagination in our perception of how the gospel lives, breathes, and takes shape in the world.

Inculturation, the venerable predecessor, has had its moment and its merits. It earnestly sought to bridge the chasm between the gospel message

PART 1: PARADIGM SHIFTS IN WORLD CHRISTIANITY

and the expressions of local culture. The Christian faith, no longer locked within the parameters of its birth culture, was translated, adapted, and reimagined in myriad tongues and expressions. Yet, for all its noble intentions, the old paradigm was still tinged with the aftertaste of colonial legacy. It often projected a one-way trajectory: from the culturally "enlightened" to the "yet-to-be enlightened," from the missionary to the mission field. Though the message was wrapped in local attire, the gift, so to speak, came from a singular, dominant storehouse.

Interculturality emerges as both a critique and a maturation of this earlier stance. It declares with firm yet humble conviction that articulating the gospel is not the sole prerogative of any culture or theological tradition. This is not a matter of mere adaptation but of mutual incarnation. The gospel doesn't just come dressed in the clothing of diverse cultures; it lives in them, learns from them, and is enriched and deepened by them. The contours of faith are carved not by monologues but dialogues, dialogues that dare to cross boundaries, listen deeply, and be changed.

The values of this seismic shift are manifold. First, interculturality plants the flag of humility in the soil of our theological cultures and imaginations. Intercultural theology contends that the mystery of the Divine cannot be fully mapped by any single cartographer or captured within the borders of any cultural or theological framework. The Revelation of God is a vast and magnificent work, encompassing various aspects of the human experience.

Secondly, this approach opens the floor for a more genuine dialogue, a two-way street paved with mutual respect and learning. No longer are some voices "normative" while others are "contextual." All stand on the level ground before the cross, and from that holy vantage point, we listen and learn from each other. The African concept of Ubuntu can teach about community, the Indian notion of Dharma can illuminate righteous living, and the Latin American liberation theology can challenge social justice—each enriching the corpus of Christian theology in irreplaceable ways.

Thirdly, interculturality enhances its global relevance by honoring the multiple contexts in which the Christian faith is lived out. A faith articulated in many cultures speaks more fluently to many cultures. In a world crisscrossed with complexities, where identities are increasingly fluid, the gospel, expressed in a polyphony of cultural idioms, finds many more openings to incarnate its liberating, life-giving message.

The shift to interculturality is not just a new chapter in missiology and theology. It is a new volume altogether. A more equitable, inclusive, and pluralistic Christian faith awaits us, a faith that mirrors the multifaceted wisdom of God and anticipates the heavenly chorus described in

Revelation, comprised of every tribe, language, people, and nation. So let us step forward into this new milieu, pens poised, ears open, hearts attuned, to inscribe this unfolding chapter in the story God is still writing through us, with us, and, most remarkably, for us.

Contributions to Interculturality: Theo Sundermeier and "Differenzhermeneutik"

In the ever-evolving scene of theological and missiological reflection, the work of Theo Sundermeier looms both foundational and transformative. Resonating through the corridors of scholarly discourse, most notably through his seminal works *Was ist Religion?* (*What is Religion?*) and *Den Fremden Verstehen* (*Understanding the Stranger*), Sundermeier orchestrated a radical reorientation in our understanding of faith's expression and mission's aim.[24] Sundermeier conceived of a polycentric Christianity—a faith without a singular cultural epicenter but a myriad of them, each as authentic in articulating the gospel as any other. He invited us to look afresh at the mission field, not as a terra incognita to be conquered or assimilated, but as a rich portrait of perspectives and practices that can deepen and refine our understanding of what it means to follow Christ. This was not mission as a monologue but as dialogue, a mutual exchange of spiritual riches where the missionary and the community are co-learners in the unfolding story of redemption.

Here, we find Sundermeier's arresting concept of "convivence," a term borrowed from the French to evoke not merely living alongside but living together. Unlike the colonial motifs that marred much of the missionary activity of previous centuries, his vision of convivial coexistence aims at a harmonious sharing of life, an intermingling of different cultural expressions of the Christian faith. This idea opens up new vistas for intercultural dialogue and mutuality, reminding us that the kingdom of God is not a gated community but a global village.

The idea of the "other," or the stranger, is central in Sundermeier's scheme. He subverts the traditional, often patronizing, tropes where the other is often considered an object for conversion rather than a subject for conversation. Understanding precedes proselytizing in Sundermeier's missiological universe; the stranger is first a fellow image-bearer to be acknowledged and respected before becoming a conversation partner in matters of faith. Here, mission isn't so much about making "us" out of "them" as it is about discovering, together, the "we" that God intends for all humanity.

24. Sundermeier, *Was ist Religion?*; Sundermeier, *Den Fremden Verstehen.*

Hermeneutics is the interpretation of sacred texts. Regarding hermeneutics, Sundermeier carves yet another distinctive niche. His so-called "hermeneutic of difference," or "Differenzhermeneutik," moves beyond a narrowly textual and egocentric interpretation. According to David W. Congdon's detailed analysis, Sundermeier's method de-centers the interpreter, placing the diversity of 'others' we encounter in our intercultural exchanges at the forefront.[25] It's a hermeneutic approach that does more than acknowledge cultural diversity; it thrives on it. This approach celebrates difference as a source of enrichment, an opening for divine surprise.

Congdon identifies a sequence of four moves within this hermeneutical model: acknowledging, living with, understanding, and finally transcending difference. This isn't about erasing lines but learning to cross them with humility, openness, and a thirst for mutual transformation. As profound as it is, Sundermeier's hermeneutic of difference could further mature towards what Congdon identifies as an "emancipatory intercultural hermeneutic." Such an approach would not only seek to understand the other but actively engage in the work of liberating unjust structures that perpetuate division and misunderstanding.

Sundermeier's vision brings us closer to the pulsating heart of the *missio Dei*—the notion that mission is fundamentally God's mission to reconcile, heal, and transform a fragmented world. But to be faithful to this divine calling, our hermeneutics must evolve further to challenge the power structures that impede God's work of reconciliation. It must become not merely intercultural but also emancipatory.

Thus, the enduring legacy of Theo Sundermeier remains not just in the doors he opened, but in the thresholds he invites us to cross. In heeding his call to a polycentric mission, to convivence, to a hermeneutic of difference, we draw nearer to a Christianity as variegated and inclusive as the manifold wisdom of God. Yet, the journey is far from complete. As we engage with the other, as we dialogue and interpret, let us do so with an eye towards the justice, reconciliation, and liberation that the gospel of Jesus Christ not only promises but demands.

Contributions to Interculturality: Henning Wrogemann

In the burgeoning fields of intercultural theology and missiology, the voice of Henning Wrogemann chimes with the clarity and urgency of a bell rung in a sacred cloister. A seasoned theologian from the academic crucibles of Germany, Wrogemann has contributed a trove of insight, encapsulated

---

25. Congdon, "Emancipatory Intercultural Hermeneutics."

most luminously in his magnum opus, the three-volume work *Intercultural Theology*.[26] With this edifice of thought, Wrogemann reshapes the environment, urging us to perceive the Christian mission as an enterprise not bound by the geographical or cultural frontiers we often take for granted.

Wrogemann's audacious claim—that the gospel of Jesus Christ is not the property of any one culture but a universal narrative accessible to all—is a corrective lens through which we may look anew at our theologies and missiologies. Unlike the fabled prodigal son, theology, Wrogemann insists, must not remain in its Western homeland but must journey to far-off countries, there to discover a plethora of theological riches. Far from a monolithic faith articulated in the stale language of colonial residue, Christian theology is polycentric—each center, whether in the bustling streets of São Paulo or the tranquil monasteries of Kerala, offers a unique refraction of the divine Light.

Herein lies Wrogemann's significant departure from the outdated concept of "inculturation," which often conjured up images of a dominating culture imposing its faith upon a passive recipient, akin to a one-way street with traffic flowing solely from West to East. In its place, he offers the principle of "interculturality," a two-way boulevard where missionaries and local communities engage in a dynamic dance of mutual enlightenment and transformation. This is no mere modification of terms but a tectonic shift in ecclesial thought that enriches the missiological endeavor with a vocabulary of respect and reciprocity.

Wrogemann convincingly reminds us that our cultural settings tint the glasses through which we read the gospel. There is no "view from nowhere," no interpretation emanating from a supposed cultural vacuum. Instead, the gospel text becomes a living expression of meaning, shaped anew by the cultures of Addis Ababa, Seoul, or Buenos Aires. Ministry, therefore, must be an exercise in cultural hermeneutics, a sensitive parsing of local narratives, idioms, and subtexts, as we proclaim the unchanging Christ who is forever new.

Wrogemann further plows the socio-political soil of the mission field. The gospel, he argues, is not merely a ticket to a heavenly future but the charter for a transformed earthly present. Personal redemption and societal reformation are not opposing categories but twin pillars holding up the architectural marvel of God's kingdom. Mission, thus, is not complete until it addresses the crying needs of justice, peace, and reconciliation.

Henning Wrogemann's work is a veritable atlas for traversing the complex terrains of intercultural theology and mission. By highlighting the

---

26. Wrogemann, *Intercultural Theology* (three volumes).

polycentric nature of Christian theology, the dialogical essence of interculturality, the critical role of cultural hermeneutics, and the undeniable social dimension of the gospel, Wrogemann not merely gives us tools but crafts for us a new epistemological and spiritual compass. His work, crucial for such a time as this, stands as both a monument and a milestone, beckoning us to travel roads less taken in pursuit of a gospel that is as wide as the world and as particular as the person next door. It challenges us to approach theology and mission with a hermeneutic of humility, a rhetoric of respect, and a praxis of profound openness to the multiplicity of voices that make up the global choir of Christendom.

Contributions to Interculturality: Gustavo Gutiérrez and Rosemary Radford Ruether

When we stand on the threshold of the twenty-first-century church, looking both inward at our traditions and outward at the manifold challenges of our world, two resounding voices echo in the corridors of our collective theological memory: Gustavo Gutiérrez and Rosemary Radford Ruether.[27] These thinkers, pioneers in their respective terrains of liberation theology and feminist theology, offer us navigational charts for a world in flux, urging us to reconceive mission as a multidimensional engagement with cultural and existential realities.

First, let us consider Gustavo Gutiérrez, the Peruvian theologian who stormed the theological stage with his monumental *A Theology of Liberation*. Gutiérrez reinterpreted the sacred story of the gospel not as a detached celestial drama but as a divine intervention in history for the poor and marginalized. In Gutiérrez's vision, the gospel emerges not as a placid theory but as a dynamic and living organism where God's love is an active force for justice and liberation. Gone are the days of mission understood merely as a proclamation pronounced from on high. What takes its place is a ground-level mission, an earthly and gritty endeavor to transform society.

In shifting our focus from a paternalistic "doing-for" to an empowering "doing-with," Gutiérrez nudges us toward a contextual theology. He insists that our reading of Scripture and our practice of faith must be imbued with the colors, textures, and contours of our specific social and cultural contexts. This is not just a footnote but a critical thesis for intercultural theology and missiology: the conviction that divine revelation is not a monologue but a dialogue within the specificity of human situations.

27. Gutiérrez, *Theology of Liberation*; Ruether, *Sexism and God-Talk*.

As we pivot from Gutiérrez, our ears catch the compelling cadence of Rosemary Radford Ruether, whose magisterial work *Sexism and God-Talk* marks a watershed moment in feminist theology. Ruether asks us to re-examine our cherished traditions, uncovering and then dismantling the scaffolding of patriarchy that has often been mistaken for the architecture of divine truth. With her, theology becomes a kaleidoscope, refracting the image of God through a broader, more inclusive lens that includes the richness and wonder of human diversity. Like a leaven in the dough, her work enriches and expands our scope of intercultural theology and missiology.

Ruether's feminist theology brings our mission and ministry to a crucible of self-examination. It compels us to strip away the gender biases that have subtly but surely colored our missional practices, inviting us to an egalitarian table where all voices are valued, and all experiences cherished. To be genuinely intercultural and inclusive, the mission must incarnate this full spectrum of human dignity.

Together, Gutiérrez's thundering cry for a preferential option for people experiencing poverty and Ruether's incisive call for gender equality provide a robust and comprehensive framework for an intercultural theology and missiology deeply anchored in justice, equality and profound respect for the symphony of human cultures and identities. These are not mere options among many; they are categorical imperatives if our mission and ministry are to flourish in a world yearning for the redemption not only of souls but of societies. As we step into this turbulent but tremendously exciting era, let us carry with us the wisdom of these guiding lights, making our theology not just an abstract set of principles but a lived response to the groaning of creation for liberation and renewal.

Contributions to Intercultural Christian Mission and Ministry

Contemplate a grand symphony, a musical opus that has evolved over centuries. The instruments are diverse, originating from every culture and continent. Yet, they contribute to a harmonious whole, a unity in diversity that profoundly enriches our auditory experience. This, indeed, is what the theological orchestra of our era sounds like, an ensemble where each theologian plays a unique but complementary role, leading us to new horizons in understanding God's mission and the gospel message in a pluralistic world.

Think of Lesslie Newbigin as the conductor of this orchestra, his baton held aloft in *The Gospel in a Pluralist Society*.[28] With a sweeping motion, he

---

28. Newbigin, *Gospel in a Pluralist Society*.

urges us to consider the context-specific nature of the gospel and how the message of Jesus takes on varied and brilliant colors depending on the cultural milieu in which it finds itself. He banishes the notion that any culture can lay exclusive claim to understanding God's mysteries. This isn't merely an idea; it's a revelation, a cornerstone for a theology that wishes to be universal and universally relevant.

Andrew Walls steps up, his composition written in the key of "translatability." With every note, he insists that the Christian faith is a message not confined by linguistic or cultural borders, a liberating proclamation that can be made native to every context. In the magnum opus of *The Missionary Movement in Christian History*, Walls attunes us to a Christianity that is ever in flux, yet eternally the same—encouraging us to be culturally sensitive missionaries, forever adaptable to God's beloved world.[29]

Now, listen to the strident chords of Soong-Chan Rah's *The Next Evangelicalism*, urging us to shift our gaze from the Eurocentric halls where the symphony was long rehearsed towards the rhythms of the Global South.[30] Rah is like a musician introducing new, unheard instruments to the orchestra, enriching the melody by adding tonalities that were always intended to be part of the composition but were hitherto marginalized.

Emmanuel Katongole contributes a soulful melody of stories, as narrated in *The Sacrifice of Africa*.[31] His approach is like jazz; it's all about improvisation within the structure, each narrative inviting us to groove along with the astonishing ways the gospel transforms and renews even in contexts of suffering and despair.

Next comes Emmanuel Y. Lartey with pastoral care as his instrument, eloquently played in *In Living Color*.[32] He doesn't just play; he teaches us to listen and attend to the harmonies and dissonances that are part of any multicultural congregation. It's a pastoral theology that stretches our horizons and enriches our communal life.

Let us not forget the compelling harmony of Judith Gruber's voice in her work *Intercultural Theology*.[33] Gruber is like a composer insisting on a dialogue among instruments, an authentic, enriching, and indispensable conversation for a symphony that aims to be truly global. Her score is written with postcolonial ink, making us aware of the past's impact on the present dialogue, forever urging us toward an ensemble performance.

---

29. Walls, *Missionary Movement in Christian History*.
30. Rah, *Next Evangelicalism*.
31. Katongole, *Sacrifice of Africa*.
32. Lartey, *In Living Color*.
33. Gruber, *Intercultural Theology*.

Henning Wrogemann adds complexity with his three-volume work on *Intercultural Theology*, much like a fugue with elaborate layers and motifs.[34] Through *The Witness of God*, John Flett reminds us of the divine Composer behind this symphony, the God whose mission (*missio Dei*) permeates and vivifies each note and instrument.[35]

Like a skilled linguist of musical notes, Lamin Sanneh emphasizes the vital act of translation.[36] He takes the sheet music and adapts it for instruments from varied traditions, thus ensuring the gospel's tune is heard universally. R. S. Sugirtharajah, on the other hand, provides a critical accompaniment, urging us to read the sacred score through the eyes of the marginalized.[37]

The final crescendo comes with postcolonial theologians like Kwok Pui-Lan and Fernando Segovia, who challenge us to rewrite the old scores penned in the ink of imperial dominance.[38] Their work calls us to a fresh composition that incorporates the sounds and rhythms of postcolonial societies.

What emerges from this remarkable symphony of theologians is not merely discordant thoughts or isolated solos but a robust and harmonious theology. It is a theology that engages every culture and every person, urging us to listen and learn, to stretch our imaginations and deepen our compassion, to embody a faith that is as diverse as the world God so loves. This, my friends, is the majestic sound of intercultural theology, missiology, and ministry—a celestial symphony urging the church toward an ever more beautiful expression of God's creative and redeeming love.

Intercultural Approaches to Christian Mission

Imagine music so rich and varied that to describe it as a mere song would be reductive, almost dismissive. In the same way that a Mozart symphony or a Bach concerto transcends the sum of its parts—each instrument, each note, each silence contributing to a more magnificent whole—so too does the burgeoning field of intercultural missiology transcend the contributions of individual thinkers, yielding an approach to theological inquiry that is as exhilarating as it is necessary. We find ourselves in a world where the

---

34. Wrogemann, *Intercultural Theology* (three volumes).
35. Flett, *Witness of God*.
36. Sanneh, *Translating the Message*.
37. Sugirtharajah, *Bible and the Third World*.
38. Kwok, *Postcolonial Imagination and Feminist Theology*; Segovia, *Decolonizing Biblical Studies*.

ever-turbulent winds of culture, language, and history meet, creating not a storm but an invitation to translate the eternal gospel of Jesus Christ into the many and varied languages of human experience.

First, consider Lesslie Newbigin, a pioneer walking ahead with a lantern in the dense fog of our pluralist society. His seminal work, *The Gospel in a Pluralist Society*, shines with revelatory clarity.[39] For Newbigin, the gospel is not a one-size-fits-all garment but a living word, ever-ready to clothe itself in the attire of each culture it encounters. He beckons us to move beyond evangelistic tourism to a deeper engagement with the terrains we traverse. Newbigin's call is not to abandon the gospel's universal truth but to understand it as a melody that can and must be played in numerous keys.

Andrew Walls steps forward like a master linguist, fluent in the dialects of global Christianity. In *The Missionary Movement in Christian History*, he expounds upon the "translatability" of our faith, the remarkable capacity of Christianity to express its essence within the manifold expressions of human culture.[40] It's as though Walls tells us that the gospel is not merely a text to be translated but a narrative to be incarnated anew in every culture and epoch.

Enter Lamin Sanneh, our skilled translator, a steward of words and meanings. His work, *Translating the Message*, underscores the sacramental nature of language.[41] Sanneh shows us that each linguistic context contains the possibility of revealing fresh aspects of the divine narrative. He contends that translating the gospel isn't merely an academic exercise but a form of worship, a way of welcoming the Word into the diverse houses of human language.

From the lively theological setting of Africa, Emmanuel Katongole's voice rises like an evocative hymn of lament and hope.[42] His work reminds us that the mission field is not an abstract battleground but a living, breathing community often marred by the scars of violence and division. Katongole urges us to think of reconciliation as the church's mission, not as a side project but as a divine mandate. In his vision, the gospel becomes a balm applied to the open wounds of a suffering world.

Henning Wrogemann, in works like *Intercultural Theology*, plays the role of the skillful conductor, one who understands that a symphony requires diverse instruments to achieve its fullest expression.[43] Wrogemann

---

39. Newbigin, *Gospel in a Pluralist Society*.
40. Walls, *Missionary Movement in Christian History*.
41. Sanneh, *Translating the Message*.
42. Katongole, *Reconciling All Things*.
43. Wrogemann, *Intercultural Theology* (three volumes).

invites us to sit at a global theological roundtable to listen and learn from the multifaceted ways God has revealed Himself across cultures and histories. His work imbues our missiological pursuits with a humility that enriches our broader understanding of what God is doing in the world.

Then comes John Flett, with *The Witness of God*, urging us to consider anew who the true Author of this missional endeavor is.[44] Flett refocuses our energies and intentions from the human-centric enterprise to the divine initiative. In his rendering, the mission ceases to be about us and becomes, first and foremost, the activity of God—the *missio Dei*—in which we are graciously invited to participate.

Together, these luminaries form a constellation that brightens the dark skies of our theological inquiry. Their distinct and interconnected contributions cast light on the undulating paths of intercultural missiology. They beckon us to a grander vision, a larger story, a more expansive room in God's kingdom. As we heed their collective wisdom, we find ourselves standing on the shores of new theological continents, poised to translate, incarnate, reconcile, dialogue, and participate in God's ever-unfolding mission in this gloriously diverse world. That, surely, is cause for both awe and hopeful action.

Intercultural Approaches to Christian Ministry

Consider standing on the threshold of a grand cathedral—a cathedral not made of stones and stained glass but of living, breathing, cultures. Picture a worship space as broad and as varied as humanity itself, where the liturgy is spoken not in one tongue but in a cacophony of languages, each enriching the other. Intercultural ministry is that cathedral, a project not of bricks and mortar but of hearts and souls. Into this variegated sanctuary, a chorus of voices has risen, each contributing a vital timbre, a unique resonance, to the melody of God's work in the world.

Here stands Emmanuel Y. Lartey, a craftsman of words and a caretaker of souls. His *In Living Color* is a narrative that utters the soul's secret language, translating the tenets of pastoral care into the rich dialects of varied cultures.[45] Lartey's work is akin to a stained-glass window, illuminating the sanctuary of ministry with hues of cultural sensitivity. His approach to pastoral care doesn't merely adapt to the complexity of cultural identity; it revels in it. For Lartey, ministry is not just about imparting spiritual truths

---

44. Flett, *Witness of God*.
45. Lartey, *In Living Color*.

but about recognizing the fertile ground in which these truths might most deeply root and fully flower.

Across the aisle, we find Judith Gruber, a herald of dialogue and a seeker of common ground. Her volume, aptly titled *Intercultural Theology*, is a homily to the power of conversation.[46] In a world where shouting is often mistaken for theology, Gruber offers a softer but far more potent invitation: to listen and speak. She reminds us that the gospel isn't a monologue to be pronounced but a dialogue to be entered. Here, in the respectful exchange of ideas and experiences, ministry becomes not just something that one does to another but something that we co-create, a spiritual space where we learn even as we teach.

Then, there's the voice of Soong-Chan Rah, resounding like a prophetic trumpet in a chamber that has for too long been an echo of Western norms. His seminal work, *The Next Evangelicalism*, serves as a sacred disruption, a call to widen our liturgical and theological horizons.[47] Rah challenges us to see the tomorrows of Christianity not as the mere extension of its yesterdays but as a dramatic reconfiguration of its geography and demography. In urging Western Christianity to become a listener rather than merely a speaker, Rah invigorates the cathedral of intercultural ministry with fresh voices and new hymns, all contributing to the complete choir of God's people.

Thus, in the hands of these scholarly artisans, the edifice of intercultural ministry rises, magnificent in its complexity and robust in its diversity. Like finely crafted mosaics, their contributions add depth and color to our collective vision of what ministry can be. Lartey, Gruber, and Rah offer us the theological tools to construct a sanctuary expansive enough to house the kingdom of God in all its breathtaking diversity. In a world often divided by walls of misunderstanding and halls of myopic visions, their writings lay the foundation stones of a cathedral where all are welcome and where the liturgy of love is spoken in as many languages as there are lips to speak and ears to hear.

So, we find ourselves, each one of us, called to join this grand, intercultural construction project. As we heed the wisdom of these architects of the soul, we discover a shared task, a mutual mission: to build not just a cathedral of stones but a living, breathing, worshiping community as diverse, as complex, and as beautifully multifaceted as the God we all seek to serve.

---

46. Gruber, *Intercultural Theology*.
47. Rah, *Next Evangelicalism*.

INTERCULTURALITY

Respecting the Marginalized and Historically-Silenced Voices and Cultures

In the arena of God's expansive narrative, where diverse cultures and histories intersect, we encounter a burgeoning field that beckons us to don the garments of humility and openness. This emerging environment is none other than intercultural theology, missiology, ministry, and missions, and it brings us into a sacred space. A space not of mere academic curiosity but of awe, reverence, and, let me stress, vital necessity.

The task before us is not merely to inscribe the marginalized into our existing theological lexicons, as though adding extra footnotes to a long-established text. No, it's a matter of granting these voices—the historically silenced, the peripherally placed—not just a seat at the table but an equal hand in crafting the agenda. To say that no one culture has a monopoly on the comprehension of the Divine is to say that each culture, including those pushed to the margins, brings irreplaceable hues to the mosaic of God's self-revelation.

We must actively incline our ears and tune our hearts to the symphonic diversity of these voices. They are not mere echoes but distinct notes essential for the full orchestration of God's grand opus. They challenge us to scrutinize the lenses through which we have traditionally viewed our faith, to interrogate the biases and blind spots that mar our vision. Our understanding of God is enriched and expanded through this unflinching self-examination and unwavering commitment to listen and learn.

Our missiological and ministerial approaches must reflect a nuanced appreciation for the richness of context. It's not about delivering a one-size-fits-all gospel but about encountering the Other in their unique geographical, cultural, and spiritual context. It's about dignifying their experiences, histories, and aspirations; it's about walking alongside them in their pilgrimage, affirming that their struggles and triumphs possess intrinsic worth in the unfolding drama of God's salvation history.

Let's recognize that intercultural theology is fundamentally a matter of posture—a posture of humility, openness, and reverent respect. In adopting this posture, let us acknowledge that every voice, particularly those from the margins, contributes something essential and vital to God's cosmic purpose. Each voice, no matter how overlooked or undervalued, is integral in shaping a more complete and beautiful depiction of the manifold wisdom of God.

PART 1: PARADIGM SHIFTS IN WORLD CHRISTIANITY

A Summary of Intercultural Christian Leadership and Ministry

The symphonic grandeur of God's kingdom is a cacophony of voices, a garment of colors, and a bouquet of fragrances—all gathering around a single table under a single banner. This is where intercultural Christian leadership and ministry come to take their stand in a dazzlingly diverse and compellingly unified backdrop. Within this framework, this splendid kaleidoscope of God's people, the church—Christ's hands and feet on earth—begins to reflect not the dull monochrome of uniformity but the variegated brilliance of unity in diversity.

The essence of intercultural leadership is not mere tolerance or even acceptance; it is a joyful embrace of the breathtaking diversity through which God chooses to reveal God's manifold wisdom. We look out over a vast ocean of human experience and culture, and we see therein a mirror of the Divine Imagination, a Creator who sculpts in myriad forms and colors, each adding an indispensable shade to God's ever-expanding palette. Intercultural leadership is akin to being a faithful steward of this divine artistry. It creates a harmonious melody out of what could easily become discord.

Listening—truly listening—is the backbone of this intercultural foray. Listening is not an act of charity but an imperative for true understanding, as the channel through which the rivers of different perspectives flow into the greater estuary of Christian community. In a setting so fashioned, dialogues become more than just exchanges; they become sacred spaces where the Spirit breathes, knitting together a community where each soul, each voice, feels deeply seen and deeply valued.

Inclusion is not a buzzword here but the lifeblood of this ministry. The aim is not merely to give voice to the marginalized but to amplify their voices into melodies, to make their perspectives not just visible but central to the communal vision. Intercultural ministry, you see, must be collaborative at its core. This shared endeavor marries wisdom from diverse quarters into a fuller, richer, and more nuanced understanding of the Divine and our communal responsibilities.

Suppose the sin of Babel scattered and divided humanity in a cacophony of misunderstanding. In that case, the Pentecostal fire of intercultural ministry seeks to heal and reunite, forging a new language of love, justice, and reconciliation. It's a project that continually learns and unlearns, dismantling barriers and prejudices, cultivating an ethos of cultural humility, and advocating for a ceaseless transformation cycle.

Through this lens of unity among diversity, we turn to the Scriptures, always sensitive to the manifold ways different cultures might interpret them. Indeed, the core values of justice, reconciliation, and compassion are not just abstract concepts but vital themes that are essential to mission, community, and ministry.

Finally, let us understand that intercultural ministry is but a chapter in the greater narrative of *missio Dei*—the mission of God. In the expansive geography of God's kingdom, the church is called polycentric, a multiple-centered reality where leadership flows from diverse sources and a chorus of voices blend into divine harmony. Intercultural ministry, then, is less about building walls than opening doors through which a cavalcade of nations will one day enter, singing their songs and telling their stories in the renewed creation God has prepared. Thus, it becomes both a present reality and a glorious hope, a signpost pointing toward the consummation of all things in Christ. It is toward this destiny that intercultural Christian leadership and ministry unfailingly guide us.

A Summary of Intercultural Service and Mission

The sphere of intercultural mission and service is where the Christian endeavor finds itself stretched, like a canvas, on a frame far broader than many had ever envisaged. There, a fresh painting of the kingdom of God is beginning to emerge, swirling with colors and forms hitherto unknown or unappreciated. Allow me, for a moment, to bring your gaze closer to this magnificent panorama, highlighting the textures and hues that form the practical application of intercultural principles within the church's global mission.

At the very epicenter of this grand endeavor stands the commitment to cross-cultural dialogue, understanding, and collaboration. Picture it as a grand symphony in which each instrument, each note, and each chord emanate from a different corner of God's variegated world, contributing to a celestial melody that rises to fulfill the divine intention for creation. Acknowledging diverse cultural perspectives, far from cluttering the piece, adds layers of complexity and beauty that make the composition resoundingly richer.

To show respect for the integrity and wisdom of all cultures is not merely a procedural nicety; it becomes the essential element that holds together this diverse and vibrant collection. Such respect births a celebration of each unique facet of divine creativity—a jubilant acknowledgment that God's presence is not confined to our narrow constructs but is vividly reflected in each culture's distinct way of life. Central here are the virtues of empathy and the art of active listening, the fine skills of cultural navigation that turn the sea of diversity from an overwhelming challenge into a navigable and enriching voyage.

Inclusion is not a footnote but a headline. The harmonizing chord in the symphony ensures that every voice, especially those hitherto pushed to the margins, can sing loudly and clearly, adding their irreplaceable tonality to the choir. In the cauldron of intercultural mission, the false dichotomy between teacher and learner evaporates. Everyone has a chair at the table; everyone contributes to and partakes in the grand feast of wisdom and understanding.

But do not mistake this flexibility for a lack of focus. The ever-urgent call for reconciliation and justice is rooted deeply in the Christian narrative. This is not just a side issue but the heartbeat, the lifeblood of intercultural missions. It brings the confrontation of injustice out of the shadows and into the light, infusing it with a prophetic imperative that cannot be ignored.

As we step back to appreciate the full scope of this intercultural masterpiece, we observe an intriguing feature: it is polycentric and polyvocal. Gone is the old vision of missions that radiates outward from a single cultural or theological epicenter. The compass now has many needles, all valid, all simultaneously pointing towards the true North, which is the accomplishment of God's ultimate mission, the *missio Dei*. It honors the diversity of voices that read, proclaim, and live out the gospel in a thousand different idioms.

Cultural humility is the posture that best suits those who find themselves swept up in this whirlwind of divine activity. No longer the colonialist venture of a bygone era, modern missions represent an open acknowledgment that we are all learners on this pilgrim journey. We are explorers in a vast continent where even the most familiar passages of Scripture take on new shades of meaning when viewed through different cultural lenses.

What's being etched out on this sprawling canvas is nothing less than the kingdom of God in its future fullness, a kingdom not confined by language, tribe, or nation. It is a vision of unity within diversity, a vision of a family drawn from every corner of the earth, a new humanity reflecting its Creator's richness. This is the lofty yet intensely practical aim of intercultural mission and service. This aim finds its ultimate consummation in God's all-encompassing love and eternal purposes.

A Summary of Intercultural Theology and Missiology

The fertile soil of intercultural theology and missiology is a field where the seeds of profound intellectual and spiritual reflection are sown, germinating into a rich harvest of understanding that nourishes not just the individual but entire communities and cultures. Allow me to guide you through this prolific terrain, lifting the leaves and uncovering the roots of practical applications that do more than merely exist—they transform, enlighten, and embody heaven's aspirations on earth.

Intercultural theology and missiology do not merely tweak the knobs of our existing theological paradigms; they invite us to an entirely new dance floor. Each culture brings unique steps and movements here, contributing to a sacred dance that redefines our concepts of God and godly action. Each twirl and leap, every moment of hand-in-hand connection, offers an opportunity to discover yet another facet of the divine character. This ever-expanding portrait defies monochrome descriptions.

At the pulsating heart of this endeavor is the commitment to dialogue, a veritable agora of theological and missiological conversation where ideas are traded, shared, tested, and collectively celebrated. This is not a debate with winners and losers but a symposium of endless enrichment, where the collective wisdom exceeds the sum of its parts.

The notion of cultural humility, a profoundly Christian virtue, moves from the margins to the center stage. It dismantles any illusion that a single cultural perspective can monopolize the wellspring of divine revelation. Instead, the panorama of cultures stands as a living testimony to the polyphonic beauty of God's discourse, each one singing a different verse of the same hymn of cosmic love.

Inclusivity, long heralded yet often misunderstood, finds its proper form here. This is not merely a polite gesture of invitation; it is a clarion call for voices from every corner of human experience to contribute to the defining narrative of God's dealings with the world. It is a round table where the last become first, and the first is humbled to discover they are not the sole bearers of divine insight.

Challenging, then, is the task before us: to confront the idol of ethnocentrism. This insidious notion, which holds one's own culture as the arbitrator of universal norms, is subjected to the intense scrutiny of an intercultural lens. The result? The unmasking of ethnocentrism as a false deity and the revealing of a richer and more diverse expression where each part contributes to the larger pattern of divine love.

Justice is not a footnote in this enterprise; it is the caption. The pursuit of justice, entangled with power, privilege, and systemic inequities, becomes an integral component of any theology or missiology worth its salt. Thus, this intertwining of cultural awareness and the quest for justice ensures a robust and actionable framework.

PART 1: PARADIGM SHIFTS IN WORLD CHRISTIANITY

The principle of polycentricity emerges like a guiding star, casting its light on multiple centers of divine activity, making the theology and mission of the church truly catholic—that is, genuinely universal. As if responding to a celestial conductor, this polycentric view blends harmoniously with a polyvocal chorus, each voice articulating the divine in idioms that enrich the whole.

The Scriptures, that ancient yet ever-new testament to God's action in history, are approached with a sensitivity to the multicolored spectrum of cultural contexts. No longer imprisoned by a single cultural lens, these sacred texts come alive with new layers of meaning, speaking anew to every culture.

The melody of reconciliation works its way through the orchestration of these disciplines. They do not shy away from the work of building bridges across the raging rivers of cultural differences. The result? A unity that does not homogenize but celebrates the kaleidoscopic wonder of global diversity.

These disciplines are not static; they are as dynamic as the cultural settings they engage. They are an ongoing adventure, a pilgrimage towards a fuller understanding of God's ceaseless activity, what we might call the *missio Dei*. It is God's project, taking root and flourishing in every cultural context, bringing together the frayed edges of a fractured world into a vision of redemption and wholeness.

We discover a divine vision for a richly diverse yet harmoniously unified community as the triune God who stands as its source and summit. In the unfolding drama of intercultural theology and missiology, it is here that every culture finds its voice and its home, united in the joyous refrain of the kingdom of God.

Table 5.1. Ten Features and Themes of Intercultural Theology

1. Cultural Contextualization: Intercultural theology emphasizes adapting theological concepts and language to various cultural contexts. This involves translating theological ideas into meaningful and relevant terms within a specific cultural framework.
2. Cross-Cultural Dialogue: The field encourages open and respectful dialogue between different religious and cultural traditions. It seeks to foster mutual understanding, learning, and cooperation among people of diverse backgrounds.
3. Inculturation: Intercultural theology often addresses the process of "inculturation," which involves integrating Christian beliefs and practices into local cultures while preserving essential theological principles.
4. Interfaith Engagement: This aspect focuses on interactions between different religious traditions. Intercultural theology explores how theological insights from various traditions can contribute to addressing global challenges and promoting peace.
5. Postcolonial Perspectives: Intercultural theology critically examines the impact of colonialism on theology and religious practices. It considers how historical power dynamics have influenced theological thought and seeks to promote more inclusive and equitable theological discourse.
6. Liberation Theology: Many proponents of intercultural theology are concerned with issues of justice, equality, and human rights. Liberation theology, which emerged from contexts of oppression, is often intertwined with intercultural theology's aims.
7. Globalization: Intercultural theology considers the world's interconnectedness due to globalization. It examines how theological ideas and religious practices influence and respond to global processes.
8. Ethics and Social Concerns: This aspect involves exploring ethical issues from a cross-cultural perspective and addressing social challenges such as poverty, environmental degradation, and discrimination.
9. Discourse Analysis: Intercultural theology often employs discourse analysis to examine how religious and theological ideas are communicated and interpreted within different cultural contexts. This approach focuses on language, communication styles, and underlying assumptions in theological discussions. By analyzing discourse, scholars in intercultural theology can uncover hidden biases, power dynamics, and opportunities for greater cross-cultural understanding.
10. Cultural Hybridity and Syncretism: Intercultural theology acknowledges the emergence of cultural hybridity and syncretism in religious and theological expressions. These concepts highlight the blending of elements from different cultural and religious traditions to create new, unique forms of spirituality and theology. Intercultural theologians examine how these hybrid forms can enrich theological thought and contribute to intercultural dialogue.

PART 1: PARADIGM SHIFTS IN WORLD CHRISTIANITY

Practical Ways We Can Apply Intercultural Approaches to Christian Ministries, Missions, and Theologies

Envision for a moment a grand symphony; each instrument tuned not to drown out others but to contribute to a harmonious blend of melodies and counter-melodies. Such is the magnificent promise of an intercultural approach to the Christian faith—a way of life and leadership that honors the manifold beauty of God's creation, even as it reflects the harmonious unity of the Creator.

As we traverse the undulating terrains of Christian leadership, churches, and ministries, it becomes immediately evident that intercultural approaches aren't just decorative frills but essential orchestrations for God's people. Through the crucible of community dialogues, the raw ore of collective wisdom is refined. Every voice—each distinct in its timbre—contributes to the decisions that shape the direction of the church. Within leadership, diversity is not an afterthought but a forethought, an intentional arrangement that captures a fuller spectrum of God's image.

Consider the Sunday worship service—not merely a habitual gathering but a sublime theatre where heaven meets earth. Intercultural principles inspire us to incorporate hymns, liturgies, paintings, and rituals from many and diverse cultures. Through such a diversity and multiplicity of expressions, we engage in a richer, fuller adoration of the God who is entirely Other and intimately Near. Cultural exchange events become sacred spaces, vestibules of mutual discovery, fostering a profound respect for the other that dignifies and elevates each participant.

When we turn to the Great Commission to go unto all nations, the richness of an intercultural approach is like a well-traveled map, guiding missions through the complex topographies of cultural, linguistic, and religious cities and countrysides. Mission ceases to be a one-way exportation of pre-packaged theological goods and becomes a dynamic interchange. Local churches in the mission field are not mere recipients but co-laborers, mutual learners in the kingdom's vineyard. A missiological approach steeped in intercultural wisdom knows to wrap the age-old message of the gospel in the local idioms, making the good news not just heard but truly understood and felt.

In the high halls of theological and missiological discussion, intercultural principles are like the varied panes of a grand stained-glass window. When light streams through, each color contributes to a dazzling spectacle that defies monochromatic description. Multicultural exegesis, far from diluting the potency of Scriptures, enriches and animates it, much like a harmonious choir elevates a singular melody. Like experienced artisans blending hues and textures, interdisciplinary approaches intertwine insights from various fields, creating a more holistic theological enterprise that rings true with the complexities of the human condition.

The journey toward intercultural competency is not an occasional sojourn but a lifelong pilgrimage. We must be perpetually committed to learning to expand the horizons of our understanding. Global partnerships become invaluable as formal alliances and living corridors for shared wisdom and mutual empowerment. Training in cultural sensitivity becomes an educational exercise and a spiritual discipline that develops the virtues—empathy, humility, and patience—that lie at the heart of the Christian life.

Above all, we are called to be ambassadors of reconciliation and advocates for justice that transcends the petty boundaries and divisions that mar God's creation. Intercultural principles are not mere options or suggestions but divine mandates echoing the apostle Paul's sentiment: "There is neither Jew nor Gentile, neither slave nor free, nor is there male and female, for you are all one in Christ Jesus" (Gal 3:28).

Thus, in this grand symphony of life, we find that an intercultural approach does not merely tolerate diversity; it celebrates it. It doesn't merely acknowledge otherness; it learns from it. It enriches our walks with God, and collectively, it allows the global body of Christ to embody the height, depth, width, and breadth of God's unfathomable love more authentically. This love transcends all cultures even as it is immanently present in each one.

Table 5.2. Fifteen Qualities of Interculturality

1. Intercultural Leadership: Guiding and influencing Christian communities in diverse cultural contexts, fostering unity.
2. Cultural Diversity Appreciation: Valuing diversity as enriching and reflecting God's creativity rather than divisive.
3. Active Listening and Open-Mindedness: Engaging in dialogue to understand different perspectives and promoting mutual understanding.
4. Respect for Cultural Differences: Prioritizing cultural, ethnic, and linguistic differences to create a community where everyone feels valued and understood.
5. Inclusivity: Inviting historically marginalized voices and promoting equitable participation and representation.
6. Collaborative Decision-Making: Encouraging collective problem-solving and decision-making using diverse perspectives and cultural insights.

> 7. Ethnocentrism and Power-Dynamic Challenge: Breaking down cultural barriers and fostering acceptance and understanding among different cultures and using discourse analysis and other mechanisms to examine how discourse dismantles or reinforces hierarchies, biases, assumptions, and ethnocentricities.
> 8. Cultural Humility: Continuously learning from encounters with others, being open to transformation through interaction.
> 9. Dynamic Adaptation: Adapting to evolving cultural contexts while rooted in gospel principles.
> 10. Intercultural Competence: The ability to interact, communicate, and build relationships effectively across cultures.
> 11. Contextually Sensitive Biblical Interpretation: Understanding and interpreting the Bible (and theology and other texts) considering cultural contexts to avoid imposition.
> 12. Reconciliation and Justice: Healing divisions, promoting fairness, confronting injustice, and fostering unity in diversity.
> 13. Polycentric and Intercultural Vision of the Church: Recognizing diverse centers of leadership and influence rather than a single dominant center.
> 14. Polyvocal Church: Welcoming diverse voices that enrich understanding of God and the church's mission.
> 15. Reflection of *Missio Dei*: Embodying God's mission by inviting all cultures and people into a loving community and the kingdom.

Interculturality: Concluding Reflections

The world is replete with varied textures, hues, and colors, each distinct yet interconnected, each contributing to the splendor of the whole. To see this world brimming with an endless diversity of cultures, faiths, and perspectives and yet to insist upon a singular, monolithic approach to theology and missiology is to partake of the tragic irony of standing before a masterpiece and praising but a single element, note, or brush stroke.

In the complex and interconnected universe God has lovingly crafted, the notion that intercultural theology is merely a "nice to have" becomes anachronistic and deeply incongruous. No, it is not an optional ornament but an urgent imperative. Far be it from us to reduce the manifold richness of Divine love to the narrow scope of a single culture, language, or interpretive lens. We are summoned to explore, to venture into the mosaic of insights, stories, and Divine footprints scattered in every culture and community.

You see, the love of God isn't provincial; it's cosmic. The Divine narrative is not a soliloquy but a grand, intertwining dialogue. In this epic, every culture, every race, every person has a role, a line, and a crucial part to play. To overlook this is not just an intellectual mistake but a spiritual shortcoming. It denies the polyphony of voices that bring us closer to the fullness of understanding the Divine—an understanding ever elusive, ever mysterious, yet ever enriched by the multiplicity of human experiences.

Imagine the faith stories that percolate in corners of the globe you may have never set foot upon. These narratives, often buried beneath the loud cacophonies of dominant cultures, are like hidden gems waiting to be discovered. Through the lens of intercultural theology, we do not merely give these sidelined voices a microphone; we give them a cathedral. It is not just the understanding of God that grows richer with their inclusion; it is also our comprehension of humanity's astonishing resilience, boundless creativity, and immeasurable capacity for love and transcendence.

What of Christian missions? Here, too, the intercultural imperative beckons us toward transformation. No longer can we be content with exporting a faith package wrapped in the paper of our own culture and tied neatly with the string of our preconceptions. An authentic mission involves a dialogue, a reciprocal exchange of gifts, and a holy conversation where listening is as sacred as speaking.

Something akin to a new Pentecost occurs when intercultural sensibilities infuse our ministries and communities. No longer confined, stale, or insular, we become, instead, dynamic and expansive, our eyes opened, as if for the first time, to the kaleidoscopic richness of the world God so loves.

So, let us revisit and resolutely espouse the central realization: intercultural theology and practice are not optional extras but the lifeblood of a faith that wishes to be truly global and truly Christian. As we open ourselves to this brimming diversity, we move closer to the heart of the gospel and, perhaps for the first time, begin to fathom the boundless dimensions—the breadth, length, height, and depth—of the love of God that surpasses knowledge (Eph 3:18–21). Herein lies our calling, our challenge, and our unbounded opportunity.

PART 1: PARADIGM SHIFTS IN WORLD CHRISTIANITY

Study Questions

1. I've summarized interculturality as "unity in diversity, embracing all cultures." How would you define intercultural theology in a simple sentence?

2. "Intercultural theology is about choosing harmony instead of assimilation, equality instead of superiority, and diversity instead of uniformity." Do you agree? Why or why not?

3. How do Acts 2:1–13, Acts 15, and Rev 7:9 shape our vision of intercultural mission, ministry, and theology?

4. Why are monocultural approaches to theology, church, and mission deficient? How might monocultural approaches entrench colonialism and cultural superiority?

5. The chapter discusses the shifts from mission, contextual, and Western-centric approaches to intercultural ones. Why are these shifts significant? What other shifts must we make?

6. Which of the "fifteen qualities of interculturality" are resisted by churches and Christian institutions and why? How do we move from resistance to a commitment to intercultural vitality?

6.

Integrality

The Fifth Paradigm Shift

IN A WORLD OF kaleidoscopic diversity and unfathomable complexity, a world where glimpses of beauty jostle with pangs of sorrow, where the breath of the divine echoes through the corridors of human endeavor and yearning, the call to integral mission emerge not as a simple "task" of the church but as its very lifeblood, its existential core. This is no small matter, for the authentic voices of global Christianity resound with a melody that sings not merely of "doing" but quintessentially of "being."

When Vinoth Ramachandra speaks of integral mission as touching the church's integrity, he draws our attention to insight as profound as it is transformative.[1] This is not merely a matter of ecclesial function but of ontological substance. The church, that mysterious and paradoxical blend of the human and the divine, stands in the world not merely as an agent of specific "activities" but as a living embodiment of the kingdom whose ultimate coming we await even as we witness its partial yet poignant inbreaking in the here and now.

To say that our mission must be "transformational and integral" is to acknowledge that the goal is nothing less than the renewal of creation itself, a theme present throughout the grand narrative of Scripture. The redemption for which we yearn and towards which we labor is not confined to isolated pockets of personal experience but is as wide as the world, as

---

1. Ramachandra, "What Is Integral Mission?"

high as the heavens, and as deep as the human heart. It seeks to touch and transform not merely individual souls but communities, not only spiritual realities but also social, economic, and ecological structures.

To be committed to an integral mission is to be drawn into the holistic character of God's redemptive plan, a plan as replete with implications for justice, culture, and relationship as it is with the promise of personal salvation and sanctification. This is the pulsating heart of the church's integrity: to be a community where "doing" flows organically, inevitably, and joyfully from "being," where the boundaries between sacred and secular blur in the dazzling light of a gospel that refuses to be confined; where the love of God and the love of neighbor are so deeply entwined that they can hardly be told apart.

So, we find ourselves back where we began, with eyes opened wider, hearts enlarged, and hands more ready for the work. Integral mission is not an add-on, a second step, or a strategy. In truth, the church is authentically what it was always meant to be: the foretaste and herald of a kingdom where justice rolls down like waters and righteousness like an ever-flowing stream. In this grand endeavor, integrity is not merely a virtue but a vocation.

Integrality can be captured in the phrase, "whole gospel, whole church, whole world, whole life." The church has integrity when it aligns its social justice and proclamation, its peace-making and teaching, its compassion and advocacy, its public and private practices, its actions and preaching, and its passion for humility, mercy, love, truth, compassion, and justice. Ramachandra says, "Integral mission is then a way of calling the church to keep together, in her theology as well as in her practice, what the Triune God of the Biblical narrative always brings together: 'being' and 'doing,' the 'spiritual' and the 'physical,' the 'individual' and the 'social,' the 'sacred' and the 'secular,' 'justice' and 'mercy,' 'witness' and 'unity,' 'preaching truth' and 'practicing the truth,' and so on."[2]

The "Micah Declaration on Integral Mission" defines *integral mission* (*misión integral*). Christian leaders, activists, and theologians from all over the world gathered to draw up this declaration. Here is some of what it says:[3]

> Integral mission or holistic transformation is the proclamation and demonstration of the gospel. It is not simply that evangelism and social involvement are to be done alongside each other. Rather, in integral mission our proclamation has social consequences as we call people to love and repentance in all areas of

---

2. Ramachandra, "Integral Mission," 45–46.
3. Micah Network, "Micah Network Declaration on Integral Mission."

life. Our social involvement has evangelistic consequences as we bear witness to the transforming grace of Jesus Christ.

If we ignore the world we betray the word of God, which sends us out to serve the world. If we ignore the word of God, we have nothing to bring to the world. Justice and justification by faith, worship and political action, the spiritual and the material, personal change and structural change, belong together. As in the life of Jesus, being, doing and saying are at the heart of our integral task.[4]

Integral mission is focused on human flourishing, freedom from oppression, and the renewal of all creation.

The Lausanne Movement defines integral mission this way:

> Integral mission is defined as 'the task of bringing the whole of life under the lordship of Jesus Christ' and includes the affirmation that there is no biblical dichotomy between evangelistic and social responsibility in bringing Christ's peace to the poor and oppressed. This was further clarified at the 2001 meeting of the Micah Network in Oxford as 'the proclamation and demonstration of the gospel,' emphasizing that it is not simply the issue of evangelism and social involvement being done alongside each other but rather that 'our proclamation has social consequences as we call people to love and repentance in all areas of life' and that 'our social involvement has evangelistic consequences as we bear witness to the transforming grace of Jesus Christ.'[5]

Mission that is truly *integral* is always *transformational*. Orlando Costas says that transformational mission always includes proclaiming, discipling, mobilizing, growing, liberating, and celebrating. These "make up the church's mission-in-life."[6] These things are always expressed in the local, messy, everyday realities of people and their churches, families, and neighbourhoods.

Transformation, in the words of Vinay Samuel, "is to enable God's vision of society to be actualized in all relationships, social, economic, and spiritual, so that God's will may be reflected in human society and his love be experienced by all communities, especially the poor."[7] *Mission as transformation* (another way of talking about integral mission) combines

---

4. Chester, *Justice, Mercy and Humility*, 19–21. See also Ma and Woolnough, *Holistic Mission*.

5. Lausanne Movement, "Integral Mission."

6. Costas, *Integrity of Mission*, xiii.

7. Samuel and Sugden, *Mission as Transformation*, ii.

evangelism and social action, secular and sacred, theory and practice, personal and communal, and more. By bringing all these things together, integral mission honors local communities and their specific concerns, frees people from oppressive use of power, enlivens people's spiritual and social lives, and inspires people to strive for God's kingdom of peace, reconciliation, love, justice, and solidarity.

Integral mission leads us to care for (to include and to be led by) the poor, marginalized, outsider, broken, and those on the periphery. Costas says we share in Christ's suffering "by serving . . . the poor, the powerless, and the oppressed."[8] Outside the gate, we "become apostolic agents in the mobilization of a servant church toward its crucified Lord, outside the gate of a comfortable and secure ecclesiastical compound."[9]

Biblical and Theological Foundations for Integral Mission and Ministry

In our Savior's divine revelation—stretching from Genesis, where creation hums with its first song, to Revelation, where the music of new creation swells—the themes of integral mission are developed intricately, deeply, and ineluctably. This is not merely a mission of words or deeds but a holistic enterprise that courses through the veins of biblical literature and the narrative of salvation history. Indeed, the mission embodies the complex harmonies of a symphony composed by the Maestro, with a sweeping range that attends to the spiritual and societal dimensions of human experience.

The ancient Scriptures speak to us not as a dissonant cacophony but as a harmonious composition in which law, wisdom, and prophecy share their melodies. In the Torah, God's covenant with Israel is neither solely a spiritual pact nor a mere social contract. It is both. It is an encompassing portrait of legislation that attends to the alien, the widow, the orphan—the marginalized of society—while also creating a hallowed space where the name of the Lord is revered and worshiped. Here, in the fiery discourse of Sinai, in the poetic justice of Deuteronomy, we hear the first refrains of integral mission.

As we move through the grand arc of Israel's narrative into the wisdom literature, we discover that the Psalms and proverbs are not just pious devotions divorced from earthly concerns. Instead, they are the merging of heaven and earth, spirituality and justice. The same voice that sings, "The

---

8. Costas, *Christ Outside the Gate*, 172.
9. Costas, *Christ Outside the Gate*, 194.

INTEGRALITY

Lord is my shepherd," also cries out for justice for the oppressed, displaying an intimate intertwining of spiritual devotion and social ethics.

The prophetic corpus is replete with this same theme. Think of Micah, who distills the divine demands into three profound imperatives: "Act justly, love mercy, and walk humbly with your God" (Mic 6:8). This is not spirituality sans social justice or social justice sans spirituality; this is a confluence of both, a testament to God who demands proper worship and right relationships.

Then, in the fullness of time, comes Jesus of Nazareth. In him, the themes of integral mission find their epitome, their most authentic expression. His ministry is both proclamation and demonstration, a gospel that is heard in his teachings and seen in his acts of compassion. Jesus's beatific vision, his inauguration of God's kingdom, is not an ethereal, other-worldly reality; it is a radical, transformative vision that touches all aspects of human existence—spiritual, physical, and social. In his profound and paradoxical teachings, compassion for the needy, and challenge to the powers that be, we see a vivid revelation of integral mission unfolding in his life, death, and resurrection.

What of the early church? It was a community animated by the Spirit, where the proclamation of the apostles and the breaking of bread were inseparably linked to the sharing of possessions and ensuring that none among them were in need. The epistles of Paul and other New Testament letters amplify this theme: faith and works, belief and behavior, personal piety, and public duty—these were not antinomies to be held in tension but facets of a singular, glorious gem. Paul's complex theologies are not lofty speculations but grounded ethics and transformative doctrines that shape individual lives and collective communities.

The Bible ends, but the song is not over. The book of Revelation paints a vivid mural where the vision of a new heaven and a new earth showcases the completeness, the integrality, of God's redemptive plan. It is a vision that spans from cosmic restoration to personal redemption.

So then, integral mission is not a modern invention but an ancient, biblical imperative. It is a rich symphony with diverse movements but a single Composer. It is a dance where both soul and body, individual and society, heaven and earth, are invited to partake in God's grand choreography of redemption and restoration. It calls us not to be mere spectators but participants in this divine drama, where the Creator is both the Author and Finisher, the Alpha and Omega. Thus, to live out the call to integral mission is to join in God's work and become co-laborers in a vineyard that extends as far as the curse is found and as close as the human heart. It is, in essence, to become the people of God, living out the life of Christ in the power of the Spirit for the sake of the world.

Organizational Contributions to Integral Mission and Theology

In the contemporary confluence of Christian theology and practice, several organizations have played key roles in shaping our understanding and application of integral or holistic missions, theology, and ministry. Their diverse resources and initiatives have created a resonant impact, emphasizing the synergy between evangelism and social responsibility, personal transformation, and societal change.

One of the foremost among these is the Lausanne Movement. Born from the International Congress on World Evangelization in 1974, this global network operates on the belief that all life is an extension of God's realm. The foundational document of the movement, known as "The Lausanne Covenant," underscores the entirety of the world as both the realm of God's actions and the context for our missionary endeavors. Further refining this perspective, subsequent declarations from the movement, notably "The Manila Manifesto" and "The Cape Town Commitment," shed light on the essence of a holistic mission. These documents champion the interconnectedness of evangelism and societal responsibility.[10] See also the Lausanne "Integral Mission" statement.[11]

Another significant contributor is The International Fellowship of Evangelical Students (IFES). Dedicated to fostering a holistic form of discipleship among global students, IFES's initiatives pivot on dual transformation: the transformation of individuals and the transformation of societies at large. Through its resources, IFES emboldens students to integrate their faith into diverse life facets and become active community contributors.

INFEMIT, or The International Fellowship of Evangelical Mission Theologians, have also enriched the discourse on integral theology and mission. Their "Transformation" publication series is a wellspring of contextual and holistic theological insights.[12] Through their consistent endeavors, INFEMIT propounds a mission encompassing spiritual, societal, and environmental dimensions.

---

10. Lausanne Movement, "Lausanne Covenant," Lausanne Movement, "Manila Manifesto," Lausanne Movement, "Cape Town Commitment."
11. Lausanne Movement, "Integral Mission."
12. See the INFEMIT *Transformation* journal.

The Micah Network, a collective of global Christian entities, champions the cause of integral missions. At the heart of their advocacy is the "Micah Declaration on Integral Mission," a profound clarion call urging the church to embody a gospel that resonates holistically in proclamation and action.[13]

Tearfund, originating from the UK, is an example of integrating holistic missions in tangible developmental efforts. This Christian relief and development agency's publications underscore the indispensability of adopting comprehensive strategies for poverty alleviation and societal development.

Lastly, World Vision, recognized as one of the world's leading Christian humanitarian organizations, exemplifies an integral mission. Their child-centric approach encapsulates holistic ideals, integrating community development, disaster response, and advocacy.

The invaluable contributions of these and other organizations to integral missions, theology, and ministry cannot be overstated. Their foundational documents, operational blueprints, and dedicated initiatives present invaluable insights. These insights collectively uphold the integral approach, epitomizing a gospel that harmonizes proclamation with social intervention and personal spiritual journeys with broader societal metamorphoses.

Scholarly Contributions to Integral Mission and Theology

In a panorama painted with the vivid colors of the human experience—interwoven cultures, clashing civilizations, yet united in a quest for the Divine—we find theologians whose minds have ventured into the deep forest of integral mission and theology. They may not all name it thus, but their pioneering spirit has expanded our intellectual horizons and molded our collective understanding of an integrated, holistic expression of faith, mission, and ministry.

Integral (holistic) mission, theology, and ministry have been significantly shaped by the contributions of Latin American scholars, practitioners, pastors/priests, and authors. These influential figures, with their diverse contexts and experiences, have provided rich insights and challenged the global church to embody a more holistic gospel. These scholars include C. René Padilla, Samuel Escobar, Ruth Padilla DeBorst, Elsa Tamez, Oscar Romero, Leonardo Boff, Jon Sobrino, Maria Clara Bingemer, Ivone Gebara, Nancy Elizabeth Bedford, Marcella Althaus-Reid, Pope Francis, and Gustavo Gutiérrez. These and many other Latin American contributors have

---

13. Micah Network, "Micah Declaration on Integral Mission."

PART 1: PARADIGM SHIFTS IN WORLD CHRISTIANITY

significantly shaped our understanding of integral mission, theology, and ministry. Their writings, teachings, and lived examples have underscored the inseparable link between the gospel proclamation and the pursuit of social justice, enriching Christian mission with a holistic perspective.

With its diverse blend of cultures and traditions, North America has contributed a wealth of voices to understanding integral (holistic) mission, theology, and ministry. Scholars, practitioners, pastors, and authors from various ethnic and cultural backgrounds have provided distinct perspectives enriching these discourses. These scholars include Ron Sider, Ruth Haley Barton, Soong-Chan Rah, Justo L. González, Ada María Isasi-Díaz, Richard Twiss, James Cone, Emilie M. Townes, Elisabeth Schüssler Fiorenza, Stanley Hauerwas, and Al Tizon. These figures have enriched our understanding of integral mission, theology, and ministry through their unique contributions. They underline the essentiality of incorporating diverse voices and perspectives in developing holistic Christian practice, underscoring the intersection of the gospel with all facets of human reality.

With their rich historical and cultural heritage, Eastern and Western Europe and the United Kingdom have contributed various influential figures to developing integral (holistic) missions, theology, and ministry. Scholars, practitioners, and authors from this region, regardless of their diverse ethnic and cultural backgrounds, have provided unique perspectives and insights that have significantly enriched these fields. These scholars include Jürgen Moltmann, Elisabeth Behr-Sigel, Kallistos (Timothy) Ware, Lesslie Newbigin, Simone Weil, Eberhard Arnold, Christine Schenk, Pavel Florensky, Dumitru Stăniloae, and Andrew Walls. These figures and their diverse contributions illustrate the depth and breadth of holistic thought in European theology and mission. Their work highlights the need for a broad understanding of the gospel that engages with the fullness of human life and the wider creation. This involves the proclamation of faith and commitment to social justice, ecological stewardship, communal living, and inclusivity.

Rich in cultural and religious diversity, the Middle East has been a fertile ground for developing integral missions, theology, and ministry. This region's scholars, practitioners, and authors have significantly contributed to these fields. Their insights, shaped by their unique cultural and sociopolitical contexts, have broadened our understanding of holistic missions. These scholars include Mitri Raheb, Elias Chacour, Martin Accad, Mona Mowafi, Najla Kassab, Naim Ateek, Atallah Mansour, Grace Zoghbi, and Isaac Munther. These individuals' diverse backgrounds and contributions significantly enhance our understanding of integral missions. Their work, deeply rooted in their unique contexts, calls the global church to engage holistically with issues of justice, peace, and reconciliation, affirming the gospel's transformative power for all dimensions of life.

Africa, a continent with a rich cultural heritage and unique Christian traditions, has birthed numerous scholars, practitioners, pastors, and authors who have contributed significantly to understanding integral missions, theology, and ministry. These scholars include Desmond Tutu, Mercy Amba Oduyoye, John Samuel Mbiti, Emmanuel Katongole, Benezet Bujo, Allan Boesak, Musimbi Kanyoro, Rene August, Kwame Bediako, Gillian Bediako, Lamin Sanneh, Tite Tiénou, John Azumah, and Femi Adeleye. Through their diverse contributions, these figures illustrate the robust nature of African engagement with integral missions. They underscore the importance of considering cultural, socio-political, and gender realities when articulating theology and carrying out Christian missions, reflecting a profoundly contextual and holistic understanding of the gospel's transformative power.

Asia, with its rich diversity of cultures, religions, and social complexities, has produced an array of scholars, practitioners, and authors contributing significantly to the understanding of integral mission, theology, and ministry. These individuals' work, deeply embedded in their contexts, helps the global Christian community understand God's work holistically in diverse Asian settings. These scholars include Kosuke Koyama, Vinay Samuel, Siga Arles, Choi Hee An, Athena Gorospe, Simon Chan, Wati Longchar, Hwa Yung, Melba Padilla Maggay, and Vinoth Ramachandra. These Asian voices provide a robust and diverse perspective on integral mission, theology, and ministry. They help construct a more comprehensive understanding of God's work, where the gospel's transformative power interacts dynamically with life's socio-cultural, economic, and ecological aspects. Through these contributions, the church can better engage with the challenges and opportunities presented in various Asian contexts and, further, in the broader global arena.

The diverse region of Oceania, comprising Australia, New Zealand, and the Pacific Islands, has produced a variety of scholars, practitioners, and authors who have significantly contributed to our understanding of integral mission, theology, and ministry. These scholars include Charles Ringma, Ross Langmead, Randall Prior, Jione Havea, Tracey McIntosh, Upolu Luma Vaai, Anne Pattel-Gray, and me, Graham Joseph Hill. These individuals, representing parts of Oceania, have shaped the understanding of integral missions by highlighting the need for holistic approaches to theology and ministry that respect and engage with diverse cultural contexts. Their contributions continue to widen the global church's perspective, helping it to address complex social, economic, and ecological challenges from a faith perspective.

With its rich history, cultural diversity, and complex socio-economic realities, the Caribbean region has offered critical voices that contribute to understanding integral mission, theology, and ministry. The unique experiences of Caribbean people—marked by colonialism, diaspora, and a montage of African, Indigenous, Asian, and European influences—inform these scholars' and practitioners' distinctive holistic perspectives. These scholars include Kortright Davis, Lewin Williams, Anna Kasafi Perkins, Dieumeme Noelliste, Ashley Smith, Marjorie Lewis, and Ivelaw Griffith. These Caribbean scholars, practitioners, and authors bring invaluable perspectives to integral mission, theology, and ministry, informed by the region's rich cultural diversity and historical experiences. Their contributions shape theological and missiological approaches within the Caribbean context and add to the global Christian discourse, encouraging the church to think holistically about its mission in diverse contexts.

Indigenous and First Nations scholars and practitioners from various backgrounds have greatly enriched our understanding of integral mission, theology, and ministry. Their unique perspectives, formed by their cultural contexts and historical experiences, contribute significantly to the global Christian discourse on holistic mission. These scholars include Ray Aldred, Randy Woodley, Anne Pattel-Gray, Terry LeBlanc, Richard Twiss, Brooke Prentis, Mark Charles, Tāwhiao Matutaera Pōtatau Te Wherowhero, Rangi Mātāmua, Atama Paparangi, Eleazar López Hernández, Aida Spencer, and the work of Daniel Oscar Plenc. These Indigenous and First Nations leaders have significantly contributed to understanding and practicing integral mission, theology, and ministry. They challenge traditional Western perspectives and call for an inclusive approach that respects and values Indigenous voices and experiences. Through their work, they continually remind us of the diverse, multifaceted nature of the global church and the importance of engaging with this diversity in our mission practices.

The Problem of the Word "Mission"

In Christian history, the word "mission" has come to occupy a curious, albeit often painful, space. The term itself, laden with echoes of imperial ambition and paternalism, has often signaled not simply the proclamation of the gospel but an agenda of domination. Within its scope lies a manifold history: one of noble intention, yes, but also, quite lamentably, of cultural eradication, coercion, and a multitude of colonizing sins.

INTEGRALITY

Many bear the scar tissue of the word, particularly those whose ancestries are inextricably tied to the story of colonized or Indigenous worlds. To them, "mission" does not merely invoke the heralding of the gospel of Jesus; instead, it recalls the displacement of ancestral wisdom, the annexing of native spiritualities, and the calculated desecration of established ways of life. The missionary zeal, which set forth from European shores with Bibles and crosses, often concealed beneath its garments the sword of empire, aimed at consolidating territories and suppressing indigenous civilizations under the banner of "civilization" and "true faith."

The memory of this cannot be disregarded, and it looms large in conversations about what it means for the church to be engaged in today's world. Language, after all, is never mere vocabulary; it is the custodian of memory, the conveyor of meaning, and the instrument of our collective imagination. What, then, are we to do with this fraught term, heavily embroidered with a narrative that too often resembles Barabbas more than Jesus?

The Scriptures offer a treasury of alternatives, words unburdened by the oppressive baggage that the term "mission" might carry for some. Consider "ministry," a term resounding with the rhythm of humble service, a term that evokes the washing of feet rather than trampling upon souls. Or think of "fellowship," a word signifying the lives of a community bound together in mutual support, service, and responsibility. The Greek term "Apostolos," from which we derive "apostolate," lends itself well; it signifies a sending, divine commissioning free from imperial ambition.

In the vocabulary of faith, we discover words like calling, commission, apostleship, witness, discipleship, service, stewardship, and testimony—each term replete with dimensions of divine assignment and purpose. They, too, originate from the biblical narrative, and like many facets of a finely cut gem, they refract the mission of God in its richness and variety.

By employing these terms, we are not merely playing with words. Instead, we exercise theological recalibration, refocusing our work in the world around the figure of Jesus, who did not consider equality with God something to exploit but emptied himself in service to all. This is not merely a cosmetic change; it is an act of repentance, a turning away from the colonial shadows that have long marred the face of Christianity. It becomes an embracing of a language of compassion, reconciliation, and hope—a language deeply embedded in God's story about the world.

Forsaking the term "mission" in favor of these others may be a way to show the gospel's ability to self-examine, reform, and offer a balm for the wounds inflicted in its name. It is to commit to a narrative of redemption, not just for those who believe but for the words that articulate those beliefs. So, let the church be ever mindful of its language, remembering that what we say and how we say it are integral to the unfolding, redemptive melody God is composing in our midst.

A Summary of Integral Christian Leadership and Ministry

In the diverse Christian ministry and leadership scene, an emerging paradigm—integral, holistic, deeply incarnational—beckons us to realize the kingdom of God fully. The Bible's most central messages inform and vivify this integral vision. This is a model that recognizes no dichotomy between the sacred and the secular, the spiritual and the physical. It speaks to us of an interconnected reality shaped and sustained by a God who is equally concerned with the sighs of the soul and the groaning of creation, the hunger for justice, and the ache for community.

Within the contours of this integral leadership, we find a robust recognition of the human person in all their glorious complexity: body, mind, and spirit. The leaders who emerge from this environment are not mere managers of religious affairs. No, they are curators of community, architects of spaces where individuals—irrespective of race, gender, or social standing—find themselves welcomed, just as they are and yet invited to become more than they dreamed they could be.

It is a leadership inflamed with the passion for justice, a white-hot yearning to see the societal scales tip away from systemic inequalities and towards the divine equilibrium of shalom. They do not merely raise their voices in sanctuaries but in the public squares, challenging the institutions that perpetuate injustice. In the most profound sense, they recognize that justice is not peripheral to the gospel but is the fruit of a gospel-rooted tree.

Let us not forget their allegiance to the earth itself. With hands dug into the soil, integral leaders know that spiritual vitality is intertwined with ecological responsibility. As stewards of God's creation, they consider the world with an ecological sensibility, understanding that the groaning of creation is not disconnected from the groaning of marginalized communities. They champion the sanctity of the earth as if their souls depended on it.

In embracing a diverse and global church, these leaders become students of culture, savoring the rich feast of languages, customs, and expressions that adorn the body of Christ. Theirs is not a monochrome ministry but a living, Christ-glorifying, and diverse expression drawn from the myriad expressions of human experience. Following Christ's footsteps, they embody servant leadership, treading the towel and basin path, elevating others over themselves, and empowering communities to become fully active in their transformation.

Theological rigor and reflection undergird their actions. These are not individuals who have merely inherited a stale, unexamined faith. They engage theologically with a broad array of perspectives, entering dialogues that are both stretching and enriching, modeling a deep and wide gospel.

Above all, their commitment to spiritual formation is more than a tagline; it's the core of their mission. They inspire souls to journey deeper into the mystery of God, not as solitary pilgrims but as a community bound for glory. They are the epitome of resilience and adaptability, with practices transparent and ethical, their very lives a parable of the gospel they preach.

In essence, the integral Christian leader stands as a torchbearer, guiding us toward a horizon where the love and justice of God are not just topics for Sunday sermons but are as real and as palpable as the bread and wine on the communion table. This integral vision is nothing less than a foretaste of the coming kingdom, an invitation to live here and now as if God's future has already begun. Indeed, in the lives and communities transformed by such leadership, perhaps it already has.

A Summary of Integral Christian Mission

The concept of "mission," in all its multifaceted splendor and challenge, beckons us into a grander vision of what Christian faith might mean for the world—a vision deeply rooted in the essence of the gospel yet expansive enough to envelop the full range of human experience. An integral Christian mission does not simply linger at the sanctuary's doors, waiting for the world to enter. Instead, it bursts forth into the highways and byways, the marketplaces and courtrooms, and the classrooms and chatrooms, propelled by God's relentless love and justice.

One finds the gospel proclamation at the heart of this paradigm. The ancient message of divine love, redemption, and renewal resounds anew, daring to speak its truth in a cacophonous world. However, let us not be misled; mere words do not exhaust the mission's breath. It manifests its vital force through decisive action, challenging the oppressive systems that stifle human flourishing and daring to envisage—and enact—a world where justice rolls down like waters and righteousness like an everlasting stream.

Mission is not a rigid structure but a dynamic organism revealing and displaying the varying cultural narratives and local exigencies. It listens before it speaks and understands before it acts. Diversity is not a problem to be solved within its embrace but a glorious reflection of God's creativity and goodness that enriches our collective journey toward the kingdom.

Regardless of background or status, each person becomes a treasured actor on the stage of God's unfolding drama.

In an era of ecological catastrophe, this mission also extends its care and concern to non-human creation. The world is not merely a stage for human action but a complex network of relationships, of dependencies and reciprocities, that calls out for wise stewardship and sustainable living. The integral mission understands that the earth is not merely the Lord's footstool to be used and abused but his creation to be loved and nurtured.

Empowerment stands as one of the mission's load-bearing pillars. This is not a ministry of handouts but hand-ups and handshakes—partnering with communities, organizations, and churches to build a future where all can flourish. Dialogue infuses and enriches through these efforts, as the mission is as much about reconciling humanity to each other as it is about reconciling humanity to God.

Marked by its nimbleness, the integral mission dances with the ever-changing tunes of global symphonies, evolving and adapting but never losing sight of its core convictions. Sustainability is not a buzzword here, but an urgent imperative, and the wisdom of local cultures is not trampled on but treasured and integrated.

In the public square, this mission does not shy away. Driven by the gospel's countercultural message, it aims to be salt and light, speaking truth to power and forming communities where the marginalized find a home and every human being is honored as an image-bearer of the divine.

Joy, the most infectious of Christian virtues, saturates this endeavor, echoing the celestial celebration over one sinner who repents, over justice that is done, over creation that is cared for, and over communities that are healed. Resilience is not merely admired but cultivated, knowing that the mission field is also a battlefield, and we are not promised an easy victory.

An integral Christian mission does not content itself with half-measures or partial visions. With its many diverse yet harmonious facets, it seeks to be a living expression of God's expansive love, a testimony to divine justice, a bearer of transformative power—a mission that reaches into the very marrow of human existence, offering healing where it is hurt, hope where there is despair and abundant life where there is decay. In this mission, we glimpse what the church can be for the world and what God has always desired the world to be—a home filled with God's children, living in love and justice, harmony and peace.

INTEGRALITY

A Summary of Integral Christian Theology and Missiology

In the labyrinthine corridors of thought where Christian theology and missiology intertwine, one may glimpse a doorway, not so much hidden as simply unopened, beckoning us to enter an even deeper understanding of God and God's cosmic, redemptive purposes. When one dares to cross the threshold into the world of integral theology and missiology, what awaits is a portrait painted in vivid hues of revelation and nuanced shades of praxis. This synthesis aims to sanctify the soul and the entire created order.

Central to this fascinating convergence is a gospel that refuses to be compartmentalized. Ah, the integrated gospel, a glorious diptych in which spiritual salvation and societal transformation are inseparable panels, illuminating each other. It insists that one can hardly speak of reconciliation with God without contemplating its societal implications and outflow into justice, compassion, and communal well-being. This calls for a profoundly contextual theology sensitive to the ambient cultures, histories, and social dynamics. To read the Bible here is to listen for the harmonics that reflect and profile local experiences, concerns, and hopes.

Yet the vista of God's mission, as envisaged by integral theology and missiology, extends far beyond the individual or societal. It encapsulates a full-throated call to social justice, an unwavering commitment to stewarding the earth—God's beloved creation—and an earnest engagement with the variegated cultures and ideas that make up our global village. This wholistic mission recalls the incarnation itself, where the divine chose not mere visitation but proper habitation, profoundly immersing in the texture of human existence.

Aspiring to global Christian unity, integral theology steers clear of a flat homogenization of religious expression and theological thought. It envisions a symphonic unity rather than monophonic—a unity enriched, not endangered, by diverse interpretations and missional engagements. The subject of reconciliation is no mere appendage to this theological project; it forms the keystone. This includes reconciliation between God and humanity, diverse peoples, and even between humanity and the natural world.

Intrinsic to this theology is an emphasis on lifting the lowly and giving voice to the voiceless, embodying God's bias toward the oppressed and marginalized. Environmental stewardship is not an optional appendage but integral to divine praxis, urging us to see the heavens and the earth as a theater for God's glory and a garden for God's children.

The word "participation" rings loudly within this paradigm, invoking the priesthood of all believers—a priesthood not confined to liturgical vestments but donned in the everyday attire of the committed Christian, each one called and equipped for mission. The richness of this approach further extends into its multidisciplinary character, inviting dialogue with arts and sciences, politics and economics, seeking a fuller, more profound understanding of God's intentions for the world.

Concrete action—embodied, enacted theology—is encouraged and insisted upon. Theoretical abstractions find their credibility in the soil of real-world practice, in justice initiatives, in empowering communities, and in alleviating suffering. This perspective finds a kinship with liberation theology, aligning with its unswerving focus on God's commitment to freeing people from existential Pharaohs.

Cooperation, partnership, and collaboration are not mere buzzwords but guiding principles. The integral mission engages in an open-handed ecumenism, believing that the Spirit of God breathes life across denominational lines, cultural boundaries, and organizational divides. This mission remains prophetic, holding a mirror to the powers and principalities while announcing the in-breaking of God's reign of peace and justice.

In sum, integrative theology and missiology offer an enriched, robust Christian faith that refuses to remain cloistered in doctrinal silos but spills over into every arena of human activity. They arm the church with the theological and missional artillery required for a high-stakes engagement with contemporary society, an engagement rooted in love, articulated in justice, and culminating in reconciliation. Here, theology is no longer merely the study of God but the active, living embodiment of God's attributes in a world crying out for divine touch.

Practical Ways We Can Apply Integral Approaches to Ministries, Missions, and Theologies

Within the broad canopy of Christianity, often scattered across diverging paths of practice and thought, a compelling vision of wholeness emerges. It's a vision that transcends parochial boundaries, stretches across the full spectrum of human experience, and captures the essence of God's kingdom project. This is the panorama of integral Christianity—a daring journey into a mode of being Christian that harmonizes spiritual development, societal renewal, ecological stewardship, and the clarion call to justice. Allow me to invite you to consider how these integral elements converge to breathe fresh life into Christian leadership, ministries, missions, and theology.

In leadership, the integral approach is like a magnificent orchestra where each instrument contributes its unique timbre to a symphony of wisdom and compassion. This orchestra comprises leaders whose rich diversity mirrors the multifaceted nature of God's creation and purposes. Lifelong learning becomes the sheet music, guiding their harmonious interplay. Here, theological education weds social and cultural literacy, equipping these leaders to steer the ship of faith through the swirling currents of modern complexities.

A Christ-like community, the envisioned telos of integral leadership, is not a monochrome painting but an astonishing mosaic. It actively invites the marginalized to the table, not as tokens but as co-authors of the community's unfolding story. Such leadership is not a dispassionate managerial task but an advocacy for social justice and ecological harmony, resonating deeply with the transformative heartbeat of the God of Israel and Jesus.

Ministry in this light becomes a multifaceted endeavor that hums with the energy of service, unity, and empowerment. A ministry that opens its doors to those who are hungry and asks why people are hungry in the first place. The central ethos is one of integral engagement, not merely offering fish but also teaching how to fish while questioning who owns the lake. Ecumenism flourishes, diverse Christian traditions are not merely tolerated but celebrated, and the whole person—body, mind, and soul—is cherished and nurtured.

Missions within the integral framework come alive with a full-bodied embrace of the gospel. These missions engage not only the soul but also the soil, the society, and the systems that underpin them. Cultural humility replaces colonial condescension, seeing the "other" as a bearer of God's image and wisdom. Sustainable change is shepherded by empowering local leadership, for the missionary does not come merely to "do for" but to "do with." Partnerships proliferate, shattering the hierarchical giver-receiver paradigm and replacing it with a narrative of mutual edification and a shared quest for justice.

The integration extends into the complex terrain of theology and missiology. These disciplines become not isolated territories but interactive contexts where diverse fields of human knowledge and global Christian experiences converse and enrich each other. The quest for theological understanding finds vitality in localized contexts while remaining open to corrective insights from the global Christian community. Integral theology invites the marginalized to speak, decolonizes inherited frameworks, and allows the Spirit to breathe through voices too long silenced.

Integral Christianity, in its fullest expression, thus becomes a grand story revealing spiritual depth, social transformation, and a robust commitment to justice. By embodying these elements, believers tap into a Christianity transcending national, cultural, and denominational boundaries. In this pursuit, the faith community becomes an agent of God's kingdom, a kingdom that is both now and not yet, where God's love flows like a mighty river through every facet of human and cosmic existence. It invites us into a dance where justice, peace, and joy swirl in the animated rhythm of the Spirit, reflecting God's endless, transformative love.

Table 6.1. Fifteen Qualities of Integrality

1. Transformational: Integral mission, ministry, and theology must lead to real, positive change in spiritual, social, and economic aspects.
2. Integrity: The church aligns its actions, beliefs, and practices coherently and consistently.
3. Social Justice and Proclamation: Social justice efforts are not separate but integral to the church's proclamation of the gospel.
4. Human and Environmental Flourishing: The focus is on holistic well-being and flourishing for all humanity and creation.
5. Evangelistic Consequences: Social involvement isn't just an act of kindness; it bears witness to the transforming grace and gospel of Jesus Christ.
6. Justice and Justification: Integral mission, ministry, and theology integrates the spiritual dimensions of faith with social action and justice efforts.
7. Worship and Political Action: Spiritual practice and social/political involvement are interwoven.
8. Personal and Structural Change: Both individual hearts and systemic structures must be addressed and transformed.
9. Community-Centric: Honors local communities and their specific concerns rather than imposing external "solutions."
10. Care for the Marginalized: Focus on those at the periphery of society, advocating for those experiencing poverty, oppression, and marginalization.
11. Collaboration: Works in partnership with other stakeholders like civil society, government, and the private sector.
12. Incarnational Approach: The church should embody its values, making the message credible.
13. Reconciliation: Works to bridge divides between communities, races, religions, economic classes, etc.
14. Resistance and Advocacy: Actively resists systemic injustices and advocates for those who cannot speak for themselves.
15. Sustainable Living: Encourages responsible and sustainable use of resources, freeing wealthier people and communities from the slavery of money and power and to generosity and contentment.

Integrality: Concluding Reflections

In the grand narrative of God's unfolding plan for creation—a tale robust with the divine richness of love, justice, and cosmic renewal—we discover the allure of an integral Christianity. It's as though we've been handed a marvelous gem, cut with multiple facets that refract the light in a dance of colors, each revealing an element of God's redemptive story. This gem—this integral approach to mission, theology, community, and ministry—is no mere academic concept. It is, instead, a breathtaking, holistic perspective that moves us to rediscover the profundities of the gospel of Jesus Christ, not merely as a spoken word but as an incarnate reality.

Herein lies the beauty and power of the gospel, where proclamation and action, theology and praxis, word and deed are related and unified. The integral vision compels us to see that the gospel is not a disembodied message floating above the fray of human experience but is instead grounded in the flesh and blood of daily life. It clamors for an incarnation of divine truths that permeate every fiber of societal structures, from the walls of our homes to the corridors of power. It beckons us to be narrators of God's story in a world not merely content with hearing but desperate for seeing, touching, and experiencing the gospel's transformative power.

This vision thrusts us into the heart of our local, national, and global communities with an expansive missional zeal. We are called not merely to offer spiritual solace but to bring the kingdom's leaven to all dimensions of human life: to heal, liberate, and advocate. We are summoned to look injustice in the eye, to dismantle the systems that perpetuate suffering, and to replace them with cruciform structures of grace and peace.

In this pursuit, we find that the Body of Christ is not a monolith but rather a new humanity of exquisite diversity. Integral approaches invite us to a grander table where varied voices and experiences are not grudgingly tolerated but passionately celebrated. Far from diluting our collective testimony, this diversity enriches it. We become, in essence, a living mosaic of cultural expressions and theological nuances, each contributing to a fuller portrait of God's kingdom.

As we examine integral mission, theology, community, and ministry, we do more than merely add dimensions to our faith; we deepen its hues, enrich its tones, and augment its reach. The world is watching, often skeptically, to see if this Jesus we proclaim can make any difference to the pain, the chaos, and the complexities of human life. Integral Christianity answers this challenge by embodying a faith proclaimed and demonstrated, not only personal but communal, not only heavenly but earthy.

So, this integral vision is not an optional accouterment to a pre-existing structure; it is, instead, foundational to the architecture of Christian faith for our age. It calls us to a faith as wide as the world and as deep as the human heart—a faith that rings with the ancient truths of the gospel yet relates to the urgencies of our contemporary crises. In embracing this vision, we renew our role as ambassadors of a kingdom that is both now and not yet, reflecting the multifaceted wisdom of God to a world that is crying out for truth, justice, and a love that heals all wounds.

Study Questions

1. "Integral mission is focused on human flourishing, freedom from oppression, and the renewal of all creation." Why do we need an integral mission that focuses on these things?

2. Integral mission combines "justice and justification by faith, worship and political action, the spiritual and the material, personal change and structural change"? What difference does such an approach make to church, mission, and social action?

3. Should we continue to use the word "mission"? Why or why not? If not, what words would we use instead?

4. "Decolonizing theology involves critiquing colonial influences and embracing marginalized voices." What is evidence that theology has been colonized? What are one or two key features of a decolonized theology?

5. How did Jesus practice an integral or holistic mission and ministry?

6. "Integral mission leads us to care for (to include and to be led by) those experiencing poverty as well as the marginalized, outsider, broken, and those on the periphery." What does this look like in practice in a local church?

7.

Pentecostality

The Sixth Paradigm Shift

PENTECOST IS THE AWE-STRIKING cradle of the church, where a gentle yet formidable wind and tongues of fire met a huddle of confused disciples and set their hearts ablaze. Here, the often-missed dynamism of Christian faith comes vividly to life. However, let us understand that Pentecost is not merely an archaic event to marvel at from a historical distance. No, it is an evergreen template, a rich paradigm pulsing through the sinews of the church, guiding it like a northern star in its endeavor to be a community of profound diversity and compelling unity.

In the book of Acts, we witness the Holy Spirit doing the miraculous, making the Galilean followers of Jesus into polyglots, able to communicate with the God-seeking diaspora gathered in Jerusalem. It was as if the Tower of Babel had been miraculously inverted—not a dispersion through linguistic confusion, but a unification through divine elucidation. Let us be clear: this was not mere spectacle but functionality. The Spirit's descent aimed not merely at dazzling the eyes but at opening the ears to hear the good news that God's love was no longer confined to a single ethnic enclave but poured out like wine at a sumptuous feast, to which all were now invited.

Paul's letter to the Galatians further deepens this theological reality. In Christ, the cultural, social, and gender divisions that have plagued humanity are dismantled; we are all one, and the Spirit at Pentecost makes this abundantly clear. Suppose God's mission was depicted as a grand design.

In that case, the elements are neither exclusively blue nor red, neither solely silk nor solely wool, but a vivid array of colors and textures, all intricately combined, emerging from a single source—the Holy Spirit.

But the mission is not merely about articulating heavenly mysteries in earthly tongues; it is about incarnating the life of heaven in the world of earth. As Paul vividly illustrates in his letter to the Galatians, the Spirit's gifts produce fruit—love, joy, peace, and so forth—that nurture the individual soul and the collective well-being. The Spirit of Pentecost galvanizes the church to be a force for comprehensive good, for an integral mission that seeks spiritual conversions, social justice, emotional healing, and physical care.

But wait, there's more: this grand design of God's does not propagate a monolithic, top-down structure but a polycentric, polyvocal community. Paul's epistles to the Romans and the Corinthians paint a portrait of a body with many parts, each equally necessary, each divinely designed to fulfill a unique function. This is God's Spirit-empowered church: polycentric in its authority, polyvocal in its testimony, as diversified in its structure as it is unified in its mission.

So, to be genuinely Pentecostal—in the broadest, richest sense of the term—is to be intrinsically intercultural, unflinchingly committed to diversity, and unapologetically integral in mission. It is to be, dare I say it, a community that mirrors the trinitarian God—distinct yet unified, diverse yet harmonious. The Spirit of Pentecost thus continues to haunt us, like a glorious refrain that we can neither ignore nor forget, urging us to new vistas of inclusion and compelling us toward ever greater arenas of love and service.

The Spirit is not just the church's inaugural gift but its abiding companion, guiding it through the labyrinthine complexities of a broken but beautiful world toward its ultimate vocation: the manifestation of God's all-encompassing kingdom. As such, Pentecost is not simply an event we commemorate but a reality we participate in—a divine empowerment for a church that aspires to be as versatile, compassionate, and radically inclusive as the God it worships.

Biblical and Theological Foundations for Pentecostal Mission and Ministry

In the sprawling narrative of Scripture—a vast and complex story that stretches from the dawn of creation to the climax of the apocalyptic vision—we find, running through it like a luminous golden strand, the constant, vivifying work of the Spirit. This is not merely a cosmic force but the very breath of God, enlivening the soil-born Adam, animating the prophets, raising Christ from the tomb, and fueling the church's mission to a fractured and fractious world.

Let us begin by turning our gaze to the Old Testament, where the Spirit is no marginal character but plays a central role in creation and redemption. There, it hovers, just above the ancient waters, in Gen 1:2, like an artist contemplating a blank canvas. The Spirit breathes, and order emerges from chaos. Similarly, the Spirit imbues Moses, Elijah, and Isaiah with wisdom, courage, and prophetic intensity. We discern, as through a glass darkly, a theme: The Spirit does not merely impart ephemeral gifts but equips individuals for their unique roles within God's broader, awe-inducing plan. This mission isn't abstract; it touches the raw nerve of ethical conduct and prophetic witness.

As we move into the sweeping pages and captivating stories of the New Testament, the Spirit's role crescendos in magnitude and beauty. According to Paul in Rom 8:11, the same Spirit resurrected Jesus Christ, making it abundantly clear that our mission is not mere proclamations but bold demonstrations of the resurrection's transformative power. In Acts 1:8, the Spirit descends not to create an enclave of enlightened spiritualists but to thrust the apostles into the breadth of the world's diverse cultures.

The theological construct of the Trinity—Father, Son, and Spirit as one God—renders the Spirit's work not as some auxiliary enterprise but as integral to the *missio Dei*, the mission of God. If we are tempted to think of mission as merely human exertion, the Trinity corrects us: this is a divine vocation, a venture rooted in the very nature of God.

The incarnation—God becoming flesh in Jesus—takes this further by showing that God is not distant but present, not unapproachable but relational. A Spirit-empowered mission is thus a holistic endeavor. It is about heralding the good news more than entering into substantive, life-giving relationships, crossing cultural boundaries, and embodying God's redemptive love and justice.

This understanding of mission is expansively polycentric and richly polyvocal. Like a multifaceted diamond reflecting a light spectrum, the Spirit's universal activity graces cultural, geographical, and even ecclesiastical contexts. Paul's account in 1 Corinthians 12 demonstrates the multiplicity of gifts and callings—each one valued and necessary. It captures a church that is not just multiethnic but also emotionally and socially attuned, seeking the full flourishing of the human family—mind, body, and soul.

Gifts of the Spirit, whether prophecy or acts of service are thus not merely spiritual accoutrements but divine tools for mission. They are complemented by the Spirit's fruit—love, joy, peace, and more—serving as the character markers of a community that isn't simply endowed with power but formed in virtue.

As the narrative of Scripture culminates in the breathtaking vistas of Revelation, the Spirit and the Bride—the church—join in calling humanity toward its true home with God. This Spirit-empowered mission is not a transient enterprise but the heartbeat of an eternal drama in which we are not merely spectators but participants.

So here we stand, at the convergence of Old and New Testaments, of creation and new creation, in the empowering gust of the Spirit's wind. We are beckoned to join a mission that is at once ancient and ever-new, a polycentric, polyvocal, intercultural, and integral mission that finds its genesis and its telos in the very life of God. In this breathtaking endeavor, we are not left to our own devices; we are accompanied by the Spirit, who equips us to be authentic witnesses in a complex and yearning world. Here, we are invited not just to read but to indwell God's grand narrative, led by the Spirit from creation to glorious new creation.

The Spirit Empowers the Church for Polycentric, Polyvocal, Intercultural, and Integral Vitality

In the grand narrative that arcs from the creation to the New Creation, a theme recurs with pulsing vitality: the church, caught up in the drama of God's love for the world, is a community empowered by the Holy Spirit. To speak of a Spirit-empowered mission is to draw deeply from the well of biblical narrative and theological tradition. Yet, this mission is not confined within narrow limits of culture, race, or socio-economic context. In its fullest sense, it is polycentric, polyvocal, intercultural, and integral. Allow me to explore this rich narrative with ornaments and portraits drawn from diverse theological vistas.

In a polycentric church, the epicenter of divine activity isn't localized to one tradition, interpretation, or cultural matrix. Herein, we detect the echoing motif of a Spirit who engages with creation at its dawn in Genesis, descends upon Jesus at the Jordan, and imbues the disciples with heavenly fire at Pentecost. This Spirit is equally at home in diverse realms and epochs, from the heights of mystical vision to the rough and tumble of grassroots church planting.

Let's lean in further. This polycentricity is not merely a theological curiosity; it invites us into a community-centered reading of the Spirit's action. The gifts bestowed by the Spirit—so vividly enumerated by Paul—are not personal possessions but shared resources for the upbuilding of the global church. Thus, whether in a charismatic congregation in Lagos or a liturgical service in Canterbury, the Spirit's diverse gifts signal that God's empowerment is as wide as the world.

But what of the polyvocal quality of the church? Here, we find not a cacophony but a symphony of voices, each contributing its distinct melody to the grand composition of God's kingdom. The Spirit, the divine conductor, harmonizes these disparate voices into a song of freedom and justice. Intersectionality—of race, gender, and religious tradition—does not dilute the church's voice but enriches its polyvocality. Indigenous spiritualities and liberation theologies, often on the peripheries of ecclesial conversation, are brought into the center, compelling us to listen to the Spirit's voice in the cries of the marginalized.

Next, the intercultural visage of the church reflects the boundary-breaking power of the Spirit. As we recall from Acts, the Spirit annihilated language barriers and cultural chasms to inaugurate a community transcending all human divisions. Evangelism here is not the imposition of one culture upon another but an intercultural dialogue underwritten by the Spirit's transformative power. The baptism of the Spirit is as much a breaking down of human barriers as it is an inauguration into divine life.

Now, to speak of an integral mission is to assert that the Spirit's work is not simply "spiritual" but spills over into every facet of human existence—physical, social, and emotional. The Latin term *missio Dei* is instructive; it speaks to God's grand mission of reconciling all things and thus summons the church to engage deeply with social justice, economic dignity, and ecological stewardship.

The Spirit, that eternal wellspring of the church's life and mission, empowers us to be a simultaneously polycentric, polyvocal, intercultural, and integral community. This is not a theological abstraction but a lived reality, a corrective lens that transforms our vision from monochromatic to panoramic. The Spirit baptizes our monocentric, ethnocentric, reductionist tendencies into a vivid new humanity in Christ reflecting God's kingdom's technicolor dream. This Spirit-empowered church thus stands as a witness in a multifaceted world, a living testament to the God who is greater than our imaginings yet ever nearer than our breath. In its truest form, it is a community marked by theological profundity, cultural diversity, vocal inclusion, and an unwavering commitment to the holistic well-being of all creation.

Table 7.1. Fifteen Qualities of Pentecostality

1. Empowerment for All: The Holy Spirit is given freely to all believers to serve in God's mission regardless of status or background. This democratizes spiritual power and makes the church inherently polycentric.

2. Spiritual Gifts: The gifts of the Holy Spirit, such as prophecy, healing, and speaking in tongues, are seen as essential tools for ministry and are intended to build up the community and serve the world.

3. Orality: An emphasis on preaching, storytelling, and other oral forms of communication. This makes the faith accessible and polyvocal, allowing multiple traditions and voices to be heard.

4. Flexibility: A Pentecostal approach adapts to different cultures and contexts, recognizing that the Spirit's work is not confined to any one expression of the church.

5. Prophetic Witness: The Spirit-empowered church speaks truth to power, engaging in spiritual and social transformation.

6. Direct Experience of God: A focus on personal, experiential knowledge of God through the Holy Spirit.

7. Communal Engagement: A strong sense of community and fellowship among believers, fueled by the Spirit to serve one another and the broader society.

8. Integrity: A holistic approach that recognizes the physical, emotional, social, and spiritual needs of individuals and communities, echoing themes from liberation theology and other integral approaches.

9. Missional and Evangelistic Zeal: An earnest desire to share the gospel, often combined with a commitment to social justice, fulfilling both the Great Commission and the Great Commandment.

10. Missional De-centralization: The understanding that every believer is a missionary, empowered by the Spirit to serve within and beyond the church walls.

11. Global Consciousness: Listening and learning from Majority World, Indigenous, First Nations, African American, and diaspora voices. This attentiveness to the global body of Christ enriches intercultural relationships and theologies, global-local mission, and Spirit-empowered ministry.

12. Authentic Worship: Worship experiences that are spontaneous and led by the Spirit, encouraging personal and communal encounters with God.

13. Culturally Adaptive: The ability to adapt and adopt various cultural forms in worship and community life, allowing for a genuinely intercultural experience.

14. Social Justice Orientation: Influenced by theologies of liberation and the understanding of the Holy Spirit as the advocate, there is a focus on social issues such as poverty, racism, and inequality.

15. Ecclesiological Diversity: Openness to various church structures and styles, from house churches to megachurches, as guided by the community's needs and the Spirit's leading.

These qualities are deeply interconnected with the Spirit's empowerment for polycentricity, polyvocality, interculturality, integrality, and diversity. They serve as foundational principles that help define what it means to be part of a Spirit-empowered community committed to the kingdom work of God in the world.

Valuing Diverse Voices in Pneumatology and Theologies of the Spirit

The Christian faith is a sprawling, ancient story often seen through a narrow lens—Eurocentric, Americentric, or Western-centric. Yet, what if I were to tell you that the church's true heartbeat lies in its marvelous diversity and uncanny ability to be simultaneously local and global? The Spirit—our subject today—brings this plurality to life, coloring outside the lines of narrowly defined borders and reaching into the diversity of human experience. Now, suppose one wishes to talk of a Spirit-empowered, life-giving faith. In that case, one must sit with the familiar voices and those from the Majority World, Indigenous peoples, First Nations, African American communities, and the diaspora.

First, let us ponder on scholarly virtues. A theology monopolized by a single cultural perspective can be likened to a grand symphony played with a solitary instrument. Yes, it can be beautiful, but think of the music we are missing! By widening the scope, by allowing other instruments into the orchestra, we gain a fuller understanding of the maestro's score—in our case, pneumatology or the theology of the Holy Spirit.

If I may continue the metaphor, these "other instruments" often strike chords unfamiliar to Western ears. Yet, precisely, these tonalities can offer innovative solutions to issues like environmental degradation, social inequality, and community-building—challenges our world faces with increasing urgency.

By including these voices, we begin to disentangle the sticky webs of power that have ensnared the church and theological academia for too long. We make room for a diversity of voices to speak authoritatively, which may have previously been dismissed or relegated to the footnotes of our theology.

But let's move from the ivory tower to the ground where theology takes on flesh. Here, we find that the liturgical wealth of Indigenous and African American communities, for instance, can rejuvenate churches that have grown arid under the oppressive heat of formalistic rituals. One can glimpse the liberating, healing power of the Spirit in community in their spiritual practices.

What of the spirituality that respects no division between the sacred and the secular? Indigenous and First Nations people remind us that the Spirit's work is not confined to the four walls of a church. It invades all of life, making our dualistic categories appear almost comical.

Finally, let us not forget the African-American church tradition, grounded in a long struggle for civil rights. This community offers a robust model of how the Spirit fuels the engine of social change; a lesson increasingly pertinent in an age hungry for justice.

Practical steps beckon us. Christian educational institutions must diversify curricula, not as a nod to fashionable trends but as a theological imperative. Churches must form partnerships along cross-cultural, racial, and national lines, for the Spirit's vibrancy is most vividly seen in such exchanges. We must engage in the social issues that affect marginalized communities, not as paternalistic saviors but as humble learners and allies. Theological work should actively invite and involve a plurality of voices from various backgrounds.

If it is indeed the Body of Christ, the church must reflect the image of a God who is infinitely diverse yet profoundly one. This is not an optional extra but a pneumatological necessity. By heeding the voices of Majority World, Indigenous, First Nations, African American, and diaspora communities, we enrich our theology and step closer to becoming the life-giving, Spirit-empowered community that the New Testament envisions. Then, and only then, can we tackle the complexities of our world in a way that mirrors God's manifold wisdom and inclusivity.

Unity and Diversity through God's Empowering Presence

The oft-sung hymn of unity is so dear to the Christian imagination yet so often misunderstood. Unity is not the dull, monochrome hue that results when all colors are mixed into undifferentiated gray. Instead, it is like a brilliant composition, where each element retains its unique shade yet contributes to a harmonious and magnificent whole. The grand composer of this divine symphony, is the Holy Spirit—God's empowering, indwelling presence in both the local church and the church universal.

Consider the marvelous symmetry of the Trinitarian God, where the Holy Spirit has often been understood as the "bond of love" between Father and Son.[1] In such a divine setting, unity does not eradicate diversity but

1. Migliore, *Faith Seeking Understanding*, 77. Also see Angelici, *Richard of Saint*

is predicated upon it. Paul's letter to the Corinthians paints a vivid picture: diverse gifts, one Spirit, diverse services, one Lord, diverse workings, and one God. Here, each spiritual gift, far from being a hierarchized token of divine favor, is granted for the common good, each one essential in contributing to the flourishing of the Body of Christ.

What a spectacle that Body is! On the Day of Pentecost, as recounted in the book of Acts, a cacophony of languages fills the air—yet comprehension dawns. The Spirit does not wash away the rich diversity of linguistic and cultural expression but instead imbues it with a transcendent harmony. This underscores the Holy Spirit as the great Equalizer. When Paul declares in Galatians that in Christ there is neither Jew nor Greek, enslaved person nor free, male nor female (Gal 3:28), he does not aim to bleach these distinctions but rather to transcend them. They are subsumed, not negated, within a more magnificent identity—that of the Spirit-empowered children of God.

Now, how does this heavenly ideal touch the earth, you ask? Consider your local congregation—a community where the Spirit's unifying power can manifest in the joyful clamor of diverse worship styles and the beauty of different cultural expressions. Here, the Spirit accommodates diversity and requires it for the Body's edification and the gospel's authentic proclamation.

However, the Spirit's work is not confined by the geographical or cultural boundaries of the local church. The Spirit is also the driving force behind global initiatives that echo this celestial harmony—ecumenical dialogues, cross-denominational conversations, and social justice movements that bridge continents and languages. The Spirit crafts a polycentric, polyvocal, intercultural, and yet integral unity in these arenas.

So, let us set aside the notion that the Holy Spirit is in the business of producing uniformity. No, the Spirit's enterprise is far more poetic: a harmonization of the many and the one, the diverse and the unified. It is an invitation to partake in a community that the world, fractured along many fault lines, desperately needs but hardly knows how to build. The local and global church, endowed and indwelt by the Spirit, stands as a living testament to this profoundly beautiful, deeply countercultural model of unity—a unity in diversity and a diversity in unity, as wondrously complex and yet as elegantly simple as the Triune God from whom it flows.

Victor.

PART 1: PARADIGM SHIFTS IN WORLD CHRISTIANITY

Pentecostality: Concluding Reflections

The stage is set: a world where diversity blooms and divisions deepen, a world that both tantalizes and terrifies with its complexity and multiplicity of cultures, ideas, and identities. Here, in this quizzical environment teeming with questions and challenges, the church is called not just to exist but to witness, shine, and sing a melody that acknowledges the many and enshrines the One. What shall guide us in this mission? As it often does when dealing with life's richest conundrums, the answer flows from the vivifying Spirit of God.

Let us begin with the splendid notion of polycentricity. The Spirit of God is not a localized phenomenon, restricted to the West's towering cathedrals or the Majority World's burgeoning mega-churches. No, the Spirit dances to a rhythm that infuses every human culture and speaks in the languages of all peoples. In recognizing this, the church is emancipated from the seductive yet destructive notions of imperialistic exclusivity. A polycentric understanding of the Spirit's work invites us to remove our cultural blinders and celebrate the variegated beauty of God's activity across the globe. In all its liberating power, the gospel refuses to be confined by any one culture but finds its home in all.

Next, let us contemplate the polyvocality of a Spirit-empowered church. It is tempting to champion a monolithic brand of Christianity, singing the chorus of orthodoxy while ignoring the many other voices that make up the ecclesial choir. Yet, from feminist theologians to liberationists, from mystics to rationalists, the Spirit anoints each voice to contribute to a harmonious and multidimensional portrayal of God's very character. This polyphony ensures a dynamic equilibrium between tradition and innovation, institution and spontaneity, the letter and the Spirit.

Now, turn your attention to interculturality, the Spirit-infused courage to cross boundaries in the service of the gospel. This isn't merely an invitation to "tolerate" or "include" the "other," as though one were doing them a favor. No, it's a divine imperative, birthed out of the Spirit's love, to grow spiritually through meaningful encounters that abolish the walls erected by ethnicity, culture, and prejudice. A Spirit-empowered church isn't a comfortable club but a lively, boundary-crossing community where the lines of "us" and "them" are constantly redrawn, redefined, and ultimately erased.

Lastly, let us linger on the Spirit's commitment to integrality. The Spirit's concern isn't merely "spiritual" if by that we mean detached from the raw, pressing issues of social justice, ecology, and human flourishing. In a Spirit-empowered theology, the scope is as broad as creation itself, reflected in the emphasis on liberation and justice that has enriched modern streams of Christianity. The Spirit is both the Breath giving life to individual souls and the Wind shaking the structures of the world.

In a world that so often seems to teeter on the brink—of division, exploitation, despair—a Spirit-empowered approach is not merely refreshing; it is essential, life-giving, and transformative. It coaxes us out of our limited perspectives and self-assured categories. It invites us into a grander narrative that is as richly textured and beautifully diverse as the world God loves. Far from diluting our essence, this approach allows us to discover it more fully, for we find ourselves invigorated, animated—yes, empowered—by the very Spirit of God for a mission as complex, as demanding, and as gloriously multifaceted as the world we are called to serve.

Study Questions

1. How does the Holy Spirit enable "unity amid diversity through God's empowering presence"?
2. How does the Spirit move the church toward polycentricity, polyvocality, integral mission, and intercultural engagement? Why does the presence and power of the Spirit move the church in those directions?
3. Why would the Spirit of Christ lead Christians to value diverse voices?
4. Why do we need Majority World, diaspora, Indigenous, and First Nations contributions to "keep in step with the Spirit"?
5. How does the Spirit bring unity, helping the church transcend the divisions and conflicts in our world?
6. "The Spirit demolishes monocentric, monovocal, ethnocentric, and reductionist tendencies, replacing them with a vitality that embraces the diversity and complexity of the kingdom of God." Write some notes about practical ways to join the Spirit in this work.

8.

Glocality

The Seventh Paradigm Shift

GOD'S GLOBAL CHURCH IS an exhilarating symphony. The worldwide church is a rich, expansive new humanity in Jesus Christ that stretches from Western urban centers to the rustic hills and bustling megacities of Majority World countries to the sacred spaces of Indigenous communities. Here is an orchestra in which each section enriches the other, where the strings of Western traditions converse with the percussive rhythms of Majority World perspectives, and where the sacred songs of Indigenous communities infuse the melody with a unique richness. But for this symphony to reach its full potential, all must play attentively, listen carefully, and contribute their unique sound.

This divine composition demands open-hearted learning, an eagerness for collaboration, and a collective alignment of our vision and values with the encompassing reign of God's kingdom. As we take up our instruments, our score is inked by insightful maestros like Kōsuke Koyama, Al Tizon, and R. S. Sugirtharajah—conductors who guide us in tuning our theological notes to the pitch of glocal resonances.

The endeavor is not just about parroting foreign melodies but rather about the delicate art of translation. How can we internalize these Majority World and Indigenous voices so that they shape our intellectual constructs and our very souls? How do we translate their insights into our unique cultural idioms without diluting their essence? How do we offer our unique theological compositions to this global ensemble, enriching a global conversation with local flavor?

Make no mistake: every local theology—Western, Indigenous, or from the Majority World—has something to offer to the global church. But these offerings must not merely exist in isolation; they must converse, challenge, enrich, and even amend one another. In this fertile intersection of global and local—that dynamic interplay between the universal and the particular—we find the true zest of "glocalized" theology and praxis.

What, then, is our task? We must cultivate a missional theology of the church that arises from these glocal conversations. Glocalization, in this context, is not a one-sided exportation of theological goods; it is a mutual exchange, an adventure in cross-cultural interpretation, fueled by the courage to listen deeply and to venture beyond our theological comfort zones.

This is not an academic exercise reserved for scholars and clergy. The roundtable must also include activists who embody their theologies in the trenches of human need, communities who live out these truths in their collective life, and ordinary believers whose daily experience provides the ultimate testing ground for our theological propositions.

How, then, shall we foster such glocal conversations? By coming together across our diverse cultures as mutual learners. Opening our hearts and minds to the surprising ways God speaks through each facet of Christ's global church. Christ calls us to harmonize our divergent voices into a unified song of praise and witness resounding throughout the earth.

In so doing, we might hear the music of God's kingdom as it was meant to be heard: a divine symphony in which every section, every instrument, every musician, contributes to a masterpiece that sings of justice, resonates with love, and harmonizes in the rich, complex key of shalom.

What is *Glocalization*?

Glocalization is a term developed by Japanese economists. Roland Robertson popularized the idea. The local (the local, contextual, homogenous) and the global (the global, universal, heterogeneous) interconnect. Our globalized world has blurred the boundaries between the local and the global. The local is a dimension of the global. Global realities and forces shape the local. The two are interdependent. They enable each other. They form each other reciprocally. While tensions exist, the global and local are not opposing forces. They connect—profoundly and inextricably. "Not only are the global and the local inseparably intertwined; they also determine each other's respective forms. From a sociological perspective, glocalization means generally the organic and symbiotic relationship between the global and the local."[1]

Al Tizon says that a transformational mission is always contextual. It is always rooted in the local and particular—as local churches embody the gospel and witness to Christ. These churches forge their theological understandings as they do missions together. They engage in transformational practices among the people in their settings. They enjoy worship, mission, and community in their local context. Ideally, the result is unique, contextual theologies and missions.

Simultaneously, global conversations form. They form because of this multitude of local theologies and practices. Local conversations inform and enrich other local conversations, catalyzing global themes and voices. Tizon observes that the global "owes its existence to local contexts . . . Shared convictions among the theologies and practices of local contextual realities give shape to its global dimensions."[2]

Majority World, Indigenous, and Western theologies are equally contextual. They are equally culture-bound. They are equally particular to their time and location. Sometimes, they are enlightened or myopic, liberating or constraining, humanizing or objectifying, beautiful or offensive, prophetic or tepid. The local and cultural shape all these theologies.

Conversely, these theologies feed and influence global conversations. There is no place for ethnocentrism, colonialism, or elitism. There is no place for theological, missional, cultural, or institutionalized arrogance.

Multiple local contexts and voices unite—intentionally or not—to form global themes and theologies. Conversely, these global realities shape local contexts. Today, local contexts must grapple with "an emerging global culture, i.e., the interacting realities of modernity, postmodernity, and the phenomenon of globalization."[3] Hence, the interdependent and symbiotic relationship between the *local/particular* and the *global/universal*. We call this interdependent relationship between the local and the global glocalization.

The global church needs a thrilling glocal exchange. We need one characterized by mutuality, respect, partnership, and symbiosis. Such exchange helps Majority World, Indigenous, and Western churches learn from each other. It enables them to pursue missional theology and practice. Together, the church becomes a "city on a hill."

---

1. Tizon, *Transformation after Lausanne*, 207.
2. Tizon, *Transformation after Lausanne*, 10.
3. Tizon, *Transformation after Lausanne*, 84.

GLOCALITY

What Requires *Glocalization*?

The glocal exchange described above needs to be broader than a transformational mission. This is necessary if the church is to develop robust, intercultural, and glocal missional ecclesiology.

In my first book, *Salt, Light, and a City*, I outlined the foundational themes of missional ecclesiology.[4] Majority World and Western leaders need to engage these themes locally and contextually. Their insights can then enrich global conversations. These global conversations, in turn, shape local understandings and practices. This way, a *global* appreciation of these themes emerges.

Local, regional, and global theologies and practices are thereby enriched. The church becomes healthier and more missional—a more authentic expression of the kingdom. The church becomes a fuller witness to Christ, his passion for the nations, and his ability to bring unity in diversity.

Stephen Bevans and Roger Schroeder outline the *six constants* of mission. These are our theologies about Jesus, the church, the end times, salvation, human nature, and culture. Bevans and Schroeder describe the relationship between these six and their historical, cultural, and theological *contexts*. This is why they call these six *constants in context*. Our understanding of these six constants develops concerning local and global movements. Sometimes, local voices influence our understanding of these six. Other times, it is regional or global voices. For all of us, local, regional, and global influences are at play at once. Collectively, they form our appreciation of the six constants of mission.[5]

Here are eight theological themes that the church can develop through processes of *glocalization*. They are vital to the church's health, mission, community, and future. We could add many other themes to these eight. But these will suffice for now.[6]

Scripture

The Scriptures are the trustworthy, authoritative word of God. Christ's Spirit has inspired them. They have absolute and final authority in all aspects of corporate and personal faith, ethics, conduct, and witness. Christians interpret and apply Scripture in local contexts and particular social settings. Conversely, we learn from the interpretations and readings of other groups.

---

4. Hill, *Salt, Light, and a City*, 149–274.
5. Bevans and Schroeder, *Constants in Context*, Part I.
6. These points first appeared in my book *Salt, Light, and a City*, xxii–xxiv.

Glocal theology asks: *How does a glocal conversation shape our local-global theology of Scripture and biblical interpretation?*

Evangelicalism, Pentecostalism, Missional Movements, and So Forth

I have charismatic, missional, and evangelical convictions. *Glocal* conversations help me understand and practice these convictions better.

I will use evangelicalism as an example. Michael Horton says that our beliefs and practices are evangelical when they are "committed to the sufficiency of Scripture, the priesthood of all believers, the total lostness of humans, the sole mediation of Christ, the gracious efficacy and finality of God's redemptive work in Christ through election, propitiation, calling, and keeping. The linchpin for all this was the doctrine of justification by grace alone, through faith alone, because of Christ alone."[7]

Such convictions are necessary to be faithful to the gospel and a biblical vision of church and mission. The gospel defines God's purposes for humanity, the church, and the universe. The triune God controls the church. God is its Lord and Savior, Sanctifier and Liberator, Master and King. God is utterly sovereign over its nature, affairs, mission, and history. God is the church's only source of grace, election, atonement, salvation, and perseverance. The church's justification and hope are by grace, faith, and Christ alone.

I remain an evangelical because of my commitment to the authority of the Bible, the centrality of the Cross, the need for personal conversion, and activism (sharing the gospel of Jesus Christ in word, sign, and action). But these very evangelical commitments (Bebbington's Quadrilateral) also make me passionate about social action, justice, reconciliation, creation care, and more.[8] I also believe that this Quadrilateral needs revision and expansion (it is more of a "theological horizon" than a definition anyway, hence the global diversity of evangelicals). Evangelicalism needs renewal and revision for many reasons, not least because this Quadrilateral of convictions has not saved evangelicalism from politicization, consumerism, racism, injustices, abuses, and other failings. I remain an evangelical while passionately believing that evangelicalism needs repentance and renewal. I love evangelicalism and its diverse faith, love, and action communities. But we need a fresh movement characterized by humility and repentance—and a more profound and regenerated biblical, social, and theological imagination.

7. Horton, "Evangelical Arminians," 17.
8. Bebbington, *Evangelicalism in Modern Britain*.

Here's the challenge I face. My understanding of evangelicalism is Western. I am a product of the Western theological tradition and my Western evangelical heritage. Much of this is terrific. But, I need Indigenous and Majority World evangelicals and others to help me expand and reshape these insights. The same would be true if I were a Pentecostal.

Glocal theology asks: *How does a glocal conversation shape our understanding of our theological traditions and convictions?*

Jesus Christ

We must center our theology on Jesus Christ, the Lord of the church. The church needs to reflect on the person and work of Christ and respond to him. This means gathering and going in the name and power of Christ. It means allowing Christ's Spirit to shape our community, identity, and mission. It means developing our Christology, ecclesiology, and missiology concurrently. The early church developed these three areas and more in a concurrent and integrated way. There was no linear progression. The same is true in the contemporary, global church.

The glocal church best explores its nature, structure, mission, and hope through the centrality and the Lordship of Christ. Majority World and Indigenous Christians help us appreciate Jesus and his mission afresh. They show how Jesus identifies with the marginalized, outcast, oppressed, rejected, and broken. He prefers them. We find him among "the least of these."

Glocal theology asks: *How does a glocal conversation shape our understanding of who Jesus Christ is? How does it help us appreciate him better? What has Jesus done for and in his church and his world? What does he care about? What personal and corporate responsibilities has he given us? How do we express these at local, regional, and global levels?*

The Spirit

Missional ecclesiology is inadequate without pneumatological foundations. In other words, our theology of church and Spirit go together. The Spirit creates and animates the church. He empowers it to witness to Jesus and his gospel. The Spirit enables the church to be a missional, transformational community. He shapes the church into an alternative society, embodying the reign of God. The church exists for the glory and mission of Christ. The power and presence of the Spirit enables this mission, worship, and glorification.

The Spirit pours gifts on the local-global church "for the common good and to prepare God's people for works of service, so that the body of Christ may be built up."[9] This includes, but isn't limited to, ministry gifts, manifestation gifts, and motivational gifts.[10]

The Spirit forms the glocal church and empowers it for service and witness. The Spirit fills the glocal church with Christ's empowering presence and leads it into the *missio Dei*—the mission of the Father, Son, and Holy Spirit.

Recently, Pentecostal and renewalist movements have grown dramatically in the Majority World. They have increased in status, size, and influence. Many have matured theologically. The churches of the West must take notice.

Glocal theology asks: *How does a glocal conversation shape our understanding of the power and presence of the Spirit?*

The Trinity

There are clear limitations to the analogy between the church and the Trinity. The church can only image the Trinity. Yet, the church is at its best when it reflects the relational and missional passion of the Trinity.

What is the source and inspiration of the church's local-global mission? Ultimately, it is the missional nature, passion, and actions of the Father, Son, and Holy Spirit. God's nature is missional. God's passion is infectious. God's actions are historical, redemptive, and eternal. The Trinity invites the church into a sending community. The Father sends the Son. The Father and Son send the Spirit. Finally, the Trinity sends the church on a mission into the world.

Glocal theology asks: *How does a glocal conversation shape our understanding of the Trinity? How does it enable our participation in the mission and community of the triune God?*

Association and Dialogue

These must happen across denominational, cultural, ethnic, gender, and theological traditions and divides. Authentic dialogue is indispensable to the health and mission of the church. What do those marginal to the church's life say to us? What do "others" have to teach us? Other ethnicities

---

9. 1 Cor 12:7 and Eph 4:12.
10. Eph 4:11–12; 1 Cor 12:7–10; and Rom 12:6–8.

and cultures? Other socio-economic groups? Other ages and both genders? Other theological and confessing traditions? Other person from times long gone?

We need to listen, share, and be vulnerable and authentic. We must be open to criticism, correction, and change. We need more than dialogue. We need communion and association. In a qualified way, it is possible to say that God is present in all the various forms of the church (i.e., the various theological, ecclesiological, socio-cultural, historical, and other permutations of the church). We discern this presence through attention to Scripture, history, tradition, culture, and the Spirit. Discernment involves critical dialogue, theological exchange, biblical study, and genuine relationships. Only the Spirit of Jesus can enable this.

Glocal theology asks: *How does a glocal conversation shape our understanding of association and dialogue?*

Mission and the *Missio Dei*

The church is missional at its core. It serves, obeys, and images a missionary God. David Bosch says, "The church's mission is not secondary to its being; the church exists in being sent and building up itself for its mission." He says, "Ecclesiology does not precede missiology; there cannot be a church without an intrinsic missionary dimension."[11]

Jesus is the Lord of his church and his world. His mission determines and forms the church. His mission shapes his church's nature, purposes, structures, ministries, and activities. Majority World and Indigenous thinkers help us understand the implications of this mission. They help us form *glocal* theologies of mission. They reveal, "Mission in context as transformation."[12]

Glocal theology asks: *How does a glocal conversation shape our understanding of mission and the missio Dei?*

Church Theology and Practice

Glocal conversations can inform and enrich many aspects of the church (when practiced well). Theologies and practices benefit from robust and critical *glocal* conversations. These conversations enrich many areas (community, spirituality, discipleship, liturgy, worship, hospitality, eco-justice,

---

11. Bosch, *Believing in the Future*, 32.
12. Tizon, *Transformation after Lausanne*, 7–9.

education, social ethics, servantship, liberation, place, suffering, beauty, and so on).

Glocal theology asks: *How does a glocal conversation shape our understanding of these many dimensions of church and mission?*

Glocal processes shape these eight themes and their practices. We need to facilitate and enable these conversations and processes. This is urgent. It must be a priority. No theology of mission or missional ecclesiology is adequate without glocal conversations.

The Local and Global Enrich Each Other

Glocalization takes the *local/particular* context and *global/universal* themes seriously. Contextual and global conversations enter an enriching and informing relationship. These two always have an active and symbiotic relationship. This is true whether we deliberately put them into conversation or not. Local realities and forces shape the global, and global dynamics shape the local. Many local voices converge to form global conversations and theologies. Al Tizon illustrates this.[13] Using the Philippines as a case study, Tizon shows the interdependence between local and global themes in mission.

Dialogue between local and global conversations is critical. Kōsuke Koyama wrote an essential contextual mission book, *Water Buffalo Theology*. Koyama is a Japanese missionary who served in Chiang Mai, Thailand. He writes of the joys and challenges of doing local water buffalo theology. He considers the relationship between local theology, holisticostal themes, and transforming cultures. "*Water Buffalo Theology* sees certain specific challenges. Contextualization of theology implies two critical movements. First, to articulate Jesus Christ in culturally appropriate, communicatively apt words; and second, to criticize, reform, dethrone, or oppose culture if it is found to be against what the name of Jesus Christ stands for."[14]

Kōsuke Koyama challenges us to recognize what we bring to the task of local theology. For him, it was doing theology in Thailand while being Japanese. We also need to notice the culture we're located in as we do the work of theology. This means we avoid speaking of "Asian theology," "African theology," and the like.[15] We need to cultivate local theologies that engage regional and global themes. But these theologies must be "distinctly local" and a "theology from below."

13. Tizon, *Transformation after Lausanne*, 7–13 and 149–202.
14. Koyama, *Water Buffalo Theology*, xiii–xv.
15. Koyama, "Asian Approach to Christ," 435–38.

Simultaneously, we need to pursue a reformation of theology and practice "in the global context." This means entering "the disturbing spaciousness of Jesus Christ." Jesus calls us to reject enmity and exceptionalism. He is present in our culture, language, stories, and relationships. But we also choose to embrace the "other." We choose to see him present in other cultures—shaping a global people to serve and worship him, joining in his mission.[16]

Kōsuke Koyama roots the gospel in the local, contextual, and particular. This is why he roots his water buffalo theology in Northern Thai culture. He is careful not to say, "Here is how you contextualize in your setting." Instead, he tells us a story. It's the story of how he contextualized theology in northern Thailand while being open to global conversations. Koyama asks us to form our local expressions of church, mission, and theology. At the same time, we must stay attentive to what God is saying and doing beyond that context. This way, local/particular and global/universal become mutually enriching conversation partners.

Glocalization and Historically Silenced Voices

Glocal theologies and conversations pay attention to voices that powers, institutions, religions, and societies have silenced. R. S. Sugirtharajah says that the church should privilege local conversations. He emphasizes the local, contextual, and *postcolonial* reading of biblical texts.

The church needs to listen. The church should be attentive to the theologies and biblical interpretations of groups that cultures and religions have ignored. Historically, powerful secular and religious forces have silenced these groups. They have marginalized, oppressed, and colonized them. It is time for the church to address this injustice. We must start listening to critical but silenced voices. We need to privilege the voices of the former victims of Western colonialism. We need to develop postcolonial biblical interpretations, theologies, and expressions of church and mission.[17]

How do we take such perspectives seriously as we develop *glocal* conversations? How do these themes help us foster vital relationships between local and global voices?

It is time for us to adopt values that enable conversations with those often ignored by the church. We need values that help us learn from these groups and individuals.

---

16. Koyama, "Reformation in the Global Context."
17. Sugirtharajah, *Asian Biblical Hermeneutics and Postcolonialism*, 15–16.

PART 1: PARADIGM SHIFTS IN WORLD CHRISTIANITY

Valuing Equal Partnership

Colonizing powers oppressed, silenced, and colonized certain groups. At times, the church was complicit. These colonized groups have now emerged. They are "confident, indomitable, and indispensable partners in the dialogue and collaboration with the dispossessed and disadvantaged in the West."[18] This calls for attentiveness to these voices and responsiveness to their prophetic challenges. It also demands a critical evaluation of colonial readings of Scripture. Colonial models of theology and church and mission are no longer the benchmark. The global church must examine them afresh.

Valuing Equal Status

Those on the margins now take their rightful place globally. They have claimed appropriate and equal status at the table. Subaltern theology, church, and mission readings are invaluable contributors to global theological conversations. This means that we esteem them. But we also test them.

What do we mean by *subaltern*? Subalterns are oppressed and silenced (or have been treated this way in the past). Dominant or colonizing groups treat them as invisible non-entities. They enjoy limited or no access to power. Sometimes, these are women, certain tribal and ethnic groups, and those considered "untouchable." In *Voices from the Margin*, R. S. Sugirtharajah provides a platform for postcolonial, subaltern readings of Scripture and theology. These readings challenge colonial—often Western—readings of the Bible, theology, and cultures. They claim equal status among other ways of doing theology.[19]

Valuing Equal Identity

People groups need freedom to explore new and emerging identities. These emerge in response to local and global influences. Local culture is not the only thing at work here. Global forces also shape identity. As do imported practices, ideas, readings, rituals, and technologies. However, each group should be free to traverse and construct their forms of Christian identity.

---

18. Sugirtharajah, *Asian Biblical Hermeneutics and Postcolonialism*, 16.
19. Sugirtharajah, *Voices from the Margin*.

Valuing Equal Interpretations

"Postcolonialism is concerned with the question of cultural and discursive domination." Colonialism led to oppressive and controlling forms of culture and discourse. These were usually not contextual or Indigenous. Western powers, for instance, brought colonial forms of theology, church, biblical interpretation, and mission.[20]

Postcolonialism calls for alternative ways of approaching these things. Those once marginalized, oppressed, and silenced must lead these fresh approaches in their settings. These, then, influence global conversations. We need to support these groups' new readings, insights, and experiments. This support must be both critical and collegial if it is to be genuine.

Valuing Equal Empowerment

R. S. Sugirtharajah says that postcolonialism is valuable when it empowers actual communities and real people. Postcolonial thought empowers when it addresses ordinary people's difficulties, hopes, and experiences. Postcolonial thought should never be about power plays and the clever use of language. It's pointless if it's obsessed with forming new—and "colonizing"—theories. It's a waste of time if it's a self-indulgent pursuit of new and hybrid identities. Instead, "The worth and credibility of postcolonial criticism will be judged by how it orchestrates the unique and fragile and imagined claims of one community against another." Empowerment happens in a variety of ways. One way is contributing equally to global conversations.[21]

Al Tizon examines postcolonialism in the Philippines. He says it can teach the global church much about healthy local-global conversations. Filipino contextual theology resists many Western forms of mission and theology. It finds them patronizing and controlling. This Indigenous theology values prophetic socio-political engagement in institutions and society at large. It emphasizes ministry to whole persons and communities. It constructs a Filipino theology of beauty and mission and worship and community. It fosters Indigenous theological approaches to the spirit world and cosmology.

Tizon says postcolonial theology has played a constructive role in the Philippines. But he is uncomfortable with the label "postcolonialism."

---

20. Sugirtharajah, *Asian Biblical Hermeneutics and Postcolonialism*, 17.
21. Sugirtharajah, *Asian Biblical Hermeneutics and Postcolonialism*, 24.

PART 1: PARADIGM SHIFTS IN WORLD CHRISTIANITY

He prefers to describe historical events "beyond colonialism." He says that global conversations enrich local theologies and vice versa.[22]

Postcolonial thought informs our understanding of the relationship between the local and global. It also shows how theology can emerge at the intersection between the local/particular and the global/universal. It reminds us that worthwhile *glocalization* listens to all voices. This includes heeding those that have been historically silenced.

Table 8.1. Fifteen Qualities of Glocality

1. Rooted Global Ideas: Glocalization emphasizes that global ideas and theologies are rooted in numerous local contexts, acknowledging the essential contribution of local communities to global theological conversations.
2. Pan-localization: This aspect ensures global conversations enrich, affirm, serve, and guide local contexts without imposition, bringing about positive accountability to diverse local contexts.
3. Value-Based Approach: Christian glocalization is anchored in core values like solidarity, understanding, mutual learning, and fellowship across cultural divides, fostering a genuine global Christian community.
4. Practical Application: Moving beyond theory, glocalization stresses the necessity of practical expressions like collaboration, cooperation, and information sharing to affirm its foundational values.
5. Humility in Dialogue: Acknowledging the interdependence of local and global contexts, glocal theology practices humility, eliminating ethnocentrism and cultural arrogance in global conversations.
6. New Global Narrative: Glocalization advocates for a new narrative that recognizes the growing Christian communities in Asia, Latin America, Africa, and beyond, shifting focus from a Euro-American-centric view of global Christianity.
7. Expansive Theological Conversations: Glocal theology commits to a broad and deliberate engagement with diverse theological topics, ensuring a holistic understanding of Christian doctrines and practices.
8. Inclusive Engagement: Glocal conversations include and esteem marginalized groups, giving dignity and voice to all regardless of societal status.
9. Embracing Diversity: Christian glocalization upholds an open, inclusive, and embracing attitude towards diverse cultural beliefs, experiences, and practices.
10. Discernment in Engagement: With discernment, glocalization ensures careful and respectful engagement with global and local ideas and practices, avoiding the commodification or misrepresentation of local contexts.
11. Avoidance of Commodification: It actively works against commodifying local and contextual practices and theologies, ensuring their original contexts and meanings are preserved and respected.

---

22. Tizon, *Transformation after Lausanne*, 102 and 167–87.

> 12. Avoidance of Homogenization: Glocalization avoids the trap of homogenizing cultures and theologies, preserving the uniqueness and significance of each local culture and theology.
> 13. Cultural Sensitivity: It practices cultural sensitivity, ensuring that engagement with global and local ideas avoids the pitfalls of cultural imposition, idealization, or demonization.
> 14. Responsive and Inclusive Attitude: Glocalization promotes a responsive, humble, and inclusive attitude to diverse cultures and contexts, fostering genuine global Christian unity.
> 15. Symbiotic Relationships: It encourages a symbiotic relationship between the local and global, acknowledging the significant impact each has on the other fostering mutual growth and learning.

Christian glocalization embodies a mutually enriching dialogue and interaction between global and local contexts, ensuring humility, inclusivity, cultural sensitivity, and the avoidance of commodification or homogenization. This respectful and discerning approach to global and local conversations fosters a rich, diverse, and unified global Christian community grounded in practical application and committed to core Christian values.

Glocalization: Concluding Reflections

How do we go about developing a model for *glocal* conversations? Al Tizon has recently provided a valuable and instructive model as we seek to learn from the Majority World. It has at least two key features.

Firstly, the local is in the global (globalization from below). Global theologies and ideas have origins in numerous local contexts. In that sense, globalization is from below. Global ideas have local roots. Ideas about integral missions, liberation theology, and missional church have local origins. They have their roots in thousands of local communities' prayers, hopes, discoveries, missions, and theologies. "The global does not, *cannot*, exist without the local—but the coming together of localities creates a global reality that becomes greater than the sum of its parts; it creates a gestalt entity to which localities make themselves accountable."[23]

Secondly, the global is in the local (pan-localization from above). The concerns and voices of multitudes of locales form global conversations. These global discussions can provide a "positive accountability" to local contexts. This is true when they enrich, affirm, serve, guide, and strengthen local contexts. It is also true when they avoid homogenization, control,

---

23. Tizon, *Transformation after Lausanne*, 210–14.

PART 1: PARADIGM SHIFTS IN WORLD CHRISTIANITY

imposition, and judgment. *Glocalization* is best when it sees itself as interdependent: deeply connected with the local.[24]

That's a helpful starting point. But we need to go further. Besides Al Tizon's proposals, I'm convinced that robust *glocal* conversations cultivate six core practices.

1. Glocal theology practices its values.

We root *glocal* theology in core values. These values include solidarity, understanding, and mutual learning. Do we value fellowship with Christians of all cultures? Do we value learning from them?

We prove our values through our practices. What practices emerge out of these values? We need to collaborate, cooperate, and share information. We must find ways to foster grassroots perspectives and local theologies. We must share stories and learnings and cultivate networks, relationships, and partnerships. We need attentiveness to local voices and global themes. We ought to find ways to put these local and global voices into conversation. Mutual learning, humility, and solidarity are key. Worthwhile *glocal* conversations can never be merely theoretical or academic. It is up to us to root our values in our practices.

2. Glocal theology practices humility (and it tells a new narrative).

We have noted that the local is in the global, and the global is in the local. The two are interdependent. They form each other reciprocally. Since this is the case, we must practice humility. There is no place for ethnocentrism, colonialism, or theological or cultural arrogance. I have seen these unhealthy postures far too often in Western settings.

Recently, I attended a missional leadership conference. On that occasion, the keynote speaker—a leading missional author and speaker—said that North American missional conversations and innovations hold the key to the future of the Western church. This Euro-American view is wrong. (I'm being kind—it's complete nonsense). It's arrogant and Euro-American-centric. It's entirely out of step with what is happening in the global church. We need a new narrative.

In June 2013, The Center for the Study of Global Christianity reported "the top 20 countries where Christianity has the highest percentage growth

---

24. Tizon, *Transformation after Lausanne*, 214–18.

rate." Nineteen of the top twenty are in Asia and Africa. Eleven of them are in Muslim-majority countries. No country from Europe or North America makes the top twenty list.[25]

It's time to cultivate a new narrative. The future of the church is emerging from the Majority World. Rather than North America, the churches of Eastern Asia, Western Africa, the Arabian Peninsula, and other parts of the Majority World reveal the future of the global church. We need the contributions of all contexts: Western, Indigenous, and Majority World. All contribute to *glocal* conversations. All are important as we learn from each other about mission, theology, and faith. But let's stop pretending that North Americans and Europeans will reveal the future of the global church. Let's start listening to what God is saying about the future of the global church. He's speaking to us through the churches of Asia, Africa, Latin America, Muslim majority settings, etc. We must cultivate a new, *glocal* narrative—one soaked in humility.

Glocal theology must be humble, meek, receptive, prayerful, dialogical, and dependent theology. Glocal theology must celebrate the interdependence between the *local/particular* and the *global/universal*.

3. Glocal theology practices expansiveness.

Glocalization is, by nature, comprehensive. Local and global influences permeate much of our lives. These *glocal* forces shape our theologies and churches, whether we like it or not.

But intentionality is also essential. We need to commit to an expansive approach to *glocal* theology. How do we *deliberately cultivate glocal conversations* in our biblical interpretation? Do we foster them in our understanding of the person and work of Christ? How does *glocalization* shape the way the Spirit empowers and constitutes the church? How can it form our understanding of the nature and mission of the Trinity? How does it influence how we practice fellowship and conversation across denominational, cultural, ethnic, economic, socio-cultural, political, gender, and theological divides? How might it shape our theologies of mission, community, beauty, spirituality, suffering, discipleship, hospitality, eco-justice, place, education, social ethics, Christian leadership, and so forth?

---

25. Mitchell, "Top 20 Countries Where Christianity Is Growing the Fastest."

4. Glocal theology practices attention.

Glocal theology doesn't need to accept all the assumptions or assertions of postcolonial or Majority World thought. But it does need to engage with them and take them seriously. Postcolonial theology, for instance, gives the marginalized, colonized, forgotten, and silenced dignity and voice. Our glocal conversations must also include and esteem these groups. We must be attentive to others: weak and powerful, female and male, dominant and downtrodden, old and young, rich and poor, privileged and marginalized, influential and subaltern, educated and illiterate. We must practice the art of attention and be incredibly attentive to those different from us.

5. Glocal theology practices embrace.

What do colonial, ethnocentric, or Western-centric perspectives do? They silence, control, commodify, institutionalize, colonize, domesticate, replace, import, and exclude. They do these things to other cultures' beliefs, experiences, and practices. A worthwhile *glocal* theology refuses to do these things. Instead, it adopts a responsive, humble, celebratory, open, inclusive, and embracing attitude.

6. Glocal theology practices discernment.

Finally, we need discernment as we engage these ideas and practices. Discernment is a vast topic that's hard to cover comprehensively in a few words. Discernment happens when the Spirit of Christ and his Word renew our minds. The Spirit grants us spiritual wisdom as we meditate on him and his Word and practice discipleship to Jesus Christ. Romans 12 provides guidance. We must be transformed by renewing our minds, serving Christ's Body, and putting love into action. Discernment also happens in conversation, both locally and globally. I pray these core values and six practices come across in the following chapters of this book.

Glocalization can never be theoretical. Are we committed to moving *glocalization* from an abstract idea to a living communion? Are we determined to construct a missional theology of the church in the context of *glocal* conversations? This must involve dialogue between Majority World, Indigenous, and Western scholars, activists, and groups.

GLOCALITY

Will glocalization be an *abstract notion*? Or will it be a formative and genuine *communion* between local, regional, and global voices? Glocal dynamics are at play whether we like it or not. They're in our churches, theologies, and missions. But we can relinquish isolationist, colonial, parochial, and arrogant approaches. Instead, we can adopt responsive, dialogical, learning, humble, and embracing postures.

Through healthy approaches to glocalization, the Spirit challenges us to value local contexts. We immerse ourselves in local communities and conversations. He inspires us to open ourselves to global theological conversations. He rouses us to value the symbiotic relationship between the *local/particular* and the *global/universal*.

Through glocal relationships, the Spirit leads us to put local, contextual theologies into conversation with global ones. He prompts us to explore how the *local is in the global* and the *global is in the local*. He persuades us to pursue collaboration, dialogue, and mutual learning. We engage with Christians from different backgrounds and cultures: ecumenicals, Pentecostals, evangelicals, etc., from Western, Indigenous, and Majority World contexts. He motivates us to express solidarity between all parties. We appreciate our unity in diversity.

Through glocal conversations, the Spirit moves us to ensure unity and solidarity emerge from a compelling vision of Jesus's kingdom, gospel, and person. He challenges us to share information, theology, and practices. He urges us to learn from each other—our successes and mistakes. We seek glocal solutions.

The Spirit calls us to develop global conversations about Christian ideas and practices. These include Scripture, Evangelicalism, ecumenism, Pentecostalism, Jesus Christ, Holy Spirit, God the Father, Trinity, community, spirituality, discipleship, liturgy, worship, hospitality, prayer, ecojustice, education, social ethics, Christian leadership, gospel and culture, beauty, place, suffering, liberation, and so forth.

Finally, through global conversations, the Spirit leads us to adopt a new posture. This is a responsive, humble, celebratory, open, inclusive, and embracing attitude to the "other." We do this as a new people, made up of every tribe and language and people and nation.

There are dangers in glocalization. R. S. Sugirtharajah warns of commodifying local, contextual practices and theologies. When this happens, they are "smoothed out of their primary contexts, concerns, and contestations, travel across borders, and become objects of analysis and scrutiny within an alien secondary context."[26]

---

26. Sugirtharajah, "Textual Take-Aways," 33 and 37; Said, *World, the Text, and the*

It's common for Western people to make mistakes when we wrestle with Majority World and Indigenous ideas. R. S. Sugirtharajah mentions our tendency to commodify, reduce, and institutionalize these ideas. We also risk doing these things. (1) We apply them in non-contextual, prescriptive ways. (2) We ignore their meanings in their original setting. (3) We glamorize or idealize their proponents or their contexts. (4) We demonize those persons or contexts. (5) We disregard them as irrelevant, rhetorical, or minority discourse.

Kevin J. Vanhoozer says we can fall into three traps when *glocalizing* theology. (1) We can underestimate the theological significance of local cultures. (2) We can homogenize cultures and theologies, exaggerating "the one." (3) We can overemphasize cultural particularity, exaggerating "the many," and pursue "theological ethnification."[27]

I hope this book does not fall into the traps R. S. Sugirtharajah and Kevin J. Vanhoozer describe. I hope that what unfolds in the following chapters is respectful and discerning. I hope it leads to further mutually enriching conversations between people of different cultures.

You, the reader, face the same challenges. You face them in your personal life, ministry context, and missional engagements. Will you treat the themes in this book as abstract, theoretical notions? Will this be a temporary infatuation, a flirtation with the "other," that dissipates as suddenly as it arrives? Or will glocal conversations become an enriching and formative orientation in your life? Will glocal conversations bring fresh approaches to theology, faith, mission, church, and worship? Will conversations with other cultures and theologies become a compelling way of life for you? I pray that glocal conversations will help the church be a global, visible, alternative "city set upon a hill."

Critic, 239.

27. Ott and Netland, *Globalizing Theology*, 125.

GLOCALITY

Study Questions

1. What's one thing that stood out to you or grabbed your attention while reading this chapter?
2. How would you define glocalization in your own words?
3. Why do local settings need global conversations, and global forums need local input?
4. Who are the oppressed and silenced in your church, ministry, or local community? How are they treated as invisible non-persons? How will you confront, expose, and challenge this situation?
5. John Macionis defines prejudice as "a rigid and irrational generalization about an entire category of people." Stereotypes, a form of prejudice, are "an exaggerated description applied to every person in some category." Which races, ethnicities, genders, socioeconomic groups, or cultures stimulate your prejudice or stereotypes? What are you going to do to address and change this?
6. Can you think of ways that people from your area involved in church, business, education, health, welfare, and industry are providing input into local, city-wide, state-wide, national, regional, or global forums? Write some notes about the interdependence between the local and global in your context.

THIRTEEN EXPRESSIONS
OF THOSE PARADIGM SHIFTS

PART 2

Renewing Our Mission

PART TWO EXPLORES HOW Indigenous and Majority World Christians teach us to renew our mission. This part outlines seven missiological expressions of the seven holisticostal paradigm shifts. These seven expressions are contextualizing mission, liberating people, showing hospitality, embracing the Spirit, caring for creation, living ethically, and transforming neighborhoods.

Among the rich metaphors offered by Jesus Christ, few captivate the imagination quite like that of light. "You are the light of the world," Jesus declares. Not merely in your secluded corner or within your tight-knit community but globally and locally—yes, you are that city on a hill. The question we must grapple with is not merely what it means to be the light but how that illuminating vocation plays out in a world choked by shadows and half-lights.

Let us make no mistake; to be the light is to dispel the darkness that shrouds our world. It is to be agents of healing in places fractured by disease, offer liberation where oppression's iron grip tightens, and participate in the grand, unfolding act of redemption that finds its source in God. Light illuminates and animates, bringing into full view the vivid hues of God's kingdom, making the invisible visible, the hidden manifest.

To speak of the church as light is thus to speak of a community—what one might dare to call a "holisticostal" community—that enters deeply into the world's suffering, joy, and mundane. This community is deeply rooted in the Spirit and, consequently, profoundly involved in God's mission to heal and redeem the world.

Given the challenges facing the church and world, a renewal of our mission becomes non-negotiable. The terrain of global Christianity is shifting, compelling us to revisit and revise our theologies and practices related

PART 2: RENEWING OUR MISSION

to mission, or as we term it, missiology. Here, we can find a fresh wellspring of wisdom by listening to our brothers and sisters from the Indigenous and Majority World traditions. They instruct us on the importance of contextualization, teaching us to articulate the gospel in the vernacular of various cultures without losing its transformative essence.

They remind us that liberation is not an adjunct to the gospel but part of its core. Liberation from sin is inextricable from liberation from societal structures that demean and dehumanize. They guide us into a more profound practice of hospitality, reminding us that our tables must extend not just to those who look and think like us but also to the stranger, the "other," who may offer us a vision of God we had not considered.

So, as we move forward, let us be keenly aware that our mission must be informed by an array of voices—polycentric, polyvocal—and must cross boundaries—intercultural. It must embrace the fullness of human life and creation—integral—and always be open to the surprising wind of the Spirit—pentecostal. This mission, rooted in a community empowered by the Spirit, will transform neighborhoods and entire disciplines of thought, society, and even creation itself.

So, let your light shine. Illuminate the dark corners of injustice, radiate warmth in the icy halls of indifference, and guide the wayward traveler. Let your light shine in patterns that reflect the manifold wisdom of God, and in so doing, bring glory to your Father in heaven. As we participate in this shining, in this glorifying, we find ourselves caught up in God's greater mission—a mission as broad as the world, as high as the heavens, and as close as your neighbor across the street. This is your calling. Be light.

9.

Contextualizing Mission

The First Expression

WHAT IS THE CHURCH, if not Christ's living, breathing body, called to incarnate the gospel in the peculiarities of our diverse contexts? The very notion of contextual mission is deeply rooted in the fertile soil of biblical revelation. But let us not be confounded by the theological jargon, for these words are signposts guiding us to the breathtaking scenery of God's kingdom, where the skies are filled with the promise of new creation and the earth teems with transformative love.

At the heart of this discourse is a vision of the kingdom of God that is as expansive as it is intimate. It is a vision revealed through the pages of Scripture, from the garden of Eden to the New Jerusalem, from the covenant with Abraham to the empty tomb of Jesus. This grand narrative shapes our approach to mission, compelling us to participate in God's ongoing restoration project in our specific locales.

Then comes the Incarnation, that sublime mystery wherein the Word became flesh and dwelt among us. In Jesus Christ, God didn't just send a message; he became the Message. He ate our food, spoke our language, wept our tears. In other words, the Incarnation was God's ultimate act of contextual mission, a divine affirmation that the gospel must always be translated into the language and culture of those it speaks to.

The Majority World Christians offer us a powerful model of what it means to do this well. They teach us that contextual mission is neither a fleeting trend nor a pragmatic strategy but an existential necessity. For the gospel to find soil where it can grow and flourish, it must be integral, touching every facet of life—social, spiritual, economic, and ecological. It must be transformational, not merely a palliative for suffering but a catalyst for systemic change.

So, when we speak of contextual mission as being "integral and transformational," we mean that our work is not done when a soul is saved or a belly filled. No, we must strive for nothing less than the redemption of the whole person, within the whole community, under the lordship of Christ. Our goal is the transformation of societies in a way that reflects the coming kingdom, where justice rolls down like waters and righteousness like a mighty stream (Amos 5:24).

In this light, the task before us is as profound as it is exhilarating: to discern what the gospel looks like in our own time and place and to live it out with the boldness and creativity that God's Spirit supplies. This chapter will, I hope, be like a compass and map for our journey, asking the all-important question: What wisdom can we glean from our Majority World sisters and brothers as we strive to cultivate a genuinely contextual mission?

Only when we learn to see through each other's eyes will we fully comprehend the magnificent new humanity God is creating. This is a story of redemption and new creation unfolding from the beginning of time and will continue until the day when God will be all in all. In that splendid vision, every voice matters, every color contributes, and the beauty of the whole is greater than the sum of its parts. It is high time we took our place in it, stitching our unique patterns into God's ever-expanding design.

Contextual Mission is Essential and Biblical

Contextualization was coined by the Theological Education Fund of the World Council of Churches in 1972. Scott Moreau defines contextualization as "the process whereby Christians adapt the forms, content, and praxis of the Christian faith to communicate it to the minds and heart of people with other cultural backgrounds. The goal is to make the Christian faith *as a whole*—not only the message but also the means of living out of our faith in the local setting—understandable."[1]

We must contextualize the gospel for cultures. We live in a time when the liberating themes of the gospel and the evolving concerns of our culture are poorly related. So, we lose opportunities to build bridges of meaning. The result is miscommunication, retreat, and mistrust. Yet the biblical and

1. Moreau, *Contextualization in World* Missions, 36.

missional underpinnings of the gospel provide a solid basis for contextualization. The church needs to examine these underpinnings and the nature of biblical contextualization. The church also needs to consider the possibilities of contextual theology and transformational mission.

There are rich resources that exist for understanding and practicing contextual missions. We can learn much from contextual missions in the Majority World. We can learn from their struggles with religious syncretism. Contextualization involves building a constructive and dynamic relationship between the gospel and culture. We should remember an important point. "Syncretism develops not because of contextualization but from a failure to contextualize."[2]

Orlando Costas of Costa Rica, Vinoth Ramachandra of Sri Lanka, and René Padilla of Argentina have all written on contextual and integral missions. All three argue the importance of such mission for transforming individuals, societies, and theology. Costas, Ramachandra, and Padilla echo a holisticostal consensus. (Yet not all agree on definitions, models, methods, and limits of contextualization). I'll be drawing on their thought throughout this chapter.

Orlando Costas says we must root our contextualization and mission in Scripture and the incarnation. Scripture, after all, is contextual. "The Scriptures are contextual from beginning to end." They show God interacting with people in context. God reveals himself contextually through their stories, worldviews, languages, situations, and settings. "He reveals himself to concrete peoples in specific situations by means of particular cultural symbols and categories." This revelation "reaches its peak" when God takes on human flesh in the incarnation.[3] "The incarnation turns theology proper and anthropology into a Christological issue. It also makes contextualization an inevitable and indispensable process for a proper understanding and communication of the Christian faith."[4]

We must contextualize offshore models and theologies of church and mission if we are faithful to the gospel and culture. We must also catalyze first-level, homegrown theology and approaches to mission and church. To do this well, we had best examine the Scriptures, traditions, and cultures. As pastors and leaders, we must exegete culture. We ought to wrestle with the relationships between theology and Scripture and the critical dimensions of our culture. We need to empower our congregations to do the same.

---

2. Ott et al., *Encountering Theology of Mission*, 266.
3. Costas, "Contextualization and Incarnation," 25.
4. Costas, *Christ Outside the Gate*, 5 and 12.

The role of Christian leaders is to identify, develop, and release contextual responses. Such responses are critical for mission, theology, and church. Transplanting offshore, non-contextualized models and reasoning into cultural contexts is irresponsible and self-defeating.

It is not enough to contextualize. As communities of faith, we must go on to develop Indigenous ways of being church. We need to cultivate homegrown approaches to mission. We need to foster Indigenous forms of theology. When we do this, we open opportunities for meaningful engagement with culture. Our contextualization has a missional drive and direction.

Contextual Mission Is Kingdom-Oriented and Incarnational

Contextual mission is rooted in missional theology. Contextualization is not always missional or kingdom-oriented. But contextualization is best when it emerges from a passion for Jesus and his mission and kingdom. It is worthwhile when it emerges from a desire to be faithful to these three in our context.

Just as the missional God reaches out to humans in contextual ways, Christians must pursue contextual mission. Orlando Costas says that Christian mission is rooted in "the missional dynamic of the Father, the Son, and the Spirit, in and for history. To understand the mission of Christians in any situation, we need first and foremost to understand God's mission as it is revealed in his trinitarian history."[5] Costas is not interested in an abstract theology of the Trinity. He values the trinitarian actions of God in human history. He cares about the pastoral and missional implications for the church. God's concrete, trinitarian actions guide the church in its contextual mission and ministry.[6]

Contextual mission is not merely about proclamation or getting people to believe propositions. I am not saying that the truths of the gospel are unimportant! But a living encounter with Jesus Christ and the power of the Holy Spirit transforms people. The Spirit of Christ enables us to embrace the values, community, justice, and transformation in Christ's kingdom. He empowers us to do this individually and in community. "As a messianic community, the church is that fellowship of men and women, both liberated and in the process of liberation."[7]

---

5. Costas, *Christ Outside the Gate*, 88.
6. Costas, *Liberating News*, 149.
7. Costas, *Christ Outside the Gate*, 90.

CONTEXTUALIZING MISSION

The missional church embraces the proclamation, demands, and priorities of Christ's kingdom. "The kingdom serves as the frame of reference for the mission of God . . . The participation of the People of God in his mission will have to be directed, therefore, by the message of the kingdom."[8] Proclamation is not just propositional and verbal. We proclaim the gospel through contextualized, Spirit-empowered, and liberating witness. Orlando Costas calls this witness a "dynamic transforming witness."[9]

Contextual mission is best when it's kingdom-oriented. René Padilla says, "Because the kingdom has been inaugurated in Jesus Christ, the mission of the church cannot be properly understood apart from the presence of the kingdom. The mission of the church is an extension of the mission of Jesus. It is the manifestation (though not yet complete) of the kingdom of God, through proclamation as well as through social service and action."[10]

The responsibilities of the kingdom of God reach beyond the personal and church-based dimensions of our lives. They reach into the social and public realms of the church's witness within societies. The church cannot avoid its political role. It cannot ignore how Jesus calls it into a transforming relationship with cultures and creation. The church must confront cultural powers and principalities. These include materialism, sexism, exploitation, lust, pride, and greed. It needs to confront these things when they are present *within* the structures and relationships of the church.

Our contextual mission is to individuals, groups, cultures, and creation. Courage, suffering, and hope characterize contextual mission. Contextual mission confronts violence and socioeconomic oppression. It affirms life and human dignity. It condemns torture and exploitation. It calls for legal and political justice. Such a mission affirms human solidarity across racial, religious, sexual, economic, and other divides. Our churches will only witness to Jesus Christ in their specific contexts when they pursue unity and reject division.

We must root our contextual mission in the gospel. Contextual mission and theology must take whole contexts, whole persons, and whole communities seriously. The church's missional nature and activities are "grounded in the mission of God and will have to be steered by the message of the kingdom."[11] God invites the church to be a *worshiping* and *missional* community within specific contexts.[12]

---

8. Costas, *Christ Outside the Gate*, 91.
9. Costas, *Christ Outside the Gate*, 92.
10. Padilla, *Mission between the Times*, 192.
11. Costas, *Christ Outside the Gate*, 94–98.
12. Costas, *Church and Its Mission*, 40.

Contextual mission in incarnational. It patterns itself after the extraordinary fact that God took on human flesh in the incarnation of Jesus Christ. For Orlando Costas, Jesus Christ's incarnation makes contextualization and mission a "theological necessity." Contextualization is an "inevitable and indispensable process for a proper understanding and communication of the Christian faith." Costas locates contextual mission within a Trinitarian frame.[13] From the beginning of history, the triune God reaches out to humanity for redemption. The words and deeds of the Father, Son, and Holy Spirit show us the ultimate form of contextual mission.

It's in the incarnation that contextual mission reaches its peak. The incarnation has missional implications for the church. It's critical for the church's mission among the marginalized, oppressed, impoverished, broken, and "powerless majority. Indeed, it was out of the mystery of the incarnation, to which Jesus' resurrection and death bear witness, that the early Christian community began to understand its mission as participation in the continuing mission of Jesus Christ."[14]

Orlando Costas says that the incarnation directs and shapes our contextual mission. In the incarnation, Jesus Christ "humbled himself to the extent that he took the form of a servant and thus the identity of the poor, powerless, and oppressed." Jesus revealed himself "within the harsh reality of the hurt, destitute, and marginated of the earth." Christ continues to be one with the marginalized, the outcast, and the oppressed. Jesus shares their experiences and is present in their suffering. He assumes their broken identity and is one with them. "We can affirm, accordingly, that Christ today is a black South African, a Latin American peasant, a Cambodian refugee, a homeless Palestinian, a persecuted Russian Jew, an orphan and homeless child, a humiliated female person. He is all these things because he is truly human and truly God, the one for others, God of the oppressed."[15]

This doesn't mean Jesus isn't present with those with financial, political, and cultural power. It doesn't mean that he's absent from those who enjoy the privileges of a particular race, ethnicity, or gender. However, Jesus reveals himself uniquely through the ignorant, exploited, humiliated, and subjugated. He calls his church to struggle against personal and systemic evil.

Samuel Escobar observes:

> Drive and inspiration to move forward and take the gospel of Jesus Christ to the ends of the earth, crossing all kinds of

---

13. Costas, *Liberating News*, 149.
14. Costas, *Christ Outside the Gate.*, 13.
15. Costas, *Christ Outside the Gate.*

CONTEXTUALIZING MISSION

geographic and cultural barriers, is the work of the Holy Spirit. There is an element of mystery when the dynamism of mission does not come from people in positions of power or privilege, or from the expansive dynamism of a superior civilization, but from below—from the little ones, those who have few material, financial or technical resources but who are open to the prompting of the Spirit.[16]

The church's contextual mission involves struggle. It confronts sexism, racism, colonialism, imprisonment, sexual violence, war-mongering, torture, exile, and exploitation. This mission includes the visible demonstration of an alternative *polis*. The church is a "city on a hill." It reflects the values of Jesus's kingdom. In its contextual mission among specific groups, the church must reveal the counter-cultural values of Jesus's kingdom. Jesus Christ's people are to embody the incarnation in their humility. They testify to the kingdom when serving the poor, powerless, silenced, and oppressed.

The incarnation shows us the person of Jesus Christ and the shape of his contextual mission. We discover "who he is (the Lord and Savior of the oppressed) in the incarnation." We see "where he is to be found today (among the poor, the powerless, and the oppressed)." We take part in "what he is doing (healing their wounds, breaking their chains of oppression, demanding justice and peace, giving life, and imparting hope)."[17]

In the incarnation, we see Jesus present among and transforming the lives of the downtrodden and the oppressed. Jesus demonstrates the definitive form of contextual mission and holistic transformation. In the incarnation, Jesus enters people's contexts. He transforms individuals and groups.

The church's contextual mission must confront systemic evil and oppression. It ought to engage in processes of transformation that lead to liberation, justice, healing, and wholeness.[18] We can only do this if we build relationships with the oppressed, marginalized, forgotten, and silenced. We must collaborate with them as they seek transformation, freedom, and justice. In the process, contextual mission transforms individuals, cultures, and churches.

Theological speculation on the incarnation isn't enough. Nor is it good enough to be missionally aware because of the incarnation. We must move from theological speculation and missional awareness to concrete practices. These practices ought to be context-specific and costly and inspired by prayer.

16. Escobar, *New Global Mission*, 19.
17. Costas, *Christ Outside the Gate*, 15–16.
18. Costas, *Liberating News*, 30.

Orlando Costas says that the church's mission is only authentic when it is concrete:

> The real issue is whether we as Christians are willing to be immersed in the concrete situations of the disenfranchised of our societies and witness to the lordship and saviorhood of Christ from within, a commitment that will have to be verified in our participation in the concrete transformation of these situations. Anything else is pure talk, and the kingdom of God "does not consist in talk but in power" (2 Cor. 4:20).[19]

A worthwhile mission isn't only contextual but also concrete, integral, and transformational.

Contextual Mission Must Be Integral and Transformational

Contextualization is transformational when we dedicate ourselves to the liberation, redemption, well-being, and transformation of whole persons, families, and societies. This contextual and integral mission is a participation in the mission of the triune God. It is dependent on the power of the Spirit of Jesus Christ.[20]

Our mission must be transformational. Transformation happens when our mission is holistic—to whole persons and communities. It also occurs when processes of critical contextualization shape our mission. Transformation occurs when believers contextualize the gospel to their settings. When they engage the gospel with their whole lives. New life occurs when individuals and groups embrace a transforming relationship with Jesus and his Spirit. Transformation happens when Jesus Christ renews individuals and communities in their totality. He does this by the power of the Spirit. Transformation occurs when the people of God are missional and courageous. It happens when we are more concerned about the extension of the kingdom, the glorification of Christ, and the well-being of people than the church's prosperity, power, or reputation.

What does it mean to say that contextual mission must be *integral*? *Integral mission* is an expression developed within the Latin American Theological Fraternity (FTL). *Integral mission* means that the church's mission is to whole persons. It's to their mind, body, and spirit. It also means the church's mission is to individuals, people groups, and whole cultures.

---

19. Costas, *Christ Outside the Gate*, 16.
20. Escobar, *New Global Mission*, 94.

Integral mission is transformational and contextual because it involves the transformation of whole persons, families, and communities.[21]

This understanding reflects the mission of Jesus and the early churches. It is more about the nature of the church than the activities of the church. Integral mission arises out of the missional nature of the triune God. Since God is missional, his church is also missional. The church's integral, transformational mission is not primarily an action, program, or strategy. It is a response to Jesus and his kingdom. It is about the missional nature and vocation of the church.

According to Orlando Costas, the church sometimes abandons this nature and call. It does this when it ignores ethics, justice, and reconciliation issues. The gospel's content then becomes "a conscience-soothing Jesus, with an unscandalous cross, an otherworldly kingdom, a private, inwardly limited spirit, a pocket God, a spiritualized Bible, and an escapist church. Its goal is a happy, comfortable, and successful life, obtainable through the forgiveness of an abstract sinfulness by faith in an unhistorical Christ."[22]

Contextual mission must be integral. If it is not integral, it has no integrity. It is distanced from the biblical picture of mission. Vinoth Ramachandra says:

> Integral mission has to do with the church's *integrity*. Integral mission flows out of an integral gospel and an integrated people. There is a great danger that we transform the mission of the church into a set of special 'projects' and 'programs', whether we call them 'evangelism' or 'socio-political action', and then look for ways to integrate them methodologically . . . The primary way the church acts upon the world is through the actions of its members in their daily work and their daily relationships with people of other faiths . . . 'Integral mission' has to do with the basic issue of the integrity of the church's life, the consistency between what the church is and what it proclaims.[23]

However, it is not enough for a contextual mission to be integral. It must also be transformational. Orlando Costas says that a transformational mission has many expressions. These include proclaiming, discipling, mobilizing, growing, liberating, and celebrating. These characteristics "make up the church's mission-in-life."[24] These aspects of mission express themselves best in local contexts.

21. Escobar, *Time for Mission*, 142–54.
22. Costas, *Christ Outside the Gate*, 80.
23. Ramachandra, "Integral Mission," 57.
24. Costas, *Integrity of Mission*, xiii.

Transformation, in the words of Vinay Samuel, "is to enable God's vision of society to be actualized in all relationships, social, economic, and spiritual, so that God's will may be reflected in human society and his love be experienced by all communities, especially the poor."[25] *Mission as transformation* constructs interdependent connections between evangelism and social action. Such transformation forges deep roots within the world. We choose not to stand apart from the world when we engage in such a mission. This is why transformation is contextual.

Transformational mission aligns theory and practice. It elevates local communities and their specific concerns. It brings freedom from the oppressive use of power. It strives for reconciliation, justice, and solidarity. It is primarily concerned with the poor and marginalized.

Transformational mission seeks community transformation. It does this by working with groups on concrete issues. (These issues include violence, addiction, sexuality, and poverty). A transformational mission has a goal. It seeks to help groups experience the liberation of the gospel, the life of the kingdom of God, and the redemption and lordship of Jesus Christ. It always does this by working with people in concrete local settings.[26]

A transformational mission is always contextual. We shape transformational missions around context and culture. "Cultures are religio-linguistic entities. They provide people with a framework for understanding their reality and a means for integrating the transcendent into daily life . . . One must look at how the gospel affects the whole of the communities' cultures, in value system, structures, and direction."[27]

Transformation is a long-term process. We cannot achieve it without the contextual and integral commitments expressed in the *Micah Declaration on Integral Mission*. Transformation involves an enduring commitment to people in local contexts. It demands immersion in particular settings.

Vinay Samuel says transformation is a long-term "commitment to community building." Transformation demands "the unity of the whole body of Christ." This recognizes the person in a community and appreciates the centrality of social units. It discerns where God is present and at work in the community. It invites people to take part in what God is already doing. Transformation invests in contexts. It builds social bonds, reconciliation, community, and transformation.[28]

---

25. Samuel and Sugden, *Mission as Transformation*, ii.

26. Samuel and Sugden, *Mission as Transformation*, 229–31.

27. Samuel and Sugden, *Mission as Transformation*, xii.

28. Samuel and Sugden, *Mission as Transformation*, 227–235; Samuel and Hauser, *Proclaiming Christ in Christ's Way*, 10–12.

Transformational mission discerns where God is at work in the world. It notices where the kingdom's values flourish—integrity, service, humility, peace, and freedom. Transformational mission seeks to develop these values. It does this through mission, discipleship, community building, and social action.

Samuel says that the values of the kingdom of God are clear. These values shape the outlook and practices of mission as transformation. They always work themselves out in context. We must contextualize these values. Samuel says the values of the kingdom of God that shape transformational missions are clear. These values become practices. The first value is human dignity. The second is freedom of conscience without threat or control. The third is participation in decisions that affect one's life and community. The fourth is the struggle against evil and injustice. Finally, the fifth is cultivating hope, respect, dignity, humility, faith, love, equity, and mutuality.[29]

The church must declare the whole gospel to the whole world. The church does this in word and action. It declares that the kingdom of God is manifest in the whole world. It announces that Jesus Christ reigns over this world and the entire cosmos. "The church in the power of the Spirit proclaims salvation in Christ and plants signs of the kingdom, always giving itself fully to the work of the Lord, knowing that its labor in the Lord is not in vain (1 Cor. 15:58)."

The church anticipates all things coming under the final rule and reign of Jesus Christ. It proclaims salvation and announces the kingdom in word and deed. The church embraces Jesus's concern for "justice and reconciliation throughout human society." It shares Jesus's passion for liberating all humanity "from every kind of oppression."[30]

The people of God engage in contextual missions in integral, transformational ways. We root these missional *practices* and *ways of being* in context. We can never divorce ourselves from context, *nor would we want to*.

Padilla writes that an integral mission must be both contextual and evangelical. We should take care that our mission is "truly *evangelical*— rooted in the gospel and consequently bringing about transformation in society."[31] Similarly, Costas affirms the emphasis on the *whole gospel* in the phrase "the whole gospel for the whole world." He challenges us to explore what we mean by the *whole world*. Hence, "a vision of 'the whole world' is essential for a faithful and relevant proclamation of the whole gospel."[32] Ac-

---

29. Samuel and Sugden, *Church in Response to Human Need*, 149–50.
30. Padilla, *Mission between the Times*, 186–99.
31. Padilla and Yamamori, *Local Church, Agent of Transformation*, 19–20.
32. Costas, *Christ Outside the Gate*, 163.

cording to Costas, the whole world is the whole gospel's object and context. Jesus gives his gospel to the world. "Hence, the whole world, the world of humans and the world of things, is the object of the gospel." The world is also the context of the gospel. "It is the context in which the good news of salvation was first given and received and is today proclaimed and heard. Outside the world, there is no gospel and certainly no Christian mission."[33]

The world is not static, rigid, or passive. It's dynamic, changing, and multidimensional. It's a world of linguistic, ideological, political, and ethnic diversity. The world is awash in myths and symbols. Connections exist between wildly differing cultures. The world is full of dynamic structures, institutions, and collective identities.

The church must contextualize the gospel in this dynamic, "crowded, complicated, and captive" environment. This way, the gospel is "made flesh in concrete situations... Hence one basic requirement of Christian mission is the immersion of the community of faith in the various situations that make up the world." This is an "experiential knowledge of human society rather than an intellectual understanding of an abstract world."[34]

To engage in *mission as transformation* in local contexts, the people of God need a missional passion for the world. We must embrace a desire for individuals' and groups' redemption, liberation, and well-being. We must commit to an integral mission expressed through service in local settings. We need "analytical tools and communication skills." These help us fulfill the missional task in particular contexts. We require prophetic courage to challenge demonic and oppressive powers, structures, and principalities. God's people must cultivate spirituality adequate for a contextual mission. We need an ability to assess the relationship between the gospel and cultures. Finally, we must form contextual responses, "incarnating the gospel in today's world."[35]

Jesus Christ died "outside the gate of the Holy City." So, the church must understand that salvation has "moved to the periphery." Our contextual mission is "outside the gates" of the edifices and institutions "that surround our religious compound and shape the structures of Christendom." Christ died outside the gate. So, we understand mission as *going out to the periphery*. A contextual mission leads to transformation when we identify with the suffering and alienation of the outsider and share in Christ's

---

33. Costas, *Christ Outside the Gate*.
34. Costas, *Christ Outside the Gate*.
35. Costas, *Christ Outside the Gate*, 164 and 172.

suffering "by serving, especially, its lowest representatives: the poor, the powerless, and the oppressed."[36]

Outside the gate, we fully understand the relationship between Jesus and the gospel and culture. Outside the gate, we can pursue a radical contextualization of the whole gospel for all persons and the world. We "become apostolic agents in the mobilization of a servant church toward its crucified Lord, outside the gate of a comfortable and secure ecclesiastical compound."[37]

Contextual Mission: Concluding Reflections

There has been a recent flood of books on missional theology and practice in the West. This is a welcome development. But much of the missional growth of the church has been in Asia, Africa, and Latin America. Conversion rates in those contexts have been astounding. Missional passion in those settings is thrilling and humbling. While missions in those settings have not always been contextual—primarily because of the influence of colonialism, globalization, and Western culture—many demonstrate what contextual and integral mission looks like.

We can learn much from the contextual and integral mission among the churches of Indigenous settings and the Majority World. We can especially learn from their focus on the kingdom of God. Their commitment to bring healing, justice, freedom, and transformation to whole persons and communities is instructive. We can also learn from their focus on incarnational immersion among the poor, exploited, and marginalized. We can learn from their missional integrity.

Here are nine things we learn from how Majority World Christians cultivate contextual mission:

1. Contextual mission understands that mission is "a permanent and intrinsic dimension of the church's life."[38]

The church is essentially missional. Mission is central, pivotal, and constitutive of its nature. David Bosch writes that "the classical doctrine of the *missio Dei* as God the Father sending the Son, and God the Father and Son sending the Spirit was expanded to include yet another "movement": Father,

---

36. Costas, *Christ Outside the Gate*, 172.
37. Costas, *Christ Outside the Gate*, 194.
38. Bosch, *Believing in the Future*, 27–32.

Son, and Holy Spirit sending the church into the world."[39] The church serves the mission of Christ. It is caught up in the missional purposes and "movements" of the Triune God. The church exists because of that mission. We exist because of God's redemptive mission to all humanity, creation, and history.[40]

Western missional thinkers often articulate this position. But many Majority World churches go further. They allow this conviction to soak every dimension of their theology, worship, prayer, and mission. Will we do the same?

2. Contextual mission focuses on the *missio Dei* and its consequences for the missional activities of the church.[41]

This includes the need for the church to stop focusing merely on mission *activities*. Instead, it should recognize that gospel proclamation, church planting, works of justice and compassion, and so forth, are all grounded in and directed toward the *missio Dei*. They are not so much missional activities as expressions of the essential missional nature of the church.

The church's mission is about the *nature* and *essence* of the church. Mission isn't merely about *adiaphora* (a thing not regarded as essential to faith or the actual nature of the church). Mission isn't only about *addresses* (that is, a message for proclamation) of the church. Mission isn't a contingent, peripheral, or optional church activity. Instead, the church "is missionary by its nature" and "exists by mission, just as fire exists by burning."[42]

It's possible to speak of mission as a set of determining goals or aims (such as in a *mission statement*). We can also view mission through our *missional actions*. However, a missional understanding of the church prioritizes the *missional nature of the church*. Missional ecclesiology proceeds from there to missional actions, systems, strategies, and structures. It's a theological vision shaped by the messianic mission of Jesus Christ.

---

39. Bosch, *Transforming Mission*, 390.
40. Hill, *Salt, Light, and a City*, 153
41. Bosch, *Transforming Mission*, 391.
42. Bosch, *Believing in the Future*, 31–32. Bosch is making his case with support from the Vatican Decree on Mission (paragraph 9) and from a quote attributed to Emil Brunner.

CONTEXTUALIZING MISSION

3. Contextual mission considers the missional "marks" of the church.

Since the Reformation, speaking of the *notae ecclesiae* (the "marks" of the true church) has been common.[43] The Reformation "marks" include faithful preaching, church discipline, and administration of the sacraments. The Nicene "marks" are unity, holiness, catholicity, and apostolicity. We must consider how we can understand these "marks" missionally. How do the *notae ecclesiae* relate to the *notae missionis* (the church's missional "marks" or the church's marks in mission)?

John Howard Yoder proposes four missional "marks" of the church. These are holy living, brotherly and sisterly love, witness, and suffering.[44] He also describes the fruit of such *notae missionis*. These are the "five sample practices of the church before the watching world." (1) We practice healthy conflict transformation. (2) We release the whole body of Christ to mission and ministry. (3) We listen to each other and the Spirit. (4) We are hospitable, and we share our resources. (5) We practice inclusivity and the transcendence of prejudices.[45] Alan Roxburgh writes that the missional church has three primary themes. (1) All cultures and societies are mission fields. (2) Mission is about the *missio Dei*. (3) The missional church is about the church being a contrast society.[46]

Having read Majority World perspectives, we must consider two critical questions. "What do I believe to be the missional marks of the church?" and "How will my church express these missional marks in my context?"

The chapters of this book give a good starting point as you form your own missional "marks" of the church. The book chapters reveal the missional "marks" that Majority World churches pursue. Here are some examples that emerge from these chapters. Missional churches cultivate *glocal* awareness and missional theology. They foster contextual and integral missions. They nurture Indigenous expressions of church, theology, and faith. Missional churches liberate the whole person. They welcome the stranger. They embrace the Spirit. They care for creation. Missional churches are ethical communities. They transform neighborhoods and seek the welfare of the city. They devour Scripture. Missional churches reimagine theological education and ministry training so that mission is central. They recover beauty—artistic, literary, natural, physical, and other forms. Their leaders

---

43. Hill, *Salt, Light, and a City*, 161.
44. Yoder, *Royal Priesthood*, 75–89; Hill, *Salt, Light, and a City*, 164.
45. Yoder, "Sacrament as Social Process," 34–39.
46. Roxburgh, *What Is Missional Church?* 5–8.

practice servantship (servant leadership). They recover authentic community. Missional churches develop missional spirituality and discipleship. Of course, you'll want to develop your list of the missional "marks" of the church over time.

4. Contextual mission immerses itself "in the concrete situations of the disenfranchised of our societies and witness to the lordship and saviorhood of Christ from within."

We verify this commitment "in our participation in the concrete transformation of these situations."[47] What does this involve? We commit to scriptural and gospel obedience and witness. We practice love, forgiveness, reconciliation, mutual accountability, hospitality, and embracing "difference." We pursue the practices of justice, peace, and mercy, even when they cost us much. We embrace a kingdom-sized vision and purpose that includes but is more extensive than the local church.

Immersed in the situations of the disenfranchised, we are a church of sinners and of grace. We are a positive contrast to racism, religious and ethnic violence, sexism, colonialism, warmongering, success orientation, manipulation, and oppression.[48] Contextual and integral mission is transformational when the love and grace of Jesus Christ saturates it.

5. Contextual mission seeks to embody the gospel of Christ in all cultures.

This includes cultivating Indigenous forms of theology, mission, worship, and discipleship. We should refuse to *merely* adapt other people's theology, mission, and worship for our setting. (We may do this occasionally, but it shouldn't be a regular practice). Instead, we must form *our homegrown indigenous* theologies and practices. This requires courage, innovation, and passion.

Contextual mission must stay true to the core of the gospel message. But it must also contextualize its mission, proclamation, discipleship, training, service, worship, etc. We must shape the choices we make in contextual missions around four things. (1) Does this contextualization glorify God? (2) Does it communicate and translate the gospel to this culture? (3) Is this a

---

47. Costas, "Contextualization and Incarnation," 23, 28, and 30; italics added for emphasis.
48. Costas, "Contextualization and Incarnation."

faithful proclamation of the gospel? (4) Does this contextual mission lead to the salvation of children, women, and men? Paul Hiebert and Scott Moreau provide us with valuable resources for *critical contextualization*.[49] In another chapter of this book, I've provided many examples of how Majority World Christians contextualize and inculturate theology, church, and mission. We can learn from these examples.

6. Contextual mission demands that we "place the totality of life under the lordship of Christ in [our] historical situation."[50]

Missional theology focuses on obedience to the lordship and mission of Jesus Christ. It places Jesus and his mission at the center of its being and organization and ministries. It expresses this complete submission to Jesus in its historical situation. Christ's incarnation, life, teaching, love, and self-sacrificial death on the cross provide us with the ultimate example of contextual mission.

We need to ask ourselves a critical question. "How do we concretely place the totality of life under the lordship of Jesus in this particular setting?" How are your mission, worship, discipleship, ministry, and fellowship under Jesus's lordship? How about your politics, aspirations, ego, finances, family, career, time, sexuality, internet use, relations with Muslims, identity, national allegiance or pride, and other areas not listed here?

7. Contextual mission translates and communicates the gospel "in the language and culture of real people in the particularities of their lives."

We aim to see the gospel "transform them, their societies, and their cultures into what God intends for them to be." We should seek "to build the bridge between Biblical revelation and human contexts." This removes "the gap between orthodoxy and orthopraxy and between truth, love, and holiness."[51]

Many people in Western contexts worry about weak government, the economy in general, unemployment/jobs, healthcare, immigration, the federal deficit/debt, and ethics/moral decline. In such a context, you

---

49. Hiebert, "Critical Contextualization"; Moreau, *Contextualization in World Missions*.
50. Padilla, "Contextualization of the Gospel," 28–30. Italics added for emphasis.
51. Tiénou and Hiebert, "Missional Theology," 225.

must translate and communicate the gospel to a culture worried about such things. In different cultural contexts, you would, of course, translate the gospel in a way that deals with the concerns of that culture.

8. Contextual mission is shaped around the kingdom of God and the incarnation of Christ.

Let's start with the kingdom of God. This kingdom is counter-cultural to many of this world's values, structures, and ethical systems. This has implications for our lifestyles, churches, and practice of mission. While recognizing and celebrating the kingdom's presence in this world, we must also renounce all that is not of the kingdom of God. We are to pursue righteousness, peace, justice, and joy. We will be misunderstood, persecuted, and even disowned at times.

That shouldn't surprise us—we're a counter-cultural messianic movement. "Today the church faces two big challenges: (1) how to make the kingdom of God understood in the different cultures of the world; and (2) how to live Jesus's own life principles of love, justice, and compassion in a world where the poor are getting poorer and the rich few are getting richer."[52]

The church is faithful to the mission of Christ and its missional nature when it's about establishing the kingdom of God. This involves redeeming individuals and entire peoples, systems, societies, and cultures. "The objective of the mission is the establishment of the kingdom of God which is the reign of God over all the forces of death, the triumph of love over all the forces of hatred, the triumph of peace over all the forces of violence and warfare. The kingdom of God is the object of the mission, and the life of Jesus Christ continues to be manifest through the church as it witnesses to, embodies and proclaims the kingdom."[53]

The church must be a "prophetic community and a sign of hope."[54] The church serves as a sign and instrument of salvation while conducting a prophetic role in the world. It's not enough for churches to be places where Christians worship, gather, and listen to preaching.[55] We must practice justice, forgiveness, compassion, love, liberation, peace, and reconciliation. We must love our neighbor and care for creation. We do this as a new creation. We're a sign, foretaste, herald, and witness to the kingdom and reign of God.

---

52. Fuellenbach, *Church*, xiii.
53. Hull, *Mission-Shaped Church*, 5.
54. Volf, "Church as a Prophetic Community and a Sign of Hope."
55. Volf, "Church as Prophetic Community," 9.

We also shape contextual missions around the incarnation. This involves patterning our mission after God becoming flesh in Jesus Christ. It means joining with the poor, powerless, conflicted, oppressed, and marginalized. We do this for empowerment, peace, justice, healing, reconciliation, and hope.

As I've already noted, this involves moving from distance to proximity, from power to weakness, from answers to questions, and from theological speculation to concrete and costly practices. Incarnational practices are always local, hands-on, costly, Spirit-dependent, and saturated in prayer.

9. Contextual mission must also be an integral mission.

What does this mean? It means the Spirit of Christ shapes us if we let him into a missional church with a transforming mission.

> When the church is committed to an integral mission and to communicating the gospel through everything it *is*, *does*, and *says*, it understands that its goal is not to become large numerically, nor to be rich materially, nor powerful politically. Its purpose is to incarnate the values of the kingdom of God and to witness to the love and the justice revealed in Jesus Christ, by the power of the Spirit, for the transformation of human life in all its dimensions, both on the individual level and on the community level.[56]

Ramachandra reminds us that *integral mission* is less about the church's *actions* and more about the church's *being*. Ramachandra says that integral mission "has to do with the church's *integrity*." The church has integrity when it brings together its public and private practices, actions and preaching, and passion for truth, compassion, and justice.

> Integral mission is then a way of calling the church to keep together, in her theology as well as in her practice, what the Triune God of the Biblical narrative always brings together: 'being' and 'doing,' the 'spiritual' and the 'physical,' the 'individual' and the 'social,' the 'sacred' and the 'secular,' 'justice' and 'mercy,' 'witness' and 'unity,' 'preaching truth' and 'practicing the truth,' and so on.[57]

As we cultivate contextual and integral missions, the words of Micah 6:8 will ring in our ears. "He has shown all you people what is good. What

---

56. Padilla, "What Is Integral Mission?"
57. Ramachandra, "Integral Mission," 45–46.

PART 2: RENEWING OUR MISSION

does the Lord require of you? To act justly, to love mercy, and to walk humbly with your God."

Study Questions

1. How is your church involved in tangible acts of service, social reform, and liberation?
2. How can we ensure our church's mission does three things? (1) Proclaim the gospel. (2) Make fully committed disciples of Jesus Christ. (3) Take part in liberation people from political, sexual, social, racial, and economic forces oppressing them.
3. Is your church or Christian organization's mission integral? Does its mission seek to integrate all three areas listed in question two?
4. Does your church engage in mission activities that are contextually relevant to your neighborhood or local community?
5. How would you define *a contextual mission* and *integral mission*?
6. How can local churches help their congregation feel empowered to join God's mission in the world?

10.

Liberating People

The Second Expression

Liberation theology, as a technical theological term, dates from the mid-1960s. It began within Latin American Roman Catholicism. By 1970, Protestant theologians were becoming involved and influential. Instead of "theology," speaking of *theologies of liberation* is more correct. This is because differences exist between writers and between regions. There are differences between Latin American and African theologians. There are unique features in South African, Asian, Northern Irish, Native American, Indigenous, feminist, and womanist liberation theologies. Even so, there are common factors in the rise of the liberation theologies. There are many similarities in approach and theology and concern.

Liberation theologies assert the value of context. The church must theologize in and serve among contexts. Theology must arise from reflection on and within the manifold contexts in which the church finds itself. Yet, theology does more than reflect. It also becomes part of transforming society and serving human liberation.

Liberation theologies arise as theology from the perspective of the poor, marginalized, powerless, silenced, and oppressed. Gustavo Gutiérrez says this well. "The starting point of liberation theology is a commitment to the poor, the non-person. Its ideas come from the victim."[1] Leonardo and

---

1. Ferguson et al., *New Dictionary of Theology*.

PART 2: RENEWING OUR MISSION

Clodovis Boff say, "Liberation theology was born when faith confronted the injustice done to the poor."[2]

The churches in Western nations must understand their role in addressing poverty, injustice, and inequality. Liberation theology arose as a response to these burdens in Latin American and African contexts. It moved later to other cultures.

Liberation theologians felt compelled to confront the legacies of imperialistic colonial domination, totalitarian regimes, revolutions, and independence. They considered the role of the colonial churches in the Majority World and Indigenous cultures. They examined the responses to Latin American and African contexts by post-conciliar Latin American and African Catholicism. They engaged the shape of faith, church, and mission amidst post-colonial deprivation. They addressed the search for hope, justice, and liberation in a world of poverty and oppression.

These liberation theologians considered the functions and demands of competing ideologies—capitalist, communist, and Marxist. They scrutinized the role of politico-economic structures in causing social division, oppression, and class struggle. They realized the importance of consciousness-raising—helping people become aware of their situation and ways out. They fostered the expansion and diversification of liberation theologies as they spread beyond Latin America and Africa. (Contextual forms of liberation theology emerged in Asia, Northern Ireland, and Eastern Europe, and in First Nation, Indigenous, feminist, womanist, and Western contexts.)[3]

Liberation theology challenges Western churches and pastors to examine our unspoken assumptions. It calls us to scrutinize our associations with power. It invites us to increase our concern for the poor and powerless. It confronts our spiritual, political, and social complacency.

Jesus Christ demonstrated a deep and responsive concern for the poor. He was passionate about the silenced, marginalized, vulnerable, forgotten, and oppressed. The Bible clearly shows God's concern for the poor and the oppressed. We must ensure that our theology and ministry are contextual, compassionate, and lived. God calls us to act justly, love mercy, and walk humbly with him (Mic 6:8).

We can express liberation theology's principles and concerns in ways relevant to our context. We can develop these themes in fresh ways and ways that are responsive to biblical analysis and the challenges of our time

---

2. Boff and Boff, *Introducing Liberation Theology*, 3; Davidson and Hill, "Liberation Theology."

3. Ferguson et al., *New Dictionary of Theology*, 387–88.

and culture. We must ask, Who is my neighbor? and act upon the answer (Luke 10:25–37).

Liberation theologies highlight the importance of mission among the margins of society. They show us ways that the church can express the priesthood of all believers (especially among the marginalized, broken, and excluded). Liberation theologies call the church to diversity and hospitality. How diverse and welcoming are our structures, language, cultures, and leadership? Other Christian traditions can explore the insights of liberation theologies. For instance, Evangelicals can explore themes concerning liberation, social justice, poverty, power, and gender. The church must become a community of partnership, hospitality, justice, equality, and welcome.

How are justice, liberation, hospitality, and inclusion missional themes? Jesus calls his church to be a community of justice and liberation. We must stand for those marginalized or silenced by religion, politics, and society.

Unfortunately, white, middle-aged, university-educated, and ecclesially employed males still headline most Western Christian conferences. This isn't just true of conferences. This group dominates various events, seminars, publications, and media. Where are the voices from the margins of this dominant culture?

In many aspects of the church, race, social status, gender, education, and theological and linguistic uniformity are central. These things shape the culture and leadership of gatherings. (This is the case even when the rhetoric suggests otherwise.) Structural complacency works against mission, hospitality, inclusion, and diversity. It works against the culture of the kingdom of God. We must examine the biblical text, Majority World, and Indigenous witness for guidance here. We need help amid these challenges to authentic church and mission. Missional churches show solidarity with those oppressed, marginalized, or excluded by societies and churches. The broken, oppressed, excluded, and vulnerable constitute many in missional churches. They are at the heart of the church. We must form missional practices and theology with attention to—and the participation of—the vulnerable and marginalized. Compassion and inclusion mark the missional church.

Missional churches must be honest about who they are as they engage in mission. We need to be honest about our presumptions, assumptions, cultural biases, prejudices, theological convictions, brokenness, and frailties. Understanding leads to repentance. Repentance leads to authentic and compassionate acts of justice, mercy, and liberation.

In this chapter, I consider the themes of liberation theology. These include focusing on context, human liberation, and solidarity with the oppressed. Liberation theologians emphasize the liberating person and work of Jesus Christ. I also outline the liberationist focus on base communities, spirituality, ecology, and dialogue. Finally, I suggest where liberation theology is headed.

Liberating Contexts: Contextual Thought and Mission

Liberation theology encourages us to remember that theology's domain is the concrete situation. Situations and contexts are formative for worthwhile theology, mission, and ministry.

If our theology is merely abstract, it's impoverished. Our theology is deficient when we remove it from concrete, genuine contexts. Liberation theology protests the abstractness of European theology. It challenges the whiteness, maleness, and parochialism of too much Euro-American God-talk.

There can be no distinction between secular and sacred history. As Hugo Assman puts it, the history of salvation is "the salvation of history."[4] All history is the history of salvation. This is true of the overarching histories of peoples and cultures and the local narratives of contexts. Human beings experience salvation now, in the present, in this context. We need to see salvation as something more than personal and individual. Salvation is also socio-political. According to liberation theologians, it is as much about redeeming the world and its systems, structures, and cultures as it is about saving individual human beings. Thus, the gospel is political. The gospel involves the redemption of the world community. The gospel leads to the radical transformation of contexts.

The biblical text is the ground and starting point for all Evangelical theology. Otherwise, as René Padilla warns, we fall into a form of historical reductionism. When we do this, historical situations determine the shape and content of all our theology. This reductionism makes our vision of the kingdom of God narrow and selective. Yet, we ignore history and contexts to our detriment.[5]

Leonardo Boff, Oscar Romero, Juan Luis Segundo, and Jon Sobrino agree on many things. They all say, for example, that "the new context for theologizing" is among ordinary people. The local context is the ideal, authentic setting for the church's mission, theology, and ministry. To do this well, the church needs an integral, holistic mission. It must make the kingdom of God central to its vision, mission, and life together. The church must commit to peace, justice, and the liberation struggle.

4. Assmann, *Teología Desde La Praxis De La Liberación*, 25.
5. Padilla, "Liberation Theology," 44.

Leonardo Boff says that the church needs to be the Good Samaritan. The church does this as it proclaims the gospel prophetically and contextually. The church is the Good Samaritan, striving for the liberation and rights of the poor and oppressed in every context, as it stands against social injustice, defends and promotes decent standards of living, and reinvents itself as a grassroots movement.

At the heart of all this is a contextually shaped church that is, at the same time, faithful to Christ and his Scriptures. This is a church with a contextually relevant theology and mission. It's a church listening attentively to the poor. It's a people pursuing justice and liberation in the world.[6]

Liberating Praxis: Cultivating Suspicion and Hope

Liberation theology is committed to leading transformational change in society. It sees itself as having a mission in the world. To bring liberation from oppression, we must scrutinize all values and presuppositions. We need to examine their contribution to liberation or oppression.

Co-opting Paul Ricoeur's language, Gustavo Gutiérrez and Juan Luis Segundo describe the role of Christian theology. They say that theology cultivates a "critical openness" and a "hermeneutic of suspicion and hope."[7] All Christians read the Scriptures through their own culture. So, we need to examine whether our culture's outlook, values, and assumptions have "bound up" our reading of the Bible. Is our biblical interpretation culture-bound? Is it open to change?

Suspicion of hidden ideologies is necessary. For example, if the God of the Bible is for the poor, why are we so undisturbed as we live among the poor? How does our whiteness, wealth, gender, privilege, or power prevent us from identifying with other people's humiliation?

There is also hope. The Scriptures rephrase our questions. The Bible changes our understanding of life, death, society, power, relationships, liberation, etc. It draws us from suspicion and despair to faith and hope and love.[8]

Liberation theologies and approaches to biblical interpretation have striking features. We can learn much from them. This is true even as we adapt and contextualize them to our cultural and theological settings.

Here are some features of liberation theology and interpretation:

---

6. Boff, *When Theology Listens to the Poor*, 32–49.
7. White, "Between Suspicion and Hope."
8. Segundo, *Liberation of Theology*, 8–9.

PART 2: RENEWING OUR MISSION

Contextual

The starting point is *the experience and cause of the oppressed*. It isn't abstract notions of liberation, justice, integral mission, praxis, etc.[9] In the words of Gustavo Gutiérrez, it's "theology from the underside of history." It's a theology focusing on "God's preferential option for the poor."[10] Since that is the starting point, this theology is *concrete and contextual*.

Orthopraxic

Liberation theology roots itself in *tangible, particular orthopraxis*, not just orthodoxy. As we practice discipleship to Jesus among the poor, marginalized, and oppressed (as we engage in orthopraxis), orthodoxy emerges to complement this praxis. This praxis focuses on human dignity and liberation. It is about social transformation. It is a "liberative praxis."[11] Gustavo Gutiérrez says that theology is "done" as a "critical reflection on praxis."[12] *Praxis* is a term borrowed and developed from Karl Marx. It means more than "practice." It is the dialectical process of action moving to reflection, to new action, to new reflection, and so on. Christians can think through their faith only as they live it. This includes the commitment to the alleviation of oppression and poverty. We cannot do this kind of reflection in the abstract. We do theology first and study it second. "It is a theology which is open—in the protest against trampled human dignity, in the struggle against the plunder of the vast majority of people, in liberating love, and the building of a new, just, and fraternal society—to the gift of the Kingdom of God."[13]

Transformational

It is a theological method characterized by transformative "seeing, judging, and acting." That is, to use more technical terms, socioanalytic, hermeneutic, and practical mediation. The *socioanalytic* mediation contemplates the world of the oppressed. It seeks to understand why the oppressed are oppressed. The *hermeneutic* mediation contemplates the word of God. It attempts to see what the divine plan is regarding people experiencing poverty.

9. Boff, "Methodology of the Theology of Liberation," 6.
10. Gutiérrez, *Power of the Poor in History*, 169–221; Gutiérrez and Nickoloff, *Gustavo Gutiérrez*, 78–148.
11. Boff, "Methodology of the Theology of Liberation," 10.
12. Gutiérrez, *Theology of Liberation*, 6; Sobrino, *True Church and the Poor*, 21–24.
13. Gutiérrez, *Theology of Liberation*, 15.

Finally, *practical* mediation contemplates the aspect of the activity. It seeks to discover how we might overcome oppression in conformity with God's plan.[14]

Interdisciplinary

The above features need this theological method to form creative, constructive interdisciplinary partnerships. These partnerships are with the social sciences and other disciplines. Liberation theology engages social analysis, sociology, politics, philosophy, economics, and modern history.[15] The contexts of liberation theology push it into these partnerships. It is from these partnerships that it understands the world. Liberation theology's connections to Marxism are not philosophical as such. However, some liberation theologians do use Marxist social analysis. This is especially true of the Latin Americans. Other forms of liberation theology have been more reluctant to embrace Marxist social analysis. African-American liberationists are an example. Marxism's demise and the collapse of socialism have undermined much of this social analysis. I will discuss this later in this chapter.

Axial

Gustavo Gutiérrez says the axis of liberation theology is "the gratuitousness and exigence of love."[16] God calls the church to be a prophetic community. We are a community characterized by gratuitousness and the freedom of God's love. We are a people that embrace the neighbor and embody the Beatitudes. We are a family that reveals the freedom, love, truth, and finality of God's kingdom. We are a people characterized by acts of love, mercy, peace, reconciliation, liberation, and justice in a broken world.

Ecclesial

We must practice Christian faith and theology in a community to address the world's needs. God calls his church to be a theologizing community. Professional theologians aren't enough. Faith communities ought to theologize

---

14. Boff, "Methodology of the Theology of Liberation," 11; Boff and Boff, *Introducing Liberation Theology*, 22–42.
15. Gutiérrez and Nickoloff, *Essential Writings*, 42–49.
16. Gutiérrez and Nickoloff, *Essential Writings*, 149–83.

together. "Theology is not an individual task but an ecclesial function."[17] Professional theologians must help pastors cultivate theologizing communities. Theologians need to do theology with accountability. They should be accountable to—and located within—dynamic, questioning, theologizing local faith communities. The community engages in the work of theology. The professional theologian contributes, facilitates, and practices accountable, community-shaped theology.

Liberation theologians cultivate suspicion of hidden ideologies and interpretive methods. They are especially suspicious of ideas and practices that foster oppression. They complement this with hope. They hope for transformed societies, renewed church structures, and fresh missional practices. They hope for gratuitous expressions of love and liberating theological methods. They hope for "seeing, judging, and acting" that results in liberation. They hope for genuine attention to the perspectives of the poor and oppressed. They hope that the church will indeed be the church envisaged by Jesus Christ.

Liberating Orientation: Solidarity with the Oppressed

Western Christians have (at times) been far too complacent about issues of poverty, exploitation, and oppression. We are wealthy, comfortable, passive, and complacent. The Scriptures challenge us to be otherwise.

Leonardo Boff describes how Christian convictions about God, Christ, Spirit, eschaton, apostolicity, church, faith, justice, love, and mission compel the church. They compel the church to show a "clear and prophetic option expressing a preference for, and solidarity with, the poor (Puebla, §1134)."[18]

Dietrich Bonhoeffer—who grew up in affluence and social privilege—wrote these words as he reflected on ten years under Hitler's tyranny. "There remains an experience of incomparable value. We have for once learned to see the great events of world history from below, from the perspectives of the outcast, the suspects, the maltreated, the powerless, the oppressed, the reviled—in short, from the perspective of those who suffer."[19]

Liberation theologians concern themselves with the liberation of the oppressed. They care about God's preference for the poor and the marginalized. This solidarity begins where the pain or subjugation is present. In Latin America, this begins with socio-economic oppression. In Africa, it is

17. Gutiérrez, *Density of the Present*, 173.

18. Boff and Boff, *Introducing Liberation Theology*, 44–46, and chapter 4.

19. Bonhoeffer, *Letters and Papers from Prison*, 17, quoted in Gutiérrez, *Power of the Poor in History*, xvi.

with colonialism and dictatorships. In African-American communities, it is with racism. Among Indigenous peoples, it is with human rights. Among feminist and womanist thinkers, it is with gender equality. We must also begin where the needs are in our setting.

Liberating Christ: The Redeeming Liberator

Christology is a fertile source for Latin American liberation theology. Most liberation theologians deal with Christological issues. They appeal to the Gospels and the theology of Jesus Christ when making a case for liberation.

Jon Sobrino exemplifies this. Sobrino offended the Vatican with his theology of Christ. He says the poor "constitute the supreme, scandalous prophetic and apocalyptic presence of the Christian God." The poor confront all Christologies with this question: "Were you there when they crucified my Lord?" The poor especially ask this question of Christologies done at a distance from the poor and oppressed.[20]

According to Jon Sobrino, people experiencing poverty are the *locus theologicus of Christology*. They tell of Christ's "self-abasement, his *kenosis*, his concealment, his cross . . . as the locus of the current presence of Christ, they are a light illuminating all things, and specifically illuminating the truth of Christ . . . as Messiah, as Liberator, and as definitive mediator of the Reign of God."[21]

In *Jesus the Liberator*, Jon Sobrino examines the relationship between the person, mission, and faith of Jesus and the nature of the kingdom of God. For Jesus, the final reality was the kingdom of God—a kingdom of and for the poor, rejected, and despised. The way of the kingdom is the way of liberation of the oppressed. It's the way of healing for the wounded. It's the way of victory over systemic and spiritual evil. It's the way of peace instead of the manifold forms of violence in this world. It's the way of welcoming sinners and hospitality toward strangers. It's the way of liberation from selfishness, exploitation, and marginalization.

Jon Sobrino also considers what the death of Jesus tells us about the nature of salvation. His death shows us what it means to be his "crucified people." Following the suffering Servant, the crucified people establish

---

20. Sobrino, *Jesus the Liberator*, 28; Ellacuria, "Discernir El 'Signo' De Los Tiempos," 58.

21. Sobrino and Ellacuría, *Systematic Theology*, 142–44. I'm not convinced by Sobrino's argument. *The poor* don't tell of Christ's abasement, his kenosis—*the gospel* tells us of those things. No *class of people* are the locus of the presence of Christ—*Christ himself* is the locus of the presence of Christ.

righteousness and justice. They embrace suffering and martyrdom. They bear the sins of the world. They are chosen for salvation. They serve as a light to the nations. They are the "martyred people." This doesn't mean that they will necessarily be martyred. They are the "martyred people" because "The essence of martyrdom is affinity with the death of Jesus."[22]

In his writings, Jon Sobrino says that we must look at Jesus through the eyes of people experiencing poverty. Looking at Jesus and Christology through the eyes and experiences of the poor, exploited, powerless, silenced, and victims achieve one central thing. "It can open our eyes to the relationship between God and what is small."[23]

Like other liberation theologians, Leonardo Boff emphasizes the importance of the historical Jesus. Boff speaks of the implications of Jesus's priorities, practices, and message about the kingdom. Jesus's values, as revealed in the Gospels, must shape our churches and discipleship. Jesus's liberating practices are the church's yardstick or measuring rod. The church's attention to *Christopraxis* accompanies its *orthodoxy* and *orthopraxis*.[24]

Boff then turns to the Cross. He reflects on its meanings for the suffering of the innocent and Jesus's solidarity with the crucified of history. He also considers the power of the resurrection. Death and suffering no longer have the last word. We "die to be raised" and "the executioner shall not triumph over the victim."[25]

Oscar Romero was a bishop in El Salvador. He was famous for his liberation theology. He was known for his ministry among the poor and his denunciation of the church's persecution. Romero was martyred in 1980 for the cause of Jesus Christ.

Liberating Community: Base Communities, and the Church

Jesus calls his church to be a transformed and transforming community. We are to lead people into his liberating power and presence. This is true for all expressions of the church: large or small, institutional or independent, local or para-local. This requires a renewal of the church. It demands a courageous examination of the church's systems and structures. It calls for a reorientation of the church's purpose, structures, mission, and ministries.

---

22. Sobrino, *Jesus the Liberator*, 267, and chapters 4 and 10.
23. Sobrino, *Christ the Liberator*, 294.
24. Boff, *Faith on the Edge*, 134–38.
25. Boff, *When Theology Listens*, 135–36.

Transformed and transforming churches orient these things around Jesus's vision of the kingdom. The church requires a "radical revision" and a "substantial transformation." It needs "courage and serenity." This is "the opposite of a facile emotionalism which leads to arbitrary measures, superficial solutions, or evasions, but avoids the search for radical changes and untrodden paths. At stake in all this is the church's faithfulness to its Lord."[26] The church is in constant need of renewal. This is so that it can be "salt, light, and a city on a hill" in every cultural context it resides.

The true church is for everyone, including the poor and the voiceless. It's a church that confronts the principalities and powers of this world. It is a scandalous church, a confronting church, and a non-violent church. It is a church characterized by the counter-cultural values of the kingdom of God. As Gustavo Gutiérrez reminds us, "This is what always happens: it is easier to point out what must be done than to do it." So, God calls us to examine the "meaning of the Church and its mission in the world."

Jesus leads us to openness to the "primordial and inescapable condition for fulfilling that mission." That condition is faithfulness to the mission of Jesus Christ. Faithfulness to that mission happens through celebrating the Eucharist, the authentic unity found in Christian *koinonia*, and active mission in the world. We pursue God's mission through the "*denunciation* of every dehumanizing situation" contrary to unity, liberty, and justice. We pursue our mission by *annunciating* the gospel that calls people to "union among themselves and communion" with the Father, Son, and Holy Spirit.[27] For Gustavo Gutiérrez, "The mission of the church, as the community of Jesus' disciples, is to communicate and bear witness to this total liberation of the human being. The church's mission is, as I said, to proclaim an integral liberation, because nothing is left untouched by the saving work of Christ."[28]

Base ecclesial communities are commonly associated with liberation theology. Yet not all base communities identify with liberation social analysis. These grassroots ecclesial communities proliferate in the Majority World. They are small groups of self-reliant believers. They meet for worship and to celebrate the Eucharist. They engage in justice, mercy, and consciousness-raising among the poor and oppressed. René Padilla rejoices in these grassroots ecclesial communities' missional, liberating, educative, and fellowshipping dimensions.[29]

26. Gutiérrez, *Theology of Liberation*, 252.

27. Gutiérrez, *Theology of Liberation*, 251–79.

28. Gutiérrez and Nickoloff, *Essential Writings*, 259 and 261; Gutiérrez, *Truth Shall Make You Free*, 141.

29. Padilla, "New Ecclesiology in Latin America," 158. See: Sobrino and Ellacuría, *Systematic Theology*, 184–91.

PART 2: RENEWING OUR MISSION

Liberating Holism: Ecology, Spirituality, and Liberation

Leonardo Boff cares about human and ecological connections. He discusses the vital relationships between liberation, ecology, poverty, and spirituality. Boff claims that it is impossible to separate three crucial things. These are authentic Christian spirituality, concern for the poor and oppressed, and ecological stewardship.

Liberation theology and eco-justice are partners. They join in responding to the needs of the oppressed. They collaborate to bridge the gap between the wealthy and the poor. They collaborate as they reclaim dignity for people experiencing poverty and the earth. The church needs an ecologically sustainable spirituality. It requires a spirituality deeply concerned with the liberation of the earth and people experiencing poverty. Christian spirituality must care about the planet's health while pursuing human freedom, dignity, and well-being.[30] Social injustice and environmental injustice are inextricably connected. So are human and ecological liberation.

For Boff, "The earth is crying out and the poor are crying out, both victims of both social and environmental injustice."[31] The answer to this problem begins with theological reflection on ecology and violence. We need an eco-social theology of liberation. We need new approaches to production. We need a socio-environmental ethic attentive to the dignity and well-being of humans and the environment. Boff says there are connections between politics, theology, ecology, poverty, oppression, and spirituality. When we see these, we can start addressing social and environmental injustice.

Boff turns to Saint Francis as a model for spirituality. Francis exemplified concern for people experiencing poverty. He sought the liberation of the oppressed. Francis practiced prayerful contemplation and a politically engaged spirituality. He was welcoming and hospitable, inviting all into the life and ministry of the church. Francis was passionate about caring for humans, animals, nature, and the planet.[32]

The church needs *political saints*. These are passionate about God. But they are also passionate for the poor, passionate for prayer, and passionate for the environment.[33] Gustavo Gutiérrez describes a spirituality of liberation in this way:

> A spirituality of liberation will center on a *conversion* to the neighbor, the oppressed person, the exploited social class, the

---

30. Boff, *Cry of the Earth, Cry of the Poor*, chapters 5 and 10.
31. Boff and Elizondo, *Ecology and Poverty*, xi.
32. Boff, *Saint Francis*.
33. Boff, "Need for Political Saints."

despised ethnic group, the dominated country. Our conversion to the Lord implies this conversion to the neighbor. Evangelical conversion is indeed the touchstone of all spirituality. Conversion means a radical transformation of ourselves; it means thinking, feeling, and living as Christ—present in exploited and alienated persons. To be converted is to commit oneself lucidly, realistically, and concretely to the process of the liberation of the poor and oppressed. It means to commit oneself not only generously, but also with an analysis of the situation and a strategy of action. To be converted is to know and experience the fact that, contrary to the laws of physics, we can stand straight, according to the Gospel, only when our center of gravity is outside ourselves.[34]

Liberating Futures: Women Extending the Conversation

Many women are expanding and revising liberation, public, and missional theologies. These women bring various cultural and theological backgrounds to these tasks.

These women often criticize liberation theology's lack of engagement with women's issues. They highlight its patriarchal assumptions and outlook. Yet, these women aren't only concerned with womanist questions. They absorb themselves in theological, ethical, justice, ecclesial, and missional enterprises. Women develop these enterprises for and with their families, communities, and societies. These women include Mercy Amba Oduyoye, Nana Amba Eyiaba, Elizabeth Amoah, Dianne Stewart Diakite, Rose Mary Amenga-Etego, Evelyn Parker, Brigilia Bam, Musimbi Kanyoro, Katie G. Cannon, Jacquelyn Grant, Letty Russell, Rosemary Ruether, Elizabeth Schussler-Fiorenza, Phyllis Treble, Rosalee Velloso Ewell, Elizabeth Petersen, Sallie McFague, Catharina Halkes, Anji Barker, Elisbeth Moltmann-Wendel, and a host of others.

Ghanaian, Liberian, Nigerian, and African-American women recently gathered in Accra, Ghana. They met for the inaugural African and African Diasporan Women in Religion and Theology Conference. Mercy Amba Oduyoye hosted this conference at Trinity Theological Seminary's Talitha Qumi Institute of African Women in Religion and Culture in Legon, Ghana. Oduyoye founded and directs this institute. The conference focused on

---

34. Gutiérrez and Nickoloff, *Essential Writings*, 288.

issues facing African cultures. It especially emphasized the need to address violence against African-descended women and girls.[35]

Mercy Amba Oduyoye inspires a younger generation of women and men to explore these issues afresh. Oduyoye says that women call liberationists and the broader church to account for patriarchal and anti-women practices, hermeneutics, and cultural sexism. She's leading the way in many areas: setting an example for other women. Oduyoye champions theological and ministerial formation among women. She retrieves the narratives and experiences of women in church and society. Oduyoye catalyzes understanding and dialogue between the genders. She addresses violence toward women and girls. She profiles women's theology. Oduyoye enhances women's and girls' health, influence, and power. Oduyoye and so many other women worldwide are helping men, the church, and liberation theology understand anew what it means to follow a just, merciful, transforming, and compassionate Messiah.[36]

Liberation: Concluding Reflections

Western Christians can learn much from liberation theology. They can learn from its solidarity with the poor and vulnerable and its passion for justice. It's time we became "liberating Christians." What does that mean? Liberating Christians join with the freeing power of Christ. They take part in his liberation of whole persons, whole communities, and the whole of creation from everything that oppresses, exploits, or dehumanizes them. They strive to see people, communities, and creation enjoy the freedom, hope, and life the Father, Son, and Holy Spirit offer.

Here are ten things we learn from how Majority World Christians pursue solidarity with the broken, oppressed, excluded, and vulnerable.

1. Liberating Christians have first enjoyed the liberation only Jesus Christ can offer.

We cannot help others find freedom unless we've experienced it. Before joining God in liberating acts, I must ask, What has Jesus liberated *me from* and *to*? How has Jesus liberated me *from* sin, oppression, lies, poverty, death, selfishness, burdens, legalism, prejudice, etc.? How has Jesus liberated me *to*

---

35. Ross, "Historic Meeting."
36. Oduyoye, *Hearing and Knowing*; Oduyoye, *Introducing African Women's Theology*.

forgiveness, hope, freedom, justice, life, love, faith, relationship, etc.? How has he liberated me to join him in bringing freedom to the world (individually and alongside others)? This doesn't mean that life is easy. It doesn't mean life is free of suffering, discrimination, and exploitation. Liberation is often an ongoing process. But, even in the face of these challenges, we know that Jesus Christ has liberated us and given us his hope.

2. Liberating Christians only offer liberation in the person and gospel of the Lord Jesus Christ.

We do not offer our liberation. We do not offer freedom and hope through other means. We recognize, in a spirit of dependency, "that all the liberating force in the world comes from Christ."[37] We proclaim and live out the gospel of Jesus Christ confidently.

3. Liberating Christians examine themselves and how associations with power and privilege shape their lives.

This is a challenge for those of us who've only known the privilege of our race, gender, or birthplace. We must scrutinize our unspoken assumptions and our associations with power. We need to consider our concern for the poor and powerless. It's time we repent of spiritual, political, and social complacency.

We need to examine our perspectives on a wide range of issues. Do these views reflect the values of Jesus Christ and his kingdom? Does Scripture shape them? Or have we allowed the values of our culture, politics, race, class, and gender to shape these perspectives? What forms our views on gender, ethnicity, the military, police brutality, race relations, money, property, immigration, healthcare, and education (to name a few)?

Jayakumar Christian engages with the work of Walter Wink when he says that the world lies about the true nature of power.[38] Here are some of these distortions of truth: Power always belongs to the powerful. Force always prevails over ideas. (The victors are those with technological, military, and economic strength.) Choice always belongs to the powerful. Power is truth. Assets are an all-important power base. (Power comes from the assets I own and the wealth I create.) Power is a zero-sum game. Powerful

---

37. Romero and Brockman, *Violence of Love*, 140.
38. Christian, *God of the Empty-Handed*.

institutions are more important than people. Finally, God is the patron of the powerful.

These are all lies. These lies shape how the world perceives, pursues, exercises, and abuses power. It's why the power of Christ is either misunderstood or an insult. Sure, power influences all human relationships. It's dangerous to deny or fail to recognize this. But we must recognize that power belongs to God (not power to the people or the powerful).

Power tempts us to play God in the lives of others—nurturing our god-complexes. We must examine our associations with power and how they shape our lives and points of view. We need to speak the truth about power. Power isn't found in resources, might, status, race, and privilege. Power belongs to God alone. He "chooses the weak things of the world to shame the strong" (1 Cor 1:27). Andy Crouch says we can use power redemptively. As we examine our views and ourselves, we can decide to use what power we have for the well-being of others. We can use power in the way of Christ—enriching human life, addressing injustice, ushering in peace, and enabling human flourishing.[39]

4. Liberating Christians are actively concerned with the poor, silenced, marginalized, vulnerable, forgotten, and oppressed.

Liberating Christians acknowledge and respond to God's concern for the poor and oppressed. They respond in concrete ways. They seek hands-on solutions to the problems of poverty, injustice, inequality, and suffering. The Spirit leads us to explore how conversion to Christ is conversion to the neighbor. We ask, "Who is my neighbor?" We act on the answer (Luke 10:25–37). We act justly, love mercy, and walk humbly with God (Mic 6:8). Sometimes, we do this in concrete and ordinary ways. Sometimes, we do it in extraordinary ways or on a larger scale.

Making a difference begins with building relationships. For most of us, friendships lead to solidarity, care, and support. But Christians should also name and confront structural injustices. These enable poverty, oppression, exploitation, and marginalization. Poverty is not merely an economic state. Systems, structures, and social forces silence and dehumanize people experiencing poverty. Poverty and oppression are scandalous and insidious forms of violence. They're a denial of the kingdom of God. They're an affront to the gospel and person of Jesus Christ. The oppressed must not give in passively to their tormentors. The church ought not to sit idly by while oppression occurs.

39. Crouch, *Playing God*.

As God's people, we must lead the way in confronting dehumanizing factors and in bringing change. The church must shape a "solid contemporary reflection on the witness of poverty."[40] This involves declaring the transformational power, presence, and kingdom of God and doing this in word and action. It means moving beyond a *notional* concern for the poor and vulnerable. Instead, we become *actively* involved in their well-being. We find ourselves transformed in the process.

5. Liberating Christians support the poor, marginalized, and silenced as they form their theologies and expressions of faith.

The poor and oppressed are not the objects of the gospel but the subjects. By the grace of God, they are calling the church back to gospel faithfulness. The theologian, pastor, and missionary must identify with the oppressed in their struggle. Poverty and oppression are never neutral. We must always oppose and confront them. We must support these groups as they form their theologies and approaches to the Christian faith.

6. Liberating Christians develop communities characterized by specific values and practices.

These practices are concrete, contextual, orthopraxic, transformational, collaborative, and communal. They're characterized by extravagant love. (See the explanations in the section "Liberating Praxis"). Together, we shape communities passionate about Christ's liberating gospel and love. We embrace neighbors. We welcome the stranger. We practice hospitality. Together, we embody the Beatitudes. We show the values of the kingdom of God through them. (The Beatitudes include humility, dependence, mourning, meekness, contentment, hunger for God, compassion, integrity, peacemaking, suffering, and witness.) Together, we practice concrete, loving, and costly deeds. These are works of mercy, peace, reconciliation, liberation, and justice in a broken world.

---

40. Gutiérrez, *Theology of Liberation*, 287–302.

PART 2: RENEWING OUR MISSION

7. Liberating Christians nurture contemplative-active spirituality that cares for humanity and the earth.

Like Francis of Assisi, our spirituality must be contemplative and active. It needs to care for the well-being of humans and the earth. We nurture the *contemplative* side of this spirituality through quiet meditation, communal prayer, immersion in Scripture, and celebrating the Word and Eucharist together. We foster the *active* side through welcome, hospitality, peacemaking, creation care, and serving the poor and marginalized. It involves helping oppressed people find freedom and justice. It means healing the broken and wounded. It includes advocating on behalf of the silenced. It's engaging in Christ-honoring political and social engagement. It's passionate care for individuals, humanity, and the earth.

8. Liberating Christians take the Scripture's focus on mercy, justice, and freedom seriously.

Over two thousand Scripture passages speak of God's attitude to poverty and injustice. Western Christians have ignored these passages too often. It's time to respond to God's passion for justice, mercy, healing, and hope. It's time to take Scripture's focus on justice and poverty seriously.

9. Liberating Christians examine the claims of liberation theology and form their conclusions.

It's essential to examine the claims of liberation theology. It's worth considering how we can contextualize its practices and theologies in our unique settings. As we do this, it's worth listening to those renewing liberation theology today.

Some suggest that liberation theology is passé. They suggest that four things have diminished the influence of liberation theology. These are: (1) The demise of socialism. (2) The marginalization of critical liberation theologians by church authorities. (3) The familiarity with liberation theology in the West. (4) The rising prosperity and middle classes in many parts of the Majority World.

These points are not groundless. Yet, I do not believe that liberation theology is passé. Liberation theology has much to contribute to our understanding of the nature and mission of the church. This theology can enrich our appreciation of what it means for the church to express the kingdom of

God. I have shown this significant, worthwhile contribution already in this chapter.

I turn to contemporary voices renewing and extending liberation theology in a moment. But before I do that, I want to identify a few difficulties with liberation theology. We need to be careful as we examine this theology. As Westerners, we are likely to look at liberation theology through the eyes of the affluent, the comfortable, the powerful, and the privileged.

Building on the work of Max Davidson—an Australian systematic theologian—I've identified five problems with liberation theology:[41]

Firstly, liberation theology concentrates too much on socio-political issues. This focus is critical to liberation theology and is one of its assets. Yet, on occasions, it leads to a loss of focus on biblical themes concerning personal, spiritual, and eternal needs. Liberation theology protests too little Evangelical involvement in the needs of the oppressed. Liberationists refuse to spiritualize the biblical idea of "the poor." Yet, the poor in the Bible are those who are not only oppressed but also remain faithful to God and seek his deliverance (see Pss 34:6 and 40:17, for example). Commitment by God to the poor does not mean the poor are committing to God.

Secondly, liberation theology locates sin and salvation in society. This is a reaction to much of Christianity's emphasis on the individual. Yet, liberation theology too often bypasses the individual. This theology can occasionally reduce the gospel to a goad to action until the church corrects the wrongs in society.

Thirdly, liberation theology identifies too readily with class struggle and socialism. Such identification gives no ultimate reason for the change. Liberation theology embraces class struggle and revolution as the means of change. In contrast, Western Evangelicals often leave the assumptions of capitalism and economics unchallenged. Marxism per se can provide no ultimate reason for change. The Bible sees history's great divisions as before and after Jesus Christ. The total perspectives of Jesus Christ—as revealed in Scripture—must determine praxis.

Michael Novak offers a scathing critique. He claims liberation theology has been too prejudiced against capitalism and favorable toward socialism. According to Novak, liberation theology has been left in a quandary since the "velvet revolution" in Eastern Europe.[42] Notions of peaceful revolution have too enamored it by throwing off the oppression of wealthy Western capitalists and their local cronies. Liberation theology didn't prepare for the rise of democratic ideals around the globe, including in Latin America. It is

---

41. Davidson and Hill, "Liberation Theology."
42. Novak, "Will It Liberate?"; Novak, "Liberation Theology."

now left trying to figure out how its theology, social agenda, and spirituality make sense in a different world. The world it is now in is post-socialist and mostly pro-democratic. Many Majority World nations are enjoying growing wealth, influence, and power. They are pursuing hybridized, contextualized forms of democracy and capitalism.

Liberation theology still has much to say to the church in a world torn by poverty and inequality. This is as true in the Western as in the Majority World and Indigenous contexts. But it must examine its identification with socialism and find fresh ways to express its theology, concern for justice, and vision for liberating mission.

Fourthly, liberation theology sometimes fails to appreciate that the biblical kingdom of God provides the basis for analyzing society, not any political analysis. Liberation theologians assume that the first step in theology is involvement in societal change processes. They base this assumption on a socialist analysis of structures and systems. Yet, they too often take this position without biblical analysis. As mentioned, this socialist analysis has unraveled in the present global context. The kingdom of God is the biblical hermeneutic of society—not any one political analysis. As Christians, we must move Jesus Christ and his kingdom to the front of our worldviews and theologies. This way, the biblical kingdom of God provides the basis for analyzing society and a vision for social change. The biblical kingdom of God is our social program.

Fifthly, liberation theology often reads Jesus and the Gospels selectively. For example, liberation theologians speak of the importance of Jesus. They often describe him as the poor and oppressed victim of his political system. But there are, of course, richer and more profound aspects to the centrality of Jesus Christ.

René Padilla says that we address the failings of liberation theology by developing a disciplined hermeneutical practice. This practice engages Scripture, the humanities, the church's praxis, and the historical situation. It puts these four things into critical, mutually enriching dialogue. None is adequate in isolation from the others.[43] We must inform this disciplined practice through an expansive, biblical vision of the kingdom of God.

How do we put Scripture, context, and practices into conversation?

> The alternative to both the "Theology of the Word" and the "Theology of Praxis" is a hermeneutical circulation in which a richer and deeper understanding of Scripture leads to a greater understanding of historical context, and a deeper and richer understanding of the context leads to a greater comprehension

---

43. Padilla, "Liberation Theology."

of Scripture from within the concrete situation and under the leading of the Holy Spirit.[44]

10. Liberating Christians extend the conversation.

In this chapter, I showed how women are broadening and examining liberation theology. Besides these fresh perspectives women offer, a new generation of liberation theologians is reframing liberationist thought for a globalized context. These thinkers are Asian, Latin American, African, African-American, and Hispanic/Latino. These younger liberationists communicate with each other in rigorous and intentional ways. This way, they bridge the divides between the diverse expressions of liberation theology.

Ivan Petrella exemplifies this new generation of liberationists. He aims to refashion "liberation theology for a new century but an old challenge, the liberation of the poor."[45] Petrella and his peers are redefining the relationships between liberation theology, capitalism, democracy, globalization, and neoliberalism.

Developing the work of Roberto Unger, Ivan Petrella says, "The task is no longer to counterpose two systems, such as capitalism/socialism or bourgeois democracy/participatory democracy, against each other but to find the gradual steps that will democratize access to political and economic opportunity."[46]

As we've seen, Western Christians can learn much from theologies of liberation. But we need to have the courage to extend the conversation. We ought to explore the connections between the ideas of liberation theology and other streams of thought. Such streams include politics, law, psychoanalysis, sociology, ethnology, post-structuralism, womanism, feminism, postcolonialism, systematic and biblical theology, missiology, etc.[47]

Are there fresh ways that we can understand Jesus Christ's church as liberating and transforming? How can we join Jesus in transforming democratic processes, political sciences, economic practices, ethno-religious conflicts, moral frameworks, civil societies, the consequences of globalization, etc.? This involves renewing ecclesial structures. It includes challenging socio-political, religious, and legal processes and structures. It means

---

44. Padilla, "Liberation Theology," 18.
45. Petrella, *Future of Liberation Theology*, vii.
46. Petrella, *Future of Liberation Theology*, ix.
47. Petrella, *Latin American Liberation Theology*, xv.

becoming *political saints*.[48] It requires we do all this within the context of the global challenges of the twenty-first century.

Isaiah draws our attention to God's concern for justice, mercy, and compassion:

> Is not this the kind of fasting I have chosen: to loose the chains of injustice and untie the cords of the yoke, to set the oppressed free and break every yoke? Is it not to share your food with the hungry and to provide the poor wanderer with shelter—when you see the naked, to clothe them, and not to turn away from your own flesh and blood? (Isa 58:6–7)

Study Questions

1. What does it mean practically for your church to be the good Samaritan?

2. How do we proclaim the gospel prophetically and compassionately, in word and deed?

3. How are you working for the liberation and rights of those experiencing poverty, oppression, and marginalization in your context? How are you standing against social injustice?

4. Ask yourself, if the God of the Bible is for those experiencing poverty, are you also disturbed by poverty in your neighborhood, community, or society? How does your ethnicity, gender, wealth, privilege or power prevent you from identifying with the humiliation or suffering of other people? How do these factors shape prejudices in you that do not honor Jesus Christ?

5. How can Scripture change your understandings of society, power and relationships? How can Scripture make you a more compassionate servant of the broken, silenced, exploited and humiliated people around you?

6. What does liberation from oppression and suffering look like in your neighborhood, town, suburb or city? How is God calling you, your family, and your church to take part in acts of liberation, justice, and compassion?

---

48. Boff, "Need for Political Saints."

11.

Showing Hospitality

The Third Expression

IN 2022, THE UNHCR released its *Global Trends Report*. The report analyzes the trends among refugees, asylum seekers, returnees, stateless persons, and internally displaced persons (IDPs) groups. The report estimated that in 2022, 108.4 million people were forcibly displaced worldwide. Persecution, conflict, violence, and human rights violations caused these people to flee their homes. Low and middle-income countries hosted 76 percent of the world's refugees. Children below 18 years make up 41 percent of the refugee population. Every year, three hundred eighty-five thousand children are born as refugees or asylum seekers.[1]

How should Christians respond to such needs? In a word: hospitality. Christian hospitality is broader than welcoming and caring for displaced persons. But it is no less than that.

Not all communities of the Majority World are hospitable. But since developing countries host the majority of the world's refugees, it should not surprise us to find acts of extravagant, self-sacrificial hospitality in the Majority World. Majority World and Indigenous cultures have known their fair share of hostility, oppression, and exclusion—within and between people groups and at the hands of colonial powers. A rich theology and practice of hospitality has developed within this context. Authentic partnership and hospitality—in church and society—can act as an antidote to exclusion

---

1. UNHCR, *Global Trends Report*.

and domination. This hospitality is demonstrated throughout Africa, Asia, Latin America, Eastern Europe, and Indigenous communities.

Scripture teaches us that God welcomes the oppressed, broken, outcast, and excluded. The church needs to reflect God's hospitality. God doesn't form a church of an elect, privileged, and powerful few. Instead, he forms his church as a diverse and hospitable people. These people show authentic unity in diversity. Hospitality is the key to the formation of wonderfully diverse yet deeply unified churches. Hospitality doesn't dominate others and doesn't demand conformity. Hospitality "creates a safe and welcoming space for persons to find their own sense of humanity and worth."[2]

Many Majority World thinkers agree that hospitality is crucial for the church's mission. The church positions itself as an alternative culture that reveals Christ's kingdom through hospitality and welcome. Such hospitality connects with the marginal, the broken, the rejected, the excluded, and the despised. It fosters a spirituality of partnership, hospitality, and inclusivity. It welcomes people into God's family. Hospitality demonstrates the extraordinary grace of Jesus Christ to the world.

We must consider its diverse expressions to appreciate hospitality in Majority World and Indigenous cultures. These include its theology, sacramentality, location, welcome, price, practices, reconciliation, and witness. I proceed in that order.

Hospitality's Theology

Christine D. Pohl provides a comprehensive treatment of hospitality. She addresses its biblical foundations, theological themes, and historical practices. Her book, *Making Room: Recovering Hospitality as a Christian Tradition*, is well worth reading.[3] Amy Oden collects early Christian texts on hospitality and its practices—letters, sermons, instructions, and community records. She presents these in her book, *And You Welcomed Me: A Sourcebook on Hospitality in Early Christianity*. Pohl and Oden offer foundational treatments of Christian hospitality in these two books. I restrict myself to briefly highlighting the theological themes shaping Majority World hospitality.

---

2. Russell, *Church in the Round*, 173.
3. Pohl, *Making Room*.

1. Biblical hospitality

Conservative biblical interpretation and passion for Scripture characterize Majority World churches. Their theology of hospitality has clear biblical commitments. This includes: (1) They pay attention to the teachings of Jesus in Matthew 25, Luke 14, and elsewhere, and the example of his life. (2) They heed Old Testament narratives, including the stories of Abraham and Lot in Genesis 18–19 and Elijah in 1 Kgs 17–18. They also take the texts about welcoming and protecting strangers, foreigners, and the dispossessed seriously. (3) They follow the New Testament emphasis on hospitality toward Christians, those in need, strangers, the broader society, and all creation. This includes Christ's call to welcome one another as he has welcomed them (Rom 15:7).

2. Trinitarian Hospitality

Leonardo Boff defines the Trinity as "Three Persons and a single communion and a single trinitarian community . . . Speaking of God must always mean the Father, Son, and Holy Spirit in the presence of one another, in total reciprocity, in immediacy of loving relationship, being one for another, by another, in another and with another."[4]

The church patterns itself, in a limited and creaturely way, after the social relations of the Trinity. Community, difference-in-relationship, unity-in-diversity, openness, reciprocity, mutuality, participation, welcome, and hospitality characterize the trinitarian church.[5] The trinitarian Persons fellowship in a free, loving, unified, and differentiated way. The church is to reflect these relations in its community and mission. Trinitarian theology shapes our hospitality by unifying, embracing, and communing. If our hospitality lacks these characteristics, it is not Christian or trinitarian.

3. Eucharistic Hospitality

Hospitality relates to the sacrament of the Eucharist. Indeed, we need a sacramental hospitality. Eating and drinking, food and wine, and fellowship around a meal table are at the heart of many Majority World cultures. This should not surprise us because these are also at the center of many Western cultures. Of course, eating and drinking together was at the heart

---

4. Boff, "Trinitarian Community and Social Liberation," 287.
5. Boff, "Trinitarian Community," 306.

of the biblical cultures and their hospitality. At the Last Supper, Jesus shows us that eating and drinking are at the heart of our relationship with him. We remember what he has done and anticipate his return. As the disciples partake in the Last Supper with Jesus, they also remember the many years of eating, drinking, and communing with him.

This theme runs throughout Jesus's ministry. Jesus invites disreputable sinners, social outcasts, tax collectors, you and me, and all who would come to table fellowship. This is scandalous hospitality. It is a divine welcome. He eats and drinks with us. Jesus amazed the disciples through the way he embraced them. He welcomed them as family. Jesus shared his life, food, Passover meal, and mission with them. He called them to imagine this divine hospitality. Jesus calls today's church to the same hospitality—to imitate him.

Majority World and Indigenous cultures prioritize table fellowship. This prioritization reminds us that eating together involves relationship, friendship, thankfulness, and welcome. It reminds us of the Last Supper and all that it signifies. This table fellowship is a sign of the kingdom of God coming among us. It is an anticipation of the coming age—of eating and drinking with our glorified Lord and each other. It is a sign of an everlasting relationship. The resurrection of Jesus means that our table fellowship with him and each other will last forever. The meals we share now—Holy Communion and enjoying food and fellowship around a meal table—anticipate the eternal feast. We have responded to Jesus's welcome at the table. We are recipients of his divine hospitality. We offer this welcome and hospitality to the world.

The Eucharist reminds us of God's welcome to humanity. How we celebrate the Eucharist says much about Christian hospitality. The Eucharist must not only symbolize divine welcome and fellowship. Eucharistic welcome must spill over into the rest of the church's hospitality.

Angel Mendez says that the Eucharist has ethical implications for the church. The Eucharist reminds us of our contingencies, embodiment, and reliance on God's nourishing grace. The Eucharist reminds us of God's generosity, superabundance, and love.

The gospel demands, therefore, that the church address hunger, poverty, inequality, and injustice. So does the Eucharist. It calls on the church to address "violence, exclusion, and destruction." The gospel and the Eucharist call for hospitality toward Christians, strangers, other cultures, the vulnerable, and creation. They remind us of divine hospitality.[6] We extend this hospitality from our homes, lands, and eschatological hope.

Hospitality's Welcome

Throughout successive generations, all over the globe, human beings have recognized the intimate connections between humanity, cultures, and the land. This theme runs throughout Majority World literature and Indigenous oral traditions. It is a theme that emerges repeatedly in Western writings, too.

We offer hospitality from our local soil, local culture, and ultimate hope. We offer hospitality *from* a particular location—our soil, home, place, culture, relationships, and eternal hope. Hospitality's location is often *the place that I love*.

Sometimes, we extend hospitality to others while *we are foreigners*, displaced, or sojourners. More often, we welcome outsiders to our local culture and local soil. Frequently, if we are hospitable, we welcome strangers and neighbors from our culture into our homes and lives. We offer hospitality *from* this location and *to* this location. We welcome others *into* our location, relationships, and place. We offer hospitality *to* that soil, that ecology, that location, and those relationships.

Ruth Padilla DeBorst shows how Israel's condition as God's people was "intertwined with that of the people and place where God had situated them. *In its welfare, you will find your welfare.*"[7] We root our hospitality and well-being in our home, land, relationships, and hope. God calls his people to be "hopeful home-builders." We nurture land, homes, gardens, children, and earth. We show hospitality to these things. We extend welcome to strangers with whom we share our lives. This requires many conversions. "Conversion from individualism to community, from autonomy to interdependence, from idolatry to true worship, from grasping to receiving, from oppressive dominion over creation to loving care of it, from indifference to passionate, prayerful action, from Western definitions of 'development' to loving participation, from competition to collaboration, from protagonism to service."[8]

Hospitality involves our relationship to our home, earth, and local places. It involves our connections to local relationships, soil, and generosity. Are we connected enough with these to be hospitable? Are we willing

---

6. Mendez, "Divine Alimentation," 14–20.
7. DeBorst, "Living Creation-Community in God's World Today," 58.
8. DeBorst, "Living Creation-Community," 60.

to welcome strangers into those places, relationships, and lands we love most? Are we willing to allow others to call our land their land and our homes their homes? We need to take these things seriously to be welcoming and hospitable. We can offer hospitality as we nurture local soils, cultures, homes, and communities. Our hospitality expresses itself in actions *toward* those things and *from* them.

Ruth Padilla DeBorst claims this involves: (1) Building homes and living sustainably. This means making these homes a refuge for people experiencing homelessness, disposed, strangers, and rural and urban poor. (The idea of homes as refuge is terrifying for most people—me included). (2) Planting gardens, caring for creation, and food sourcing. We must recover "our relationship to the earth in the creation-community." (3) Cultivating families and churches that provide "fertile ground for converted covenantal relations." We form these relationships through intimacy, simplicity, hospitality, collaboration, and inclusion. (4) Seeking the welfare of the city. This includes ecology, built environment, socioeconomic elements, human connections, and marginalized persons.[9]

Hospitality is often richest in the context of *shared history* and *generous inclusion*. Such shared history with people, places, and lands is not always possible. But it can provide a remarkable environment for hospitality and inclusion when possible and valued. What does it mean to enrich shared history through inclusion? It means welcoming others into our lovingly nurtured homes, lands, cultures, and communities. It means recognizing the importance of shared history and the welcome of the outsider.

We open this shared history so that the outsider can become an insider. It is an intentional openness to others entering our lives. Our hospitality needs to be free, generous, and active. John Chrysostom, fourth-century Archbishop of Constantinople (in modern-day Turkey), charges the church to *be committed* to hospitality.[10] We welcome people into our homes in hopeful anticipation of our ultimate home. In welcoming them, we welcome Jesus Christ.

Hospitality will often disappoint us. People will wound us, use us, and let us down. They will betray our trust and refuse to reciprocate in kind. Hospitality will be a "now/not yet" experience. Sometimes, it will be as unpleasant as foot washing. Some will offer us hospitality, enriching our lives more than we could have imagined. It was like that for Jesus. But hospitality makes us fuller, richer, more Christ-like people. We welcome people into our homes, lives, and lands in anticipation of the home and the age to come.

---

9. DeBorst, "Living Creation-Community," 62–69.
10. Chrysostom, "Homily 21 on Romans," 505. Italics added for emphasis.

In doing so, we are a foretaste of our ultimate home and the age to come in Christ Jesus.

Hospitality's Price

Sometimes, we think of hospitality as a soft, easy practice. Nothing could be further from the truth. Churches that practice hospitality are courageous communities. Generous people fill these churches—practicing hospitality at personal cost.

The Asia-Pacific is experiencing a dramatic rise in asylum seekers and refugees. This wave of displaced persons affects all countries in our Asia-Pacific region. Recently, a debate about asylum seekers has flared up in my country, Australia. Our main political parties seek to win votes through harsh policies directed at refugees and asylum seekers. The United Nations refugee agency, the UNHCR, and Amnesty International have criticized these policies. The concern is that Australia's harsh policies flout critical articles of the Refugee Convention. This includes Article 31, which forbids discrimination against asylum seekers based on how they arrive.

Church groups have joined in the condemnation of Australian policies. Christian leaders and young people are in our news for showing love, welcome, generosity, and practical support to asylum seekers. They are swimming against the tide of Australian opinion in response to the compassion and gospel of Jesus Christ.

Looking around Africa, Asia, and Latin America, we see countless stories of costly hospitality. Churches in Indigenous and Majority World settings know about hospitality's *price* and *practices*. Stephen Liggins, for example, tells of an experience he had while teaching in Africa. "I once traveled down into Rwanda for a couple of days after teaching in Uganda. By arrangement, I was met at the border by a Rwandan Christian. Making general conversation, I asked about his family and how many children he had. His answer was something like: 'One of my own, and 35 others.'"[11] Hospitality is costly if we do it in the way of Christ.

Hospitality's Practices

These stories cause us to consider hospitality's practices. What practices sustain such costly hospitality? What practices help us cultivate communities of hospitality, welcome, and inclusion?

---

11. Liggins, "What We Can Learn from African Christians."

PART 2: RENEWING OUR MISSION

Wesley Ariarajah says the church needs practices that cultivate unity and harmony in diversity. This is especially true when we welcome people into our homes, lands, and cultures. Ariarajah proposes six practices. I list these here and supplement them with fourteen other practices in Majority World and Indigenous cultures.

We see extraordinary hospitality all over the Majority World. Malaysians welcome refugees from Myanmar. Tanzanians offer *Karibu* to foreigners. Brazilians deconstruct divisions on the Mexican border. Rwandans take in orphans after the Rwandan Civil War. Indigenous Australians seek reconciliation with their colonizers. There are a multitude of other examples. Twenty practices emerge repeatedly.

These settings know their fair share of hostility, alienation, division, exclusion, and prejudice. Amos Yong makes this clear in his Sri Lankan, Nigerian, and North American case studies in *Hospitality and the Other*. Yong also shows how hospitality and reconciliation can emerge even in violent and conflicted contexts.[12]

Here are twenty practices the church in Western settings must pursue if it is to reflect the best of hospitality in Majority World and Indigenous cultures:[13]

1. Welcome plurality of "peoples, cultures, and ways of thinking." This means embracing "many-ness" as a blessing and promise.

2. Affirm the diversity of identities that contribute to plurality.

3. Embrace common commitments of respect and acceptance. "The communities that have successfully dealt with plurality have learned the art of weaving plurality into a coherent whole without, at the same time, abolishing, undermining or suppressing any of the elements that contribute to its richness."

4. Ensure justice for all. "Just relations, just ways of sharing power, and economic justice, are crucial in pluralist situations."

5. Construct mechanisms for reconciliation. These help address those times when conflict, misunderstanding, and division occur.

6. Reject violence, in all its forms, to resolve conflict. Violence only "polarizes people, deepens grievances, and destroys community."

---

12. Yong, *Hospitality and the Other*, 1–37.
13. Ariarajah, "Challenge of Building Communities of Peace for All." The first seven points, including the quotes, come directly from Ariarajah's article.

7. Nurture a spirituality of plurality and hospitality. This "equips us with the wisdom to deal with differences." A spirituality of "inclusion of all, freedom for all, and participation of all."
8. Warmly greet and welcome people *as we receive* the other.
9. Move out of our comfort zones into other cultures and groups *as we go* to the other.
10. Welcome and advocate for the displaced, dispossessed, marginalized, needy, alienated, homeless, victimized, silenced, and those with disabilities. Welcome them into our homes, churches, and lives.
11. Wash feet and conduct other acts of humility and service.
12. Pray for the church, strangers, neighbors, foreigners, and other cultures.
13. Reconstruct church small groups so that they are missional, outwardly focused, and hospitable.
14. Pursue interreligious dialogue as a demonstration of God's hospitality.
15. Invite people into the nucleus of our culture, soil, and place—*the home*. Do we only invite friends and family into our homes? Do we invite strangers and foreigners into our homes?
16. Provide food, clothing, accommodation, protection, medical care, funds, sanctuary, advocacy, and access to the host culture.
17. Allow Holy Communion to shape a lifestyle of table hospitality. This is one where we connect over food and drink. We welcome the stranger to our table. We evaluate our consumption. We address human hunger.
18. Reclaim spiritual friendship as a form of hospitality, as Jesus has made us his friends.
19. Cultivate hospitality as a *way of life* and *being*, not just a set of practices.
20. Revisit the structures that sustain or prevent hospitality. We must embed this list of practices in the Christian community. This happens through institutional attention to practices. It also requires renewing our systems, structures, ministries, and mission. We renew these to be genuinely hospitable—witnessing Christ's astonishing, incomparable welcome.

These practices are crucial for the church's witness as a reconciling community.

PART 2: RENEWING OUR MISSION

Hospitality's Reconciliation

Amos Yong reminds us that hospitality practices will vary according to context and the movement of the Spirit. Yong has distinguished himself as a leading Asian Pentecostal scholar. His basic thesis is that pneumatology—our theology of the Holy Spirit—is a point of contact with other religions.[14] Pneumatology opens space for hospitality, reconciliation, and understanding. Yong believes this is true for relationships in general and for interfaith relations in particular.

Yong develops a Spirit-centered theology of hospitality. He then makes Christian practices the key to understanding how the Spirit enhances hospitality. Yong says that Jesus Christ is the paradigmatic host and guest. He offers God's hospitality to humanity and comes to us as a guest.[15] The gift of the Holy Spirit "signifies the extension of God's abundant hospitality into the whole world."[16] Practices of hospitality embody trinitarian hospitality. "What is being given and what is being received is not any *thing*, but the triune God as manifest in the body of Christ and animated by the power of the Spirit."[17]

Practices of hospitality are participations in divine hospitality. God calls his people "to discern the Spirit's presence and activity so that we can perform the appropriate practices representing the hospitable God. Which tongues we speak and what practices we engage in will depend on where we are, who we are interacting with, and what the social, political, and economic structures are that give shape to our encounter." Hospitality can take many forms. These include "signs and wonders and works of mercy and compassion and acts of social liberation. The hospitality of God is thus embodied in a hospitable church whose members are empowered by the Holy Spirit to stand in solidarity and serve with the sick, the poor, and the oppressed."[18]

According to Yong, the following things are all pneumatological practices: (1) interreligious dialogue, (2) Christian mission, and (3) the pursuit of reconciliation, peace, and justice. They demand that the church be both guest and host. They show the trinitarian hospitality of God. Hospitality is an indispensable foundation for many things. This includes interreligious dialogue and missional expressions of the church. It also includes deeds of

14. Yong, *Discerning the Spirit(s)*; Yong, *Hospitality and the Other*; Yong, "Spirit of Hospitality."
15. Yong, "Spirit of Hospitality," 62.
16. Yong, *Hospitality and the Other*, 126.
17. Yong, *Hospitality and the Other*, 127.
18. Yong, "Spirit of Hospitality," 63.

reconciliation, mercy, justice, and peace. Hospitality is crucial to "keeping in step with the Spirit."[19] Yong claims, "Christian mission is nothing more or less than our participation in the hospitality of God."[20]

Hospitality's Witness

The trinitarian mission is a movement of extravagant hospitality. The church does not have its mission. Instead, it participates in God's hospitality. Following the hospitality of God, the church must offer this hospitality to the most unlikely people and in the most unexpected places. Ruth Padilla DeBorst says God calls his church to welcome "unexpected guests" at God's multicultural, multi-faceted banquet table.

The church's witness is more than word or deed—it witnesses to Christ in its total life *together* and *toward* the world. It testifies to Jesus's passion and power and welcome in its *being*. The church *is* hospitable because God *is* hospitable. "In so doing, or rather in so *being*, the church—the multi-faceted community of Jesus's disciples, gifted in 'many tongues' by the Spirit—indwells God's story, she takes on God's mission in the midst of clashing and blending human cultures and is used by God to unite those strands into meaning and life-granting wholes."[21]

The church's hospitality is a participation in the mission of God and an expression of its hopeful expectation. Hospitality gives us a taste of that which is to come. We are welcoming the stranger and neighbor to God's banquet table. This table is where all socio-cultures, ethnicities, languages, and people groups are welcome. They are welcome to take part in the hospitality of God. An inclusive church embodies this hospitality. More broadly, Jesus Christ reveals this hospitality wherever his inaugurated kingdom is present.

Tobias Brandner, who teaches at the Divinity School of Chung Chi College in Hong Kong and ministers among prisoners in that city, writes of "hospitality as an emerging paradigm in mission." Hospitality transforms the church into an "open church." The open church shares in "joint celebration and joint meals." It renews its language and liturgy to make communication, understanding, and inclusion possible. It welcomes the interruption of the guest and grows as a result. The "missionary encounter thus *transforms both sides, hosts, and guests*." We are at once both host and guest. There is only one true host, Jesus Christ. "Host-missionaries who keep their status

---

19. Gal 5:25.
20. Yong, *Hospitality and the Other*, 131.
21. DeBorst, "'Unexpected' Guests at God's Banquet Table," 74.

as guests in mind will not be concerned about losing power or mastery. They will allow guests/strangers to become fellow citizens and part of the family."[22] The church must develop a "centripetal mission or evangelization by hospitality" to reflect God's hospitality.[23]

Mortimer Arias writes that Latin Americans have a reputation for generous hospitality. But migration into that region, especially from Asia, has tested this in recent years. Human displacement has also tried this hospitality. "Need, oppression, repression, and persecution" have driven people from their lands. "What used to be 'lands of refuge' became hunting grounds of political prisoners, nonconformists, and those suspected of independent ideas and wrong associations."[24]

Arias says *centrifugal mission* is necessary—this term means radiating from the church into the world. But *centripetal mission* becomes especially important when groups of people move within and between nations. Centripetal mission means drawing people into the welcoming church. It means witnessing to Jesus by welcoming people into a community. Centripetal mission is about being the hospitable people of God. It "has to do with quality, authenticity, and being."[25]

Hospitality: Concluding Reflections

This chapter began with a discussion about asylum seekers and refugees. Mortimer Arias says that such migrations provide opportunities for missional hospitality. They offer distinct occasions for the church to *be* the church. "Can we see in the faces of contemporary Asians, Latin Americans, and Africans, pushed from their lands and attracted to our shores, the potential glow of the angel of the Lord—the Lord of migrants who transforms and moves history through migrant peoples, and raises his people as a pilgrim church among many diverse peoples?"[26]

Orlando Costas says that when we show hospitality to others, we also discover that the church has *come to us*. The church that welcomes the periphery discovers that the church is at the periphery. Consequently, we enjoy the renewal of the church.

---

22. Brandner, "Hosts and Guests," 102.
23. Arias, "Centripetal Mission or Evangelization by Hospitality," 69.
24. Arias, "Centripetal Mission or Evangelization by Hospitality," 73.
25. Arias, "Centripetal Mission or Evangelization by Hospitality," 75.
26. Arias, "Centripetal Mission or Evangelization by Hospitality," 77.

Black, Hispanic, Asian, and Native American churches and Christians, in partnership with a minority from the mainstream society that has identified itself with the poor, the powerless, and the oppressed of the land, are witnessing to the new world order announced in the gospel—outside the realm of economic wealth, military might, and political power, and inside the world of millions who are being wasted by numerous forms of social, economic, and political evils.[27]

It is time for us to learn from hospitality in Majority World and Indigenous cultures. We must consider hospitality's theology, sacramental dimensions, location, welcome, price, practices, reconciliation, and witness.

Here are eight things we learned from how Majority World Christians practice hospitality and welcome.

1. Hospitality requires biblical and theological foundations.

Our hospitality needs robust biblical and theological foundations. It needs them to meet the challenges of exclusion, violence, fear, indifference, idolatry, siege-mentalities, and oppressive dominion. When a group moves into your neighborhood and threatens its homogeneity and sense of security and identity (let's say, for instance, a prominent Muslim group moves into your area), you need to ask yourself a question. Is my theology and practice of hospitality up to the task? I've outlined some biblical teachings and stories that undergird Christian hospitality in this chapter. I've shown how trinitarian and Eucharistic theology helps construct a theology of hospitality. These are starting points. It's up to you to build solid theological foundations—and personal commitments—that nurture and sustain Christian hospitality.

I don't remember studying a theology of hospitality when I went to theological college. This is strange, given hospitality's prominence in Scripture and the mission of God. The church needs "a radical theology of hospitality that might take the stranger and the poor into greater consideration." This theology is lived out in the world. We "live a radical hospitality." This includes avoiding the "rigidity of place, sacramental understanding, and liturgical practice." It means "venturing into a world yet to be created."[28]

Let's take our theology of the Eucharist (Holy Communion or The Lord's Supper) as *one* example. Latin American missional leaders saturate

---

27. Costas, quoted in Arias, "Centripetal Mission or Evangelization by Hospitality," 80.

28. All quotes in this paragraph are from Carvalhaes, "Borders, Globalization and Eucharistic Hospitality," 54.

their theology of the Eucharist with a theology of hospitality. Claudio Carvalhaes, for instance, says that the church should "welcome people in and around and through the Eucharistic sacrament." Through the Lord's Supper, we "gather with one another to be with one another and issue this constant call of welcome to whoever wants to come and eat."[29]

Carvalhaes writes that his family practiced constant hospitality when he was a child in Sao Paulo, Brazil. They welcomed neighbors, those in need, and strangers. He carried this hospitality into his pastoral ministry in the shantytowns of Sao Paulo. Later, he practiced hospitality among poor immigrants on the Mexico—United States border. Carvalhaes says that on the Mexican border, he discovered how the Eucharist reveals other "borders"—church, theological, socio-economic, and political. Christ calls us to transcend them for his sake.[30]

2. Hospitality involves conversion.

When we decided to follow Jesus, most of us didn't fully understand the breadth and depth of conversion. There's no such thing as a partial conversion. We're tempted to think that there is. We say my Sundays are converted, but not my Mondays. My tithe is converted, but not the rest of my finances and spending habits. My reading is converted, but not my Internet use. My attire is converted, but not my consumerism and autonomy. My church building is converted into a welcoming place, but not my home. My singing of praise songs is converted, but not my welcome of foreigners and strangers into my home, land, and nation. My Bible memorization is converted, but not my care for creation or the most vulnerable in my neighborhood. My care for my home is converted, but not my concern for the cries of the earth and people experiencing poverty. My hard work at my job is converted, but not my politics and nationalism. Am I willing to let God convert my civil religion?

Jesus demands our complete conversion. We will only exercise his hospitality in the world when we allow him to convert us to himself and his hospitality fully. We need to be converted from "individualism to community, from autonomy to interdependence, from idolatry to true worship, from grasping to receiving, from oppressive dominion over creation to loving care of it, from indifference to passionate, prayerful action, from

---

29. Carvalhaes, "Borders, Globalization and Eucharistic Hospitality," 45.
30. Carvalhaes, "Borders, Globalization and Eucharistic Hospitality," 46.

Western definitions of 'development' to loving participation, from competition to collaboration, from protagonism to service."[31]

3. Hospitality welcomes others into our homes, families, land, churches, and cultures.

We offer hospitality from this location and to this location. We welcome others into our place, relationships, soil, and homes. We do all this in hopeful anticipation of our ultimate home. As we've seen, Ruth Padilla DeBorst encourages us to build homes and live sustainably in them. We should make them a refuge for the homeless, disposed, strangers, and rural and urban poor.[32] This includes planting gardens and caring for creation. It means recovering "our relationship to the earth in the creation-community." We cultivate families and churches that provide "fertile ground for converted covenantal relations." We express these relations through intimacy, simplicity, hospitality, collaboration, and inclusion.

Evelyn Parker, who calls herself an African of the Diaspora, writes of her experience of Tanzanian hospitality. African hospitality overwhelms her. Hospitality that is sacrificial and unconditional

> redefines what it means to welcome the stranger. As I reflect on the significance of my sojourn in Moshi, Arusha and other parts of northeast Tanzania . . . I realize [that the people of] Moshi modeled receiving the stranger unconditionally . . . This [sacrificial] hospitality changes our priorities from self-serving and individualistic concerns to true *Koinonia* . . . Persevering hospitality that the Moshi community modeled calls us to the responsibility of persistently pursing ways to compromise and reconcile so that all the world will see our oneness in Christ Jesus. Persevering hospitality fortifies our efforts for overcoming the sins of racism, classism, and sexism that hinder genuine visible Christian unity. This new meaning of hospitality as unconditional, sacrificial, and persevering, is captured in the phrase *incarnational hospitality*. This means the embodiment of divine practices for entertaining strangers . . . The people of Moshi and northeast Tanzania call it *Karibu*.[33]

---

31. DeBorst, "Living Creation-Community," 60.

32. In these next four points I'm quoting directly from DeBorst, "Living Creation-Community," 62–69.

33. Parker, "Karibu," 19.

PART 2: RENEWING OUR MISSION

4. Hospitality cultivates a spirituality of embrace.

Christian spirituality is welcoming, open, inclusive, and embracing. This means welcoming people and demonstrating to the world the extravagant grace of Jesus Christ. A hospitable spirituality addresses hunger, poverty, inequality, injustice, "violence, exclusion, and destruction." We practice hospitality toward Christians, strangers, other cultures, the vulnerable, and creation. We offer welcome to our homes, lands, relationships, churches, soil, and eternal hope.[34] Together, we live out the twenty practices of hospitality (see them listed under "Hospitality's Practices" above).[35] They shape a spirituality of welcome and embrace.

It's time to multiply the practices of hospitality and welcome. This includes "signs and wonders and works of mercy and compassion and acts of social liberation. The hospitality of God is thus embodied in a hospitable church whose members are empowered by the Holy Spirit to stand in solidarity and serve with the sick, the poor, and the oppressed."[36] A hospitable spirituality welcomes "unexpected guests" at God's multicultural banquet table. It witnesses to Jesus in our life *together* and *toward* the world. We *are* hospitable because God *is* hospitable.

5. Hospitality is courageous and costly.

It takes courage to be hospitable when others are hostile and exclusive. You risk being excluded, too, or worse. Genuine hospitality always comes at a price. It takes effort. We risk losing status and comfort. For a season, we may lose our sense of identity and belonging. Hospitality costs us our pride, control, and dominance. On some occasions, it costs people their homes and lives. What are you willing to do to show the hospitality of God? What are you willing to lose? What price are you willing to pay? We pay this price considering the eternal treasure.

6. Hospitality seeks the welfare of our immediate neighborhood and our broader town or city.

Most of the time, I find it easy to pursue my family's and church's well-being. But do I seek the welfare of my neighborhood and town and city?

---

34. Mendez, "Divine Alimentation," 14–20.

35. Ariarajah, "Challenge of Building Communities of Peace for All." The first seven points, including the quotes, come directly from Ariarajah's article.

36. Yong, "Spirit of Hospitality," 63.

Christian hospitality demands that I do. This includes their built environments, ethnicities, race relations, marginalized and impoverished persons, socioeconomics, human connections, and ecologies. Love your neighbor. Seek the welfare of your city. Pray for your city. Bring peace and reconciliation. Know your neighbor's names. Welcome strangers. Care for creation and green space. Contribute positively to politics and community organizations. Support positive urban planning projects, local economic initiatives, and neighborhood and community organizations. Help create "urban sanctuaries." (Urban sanctuaries are spaces for peace, recreation, and community in urban centers: community gardens, green belts, nature corridors, recreation spaces, etc.) The Spirit calls us to actions that bring peace and well-being. Hospitality seeks human flourishing, healthy cities, and the prosperity of nature.

7. Hospitality is essential to reconciliation and mission.

Without hospitality, there is no peace and reconciliation. Forgiveness, understanding, and welcome require hospitality. Repeatedly, Australian Aboriginal communities have invited me into their lands and homes. They do this, even though—as a white man—I symbolize the colonizer and invader. Their generous hospitality offers reconciliation, forgiveness, peace, and a warm welcome.

Hospitality is essential for mission. Just as God invites us into his love, kingdom, and future, so we must be hospitable. Let me illustrate how hospitality relates to mission through a brief story. John Ong is a friend of mine who ministers among migrants, refugees, and asylum seekers in Malaysia and surrounding countries. Twelve years ago, John established a network among churches of different denominations. This network ministers among refugees from eight nationalities. John set up a school for two hundred and fifty refugee children aged five to seventeen. These children come from Myanmar (Chin, Rohingya, and other tribal groups), Sri Lanka, Pakistan, and Cambodia. This school comes under the supervision of UNHCR. The school has a center that produces handmade soap and textiles. This employment helps refugee women support their families. It enables them to buy food, secure accommodation, and enjoy education.

John's team also operates several drop-in centers. These enable displaced migrants to find support in disputes with employers or property owners. They have other centers for persecuted groups, vulnerable, single, refugee women, and families with young girls. These refugee support centers are open to all, regardless of ethnicity, religion, or gender. Local churches and not-for-profits support these centers. They are a demonstration of authentic Christian hospitality. This is a mission inspired by God's extravagant hospitality in Jesus Christ.

8. Hospitality follows Jesus's example and teaching.

Examples here are too numerous for this chapter. Jesus extolled the virtue of hospitality. He revealed God's hospitality in the incarnation. He showed it by embracing the sinner, outcast, diseased, unclean, and marginalized. We must go and do likewise.

Study Questions

1. What stood out to you while you read this chapter?
2. Hospitality involves our relationship to our home, the earth, and local places. We invite people to share our local relationships, our local lives, our local soil, and our local faith. Are you connected enough with these to be hospitable?
3. Are you willing to welcome strangers into those places, relationships, and lands you love the most?
4. Are you willing to allow others to call your land their land and your homes their homes?
5. Is your family and church given to hospitality? Are you? Or is it an incidental, peripheral, and optional activity?
6. Look at the twenty practices of hospitality. Western churches must embrace these if they are to reflect the best of hospitality in the Majority World. How will your church, ministry, and family practice these over the next few years and beyond?

12.

Embracing the Spirit

The Fourth Expression

RENEWALIST CHURCHES REFER TO Pentecostal, charismatic, neo-charismatic, and "third-wave" churches. These churches are broader than classical Pentecostalism but incorporate it. They are diverse. They often take on characteristics of their host culture.

These renewalist churches have grown and multiplied in the Majority World. This is especially the case in the Global South. These churches emphasize baptism with the Holy Spirit. They also focus on divine healing, spiritual gifts, and Spirit-empowered witness. They "agree on the presence and demonstration of the charismata [spiritual gifts] in the modern church, but beyond this common agreement, there is much diversity as in all the other branches of Christianity."[1]

Since these renewalist churches are so diverse, measuring their growth is difficult. In 1970, there were around 15 million Pentecostals and 60 million other renewalists worldwide. Now, researchers estimate that around 600 million people are in renewalist churches worldwide.[2] Pew Research claims Pentecostal and charismatic Christians comprise about 27 percent of all Christians. They make up more than 8 percent of the world's total

---

1. Hollenweger, *Pentecostalism*, 327.
2. Dunn, *Christ and the Spirit*, 86.

population. Pew puts Pentecostal Christians at 279 million and charismatic Christians at 305 million.[3]

Gordon-Conwell's Center for the Study of Global Christianity (CSGC) recently released a critical report. They called it *Christianity in its Global Context, 1970–2020*. Their findings relating to renewalist churches are striking:

> Renewalists numbered 62.7 million in 1970. They're expected to grow to 709.8 million by 2020. In 1970, Renewalists were 5.1% of all Christians. But by 2010, they had grown to 25.8% (averaging 4.1% growth per year between 1970 and 2010). Looking forward to 2020, Renewalist movements will grow almost twice as fast as global Christianity as a whole. They'll represent 27.8% of all Christians. Renewalists grew the fastest in Asia and Latin America over the 40-year period. They'll grow most rapidly in Asia and Africa over the next 10-year period. In 1970, the three largest Renewalist populations were in the United States, Brazil, and the Democratic Republic of Congo. In 2020, the countries with the most Renewalists will likely be Brazil, the United States, China, and Nigeria. The growth of Renewalist Christianity in Asia, Africa, and Latin America has been astounding. They've grown from 18.8 million in 1970 to 226.2 million by 2020 in Africa, from 12.8 million to 203.1 million in Latin America, and from 9.3 million to 165.6 million in Asia.[4]

Patrick Johnstone says that renewalists will number 1 billion by 2050 at current growth rates. That will be "one-third of all Christians and one-tenth of the world's population."[5]

Amos Yong is a Malaysian-born, Asian-American scholar. He writes that there are 400-plus million renewalists in the Majority World. This number will likely grow to around 710 million by 2020 and 1 billion by 2050. 76% of all renewalists are in Latin America, Asia, and Africa.

> Clearly, the most vibrant Pentecostal communities are now in the Southern and Eastern Hemispheres, although traffic from South to North, from East to West, and vice versa is now busier than ever before, especially given the telecommunications revolution . . . [Philip Jenkins] suggests that the coming Christendom will be radically pluralistic, centered not in Rome or

---

3. Pew research uses data supplied by the Center for the Study of Global Christianity at Gordon-Conwell Theological Seminary.

4. Center for the Study of Global Christianity, *Christianity in Its Global Context, 1970–2020*, 7, 8, and 19.

5. Johnstone, *Future of the Global Church*, 125.

Canterbury but variously in Seoul, Beijing, Singapore, Bombay, Lagos, Sao Paulo, and Mexico City.[6]

The Spirit is being "poured out on all people."[7] These statistics show that Majority World Christians have much to teach the West. We can learn from them about ministry and mission in the power of the Spirit. Statistics measuring the growth of renewalist churches provoke us. They make us consider the *influence* of this mode of church. These statistics challenge the assumption that the Western church is the thriving church.

This focus on the Spirit and his role in mission isn't prominent in Western missional conversations. This must change. Charismatic and Pentecostal churches have much to teach missional movements and vice versa.

The growth of Pentecostal Christianity in the Majority World has given these churches a global voice. But some issues have emerged. Some Western churches ignore God's empowering presence. But many Majority World renewalist churches overestimate the missional value of charismatic expressions. These churches are often missional yet may uncritically embrace elements of their host cultures. Similarly, the challenge for Western churches is their adoption of rational and secular assumptions.

The churches of the West, Indigenous cultures, and the Majority World can learn much from each other. This includes learning from each other about what it means for the Spirit to empower the church's mission. To date, the Western missional conversation hasn't prioritized pneumatology. It hasn't paid enough attention to the role of the Spirit's empowering presence and gifts in mission. This is strange since the Spirit empowers the church for mission and witness. Western missional conversations haven't focused enough on the role of the Spirit. They haven't prioritized the Spirit's role in the church's mission, discipleship, and community.[8]

Missional theology needs to reclaim the role of the Spirit. Jesus Christ sends his church into the world for the glory of the Father. The Spirit empowers the church for faithful witness to the Father, Son, and Holy Spirit. The Spirit enables the church to witness to the kingdom of God, inaugurated by Jesus in the incarnation and at Pentecost. The church needs a rigorous discussion about its role in Jesus's healing and reconciling mission. This demands greater attention to a theology of the Spirit.

---

6. Yong, *Spirit Poured out on All Flesh*, 19–20.

7. Joel 2:28 and Acts 2:17.

8. Two exceptions are worth noting. The first is my chapter "The Spirit-Empowered Church" in Hill, *Salt, Light, and a City*, 205–29. The second is Michael Frost's chapter in Barker, *Following Fire*, 33–41.

This chapter considers the growth of Majority World renewalist and Pentecostal churches. It examines their emphases, worship, spirituality, contextualization, mission, challenges, and future.

Spirit-Constituted Churches

The rise of the Pentecostal-charismatic churches in the Majority World has been extraordinary. The growth of the churches in those cultures is a move of the Spirit. It is an expression of their dependence on the Spirit's power, presence, and provision.

In my book *Salt, Light, and a City*, I described the connection between the Spirit and mission.[9] A missional understanding of the church requires a deep commitment to the Spirit. A missional view of the church is only as good as its theology of the Spirit. The church needs a *missional pneumatology* and a *pneumatological mission*. A missional understanding of the church takes the Spirit seriously.[10]

The Spirit creates, fills, and animates the church—he causes it to come into being. The church is the "people of God who the Spirit creates to live as a missionary community."[11] The Spirit creates and empowers the church so that it is a unique, spiritual community. The Spirit "creates, leads, and teaches the church to live as the distinctive people of God."[12] The Spirit is essential to the *being* of the church. "The church is and is visible because God the Holy Spirit is and acts."[13] The Spirit creates the church and fills it with his grace and gifts. He empowers the church to serve the messianic mission and the kingdom of God. The Spirit is present in the church's sacraments, ministries, missions, and structures. The church's dimensions are "conceived in the movement and presence of the Spirit." The Spirit shapes all aspects of the church for the glory and mission of the Trinity.[14] The Spirit renews the church as the triune God's ongoing creation. The Spirit forms the community of faith into a counter-cultural community embodying the reign of God. The Spirit is the advocate-helper of the church who helps it be faithful to the redemptive reign of God. He indwells it with his power

---

9. Hill, *Salt, Light, and a City*, chapter 16.
10. Hill, *Salt, Light, and a City*, 205.
11. Van Gelder, *Essence of the Church*, 25.
12. Van Gelder, *Essence of the Church*, 31.
13. Webster, "Visible Attests the Invisible," 104; Hill, *Salt, Light, and a City*, 216.
14. Moltmann, *Church in the Power of the Spirit*, 289; Hill, *Salt, Light, and a City*, 206.

and presence. The Spirit works in the church so that it is holy. The Spirit establishes the marks of the true church and enables its mission.[15]

Hans Küng says:

> If there is no Spirit, it does not mean that the community lacks its missionary commission, but that there is no community at all . . . The church is filled and vivified, sustained, and guided by his Spirit, the power and strength of God. The church owes to the Spirit its origin, existence, and continued life, and in this sense the church is a *creation of the Spirit*.[16]

The church is one, holy, catholic, and apostolic, in the power of the Spirit. The Spirit uses these four attributes for the glory of Christ and his kingdom.[17] The Spirit uses these attributes for the sake of the mission of God. He uses them to bring the world liberation, healing, justice, mercy, and hope.[18]

The Spirit fills the mission of God's people. This Spirit-empowered mission alerts people to the universal reign of God through Christ. The church, in the power and presence of the Spirit, exists for the mission of Christ. The Spirit empowers the church's mission. He does this for Christ's mission and the Father's glory. The Spirit empowers the church for Christ-honoring mission, service, love, and compassion.[19]

Majority World churches are aware of this empowerment. They rely on the Spirit's renewal and re-missionalization of the church. Singaporean theologian Simon Chan says that our theology of the Spirit needs to be more communal. It must be less individualistic. "To be baptized into Christ is to be incorporated into a Spirit-filled, Spirit-empowered entity. Spirit-baptism is first an event of the church prior to its being actualized in personalized Spirit-baptism."[20]

Chan develops what he calls an *ecclesial pneumatology*. He is talking here about a theology of the Spirit shaped around the Christian community. Chan says that the Spirit forms the church. The Spirit does this in an ongoing way. He forms the church as it worships, celebrates the Eucharist, and

---

15. Van Gelder, *Essence of the Church*, 42–44, 78–81, 86, 112–18, 142–62, and 180.
16. Küng, *Church*, 165 and 172.
17. Moltmann, *Church in the Power*, 337–38; Hill, *Salt, Light, and a City*, 207. Amos Yong provides a Pentecostal "re-reading" of the marks of the church in Yong, "Marks of the Church."
18. Moltmann, *Church in the Power*, 361.
19. Moltmann, *Source of Life*, 55–69.
20. Chan, "Mother Church," 180.

joins Christ in his mission. The Spirit enables the church to be a dynamic catholic, healing, truth-traditioning, and eschatological community.

A dynamic catholic community: The Spirit of Christ makes the church *whole* and *one* in its local and universal expressions.

A healing community: The Spirit creates a church that transcends "all social, cultural, and historical boundaries." He forms a church "characterized chiefly by its work of reconciliation and healing."[21]

A truth-traditioning community: The Spirit "constitutes the church dynamically." He also "makes the church the place where truth exists dynamically." There is a profound connection between Christ the Truth and the action of the Spirit. This connection "makes possible the ongoing traditioning of Christ the Truth in the church." What does this mean? "Christ the Truth is made present in the church by the action of the Spirit in the preaching of the Word and in the sacrament."[22]

An eschatological community: The Spirit enables the church to join in historical events. These include the incarnation, the resurrection, and Pentecost. The Spirit forms the church for the present witness and the age to come. The Spirit helps us to appropriate the inaugurated kingdom and the future reign of Christ in the present age. This is true even when we only have a foretaste, measure, and glimpse of the age to come.[23]

Julie and Wonsuk Ma claim the church and its mission are naturally renewalist. The church is "charismatic if left with little theological 'assistance.'" They argue:

> The church birthed in Jerusalem was highly charismatic . . . Indigenous Pentecostal churches throughout the world are another sure proof of this contention. Completely unconnected with the modern Pentecostal tradition, there are countless number of "Indigenous" churches, particularly in the non-Western world, that has made scholars revise the one-fountainhead theory of modern Pentecostalism. Healing, prophecy, miracles, exorcisms, and tongues are naturally practiced.
>
> In Asia, the Chinese house church movement provides another excellent example. After a generation without any outside "assistance," today's Chinese Christianity is strikingly charismatic. With this in mind, Pentecostals can encourage the churches to become closer to what has been intended for from the beginning.[24]

21. Chan, "Mother Church," 188.
22. Chan, "Mother Church," 191.
23. Chan, *Pentecostal Theology and the Christian Spiritual Tradition*, chapter 4.
24. Ma and Ma, "Jesus Christ in Asia," 503.

Spirit Baptism and Power

Majority World renewalist churches emphasize Spirit baptism—with varying definitions of this term. Spirit baptism is the hub of renewalist thought and praxis. They connect Spirit baptism with emphases on divine healing, spiritual gifts, demons, angels, deliverance, spiritual warfare, and the Spirit's power.

Chan says that renewalist churches diverge on a range of issues. But "what comes through over and over again in their discussions and writings is a certain kind of spiritual experience of an intense, direct, and overwhelming nature centering on the person of Christ which they schematize as 'baptism in the Holy Spirit.'"[25]

Yong writes that renewalists don't understand Spirit baptism in a homogenous way. Even so, "it probably best symbolizes the distinctive orientation of the Pentecostal-charismatic imagination . . . [Spirit baptism] has great theological import for the global movement . . . and brings us closest to what, if anything, can be termed the 'essence' of the Pentecostal-charismatic experience."[26]

Allan Anderson describes the various theologies of Spirit baptism. Classical Pentecostal, charismatic, neo-charismatic, "third wave," and Catholic charismatic views diverge. These groups debate how to understand Spirit baptism in the light of Scripture and experience. Questions on the connection between Spirit baptism and conversion come from this contested center. For example, "What is normative about this experience and its expressions? Is "speaking in tongues" inconsequential, normal, or normative?"[27]

David Yonggi Cho is the pastor of Yoido Full Gospel Church in Seoul, South Korea. This is the largest Pentecostal church in the world. It has more than one million members. Cho typifies the classical Pentecostal view on Spirit baptism. For Cho, baptism in the Spirit is necessary—spiritual power, supernatural gifts, effective prayer, and church growth evidence Spirit baptism. The Spirit baptizes and gives spiritual gifts. There are many spiritual gifts. *Revelatory gifts* include knowledge, wisdom, and discernment. *Vocal gifts* include tongues, interpretation, and prophecy. *Power gifts* include faith, healing, and miracles. Cho claims that established churches resist the Holy

---

25. Chan, "Evidential Glossolalia and the Doctrine of Subsequence," 196.
26. Yong, *Discerning the Spirit(s)*, 165.
27. Anderson, *Introduction to Pentecostalism*, 192–95.

Spirit. He says they encourage wrong doctrines and persecute renewalist churches.[28]

Korean theologian Koo Dong Yun has a more open position than David Yonggi Cho. Yun undertakes a fascinating treatment of Spirit baptism. He notes the centrality of Spirit baptism to renewalist churches. He says, "The Classical Pentecostal view of Spirit baptism is characterized by (1) the Lukan orientation, (2) the vitality of experience, and (3) the verifiability of Spirit baptism."[29]

Yun goes on to examine nine divergent theologies of Spirit baptism. He does this to enrich doctrine and ecumenical understanding. Yun sees the essence of Pentecostalism in its pragmatic orientation. He contrasts this with Simon Chan's articulation of Pentecostalism's essence. For Chan, Pentecostalism's essence is a desire for the miraculous, surprising, and unexpected. However, according to Yun, pragmatism is at the heart of Pentecostalism. This pragmatism allows it to revise and expand its understanding and practice of Spirit baptism. This is good news. It allows global Pentecostalism to form a new theology of Spirit baptism. This theology will be holistic, open, and ecumenical. An array of cultures, experiences, Christian traditions, and biblical texts will inform it.[30]

Renewalist churches in the Majority World seek the Holy Spirit's power, presence, and provision. They long for the Spirit of Christ to fill them with power for faith and mission. Their experience of the spirit world convinces them of the necessity and power of the Holy Spirit. (Such experience includes exposure to animism, ancestral spirits, cults, magic, divination, demonic powers, "gods," miracles, and traditional religions.)

Renewalist churches are not content with what they consider a powerless Christianity. These Majority World believers ask critical questions. "If God's Spirit is supreme, why shouldn't healings, signs, wonders, miracles, and supernatural gifts follow? Why shouldn't our experience of the Spirit mirror that of the early church—especially when our lives are like those in the Bible? Since we know the spiritual world is real and full of powerful spiritual beings, why shouldn't we expect the Holy Spirit to reveal Jesus Christ? Why wouldn't he reveal Jesus in holiness and power and wonder? Didn't Jesus Christ promise to fill us with the Holy Spirit and power?"

Malaysian theologian Hwa Yung says these churches call the global church to "recover the supernatural." This includes "addressing the demonic

---

28. Cho, *Holy Spirit, My Senior Partner*, 182.

29. Yun, *Baptism in the Holy Spirit*, vii.

30. Yun, *Baptism in the Holy Spirit*, 147–62; Yun, "Water Baptism and Spirit Baptism," x.

at both the personal and cosmic levels." It means fitting "signs and wonders of the Holy Spirit" into our theological frameworks.

Yung arrives at clear conclusions. "A 21st-century reformation will demand reinserting the supernatural into the heart of Christianity. This will result in a sounder biblical theology and a more powerful missional church. The world will then understand what Jesus meant when he said, 'But if it is by the Spirit of God that I cast out demons, then the kingdom of God has come upon you' (Matt. 12:28)."[31] Spirit-constituted churches are attentive to the Spirit. They "recover the supernatural" together. They embrace the Spirit's power in culturally appropriate worship and mission.

Spirit-Infused Cultures and Contexts

Many Majority World thinkers appreciate that aspects of their cultures and contexts are Spirit-infused. The Spirit is present in these cultures, inspiring repentance and renewal, among other things. These thinkers and practitioners also know that a theology of the Spirit must be contextual. It must be relevant to its setting to align with what the Spirit of Christ is doing there.

Veli-Matti Kärkkäinen acknowledges this. He dedicates a third of his book, *The Spirit in the World*, to "The Spirit Among Cultures."[32] In that section, Asian and African thinkers describe the relationships between renewalist theology, practice, and cultural diversity. Paulson Pulikottil considers native Pentecostalism in Kerala, India. Koo Dong Yun examines Minjung's thought and Asian Pentecostalism. Deidre Helen Crumbley studies gender and Afro-Christian renewalist churches. Ogbu U. Kalu considers Pentecostalism and African cultural heritage. All these authors show how the Spirit is present in their cultures and how Christians respond in context.

Let's consider Yun's treatment of Minjung liberation and Asian Pentecostal theology. Koo Dong Yun notes a recent shift in scholarship examining the origins of global Pentecostalism. Recent scholarship has questioned American-centric descriptions of the origins of Pentecostalism. These descriptions usually trace Pentecostal origins to the Azusa-related churches. Today, it is becoming more common to trace Pentecostalism in Asia and Africa to different origins. Scholars note origins within those cultures predating the Azusa-related missionaries' arrival.

Westerners often entertain a flawed notion about the origins of global Pentecostalism. They believe that America is the main birthplace of the global Pentecostal-charismatic movement. Yun writes, "I want to refute this

31. Yung, "Recover the Supernatural," 32–33.
32. Kärkkäinen, *Spirit in the World*.

kind of narrow, colonial, egotistical, Western definition of Pentecostalism and try to reinterpret Pentecostalism from an Asian *minjung* perspective... From the very beginning, modern (or twentieth-century) Pentecostalism has been multicultural and global."[33]

Minjung is a collective noun. It refers to a group of people who are marginalized, victimized, oppressed, and exploited. Yun says it is difficult to translate the meanings of *minjung* well into English. Even so, "A theological translation of *minjung* refers to *the people of God* who do not possess political power, economic wealth, social status, and advanced education in contrast to the wealthy and dominant class."[34]

In that sense, minjung transcends culture, gender, and nationality. We can apply the concept in non-Korean settings. For example, Yun considers the Azusa Revival in America a "black *minjung* movement." He shows how Pentecostalism took hold in poor and marginalized cultures across the globe. It had a natural home among *minjung* groups worldwide, including South Korea.[35]

Many examples of contextually shaped theologies of the Spirit in the Majority World exist. I detail examples from Africa, Asia, Latin America, and Indigenous cultures in another chapter of this book. Western churches cannot duplicate these Indigenous, contextualized expressions. As Western Christians, we must find fresh, innovative ways to contextualize our theology of the Spirit. At the same time, we need to notice where the Spirit is already at work in our cultures and contexts. How is the Spirit meeting people in our context? How do we engage in a Spirit-empowered mission?

Spirit-Empowered Mission

What is the shape of a Spirit-empowered mission in Western contexts? How do we contextualize Western theologies of the Spirit for our own cultures? How do we contextualize these theologies for the sake of the mission of Jesus Christ? These are not easy questions. But the answers are essential for Spirit-empowered missions in Western settings. Why is a Spirit-empowered mission critical in the West? Today, many Westerners find spirituality and the spiritual world fascinating.[36]

Majority World, Indigenous, and Western cultures are spiritual contexts. Doing mission in them requires the power of the Spirit. The Spirit

33. Kärkkäinen, *Spirit in the World*, 91.
34. Kärkkäinen, *Spirit in the World*, 95.
35. Kärkkäinen, *Spirit in the World*, 114.
36. Theos, "Spirit of Things Unseen," 7–9.

propels the church into mission. He empowers it for the mission of God. The church is dependent on the Spirit's presence in its mission. The Spirit *precedes* the church's mission. He is active and present in the cultures and peoples of the world. He is preparing the soil for the church's missional efforts and gospel proclamation. The Spirit is *present* in the mission of the church. He enables the church to take part in the *missio Dei*. The Spirit *prevails* even where the church can no longer be present. He prevails even when the church has had to withdraw from a culture or people or when the church is not present anymore. The Spirit continues God's sovereign purposes in the world. The Spirit *persists* in convicting hearts, transforming lives, and confronting principalities and powers. He leads toward repentance and discipleship to Jesus Christ. The Spirit does this *before* the church arrives, *while* the church is on mission, and even *after* the church has withdrawn. A missional theology of the Spirit does not minimize the importance of the church in mission. But it does frame this mission with attention to the sovereign and powerful work of the Spirit.

The Spirit is the fulfillment of God's promise. The Spirit is his life-giving breath, power-in-weakness, and personal presence. The Spirit is his assurance of what is to come. God empowers the church's proclamation and action through the Spirit. The Spirit guides the church into the witness that is only possible through holiness, unity, catholicity, and apostolicity. The Spirit distributes his supernatural gifts for the edification of the church. The Spirit gives these gifts for the glorification of Jesus Christ. The Spirit pours these gifts upon people, enabling bold, passionate, and compelling witnesses. The church and its mission depend on the Spirit, who creates, fills, and empowers it.[37]

What do we learn from Majority World churches about Spirit-empowered mission? What are the missional characteristics of these Majority World renewalist churches?

Ma and Ma provide the most thorough treatment of these questions. Stephen Bevans calls their book *Mission in the Spirit* a *summa missiologiae pentecostalis*.[38] These Korean scholars assert that empowerment, creation, eschatology, and practices characterize Majority World Spirit-empowered mission.

---

37. Hill, *Salt, Light, and a City*, 226–27.
38. Ma and Ma, *Mission in the Spirit*.

PART 2: RENEWING OUR MISSION

1. Empowerment

"For Pentecostal theology, the most influential theological ground [for Christian mission] is its theology of empowerment, often anchored on the unique experience called baptism in the Holy Spirit."[39] Renewalist mission emphasizes supernatural empowerment. It seeks Spirit-emboldened witness. Renewalist mission focuses on divine gifts of healing. It longs for the Spirit to provide supernatural power, deliverance, and restoration.

2. Creation

A Spirit-empowered mission includes a theology of creation. This is because mission is the "restoration of God's creation." The Spirit of creation calls the church to a Spirit-empowered restoration of the whole creation.[40] A theology of creation places mission at "the center of God's activity in human history." Creation theology shapes the church's mission. This mission must seek to restore all creation. Creation theology leads to a mission that addresses *anti-creation* in human cultures. Anti-creation includes injustice, poverty, oppression, exploitation, and so forth. Creation theology sees mission as restoring human and divine-human community.

3. Eschatology

Eschatology studies the "last or end times" when Jesus Christ returns, restores, and reigns. All Spirit-empowered mission

> is an attempt to bring a 'foretaste' of kingdom life through proclamation, serving, and miracles . . . Pentecostals have an understanding that the advent of the Spirit in the modern times is the sign of the beginning of the end of time, *vis-à-vis* the first outpouring of the Spirit being the beginning of the end. Consequently, their mission engagement should be the expression of their eschatological conviction.[41]

---

39. Ma and Ma, *Mission in the Spirit*, 27.
40. Ma and Ma, *Mission in the Spirit*, 18–27.
41. Ma and Ma, *Mission in the Spirit*, 27.

4. Practices

Ma and Ma say that Majority World Christians express Spirit-empowered mission through various practices. What are some of those practices? Here's a snapshot. They democratize ministry—the whole community participates in mission and ministry. Their missional zeal and commitment are palpable—passion for mission is a primary characteristic of many churches. They are willing to suffer considerable personal loss for the sake of mission. They link mission with healing, miracles, and the supernatural. Renewalist churches grow through missional planting and innovation. Gospel proclamation, power evangelism, Indigenous leadership, prayer, and continual reproduction characterize this church planting and missional innovation. Such reproduction happens through the multiplication of disciples and churches.

Other practices are evident in the Spirit-empowered mission in the Majority World. Pastors expect Holy Spirit manifestations to go with their preaching (this includes divine healing, speaking in tongues, miracles and wonders, prophecy, and other manifestations). Missionaries expect to have power encounters with angels and demons. The spirit-empowered mission focuses on spiritual warfare and deliverance from evil. This mission prioritizes *both* inner change and societal transformation. It emphasizes *both* evangelism and social concern. Spirit-empowered mission in the Majority World adapts its expressions and mission to Indigenous contexts. It often pursues ecumenical, interracial cooperation and leadership. It's characterized by local, regional, and global networking in mission. It integrates Spirit-empowered mission into ministry training and theological curriculum. This integration is central to theological and ministry education in Majority World renewalist churches. Such a Spirit-empowered mission engages with other religious, spiritual, and secular worldviews. (In Asia, this is especially Animism, Buddhism, Confucianism, Hinduism, Islam, and secular perspectives). It has also become more common for such missions to address the plight of women and girls in the Majority World. These face degeneration, violence, rape culture, and poor educational opportunities.

So much can be said about the practices of Spirit-empowered mission in the Majority World. Its mission is characterized by enthusiastic, spontaneous, participatory, experiential, and community-centered worship, prayer, and spirituality. This defining feature of renewalist churches is critical to their missional vitality.[42]

---

42. Ma and Ma, *Mission in the Spirit*, 8–9, 49–58, and 65–272; Ma, "Pentecostalism and Asian Mission," 32–34.

Anderson examines Pentecostal-charismatic churches and missions in the Majority World. He lists the missional practices of Spirit-empowered churches. Anderson says that they practice a Spirit-centered mission. They embrace dynamic and contextual missional forms. They focus on evangelism and church planting. They shape contextualized missional leadership. They throw enormous energy into mobilization in (and for) missions. Often, premillennial and dispensational eschatologies go with such mission. (That is, a belief in the imminent return of Christ that inspires a passionate mission). Mission among Majority World renewalist churches is often pragmatic and contextual. It addresses "sickness, poverty, unemployment, loneliness, evil spirits, and sorcery."[43]

What does all this mean for the global church? Yong writes that the global church must develop a Spirit-centered theology and practice of mission. This missional theology and practice must (1) deal with its "social and political locations." This includes its relationship to Christendom, Colonialism, and Pentecostalism. (2) It must depend "on the church being a body of Spirit-empowered people who embody and invite an alternative way of being in the world." This is crucial—especially if this Spirit-centered theology and practice are to be post-Christendom, postcolonial, and Spirit-focused. (3) It must focus on the many cultural, ethnic, and other voices and "practices of the Spirit-filled people of God." That way, it remains dialogical, dispersed, multicultural, and multi-voiced.[44]

Ghanaian pastor Opoku Onyinah writes about the extraordinary growth of African renewalist churches. He describes Spirit-centered and Spirit-empowered foundations for mission. Onyinah says that the Holy Spirit "is a missionary Spirit. He is the motivating force behind every activity that the believer undertakes. The climax of his work in the believer is baptism in the Holy Spirit, whose main purpose is to witness for Christ."[45]

We can learn from what these Majority World writers say about Spirit-empowered missions. This is a dynamic picture of mission. It's Spirit-empowered. It's unmistakable that God is moving through this. The Western church needs to listen and learn.

The church's role is to join the Spirit of Christ in his mission. This participation includes liberating individuals, people groups, societies, and creation. We join with the Spirit in restoration, healing, and salvation.

---

43. Anderson, "Towards a Pentecostal Missiology for the Majority World," 8; Anderson, *Introduction to Pentecostalism*, chapter 11.

44. Yong, "Many Tongues, Many Practices," 43–58.

45. Onyinah, "Pneumatological Foundations for Mission," 334.

The Spirit and Liberation

Renewalist churches in the Majority World are not always interested in socio-political matters. Many focus on proclamation, evangelism, and personal salvation. However, there is a growing global trend for renewalist Christians to focus on evangelism and social action. These renewalists ask an essential question. "What might it mean to address issues of justice, liberation, poverty, and social action in the power of the Spirit?"

Chilean theologian Juan Sepulveda serves as an example. He compares Indigenous Latin American Pentecostal communities and liberation theology. He primarily focuses on Base Ecclesial Communities (BECs). Sepulveda describes how each may learn from the other. They both engage in Spirit-empowered service with and among people experiencing poverty. Latin American Pentecostalism and BECs are at home among the poor and marginalized. They both encourage a direct encounter with the Spirit. They both make the Christian Scriptures accessible to ordinary readers.

Both communities see the church as a healing presence in the world. They believe the Spirit empowers the church for mission, justice, restoration, and healing. So, while Pentecostalism focuses on the Spirit and BECs on liberation, there are many points of connection—the cross-pollination between the two results in richer forms of mission and church and social action.

José Comblin describes the relationship between the Holy Spirit and liberation. Comblin was known throughout Latin America for his sharp theological mind and service among people experiencing poverty. He opposed military dictatorships in the region. Military dictatorships expelled him from Brazil and Chile for his views. He died in 2011. He was buried in a small town in the impoverished Brazilian state of Paraíba, also in the state of Bahía, where he lived. Comblin was a passionate defender of human rights. He proclaimed Jesus's option for people experiencing poverty. He complemented his defense of liberation theology with his vigorous opposition to military dictatorships. Comblin served tirelessly among poor peasant communities in northeastern Brazil.

Comblin's best-known book is *The Holy Spirit and Liberation*. Comblin argues that renewal in the Spirit leads to service among the poor, marginalized, and oppressed. The outpouring of the Spirit can have many manifestations. This includes the renewal of worship, the charismatic gifts, and the gospel proclamation. But compassion, justice, and mercy also flow from any true renewal in the Spirit.

The Spirit leads us into service among and with the poor, wounded, broken, forgotten, and oppressed. In the words of Jesus: "The Spirit of the

Lord is on me because he has anointed me to proclaim good news to the poor. He has sent me to proclaim freedom for the prisoners and recovery of sight for the blind, to set the oppressed free, to proclaim the year of the Lord's favor" (Luke 4:18–19).

Comblin says the Spirit liberates all creation—not just the church or individuals. The church's mission is to cooperate with the Spirit in his work of new creation. The Spirit invites us to join him in making new creations of all things. This includes persons, churches, cultures, creation, and history. The church does this best when it is self-giving and dispersed and serving.

Jose Comblin comes to the following conclusions about the Holy Spirit, justice, and liberation:

The Spirit in focus: Western churches have given too little attention to the Spirit. "There was one Easter; there are millions of Pentecosts."[46]

The Spirit in the church: The global Pentecostal phenomenon is God's renewal of the church. It calls the church away from a materialistic, "rationalized, intellectualized, and institutionalized" existence. It calls the church to a living and transforming experience and community.[47]

The Spirit in the world: The Spirit is at work in the world. He calls the church to join with him. The Spirit is ushering in resurrection life, the kingdom of God, the new creation, and "the birth of a new humanity." We get to take part in this mission![48]

The Spirit and those experiencing poverty: The Spirit is among people experiencing poverty and their liberation struggle. As the church recognizes and celebrates this, it experiences a just and Christ-like spirituality.

> The Holy Spirit lies at the root of the cry of the poor. The Spirit is the strength of those who have no strength. It leads the struggle for the emancipation and fulfillment of the people of the oppressed . . .
>
> The signs of the action of the Spirit in the world are clear: the Spirit is present wherever the poor are awakened to action, to freedom, to speaking out, to community, to life . . .
>
> A new spirituality is being born under the impulse of the Spirit, among elites placing themselves at the service of the poor, and among the poor themselves who are irrupting on to the stage of history.[49]

---

46. Comblin, *Holy Spirit and Liberation*, 184.
47. Comblin, *Holy Spirit and Liberation*.
48. Comblin, *Holy Spirit and Liberation*, 185.
49. Comblin, *Holy Spirit and Liberation*, 184–86.

Many Majority World theologians challenge us to see the connection between our theologies of liberation, justice, and Spirit. These include Sepulveda, Comblin, Marthinus L. Daneel, Katy Attanasi, and M. M. Thomas. They do not minimize Spirit-filled worship and spirituality. After all, these are hallmarks of Pentecostal-charismatic faith. But they assert that an authentic experience of the Spirit leads to Spirit-empowered social action and concern.

Spirit-Filled Worship and Spirituality

What can the Western church learn from renewalist worship and spirituality in the Majority World? I'll begin with worship and move on to spirituality.

Certain features characterize renewalist worship in Asia, Africa, Latin America, and Indigenous settings. The importance and shape of each feature will vary according to context. Many Majority World congregations embrace renewalist expressions as "normal Christianity." What Westerners consider "Pentecostal," "over the top," or "ecstatic" they see as ordinary faith.

Simon Chan is a Singaporean theologian. He provides a thorough treatment of Pentecostal-charismatic worship and spirituality.[50] Chan shows how contemplative, social, Word-centered, and charismatic spiritualities can come together. These four spiritualities come together in Spirit-graced dialogue and Spirit-enabled *practices*. These practices are many. They include contemplative and self-examining prayer. They incorporate the art of "practicing the presence of God." They also include spiritual reading, biblical meditation, and spiritual friendship. We can add social action, spiritual direction, and corporate and personal discernment to these.

The Spirit leads the church into complementary spiritual practices and dialogue.[51]

Spirit-Graced Conversations

Renewalist churches do not always value conversation with other groups. Suspicion of other groups was a defining feature of the Pentecostalism I experienced in my twenties. But renewalist churches have a long history of positive ecumenical and interreligious engagement. Walter Hollenweger outlines "four phases of ecumenical development" in Pentecostalism.

---

50. Chan, *Pentecostal Theology*.
51. Chan, *Spiritual Theology*, Part 2.

Through these phases, Pentecostal churches return to their original ecumenical roots.[52]

Timothy Tennent describes how Latin American Pentecostals have rediscovered the value of ecumenical cooperation. He notes their positive contribution to ecumenical spirituality and mission. "The term [ecumenical] has come full circle to refer to the emergence of global Christianity of which we (despite our various denominations) are all participants."[53] This emerging unity is not based on an *identical theology*. Unity emerges through a *shared passion* for Jesus Christ and his Body, mission, kingdom, and Spirit.

There is a growing ecumenical drive among Majority World renewalists. This involves conversations with other Christian groups and religious faiths and worldviews. Koo Dong Yun and Grace Si-Jun Kim are examples of this inter-religious and ecumenical conversation. Yun constructs an elaborate ecumenical theology of Spirit baptism. He developed his theology of Spirit baptism in conversation with nine theologians, including Karl Barth. Yun believes that a deep understanding and experience of Spirit baptism requires conversation. It requires dialogue with different cultures, spiritual experiences, and theological traditions.[54] Grace Si-Jun Kim believes we need a "global understanding of the Spirit." This results from authentic conversation. Kim believes that we need to listen to others as we develop a theology of the Spirit.[55]

Yong is prolific on this topic. No one else makes such a contribution to "a Pentecostal-charismatic Christian theology of religions." Yong believes that the church, empowered by the Spirit, must engage other religions. Here are seven of Yong's key assertions:

1. A pneumatological theology of religions

We need a "robust pneumatological theology of religions." How is a theology of religions robust and Spirit-graced? It is robust because of its systematic engagement with trinitarian theology and other worldviews. It is Spirit-graced through its attention to the Spirit in Christian faith and experience. It is robust through "the emergence of a new set of categories that may chart the way forward." It is Spirit-graced through its attention to the Spirit's voice in other faiths.

---

52. Hollenweger, *Pentecostalism*, 334–87.
53. Tennent, *Theology in the Context of World Christianity*, 184–89.
54. Yun, *Baptism in the Holy Spirit*.
55. Kim, "Global Understanding of the Spirit," 20–21.

Yong writes, "In brief, a pneumatological theology of religions begins with the doctrine of the Holy Spirit as the universal presence and activity of God and attempts to understand the world of the religions within that universal framework."[56]

2. Discernment

We must root our engagement with other religions in trinitarian thought. "The Pentecostal narrative of Acts 2" grounds our discernment. It considers all the ways the triune God reveals himself—manifesting his power, presence, and voice. God pours the Spirit out "on all flesh" (including the world of religions). "Hence, the pentecostal narrative can be understood to redeem not only human languages and cultures, but also human religiosity. However, just as this does not mean that all human words and all aspects of human culture are holy without qualification, so also it does not mean that all human religiousness is sanctified."[57]

We must learn to discern the voice of the Spirit in those religious traditions. This happens through developing sound trinitarian and biblical theology. This Christian theology serves as our foundation. Our discernment increases through prayerful attention to the Spirit in all cultures. We also need thoughtful guidelines and categories.

3. Guidelines and categories

We need guidelines for discerning the Spirit's voice in other religions, cultures, and theological traditions. This voice may challenge our understanding of what the Spirit is doing in the world. Amos Yong offers guidelines and categories. I won't list them here, but I encourage you to read his book. Yong says we need "dynamic categories for comprehending the phenomena of religion and religiosity." We then see "the openness and unfinished character of religious traditions and human religiousness."[58]

---

56. Yong, "P(new)matological Paradigm for Christian Mission in a Religiously Plural World," 175.

57. Yong, "P(new)matological Paradigm for Christian Mission in a Religiously Plural World," 177.

58. Yong, "P(new)matological Paradigm for Christian Mission in a Religiously Plural World," 179.

PART 2: RENEWING OUR MISSION

4. Moving beyond exclusivism or inclusivism

We must move beyond *exclusivism* (we have the truth, and no other religion does). We need to reject *inclusivism/pluralism* (everyone has the truth). Instead, we need a *pneumatological theology of religions*. This is a discerning engagement with other religions. The Spirit enables this engagement. We must shape it around clear guidelines and categories.

5. Attention to the other

We must hear other religious faiths on their terms. We should listen to them as they "define themselves in their own voices."[59]

6. The middle way

We need to "find a middle way between the Scylla of subordinating the Spirit to the Word (the perennial failure of the classic theological tradition) and the Charybdis of disengaging the Spirit from the Word altogether (the perennial temptation of the tradition of enthusiasm)."[60]

7. Interreligious dialogue

"Christian mission should include both authentic dialogue and sincere proclamation as two sides of the one coin. Dialogue and proclamation together constitute authentic interreligious engagement (i.e., authentic engagement between individuals from different religious traditions)."[61] If authentic, this dialogue will lead to "conversion to the other." This does not mean abandoning Christ or his gospel. But it does mean that all dialogue partners open themselves up to the transforming, converting work of the Spirit.

As we discern the Spirit in this interreligious dialogue, he transforms us. He renews us spiritually, theologically, relationally, and morally. Our Christian faith experiences the benefit of the cross-fertilization of religions. The Spirit guides us into constructive conversations between various

---

59. Yong, "Beyond the Impasse?" 281.

60. Yong, "Beyond the Impasse?"

61. Yong, "P(new)matological Paradigm for Christian Mission in a Religiously Plural World," 182.

religious faiths. The Spirit leads toward constructive, healthy cooperation between Christian traditions.

People like Samuel Solivan are working to construct a Pentecostal approach to inter-religious dialogue.[62] We may not embrace all the perspectives of people like Grace Si-Jun Kim, Samuel Solivan, Amos Yong, or Koo Dong Yun. But they give us a window into a burgeoning conversation in the Majority World and beyond. They show us the characteristics and concerns of this conversation.

Clark Pinnock writes, "One might expect the Pentecostals to develop a Spirit-oriented theology of mission and world religions because of their openness to religious experience, their sensitivity to the oppressed of the Third World where they have experienced much of their growth, and their awareness of the ways of the Spirit as well as dogma."[63]

Spirit, Atonement, and Healing

I presented at a Baptist theological conference on the Holy Spirit in 2013. The conference theme was *In Step with the Spirit*. The Baptist World Alliance held it in Ocho Rios, Jamaica. Participants came from all over the world. Presenters came from Australia, Canada, Jamaica, Nigeria, Romania, the Philippines, and the United States. The organizers gave me the topic "The Atonement and Healing." They gave me this theme for a specific reason—emphasizing atonement and healing in the Majority World.

I came to a personal faith in Jesus Christ in my late teens. Having grown up in a Reformed, Free Church, congregational church, I decided to follow Jesus in an Australian Pentecostal church. I embraced the biblical foundations of my childhood and the spiritual enthusiasm of Pentecostalism. Then, in my early twenties, I experienced a spiritual crisis.

The Pentecostal church I attended taught that God guarantees physical healing in the atonement. God will heal all those who have enough faith. This church told me that the following things guarantee healing: (1) the personal faith of the sick person; (2) the faith of the believing congregation; (3) the spiritual gift of the charismatic leader; (4) the atoning work of Jesus Christ; and (5) the biblical guarantee of present physical healing. Even as a young person, I struggled with this theology. I could not reconcile this theology with Scripture, modern medicine, and human experience.

Then, in the early 1990s, two Pentecostal Christian leaders I knew died from cancer in the same year. Both were certain that God would heal them

---

62. Solivan, "Interreligious Dialogue."
63. Pinnock, *Flame of Love*, 274.

from their cancer in this life. I watched as their congregations tried to make sense of their deaths (which was at complete odds with their theology). I decided that I would allow Scripture to speak for itself. I began to investigate the biblical relationship between atonement and physical healing.

Some Pentecostal, neo-Pentecostal, and charismatic movements have linked physical healing with atonement. They do this by appealing to Isa 53:4–6; Matt 8:16–17; and 1 Pet 2:24. This is common in the Majority World. This theology has also influenced Evangelical, Free Church, and mainline Protestant churches. This is especially true in the Majority World and among churches with charismatic leanings.

Rigorous debates have concerned the associated theological, biblical, and pastoral issues. On one end of the spectrum are those who believe God guarantees physical healing in the atonement (e.g., A. B. Simpson, Kenneth Hagin, and Kenneth and Gloria Copeland). At the other end are those who reject any such notion. This latter group focuses on how the atonement deals with sin (e.g., B. B. Warfield, Merrill F. Unger, John MacArthur, and Richard Mayhue).

There is, of course, a long tradition of linking *healing* with *atonement*—with variations on what groups mean by healing and atonement. Roman Catholic theologians often have healing at the center of their view of atonement. The Patristic era produced atonement theories that were healing-based (to call them theories may be overstating the case). This is also true of Eastern Orthodox theology—*theosis* being the critical lens for such treatments. *Theosis* is the theology of spiritual and holistic healing and transformation. Christians experience this transformation in union with God and the attainment of his likeness. *Theosis* has three main stages: (1) purification of body and mind (*catharsis*), (2) spiritual contemplation and illumination (*theoria*), and (3) union with and likeness of God found in sainthood (*theosis*). Other theologians link spiritual healing and the atonement. These include Athanasius, Clement, Irenaeus, and Origen.

Why is this theology emphasized in renewalist churches in the Majority World? The answer to this question resides in the physical sickness and impoverishment in so much of the developing world. The emphasis also emerges from the focus on divine spiritual encounters in Pentecostal-charismatic churches. There is a heightened attention to the spiritual, metaphysical realm in the Majority World. The eschatology of these renewalist churches focuses on present-day healing and deliverance. Finally, this theology grants some sense of control and influence on people who feel powerless.

So, what do we make of the focus on atonement and physical healing in many renewalist churches in the Majority World? There isn't space to examine the key passages (Isa 53:4–6, Matt 8:14–17, and 1 Pet 2:21–25). When we examine these texts, we arrive at a clear conclusion. The atonement includes the possibility of physical healing in the present. But we can't demand it "any more than we have the right and power to demand our resurrection bodies."[64] Only in the age to come, are we completely healed and receive our promised resurrection bodies.

Inaugural eschatology affirms that the kingdom of God has *present* and *future* dimensions. The end is already here. The kingdom is already inaugurated through the life, death, and resurrection of Jesus Christ. But we are yet to experience the final consummation. It is *now, but not yet*. The person and work of Jesus Christ brought the ultimate future reality into the present. He demonstrated the *current presence* of the kingdom in his life, death, and resurrection. But it is only in the *final consummation* that all disease, suffering, conflict, and death end (Rev 21:4).

Because the kingdom is *present*, God heals believers from their sins and unrighteousness. He also heals them physically on occasion. Because the kingdom is *future*, our ultimate physical healing, like our resurrected bodies, awaits the final and decisive reality. The life, message, and resurrection of Jesus witnesses to this present and future healing. So, we are "confidently restless." We wait for the final restoration of all things—including our bodies.

We can associate bodily healing with the atonement, just as we can link every other blessing promised by God. People experience divine healing on occasion. We can relate this to Christ's atonement for our sins. But "God has not seen fit to shower us with all physical blessings now in the way he has with spiritual blessings (Eph 1:3); we await the final consummation of God's redemptive plan, and this is our 'blessed hope'—the glorious appearing of our great God and Savior, Jesus Christ (Titus 2:13)."[65]

The Spirit: Concluding Reflections

The Spirit of Christ is sovereign over the global church's past, present, and future. God has tied the future of the global church to the worldwide emergence of renewalist movements. The West can learn much from the growth of the Pentecostal and renewalist churches in the Majority World. The West can learn from renewalist emphases, worship, spirituality, contextualization, mission, and challenges.

---

64. Carson, *Matthew*, 207.
65. Bokovay, "Relationship of Physical Healing to the Atonement," 37.

Here are nine things we learn from how Majority World Christians embrace the Spirit.

1. Spirit-empowered Christians depend on the Spirit's power, presence, and provision.

We tend to rely too heavily on our resources and finances in the West. We trust our programs, academic training, conferences, and personalities. As I travel through Majority World and First Nation cultures, I notice a striking thing repeatedly. They often have few resources and little money. But they depend on the Spirit for provision, empowerment, and mission. Their dependency is evident in their corporate prayer and expectant worship. It shows in their confrontation of the "principalities and powers of this world." It's revealed in their courageous witness. The fruit is abundant—fruit that will last.

2. Spirit-empowered Christians develop their mission and attention to the Spirit simultaneously.

For too long, a focus on how the Spirit forms the church and empowers it for mission has been (mostly) absent from Western missional conversations. For too long, renewalist churches have overestimated the missional value of charismatic expressions. They haven't been attentive to the insights of missiology. It's time for this to change. We need a theology of the Spirit focused on God's mission. We need a theology of mission that's shaped through attention to God's empowering presence.

In the Majority World, Spirit-empowerment and mission are inextricable. Let's make this so in the West, too. We must live as Spirit-empowered missionary communities. We do this by examining our theology and practices of empowerment, Spirit, mission, creation care, the end times, justice, peacemaking, etc. As Amos Yong says, a Spirit-centered mission is conversational, dispersed, multicultural, and multi-voiced.[66]

Michael Frost challenges us to see the place of the Spirit in mission. It's time we rediscovered the Spirit in dialogue, (2) the Spirit beyond the church, (3) the Spirit within the local congregation, (4) the Spirit and justice, (5) the Spirit and creation, and (6) the Spirit and the world. Elsewhere, I've written that the missional church recovers: (1) its Spirit-constituted being, (2) its Spirit-filled structures, (3) its Spirit-formed communities, (4) its

---

66. Yong, "Many Tongues, Many Practices," 43–58.

Spirit-shaped theology, (5) its presence within a Spirit-infused world, and (6) its Spirit-empowered mission.[67]

3. Spirit-empowered Christians invite the Spirit to empower them for ministry, mission, and life.

The Spirit of Jesus moves us to foster spiritual expectations. He empowers us for ministry, mission, and life. We must be open to "the invasion of the Spirit" and to encounter with him. Do we desire Jesus to reveal himself through the ordinary moments of life and through the miraculous, surprising, and unexpected? Do we long for the Spirit of Christ to fill us with power for faith and mission? Do we expect Jesus to reveal his holiness, power, love, and truth in every aspect of our lives, mission, and gathered worship? Are we content with a powerless Christianity? Or are we actively seeking God's empowering presence?

4. Spirit-empowered Christians believe the Spirit fills their entire life together and on mission, enabling them to recover the supernatural power of the Spirit.

We should invite the Spirit's presence in our sacraments, ministries, missions, and structures—more than that. We must see how the Spirit forms, animates, and sanctifies these things for the glory of God the Father. Jesus promised to fill us with the Holy Spirit and power. We should expect that in every dimension of our service, worship, mission, and life together. (At the same time, we recognize our frailties and faults).

We must commit to the supernatural's recovery in our worship, mission, and prayer. This means inviting the "signs and wonders of the Holy Spirit" into our theological frameworks and ministry training and this power into our gathered worship, organizational structures, and mission. We need to recover the supernatural power of the Spirit in our churches, worship, and mission (with contextual and cultural sensitivity).

---

67. Hill, *Salt, Light, and a City*, 205–29; Frost in Barker, *Following Fire*, 33–41.

PART 2: RENEWING OUR MISSION

5. Spirit-empowered Christians bring liberation, healing, justice, mercy, and hope in the power of the Spirit.

Jesus leads us to seek Spirit-enabled reconciliation and healing in the world. When God pours out his Spirit, he renews worship and empowers mission. He releases the charismatic gifts and emboldens gospel proclamation.

But he doesn't stop there. Compassion, justice, liberation, and mercy also proceed from all genuine movements of the Spirit. The Spirit of Jesus Christ—the companion of sinners and outcasts—leads us into service with the poor, wounded, forgotten, and oppressed. We look for signs of hope where the Spirit is already at work in our neighborhoods, families, and cities. We join with him in processes of healing and hope and reconciliation and justice and liberation and renewal.

6. Spirit-empowered Christians are attentive to the voice and presence of Jesus Christ in other Christian traditions and the world.

God is present in every expression of his church. This demands qualification. On the one hand, there is a sense in which God is present everywhere, outside and within the church. We must look for signs of hope in cities, neighborhoods, and churches. This way, we discern where God is already at work and join with him. But, as David Starling points out, there is the terrible possibility that some forms of the church and its mission can become apostate structures:

> They are edifices in which the form of godliness is present, but the power has departed. These are places where the Spirit of Christ is no more present than he is at a football game or the shopping mall. For all the discontinuities and differences within the history of the last 2000 years of Christianity, the New Testament nevertheless reminds us that our identity as the church is created by our union with Christ, a union that we possess in common with believers of all times and places.[68]

Being attentive to the Spirit in other Christian traditions and the world requires courage, humility, wisdom, and discernment. I have offered Amos Yong's seven guidelines in this chapter. They're helpful. It takes courage to listen to others. It takes wisdom and discernment to know what to offer and receive.

68. Starling, "Theology and the Future of the Church."

7. Spirit-empowered Christians integrate Spirit-empowered missions into ministry training and theological education.

It's common for theological colleges to speak of equipping heads (theology), hands (competency), and hearts (spirituality). Colleges often do well in the first and second areas and struggle to do the third. But I repeatedly hear graduates lament that colleges don't prepare them to serve in the power of the Spirit. They go into mission and ministry and discover they're at war with principalities and powers. They need to rely on God's empowering presence in mission and service. Theological colleges and churches must return this theme to the heart of ministry training.

8. Spirit-empowered Christians join with the Spirit wherever he is at work.

This involves preparing and ushering in resurrection life, the kingdom of God, the new creation, and the birth of a new humanity. Stop behaving as though the Spirit was absent before we arrived. Start discerning his presence in the world. Start joining him in bringing resurrection life, the new birth, the new creation, and the kingdom of God. Courageously proclaim and live out the gospel of Jesus Christ.

9. Spirit-empowered Christians must think critically and biblically about their theology of healing and atonement.

The church must develop a broader understanding of healing and its relationship to atonement. Craig Keener writes, "Matthew informs his audience that healing was part of Jesus' mission, which God provided at great cost to Jesus (8:17)." We need to consider the various dimensions of healing associated with the atonement. Healing is also linked with Christ's empathy with our human condition. Jesus exemplifies this empathy and identification in his incarnation. But we must also recognize that ultimate healing is in the coming age.

What does it mean for humans to experience complete healing? How is healing physical, emotional, relational, and spiritual? How do the atoning life, passion, death, and resurrection of Jesus Christ heal us?

We need to be careful here—very careful. Atonement is primarily about the cancellation of guilt. It is about God's work liberating individuals, the church, and the created order from guilt and sin. But our theology of the atonement can expand our understanding of the nature and scope of healing. We can see the connections between the atonement, the incarnation, and the resurrection.

We have seen that physical healing is available to all through the atonement. But, thanks to the *already but not yet* nature of the kingdom, it is not available to all in this present life. It is only guaranteed in the age to come. Ultimate bodily healing is in the resurrection of our bodies, but God can heal bodily if he chooses to do so. So, we shouldn't neglect to pray for those who are sick.

We must also explore the nature of healing associated with atonement in its broadest sense. How is healing liberation from sin? How is it restoration of relationships? How is it freedom from addictions and slavery? How is it a rejection of idolatry? How are healing, peace, freedom, and joy in the emotional, psychological, and spiritual dimensions of our lives?

The church joins in this healing ministry—as a sign, foretaste, herald, and witness to the *now but not yet* kingdom. It participates in human healing for the sake of Jesus Christ and his mission in the world. God calls his church to express this healing in its corporate life, ethics, public witness, and service. To be a healing presence in the world, the church must pursue the healing mission of God. The church does this best with a mature and biblical view of the kingdom of God. Its grasp of the kingdom—and the kingdom's *present* and *future* aspects—enables healing ministries. The Spirit gives us a foretaste of Christ's reign and the church's future.

Western churches can learn much from renewalist churches in the Majority World. We cannot ignore the enormous growth of these churches in Latin America, Asia, and Africa. They are having a global and local influence. These churches are missional and empowered by the Holy Spirit. It is up to us to adapt these Spirit-centered commitments to our setting. Adopting the lessons outlined above prioritizes the Spirit in our way of doing church. I don't want churches to conform to *this* image of church. Instead, I want the renewalist movement to challenge us to do church differently. We do this by adapting aspects of renewalist churches to our setting. Thankfully, we are not alone in this task. We can rest in the presence of the Spirit of grace, power, and truth.

Study Questions

1. How can your congregation use the spiritual gifts as missional gifts (that is, as gifts for outreach and mission)?
2. Is God's empowering presence enabling your mission? What can you change about your mission activities to depend on this divine presence?
3. How do we recognize the Spirit's presence beyond the church's walls? Where is the Spirit present in popular spirituality, contemporary spiritual quests, consumer culture, film and media, and sports and recreation?
4. How do we join with what the Spirit already does in those places?
5. How will you increase your spiritual expectations? How will you foster your openness to the Spirit and encounter with God?
6. How will you help your congregation, small group, family, friends, tea, or ministry increase spiritual intensity and expectation?

13.

Caring for Creation

The Fifth Expression

THE GROWTH OF MANY Majority World economies has been extraordinary (take China, for example). This growth has often paralleled the growth of the Majority World churches. Majority World middle classes are as enthusiastic about material accumulation as the Western middle classes—global growth in middle-class consumerism results in increased pressure on the environment. Majority World leaders are seeking solutions and responses. These leaders include economists, environmentalists, businesspeople, religious leaders, and politicians.

Western churches can learn much from Majority World and Indigenous thinking about ecology. We can learn from their eco-theology and eco-justice. Humanity faces terrible ecological challenges. These include global warming, climate change, deforestation, and desertification. Pollution, water deterioration, habitat destruction, and species extinctions are serious problems. Humans have depleted natural resources. Global population growth is putting the earth under pressure. It is time to learn from each other about creation care. It is time to act.

This chapter considers Majority World ideas about eco-theology, eco-justice, eco-feminism, eco-Indigenous movements, and eco-practices. I proceed in that order. Churches and individual disciples need to take responsibility for the environment. We need to act for its well-being and future generations' sake.

We must pursue constructive environmental solutions as proactive stewards of the earth. God has entrusted the earth to our care.

Eco-Theology

Indigenous writings contain substantial eco-theological reflections. It is not possible to treat such eco-theology in detail here. However, it is possible to summarize some of the central eco-theological proposals and considerations.

1. Eco-theology is a global, multivocal dialogue.

David G. Hallman edits a volume called *Ecotheology*. In that book, he shows that we do the best and richest eco-theology in dialogue. Our eco-theology flourishes in a dialogue between Majority World and Indigenous and Western voices.[1] Hallman constructs a global, multi-voiced, and dialogical eco-theology. He considers the biblical witness—creation, covenant, prophets, Psalms, Gospels, Romans, and eschatology. His eco-theology covers the theological challenges and the shape of eco-feminist theology. He unpacks Indigenous perspectives and investigates ethical implications.

This book exemplifies the future of multi-voiced and global eco-theology. All eco-theology is at its best when we construct it globally and multifocally. Why is this the case? Only a globalized approach to eco-theology is adequate for the vast challenges of climate change and environmental degradation. Christians have done minimal work on eco-theology—so we need to get on with this and learn from voices from all over the globe. The globalized nature of the modern world demands a globally shaped eco-theology. Rich possibilities reside in a global eco-theological conversation.

This dialogue will not only be between individuals and cultures. It will also be between theological traditions, the sciences, the biblical witness, and the humanities. It will involve discussions and actions dealing with the environmental crisis.

2. Eco-Theology is obedient to the biblical witness.

In recent years, Christian scholars have examined Scripture for ecological themes. The *Earth Bible* is one example. This Bible examines Scripture for eco-justice themes. It contributes to current debates on ecology,

---

1. Hallman, *Ecotheology*.

eco-theology, and eco-ethics. Its interpretations range from brilliant to dubious. However, it contributes to ecological hermeneutics (i.e., interpreting the Bible through an ecological lens).

Ken Gnanakan is a theologian based in Bangalore, India. He writes books and articles on a biblical theology of the environment. These include pieces for the World Evangelical Alliance Theological Commission. Gnanakan calls evangelicals back to "responsible stewardship of God's creation." This stewardship responds to an eco-theology constructed upon a careful interpretation of Scripture.

The Bible testifies that the earth belongs to the Lord: sin and the Fall affect humans and all creation. The Bible also calls humanity to responsible stewardship of the earth. God gives us dominion over creation. But it is a role characterized by care, nurture, and protection. It is an earth-enriching, "creation care" role. Christians must reject all forms of earth-destroying domination. We must see ourselves as stewards of God's creation. God connects us intimately with creation. He charges us with nurturing and protecting it. We share our final redemption and healing and resurrection and renewal with creation.

As the resurrection community, God calls us into a just, responsible, and loving relationship with creation. We worship, witness, and reveal true community and stewardship in our care for the earth. This stewardship is characterized by commonality, love, responsibility, interdependence, servanthood, respect, worship, mission, and eschatological vision.[2]

3. Eco-theology is connected to justice, liberation, and spirituality.

Leonardo Boff connects ecological justice with justice for people experiencing poverty. He links the cries of people experiencing poverty with the cries of the Earth. Boff draws on James Lovelock's *Gaia Theory* elements to construct an eco-theology.

Gaia Theory takes both rational and mystical forms. It suggests that all the Earth's geological, physical, chemical, and biological dimensions interpenetrate each other. This interpenetration or interdependence regulates the planet. It makes Earth an optimal habitat for life. For James Lovelock, "We define Earth as Gaia because it presents itself as a complex entity embracing the biosphere, the atmosphere, the oceans, and the land; in their

---

2. Gnanakan, *God's World*.

totality, these elements constitute a cybernetic or self-sustaining system that provides an optimal physical and chemical medium for life on this planet."[3]

As I noted, Gaia Theory has both scientific and mystical forms. Science has verified some aspects of the theory, while other features remain untested or unverifiable. Leonardo Boff claims that this interdependency between humanity and the earth provides an ethical and spiritual challenge for Christians. Like Francis of Assisi, we are to recognize our interdependent responsibility for the earth and the terrestrial community—soil, subsoil, air, plants, animals, birds, fish, biodiversity, and the rest of the planet. We have ethical, spiritual, and practical responsibility for these things.[4]

Boff believes this "experience of radical communion with the Earth," united with an experience "of the Father of limitless love and goodness, will open us up to a more global and all-embracing experience of the mystery of God."[5] All genuine eco-theology will lead to radical eco-justice, eco-ethics, and eco-politics. True eco-theology leads to innovative eco-technologies. It results in constructive social and interpersonal approaches to ecology. We reveal authentic eco-theology in our eco-spirituality and eco-communities. Our daily habits show whether we mean what we say when we do eco-theology.[6]

Boff's eco-theology is a form of Christian Panentheism. Panentheism is the idea that God is greater than the universe and that he transcends nature—but God also interpenetrates every part of nature. God fills creation with his presence. He draws it into his divine and final purpose. Process (Whiteheadian) Theology and Creation Spirituality are related to Panentheism. Note that Panentheism is not Pantheism. Panentheism doesn't believe that everything is God. It acknowledges that God is distinct from—and revealed in—creation.

Like Jürgen Moltmann, Leonardo Boff builds trinitarian dimensions into this panentheistic eco-theology. Boff proposes an ecologically active God. "The world, indeed, is complex, diverse, one, united, interrelated, because it reflects the Trinity. God invades every being, enters every relationship, erupts into every ecosystem."[7]

---

3. Lovelock, quoted in Boff, "Earth as Gaia," 27.
4. Boff, *Ecology and Liberation*, 52–54.
5. Boff, "Earth as Gaia," 31.
6. Boff, *Ecology and Liberation*, 9–54.
7. Boff, *Ecology and Liberation*, 48.

PART 2: RENEWING OUR MISSION

4. Eco-theology is multidimensional.

Majority World eco-theology engages in a vast array of theological themes. These include creation, Christ, salvation, ethics, church, Spirit, Trinity, ecology, and eschaton.

For example, Ferdinand Nwaigbo writes that the Trinity's communion provides a model for communion between humans and creation. How do we know what good "creation care" looks like? We turn to the trinitarian mutual indwelling and missional actions. Trinitarian relations guide us toward communion with creation. Trinitarian mission compels us to act for the sake of creation's wellbeing. The Trinity is our model and motivation. The Trinity leads us toward "ecological-hearted community and inclusiveness." The Trinity inspires us to embrace ecological responsibility for persons, creation, societies, and the planet. Nwaigbo centers his eco-theology on Christ. His eco-theology highlights the power and presence of the Spirit in creation. Nwaigbo shapes his eco-theology with attention to the mission of God and his church. He peppers it with African socio-cultural and theological perspectives.[8]

Similarly, M. L. Daneel, Kok-Weng Chiang, and Geoffrey Tan show that a theology of the Spirit must have ecological implications. This is because the Spirit participates in the work of creation. The Spirit heals and protects humanity and nature. The Spirit brings justice and liberation. All Spirit-human-creation relationships are a work of the Spirit. He leads toward a "Spirit-driven, human-responsible, earth-friendly" eco-theology. Such eco-theology is dynamic and multifaceted.[9]

Eco-Justice

Eco-theology leads to ethical and just considerations and actions. Leonardo Boff makes this case when he speaks of ecology and poverty as the cry of the earth and those experiencing poverty. Liberation and ecology bridge the concerns of the Majority World and Western cultures, the North and South. This is because the destiny of the world's poor and the destiny of the world's climate and ecosystems affect us all.

The poor need liberation from oppression and marginalization. The earth needs liberation from exploitation and degradation. We all need liberation from "a paradigm that places us—against the thrust of

---

8. Nwaigbo, "Cosmic Christology and Eco-Theology in Africa."

9. Daneel, "African Independent Church Pneumatology and the Salvation of All Creation."

the universe—over things instead of being with them in the great cosmic community."[10]

Jayapaul Azariah is an Indian marine scientist, bioethicist, and theologian. He writes passionately about the ethical management of natural resources. These include renewable and non-renewable resources, natural ecosystems, human-produced resources, and human resources. By human resources, Azariah means our care for humans' health, dignity, and well-being. Azariah says Christians should lead the way in the ethical care and management of creation.[11]

Paul G. Harris teaches at the Hong Kong Institute of Education. Harris examines the relationships between ethics, global justice, urban settings, built environments, international politics, poverty, and climate change. Those who suffer most from climate change contributed the least to it. They have little ability to mitigate or adapt to its effects. Those who benefited the most from the practices that caused climate change have obligations. They must care for those who suffer the most from climate change. They must protect the vulnerable. They must commit themselves to "climate justice."

Economic globalization and environmental interdependence demand international environmental justice. Paul G. Harris cites examples of such international ecological justice. Examples include the *Stockholm Conference on the Human Environment*, the *Law of the Sea*, the *Montreal Protocol*, the *Earth Summit*, the *Biodiversity Convention*, and agreements like the *1992 Framework Convention on Climate Change* and the *1997 Kyoto Protocol*. All nations and states have responsibility. But responsibility increases according to a nation's contribution to the problem. It also increases concerning a nation's level of development. In other words, some nations have greater responsibility than others.

Harris argues for "cosmopolitan justice." He doesn't discount nation-state organizations pursuing international justice. However, he argues that the best approaches to global environmental justice happen at local and regional levels. This is true in both developed and developing nations.

Who should champion global eco-justice? Poorer people have a role to play. They show the effects of climate change on the rest of the world. They demonstrate generosity and contentment. They often exemplify creation care. But wealthier people have a role to play, too. More affluent people have the financial means to make a difference and contribute to solutions. They have the resources to help those that climate change has ravaged. Wealthier

---

10. Boff, *Cry of the Earth, Cry of the Poor*, xii and 104–14; Boff, *Ecology and Liberation*, 131–36; Boff and Elizondo, *Ecology and Poverty*, xi–xii.

11. Azariah, "Ethical Management of Natural Resources."

PART 2: RENEWING OUR MISSION

groups must cultivate sufficiency, generosity, service, justice, and contentment. They need to collaborate with people experiencing poverty in climate justice and creation care.[12]

Gnanakan roots eco-justice in biblical theology. He shows how eco-justice, sustainable development, and environmental sustainability develop from Scripture. Eco-justice emerges from biblical notions of Creation, solidarity, equity, justice, Sabbath, Jubilee, and restoration. Eco-justice develops out of our theology of the nature and mission of God.[13]

As the Micah document on "Creation Stewardship and Climate Change" asserts, the people of God are responsible for pursuing eco-justice. We must engage with politics, development, and economics for the planet's sake. God calls us to put faith into action. Now is the time to develop sustainable practices and lifestyles and churches. We must seek justice for those that climate change and ecological degradation have ravaged. It is time to take responsibility for implementing the seventeen United Nations "Sustainable Development Goals (SDG)." We do this individually and collectively.

1. No poverty (SDG 1)
2. Zero hunger (SDG 2)
3. Good health and well-being (SDG 3)
4. Quality education (SDG 4)
5. Gender equality (SDG 5)
6. Clean water and sanitation (SDG 6)
7. Affordable and clean energy (SDG 7)
8. Decent work and economic growth (SDG 8)
9. Industry, innovation and infrastructure (SDG 9)
10. Reduced inequalities (SDG 10)
11. Sustainable cities and communities (SDG 11)
12. Responsible consumption and production (SDG 12)
13. Climate action (SDG 13)
14. Life below water (SDG 14)
15. Life on land (SDG 15)
16. Peace, justice, and strong institutions (SDG 16)

12. Harris, *World Ethics and Climate Change*.
13. Gnanakan, *Responsible Stewardship of Creation*, 115–16.

17. Partnerships for the goals (SDG 17)

Eco-Equality

Aruna Gnanadason coordinates the World Council of Churches team on Justice, Peace, and Creation. She constructs a holistic theology of creation-stewardship in her small but profound book *Listen to the Women! Listen to the Earth!* Gnanadason exemplifies the environmental and social consciousness in postcolonial eco-feminist theology. She connects the liberation of women and creation and people experiencing poverty. The bondage of one of these three always leads to the bondage of the others. We must seek the liberation of people experiencing poverty from marginalization and oppression. We need to work for the liberation of *creation* from degradation and exploitation. We should ensure the liberation of *women* from patriarchal, abusive systems.

Gnanadason draws on stories of women and Indigenous people who struggle on behalf of the poor and females and creation. She challenges her readers to learn from these *eco-systems peoples*. She Gnanadason notes the different concerns of Western, Indigenous, and Majority World eco-feminists. She says that Euro-American eco-feminists make an essential contribution. But they often indulge in psycho-spiritual issues. Gnanadason quotes Rosemary Radford Ruether here. Western eco-feminists fail "to make real connections between their own reality as privileged women, and racism, classism, and impoverishment of nature."[14]

In contrast, Majority World eco-feminism cares about "intentionally created poverty and wealth." It concerns itself with "poverty that afflicts whole communities (particularly women and children)." It seeks the recovery of pre- and post-colonial "patterns of spirituality that connect them to their Indigenous roots—a past that is still present in the lives of communities, as women care for the earth."[15]

Rosemary Radford Ruether's book *Women Healing Earth* contains the writings of sixteen Latin American, Asian, and African eco-feminists. There are five from each continent, plus Ruether. Each contributor writes about the struggle for eco-justice. They construct fresh eco-theologies. This

---

14. Gnanadason, *Listen to the Women! Listen to the Earth!*, 32; Ruether, *Women Healing Earth*, 5.
15. Gnanadason, *Listen to the Women! Listen to the Earth!*, 32.

eco-feminism is not homogenous. So, we need to differentiate "between women of different classes, castes, races, ecological zones, and so on."[16]

Such diverse, postcolonial, Indigenous, and Majority World eco-feminism asks essential questions. "Have women been colonized by patriarchy? Do women's bodies and labor function as the invisible substructure for wealth extraction? How does the positioning of women as caretakers in the family make this work inferior? How does this identify women with the non-human world that is also given an inferior status?"[17]

Gnanadason builds an eco-feminist theology. She does this by developing an integrated theological understanding of grace. Gnanadason incorporates ecological perspectives on grace—*green* grace, *red* grace, and *brown* grace. This notion of green, red, and brown grace draws on the work of Jay McDaniel and Indian eco-feminists.

Green grace is about the wisdom, healing, and integrity of creation. It sees nature as an integral, self-organizing, and beautiful gift from God.

Red grace is about the love of God demonstrated on the Cross. It highlights the human and ecological responsibilities we share as the people of the Resurrection.

Brown grace is about learning from the "traditions of prudent care." Indigenous, eco-systems peoples have handed down these traditions to humanity. Brown grace is about seeing these practices as a grace from God.[18] This brown grace does not idealize Indigenous and First Peoples as ecologists. Instead, it seeks to assess their contributions. It regards Indigenous practices as a grace for our planet and environmental stewardship.

Eco-feminist theology develops metaphors for God that inform and inspire creation care. For example, God's trinitarian communion helps us understand our connection with him, others, and creation. We can build "a holistic vision" of the interdependence between all created things. All things are intimately connected—animate, inanimate, human, and the rest of creation.[19]

Gnanakan claims that eco-feminism features the spirituality of Indigenous communities. It also emphasizes the ecological perspectives in Scripture. Eco-feminism calls on the church to consider women's concrete and daily and local struggles. These are struggles for justice and wholeness and liberation and dignity. We need to learn from these women. Gnanakan

---

16. Bina Agarwal, quoted in Gnanadason, *Listen to the Women! Listen to the Earth!*, 35.

17. Gnanadason, *Listen to the Women! Listen to the Earth!*, 33.

18. Gnanadason, *Listen to the Women! Listen to the Earth!*, 81–106.

19. Gnanadason, "Women, Economy and Ecology," 184.

provides examples from the Vacaia Project in Brazil, tribal women in Iran, and the Chipko women of India.[20]

Eco-feminism calls the church to action. It invites people into just relationships with each other and creation. In the words of Rosemary Radford Ruether, "a healed ecosystem—humans, animals, land, air, and water together—needs to be understood as requiring a new way of life, not just a few adjustments here and there . . . One needs pioneering ecological communities that demonstrate a new way of life in which the community as a whole lives in an ecologically sustainable way."[21]

Eco-Indigenous Contributions

In my country, Australia, there is an ongoing discussion about what we can learn from Indigenous practices. What can Aboriginal and Torres Strait Islanders teach about caring for the planet and its ecosystems? What can we learn from their sustainable practices and land care and conservation? A conversation is developing between Indigenous peoples and contemporary land care and sustainability models.

The Australian ecological landscape is fragile. My country needs to respond urgently. We face serious problems—environmental degradation, pollution, endangered ecosystems, and species extinction. The Australian Government's Threatened Species Scientific Committee (TSSC) claims that hundreds of species—and many ecological communities—have become extinct or endangered over the two hundred years since European settlement. This is due to "loss, change, and fragmentation of habitat; the effects of invasive plants, animals, and diseases; and direct effects of human activities."[22]

In contrast to European settlement's ecological devastation and exploitation, Aboriginal and Torres Strait Islander people maintained a deep and spiritual connection with the land. They saw themselves as created, along with the land, by the Creator Spirit. This Spirit provided for them through nature's abundance. He gave them a sacred responsibility to nurture, protect, and sustain the land. Indigenous Australians cultivated an understanding of the needs of local ecosystems. They only took from the land what they needed. For countless generations, they cared for specific, local areas. They developed sustainable practices—handed down from generation to generation. Indigenous Australians developed a creation-based, nature-nurturing,

---

20. Gnanakan, *God's World*, 150–65.

21. Ruether, "Religious Ecofeminism," 373.

22. Australian Government, "Threatened Species and Ecological Communities in Australia."

and ecologically attentive spirituality. They shaped this spirituality around sacred sites, ancestral lands, myths, rituals, and hunting and farming. They fashioned all these around care for the land.[23]

Graham Harvey says that environmental concern is crucial to the construction of indigeneity. Sacred places and lands play an essential role in constructing Indigenous environmentalism. Indigenous peoples both damaged and sustained their environments. We need to remember this and avoid idealism or romanticism. However, Harvey shows the ecological concerns embedded in Indigenous cultures. Indigenous people shape their cosmologies, myths, narratives, sacred sites, and communities around the earth. We cannot develop forms of holistic environmentalism without Indigenous outlooks and practices. Jacob K. Olupona of Nigeria and George E. Tinker of the Osage-Cherokee make this point strongly.[24]

All over the globe, contemporary ecologists are conversing with Indigenous communities. These ecologists aren't discarding modern eco-sciences or ecologically sustainable practices. They are enriching these through conversation with the wisdom of Indigenous peoples. Rob Cooper is a Maori of Aotearoa-New Zealand. He writes, "The coupling of technological, scientific, and Indigenous experiences and skills is not merely desirable but essential. To achieve this will not be easy, but we must try. The whole earth is the Lord's, and we are called to co-operate with this wonder in creation and re-creation."[25]

Boff invites his readers to learn from Indigenous people. We learn from their ancestral wisdom and their love for nature. We're challenged by their approaches to work, production, sustainability, dance, community, and celebration. Boff quotes the Villas-Boas brothers, who worked among Indigenous groups in the Amazonian rainforests for fifty years. "If we want to be rich, accumulate power, and rule the Earth, there is no point in asking the native peoples. But if we want to be happy, combine being human with being [spiritual], integrate life and death, put the person in nature, connect work and leisure, harmonize relations between generations, then let us listen to the Indigenous peoples. They have wise lessons to impart to us."[26]

George E. Tinker is an Osage-Cherokee scholar who writes extensive Native American theology. Tinker examines "missionary conquest" and Western categories of thought. He also calls the Christian church to

---

23. Adrahtas, "Perceptions of Land in Indigenous Australian Christian Texts."

24. Harvey, "Sacred Places in the Construction of Indigenous Environmentalism"; Olupona, "Spirituality of Matter."

25. Hallman, *Ecotheology*, 212.

26. Boff, *Cry of the Earth, Cry of the Poor*, 123.

eco-justice and concern for the integrity of creation. Tinker invites us to embrace the responsible and balanced nurture of ecosystems. Tinker calls the church to listen to Indigenous environmentalism. He wants us to do this without succumbing to racism or romanticism. Racist views dismiss native perspectives. Romanticized and idealized acclaim of eco-Indigenous practices is also unhelpful. We must listen to Indigenous perspectives on creation care without committing these errors.[27] For Tinker, God calls human beings to *world-balancing* and *world-renewing* practices. Eco-balance and renewal occur when we understand and respond to reciprocity, spatiality, connections, community, integrity, and grace. Let me explain how these relate to ecological well-being.

> *Reciprocity*: We recognize our reciprocity with the earth and each other and act accordingly. We care for the earth and its people.
>
> *Spatiality*: We focus on temporality (time) and spatiality (place). This emphasizes historical and eschatological processes (time) and our concrete location in a place. Place includes family, tribe, culture, land, and ecosystem. We prioritize and nurture specific "animals, birds, plants, rocks, rivers, and mountains" in our place.
>
> *Connections*: We see the connections between ecological, social, ethnic, class, gender, and socio-economic injustices. We recognize the relationship between ecological injustice and the subjugation or extinction of cultures.
>
> *Community*: We relinquish some dimensions of Western individualism. We embrace ecological solutions. We find these collectively, within a community, and in intercultural dialogue.
>
> *Integrity and graces*: We honor the integrity of creation. We respect the spiritual and ecological gifts of Indigenous peoples. These are graces to us amidst the current ecological crises.

Eco-Praxis

Our concern for the environment cannot remain merely theological or ideological. We must work it out in our practices. The Brazilian educator and philosopher Paulo Freire defined praxis as "reflection and action upon the world in order to transform it."[28] We must express our eco-theology in our discipleship, spirituality, ethics, community, worship, mission, and service.

27. Tinker, "American Indian Theological Response to Ecojustice," 86.
28. Freire, *Pedagogy of the Oppressed*, 36.

PART 2: RENEWING OUR MISSION

Spirituality and Discipleship

Leonard Boff has put a lot of thought into the shape of eco-spirituality. Boff believes "a new spirituality, one adequate to the ecological revolution, is urgently needed."[29] This spirituality is less anthropocentric (i.e., it doesn't place human beings at the center of everything). It prioritizes eco-stewardship and the restoration of creation. It is a spirituality characterized by simplicity, active awareness of our ecological interdependency, and celebration, reverence, and thankfulness for creation's wonder, beauty, and sacredness.

This spirituality doesn't replace Christ and the gospel with creation. Instead, it is a spirituality that sees Christ present in all creation. It understands creation's importance in Christ's redemptive plan and history. It commits to creative ecological stewardship and the worship of the Creator God. It demonstrates the values of the kingdom of God through environmental care.

We need models of such spirituality and discipleship to Christ. Leonardo Boff turns to St. Francis of Assisi as an exemplar of such spirituality. St. Francis exemplifies "all the cardinal ecological virtues."[30] St. Francis demonstrated the fusion of *outer and inner ecology*. He merged his compassion for the poor and the earth with his rich spiritual life. He cared about human and ecological liberation. He sought the health and well-being of creation. He proclaimed the gospel in prayer, word, and action. He showed sustainable, earth-renewing, human-liberating, outwardly engaged Christian spirituality.[31]

Outer ecology is "harmony with nature and its rhythms" and concern for the well-being of humanity.

Inner ecology is a prayerful, spiritual, and joyful integration of critical aspects of our inner lives. These include environmental concern, social compassion, intellectual curiosity, and emotional and psychological wholeness.

This fusion of outer and inner ecology is displayed in St. Francis's "Canticle to Brother Sun."[32] It is never experienced in isolated contemplation. It is always experienced in communion between humans and nature and God.

Affirming these ideas, Neil Darragh describes a "Christian Earth Spirituality" that values the sacramentality of all things. It views creation

---

29. Boff, *Cry of the Earth, Cry of the Poor*, 189.
30. Boff, *Cry of the Earth, Cry of the Poor*, 203–20.
31. Boff, *Ecology and Liberation*, 52–54.
32. Boff, *Cry of the Earth, Cry of the Poor*, 216.

through eschatological eyes. It participates in the redemptive work of the triune God in humans and nature.

It also seeks justice and righteousness in practical ways. "Christian Earth Spirituality" works toward *justice* for people and nature. It pursues the *common good* of all beings and eco-processes and eco-systems. It initiates *sustainable practices* that benefit humans and allow nature to regenerate. It embraces *solidarity* with marginalized people and endangered species.[33]

The Guatemalan theologian Julia Esquivel Velasquez describes this spirituality. He says it's "experiencing grace, gratitude, and free giving." It's "healing and growing to assume our responsibility." It's "praising and communing with all creation."[34]

David Hallman wrote *Spiritual Values for Earth Community*. He says that eco-spirituality is characterized by gratitude, humility, sufficiency, justice, love, peace, simplicity, faith, and hope.[35] Are we developing such disciples in our churches, seminaries, and colleges? Do they show the *ecological virtues* and the *inner and outer ecology* of St. Francis of Assisi?

Mission and Witness

Our theology and practices of creation care directly influence our witness before a watching world. Our societies and communities examine our engagement with human and ecological issues. Do Christians have a concern and theology and response to environmental issues? Are they disinterested and environmentally irresponsible? Are they developing sustainable practices? Are they leading the way in environmental innovation and responsibility? What does this say about the Christ they follow? How does it reveal his relation to humans and the planet?

Geevarghese Mor Coorilos is an Indian church leader and theologian. He develops a missiology that begins with creation and postcolonial mission perspectives. Mor Coorilos says the church is guilty of colonizing people and dominating the earth. It often does this while "on mission." Mor Coorilos proposes a different missiology. "A missiology grounded in biblical creation theology, with creation as a harmonious act of God who brings about life in abundance and preserves it, will be a missiology that is life affirming." Furthermore, "Mission theology cannot ignore these concerns [i.e., climate change, global warming, deforestation, desertification,

---

33. Darragh, "Ascetic Theology, Spirituality, and Praxis," 80.
34. Boff and Elizondo, *Ecology and Poverty*, 58–66.
35. Hallman, *Spiritual Values for Earth Community*, 33–124.

pollution, and destruction of land and water and biodiversity] because *missio Dei* encompasses the entire creation of God."[36]

Mor Coorilos develops a missional theology and praxis of self-emptying. He calls Christians and churches to divest and empty and sacrifice themselves. To do this for the sake of humanity and creation. This is a *kenotic* and *creation-oriented* missiology. Our gospel proclamation must be "creative, affirming life, and encompassing the entire creation." We ought to shape our mission around an awareness of the trinitarian presence in creation (*perichoresis*). God calls us to be a peaceable kingdom. We are to direct our missional practices toward the redemption of human beings and the restoration and integrity of all creation.[37]

Creation Care: Concluding Reflections

The earth is crying out for justice and healing. The church cannot stand on the sidelines as a neutral or disinterested observer. We must make fresh commitments to eco-justice, eco-theology, and creation care.

Here are nine things we learn from how Majority World Christians care for creation.

1. Creation care nurtures a just, responsible, and loving relationship with all creation.

Our care for creation does this in recognition of our God-given stewardship. As outlined in the chapter, we have a biblical and theological mandate to act justly, conscientiously, and lovingly toward all creation.

This includes taking environmental and climate change science seriously. Naturally, this includes the IPCC reports and recommendations. I'm not advising we accept all science uncritically. But we must listen to the consensus from international scientific institutions. NASA reports the following. "Ninety-seven percent of climate scientists agree that climate-warming trends over the past century are very likely due to human activities. Most leading scientific organizations worldwide have issued public statements endorsing this position." NASA then provides a partial list of these organizations. They offer "links to their published statements and a selection

---

36. Mor Coorilos, "Toward a Missiology That Begins with Creation," 310 and 315.
37. Mor Coorilos, "Toward a Missiology," 321.

of related resources."[38] You can see the list and statements in the footnoted link I've provided.

But we don't stop at climate change. Our creation care must also address resource depletion, toxicants, and environmental degradation. We tackle pollution and other environmental problems. We pursue cleaner production and climate change mitigation. We support reforestation and the preservation of marine environments. We invest in industrial ecology, organic agriculture, and restoration ecology. We applaud waste minimization and sustainable consumption.

2. Creation care develops robust eco-theologies.

These eco-theologies must also be fresh, courageous, and biblically faithful. In this chapter, I've also outlined how these eco-theologies must be *glocal*, biblical, liberationist, trinitarian, practical, and public.

Recently, a group of Australian Baptists got together to summarize our climate change position into a concise statement. Eco-theology needs to be more robust than this statement. But this "Statement on Climate Change" does summarize our theological and biblical convictions. You can see the statement here https://www.baptist.org.au/statement-on-climate-change-by-the-baptist-union-of-australia/.[39] As you can see from this statement, the eco-theology we outlined—albeit briefly—is rooted in Scripture and speaks with prophetic passion to the world and humanity's treatment of creation. I encourage you to develop your statement. Include a call to action for your nation's government, citizens, businesses, not-for-profits, and churches.

3. Creation care protects the planet's well-being and against climate change and environmental degradation.

Eco-theology must lead to action. Action must inform eco-theology. Ideally, eco-theologies lead to radical actions against environmental degradation and climate change. These actions should facilitate eco-justice and eco-ethics. Preferably, these actions lead to innovative eco-technologies. They result in social systems that nurture and protect the environment.

---

38. NASA, "Climate Consensus: Earth's Climate is Warming."

39. Australian Baptist Ministries, "Statement on Climate Change by the Baptist Union of Australia." November 24, 2006.

PART 2: RENEWING OUR MISSION

Some actions are small and every day. But they make a difference if we all contribute. Use compact fluorescent bulbs. Turn off electronics at night. Plant a tree. Compost. Recycle glass, aluminum, paper, and other products. Use a cloth or environmentally friendly disposable diaper. Hang dry clothes. Use both sides of the paper. Unplug devices when possible. Stop using bottled water. Eat less meat. Avoid fast food. Take shorter showers. Buy local. Buy secondhand. Turn off the lights. Install skylights and solar tubes. Stop using electronic exercise equipment. Conserve water. Walk or cycle to work. Use public transport. Carpool. Buy a fuel-efficient car. Telecommute. Insulate exterior doors and windows. Install window treatments. Reduce junk mail. Stop using plastic bags. Pay bills electronically. Share and reuse. Start or join a community garden. Use renewable energies. Consume mindfully.

Other actions are corporate and demand the commitment of institutions. There are actions on behalf of the planet that are brave and costly. I'll illustrate this with a story from Brazil. It's a story of fearless and costly advocacy for eco-justice. It's an example of godly, ecological martyrdom.

They Killed Sister Dorothy is an enthralling, award-winning documentary. It considers the February 12, 2005, murder of the seventy-three-year-old Sister Dorothy Stang. Assassins murdered her on a muddy road in the Brazilian Amazon.[40] The film traces the life and work of Sister Dorothy. It examines who murdered her and why they committed this horrific act.

Sister Dorothy was a nun from Ohio and a naturalized Brazilian. She worked alongside Indigenous peoples in the Amazon. Sister Dorothy supported sustainable agricultural projects. She advocated for the protection of native peoples and their cultures. She assisted native peoples in reclaiming land that others had taken through violence and force. The film follows the trials of her killers. It considers Sister Dorothy's mission to protect the people and ecology of the Brazilian rainforests.

The Brazilian theologian Luiz Carlos Susin has written a book chapter called "Sister Dorothy Stang: A Model of Holiness and Martyrdom." Susin writes of the clash between the traditional way of life of the Indigenous Brazilian forest peoples and the forces of globalized agri-business. This results in the possession of land through violence. It leads to the murder of countless innocents and the rape of the Brazilian rainforests. It results in slave labor and the destruction of Indigenous cultures. Christians and others are murdered when they oppose these forces. Martyrs include Sister Dorothy, Sister Adelaide Molinari, and the young priest Josimo Tavares.

---

40. Junge, *They Killed Sister Dorothy*.

After receiving death threats, Sister Dorothy said, "I don't want to flee, nor do I want to abandon the battle of these farmers who live without any protection in the forest. They have the sacrosanct right to aspire to a better life on land where they can live and work with dignity while respecting the environment." Her assassins were paid the equivalent of twenty US dollars.

Following Sister Dorothy's murder, some influential Brazilians set up a "Dorothy Committee." These people came from a wide range of professions in Brazil. They dedicated themselves to the preservation of the rainforests. They committed themselves to the survival and flourishing of the peoples and cultures of the Amazon. Luiz Carlos Susin concludes that Sister Dorothy "loved the people and the forest, biodiversity, and justice, with the same love, her love for God. She ended by helping to overthrow, or at least shake, the ranks of profiteers who desecrate [creation] and make the people desolate. For that, she was executed."[41] Whether our actions are small and everyday, corporate and institutional, or brave and costly, we must all do our part for the planet's sake. It's time to be good stewards of what God has given us.

4. Creation care fosters Christian eco-spirituality.

This Christian eco-spirituality seeks the well-being of humans and creation. St. Francis of Assisi models it for us. Ecological stewardship and creation care are intrinsic to Christian spirituality. We sustain this passion for creation care through prayer and contemplation. We fuel it through theological inquiry and action in the world. We seek to help people in our churches develop this conviction and associated practices. Or *inner and outer ecologies* witness to the Creator God who redeems and restores creation and humanity.

5. Creation care seeks justice for those displaced, disadvantaged, or ravaged by climate change and ecological degradation.

Creation care pursues eco-justice. It seeks *justice* for both people and nature. It works for the *common good* of all beings and eco-processes and eco-systems. It develops *sustainable practices* that benefit humans and allow nature to regenerate. It embraces *solidarity* with marginalized people and

---

41. Susin, "Sister Dorothy Stang," 112–13.

endangered species. It works for their healing, justice, and hope.[42] Such advocacy may come at a personal cost. But it's a price we must pay. In the long term, the cost of doing nothing is far greater. (Doing nothing always costs humanity, creation, discipleship, and integrity.)

6. Creation care does its part, individually and collectively, toward implementing the seventeen Sustainable Development Goals.

We aim for these goals for the sake of humanity and creation. Recently, my friends and I sat down to plan how to contribute toward reaching these goals. We asked each other what we'd each do. We asked what we'd do together in our families, churches, and organizations. You can do the same.[43]

7. Creation care practices green grace, red grace, and brown grace.

As Aruna Gnanadason says, we need an integrated theology of grace.[44] How is God's grace expressed in creation, Cross, science, and Indigenous traditions of creation care? How can we join with him in these graces for the sake of humanity and the planet?

8. Creation care listens to Indigenous and Majority World environmentalism.

What can we learn from Indigenous and First Nations' environmental practices? What can Westerners learn from ecological perspectives in the Majority World? I've summarized some eco-Indigenous and Majority World contributions in this chapter. But we need to learn from these people without succumbing to either racist dismissal or romanticized acclaim.[45]

---

42. Darragh, "Earth as Gaia," 80.
43. The United Nations "Sustainable Development Goals."
44. Gnanadason, *Listen to the Women! Listen to the Earth!*, 81–106.
45. Tinker, "American Indian Theological Response to Ecojustice," 86.

9. Creation care enhances the church's witness through its response to environmental issues.

Creation care is missional. The world is watching. Do we exercise loving care of the planet? Are we concerned about those made vulnerable through environmental degradation and climate change? Do we engage in ecological responsibility and innovation? Do we cultivate sustainable practices and simple lifestyles? Do we testify to Jesus Christ through our caring relationship with humans and the planet? Our creation care can witness to Jesus Christ, his gospel and kingdom, and his restoration of all things.

The Lausanne Movement and the World Evangelical Alliance recognize the missional importance of creation care. They organized the Lausanne Global Consultation on Creation Care and the Gospel in Jamaica in November 2012. Fifty-seven women and men from twenty-six countries participated. These included theologians, church leaders, scientists, and creation care practitioners. They came from the Caribbean, Africa, Asia, Latin America, Oceania, North America, and Europe. After reflecting on Scripture and discussing the issues, the group formed two significant convictions.

First, creation care is a

> gospel issue within the Lordship of Christ. Informed and inspired by our study of the scripture—the original intent, plan, and command to care for creation, the resurrection narratives, and the profound truth that in Christ all things have been reconciled to God—we reaffirm that creation care is an issue that must be included in our response to the gospel, proclaiming and acting upon the good news of what God has done and will complete for the salvation of the world. This is not only biblically justified, but an integral part of our mission and an expression of our worship to God for his wonderful plan of redemption through Jesus Christ. Therefore, our ministry of reconciliation is a matter of great joy and hope, and we would care for creation even if it were not in crisis.

Second,

> We are faced with a crisis that is pressing, urgent, and that must be resolved in our generation. Many of the world's poorest people, ecosystems, and species of flora and fauna are being devastated by violence against the environment in multiple ways, of which global climate change, deforestation, biodiversity loss, water stress, and pollution are but a part. We can no longer afford

complacency and endless debate. Love for God, our neighbors and the wider creation, as well as our passion for justice, compel us to urgent and prophetic ecological responsibility.[46]

The group then outlined specific responses. These ten responses included a commitment to a simple lifestyle and further theological work. It involved a commitment to action to address climate change and its consequences. The group also recognized the need for leadership on this issue from the churches of the Majority World.

My prayer is that the global church will cooperate to confront climate change. I pray that the global church will advocate for the environment. I pray that it will commit to simplicity and sustainability. I pray that it will develop fresh and vigorous theologies of creation care. This will involve cooperation between governmental, business, non-profit, academic, scientific, religious, and other groups. We can find solutions through collaboration. It will involve committing to care for the world God has given us. We must work in harmony with each other and with God's creation.

In the words of the consultation:

> Each of our calls to action rests on an even more urgent call to prayer, intentional and fervent, soberly aware that this is a spiritual struggle. Many of us must begin our praying with lamentation and repentance for our failure to care for creation, and for our failure to lead in transformation at a personal and corporate level. Then, having tasted of the grace and mercies of God in Christ Jesus and through the Holy Spirit, and with hope in the fullness of our redemption, we pray with confidence that the Triune God can and will heal our land and all who dwell in it, for the glory of his matchless name.

---

46. Lausanne, "Creation Care and the Gospel."

Study Questions

Lausanne Movement "Creation Care and the Gospel: Jamaica Call to Action," here https://lausanne.org/content/statement/creation-care-call-to-action. Then, discuss the following questions with your family, in small groups, as an entire congregation, or with your leadership team.

1. Many people turn to Genesis 1–3, Psalm 8, and Romans 8 when considering a Christian response to caring for creation and the environment. What verses or passages of Scripture inform your understanding and responses?

2. Do you agree that creation care is a "gospel issue within the lordship of Christ"?[47] Why or why not?

3. "We are faced with a crisis that is pressing, urgent, and that must be resolved in our generation." What practical things can your group do to advocate for practical Christian and secular responses to climate change?

4. How will your group or congregation address ecological degradation in your local area?

5. What are ways you can adopt a simple lifestyle?

6. How does responding to climate change and engaging in local expressions of care enhance the church's witness to Christ and the gospel?

---

47. All quotes in these questions come from Lausanne, "Creation Care and the Gospel."

14.

Living Ethically

The Sixth Expression

THE WORLD RECENTLY MOURNED the loss of Nelson Mandela. Mandela was a remarkable ethical leader. He paid a high personal price for his fight against injustice, discrimination, and apartheid. Mandela was released from prison in 1990. He won the Nobel Peace Prize in 1993 and became the first democratically elected president of South Africa in 1994. Mandela's autobiography, *Long Walk to Freedom*, had a profound and lasting effect on me when I read it in 1995.

Nelson Mandela advocated *ethical leadership*. He called a generation of African and world leaders to *ethical* leadership. Leaders behave ethically when they pursue justice, freedom, reconciliation, peace, equality, and mercy:

> It was during those long and lonely years that my hunger for the freedom of my own people became a hunger for the freedom of all people, white and black . . . The oppressed and the oppressor alike are robbed of their humanity. When I walked out of prison that was my mission, to liberate the oppressed and the oppressor both . . . For to be free is not merely to cast off one's chains, but to live in a way that respects and enhances the freedom of others.[1]

---

1. Mandela, "Nelson Mandela Reflects on Working toward Peace."

Archbishop Desmond Tutu is another well-known anti-apartheid figure. Tutu defended human rights during apartheid. He has continued to do so since the demise of apartheid. He received the Nobel Peace Prize in 1984. Since then, he has won other international peace prizes. Desmond Tutu challenges world and church leaders to *ethical leadership*—a term he uses often. Tutu says that ethical leaders stand *for* justice, peace, and reconciliation. They stand *against* violence, discrimination, disease, poverty, racism, sexism, and exploitation. They have ethical roles, including the following: (1) advocating for the powerless, marginalized, and silenced; (2) communicating ethical principles; (3) warning against war and violence; (4) upholding human dignity; (5) seeking truth and reconciliation; (6) foreseeing and naming ethical challenges; (7) standing with victims; (8) demanding action; (9) respecting and enhancing human, animal, and ecological freedom; and (10) urging the pursuit of justice, truth, reconciliation, and peace.[2]

Christian ethics is about what is *good* (virtuous, noble, and worth valuing) and what is *right* (right individual and corporate moral behavior). Arthur F. Holmes says that Christian ethics "examines alternative views of what is good and right; it explores ways of gaining the moral knowledge we need; it asks why we ought to do the right; and it brings all this to bear on the practical moral problems that arouse such thinking in the first place."[3]

Christian ethics explores these questions about the good and right through critical sources. These include the Bible, Christian theology, and tradition. Christian ethics also consult philosophical, scientific, religious, cultural, and other relevant sources (i.e., human knowledge and experience of the world). Christian ethics consults ethical traditions and fields. There are too many to name. But *virtue ethics* is a good example (how your character and virtues shape your behavior), and so is *bioethics* (the ethics of medicine and the biological sciences).

The West has much to learn about ethics from Indigenous cultures and the Majority World. They can teach us about the cultivation of *applied ethics* (ethics associated with politics, power, war and peace, sexuality, family, criminal restoration, truth-telling, religion, medicine, finance and economics, globalization, and care of creation). Majority World thinkers often link mission and ethics.

The missional church pursues the ethics of the kingdom of God and the Sermon on the Mount. The ethical church is mission-oriented. It stands for justice, liberation, and peace. Louise Kretzschmar of the University of South Africa writes, "Theological ethics is inescapably linked to the missio

---

2. Tutu, "Who Will Lead Syria Out of Crisis?"
3. Holmes, *Ethics*, 10.

Dei, the mission of God in the world." She says that the task of ethics is, therefore, fourfold. It analyzes "the nature, extent, and causes" of global ethical problems. It proclaims salvation. It pursues human freedom and liberation. It acts in ways that lead to transforming individuals and societies. "Theological ethics, therefore, adopts a world-transforming rather than a world-escaping approach to social and physical realities."[4]

This chapter considers how Indigenous and Majority World writers approach these ethical themes: biblical theology, culture, inter-religious relations, church, personal integrity, politics, sexuality, medicine, commerce, ecology, and ethical commitments. I proceed in that order.

Biblical Ethics

Majority World thinkers and pastors often discuss applied ethics. But they pursue the specialized discipline of theological ethics less commonly. People like Vimal Tirimanna (Sri Lankan), Nimi Wariboko, and Samuel Waje Kunhiyop (both Nigerian) are exceptions to the rule.

Most Majority World Christian leaders who examine ethical issues are not trained as ethicists. They have trained as biblical scholars, theologians, or pastors. A level of expertise is lost when this is the case. On the positive side, ethical reflection in the Majority World has many qualities. It is often biblically faithful, culturally sensitive, prophetic, and concretely applied. This is true even when theological and philosophical sophistication is lacking.

Recently, I spent a day listing the ethical concerns of Majority World Christian literature. I also listed the theological themes associated with those concerns. Imagine my surprise when a friend gave me a copy of Christopher Wright's *Old Testament Ethics for the People of God*. The ethical concerns I had listed and their associated theological themes appear in Wright's chapter headings.

Old Testament and Majority World ethics are the *theological* grounds for ethics, primarily found in God's actions, words, sovereignty, and holiness. They treat the *social* location of ethics (how do we think and act ethically together?). They deal with the *economic* dimension of ethics (land, wealth, generosity, stewardship, etc.). They cover the *applied* scope of ethics (both bodies of literature focus on ethics relating to ecology, economics, poverty, justice, the land, truth-telling, politics, war, violence, legal systems,

---

4. Villa-Vicencio and De Gruchy, *Doing Ethics in Context*, 2–23.

culture, love, race, nation, marriage, family, divorce, domestic violence, sexuality, rape, prostitution, witchcraft, corruption, power, etc.).[5]

This is not news. Philip Jenkins, for instance, demonstrates how Old Testament themes and stories resonate with Christians of the Global South.[6] To my delight, I discovered significant correspondence between the ethical concerns of the Old Testament and those of the Majority World. Of course, the New Testament deals with these themes too. Glen Stassen and David Gushee show us how the teachings and practices of Jesus deal with ethical themes. This is especially true in Jesus's teaching on the kingdom of God and during the Sermon on the Mount.[7]

Samuel Waje Kunhiyop draws on theological themes in the Old and New Testaments to build a biblical foundation for African Christian ethics. He provides an example of how biblical and cultural themes can converse as we construct culturally appropriate ethics. Kunhiyop puts African ethics—based on African customs, stories, taboos, oral traditions, and communities—into conversation with biblical ethics. He shows how community is central to both African and biblical ethics. We must root our biblical ethics in the trinitarian and human community. African ethics are inconceivable outside of the human community.[8] The correspondence between biblical and Majority World ethics concerns is striking.

Cultural Ethics

It should not surprise us that ethics shape and are shaped by their cultural context. We make individual and corporate ethical decisions by putting these things into conversation: the Bible, theology, reason, experience, tradition, culture, and the guidance of the Holy Spirit. Culture affects our interpretation of the Bible. Our application of Scripture to ethical problems is always socio-cultural. This is why we must listen to many cultures as we construct Christian ethics.

M. Daniel Carroll is a Guatemalan theologian. He notes the importance of cultural conditioning for Christian social ethics. Quoting Lausanne, Carroll says that Christian social ethics must do three things: (1) recognize cultural conditioning; (2) appreciate cultural variety; and (3) put

---

5. Wright, *Old Testament Ethics for the People of God*.
6. Jenkins, *New Faces of Christianity*.
7. Stassen and Gushee, *Kingdom Ethics*.
8. Kunhiyop, *African Christian Ethics*, 65–66.

the Bible and theology into conversation with these cultural values and behaviors and ethical challenges.⁹

Cultures wrestle with their ethical issues. Particular ethical problems take center stage from culture to culture. Global ethical issues inform these cultural challenges and vice versa. For example, a team from the International Baptist Theological Seminary in Prague, Czech Republic, recently conducted a major research project: *A Comparative Mapping of Baptist Moral Concerns and Identity in Six Regions of Europe and Central Asia*. Their study considers how different cultures prioritize ethics concerning sexuality, marriage, church unity, war, violence, medicine, speech, poverty, justice, and refugees and asylum seekers.

The findings are fascinating. For example, Moldovan Baptists emphasize ethics concerning divorce and remarriage. Bulgarian and Polish Baptists focus on ethics to do with poverty and justice. Baptists from Omsk Oblast (southwestern Siberia) believe the fundamental ethical issue of our time is refugee and relief work.¹⁰ There is much to explore here. Why do these different Eastern European and Central Asian cultures prioritize some ethical issues? Culture plays a significant role in ethical consideration and prioritization. These cultures and their ethics usually focus on community.

Community-Based Ethics

In *African Christian Ethics*, Samuel Waje Kunhiyop describes the role of church and community in African traditional and Christian ethics. It is one of the most precise treatments of the role of relationships, community, and church in non-Western Christian ethics available.

Kunhiyop quotes John Mbiti when he describes the centrality of community in traditional cultures. Mbiti says that people see themselves entirely within the community context in traditional life.

> In traditional life, the individual does not and cannot exist alone except corporately . . . The community must therefore make, create or produce the individual; for the individual depends on the corporate group . . . Whatever happens to the individual happens to the whole group, and whatever happens to the whole group happens to the individual. Therefore, the individual can only say, 'I am because we are, and since we are, therefore, I am.'¹¹

---

9. Carroll, "Relevance of Cultural Conditioning for Social Ethics."
10. Wink, *Engaging the Powers*.
11. Kunhiyop, *African Christian Ethics*, 21; Mbiti, *African Religions and Philosophy*,

In this context, morality and ethics are entirely social, even when practiced by an individual. Individuals practice morality within broader social contexts. These include families, groups, villages, tribes, clans, societies, nations, and humanity.

Kunhiyop proceeds to construct a theology for Christian ethics. He places community and relationships at its core. He starts with the Trinity. When it comes to Christian ethics, God the Father is the *norm*. Jesus Christ is the *model*. The Holy Spirit is the *power*.

Trinitarian relationships and actions shape our understanding of ethical community. Trinitarian relations exemplify love, service, sacrifice, reciprocity, mutuality, and self-giving. The Trinity's love and mission show us the shape of authentic community, witness, and ethics. Kunhiyop says that our desire for community results from God creating us in his image. He places us within relationships and redeemed communities. We will enjoy community with each other and with the Trinity eternally. Human and divine relationships form our convictions about what is good and right. By the grace of God, we have entered an ethical community. Together, we pursue the ethics of Christ's kingdom. Together, we form ethical, Trinity-imaging relationships.[12] When the church is indeed the church, it's an ethical community. The church reveals *kingdom ethics* as a foretaste of Jesus's inaugurated kingdom.[13]

This obedience to Jesus results in *lived ethics*. We are witnesses to Jesus and his kingdom and the new humanity. This means that our personal and corporate *integrity* supports our ethical positions. Our lives testify to the goodness, righteousness, and justness of the ethics we embrace—the ethics of the kingdom of God.

Ethical Integrity

Ethical teachings and positions are meaningless without ethical integrity. If we contradict our teachings throughout our lives and behaviors, our ethics lack credibility. This principle is valid in all cultures: the most persuasive moral voices live consistent moral lives. Their private and public integrity confirms their articulated ethics. They show ethical integrity. Many people see it, admire it, and aspire to do the same (or it outrages them).

The lives of many Christian leaders illustrate this principle. Oscar Romero is a prime example. His moral voice was persuasive because of his

---

108–9.

12. Kunhiyop, *African Christian Ethics*, 7–71.
13. Padilla and Yamamori, *Local Church, Agent of Transformation*, 33, 34, and 49.

integrity. Tod Swanson writes, "Romero had integrity as a public figure. He lived in such a way that his life, and especially his death, became an exemplary embodiment of the larger religious narrative that both grounded his ethics and gave meaning to the nation."[14]

Swanson describes how Oscar Romero's "moral reasoning resonated with Salvadoran identity." Romero's "moral judgments were timely." His ethical position on institutionalized, political, and military violence was apt for San Salvador. Finally, his life was a public testimony to his ethics. Forces assassinated him because of his public message, integrity, and the alignment between his actions and message. His ethical integrity cost him his life. This integrity drove home his message about peace and justice.[15] This alignment between life and speech is a pressing issue for the global church. It is one thing to speak about holiness and ethics. It is another to support this message through credible witnesses and ethical integrity. Romero and others show us that our integrity must confirm our positions on applied ethics (politics, sexuality, family, bio-technologies, economics, the environment, etc.). Our applied ethics are not merely theoretical or theological. We ought to align them with our personal and corporate ethical practices.

Applied Ethics

Indigenous and Majority World Christians focus on applied ethics. Here, I survey a few of the key themes in these practical ethics: (1) political ethics; (2) financial ethics; (3) scientific and bio-medical ethics; (4) sexual and familial ethics; (5) and ecological ethics.

1. Political Ethics

Political ethics are ethics involving states, governments, and political agents. Political ethics includes these political agents' philosophies, actions, processes, and policies. Christian political ethics is about the church's relation to these in the light of the rule and reign of Jesus Christ.

God is sovereign over the world. He has charged human beings with its care. But we care for a world marred by sin. Sin has widespread consequences, including the corruption of human relations. These relations need external human management because of sin. God allows governments to

---

14. Swanson, "Civil Art," 127.
15. Swanson, "Civil Art," 142–43.

rule and to restrain or punish socially damaging expressions of sin. Governments exist for the benefit and good of human societies.

God charges Christians with challenging and supporting this governmental rule. We challenge this rule when it is oppressive, perverted, demonic, idolatrous, and self-deifying. We will resist and even die when necessary. We resist governmental exploitation or neglect of the silenced and powerless. We call on governments to care for the most vulnerable, neglected, and invisible in their societies. We resist governmental injustice and violence.

Christians also support governments and their efforts toward peace, justice, and law and order. We respect their limited and provisional rule. We offer submission to all rules exercised within God's mandate for governments. We cultivate loving, just, peaceful, and righteous relationships with each other and our societies. We support law and order. We pursue reconciliation and peace between peoples. We acknowledge the mistakes the church has made in the past. We accept responsibility for them. We seek justice for those who have suffered at the hands of the church and its members and leaders. We seek forgiveness for these mistakes and abuses. We recognize governments and their agencies as gifts from God. We embrace our prophetic role. This involves challenging the powers and principalities. It means keeping a vigilant eye on governmental behavior. It involves witnessing to the rule and reign of Christ.

Christians witness to another kingdom. We prefigure and embody the reign of God in our love, justice, peace, and righteousness. We find ways to advance this kingdom and proclaim the gospel as we await Christ's return. We fix our eyes on his final and total transformation of the world. Christians must diligently protect their political independence. Our complete submission is only to the Lordship and rule of Jesus Christ. We ought to determine the best way to engage relevant political challenges. These include the relationship between church and state and our position on war and violence. We must determine the nature of our political engagement, especially on contested moral and social issues.

Kunhiyop provides a detailed treatment of the relationship between church and state. He outlines the historical positions on this question. He examines these position's expressions in Western and African settings. Kunhiyop concludes, "Three important principles should govern the relationship between church and state: separation, transformation, and involvement."[16] Church and state must remain separate. The church needs to seek the transformation of the world, including its ethics and political

---

16. Kunhiyop, *African Christian Ethics*, 104–6.

systems. The church must be deeply involved in the world for its healing and transformation.

Majority World and Indigenous ethicists remind us that our involvement in political ethics is crucial. I briefly outline two areas here. The first is conflict, peace, and reconciliation. The second is human rights and political oppression.

Conflict, Peace, and Reconciliation

The church must address war, violence, and ethnic and religious conflict. Consider the ongoing conflicts in Afghanistan, Pakistan, Syria, Sudan, Israel/Palestine, the Democratic Republic of Congo, the Korean Peninsula, and Northern Mali. This is without counting the regions struggling for independence or the countless conflicts between militia-guerrilla, separatist, insurgent, and anarchic groups. Between 794,000 and 1,115,000 people died in 2012 in one hundred and thirteen armed conflicts.[17] This requires the church to be about peacemaking, healing, and reconciling. The words of Jesus challenge us to be courageous peacemakers. "Blessed are the peacemakers, for they will be called children of God."[18]

Emmanuel Katongole and Chris Rice describe how reconciliation is at the heart of the gospel. The church ought to recover "reconciliation as the mission of God."[19] Christian reconciliation begins with God and is his "gift to the world."[20] Reconciliation is primarily a theological and interpersonal journey. God's reconciliation of all things in the new creation is the final purpose of this ministry. Reconciliation requires lament for past conflicts and the world's brokenness. It has eyes to see God's seeds of hope. Reconciliation requires memory, truth-telling, and forgiveness. It's served by the ability to imagine a better future. Reconciliation means conversion to God's reconciling grace.

Moreover:

> Reconciliation needs the church, but not as just another social agency or NGO ... To be a sign and agent of reconciliation, the church must inspire and embody a deeper vocation of hope in broken places. We do this through our presence in local places and in the everyday and ongoing practices of building community, fighting injustice and resisting oppression, while also

17. Amnesty International, *Annual Report 2013*.
18. Matt 5:9.
19. Katongole and Rice, *Reconciling All Things*, 147.
20. Katongole and Rice, *Reconciling All Things*.

offering care, hospitality, and service—especially to the alien and the enemy.[21]

Christian reconciliation "calls forth a specific type of leadership that is able to unite a deep vision with the concrete skills, virtues, and habits necessary for the long and often lonesome journey of reconciliation."[22]

Human Rights and Political Oppression

Amnesty International says that in 2012, one hundred and twelve countries tortured their citizens. One hundred and one countries repressed their people's right to freedom of expression. Eighty countries conducted unfair trials. Christians need thoroughly Christian responses to such abuses.

Vinoth Ramachandra says that Christians need to reclaim biblical perspectives on human rights. These must inform their actions. "A rigorous argument for human rights (as in a Christian theological perspective) will radically expose the hypocrisies and double standards of those powerful nations whose domestic and foreign policies run counter to their lip service to universal norms."[23]

Melba Maggay speaks of the church's role in confronting political oppression and violence. "Fresh in the memories of the peoples of the Philippines, Latin America, and Eastern Europe is the church as refuge, sanctuary to dissidents hunted down by repressive regimes, the last stronghold against the menace and madness of political powers gone haywire."[24]

2. Financial Ethics

By *financial ethics*, I mean ethics to do with finances and economies. Financial ethics includes poverty, aid, development, economics, business, markets, globalization, and business. Majority World ethicists write a lot on financial ethics. They mainly write about themes to do with globalization and poverty.

Globalization has ethical implications. It raises many ethical problems. Globalization affects economies, cultures, churches, politics, and creation. It has the potential for good and for creating prosperity. But it

---

21. Katongole and Rice, *Reconciling All Things*, 150.
22. Katongole and Rice, *Reconciling All Things*.
23. Ramachandra, *Subverting Global Myths*, 125.
24. Maggay, *Transforming Society*, 36.

also reinforces the negative dimensions of Western cultures. These include enthusiastic consumerism and individualism.

Samuel Escobar says that globalization has helped some impoverished societies prosper. But it has also accentuated existing social inequalities and disparities. Some have gotten rich through globalization. The middle classes of Asia, Africa, and Latin America are growing astoundingly. Five hundred twenty-five million Asians are now middle class. Homi Kharas of The Brookings Institute says that by 2030, 64 percent of the world's middle class will live in Asia.[25] By 2030, almost five billion people will be middle class.

There is another side to this story. While many have been getting wealthier, a "proportion of people are being driven into extreme forms of poverty."[26] In 2013, the Asia Development Bank (ADB) reported that the gap between rich and poor is widening globally. The Worldwatch Institute summarizes the ADB findings on the widening income inequality in Asia this way:

> Although poverty rates in Asia are declining and inequality rates in the region are lower than in parts of Latin America and sub-Saharan Africa, 15 of the 21 countries the ADB surveyed experienced a proportionate widening in people's incomes since the early 1990s . . . Among the worst affected were Bangladesh, Cambodia, China, India, Laos, Nepal, and Sri Lanka . . . Meanwhile, "absolute" inequality—the actual dollar differences in incomes—increased virtually everywhere in Asia between the 1990s and 2000s.[27]

The ADB calls on Asian governments to work against this inequality by investing in education, training, and health care. This is not just an Asian phenomenon. The inequality gap also widens in countries like the United States and Australia. Jon Sobrino suggests that the victims of globalization can be its redemption. They summon the world to truth, solidarity, and poverty.

The victims of globalization summon the world to *truth*. They call the world to the truth revealed in Jesus Christ. They reveal the way globalization has positive and destructive elements. They summon the world to acknowledge injustice, inequality, and suffering. "This suffering is on a massive scale, unjust and cruel; it battens on innocent, defenseless people, and is a product of the world of power (economic, military, political, media,

---

25. Reuters, *Swelling Middle*.
26. Escobar, *Time for Mission*, 61.
27. Worldwatch Institute, *Inequality Gap Grows in Asia, United States*.

LIVING ETHICALLY

sometimes even church and university)."[28] The victims summon the world to mercy, compassion, justice, and equality by revealing the truth.

The victims of globalization summon the world to *solidarity*. Solidarity means identification, support, and closeness to the weak, victimized, ignored, and impoverished. The wealthy support the poor, and the poor support the rich. "The victims can convert 'a globe' into 'a family,' 'a giant supermarket' into 'a home.' They can also bring in something that, to our great detriment, is virtually absent from present-day civilization: grace."[29]

The victims of globalization summon the world to *poverty*. Jon Sobrino does not mean the poverty typified by oppression, bondage, and deprivation. He means generosity, contentment, and a way of life, contrasting a world obsessed with capital, wealth, and individuality. He means a way of life that is humanizing rather than consuming, greedy, and individualistic.

Majority World thinkers write so much on financial ethics that I could not cover it all here. They address poverty, wealth, corruption, employment, strikes, aid, development, economics, and globalization. Jayakumar Christian is one of the most articulate voices regarding "poverty, power, and the kingdom of God." Recently, I had the privilege of hearing Jayakumar Christian teach on serving among the urban poor. Christian offers seven themes on "developing a kingdom-based paradigm for responding to the powerlessness of the poor." A kingdom-based response: (1) reverses the process of disempowerment; (2) confronts the god-complexes; (3) heals persons in poverty relationships; (4) addresses inadequacies in worldview; (5) challenges principalities and powers; (6) establishes truth and righteousness; and (7) proclaims that all power belongs to God.[30]

Pope Francis has recently written on the church's missionary transformation. Francis describes the relationship between the church's mission and its social action. This Argentinian Pope addresses social, financial, and political ethics. He passionately advocates for those experiencing poverty, powerlessness, and economic injustice. He reminds the global church that it cannot ignore financial ethics. Francis writes, "As long as the problems of the poor are not radically resolved by rejecting the absolute autonomy of markets and financial speculation and by attacking the structural causes of inequality, no solution will be found for the world's problems or, for that matter, to any problems."[31]

---

28. Sobrino, "Redeeming Globalization through Its Victims," 110.
29. Sobrino, "Redeeming Globalization through Its Victims," 112.
30. Christian, *Empty-Handed*, 212–13.
31. Pope Francis, *Evangelii Gaudium*.

PART 2: RENEWING OUR MISSION

3. Scientific and Bio-medical Ethics

Scientific and bio-medical ethics include ethical issues associated with science, medicine, healthcare, infertility, reproductive technologies, contraception, bio-medical technologies, life and death responsibilities, genetically modified foods, and disease treatment and prevention.

These issues do not receive the same breadth of ethical consideration in the Majority World as in the West. But this is changing. Asian, African, and Latin American ethicists provide fresh perspectives on bioethics. Some issues receive substantial ethical treatment in those settings. HIV/AIDS is an example.

Ramachandra of Sri Lanka provides a fascinating treatment of the "myths of science." He shows how these myths have influenced humanity. He unpacks the political ideologies of science. Quoting Mary Midgley, Ramachandra says that science offers a value-laden system. This system serves as a "moral signpost that could replace religion."[32] Its values are rational observation, theory formation, clinical experimentation, and intellectual respectability. Ramachandra doesn't decry all these values. But he does say they are political ideologies. They are "dominant social myths." These myths compete with other perspectives. They are often squash alternative ways of seeing the world. Ramachandra describes the moral responsibilities associated with scientific research. He especially considers genetic engineering, eugenics, biomedical advances, and artificial intelligence.

What is Vinoth Ramachandra's main point? He wants us to realize that we don't have to choose between being "gods or nothings." We aren't *nothings* that have evolved in a vast, uncaring universe. We don't have to be nihilistic about our existence. But we are also not *gods*. We don't have "unlimited capacity for self-design on the part of the technocratic magi of the future." We aren't supreme over creation.[33] Ramachandra concludes, "A Christian theological anthropology recognizes the multidimensional nature of human experience."[34] Christians believe faith, theology, science, medicine, and ethics need each other. Together, they offer human well-being.

HIV/AIDS is a topic in this area that receives a lot of consideration. The World Health Organization provides these critical facts on the epidemic. "HIV remains a major global public health issue, having claimed 40.4 million [32.9–51.3 million] lives so far with ongoing transmission in all countries globally, with some countries reporting increasing trends in

32. Ramachandra, *Subverting Global Myths*, 174.
33. Ramachandra, *Subverting Global Myths*, 213.
34. Ramachandra, *Subverting Global Myths*, 214.

new infections when previously on the decline. There were an estimated 39.0 million [33.1–45.7 million] people living with HIV at the end of 2022, two-thirds of whom (25.6 million) are in the WHO African Region."[35]

HIV/AIDS has infected at least 10 percent of the populations of Botswana, Lesotho, Malawi, Mozambique, Namibia, South Africa, Swaziland, Zambia, and Zimbabwe. The spread of the disease has remained stable in most of Asia and Latin America. But there has been a recent increase in Eastern Europe and Central Asia.

The AIDS epidemic, especially in parts of Africa, raises many ethical questions concerning sexuality, medicine, poverty, and society. A person's lifestyle will determine whether they are at a high or low risk of infection from HIV. High-risk groups include homosexual and bisexual men with many partners. They include intravenous drug users who share needles indiscriminately, frequently, or rarely. People who receive blood transfusions, such as hemophiliacs, are also at risk. The sexual partners of those in high-risk groups are also at risk. Children born to those infected with HIV or born to parents who are in the high-risk groups are at risk. There are many ethical issues associated with this disease. These include ethics concerning sexuality, poverty, marginalized persons, social taboos, access to medicines, and care for the sick and dying.

Kunhiyop says, "The Christian response to HIV/AIDS must be multifaceted, focusing both on the church and the community." Pastors and congregations must care for those living with and dying from the disease. Educators need to help individuals and communities develop healthier sexual and lifestyle practices. Spouses face ethical dilemmas. Can they continue to have sexual intercourse with an infected partner? A host of other ethical issues arise. Kunhiyop provides a moving example:

> I know if a young woman whose husband had died of HIV/AIDS and left her HIV positive. Another young man proposed to her and was told her HIV status but insisted on marrying her all the same. Some pastors would refuse to officiate at such a wedding because it would likely lead to the untimely death of the groom. Others might be prepared to officiate, provided the couple were given full counseling about the risks they are running and about how to have the safest possible sex within marriage.[36]

There is often discrimination against those infected with HIV. This is especially the case in employment, accommodation, education, and

---

35. World Health Organization, "HIV and AIDS."
36. Kunhiyop, *African Christian Ethics*, 328.

provision of social services. Sufferers experience discrimination in everyday social interactions. Discrimination is often directed against men who are homosexual or who may appear to be homosexual. Discrimination affects those who live in the same household as these individuals. Some direct their discrimination toward hemophiliacs. Cultures may discriminate against ethnic minorities who suffer from the disease. People may discriminate against healthcare professionals who work with those infected with HIV.

The theological debate's focus on the AIDS epidemic in parts of the Majority World has been fourfold. It focuses on a Christian response to homosexuality. It emphasized a Christian view of marriage and sexuality. It highlights the relationship between poverty and societal problems and disease. It explored God's role in the AIDS epidemic (and in general epidemics).

The incarnation and the Cross reveal a compassionate God who identified with a suffering world. Jesus Christ shows supreme love, self-sacrifice, and identification with the broken, suffering, and stigmatized. He is our example. He reveals the ethical approach to HIV/AIDS. The incarnation, Cross, and resurrection are about compassion, sacrifice, grace, mercy, reconciliation, truth, forgiveness, and human value. They speak of our resurrection to new lives and bodies. These qualities must characterize our ethical response to those infected with HIV.

John Mary Waliggo of Uganda speaks of losing a generation to HIV/AIDS. He then provides a detailed plan of action for the church. The plan is too comprehensive for me to detail here. But I will summarize its main points. It focuses on the vulnerability of girls and women.[37] It develops the church's health, social, and education services to respond to the epidemic. It advocates for those who are too poor to access treatment. It promotes partnerships between churches, governments, NGOs, businesses, the United Nations, and so on (and does this to provide collaborative solutions). Waliggo's plan addresses the damaging stigma and discrimination experienced by sufferers. It trains pastors and congregations to care for sufferers and their families. It welcomes sufferers and their families into "warm, non-judgmental and compassionate" churches and homes.[38]

Musa Dube of Botswana calls the church to see this epidemic as more than a matter of medicine and individual morality. We must address poverty and discrimination in this epidemic and other global healthcare issues. We need to pursue a plan of action like the one outlined by John Mary Waliggo. We must develop churches that can interpret Scripture among

---

37. Dube, "Reducing Women's Vulnerability and Combating Stigma."
38. Waliggo, "Church and HIV/AIDS," 29–34.

and with sufferers. These churches and their leaders will help communities explore key biblical and social themes. These themes include suffering, justice, sexuality, discrimination, poverty, gender inequality, healing, hope, and resurrection. The church must learn to listen to sufferers as it interprets Scripture with them and develops its ethics.[39]

Kay Lawlor of Kitova Hospital in Uganda calls this ethic the *Way of the Cross*. Using the *Stations of the Cross*, Kitova shows how we meet Jesus Christ as we minister among and with those who suffer. We encounter Jesus as we practice his compassionate ethic. We meet him at the Cross. "We make the way of the Cross in the homes and at the bedsides" of those who suffer. In our care for them, we image the radical ethic of Jesus Christ.[40]

4. Sexual and Familial Ethics

Many Majority World cultures are changing. Globalization, Western media, economic prosperity, and political and cultural power shifts influence them. This affects perspectives on sexuality, gender, and family. Cultures once sexually conservative—with clear gender roles and family cohesion—are now changing. This leads to much discussion about sexual, gender, and family ethics.

Majority World ethics cover such issues as patriarchy and matriarchy, masculinity and femininity, feminism and womanism, misogyny and sexism, abortion and contraception, and parenthood and marriage.[41] They address culture and its relation to sex, gender, and family. They tackle issues to do with pornography, rape, sexual exploitation, incest, predatory violence, human and sex trafficking, prostitution, female circumcision, and pedophilia.[42] These ethics explore the intersections of gender, religion, race, poverty, and class. They cover sex education for young people. They address marriage as between a man and a woman (dominant Western view) or marriage as between families and families (common Majority World view).[43] They tackle monogamy and polygamy, divorce and remarriage, and widows and orphans. These ethics explore the gendered division of labor and family responsibilities. They challenge systemic gender violence and propose intervention programs. They look at gender inequality and issues concerning human rights—especially the neglected or violated rights of women and

39. Dube, "Go Tla Siama. O Tla Fola," 212.
40. Lawlor, *AIDS Way of the Cross*.
41. Richardson, *Peace Child*.
42. Kunhiyop, *African Christian Ethics*, 271–311.
43. Kunhiyop, *African Christian Ethics*, 190.

children. They cover sexual orientation, homosexuality, and bisexuality. These ethics address issues to do with political instability, war and violence, and the unique vulnerability of women and girls. They examine HIV/AIDS and other epidemics and how they affect families and genders. They consider the relationships between education, healthcare, employment, and gender. They analyze the connections between gender and religious ideologies. Importantly, these ethics deal with the church's role in perpetuating, challenging, and healing these issues.

I cannot cover all these issues here. So, I will focus on ethics to do with the protection of women and children. Writing from the Ugandan context, John Mary Waliggo and Benedict Ssettuuma write about the plight of women and children in armed conflicts. After caring for women and children in African warzones, Waliggo describes, "Abduction, rape, defilement, forced marriages, brutal beatings, widowhood, loss of life, inability to provide for the family, displacement, mental and psychological torture, trauma, mistrust, feelings of revenge, sense of helplessness, dehumanization, and constant fear."[44]

Waliggo calls on African churches to take joint action to address these issues. They must join with each other and government and other agencies to find solutions. He describes churches' actions as addressing issues such as child soldiers and the rights of women and children. Waliggo shows how many African churches are peacemaking. These churches also address the rural-urban migration of vulnerable people.

In *The Rights of a Child*, Waliggo says the church must protect women, children, and families. We must denounce "all policies, practices, and attitudes which undermine children's full and holistic growth."[45] We must take practical actions to address war, violence, poverty, corruption, and HIV/AIDS. We should address moral decline, environmental degradation, and harmful or exploitative cultural practices. Waliggo lists ways churches and societies must work together in this cause. These include supporting human rights, advocating for the victimized, and providing pastoral care and healing programs. Churches, governments, and agencies need to collaborate. Partnerships help develop constitutional, governmental, policing, and community safeguards and protections.

June O'Connor gathers the stories of Latin American women. She details their experience of sexual violence, poverty, inequality, family, and politics. "These women want us to see the ways in which our lives are

---

44. Waliggo, "Plight of Women and Children in Areas of Armed Conflicts in Uganda," 375.

45. Ssettuuma and Waliggo, "Rights of a Child," 62.

implicated in theirs. In this lies the problem but also their hope: because we North Americans are part of their problem; we can also be part of the solution."[46]

These and other solutions are difficult in societies ravaged by war and violence. But the church must take an active part in protecting and nurturing women and children. It must especially seek the welfare of the most vulnerable. The church ought to work within societies and cooperate with governments, NGOs, and other agencies. We aim to ensure everyone receives "love and security, food, clothes, shelter, medical care, and education."[47]

5. Ecological Ethics

I have dedicated a chapter of this book to Indigenous and Majority World perspectives on care for creation. Creation care raises many ethical issues. Members of the Micah Network met at Limuru, Kenya, from July 13–18, 2009. They discussed creation stewardship and climate change. Participants came from thirty-eight countries from all five continents. Latin American theologian Rene Padilla published the "Declaration on Creation Stewardship and Climate Change."[48]

The declaration covers the church's ethical responsibility to pursue faithful stewardship of creation. As the church, we must confess and repent of our exploitation, abuse, and neglect of creation—and our greed, arrogance, and self-centeredness. We must "repent of our self-serving theology of creation and our complicity in unjust local and global economic relationships."[49] We should "acknowledge that industrialization, increased deforestation, intensified agriculture and grazing, along with the unrestrained burning of fossil fuels, have forced the earth's natural systems out of balance."[50] The Spirit calls us to change our lives so that we live sustainably—practicing God-honoring creation stewardship. This involves rejecting consumerism, greed, and environmental exploitation. It means bearing witness to God's love for creation and his redemptive purposes for all creation. It includes interceding on behalf of humanity and creation. The church must collaborate with governments, NGOs, other agencies, and the United Nations in addressing climate change and ecological destruction.

46. World Council of Churches, "Together Towards Life," 290.
47. Ssettuuma and Waliggo, "Rights of a Child," 61.
48. Padilla, "Declaration on Creation Stewardship and Climate Change."
49. Padilla, "Declaration on Creation Stewardship and Climate Change," 77.
50. Padilla, "Declaration on Creation Stewardship and Climate Change," 76.

We have a responsibility to partner with those organizations to invest in solutions. We can advocate for people experiencing poverty and the vulnerable—who are most likely to suffer from climate change. Finally, we must stop further denying or delaying our ethical responsibilities. "We will labor with passion, persistence, prayer, and creativity to protect the integrity of all creation and hand on a safe environment and climate to our children and theirs."[51]

Korean theologian Jo Yong-Hun puts Hindu, Buddhist, and Chinese views of nature into conversation. The goal is to show how Christian creation care can speak with other views of nature in Asian thought. Yong-Hun believes cooperation between religions, worldviews, and cultures is necessary to preserve nature. "Although Christianity cannot accept the Asian worldview without a critique, ideas from the Asian religions will be helpful to create a global environmental ethos for the preservation of the integrity of creation."[52]

Yong-Hun notes the significant differences between Christianity and Asian religions regarding nature. For example, Christianity has a theology of radical transcendence, but Buddhism does not. Christianity has a theology of God as Creator, but Confucianism does not. God is sometimes identified with the universe in Hinduism, but he is not in Christianity. Still, dialogue and cooperation with other religions and worldviews are necessary to address the present climate and ecological crisis.

South African theologians John De Gruchy and David Field claim that Christian ethics must address Christianity's role in our ecological crisis. Christianity played a role in developing "modern science, technology, capitalism, and the ideology of progress." These "provided an environmentally devastating combination."[53] But Christians have also valued, nurtured, and protected creation.

Historically, Christianity has been ambiguous toward the environment. Some Christians oppose environmentalism, while others engage with environmental issues. John De Gruchy and David Field say that Christian ecological ethics must consider Christianity's critique of the consumer society and present inequalities. Such ecological ethics must consider Christianity's views on the ethical status of non-human life and ecosystems. These ethics must consider Christianity's approach to reproductive responsibility. The human population's exponential growth has severely impacted ecosystems and biodiversity. Finally, such ecological ethics should examine

---

51. Padilla, "Declaration on Creation Stewardship and Climate Change," 78.
52. Crouch, *Playing God*, 407.
53. Mangalwadi, *Truth and Social Reform*, 203.

Christianity's understanding of the relationship between ecological ethics and the Christian mission.

The last point is an especially important one. Creation care is integral to our "witness to the creative and salvific reign of God. As the church has been forced to reexamine its witness in relation to the oppression of human beings, so it is now called to do so in the light of the devastation of the environment. In doing so, the church needs to get its own house in order, as well as to issue a prophetic call to society."[54]

Ethics: Concluding Reflections

Christian ethics, community, and mission are closely linked. Christ-honoring churches reveal the ethics of the Sermon on the Mount. These churches do this in their life together and their missional practices. Ethical churches witness to Jesus Christ. They do this through their commitment to justice, holiness, truth, love, and peace.

Here are ten things we learn from how Majority World Christians express the ethics of Christ and his kingdom.

1. Christian ethics are based on Scripture, faith, and the values of Christ's kingdom.

Faith, not culture, is the primary source of Christian ethics. Christian faith submits to the authority of Scripture. Christian ethics embrace the values of the kingdom of God. (The Beatitudes, for instance, give us a window into these values).

I have noted the complex relationship between faith and culture in ethics. But Paulinus Ikechukwu Odozor laments the common temptation to prioritize culture over faith and Scripture. All groups are tempted to do this. However, this elevation of culture over faith can often occur when people feel that forces have marginalized or colonized their culture. Odozor writes:

> The Christian faith, not cultural pattern, should provide the theologian with the primary lens through which to view life and reality in general. Only in this way can the theologian perceive the strengths and the distortions and evil in any culture . . . The Christian story is not an arcane or exclusive source of moral

---

54. Villa-Vicencio and De Gruchy, *Doing Ethics in Context*, 208.

insight, even though, for the Christian, it should be the primary criterion for measuring the soundness of any other source.[55]

We must scrutinize all cultural ethics, practices, and values in the light of Scripture and the values of the kingdom of God revealed in Christ Jesus. This takes courage and honesty. We don't usually like examining ourselves. We often avoid scrutinizing what our culture has endowed us with. It's hard and uncomfortable work. But we must scrutinize our ethics in the light of Christian faith and Scripture.

Scripture and the values of the kingdom of God shape all proper Christian faith-based ethics. We need to communicate our culture's ethics with biblical and kingdom ethics. This means that we will recognize our cultural conditioning and appreciate cultural variety. We'll put Scripture into conversation with these cultural values and behaviors and ethical challenges. We'll courageously explore what emerges.[56]

2. Christian ethics are inculturational.

What do I mean by *inculturation*? Inculturation is the adaptation of Christian teaching and ethics for cultures. It's the subsequent influence of those cultures on these things.

This is important for much Majority World Christian ethics and theology. Inculturation is an effort to form Indigenous Christian ethics. It seeks to evaluate colonial and Western legacies. It hopes to transform culture. Odozor writes, "Inculturation is a continuous process of dialogue between faith and culture." Its goal is a "symbiotic fusion, as it were, of culture and faith into a new creation that is Christian because it is totally permeated by the Spirit and teaching of Jesus Christ." Odozor proceeds to quote Pedro Arrupe when he describes inculturation. Inculturation is not merely about adapting theology and ethics to a culture. It is much more than that. It is "*a principle that animates, directs, and unifies the culture, transforming it and remaking it to bring about a 'new creation.'*"[57]

Take the HIV/AIDS epidemic in Africa as an example. Christians shape ethical responses to this outbreak with attention to culture, science, and Scripture. But such responses should also lead to the animation, healing, and transformation of the cultures affected by HIV/AIDS. That is, to the birth of a "new creation." John Mary Waliggo asserts that Christian

---

55. Odozor, "African Moral Theology of Inculturation," 601.
56. Carroll, "Relevance of Cultural Conditioning."
57. Odozor, "African Moral Theology of Inculturation," 585.

ethics must engage specific cultural dynamics when responding to HIV/AIDS. We engage in inculturation as we form ethical responses to these cultural challenges. I list some of these challenges here: (1) African traditional customs and practices ("funeral rites, traditional marriages, initiation, and circumcision rites"); (2) traditional healing, spiritual practices, and attitudes to modern medicine; (3) social hierarchies, the exploitation of the vulnerable, and the marginalization of the sick; (4) community, neighborliness, and social cohesion; (5) a "sub-culture" of "defilement, incest, and rape"; (6) polygamy and polygyny; (7) the sex trade, human trafficking, and pornographic consumption; (8) global attitudes to human sexuality, homosexuality, marriage, and family; and (9) issues of justice, mercy, peace, forgiveness, and reconciliation.[58]

What are the ethical challenges in your situation? What cultural dynamics undergird them? How will you adapt Christian teaching and ethics to your culture? How will your culture positively influence your understanding of Christian ethics? Will you have the courage to form ethical views and responses that are both *Indigenous* to your setting and *adequate* for your culture's ethical challenges?

3. Christian ethics are political.

Christian ethics have political dimensions and repercussions. Christian ethics challenge the cultures, powers, and systems of the world. They witness to an alternative politic. They testify to the kingdom of God.

People like Oscar Romero give us a marvelous example of Christian political ethics before a watching world. Romero was the former archbishop of San Salvador. He was assassinated on March 24, 1980 for his Christlike political ethic.[59] Solidarity with those on the periphery is central to such an ethic. When Christians form ethical positions on bioethics, the environment, economics, sexuality, family, human rights, war, and refugees and asylum seekers, they are constantly engaged in politics. This is even more so when the goal is social and structural transformation.

Jesus's life, work, and teaching must shape our social and ethical behavior. When we take Jesus seriously, we practice political ethics. This is because our ethics confront power, freedom, justice, relations, and status issues. We engage social, ethical, and political issues in word and deed. We tackle them individually and corporately. We address conflict, peace, reconciliation, human rights, political oppression, migration, persecution,

---

58. Waliggo, "Inculturation and the HIV/AIDS Pandemic in the African Region."
59. Swanson, "Civil Art."

PART 2: RENEWING OUR MISSION

displaced persons, economic systems, ethno-religious violence, racial discrimination, gender inequality, ecological responsibility, sexuality, family, scientific and bio-medical advances, and the dynamics of globalization. So, our ethics are inevitably political. We witness to the resurrected Lord and his gospel and kingdom.

4. Christian ethics are transformational.

Christian ethics have the power to transform people and cultures. So, we must examine the nature, extent, and causes of global and local ethical problems. We proclaim salvation. We pursue justice, freedom, liberation, and transforming individuals and societies. We adopt "a world-transforming rather than a world-escaping approach to social and physical realities."[60]

The Ghanaian theologian Simon Kofi Appiah calls on Christian ethicists to pay attention to Scripture, theology, culture, and the human sciences. He invites Christian ethicists to do this for cultural transformation. Christian ethics can help cultures "make sense of their past and present cultural, historical, religious, and anthropological experiences." But it can only do this if it calls cultures to "a radical renewal of memory." These cultures make sense of their past and present values, experiences, and challenges in the light of the gospel. The gospel speaks to a culture's history, values, and sins. The gospel reveals possibilities for renewal and conversion. Christian ethics need this transformational dimension. Otherwise, contextualized Christian ethics are "a masque that covers the concrete situation" of cultures.[61]

Christian ethics must tackle the pressing issues that cultures face. Let's look at an example from Africa and one from Asia. Let's start with Africa. Agbonkhianmeghe E. Orobator shows how Christian ethics must engage and transform Africa's *five significant* moral issues. The first issue is the "lion" of *governance* (ethical approaches to politics, law, policing, military, human rights, poverty, corruption, social inequality, displacement, peace, justice, and reconciliation). The second is the "elephant" of *creation care* (ethical approaches to climate change, global warming, natural disasters, and sustainable care for the earth). The third is the "rhinoceros" of *genetically modified foods* (ethical approaches to biotechnologies in the light of hunger and scarcity). The fourth is the "buffalo" of *resource extraction* (ethical approaches to mining, water use, and extracting precious, mineral, and natural resources). The fifth is the "leopard" of *domestic justice* (ethical approaches to human morality—including marriage, sexuality, and

60. Villa-Vicencio and De Gruchy, *Doing Ethics in Context*, 2–23.
61. Greenman and Green, *Global Theology in Evangelical Perspective*, 278.

family life—and justice for those experiencing poverty, exploitation, and voicelessness).[62]

Now, let's turn to an example from Asia. Muriel Orevillo-Montenegro shows how Christian ethics must have a transformational role. This is especially the case when Christian ethics address the marginalized women of Asia. She shows how Asian women are developing Indigenous Christologies and associated ethical practices. These can transform women in India, Korea, the Philippines, and Hong Kong. For example, Orevillo-Montenegro writes of the plight of many young girls in the Philippines. Cartels traffic these girls for sex with foreign tourists. The legal and policing systems that should protect these girls ignore and abuse them. She writes about how Filipino women's voices are rising. They are seeking justice.

Orevillo-Montenegro shows how Filipino women are exploring the person and work of Jesus afresh. They are meeting Jesus, the Wounded Healer, as wounded healers. "Filipino women must face the challenge to keep going, to embody Christ in accompanying the people in their journey out of the bondage of evil. Her prophetic ministry, her dances, her songs and rituals, must provide healing and inspiration to the wounded spirits out there."[63]

What are your culture's pressing moral, social, and political issues? How will you and your church provide ethical responses? Will these help lead toward the well-being, liberation, healing, and transformation of people in your setting?

5. Christian ethics are dialogical.

Christian ethics must speak with their religions and worldviews to engage cultures fully. Interreligious dialogue is vital. It helps Christian ethics be relevant to cultures, histories, experiences, and values.

Comparative ethics—comparing ethics across religions and worldviews—is common in the Majority World. These cultural and religious melting pots lead to fruitful interreligious, comparative ethics. Majority World ethicists cannot ignore the Abrahamic, Taoic, Dharmic, Shamanic, Animistic, philosophical, and secular traditions around them. Majority World Christian ethicists often engage in these traditions. They do this to make an impact on their cultures for the sake of Christ.

The same is now true in the West. We do Christian ethics in a pluralistic, global setting. This demands inter-religious dialogue, comparison, and

62. Hastings, *Missional God, Missional Church*.
63. Orevillo-Montenegro, *Jesus of Asian Women*, 157.

learning. We must do this without surrendering, minimizing, or apologizing for our distinctive Christian beliefs.

Michael Amaladoss and Peter Phan write much on comparative religious ethics and inter-religious dialogue. They examine how the religions might share insights on peace, justice, and reconciliation. Amaladoss and Phan say that the September 11, 2001, events demand more conversation between the world's major religions. We need more cooperative peacemaking, healing, and reconciliation.

Hans Küng's famous dictum says, "No peace among nations without peace among the religions. No peace among the religions without dialogue between religions. No dialogue between the religions without investigation of the foundation of the religions."[64] Phan expands Hans Küng's dictum: "Most importantly, no reaching the foundation of religions without a dialogue of life, action, theological exchange, and, above all, religious experience and prayer."[65] I would add that while seeking peace among nations and religions is a worthwhile and noble expression of our ministry of reconciliation and peacemaking, ultimate peace will only come when Jesus Christ returns in all his love, power, and glory. Christian peacemaking emerges from Christ-centredness and eschatological hope.

6. Christian ethics are anamnetic.

Benezet Bujo describes how traditional African ethics are *anamnetic*. By this, he means Africans shape their ethics around memory and solidarity with the past. Bujo says, "The ancestors' words and deeds, the norms they set, are made available to the current generation so that it has life and continues to look after the deceased, and so that it prepares the future of the not-yet-born."[66]

I agree with Odozor that all Christian ethics must be anamnetic. All Christian groups remember. We remember our unique cultural and Christian heritage. We also remember our Christian story (the stories, persons, and drama of Scripture). We recall God's saving deeds. We remember Jesus's example, teaching, ethics, passion, resurrection, and ascension. We construct Christian ethics as we remember.[67]

---

64. Küng, *Global Responsibility*, xv.
65. Phan, "Global Healing and Reconciliation," 105.
66. Bujo, "Differentiations in African Ethics," 433.
67. Odozor, "African Moral Theology of Inculturation," 609.

7. Christian ethics are relational and community-based.

Majority World and Indigenous ethics show that Christian ethics must be relational and community-based. Desmond Tutu and Nelson Mandela popularized the Nguni Bantu term *Ubuntu*. *Ubuntu* means that our bonds with others form and express our human nature.[68] Similarly, as Christians, we must construct our ethics around human and divine community notions.

Christian ethics are relationship-centered and community-based. As Samuel Waje Kunhiyop says, Christian ethics must image trinitarian relations. They're loving, self-sacrificial, reciprocal, and mutual. Christian ethics concern the well-being of the church, humanity, and all creation. This causes these ethics to emphasize reconciliation, peace, love, and freedom. Christian ethics seek the transformation and well-being of local and global cultures. Majority World and Indigenous Christians root their ethics in church, relationships, and community. Western Christians must do the same.

8. Christian ethics are foundational for Christian ministry and leadership.

We must cultivate *ethical leadership*. We need leaders who stand for justice, peace, and reconciliation. We need leaders who oppose violence, discrimination, disease, poverty, racism, sexism, and exploitation. It's time to foster "a specific type of leadership that can unite a deep vision with the concrete skills, virtues, and habits necessary for the long and often lonesome journey of reconciliation."[69] This includes dedicating ourselves to peacemaking, healing, and reconciling.

9. Christian ethics are integral.

Christian ethics are about living with integrity. Our private and public integrity needs to confirm our articulated ethics. Integrity must be present in all dimensions of individual and corporate life. This involves removing the distinctions between sacred and secular, physical and spiritual, private and public, evangelism and social action, and so on. It means cultivating individual and corporate integrity—being an *integral* people. We do this through complete submission to Jesus Christ. We do this through discipleship, love,

---

68. Tutu, "Passion for Justice," 17.
69. Katongole and Rice, *Reconciling All Things*.

justice, holiness, reconciliation, and peace. Our *lived* ethics must confirm our *proclaimed* ethics.

10. Christian ethics are holistic and glorifying.

By *holistic*, I mean that Christian ethics seek the well-being of whole persons, whole families, whole churches, whole cities, whole cultures, and the whole creation. More simply, Christian ethics pursue the welfare of all humanity and all creation. What are some ways that we do this? We are compassionate and welcoming. We welcome sufferers and outcasts into "warm, non-judgmental, compassionate" churches and homes.[70] We "make the way of the Cross" with those who suffer. We stand with those whom the church and society shun or discriminate against. In our solidarity with them, we image the radical ethics of Jesus Christ. We are a counter-cultural people—salt, light, and a city on a hill—showing the ethics of the kingdom to a watching world. We care for creation. We change our lives so that we live sustainably. We practice God-honoring creation stewardship. We reject consumerism and greed. We bear witness to God's redemptive purposes for humanity and all creation.

By *glorifying*, I mean Christian ethics bring glory to the Father, Son, and Holy Spirit. Our upright, holy, and ethical lives and communities exist to glorify the Triune God.

As a glocal faith community, we shape our ethics to live as those made alive in Jesus Christ. We embrace these ethics in our community life and service to Christ and his world. We seek to bring praise, glory, and worship to God through our individual and corporate ethics.

---

70. Waliggo, "Church and HIV/AIDS," 29–34.

Study Questions

1. How does the Bible relate to social justice, action, and concern?
2. How do people's roles in institutions affect their ethical decisions and character? What are the implications of this for your organization?
3. Can we speak of sinful social structures and political systems or only personal sin?
4. What ethical challenges do your culture, family, and congregation face? How will you help others deal with these challenges?
5. How are you helping people in your family or church face ethical issues prayerfully, thoughtfully, courageously, biblically, and ethically? (Choose one ethical issue and reflect on this question.)
6. Christian ethics are faith-based, inculturational, political, transformational, dialogical, anamnestic, integral, holistic, glorifying, community-based, and foundational to Christian leadership and ministry. Pick one or two of these and ask, does this describe my ethics?

15.

Transforming Neighborhoods

The Seventh Expression

THE CHURCH CAN BE God's instrument of transformation in neighborhoods. We need kingdom-oriented approaches to neighborhood transformation and community building. Our churches must address need, addiction, violence, and racial tension. We need to be agents of change, reconciliation, and transformation. This chapter invites the church and the reader to consider four essential issues. What does it mean to be urban neighbors of hope? How can we be converted to the neighbor? How is the church God's instrument of transformation? How can we be involved in kingdom-based struggles for justice?

Being Converted to the Neighbor

The church needs a *conversion to the neighbor* to embrace God's love and compassion and pursue *mission as transformation*.[1] Vinay Samuel describes transformation like this: "*Transformation* is to enable God's vision of society to be actualized in all relationships, social, economic, and spiritual, so that God's will may be reflected in human society and his love be experienced by all communities, especially the poor . . . Fundamentally, *Transformation* is

---

1. Gutiérrez, *Theology of Liberation*, 194.

the transformation of communities to reflect kingdom values."[2] The church mainly pursues transformation and its practices in local communities and neighborhoods.

Gustavo Gutiérrez claims that we encounter God in human relations. This encounter especially happens as we engage with human beings in church, community, and society. God loves and reveals himself through our neighbor—so we need a "conversion to the neighbor, to social justice, to history."[3] To love God is to seek justice, healing, and liberation for our neighbor. It is to join God's reconciliation ministry—bringing justice, salvation, beauty, and wholeness. The incarnation of Jesus Christ compels us to embrace our neighbor. It moves us to enter our neighbors' lives and seek their well-being, salvation, and liberation.

Gutiérrez unpacks the parables of the Last Judgment (Matt 25:31–46) and the Good Samaritan (Luke 10:29–37). He shows, "The neighbor was the Samaritan who *approached* the wounded man and *made him his neighbor*. The neighbor, as has been said, is not the one whom I find in my path, but rather the one in whose path I place myself, the one whom I approach and actively seek."[4] Gutiérrez challenges those of us who know power, privilege, inclusion, access, or wealth to make the difficult choice to be "converted" to the service and love of the poor, abused, needy, neglected, despised, wounded, and marginalized neighbor:

> It is not enough to say that love of God is inseparable from the love of one's neighbor. It must be added love for God is unavoidably expressed *through* love of one's neighbor. Moreover, God is loved in the neighbor . . .
>
> The conversion to the neighbor, and in him to the Lord, the gratuitousness which allows me to encounter others fully, the unique encounter which is the foundation of communion of men among themselves and of men with God, these are the source of Christian *joy*.[5]

Love for God is always expressed through the love of our neighbor. Kosuke Koyama speaks of *neighborology*. While our neighbors may not care about our theology, they are often interested in our neighborology. In Luke 13:11–16, we have the story of Jesus healing a sick woman on the Sabbath. The religious rulers are enraged that Jesus does this on the Sabbath. Jesus exposes their hypocrisy and misunderstanding of the Scriptures and

---

2. Samuel and Sugden, *Mission as Transformation*, ii and xii.
3. Gutiérrez, *Theology of Liberation*, 205.
4. Gutiérrez, *Theology of Liberation*, 198.
5. Gutiérrez, *Theology of Liberation*, 200 and 207.

the kingdom of God. Koyama writes, "The uncushioned neighborology of Christ cuts like a knife through the cushioned neighborology of the ruler of the synagogue." Jesus Christ is the "uncushioned *neighbor* to us all."[6]

The church needs to be present with people. For Kosuke Koyama, "Christian presence, which is rooted in and participates in the crucified Christ, must demonstrate the quality of Christ's glory in suffering, his exaltation in rejection."[7] Koyama says that this presence among our neighbors—this personal identification with the world—has at least three modes. It's a stumbling presence, a discomforted presence, and an unfree presence.

Stumbling presence: "Can unstumbling Christians point to the shaking of the foundations caused by the crucified Lord? Can Christians bear witness to Christ's crucified lordship unless they themselves stumbled at it? Can a house unshaken bear witness to the earthquake which is going on?"[8]

Discomforted presence: "Can Christians who do not involve themselves in the great "discomfort" of the nailed Christ point to the source of all comfort? Isn't it true that precisely because they are comforted by the crucified Lord, they are inescapably involved in the "discomfort" of the crucified Lord?"[9]

Unfree presence: "We are called to participate in all situations of life as the Incarnate Lord fully did. Yet this participation must not lead them to 'drink the cup of demons.'"[10] We're not so free that we are free to sin.

Our conversion to the neighbor leads to transformation and hope when we practice Christ-centered presence.

Being Involved in Struggles for Justice

In *Transforming Society*, Melba Padilla Maggay challenges the church to participate in justice struggles. She examines biblical and historical models for effective Christian involvement in social transformation. Maggay says the church has usually engaged in four approaches to social transformation:

The first is being an alternative, exemplary, and *counter-cultural community*. This involves witnessing to the gospel and the kingdom by being "salt" and "light." The Anabaptists, Mennonites, and Quakers exemplify this approach.

---

6. Koyama, *Water Buffalo Theology*, 67.
7. Koyama, *Water Buffalo Theology*, 160–70.
8. Koyama, *Water Buffalo Theology*, 163.
9. Koyama, *Water Buffalo Theology*, 166.
10. Koyama, *Water Buffalo Theology*, 170.

The second is *influencing power structures* and appealing to them by promoting Christian ideals and principles. Christian political parties took this approach, the dominant approach in Western Christendom.

The third is being a *liberationist community* concerned with solidarity and freedom and a church that seeks the liberation of the oppressed, marginalized, impoverished, and powerless. Liberation theology embodies this approach.

The fourth is being a *compassionate presence* in the world. This involves witnessing to Christ through compassionate care of the sick, wounded, and broken. Catholic orders, like the one established by Mother Teresa, epitomize this approach. So do multinational Christian aid and development agencies.[11]

Maggay seeks to integrate these approaches through the metaphors of *prophet*, *priest*, and *king*. The church has a prophetic role ("bringing the Word of God to the world"—including the political arena). It has a priestly role ("bringing the world's need to God and the power of God to the world"—through compassion, liberation, and care). It has a kingly role ("managing the world under God"—by participating in technological, economic, and developmental advancement).[12]

Whenever the church participates in social transformation, it finds itself going through a change process. This change can be renewing or retrograde. Change occurs no matter what approach the church adopts. Maggay is careful to note this. So is Jayakumar Christian in *God of the Empty-Handed*. Christian examines the strengths and weaknesses of various Christian approaches to social transformation. He considers developmental, liberationist, counter-cultural, and evangelical models. Christian then discusses a recent development in social transformation in the Majority World (especially in India). Mega-churches, church plants, mainline churches, Pentecostal churches, and parachurch groups are focusing on neighborhoods. They are putting an enormous, concentrated effort into changing local neighborhoods. They are joining with community leaders and organizations to address the concrete needs of neighborhoods. This includes poverty, crime, employment, infrastructure, housing, family, youth, etc. Christian notes the importance of carefully considering our approaches to social transformation—since the church is both transforming and transformed in the process.[13]

---

11. Maggay, *Transforming Society*, 46–67.
12. Maggay, *Transforming Society*, 68–75.
13. Christian, *Empty-Handed*, 19–166.

Maggay says that we shape the best responses around a theology of the Cross. The Cross leads us to a self-emptied, Christ-centered, obedient, and sacrificial confrontation with powers and principalities. The way of the Cross binds us to people and their needs and neighborhoods. We must develop approaches focusing on strategic minorities (i.e., those who influence their communities). We need to address local people's practical needs, concerns, and interests. These strategies pay careful attention to personal and community flourishing and well-being. These responses practice "radical pessimism" (they take evil seriously). They practice "radical hope" (they believe in the possibility of transformation, as those who have an ultimate hope).[14] René Padilla and Jayakumar Christian put it this way:

> The kingdom demands at this critical moment of history nothing less than a revolution of values for the fostering of justice and peace; a restructuring of the church as the community that exists for sacrificial service to the gospel of Jesus Christ, and a renewed spirituality that brings together worship and public life, evangelism and social responsibility, personal faith and kingdom service.[15]

> Kingdom-based response can reverse the process of disempowerment, confront the god complexes, heal persons in poverty relationships, set right inadequacies in the worldview of a people, challenge principalities and powers, establish truth and righteousness, and proclaim that all power belongs to God . . . Mission is a response in which the kingdom community's involvement at the micro level influences macro-global dimensions at cosmic levels.[16]

Place Making: Concluding Reflections

As God's people, we must seek a Christ-glorifying transformation of communities and neighborhoods. We do this through meaningful presence, practices, and proclamation. We commit to a place. Through these, we witness to the hope, power, liberation, reconciliation, wholeness, love, and beauty of God's kingdom. We find that neighborhoods *and* the local and global church are renewed as we do this.

---

14. Maggay, *Transforming Society*, 78–108.
15. Samuel and Sugden, *Mission as Transformation*, 449.
16. Christian, *Empty-Handed*, 223.

TRANSFORMING NEIGHBORHOODS

Here are eight things we learned from how Majority World Christians transform neighborhoods and engage in place making.[17]

1. Place making is key to transforming neighborhoods.

Place making means immersing oneself in a local neighborhood or community for the long haul. It's about capitalizing on that place's assets, relationships, dreams, imagination, and potential so that it becomes what God intends. It's about helping a neighborhood see where God is already at work, bringing hope, peace, love, and renewal. Place making seeks a place's welfare, transformation, and flourishing.

Neighbors transform neighborhoods from the inside. That's why place making is critical. Local people must cooperate for the renewal and future of their area. Otherwise, change isn't long-term. Place making is about collaboration. It's people working together over an extended period for the well-being of a local community and doing this through community-based and community-initiated strategies and relationships. Place making seeks "his kingdom come, and his will be done, on earth as it is in heaven" (Matt 6:10).

2. Place making nurtures local ecology, economy, community, and faith.

In many cities today, people are localizing their lives. They're tired of feeling disconnected. People are planting urban gardens and serving with community-based organizations. They're exploring sustainability and simpler lifestyles. They buy, build, or rent properties, facilitating shared lives and community living. Extended-family and multi-family households are increasingly common. People are buying locally. They're supporting neighborhood causes, organizations, and sporting teams. They are getting rid of cars, catching public transport, or walking and cycling to work. Many people in my Sydney suburb are urban homesteading. People are becoming *locavores*—growing, buying, and consuming fresh, local produce. They're collecting rainwater, keeping urban livestock, canning and preserving foods, and growing household, street, and community vegetable gardens. People are becoming increasingly passionate about living, working, spending, loving, serving, and growing locally.

---

17. More than a few of these are direct quotes from the *Urban Neighbours of Hope* (UNOH) covenant.

God's people have a unique opportunity to be at the forefront of this. But we must prioritize local worship, mission, community, ministry, and discipleship. Too many Christians commute out of their suburbs for church and ministry. Root yourself deeply in your suburb. Get to know the families, personalities, issues, and hopes. Worship Christ locally. Serve Christ locally. Be discipled to Christ locally. Eat, love, produce, laugh, mourn, spend, grow, and pray locally. As stewards of God's creation, we need to nurture local ecologies. These include green spaces, community gardens, and the plants and animals unique to our area. Finally, local churches need to invest in local economies. Encourage the well-being and prosperity of local establishments and those who own and work in them.

Place making is often wonderfully missional. But it demands a movement away from autonomy, disconnectedness, and anonymity. Instead, we make the most of place making's missional potential through rootedness, stability, localization, and deep, long-term relationships. *Staying is the new going*. We choose to stay in *this* local place and in *these* local relationships. We see God's grace manifested in the change and transformation of local neighborhoods. In this local place, we grow in loving obedience, missional service, prophetic advocacy, generosity, and contentment. A simpler, local lifestyle enhances our mission.

3. Place making is collaborative transformation.

Place making involves *serving alongside* the people who live and work in our neighborhood. We collaborate with others to release neighborhoods from urban poverty. We join with them to facilitate healing from woundedness and dysfunction. We partner with others so that we might move toward holistic prosperity. (By this, I mean the well-being of whole persons and communities through the whole gospel.) This involves the collaboration of churches, governments, businesses, community organizations, developers, etc. We work together for the well-being and transformation of neighborhoods.

We have a responsibility to help the Body of Christ take God's particular concern for those experiencing poverty as seriously as Jesus does. We can never address poverty, oppression, exploitation, and disadvantage alone. We need to collaborate. This involves inviting the broader church to mission and ministry with Jesus among those experiencing poverty. It means cooperating with other groups and organizations.

Seeking "God's kingdom come"—sharing Jesus and his gospel in word, deed, and sign—is a collaborative affair. We partner with each other, with our community, and with Christ. This starts by asking the right questions and having the courage to respond to the answers. For example, how can we be Christians who engage missionally with our neighborhoods? How do we do this collaboratively, not colonially? How can we join others in healing, renewing, and transforming our neighborhood? How do we shape churches that join Jesus in transforming and releasing neighborhoods from the bottom up? How do we pursue cooperative, kingdom-based responses that "reverse the process of disempowerment, confront the god complexes, heal persons in poverty relationships, set right inadequacies in the worldview of a people, challenge principalities and powers, establish truth and righteousness, and proclaim that all power belongs to God"?[18]

4. Place making serves as hope enfleshed.[19]

What does it mean to say that the church needs to be *hope enfleshed*?[20] The church testifies to the new creation. It does this through its message, love, service, faith, and hope. The church testifies—in word and deed and sign—to the hope of Jesus Christ. We root our hope in his incarnation, life, death, resurrection, and glorification. As we immerse ourselves in our neighborhoods—collaborating with the Spirit's work, connecting deeply with people, and witnessing to the new creation—we embody the hope of Christ. By the grace of God, we are *hope enfleshed*.

Tetsunao Yamamori and René Padilla bring together a host of Latin American thinkers and practitioners in *The Local Church, Agent of Transformation*. These leaders address how churches can pursue integral missions and community transformation. The book establishes a theological basis for local churches as agents of transformation. God calls his church to be a transforming presence within neighborhoods and a sign of hope.

In that book, Padilla describes how the church he pastored sought transformation in its neighborhood. They became a sign of hope. In an urban slum, Padilla discovered that being hope enfleshed means being committed to people experiencing poverty. It's being

> a sign of the new creation that burst into history in the person and work of Jesus Christ—a sign of hope during despair. So, it is important that we should have a teaching ministry which combines theory with practice and is oriented toward creating,

---

18. Christian, *Empty-Handed*, 223.
19. Barker, *Slum Life Rising*, 21–22.
20. Barker, *Slum Life Rising*, 21–22.

in the whole church and in each of its members, the Christian mind—a mind that conceives of the totality of human life as the locus of God's transforming work. We can find many good reasons to criticize the church. Far too often it has been the primary cause of people's turning their back on God because they believe that the Christian faith has nothing to offer them. Often that is true. But it also is true that whenever the church opens itself up to people who are marginalized and poor, God surprises it, making it a Good Samaritan who responds to the needs of the neighbor with the resources of the Kingdom of God: faith, hope, and love.[21]

5. Place making is welcoming and welcomed.

By *welcoming*, I mean we find and invite Jesus, disguised as "the least of these," into our lives, homes, lands, families, friendships, and churches.

By being *welcomed*, I mean we're willing to let others welcome us into their lives. We're humble enough to be a guest. We don't always need to be the host. We're willing and eager for the people Jesus fellowships with to welcome us into their lives and homes. He communes with the powerful and the weak, the sober and the drunk, the dignified and the prostitute, the religious leader and the tax collectors. He prefers the humble, poor in spirit, meek, despised, foolish, weak, and marginalized. Are we humble enough to let others receive and welcome us?

6. Place making is conversion to Christ and to the neighbor.[22]

Jesus Christ converts us to himself. He converts us to our neighbors. Jesus converts us to loving and serving our neighbors and seeking their well-being and relationship with him. This conversion leads us to pursue our mission through the transformation of neighborhoods. It also involves allowing Jesus to convert us to the service and love of our neighbors experiencing poverty, abuse, need, neglect, woundedness, disdain, and marginalization. We also care for the prosperous, powerful, and privileged neighbor.

People will judge the gospel's truth by our love for each other, neighbors, and neighborhoods. They will especially notice our love for our

---

21. Padilla and Yamamori, *Local Church, Agent of Transformation*, 299–300.
22. Gutiérrez, *Theology of Liberation*, 194.

unlovable, offensive, stigmatized, or immoral neighbor. They will notice the love we show the neighbor who is different from us (class, ethnicity, politics, sexuality, religion, worldview, etc.). Loving people like us, who share our values, beliefs, and race, is easy. But can I love and serve that *particular person*, right there in front of me, who stands in contrast to my race, religion, values, politics, sexuality, or beliefs? Can I love and serve *that* person?

Vinay Samuel puts it this way:

> One sign and wonder, biblically speaking, that alone can prove the power of the gospel is that of reconciliation . . . Hindus can produce as many miracles as any Christian miracle worker. Islamic saints in India can produce and duplicate every miracle that has been produced by Christians. But they cannot duplicate the miracle of black and white together, of racial injustice being swept away by the power of the gospel . . . Our credibility is at stake . . . If we are not able to establish our credibility in this area, we do not have the whole gospel. In fact, we have not got a proper gospel at all.[23]

Our conversion to the neighbor testifies powerfully to our conversion to Christ.

7. Place making develops neighborology and a theology of place.[24]

Our theology is more appealing if we are loving neighbors. Hospitality is missional. Love for God and love of neighbor are inseparable. What price am I willing to pay for the well-being and transformation of my neighbor and neighborhood? Ridicule? Exclusion? Discomfort? Persecution? Poverty? Slander? What price did Jesus pay for his "uncushioned neighborology"?

Place making requires a theology of place. I don't have the space to develop a theology of place here. But I highlight some key themes. Firstly, Christians and Jews have a long history of describing the sacred relationship between God, people, and place. Secondly, place is essential in Scripture. This theology of place is present in biblical notions of creation, covenant, exile, pilgrimage, land, Israel, and holy places. Thirdly, Jesus Christ was God incarnate in a particular body, time, culture, and place. Fourthly, God calls us to worship and serve with a particular people in a specific place—hence the importance of the local church. Fifthly, the Eucharist is a remembrance

---

23. Samuel, *Lausanne II Conference on World Evangelism*.
24. Koyama, *Water Buffalo Theology*, 160–70.

of Christ's bodily death and resurrection in a particular place and time. The sacraments celebrate his presence with us in this place now. Sixthly, a theology of God's kingdom contributes to a theology of place. The kingdom of God is "God's people in God's place under God's rule."[25] It's manifest in particular places as Christ reigns in human history, liberating people from sin and darkness and establishing the rule of God on earth. Lastly, our ultimate hope includes resurrection to a particular, physical place.

What does all this mean? We must root Christian place making in a theology of place. Consequently, our place making is rich in practice and theology.

8. Place making must be saturated in prayer.

Immerse yourself in your neighborhood and pray. Nurture that place's assets, relationships, and imagination, and pray. Help people see where God is already at work in your neighborhood and pray. Seek your neighborhood's welfare, transformation, and flourishing, and pray. Collaborate with others for the well-being of your community and pray. Champion justice, hope, faith, and love in your local place, and pray. Serve with your neighbors and pray. Promote a culture of peace and prayer. Celebrate and grieve with neighbors and saturate every dimension of your place making in prayer.

As we engage in place making and transforming neighborhoods, Jesus's example and words chart our course:

> On one occasion an expert in the law stood up to test Jesus. "Teacher," he asked, "what must I do to inherit eternal life?" "What is written in the Law?" Jesus replied. "How do you read it?" He answered, "'Love the Lord your God with all your heart and with all your soul and with all your strength and with all your mind'; and 'Love your neighbor as yourself.'" "You have answered correctly," Jesus replied. "Do this and you will live." (Luke 10:25–28)

---

25. Goldsworthy, *Gospel and Kingdom*, 53.

Study Questions

1. What stood out to you in this chapter? Journal some reflections on that idea, insight, or impression.
2. Do you know your neighbors? What are their concerns, joys, fears, hopes, and dreams? What concrete things can you do to get to know your neighbors and be a genuine part of their lives?
3. What would it mean for you and your church to do the following?
4. Live out our passion for loving God and neighbor.
5. Focus on releasing our neighborhood from poverty or some other bondage or ailment.
6. Grow by equipping each other, neighbors, and the broader church to follow Jesus and join God's kingdom.
7. How does your church seeking God's kingdom come into your neighborhood through word, deed, and sign?
8. Has your church experienced a *conversion to the neighbor*? How can you seek out the wounded, overlooked, and marginalized together and make them your neighbors?
9. How would you define *place making*? How can you get involved in *place making* in your neighborhood?

PART 3

Revitalizing Our Churches

PART THREE SHOWS HOW Indigenous and Majority World Christians teach us to revitalize churches. This part outlines six ecclesiological expressions of the seven holisticostal paradigm shifts. These six expressions are inculturating faith, devouring Scripture, renewing education, practicing servantship, recovering community, and developing spirituality and discipleship.

"You are a city set on a hill," Jesus tells us, echoing a vision that would have resonated deeply with his first-century Jewish audience—an elevated city, impossible to ignore, radiating light across the landscape, a people of justice and mercy amidst the chaos and confusion of a world spinning out of kilter. But do we realize the monumental implications of being globally and locally this luminous city? Indeed, to be a city set on a hill is to be nothing less than an alternative society—an "altera civitas" in a world all too enamored with the politics of empire, with the idolatries of consumerism and nationalism.

It is to say that we stand as an alternative and counter-cultural force, not in the sense of rejecting everything 'worldly,' but in the sense of fulfilling the world's deepest dreams by living under the Lordship of Christ. We are a people apart, not by our exclusion, but by our inclusion of every tribe and tongue, drawn together by the Spirit into a life so distinctive that the watching world takes note. We are "in the world but not of it," a phrase that does not speak to isolation but to vocation. We are in the world for the sake of the world, even as we are distinct from the world.

Yet, suppose we are to embody this alternative existence, this city on a hill. In that case, it will require nothing less than a wholesale renewal of our mission, shared life, ethical bearings, and worship. Our churches must become revitalized expressions of this alternative city. How? Here, the witness of Indigenous and Majority World Christians beckons us forward. They teach us the art of inculturating faith, of so steeping the gospel in local cultures that it becomes a living stream within them. They draw us back to the deep wells of Scripture, urging us to devour it as daily sustenance. They insist upon a renewal of education that forms whole persons rather than merely stuffing heads full of abstract principles.

A "city set on a hill" is essentially a holisticostal community imbued with the renewing energy and love of the Spirit. In that Spirit, we learn the art of servant leadership—leading by serving, serving by leading. We recover the essence of community, remembering we were saved as individuals and people. We deepen our spiritual practices, not as an end in themselves but as how we grow into Christlikeness.

This holisticostal vision must transform our ecclesiological practices related to the church's life. They must be polycentric, acknowledging the myriad ways God is at work around the world. They must be polyvocal, ready to hear the Spirit's voice in unexpected quarters. They must be intercultural, embracing the full spectrum of human culture as arenas for the gospel. They must be integral and concerned for both soul and body and heaven and earth. They must be Pentecostal, open to the ever-new work of the Spirit who enlivens, empowers, and sends us out.

In the final chapter, I challenge the reader to embrace a world Christianity narrative shaped around holisticostal commitments. As we arrive at the end of our exploration—a journey through tectonic shifts and tumultuous challenges—I invite you to this vision. It is a vision of being a city set on a hill, a holisticostal community that challenges every lesser loyalty and lesser hope. In such a community, in such a city, the world may yet see a hint, a foretaste, of the city that is to come. Perhaps, by finding its true end and beginning in that vision, the world itself may be transformed.

16.

Inculturating Faith

The Eighth Expression

ALAN TIPPETT WAS AN Australian missionary to the Fijian islands for over twenty years. He then served as a professor of missiology at various universities in the United States. Tippett's work among Fijian peoples led him to a firm conviction. "The truly indigenous church is an ideal for which we strive—something truly a church and truly indigenous."[1]

What does it mean to say a church is *inculturated* (or *indigenous*, to use Tippett's term)? Alan Tippett answers this question. "When the indigenous people of a community think of the Lord as their own, not a foreign Christ; when they do things as unto the Lord, meeting the cultural needs around them, worshiping in patterns they understand; when their congregations function in participation in a body which is structurally indigenous; then you have an *indigenous* church."[2]

I consider the terms *inculturation*, *indigenization*, and *contextualization* to be (basically) synonymous and interchangeable. This is the case even though these terms have different nuances in meaning. There is ongoing debate about the meaning of these three concepts and which is better to use. Some prefer indigenization (e.g., James Buswell and Charles Kraft). Others prefer contextualization (e.g., Shoki Coe, Charles Taber, and the Theological Education Fund). Others prefer inculturation (e.g., Pedro Arrup, John

---

1. Tippett, *Introduction to Missiology*, 381.
2. Tippett, *Introduction to Missiology*.

Walligo, and many Catholic theologians). Some use the terms interchangeably (e.g., Saphir Athyal, Rene Padilla, and Daniel Von Allmen).

As you read the examples of theologies and practices in this chapter, you may prefer to think of them as examples of inculturation, indigenization, or contextualization (or all three). I am not fussed and will leave it to you to make your conclusions. As Bruce Nicholls says, "In the end, it is not so much the word used as the meaning that grows up around that is important."[3]

While I once preferred indigenization, I now use inculturation out of respect for Indigenous peoples, including Aboriginal and Torres Strait Islanders in my country.

How are these three terms defined? I've dedicated an entire chapter of this book to *contextualization* and contextual mission, defining what these mean. That chapter shows how Majority World and Indigenous churches define and express such *contextualization*. Alan Tippett has defined *indigenization* already in this chapter.

Pedro Arrup defines *inculturation* this way: "The incarnation of Christian life and of the Christian message in a particular cultural context, in such a way that this experience not only finds expression through elements proper to the culture in question (this alone would be no more than a superficial adaptation) but becomes a principle that *animates, directs, and unifies the culture*, transforming it and remaking it so as to bring about a 'new creation.'"[4]

This chapter considers what we can learn from inculturated expressions of faith in Africa, Asia, and Latin America. We can learn from *what* Christians in those settings have to say to us. Inculturated theological perspectives enlarge our theological imagination. We can also learn from *how* believers in those settings inculturate their spirituality, worship, mission, and churches.

It is impossible to thoroughly survey inculturation in Africa, Asia, and Latin America in a chapter this size. Instead, I provide some *brief* examples of inculturated *theology* and *practices* from those settings. I don't have space to consider inculturation in Eastern Europe, the Middle East, Muslim settings, and among Indigenous peoples. On my website http://www.grahamjosephhill.com, I list books and articles dealing with Christian contextualization and inculturation in Africa, Asia, Latin America, Eastern Europe, Muslim settings, the Middle East, Western cultures, and Indigenous peoples.

---

3. Nicholls, *Contextualization*, 21.
4. Arrupe, "Letter to the Whole Society on Inculturation," 172.

I am concerned that this chapter will feel like a list of inculturated theologies and practices in the Majority World. So, how can you make the most of this chapter? Ask yourself: "What can I learn from these theologies and practices? What can they teach me, my culture, and the global church? What can these inculturated expressions teach us about Jesus, mission, worship, spirituality, and the church?"

Inculturated expressions of faith are present throughout the global church. They are reactivating the church. Ask yourself, How inculturated is my theology and my church? How can my church develop inculturated theology and homegrown practices? How can these grassroots theologies and practices develop "from below"? How can Christians inculturate their faith in their everyday lives?[5] How can our church and theology become inculturated to our particular culture at this particular time?

1. Inculturation in Africa

During the last sixty years, African Christian theologies and expressions of faith have multiplied. The African churches have sought to shake off colonial influences. They're forming inculturated churches and theologies. They're innovating theologically and practically. Africans link this creativity to local concerns and inculturated expressions. This innovation is also associated with globalization's (positive and negative) influence on inculturated cultures. Globalization shapes the prioritization, health, and revival of inculturated cultures. This melting pot of theological and practical experimentation is diverse and astonishing.

African Theologies

Diane Stinton teaches theology in Nairobi, Kenya. She highlights four features of African Christian theologies:[6]

The first is *formality and informality*. African theologies express a duality of "formal and informal expressions." Systemic, propositional theology is present in Africa. But Africans complement formal theology with informal theology. Such informal theologizing happens through art, dance, music, painting, liturgy, drama, and oral traditions.

The second is *community*. African theologies focus on "the community of faith in their formulation." Theology is often done within a community.

---

5. Bevans, *Mission and Culture*, 115.
6. Stinton, "Africa, East and West," 107–10.

An entire community often theologizes together. Stinton provides many examples of this. The most striking is the work of Cameroon theologian Jean-Marc Ela. Ela calls for "shade-tree theology." This is a theology that, "far from the libraries and the offices, develops among brothers and sisters searching shoulder to shoulder with unlettered peasants for the sense of the word of God in situations in which this word touches them."[7] The theologian roots their role in community, praxis, and specific locations.

The third is *contextuality*. African theologies have a "contextual nature." Inculturated African theologies deal with contextual problems (social, political, sexual, economic, and religious). These problems and contexts are often different from those faced by Western Christians. So, contextual African theologies often take a different form.

The fourth is *plurality*. African theologies have "many articulations." Africa is a large and diverse continent with many cultures. It should not surprise us that African theologies are many and diverse.

Kenyan theologian James Kombo takes a different approach. Kombo categorizes African theologies into four types:[8]

Identity theologies explore the continuities between biblical ideas about God and the perspectives of African primal religions (see the work of Bolaji Idowu, John S. Mbiti, Gabriel M. Setiloane, Charles Nyamiti, Ajayi Crowther, and Kwame Bediako).

Incarnational theologies cultivate homegrown Christian theologies that are entirely "African" and inculturated (see the work of Placide Tempels, Alexis Kagame, John S. Mbiti, Kwame Bediako, Lamin Sanneh, and Andrew Walls).

African/World theologies shape theologies attentive to inculturated needs and primal religious connections. They're globally influential. These theologies commit to an African Christianity that isn't second-rate to Western forms or theologies. They see these theologies influencing and shaping a new, global "world Christianity." Their conviction is that—given the explosive growth of the church in the Majority World—Christianity is now a religion of the Global South. They believe a new era of Christianity is emerging—one that the Global South is shaping. "What happens within the African churches in the next generation will determine the whole shape of Church history for centuries to come . . . What sort of theology is most characteristic of the Christianity of the twenty-first century may well depend on

---

7. Ela, *African Cry*, vi.
8. Kombo, *African Theology*, 134–47.

what has happened in the minds of African Christians in the interim"[9] (see the work of Lamin Sanneh, Andrew Walls, and Kwame Bediako).

Contextual theologies contextualize African Christian theologies and expressions. Examples include apartheid-related theology, inculturation theology, and South African black theology. African womanist and liberation theologies are also examples. The proponents of African contextualized theologies and practices are too many to name. Some notable persons include Desmond Tutu, Byang H. Kato, Jean-Marc Ela, Benezet Bujo, Marcy Amba Oduyoye, Emefie Ikenga-Metuh, Victor Chendekemen Yakuba, Laurenti Magesa, Isabel Phiri, Yvette Akle, and Anne Nasimiyu-Wasike.

As you can see, African theologies are many and diverse. So are the practical expressions of mission, church, and worship that arise from them.

The late Byang H. Kato supported these developments, especially contextualization. But some developments in African inculturated theology and practice concerned him. These included the rise of universalism and the syncretistic elevation of primal religions and practices. Kato wrote that biblical perspectives were too often devalued in these settings.

Kato developed ten principles for safeguarding biblical Christianity in Africa to counter this. I will not list them all here. But Kato called the African churches to adhere to the core tenets of historic Christianity. He challenged them to train African leaders in biblical exegesis and original languages. Kato acknowledged that culture and Scripture are mutually interpreting. But he maintained that Scripture has authority over culture.[10]

Inculturated Christian theologies and practices are best when they have a dynamic relationship with historical and global Christianity. These inculturated expressions also need deep biblical foundations.

There is no space here to deal with a wide range of inculturated forms of African theology. Instead, I highlight the inculturation of two areas. These are *Christology* (reflections on Jesus Christ) and *ecclesiology* (reflections on the church as an extended family). As you read them, I invite you to consider them in light of Dianne Stinton's *four features* and James Kombo's *four types* of African Christian theologies.

Let's start with Jesus Christ in African theology (*Christology*). Kwame Bediako lists some ways African Christians use inculturated ideas, analogies, and metaphors to understand the person and work of Jesus.[11] Jesus is the "Grinding Stone," who sharpens us for service. Jesus is the "Sword Carrier" (the *nkrante brafo*). He's the "Hero Incomparable" (the *Okatakyi*

---

9. Walls, quoted in Bediako, "Significance of Modern African Christianity," 51.
10. Kato, *Theological Pitfalls*, 181–84.
11. Bediako, *Jesus in Africa*, 1–33.

Birempon). He's victorious in battle. Jesus is the "Hunter" who leads us deep into the dangerous forest and removes the heads of evil spirits. He kills the *sasabonsam* and the *mmoatia*, those evil spirits that haunt humans and forests. Jesus is the "Great God" (the *Onyankopon*) to whom all lesser spirits and gods must submit. Jesus is the "Lion of the grassland" who defeats Satan. He "tears out Satan's entrails and leaves them on the ground for the flies to eat." "Jesus of the Deep Forest" provides shelter, food, water, healing, wholeness, and new life. Jesus is the "Fearless One" (the *Tutugyagu*). He's the "Strong-armed One" (the *Adubasapon*). He defeats our terrors. Jesus protects us from war, famine, illness, and deadly beasts. He gives us courage in the face of these things. Jesus is the "Savior of the Poor." He's the "Great and Dependable Friend" (the *Damfo-Adu*). We rely on him "as the tongue relies on the mouth." Jesus is the "Great Rock" whom we hide behind. He's the "Magnificent Tree" who shelters us and causes "luxuriant growth below." Jesus is the "Tall Mountain" (the *ekyere buruku*). He shows the nations his glory and points us to God. Jesus is the "King of the Nations" (the *amansanheme*). He's the "Chief of the Valiant" (the *owesekramofohene*). He "brings nations together, milk and honey flow in his vein."

In *Jesus of Africa*, Diane Stinton comprehensively surveys African Christologies. Stinton unpacks contemporary African images of Jesus. These images include Healer, Life-giver, Mediator, and Ancestor. Other images include Loved One, Family Member, Friend, King/Chief, and Liberator. Stinton examines the cultural origins of these metaphors. She demonstrates their interconnections. She studies both their beneficial and controversial aspects. For example, there is division among African theologians about whether Africans should view Christ as "Ancestor."

Let's consider the church as *an extended family* in African theology (*ecclesiology*). Besides reflecting on the person and work of Christ, Africans think a lot about the church. This consumes much of their theological energy. They're concerned about the church's community and mission.

Africans often view the church as an extended family (in theology and practice). African understandings of *church-as-family* resonate with trinitarian communion ecclesiology. But, just as importantly, Africans express church-as-family in the practical ways they do church. Africans prioritize community, union, intimacy, and relationships. Relationship surpasses institution. Relationships lead to a passionate mission.

John Waliggo writes:

> The *koinonia* practiced in the early church is nothing but familial relationship. Every believer is a brother or sister to the other. It was only through the subsequent development of the church

that this relational and charismatic model became weak and was gradually substituted with the institutional model. One of the signs of the times in the church has been the reawakening of this familial model through small groups, charismatic groups, and others.[12]

Tite Tiénou examines African notions of the church as a family or clan. Tiénou is supportive of the image. He believes it has biblical roots and favorable consequences for mission and community. But he is also critical of its emphasis on ancestors. He disagrees with its prioritization of "Christ as Ancestor" over biblical images.[13]

Tite Tiénou, Waliggo, and many other African theologians believe Christian participation in the church-as-family should supersede ties to the natural family. Christian communion and mission depend on deep, authentic relationships in the local church.

As in many other contexts, local practices complement inculturated theologies in Africa.

African Expressions and Practices

There are a multitude of creative, inculturated expressions in Africa. Some are innovative in pointing Africans to Jesus and his gospel. These expressions allow Africans to worship in inculturated ways. Other practices are problematic. African evangelicals question the assumptions, validity, and consequences of these practices.

I will not be scrutinizing the value of these expressions and practices. I will merely provide a taste of the breadth and creativity of inculturated worship, community, and mission in Africa.

Relational Expressions of Church

As mentioned earlier, Africans view the church as an extended family or clan. It is common for Africans to think of family as "extended" rather than "nuclear," so this is a natural development. Jesus Christ is the "ruler/chief/elder" or "proto-ancestor." Africans tend to pursue deep relationships. They see the church as an extended and prioritized family group.

Solidarity, unity, and community characterize this *koinonia*. Natural families and the church-as-family celebrate communal feats and rites of

---

12. Waliggo, "African Clan as the True Model of the African Church," 125.
13. Tiénou, "Church in African Theology," 162–63.

passage together. These include births, deaths, marriages, and coming of age.

Stinton quotes John Mbiti and Anne Nasimiyu Wasike to illustrate this point. She shows the centrality of community in African culture and faith. "The individual can only say: 'I am because we are and since we are, therefore, I am.'"[14] "Community participation is a very prominent value among the African people. It permeates all life; it is the matrix upon which all the human and social values, attitudes, expectations, and beliefs are based, and it is the foundation of an African theology, catechesis, and liturgy."[15]

Since this is true, it is easy to see why relational expressions of the church are the foundation for other inculturated expressions and practices. For example, Stinton notes the consequences of *church-as-family* for African understandings and practices. These include Jesus as a family member and proto-ancestor, paternal and maternal images of Christ, and the Eucharist as a communal meal. *Church-as-family* influences how many Africans see other denominations as "true relatives in the wider clan." They see the Christian mission as a social, communal, and familial transformation.[16]

Liturgical Innovations

Many African Christians experiment with inculturated forms of worship. They inculturate baptism, the Eucharist, penance, marriage, ordination, and consecration. Many African churches inculturate these liturgical and sacramental dimensions of the church.

For example, many Africans celebrate the Eucharist through dance and drama. The Eucharist focuses on caring for the environment. It draws the worshiper's attention to the ancestors and the Great Ancestor. Africans often celebrate the Eucharist within the context of food, wine, and feasting. They associate the Eucharist with agricultural and hunting motifs, struggles with famine and drought, and rites of passage.

F. Kabasele Lumbala is a Congolese theologian. He describes how Africans innovate with a wide range of liturgies and sacraments. This innovation has a few key features. They inculturate liturgies, sacraments, blessings, prayers, and rites to African cultures. They recognize the holiness of the "other" (humans, rituals, creation, and spiritual beings). There's a desire for harmony with the universe and creation. They remember ancestors (who are the "living past"). Africans often celebrate the holiness of embodiment

---

14. Mbiti, *African Religions and Philosophy*, 107–8.
15. Wasike, "Vatican II," 258.
16. Stinton, "Africa, East and West," 129–31.

(bodily holiness). They connect worship with social harmony and interpersonal connection. They seek to release the power of human imagination and language.[17]

Explosive Growth of Inculturated, Independent Churches

Three groups are significant forces in African Christianity today:

1. The African Independent/Initial Churches" (henceforth AICs).
2. The Roman Catholic "Small Christian Communities" (henceforth SCCs).
3. The newer "Independent Pentecostal/Charismatic Churches" (henceforth (IPCCs).

Even though I focus on the AICs and IPCCs here, the Roman Catholic SCCs are essential, too. African Catholic believers developed the SCCs as a pastoral priority to meet local needs. In the SCCs, local people determine who celebrates the sacraments. There is space for polygamous and female leaders. The SCCs are self-governing, self-ministering, and self-supporting. The parish is a communion of SCCs. As you might imagine, these developments threatened the Roman Catholic Church. The priests and bishops set out to quash the SCCs. The result is that they are not as numerous or vibrant as they once were.[18]

The AICs and IPCCs have been much more successful. Harold Turner and Allan Anderson have written extensively on their characteristics and growth. Anderson writes, "Observers have long recognized that the AIC movement amounts to a fundamental reformation of African Christianity, a movement of such momentous significance that it can truly be called an African Reformation. It must be taken seriously by anyone interested in African Christianity and the globalization of Christianity."[19] The *World Christian Encyclopedia* puts the number of AIC participants in Africa at 83 million. It estimates IPCC participants at 126 million.[20]

Allan Anderson cautiously divides these churches up into three main types:[21]

---

17. Lumbala, *Celebrating Jesus Christ in Africa*, ix–xiv.
18. Mellor and Yates, *Mission and Spirituality*, 103–6.
19. Anderson, "Types and Butterflies," 107.
20. Barrett et al., *World Christian Encyclopedia*, 1:13 (Table 14).
21. Anderson, "Types and Butterflies," 109–12.

PART 3: REVITALIZING OUR CHURCHES

The first type is the *African/Ethiopian Churches*. The leaders of these groups shaped them after European mission churches. They do not have the spiritualist and charismatic elements of other independent churches. In southern Africa, people often call them "Ethiopian" or "Ethiopian-type" churches. In Nigeria, people often call them "African" churches. They are older than other forms of AICs and are not as numerous.

The second type is the *spiritual/prophet-healing churches*. These are like Western Pentecostal/charismatic churches. But they have shaped their worship around African cultures. They claim an inculturated Pentecostal heritage. They focus on spiritual power. Some are small. Others are huge. Allan Anderson includes a broad range of AICs in this group.

> They are particularly difficult to describe, for they include a vast variety of some of the biggest of all churches in Africa—the Kimbanguists and the African Apostolics in central Africa; the Christ Apostolic Church, the Aladura churches, and the Harrist churches in West Africa; and the Zion Christian Church and the Amanazaretha in southern Africa. These are all churches with hundreds of thousands of members, and in at least the cases of the Kimbanguists and Zionists, several million.[22]

These churches have sought to engage and express their inculturated cultures. There is a focus on healing, deliverance, prayer for the sick, and miraculous works. These churches link these practices with "the use of various symbolic objects such as blessed water, ropes, staffs, papers, or ash."[23] Members wear uniforms—often white robes with colored sashes. These AICs have "adapted themselves to and addressed the popular African worldview."[24] They portray Jesus as the suffering and healing chief. They emphasize story (rather than proposition). They enjoy song and dance and drama (rather than apologetics). They practice healing (rather than hermeneutical analysis). They embrace the prosperity gospel, focusing on health, wealth, and general prosperity. Their leaders are frequently seen as apostles and prophets. These churches often equate these "big men" (usually men) with the chiefs of African settings.

The third type is the *newer Pentecostal/charismatic/renewalist churches*. These also emphasize the Holy Spirit's power, gifts, and healing. But they refer to themselves as "charismatic" rather than "Pentecostal." They view themselves as "Evangelical" rather than "independent." These are proliferating. They tend to maintain strong connections with the West. Anderson

---

22. Anderson, "Types and Butterflies," 109.
23. Anderson, "Types and Butterflies," 110.
24. Anderson, "Types and Butterflies."

includes the following churches in this group: "The Deeper Life Bible Church in Nigeria, led by William Kumuyi; the Zimbabwe Assemblies of God, led by Ezekiel Guti; and the Grace Bible Church, led by Mosa Sono in South Africa."[25]

These newer charismatic/evangelical AICs have less inculturated expressions than the spiritual/prophet-healing churches. They seek to be relevant to their cultures. But they are more wary of African primal religion and practice than are the spiritual/prophetic-healing churches. Africans led them all. While they connect with the West, they are fiercely independent and "African." They are critical of established African churches and denominations. These newer churches tend to see the established churches as non-inculturated and lukewarm. They see real connections between biblical cultures and their own (especially Old Testament cultures). They address these biblical themes by showing that African and biblical cultures deal with similar problems—war and violence, family and ancestors, genocide and rape, poverty and corruption, famine and disease, procreation and infertility, polygamy and marriage, widows and orphans, prostitution and sex trafficking, displacement and migration, sickness and oppression, witchcraft and substance abuse, and spirits and deliverance.

Inculturated theology, worship, community, and mission in Africa are diverse. I find it inspiring. Diane Stinton describes how African-inculturated Christian theologies and practices influence the global church. Stinton quotes John Pobee as she describes the prophetic voice of the African church in this area.

> The test of any cultural construct of the gospel is whether it enables growth, change, and transformation in and into the image and likeness of God through Christ . . . The Akan have a saying, "The mother feeds the baby daughter before she has teeth, so that the daughter will feed the mother when she loses her teeth." The old church has lost her teeth. Evidence: empty churches. This new church, the younger church, is now the vibrant part. It owes it to the so-called mother churches to share its insights, so that together they may be renewed and transformed.[26]

---

25. Anderson, "Types and Butterflies."
26. Stinton, *Jesus of Africa*, 250–53.

PART 3: REVITALIZING OUR CHURCHES

2. Inculturation in Asia

Asia is a vast melting pot of cultures. There are almost fifty countries in Asia. Two-thirds of the world's six billion people live in Asia (almost four-and-a-half billion people). Asians speak 33 percent of the world's languages (more than two thousand). So, Asian Christianity is diverse.

Two books illustrate this well. Peter Phan edits the first book, called *Christianities in Asia*. Each contributor traces the unique shape and development of Christianity in particular parts of South Asia, Southeast Asia, Northeast Asia, and Southwest Asia. They show the unique expressions of Christianity in more than twenty countries. They consider significant churches and denominations. They outline missionary figures and the role of women in Asian churches. They give us a window into Asian martyrs, persecution, and relations with other religions. They profile Asian theologians and theological trends. They tackle church-state relations and prospects for the Asian church. Finally, they reveal inculturated and contextualized mission, worship, and spirituality expressions.

Phan's book is the best treatment I have seen on "how Christians in Asia have received and transformed Christianity into a local or inculturated religion, with their ecclesiastical structures, liturgy and prayers, spirituality, theology, art and architecture, music and song and dance, often in dialogue with Asian cultures and religions."[27]

The second is by Muriel Orevillo-Montenegro (a Filipino theologian). The book's title is *The Jesus of Asian Women*. Orevillo-Montenegro considers how many Western Christologies imported into Asia were inadequate for Asian challenges. These Christologies were irrelevant to Asian cultures. She says that Westerners underestimated the diversity and complexity of Asian cultures and religions.

Orevillo-Montenegro then considers the diverse and inculturated Christologies developed by Asian Christian theologians. She is especially interested in those developed by Indian, South Korean, Filipino, and Hong Kong Chinese women.

> Indian women's Christologies criticize Christianity's use of Jesus' maleness as a norm. These Christologies reveal these women's view of the cross considering Indian women's experience of complex suffering at the intersection of caste, ethnicity, religion, gender, race, and poverty. Indian women also explore

---

27. Phan, *Christianities in Asia*, 4.

the meaning of Jesus the Christ in connection with the degradation of women and the exploitation of nature.[28]

South Korean women develop Christologies that converse with Korean inculturated religions. They value creation care. Filipino women develop Christologies in the context of political struggle and upheaval. These reflect Asian womanist liberation theologies. Hong Kong Chinese women are developing hybridized Christologies. These consider Chinese and Western ideas and postcolonial theology.

Orevillo-Montenegro concludes with the following. "Overall, the Jesus of Asian women is the Asian Christ who accompanies them in their daily struggles for liberation from oppression and suffering. This Christ seeks to engage with religions, cultures, and inculturated spiritualities to make life flourish for every living being."[29]

Inculturated Asian theologies and practices take many forms. Let's consider some examples and what we can learn from them.

Asian Theologies

There have been various attempts to categorize inculturated Asian theologies. Asian evangelicals have sought to analyze these theologies in the light of Scripture and evangelical convictions. See, for example, the 1982 *Seoul Declaration: Toward an Evangelical Theology for the Third World*.[30]

Bong Rin Ro provides the best-known categorization of Asian theologies. He lists four types. I list these types here and include the examples Ro provides and some of my own examples.[31]

The first type is *syncretistic theologies*. These are Asian theologies that have moved beyond inculturation and are syncretistic (e.g., Raymond Panikkar's *The Unknown Christ of Hinduism*).

The second type is *accommodation theologies*. These are Asian theologies that seek to accommodate good ideas from other religions while preserving Christian belief (e.g., Kosuke Koyama's *Waterbuffalo Theology* and Batumalai Sadayandy's *A Prophetic Christology for Neighborology*).

The third type is *situational theologies*. These are Asian theologies that arise from and speak to concrete situations in Asia (e.g., Kazoh Kitamori's *Pain of God Theology*, Kim Yong Bock's *Minjung Theology*, liberation

---

28. Orevillo-Montenegro, *Jesus of Asian Women*, 7.
29. Orevillo-Montenegro, *Jesus of Asian Women*, 194.
30. Ro and Eshenaur, *Bible and Theology in Asian Contexts*.
31. Ro, "Theological Trends in Asia."

theologies in India and The Philippines, Minjung Theology in South Korea, and Asian postcolonial, ecological, and womanist theologies).

The fourth type is *biblically oriented Asian theologies*. These are Asian theologies that prioritize evangelical commitments (e.g., The 1982 *Seoul Declaration*, Bong Rin Ro and Ruth Eshenaur's *The Bible and Theology in Asian Contexts*, Ken Gnanakan's *Biblical Theology in Asia*, and Vinay Samuel and Chris Sugden's *Sharing Jesus in the Two-Thirds World*).

Let me introduce a few examples of creative, inculturated Asian theologies. These are *Dalit* theology from India, "pain of God theology" from Japan, "Waterbuffalo theology" from Thailand, *Minjung* theology from South Korea, and "story theology" from China.

1. *Dalit theology (India).* Like liberation theology, Dalit theology is for and by the poor and oppressed. It seeks liberation from oppressive forms of the Indian caste and political system. 70 percent of Indian Christians are lower-caste Dalits. But they have often felt marginalized and silenced by church and society.

    Dalit theology does not draw on Marxist philosophy like Latin American liberation theology. Instead, it seeks inspiration from biblical motifs that resonate with the experience of the Dalits. These motifs include suffering, incarnation, service, and freedom. Arvind P. Nirmal wrote that the suffering servant of Isaiah 53 reveals Jesus Christ as a Dalit. Jesus exists in solidarity with the downtrodden, suffering, and oppressed.[32] Dalit theology is closely associated with *subaltern theology*—theology done by those at the margins of society. In Asia, this includes many women and groups like the Indian Dalits and the Japanese Burakumin.

2. *Pain of God theology (Japan).* This theology grew from Kazoh Kitamori's book, *Theology of the Pain of God*. Kitamori shows how God suffers. God roots his love in his pain. God draws us into communion with his pain. In doing so, he heals and transforms human suffering, making it meaningful.

    Kitamori draws on biblical, Japanese, and Buddhist ideas of suffering to develop his theology. Kitamori wrote *Theology of the Pain of God* during World War II. He published the book just after the Japanese defeat and the atomic bombings of Hiroshima and Nagasaki. It struck a chord with a world in terrible suffering and pain.[33]

---

32. Oommen, "Emerging Dalit Theology"; Nirmal and Devasahayam, *Reader in Dalit Theology*.

33. Kitamori, *Theology of the Pain of God*.

3. *Water buffalo theology (Thailand)*. This theology developed out of Kosuke Koyama's book, Water Buffalo Theology. Koyama was a Japanese theologian who served as a missionary in Northern Thailand. Koyama rejected abstract, academic theology. He developed a way of talking about Jesus that he rooted in the experience of Thai peasants. He also sought to bridge Buddhist and Christian thought. Koyama called this blending Western Aristotelian theological "pepper" with Eastern Buddhist philosophical "salt."

   Koyama rooted his theology in Thai history and Asian Buddhist culture. He believed "neighborology" was necessary for Asian missions as proclamation or apologetics. Christians do their mission best in Asia through intimate, self-sacrificial, honest, and neighborly relationships.[34]

4. *Minjung theology (South Korea)*. Byung-Mu Ahn was the best-known proponent of this theology. Minjung is a movement seeking social justice for the poor and marginalized and silenced members of Korean society. It is a movement for the people and of the people. Jesus's experience is not only the hope of the Minjung—it is the experience of the Minjung. Minjung's popularity has waned since Korea became democratic and economically prosperous.

5. *Story theology (Chinese)*. Choan-Seng Song typifies this theology. Drawing on Chinese ideas, Song shows how imagination, relationships, and stories birth theology. Song says that theology must have four ingredients.

   > (1) It is the power of *imagination* given to us by God, who created us human beings in the divine image. (2) It is the *passion* that enables us to feel the compassion of God in us and others. (3) It is the *experience of communion* that makes us realize we are responsible for one another and God. (4) It is the *vision* of God's redeeming presence in the world, enabling us to envision a new course for theology.[35]

   Song claims that inculturated Asian theology is always rooted in story. Asian theology must be *story theology*. Good theology emerges from the intersection between *my* story, *our* story, *Christ's* story, *our culture's* story, and *countless* life stories. "In the beginning were stories, not texts."[36]

---

34. Koyama, *Water Buffalo Theology*.
35. Song, *Theology from the Womb of Asia*, 3.
36. Song, *Theology from the Womb of Asia*, 3.

PART 3: REVITALIZING OUR CHURCHES

Asian Christians often complement theological creativity with inculturated Christian practices.

Asian Expressions and Practices

Each of the five Asian theologies mentioned above has associated practices. These theologies lead to concrete Christian expressions. All over Asia, Christians shape inculturated expressions of church, worship, mission, and spirituality.

Balinese Christianity serves as an example. Christianity has struggled to get a foothold in Bali. Hinduism has been extraordinarily successful in winning over the Balinese. Some say this is because Hinduism presented itself as an Asian religion. It adapted itself to inculturated Balinese animism. I. Wayan Mastra writes, "The success of the Hindus in winning Balinese for Hinduism was the result of their efforts in introducing Hinduism not in the form of a foreign religious and cultural invasion, but as a seed planted in Balinese soil and growing up in its way."[37]

During the last few decades, many churches have sought to move Christianity away from its perception as a foreign religion. These Christians have done this through inculturation. This includes building churches in Balinese style. Balinese art, color, architecture, symbols, paintings, and decorations adorn the churches. The worship services have incorporated Balinese dance and dramatic opera (tembang). Church leaders dress in Balinese clothes and wear colors that speak of life, freedom, and joy in Balinese culture. Churches engage in social action and cultural enhancement. This includes supporting Balinese agriculture, fishing, medicine, families, and education.[38]

We see similar approaches to inculturation in Japan. In *Developing a Contextualized Church*, Mitsuo Fukuda shows how Japanese Christians attempt to communicate Christianity with the Japanese worldview and its religious rituals. Building on Japanese supernaturalism, ritualism, and groupism, many Japanese churches are redefining themselves as "divine families" and "holy places." Japanese culture values form and mysticism and ritual and relationship. So, inculturated Japanese churches are prioritizing these in their worship. They also emphasize these in small groups, mentoring, rituals, and ceremonies. These Christians keep church buildings open, like Shinto shrines and Buddhist temples.

---

37. Coote and Stott, *Down to Earth*, 265–66.
38. Coote and Stott, *Down to Earth*, 269–72.

Mitsuo Fukuda calls this *Japanese ethno-ecclesiology*. "Seeking inculturated church forms for the Christian church in Japan is a pioneering work . . . Our conviction is that through working with the Holy Spirit, we can discover God's redemptive gift within Japanese culture and employ it for a better church ministry."[39]

Another example is the Mukyokai Non-Church Movement, which began in Japan. Founded by Uchimura Kanzo, it now boasts thirty-five thousand participants across Japan, Taiwan, and South Korea. The movement has no church buildings, clergy, liturgy, or sacraments. Groups meet in homes, and people with pastoral gifts continue full-time secular work. The movement practices scholarship, social criticism, and sophisticated theological conversations. It speaks out against Japanese nationalism and militarism. It also seeks harmony between Asian cultures.

Mukyokai believes the church and Christian faith should be spiritual, relational, and life-affirming. Mukyokai holds that Christianity shouldn't be institutional or structural. Christians experience *koinonia* in deep community. All believers are ministers. The whole congregation teaches and leads. The church is a dynamic and living organism—not a static institution. It is forever being reborn and renewed. "The church is forever constructed and forever destroyed."[40]

In China, many Christians are contextualizing the Chinese New Year Festival. They are adapting their Christian practices at this time of the year. This way, Christian New Year festivities are inculturated. Christian Chinese New Year Festivals involve valuing kinship groups, elders, and extended families. They include honoring the ancestors (Christian and otherwise). They entail culturally appropriate greetings, visitations, and exchanging of gifts.[41]

What does a genuinely inculturated Asian Christianity look like? The Federation of Asian Bishops offered a description when they met in Samphran, Thailand, in 2000. While they are only one group in Asia (albeit a significant group—there are 137 million Catholics), they highlight salient features of an Asian inculturated church. They examined what the Spirit has been saying to their churches for over thirty years. They desired to be faithful to Christ through an inculturated Asian vision of a renewed church. This is instructive for us in our settings.

---

39. Fukuda, *Developing a Contextualized Church as a Bridge to Christianity in Japan*, 240.

40. Norman, "Kanzo Uchimura," 358–60.

41. Tan, "Contextualization of the Chinese New Year Festival."

So, what did they conclude? They observed, "eight movements that as a whole constitute an Asian vision of a renewed Church." A renewed Asian church is a church of the poor and the young. It's a truly local church with a profound interiority. It's an authentic faith community with an active and integral mission. It empowers men and women. It serves and generates life. It enters a dialogue with other faiths, people experiencing poverty, and Asian cultures.[42]

What will a genuinely inculturated church look like in your setting? Will it be a church of those experiencing poverty and the young that is inculturated to its culture? Will it practice deep interiority and authentic community? Will it embrace an active, integral mission and empowerment of women and men? Will it confront your culture's sin? Will it promote creation care, religious dialogue, and ethnic harmony? Will it value human dignity, life, peace, and solidarity? Or will a genuinely inculturated church be evident through other distinctions and characteristics?

3. Inculturation in Latin America

Like Africa and Asia, inculturation in Latin America is widespread and diverse. Latin Americans have found innovative ways to meet the challenges and opportunities of their cultural contexts.

Latin American Theologies

I have devoted an entire chapter to liberation theology and associated Latin American Christian perspectives in this book (see the chapter called *Liberating People*). In that chapter, I demonstrated that liberation theology has various recognizable features. These qualities are often shared with other expressions of Latin American contextual theology.

Liberation theology shares many features and perspectives with other Latin American theological movements. But it isn't the sum of inculturated Latin American theology. We must avoid caricaturing Latin American theology into one homogenous type. In Latin America, *liberation* theology, *Pentecostal* theology, *mujerista* theology, *base ecclesial* communities, *integral mission* movements, and *evangelical* groups are all unique. Each has forms of worship, theology, and leadership.

There are also unique forms of theology developing among Latino Jewish Christians, Afro-Latinos, and Amerindians (to name a few). But

---

42. Eilers, *For All the Peoples of Asia*, 3–4.

even though these theologies are unique, they share certain features and perspectives. They're committed to Scripture and social transformation. They combine evangelistic passion and integral mission. They enjoy deep personal spirituality and counter-cultural lifestyles. They cultivate private piety and immersion in the community. They embrace contextual theology and grassroots missional practices. There is theological diversity here, but also commonalities.

Here are some features of Latin American contextual theologies (not merely what we have come to know as "liberation theology")

Liberating Scripture and theology. There's a focus on renewing theology and theological method. Theologizing practitioners, pastors, congregations, and missionaries do theology together. They prefer this to outsourcing theology to "professional theologians." The whole community does theology together. The powerful and wealthy do theology alongside the marginalized and poor. Latin American contextual theologies are, of course, culture-specific. They recognize their social location and theologize within contexts. They immerse themselves in a human community.

Liberating contexts. There's an emphasis on transforming concrete situations. Contextual theologies form theology and mission and church that's specific to contexts.

Liberating praxis and interpretation. There's a suspicion of oppressive ideologies. Certain practices complement this suspicion. These include seeking social transformation and renewing church structures. They confront unjust political and social systems. They parallel suspicion of ideologies with innovation in church and mission. Later in this chapter, I provide examples of Latin American inculturated innovations in such areas. L Juan Luis Segundo speaks of the hermeneutical circle. This circle involves at least three steps. (1) Scrutinizing received interpretations with holy suspicion. (2) Being open to paradigmatic and interpretive upheaval and change. (3) Practicing circumstance-defying hope.[43]

Liberating orientation. There's solidarity with the poor, marginalized, and oppressed.

Liberating mission. There's an emphasis on mission. They see mission as participation in the *missio Dei*. Mission is liberation to the fullness of life. It is participation in the extension and proclamation of Christ's

---

43. Vaage, *Subversive Scriptures.*

inaugurated kingdom. Mission is healing, redemption, and liberation of whole persons, cultures, and the world. Mission is *integral*. This means that mission involves holistic transformation and social responsibility. It means that mission calls people to personal conversion and discipleship. It means that mission places everything within the context of the liberating mission, love, and kingdom of God.

Liberating Christ. These contextual theologies focus on Jesus. They form inculturated Christologies that are true to Scripture and relevant to the culture.

Liberating Trinity. There's an aversion to dry, abstract, academic doctrine. Instead, trinitarian theology provides meaning and impetus for fresh theological understandings and explorations of Christian community, mission, faith, and praxis. Juan Luis Segundo and Leonardo Boff show how trinitarian perspectives give these things deeper foundations.

Liberating Spirit. Pentecostalism has grown exponentially in Latin America. Latin American liberation and Pentecostal and evangelical theologies focus on the Spirit. They emphasize the person and work and empowerment of the Spirit (pneumatology).

Liberating kingdom. There's an effort to understand faith and church and mission in the light of the kingdom of God. God inaugurated this kingdom in the incarnation, life, death, resurrection, and glorification of Jesus Christ.

Liberating community and church. There's a desire to reactivate the church. This includes grassroots communities that worship together. They do missions together and engage in justice, mercy, and consciousness-raising among the poor and oppressed.

Liberating holism. There's a focus on holistic practice and theology. This involves describing the connections between liberation, eco-theology, poverty, economics, and spirituality. It also means pursuing appropriate actions.

Liberating dialogue. There's an effort to put key things into critical and enriching dialogue. These include Scripture, theology, the humanities, the church's practices, and the historical situation.

Liberating futures. There's a focus on meeting the present challenges within Latin America. This involves listening to the voices of women and children. It also involves paying attention to a younger generation of theologians. These emerging thinkers are influencing global conversations. They come from many settings—Asian, Latin American,

African, Eastern European, Middle Eastern, Indigenous peoples, and more. They don't ignore Western voices. But Western voices have been dominant for so long. Latin American thinkers know it is time to pay attention to voices and practices from the Majority World.

Almost all forms of inculturated Latin American theology contain a common feature. They integrate theology and practice into Christian social action, community, and mission.

Latin American Expressions and Practices

I consider four inculturated expressions of Latin American faith here: *mujerista* theology, basic ecclesial communities (BECs), autochthonous Pentecostal churches (LAAPs), and integral mission movements.

1. Mujerista Theology (Latina/Hispanic Womanist Theology)

Mujerista theology emerges from the life experiences and theologies of Latin American and US Hispanic women. It sees itself as womanist, not feminist. *Mujerista* theology integrates Latin American liberation theology, Latin American and US Hispanic womanist theology, and cultural studies.

Mujerista is a grassroots Latina ecclesiology. It seeks the liberation of the church and its mission from forms of oppression based on gender. It has a communal focus. *Mujerista* prefers the theological perspectives of black and Hispanic/Latina women (*mujeres*). It encourages Latina women to rediscover the Bible for themselves in small reading groups.

Mujerista is also characterized by:

- A preferential option for women and people experiencing poverty.
- The pursuit of justice and liberation for women and people experiencing poverty.
- The development of a unique Latina theology.
- Practices are outworked throughout the community.[44]

---

44. Isasi-Díaz, "Mujeristas," 560.

PART 3: REVITALIZING OUR CHURCHES

2. Basic Ecclesial Communities (BECs)

These are small, basic, grassroots, autonomous, self-reliant, rural, and urban Christian groups.

BECs emerged in Brazil in the 1960s. They spread throughout Latin America, Asia, and Africa. They are often associated with liberation theology. BECs focus on solidarity with the marginalized and poor. They enjoy participatory forms of ministry, decision-making, and governance. Liberation theologians popularized BECs. The 1968 meeting of the Latin American Council of Bishops (CELAM II, Medellín, Colombia, 1968) brought them to the world's attention. These BECs sought fellowship within the Roman Catholic churches of Latin America after Medellín. Post Vatican II, modernizing impulses helped this shift. The vision for renewal expressed in the Vatican II documents *Lumen Gentium*, and *Gaudium et Spes* provided further momentum for these basic communities.

Boff is an enthusiastic supporter of BECs. Boff encourages new forms of church "from below." Hence, his book *Ecclesiogenesis: The Base Communities Reinvent the Church*. These churches "from below" are autonomous, multi-voiced, and self-governing. They're *of* people experiencing poverty and *for* people experiencing poverty. Boff says that cclesiologies must replace universal cclesiologies. Our vision for the kingdom of God must be greater than our commitment to the institutional church.

For Boff, BECs are reinventing the church. They're forging new ways of being church and growing beyond current church structures. They give space for oppressed people to organize for liberation. They encourage people to question the institutions of the church. Lay people can coordinate the celebration of the Lord's Supper as "an extraordinary minister of the Lord." BECs open possibilities for women's priesthood.[45]

Occasionally, Catholic Church leaders have criticized the theology, deinstitutionalization, and practices of BECs. But, in Redemptoris Missio, Pope John Paul II affirmed BECs:

> BECs are centers for Christian formation and missionary outreach. They are a sign of vitality within the Church, an instrument of formation and evangelization, and a solid starting point for a new society based on a "civilization of love." BECs decentralize and organize the parish community to which they remain united. They take root among the less privileged. They become a leaven of Christian life, care for the poor, and commitment to the transformation of society . . . They are a means of evangelization and the initial proclamation of the Gospel—a

45. Boff, *Ecclesiogenesis*.

source of new ministries. They are a true expression of communion and a means for constructing a more profound communion. They are a cause for great hope for the life of the Church.[46]

Writing to the *13th Interecclesial Meeting of the Basic Ecclesial Communities* (December 17, 2013, Brazil), Pope Francis expressed support for BECs. He said they "bring a new evangelizing fervor and a new capacity for dialogue with the world whereby the Church is renewed." He challenged them to pursue fellowship with the rest of the church. He urged them to be "missionary disciples who walk with Jesus, proclaiming and witnessing to the poor the prophecy of a new heaven and a new earth."[47]

Basic ecclesial communities have not received much attention recently. They have suffered from the rise of neo-liberalism and the decline of socialism in Latin America. They have also struggled under the resurgence of conservatism during the pontificates of John Paul II and Benedict XVI.

This does not mean that BECs are insignificant—millions of people are members of them in Brazil alone.[48] It will be interesting to see whether they experience a resurgence during Francis's pontificate.

3. Latin American Autochthonous Pentecostal Churches (LAAPs)

These are Pentecostal churches that originated in Latin America. They're *autochthonous*. This means they're not missionaries, and they're not transplanted from elsewhere. They're typically independent of denominations or mission agencies. Like the BECs, they are Christian communities formed "from below." They are grassroots, locally-led, self-supporting, and inculturated. Unlike most of the BECs, they are Pentecostal.

The LAAPs are fringe to Latin American denominational Pentecostalism. They're separate from Western planted and led Pentecostal movements. LAAPs are more resistant than BECs to Protestant and Catholic denominational cultures and institutions. LAAPs are restorationist. They value Pentecostal holiness, biblical primitivism, and literalism. They elevate non-professional leadership. They practice solidarity with people experiencing poverty. They've been more successful than missionary-led, Western forms of Latin American Pentecostalism. They often view Western Pentecostalism as foreign, professionalized, elite, and dependent on Western support.

---

46. Pope John Paul II, *Redemptoris Missio*, 51.

47. Pope Francis, *Letter to Participants in the 13th Meeting of the Basic Ecclesial Communities in Brazil.*

48. Berryman, *Religion in the Megacity*, 63–70.

Clayton L. Berg Jr. and Paul E. Pretiz are missionary researchers in Latin America. Their book *Spontaneous Combustion* considers the explosive growth of LAAPs in Latin America.[49] These LAAPs correspond to the "African Independent Churches" (AICs). They're especially like the "Independent Pentecostal/Charismatic Churches" (IPCCs).

In 1980, LAAPs constituted around 40 percent of Protestants in Latin America. Today, more than 50 percent of Latin American Protestants are in LAAPs. Berg and Pretiz say that LAAPs are breaking the non-inculturated stereotype of Latin American Protestantism. They reveal fresh, inculturated, contextual forms of Protestant Pentecostalism in Latin America.

Occasionally, researchers compare Latin American Pentecostal churches with BECs. The stereotype is that Latin American Pentecostalism is "otherworldly" and tied to the West. They're portrayed as disinterested in the plight of people experiencing poverty or in social transformation. BECs are stereotyped as the opposite of this.

But LAAPs are challenging the stereotypes. LAAPs are Pentecostal churches committed to indignity, independence, and solidarity with the poor. They pursue social transformation and political activism. LAAPs break the stereotype of "otherworldly," "materialistic," or "Western-dependent" Latin American Pentecostalism.[50]

4. Integral Mission Movements

I have discussed integral missions in the chapter *Contextualizing Mission*. The chapter contains the definition, key personalities, and characteristic practices of integral missions.

This *approach to* and *theology of* mission is often associated with liberation theology. But many others practice, embrace, and advocate integral missions—both in and outside Latin America. Many who do not self-identify with liberation theology do, in fact, practice and support integral missions. This is as true in Latin America as it is elsewhere. An integral mission is always best practiced in inculturated and contextual ways.

In *Serving with the Poor in Latin America*, C. René Padilla, Tetsunao Yamamori, and others provide examples of integral missions in Latin America. Here are five examples:

---

49. Berg and Pretiz, *Spontaneous Combustion*.

50. Bergunder challenges these stereotypes and shows how Latin American Pentecostalism is evolving into a movement for social transformation, in: Bergunder, Woodhall, and Anderson, "Pentecostal Movement and Basic Ecclesial Communities in Latin America."

1. The Evangelical Hospital in Honduras doesn't just provide hospital services. It offers economic contributions to the local community. It assists with the transformation of the national health system.

2. The Redeemer Project in Brazil works in the major cities. It cares for homeless people, prostitutes, addicts, adolescents, trafficked persons, and battered women.

3. The Child Wellbeing Project in Brazil helps disadvantaged children through holistic measures. These initiatives address poverty, illiteracy, crime, gangs, addiction, and family breakdown.

4. The Assemblies of God in Nicaragua engage in soil regeneration and environmental conservation enterprises. These have positive social consequences. This group invests in soil conservation, enrichment, and reforestation. They build family and communal gardens. They improve traditional and non-traditional crops. They rebuild local communities by supporting connections between people and lands and Christ.

5. Finally, Colombia's Christian Office for Social Advancement and Development is getting women and men out of poverty and the drug trade. They invest in microenterprise and education. They help churches serve their communities. This NGO encourages churches to invest in local businesses, families, social networks, and education.

Padilla and Yamamori offer other case studies of integral missions in their book. In each case, local people find inculturated ways to be church and do mission. Local Christians are helping transform their locations.[51]

Inculturation: Concluding Reflections

In this chapter, I've outlined the diverse inculturated expressions of faith in Africa, Asia, and Latin America. I've examined what we can learn from their unique and inculturated theologies. I've considered what we can learn from how they inculturate their faith. I've shown how they inculturate their spirituality, worship, mission, and church. I've asked the reader to take note of these things and learn from them.

These examples of inculturated theology and practice should inspire us. They should motivate us to shape *our* inculturated ways of being God's people in our setting. How can your church be inculturated? How will you and your Christian community develop a grassroots and inculturated

51. Yamamori et al., *Serving with the Poor in Latin America*, 11–84.

theology? What church, mission, and theology forms will emerge in your setting? How will they be relevant and inculturated to your culture?

Here are thirteen things we learn from how Majority World Christians inculturate faith:

1. Inculturated churches evidence the six marks of inculturation.

Alan Tippett's six marks of a genuinely inculturated church are helpful. He developed this while doing mission among the Fijian islands. The first is *self-image*. An inculturated church knows it's *the* church of Jesus Christ in its local situation. It knows it's not a poor imitation of the true church elsewhere or in another culture.

The second is *self-function*. Inculturated people *take part in* and *lead* the ministries and mission of the church. They *own* those ministries, missions, and expressions of the church under the Lordship of Jesus Christ.

The third is *self-determination*. An inculturated church makes its own decisions and determines its own structures. It forms its own theology. It shapes its own ministries. It develops inculturated expressions of worship. It leads its own process of *self-contextualization* or *self-inculturation*. It does all these things in a way that is inculturated to its culture so that its witness and worship make sense to that culture.

The fourth is *self-support*. An inculturated church raises and administers its own finances. It carries its own financial burdens. It funds its own local ministries, service projects, and missions.

The fifth is *self-propagation*. An inculturated church multiplies itself by planting and raising its own missionaries. It does not rely on missionaries from elsewhere but becomes a missional movement.

The sixth is *self-giving*. Inculturated people seek to transform their own cultures. They engage the political, social, and relational challenges of their setting. They serve their own cultures in ways that are inculturated and transformational.[52]

How do you know if your church is inculturated to your culture? Ask yourself whether it displays these six qualities.

---

52. Tippett, *Introduction to Missiology*, 377–81.

2. Inculturated churches fuel theological imagination.

As you've read this chapter, you may have noticed the theological creativity in Asia, Africa, and Latin America. Theological originality is a hallmark of inculturation. Duplicating the theology of others never leads to inculturated churches. Truly inculturated churches throw fuel on the fire of theological imagination. This theological experimentation listens to history and tradition. It respects the authority of Scripture. It pays close attention to the interpretations of other cultures and groups. But it's still theologically imaginative. It strives for theological innovations, interpretations, and explorations. These challenge *and* communicate to its culture. It gives fresh meaning to cultural narratives, images, rituals, rites, myths, and practices. It puts these into a dynamic conversation with a Christian worldview. This way, we understand and reshape *both* Christian theologies and cultures. We do this in fresh and mutually enriching ways.

3. Inculturated churches are relevant and prophetic.

They do worship and mission in ways that are inculturated to their culture. They're relevant. Their language, practices, and analogies are meaningful to their culture. But they're also confrontational and prophetic. They proclaim the gospel, in word and deed, without compromise. They pursue Christ-honoring worship, preaching, service, mission, and discipleship that call their culture—and people within that culture—to repentance and discipleship.

Truly inculturated churches are relevant and prophetic and committed uncompromisingly to the gospel. Inculturated forms and analogies can be counter-cultural. But only when they witness to the values, holiness, faith, hope, love, gospel, and person of Jesus Christ. They stand within culture but witness to the One who transcends all cultures and persons, calling them to faith and repentance.

4. Inculturated churches engage local people's hearts, minds, and hands.

I've seen too many churches and theological colleges worldwide that expats start, lead, and fund. Recently, I spoke at a large church in Malaysia. Westerners planted the church (I won't say which nationality). After twenty years of operation, these non-Malaysians still filled almost all senior positions in that church. That makes no sense to me. Here's another example.

PART 3: REVITALIZING OUR CHURCHES

Six months ago, I spent a few nights with friends in a Cambodian village. These Cambodian Christians serve among the poorest of the poor. They live among slum dwellers whom the Cambodian government had forcibly removed into a rural area. These Cambodian Christians collaborate with this poor community to develop its educational, health care, employment, and micro-enterprise opportunities. They also partner with the community to grow its spiritual capacities and receptivity to Christian faith. But recently, a wealthy church from another Asian nation "planted a church" in that village. They built an expensive building and started paying people to come to church. They offered food, clothing, and money to people who turned up to church services. The leaders of the poor community went to the Cambodian Christians in distress. They said, "What are these Christians doing? They're turning Cambodians into beggars. Our people are losing all self-respect."

Local people form and lead inculturated churches. These locals ensure that other local people *take part* in and *lead* the ministries and mission of the church. They help them *own* these ministries, missions, and expressions of the church—under Christ's Lordship. Inculturated churches engage the hearts, minds, and hands of local people. We must entrust the inculturated church to them. This includes its theology, leadership, funding, identity, governance, propagation, etc.

5. Inculturated churches proclaim the gospel in inculturated ways.

We must use inculturated ideas, metaphors, and analogies to help all people understand the person and gospel of Jesus Christ. The best people to determine and shape these are inculturated into the receiving culture.

The classic story missionaries use to illustrate this point is the *Peace Child*.[53] Don Richardson was a missionary among the tribes of New Guinea, Indonesia. He lived among the Sawi tribe, who were cannibalistic headhunters. For a long time, he tried to communicate the gospel with them. However, cultural barriers prevented its reception. This tribe considered betrayal advantageous. So, they saw Judas as a clever hero and Jesus as weak. That was until Richardson stumbled upon the image of the "peace child." During times of tribal warfare, warring sides would sometimes exchange children to make peace. A fierce chief would offer up his son to another tribe as an ultimate sacrifice. He would offer his precious child as a peace offering. This image presented a window for the Sawi people into the substitutionary

---

53. Richardson, *Peace Child*.

atonement of Jesus Christ. Richardson called it a "redemptive analogy." He proposed that such redemptive analogies exist in all cultures. We can use them to illustrate the meaning of the gospel of Jesus Christ to people groups.

Don Richardson found a "redemptive analogy" that made sense to the Sawi. But once the Sawi became Christian, they needed to explore their own cultural analogies. Only this way would they shape their own inculturated faith. This is always the case. What redemptive analogies exist in your culture and the cultures around you? How will you empower "cultural insiders" to use inculturated stories, analogies, and ideas to shape their own theologies?

The goal isn't inculturation. The goal is the reception of the gospel and the person of Jesus Christ. The Balinese theologian I. Wayan Mastra outlines the role inculturation plays:

> Let us be clear that "indigenization" is not the goal of the church. We are not embarked on an effort to make an indigenous church just for the sake of making an indigenous church, nor for the sake of preservation of the culture . . . No, the process of making an indigenous church is undertaken for the sake of making the Gospel relevant to the people in a certain place at a particular period. It is a strategy of its mission, so that Christianity can have a home base and be rooted in the soul of a society, so that the Christians will not be foreigners in their own country, so that then Christ can be truly felt by all people to be the Savior of all the nations of the world.[54]

6. Inculturated churches experiment with forms of liturgy and sacrament.

They shape inculturated prayers and liturgies. They cultivate inculturated forms of baptism, the Lord's Supper, ordination, blessings, consecrations, and other Christian rituals. We must inculturate these and other liturgical and sacramental dimensions of our churches.

7. Inculturated churches import critically.

They refuse to mindlessly import theologies, church models, governance structures, mission programs, preaching guides, and worship expressions. Sometimes, these resources can help us. After all, that's one of the benefits

54. Mastra, "Christianity and Culture in Bali," 399.

of glocalization. We gain from a mutual exchange of ideas, resources, and practices. Glocalization means that the global is in the local, and the local is in the global. But we make a grave mistake when we adopt these things uncritically and without contextualizing them.

Instead, we must make our own local and inculturated decisions. We determine our own structures. We form our own theologies. We shape our own ministries. We set our own curriculum. We choose our own analogies and metaphors. We develop our own expressions of worship. We seek to make these dimensions of our churches relevant and transforming for our contexts. We make them truly inculturated to our cultures.

8. Inculturated churches take a long-term view.

They scrutinize what the Spirit has been saying to their churches and culture. Earlier in this chapter, I showed how Asian Bishops explored what the Spirit had been doing among their churches over thirty years. The goal was to discern what Jesus was doing in their Asian cultures and join him. We also need to take a long-term view. What has Jesus been doing in your church over the past ten, twenty, or thirty years? How will you join with him? How will you respond in obedience—developing inculturated theologies and practices that lead to renewed churches?

9. Inculturated churches make holistic commitments.

We need to proclaim the gospel in word and deed and sign. We should reject dualisms and pursue holism in our unique settings. This means seeking inculturated expressions of holistic commitments. What do I mean by this? I mean that we must find inculturated ways to combine these kinds of things: (1) gospel proclamation and social transformation; (2) evangelistic passion and integral mission; (3) cultural relevance and counter-cultural lifestyle; (4) private piety and public witness; (5) personal spirituality and immersion in community; (6) contextual theology and attention to history and tradition; (7) national political action and grassroots mission, and; (8) passion for Scripture and reliance on God's empowering presence.

10. Inculturated churches seek the transformation of their cultures and societies.

They seek to transform, heal, liberate, and unify their culture. Of course, this usually starts with individuals, families, and small groups within a society. Inculturated churches don't pursue transformation in their strength. They don't do this through their clever plans and initiatives. Instead, they seek to bring transformation through the power, gospel, and Spirit of Jesus Christ. Sure, we must plan, strategize, and work wisely within the systems of this world. But transformation can't rely on such things. Regeneration and renewal aren't by might or power but by the Spirit of Christ.

11. Inculturated churches test their inculturated forms.

They test them according to John Pobee's criteria. "The test of any cultural construct of the gospel is whether it enables growth, change, and transformation in and into the image and likeness of God through Christ."[55] Here are other necessary tests. Does this cultural construct proclaim the true gospel of Jesus Christ? Does it lead to the glory of the Father, Son, and Holy Spirit? Does it look like the Beatitudes? Does it cause people to seek God's kingdom and righteousness first? Does it inspire them to love the Lord their God with all their heart, soul, mind, and strength and love their neighbor as themselves?

12. Inculturated churches care about the local and global.

In one of the first chapters of this book, I discussed the importance of the *glocal* church. Healthily inculturated churches understand the importance of local and global exchange. They pursue the well-being of both expressions of the church. They invest in the welfare of their own church and culture. They look for ways to enrich the global church and contribute positively to the whole world.

13. Inculturated churches are flowerpot-breakers and seed-sowers.

How do we know if our church and theology are truly inculturated? Here are the signs. Firstly, we know that Jesus is the Lord and Savior of our culture

---

55. Stinton, *Jesus of Africa*, 250.

and church (and not some imported God from another context). Secondly, we fashion churches, missions, and services that meet the needs of our culture. Thirdly, we worship in ways that are inculturated into our culture. This worship makes sense to believers and non-believers alike. This is the case even when our worship contains elements that challenge our culture. Fourthly, our congregations are places where local people *take part* in and *lead* the ministries and mission of the church. They *own* these ministries, missions, and expressions of the church (under Christ's headship). Fifthly, we refuse to unthinkingly import theologies, church models, governance structures, and worship expressions. Instead, we make our own decisions and determine our own structures. We form our own theologies and shape our own ministries. We develop our own expressions of worship. We seek to make these dimensions of our church relevant and transforming for our context. These things are genuinely inculturated to our culture. Sixthly, we carry our own financial burdens and multiply inculturated churches and ministries. Seventhly, we seek to transform, animate, direct, and unify our own culture. (We do this through the power of the gospel and the Spirit of Christ). Eighthly, we do all these things not only for the sake of our own culture but also for the sake of the whole world. We seek to enrich the church locally and globally.

Lastly, our churches are flowerpot-breakers and seed-sowers. The Sri Lankan preacher and evangelist Daniel Thambyrajah Niles put it this way.

> The gospel is like a seed, and you must sow it. When you sow the seed of the gospel in Palestine, a plant that can be called Palestinian Christianity grows. When you sow it in Rome, a plant of Roman Christianity grows. You sow the gospel in Great Britain, and you get British Christianity. The seed of the gospel is later brought to America and a plant grows of American Christianity. Now when missionaries came to our lands they brought not only the seed of the gospel, but their own plant of Christianity, flowerpot included! So, what we must do is to break the flowerpot, take out the seed of the gospel, sow it in our own cultural soil, and let our own version of Christianity grow.[56]

Will you and your Christian community do the following? "Break the flowerpot, take out the seed of the gospel, sow it in your own cultural soil, and let your own version of Christianity grow."

---

56. Niles is quoted in Núñez, *Crisis and Hope in Latin America*, 332–33.

Study Questions

1. Investigate the meanings associated with the terms inculturation, inculturation, and contextualization. Which do you prefer? Do you agree that they are (basically) synonymous? How do you arrive at your conclusion?

2. What are examples of inculturated ministries, missions, theology, and worship in your setting? Why do you believe that these are authentically inculturated?

3. Has your church or denomination blindly imported theologies, church models, governance structures, and worship expressions? How successful have these been (regarding relevance for and mission to people in your particular setting)?

4. Is your church or ministry shaping your own forms of theology, church structure, ministry, worship, and mission? If not, why not?

5. How can your church or ministry move toward homegrown, inculturated theologies and innovations?

6. How would the forms and practices of your church change if you do the following? "Break the flowerpot, take out the seed of the gospel, sow it in your own cultural soil, and let your own version of Christianity grow"?

17.

Devouring Scripture

The Ninth Expression

As THE CHURCH GROWS in the Majority World, it must wrestle with its *multi-voiced* and *multi-peopled* nature. This global and diverse nature is reshaping its understanding of mission, church, and biblical interpretation. Western cultures no longer define how Christians should understand, believe, and interpret the Bible. Interpretive approaches in the West are now part of a global conversation. This conversation is broadening and enriching the way Christians believe and apply Scripture. This global exchange is heralding a transformation of the church. Christians in the Majority World believe and interpret the Bible in fresh, dynamic ways. They're influencing the Western and the global church.

Global ethnic diversity is de-westernizing the global church. Global and local conversations about biblical interpretation are de-westernizing hermeneutics. *Hermeneutics* is the branch of theology that deals with the interpretation of Scripture. The way the church interprets and applies Scripture, in global situations, will witness to the power of the gospel. Biblical belief will determine the church's shape and missional vitality.

Majority World and Indigenous voices can teach the global church further practices of biblical faithfulness. They can help the worldwide church discover further multi-voiced and multi-peopled approaches to interpreting and believing the Bible. What characterizes these approaches? People believe in the absolute authority of Scripture. They passionately apply the Bible to everyday life. They put their interpretations into a living conversation with their cultures. They identify personally with the biblical text and its stories.

How can we nurture communities characterized by dynamic biblical interpretation and belief? What can we learn from Christians in the Majority World and Indigenous cultures about reading the Bible? How can they help us interpret Scripture missionally, faithfully, and expectantly?

This chapter considers how many Majority World believers complement conservative Scripture readings with innovative applications. I examine the many contextual, popular, and communal Scripture readings in the Majority World. From there, I consider various other approaches to interpreting Scripture in those cultures. These include sociopolitical, active, supernaturalist, and Pentecostal readings.

Conservative Readings—Radical Applications

Philip Jenkins describes the conservative approach to Scripture in the Global South. He contrasts this with liberalizing tendencies in Anglo-European contexts. Majority World Christians often see Scripture as an inspired, infallible, authoritative, and sacred text.

Liberal Majority World scholars don't tend to represent belief and interpretation in the churches. The writings of such Majority World academics may give a distorted view of belief and practice in those churches. Jenkins writes that average Asian, African, and Latin American believers have views on Scripture: (1) They respect "the authority of Scripture, especially in matters of morality." (2) They honor "the Bible as an inspired text," and tend to literalism. (3) They have "a special interest in supernatural elements of Scripture, such as miracles, visions, and healings." (4) They believe "in the continuing value of prophecy." (5) They venerate "the Old Testament, which is considered as authoritative as the New."[1]

Fernando Segovia surveys Asian biblical hermeneutics, including how ordinary Asians read the Bible. He describes a high regard for the Bible as the word of God. "The biblical texts are regarded as a locus of unquestionable truth and liberation."[2]

These Majority World believers are redefining terms like *liberal* and *conservative*. Their faith in the authority of Scripture doesn't prevent "a

---

1. Jenkins, *New Faces of Christianity*, 4.
2. Segovia, "Emerging Project of Asian Biblical Hermeneutics," 372.

creative and even radical exegesis." These Christians often apply biblical texts "to contemporary debates and dilemmas."³

Many Majority World believers complement their trust in Scripture's authority with imaginative applications. They believe in the authority of Scripture. They apply Scripture creatively to sociopolitical and postcolonial issues. They also apply the Bible innovatively to moral, supernatural, sexual, and environmental issues. We see this throughout the Majority World. Sherron Kay George says that Latin American Pentecostals exemplify this. For them, the Bible is "a constant companion and identifying sign." Scripture "provides models, examples, and solutions for the contemporary Christian. It is used extensively in church services, healing, exorcism, testimony, daily witness, street-preaching, problem-solving, and vehement apologetics."⁴

It's like a breath of fresh air to read of those who trust and use the Scriptures so, well, trustingly. How will Western Evangelicals react? We will probably applaud the adherence to Scripture's authority. But we'll probably also be wary of what we would label "superstitious" uses of the Bible and passages. But is that just two centuries of critical scholarship affecting our thinking unawares?

Religious plurality sharpens this biblical interpretation in the Majority World. Social and political upheaval sharpens it, too. Anglo-European Christians have often underestimated the ability of conservative exegesis to address contemporary issues. Such conservative readings can lead to transforming applications. We'll see this as this chapter unfolds. Such readings can lead to naming and confronting the principalities and powers in societies. These innovative readings of the Bible are often carried out with careful attention to culture and context.

Contextual and Inculturational Readings

Contextualization and inculturation characterize Majority World interpretations of Scripture. *Contextualization* means shaping an idea or practice for a particular context. *Inculturation* is about adapting ideas, practices, and teachings for cultures. It is about the influence of these cultures on the evolution of these aspects of the church.

Majority World readers often contextualize their reading of Scripture for their setting—those cultures, in turn, shape Majority World biblical interpretation, theology, and practice.

---

3. Jenkins, *New Faces of Christianity*, 12.
4. George, "From Liberation to Evangelization," 367.

What are some examples of contextual, inculturational readings of Scripture? In his writings, R. S. Sugirtharajah roughly puts Majority World and Indigenous contextual interpretations into five groups. These are subaltern, postcolonial, inter-textual, popular, and numerous readings.

Subaltern readings are those of the rejected, subservient, oppressed, lowly, and marginalized. These groups are not homogenous. So, they develop a contextual reading for their circumstances. For example, the *Dalit* peoples of India have cultivated a contextual reading distinct from those living with HIV/AIDS in Uganda.

Postcolonial readings are those from former colonial contexts. These include Australia, Brazil, Congo, Guinea, Hong Kong, India, Indigenous peoples, Indonesia, Jamaica, Macau, Mozambique, Philippines, Sri Lanka, and Taiwan. These postcolonial readings ask questions about "empire, religion, and the role of the Bible in the imperial cause." They also examine "the colonial and neo-colonial power operating in biblical interpretation."[5]

Inter-textual readings seek to compare the Christian Scriptures with the sacred texts of Judaism, Hinduism, Buddhism, and Islam.

Popular readings are those of the ordinary reader. Truly contextual interpretation puts biblical scholarship into conversation with local issues and voices. It regards the "religio-spiritual interests and aspirations of the grassroots and their communitarian readings."[6] R. S. Sugirtharajah provides examples from Latin American Pentecostal congregations. He also considers African non-literate communities. He offers examples from post-Apartheid black non-academic women and Southeast Asian rural churches. These non-academic groups read the Bible in fresh, grassroots, and relational ways. They usually do this within local communities and congregations.

Numerous readings refer to the breadth of contextual interpretations in the Majority World. We see Latin American, Asian, Palestinian, Indigenous, womanist, and many more interpretations. I only have space here to give a few examples. In *An Introduction to Third World Theologies*, John Parratt draws together thinkers from across the globe. Latin Americans, Indians, Asians, Africans, and Caribbeans unpack unique contextual theologies from their settings. They describe the unique ways they interpret and apply Scripture in their cultures. Edmond Tang's chapter on East Asia exemplifies the rich contextual theologies growing in each continent. Tang writes of the relationship between biblical interpretation and the support of Confucian virtues in Chinese churches. He explores the relationship between biblical interpretation and cultural notions of human suffering in

---

5. Sugirtharajah, *Voices from the Margin*, 8.
6. Sugirtharajah, *Voices from the Margin*, 9.

Japan. He shows how storytelling and "the reconstruction of history from below" shapes biblical interpretation among the *Minjung* of South Korea.[7] In a different book, Nestor Miguez analyses the various Latin American approaches to interpreting Scripture. He writes of the diverse interpreters of the Bible. These include "African descendants, aboriginal peoples, mestizos, women, campesinos, etc." These show that "there is no 'simple poor,' but a complexity of reading locations."[8]

Contextual Bible reading involves rereading the Bible through the lens of our own culture. It is not about ignoring perspectives from other cultures and societies. We critically engage those perspectives. But we develop forms of interpretation relevant to (and shaped within) our own culture.[9]

In the Majority World, people who closely identify with the Bible also do contextual theology. They identify with biblical stories and concerns. They interpret Scripture in communities. They identify with the world of the Bible together.

Popular and Communal Readings

Jenkins describes how Majority World Christians identify with biblical themes and stories. The Bible describes a world they know well. It's a world of poverty and wealth, injustice and reconciliation, evil and good, demons and angels, sickness and healing, exorcism and deliverance, suffering and liberation, famine and plague, war and sexual violence, occupation and colonialism, persecution and retribution, corruption and integrity, privileged and marginalized, holy sites and pilgrimage, and rituals and sacred texts.

This identification with the Bible leads to profound *popular* or *ordinary* readings. This identification with the ancient world and stories of the Bible is *communal*. It is more communal than individual. These themes resonate with entire communities. They touch their beliefs, concerns, and experiences.[10]

How does personal and communal identification with Scripture shape biblical interpretation in much of the Majority World? How does trust in the Bible's absolute authority influence interpretation? It leads to communal, relevant, Christ-centered, Spirit-oriented, obedient, practical, literal, and multi-voiced readings.

7. Parratt, *Introduction to Third World Theologies*, 74–104.
8. Míguez, "Latin American Reading of the Bible: Experiences, Challenges and Its Practice," 126.
9. Ukpong, "Rereading the Bible with African Eyes," 5.
10. Jenkins, *New Faces of Christianity*, 68–69.

Here, I use African churches as an example. In four separate articles, Zablon Ntamburi, Daniel Waruta, Fergus King, Gerald West, and Fidon Mwombeki list the assumptions and practices of popular African Bible reading.

Let's start with a group of popular African convictions, which Zablon Ntamburi and Daniel Waruta notice:

> The Bible is a document which shapes communities, not just individual faith. The meaning of the Bible is both historical and contemporary. The Bible presents a message that is to be obeyed. The Bible is practical and involving. The Bible gives news of salvation from all kinds of catastrophes, physical, political, and spiritual. The Bible gives counsel and enlightenment. The Spirit of God speaks directly to us from Scripture. The Bible's message is clear and to the point. The literal sense is a necessary precursor of any allegorical interpretation. The Bible's message is not always positive: it can warn, condemn, curse, and threaten, as well as bless.[11]

Mwombeki adds that African interpretation has critical features.[12] (1) Africans see the Bible "as a symbol of God's presence and protection." (2) They read the Bible for its practical use. "It is a book of life, neither a book of fiction nor one of history. It is not read for curiosity or fun. In this book, the reader listens to God speaking: giving comfort, instruction, exhortation, even condemnation." (3) The Bible "does not always have to be understood rationally." Many Africans appropriate their biblical reading "spiritually, emotionally, and mystically. The historical setting of the text is not significant, and even less the identify of its author." Often, many Africans appropriate the Bible worshipfully: "by heart, not necessarily by mind." (4) Many Africans apply the Bible to contemporary problems through communal discussion. (5) "There is a strong affinity between the religious and cultural context of the Bible and contemporary Africa." (This includes issues surrounding poverty, famine, child mortality, begging, prostitution, fishing, exclusion of women and children, demon possession, and so on.)

King describes other qualities of popular African biblical interpretation.[13] The "Christocentric interpretation of the Old Testament is often seen as standard" (i.e., many Africans prefer a Christ-centered interpretation over the historical meaning of the text). Additionally, many Africans memorize

---

11. Ntamburi and Waruta, "Biblical Hermeneutics in African Instituted Churches," 48 (points 1–10).

12. Mwombeki, "Reading the Bible in Contemporary Africa," 121–23.

13. King, "Across the Great Divide," 20.

and quote the Bible directly. "Instead of paraphrases or explanations, the interpreter will encourage reading the text itself." This comes with the assumption that "There is an authority in the words of Scripture themselves, and they must be used accurately." Many Africans change their interpretations according to their context and setting. They subject the Bible to a "plurality of interpretations," depending on the situation's needs. They give Scripture "fresh layers of meaning within new circumstances."

Many Africans interpret the Bible for personal and societal transformation. "Biblical interpretation is always about changing the African context. This is what links ordinary African biblical interpretation and African biblical scholarship." It is "a common commitment to 'read' the Bible for personal and societal transformation."[14] Often, local African congregations hold African biblical interpreters accountable. These theologians interpret within communities. Their churches hold them accountable for their accuracy, application, and spiritual vitality.

Identification with the Bible extends beyond Majority World scholarship into popular readings. These are readings by ordinary local believers. They are often conducted within congregations, families, and communities. For example, Miguez describes how many Latin American Christians developed popular, communal readings of the Bible within the context of repression. Their readings emerged as a response to persecution, torture, and harsh repression. This resulted in contextual and complex readings within Latin America. These developed at both popular and critical levels.

Musimbi Kanyoro says this identified, literal, communal reading has strengths and challenges. A literal reading will often mean an unwillingness to challenge the cultures of the Bible. They may consider doing this sinful.

> This points to a central task for those who read the Bible in cultures whose practices closely mirror those of Bible times. We can easily justify our behavior simply because we think we are in good company with the biblical culture. On the other hand, those cultures that are far removed from biblical culture risk reading the Bible as fiction. Cultural hermeneutics scrutinizes every culture with the intention of testing its liberative potential for people.[15]

Identification with the Bible can be as risky as distance from the Bible. Both have possibilities for interpretation and application. But we need to examine ourselves, the text, and our context. Both distance and proximity

---

14. West, *Biblical Hermeneutics in Africa*, 2 and 9.
15. Kanyoro, "Reading the Bible from an African Perspective," 20.

from the world of the Bible require us to examine our reading and use of Scripture.

Sociopolitical and Active Readings

Sociopolitical and active readings are common in the Majority World and Indigenous cultures. By *sociopolitical*, I mean reading the Bible to transform social and political realities. I also mean interpreting the Bible in the light of those realities. This is a dynamic engagement between Scripture and social factors. It involves appropriating the Bible in social and political contexts. By *active*, I mean a *dialogue* between crucial things:

- Reason and action
- Interpretation and application
- Theology and praxis
- Thought and social transformation
- Biblical interpretation and mission
- Scholarship and congregational practices

Our actions interrogate our use of Scripture. This includes our mission, ministry, politics, and service. Our interpretation of Scripture scrutinizes our actions.

In Majority World theology, sociopolitical and active readings are prophetic, creative, and numerous. Let's look at four examples. These are liberationist, feminist/womanist, postcolonial, and subaltern/marginal interpretations. These four are often integrated in sociopolitical readings in the Majority World.

1. Liberationist Readings

I deal with liberation theologies in another chapter of this book. Liberationist readings focus on liberation from all forms of oppression. They seek freedom from economic, social, political, religious, colonial, sexual, and racial domination.

Some liberation theologians are well-known. These include Gustavo Gutierrez, Juan Luis Segundo, Jose Porfirio Miranda, Jose Miguez Bonino, and Fernando Belo. They have particular ways of interpreting and applying Scripture. This is perhaps best articulated in Segundo's "hermeneutic circle." But here, I've tried to summarize their combined thought on biblical interpretation.[16]

> *Suspicion.* Reasonable interpretation begins with *suspicion*. We are skeptical of our inherited narratives, interpretations, ideologies, and traditions.
>
> *Praxis.* The Bible is always interpreted in *context*. We study Scripture in the context of *praxis*. Praxis is the outworking of our theories in customs, practices, habits, and applications. The relationship between praxis and interpretation is complex and critical. It is also mutually informative.
>
> *Transformation.* The Bible is best interpreted alongside a commitment to personal and social *transformation*. The Scriptures are best studied within the context of transforming practices. These include efforts to address poverty, injustice, and conflict. The church can learn much from the readings of oppressed people who struggle for liberation and justice. We form liberating interpretations in the context of struggle, mission, and praxis. Our readings transform individuals, churches, and societies when they commit to liberation.
>
> *Examination.* We must *examine* all interpretations concerning their context. All readings emerge from contexts, cultures, and practices. This is true of the *biblical* socio-economic, theological, and historical contexts. It is just as valid for the *contemporary* contexts and practices in which people interpret and apply the Bible.
>
> *New orthodoxy and orthopraxis.* The Bible interprets our contemporary praxis. Our praxis interprets Scripture. This exchange leads to new beliefs and praxis. This results in new *orthodoxy*—proper, liberating interpretation and belief. It leads to new *orthopraxis*—proper, liberating praxis. This ongoing exchange anticipates renewal of interpretation, belief, and practice.

2. Feminist and Womanist Readings

Women are not immune from exploitation and oppression in the churches of the Majority World. Repressive cultures often find expression in oppressive churches. Repressive, unjust cultures may seek to fashion conservative interpretations in their image. But, conservative biblical interpretation is

---

16. Segundo, *Liberation of Theology*, 9.

not always the culprit. Often conservative, complementarian Bible readings challenge repression. They support distinct gender roles in society. But they emphasize women's care, nurture, protection, and flourishing. The picture is complex. We need to be careful not to read Western assumptions into our examinations of the cultures of the Global South.

Majority World Christianity has nurtured the rise of distinct female voices. These challenge the political, economic, gender, and religious status quo. They are paving the way for the global church. They are tackling significant issues to do with society and gender. They are doing this courageously. These women include Maricel Mena Lopez, Mercy Amba Oduyoye, Kwok Pui-Lan, Elsa Tamez, Saroj Nalini Arambam Parratt, Yuko Yuasa, Virginia Fabella, Elina Vuola, Ruth Padilla Deborst, Azza Karam, Yong Ting Jin, Pauline Hensman, Denise Ackermann, and Musa Dube. They are forging ahead with innovative and distinct forms of biblical interpretation. They are pursuing gender equality and social justice. They are leading the way with missional and ministry practices.[17]

Kwok writes about how these women challenge the church's patriarchy. They disciple both women and men. They call for the equal partnership of women. These women develop distinct sociopolitical readings of the Bible from the perspective of women. They interpret colonial and patriarchal repression through the experience of women. They address issues surrounding the cessation of the exploitation of women and children. They call for the abolition of sexism and discrimination. They seek the rise of grassroots, participatory movements. They dream of a church that represents God's liberating reign. They work for a church that pursues peace, anti-militarization, and justice. They describe and create churches characterized by intercultural, interfaith, and inter-gender shalom.

Kwok describes how Majority World womanists often distance themselves from Western feminists. They are uncomfortable with the views and hermeneutics of Euro-American feminists. She describes the breadth of women's theology in Asia, Africa, Latin America, African-American, and Indigenous settings.[18]

---

17. Oduyoye, "Feminist Theology in an African Perspective," 179.
18. Kwok, *Introducing Asian Feminist Theology*, 112.

PART 3: REVITALIZING OUR CHURCHES

3. Postcolonial Readings

These are biblical interpretations from former colonies. They "emerge out of liberation hermeneutics, or extra-biblical Postcolonial Studies."[19] *Postcolonial* literature is massive, growing, and contested.

Postcolonial biblical interpretation is "diverse and hybrid."[20] These interpretive readings examine the relationship between empire, power, religion, and biblical interpretation. They do this in matters that are diverse yet interwoven. These include gender, liberation, race, ethnicity, marginality, power, geopolitics, social theory, church-state relations, globalization, and exclusion of the "other."

R. S. Sugirtharajah is probably the most widely read postcolonial theologian. He has written much on postcolonial biblical reading. So, I will focus briefly on his thoughts here. Sugirtharajah defines postcolonial biblical interpretation.

> Postcolonialism is roughly defined as scrutinizing and exposing colonial domination and power as these are embodied in biblical texts and in interpretations, and as searching for alternative hermeneutics while thus overturning and dismantling colonial perspectives. What postcolonialism does is to enable us to question the totalizing tendencies of European reading practices and interpret the texts on our own terms and read them from our specific locations.[21]

This project is about rejecting colonial, Western interpretations of Scripture. Or it is at least about modifying Western readings for the Majority World. Postcolonial theologians cultivate specific and local and postcolonial readings. The kind of postcolonial interpretations R. S. Sugirtharajah champions include those by outcast, subaltern groups in the Majority World. (E.g., The *Dalits* of India). They include the interpretations of Indigenous cultures and First Nations. They include the interpretations of oppressed, silenced, or marginalized women and children. They incorporate Majority World and Indigenous postcolonial interpretations of Scripture (e.g., *A Postcolonial Commentary on the New Testament Writings*).[22] They encompass the work of Majority World scholars pursuing inter-textual interpretations. These put non-Christian sacred and secular texts into postcolonial conversation

19. Moore and Segovia, *Postcolonial Biblical Criticism*, 5–6.
20. Moore and Segovia, *Postcolonial Biblical Criticism*, 6.
21. Sugirtharajah, *Postcolonial Bible*, 16.
22. Segovia and Sugirtharajah, *Postcolonial Commentary on the New Testament Writings*.

with the Christian Scriptures. Additionally, some postcolonial theologians develop Indigenous and Majority World images and understandings and contextualizations of Jesus (e.g., Relevant images of Christ for Buddhist, Islamic, Hindu, Sikh, pluralistic, and Indigenous contexts).

Having put together this list, one must be careful. R. S. Sugirtharajah addresses the dangers associated with exoticism and reception and power.

The issue of exoticism: "The practice of treating American and European interpretation as *the* interpretation and labeling the enterprise of others "Asian," "African," and so on, or of using gender or ethnic terms persists. Those who work on the margins cannot shake off the exotic tag attached to them."[23]

The issue of reception: "Those who act as the interpreters of minority communities find themselves in the strange situation of working with a troubled awareness that their productions will be less appreciated by the minorities themselves than by the outsiders who want to know about the 'other.'"[24]

The issue of power and the center: "Do we want to replicate the colonial game of occupation and capture the center in the name of the oppressed, or do we want to demolish the center itself and redraw its parameters? The next set of questions will be: How many centers should we have? Who will provide the parameters? Whose resources will we draw upon to redesign them?"[25]

4. Subaltern and Marginal Readings

Subaltern readings are those by groups, cultures, and subcultures that have been marginalized. Within their settings, they are considered outsiders, subservient, undesirable, and on the margins.

As I indicated earlier, these groups are numerous and diverse. They live in many Majority World and Indigenous contexts. These include poor, rural, illiterate women; small-scale agrarian workers; those who have HIV/AIDS; Indigenous and aboriginal groups; asylum seekers and refugees; immigrant laborers; the Dalit in India; the Burakumin in Japan; the Roma in Europe; the Baekjeong in Korea; the Midgan in Somalia; the Al-Akhdam in Yemen; homeless people and alcoholics and prostitutes on the streets of major cities; the incarcerated; and those with skin or sexual or other diseases.

---

23. Sugirtharajah, *Voices from the Margin*, 1.
24. Sugirtharajah, *Voices from the Margin*, 9.
25. Sugirtharajah, *Voices from the Margin*.

Christians among these groups often grow biblical interpretations and applications for their situations. These can have significant implications for the global church and humanity. They often challenge the sociopolitical, religious, economic, and racial status quo. They foster unique understandings of the message of Jesus. They grasp a vision of the kingdom of God rarely seen in less marginal groups.

One example will need to suffice. Joel Van Dyke lives in Central America. He directs a grassroots training initiative called *La Estrategia de Transformacion*. This involves ministering to gang members, prostitutes, and their families. His organization works in some of Central America's most notorious men's prisons. He writes of the lonely, marginalized girlfriends, wives, mothers, and sisters of these prisoners. These women sleep on the hard, concrete floors of the prisons. The prisoners and authorities often abuse, violate, and treat them like property.

In one prison, his team decided to lead a conversation with these women centered on the story of Hagar in Genesis 16. "The women quickly applied the story personally." In Hagar's story, "the women found their story. Reading the Bible with those we serve means we learn to take the stained glass off the text of Scripture and begin reading from the perspective of those who have been crushed by life. It's an adventure in mining good news out of the holes in Scripture that the church typically refuses to climb down into."[26]

Hagar calls God *El Roi*, "the God who sees me." The women in the prison were so gripped by the idea that God "sees them"—forgotten, rejected, violated, and invisible—that they painted a mural of Hagar's story on a prison wall. They made the focal point of the mural the words *El Dios Que Me Ve* ("the God who sees me").

> The larger missional implication is that Hagar grasps something about God that Abraham is not able to confess until six chapters later. In Genesis 22:14, Abraham names Mount Moriah *Jehovah Jireh* ("the God who provides"), using the verb *ra'ah*, the same one that Hagar used in naming God. This leads us to marvel that perhaps the Hagars of the world can recognize the gospel long before the Abrahams do.[27]

---

26. Van Dyke and Rocke, "Asking the Beautiful Question," 46.
27. Van Dyke and Rocke, "Asking the Beautiful Question" 46.

Supernaturalist, Mystical, and Pentecostal Readings

Majority World and Indigenous cultures identify closely with the world of the Bible. Its supernatural and spiritual dimensions ring true to their experience. They're familiar with a world of healings, demons, exorcisms, angels, witches, shamans, and cults. They believe in the power of prayer, dreams, visions, and spiritual warfare. They've experienced charismatic renewal and Pentecostal power.

This means that their interpretations of Scripture are often *supernaturalist*. They shape these interpretations around an experience of the spiritual world. They form them around their identification with the spiritual world of the Bible's cultures. This is especially true of ordinary, popular interpretations in grassroots congregations.

By *mystical*, I mean that ordinary Majority World readings are mystically oriented. They are often saturated in prayer and spiritual hunger. An expectation of Pentecostal experiences and power goes with these readings of Scripture. This mystical, prayerful, charismatic reading engages and anticipates these supernatural realities.

These churches believe in supernatural agencies that intervene in the natural world. They find support for this belief in the narratives and themes of Scripture. Their experience of these supernatural forces corresponds with those of biblical cultures. So, the biblical witness does not surprise them at all.

Jenkins has made much of this supernaturalist tendency in the Global South. "The supernatural approach certainly harks back to the ancient roots of Christianity." For millions of Majority World believers, "proclaiming the power of Jesus means declaring his victory over conquered forces of evil."[28]

An example of such readings comes from Kenya. John Mbiti writes of the encounter between biblical ideas and traditional beliefs among the Akamba of Kenya. He also draws on material from other parts of Africa. The Akamba see the spirit world as pervasive. They consider distinctions between the visible and invisible as inconsequential. "Magic, witchcraft, and sorcery play a prominent role in Akamba life. The people are saturated with beliefs, fears, and superstitions connected with these practices. Every Mukamba, whether Christian or otherwise, has a dormant or active share of these beliefs."[29]

The Akamba believe in the active presence of *Mulungu* or *Engai*, the Creator God. They fear demonic and angelic spirits and magic and sorcery.

---

28. Jenkins, "Believing in the Global South," 16.
29. Mbiti, *New Testament Eschatology in an African Background*, 9.

They look for the "living-dead" (those who have died up to three or four generations ago). They revere the *Aimu* (spirits of ancestors who have died many generations ago, whom none remember). These beliefs permeate Akamba life, language, social relations, and churches. They demand a response from Christianity—its spirituality, eschatology, and biblical interpretation.[30]

Mbiti constructs such a response. He shows the divergences and similarities between Akamban and biblical views of the spirit world:

> As the Akamba feel themselves surrounded by innumerable 'spirits' (the living-dead and the Aimu), so do the Christians with their great cloud of witnesses (Heb.12:1), angels, the Church of the firstborn, and the spirits of just men (sic) (12:22ff.). But whereas the spirit world of the Akamba is conceived physically and anthropocentrically, the N.T. view is 'spiritual' and Christocentric.[31]

Mbiti shows how Akamba Christians appropriate these understandings. They then express their Christianity responsively. Cultural and biblical views of the spiritual world enter dynamic conversation. Akamban Christians expect the spirit world described in the Bible to infuse their prayer, worship, miraculous works, and mission. This is because they've seen the nearness of the spirit world in pre-Christian Akamban culture.

Pentecostal hermeneutics is another example of supernaturalist interpretation. Pentecostalism is enormous and diverse in the Majority World.[32] Amos Yong notes that Pentecostal theology has a biblically grounded hermeneutic. Pentecostal theology has a deep respect for the authority of the Bible. It also has a reliance on the Spirit in the interpretive task. It seeks Spirit-empowered application. It expects many things to go with faithful biblical application. These include signs, miracles, wonders, hearings, manifestations, dreams, and visions.

According to Amos Yong, Pentecostal readings of Scripture have three features. They have a Lukan interpretation, a pneumatological framework, and an experiential and practical base.

Lukan interpretation. Pentecostal interpretation of Scripture is "informed explicitly by Luke-Acts." This Pentecostal hermeneutic "is animated by the conviction that the accounts in the book of Acts (especially) are not

---

30. Mbiti, *New Testament Eschatology in an African Background*, 9–10.
31. Mbiti, *New Testament Eschatology in an African Background*, 154.
32. Yong, *Spirit Poured Out on All Flesh*, 19–20.

merely of historical interest but an invitation to participate in the ongoing work of the Holy Spirit."[33]

Pneumatological framework. Pentecostal interpretation of Scripture is pneumatological. This means that it focuses on the power and presence of the Holy Spirit. It relies on God's empowering presence for ministry and theology. It seeks to rethink "traditional theological loci from the starting point of pneumatology." Pneumatology "provides the orienting dynamic for this theology, Christology provides the thematic focus."[34]

Experiential and practical base. Pentecostal interpretation of Scripture is rooted in the experience of the Holy Spirit. Conversation between theology, praxis, prayer, and spiritual experience shapes these interpretations of the Bible.

Many Majority World and Indigenous Christians identify with the spiritual world of the Bible. They expect the Spirit to act with signs and wonders. They complement their reading of Scripture with passionate prayer and spiritual hunger. They expect the Bible to open a world of supernatural revelation and Pentecostal power.

Scripture: Concluding Reflections

Typically, Christians in the Majority World are passionate about Scripture. Innovative applications often complement Conservative readings of the Bible. We can learn much from the love for Scripture in the Majority World. But these believers don't just love the Bible. They're passionate about Jesus Christ, revealed in Scripture.

Here are ten things we learn from how Majority World Christians devour and interpret Scripture.

1. The Bible must be devoured to know, love, serve, and glorify Christ.

A trend strikes me as I serve among churches in Australia, North America, Europe, and the United Kingdom. Western Christians seem to have a declining passion for memorizing, contemplating, interpreting, and applying Scripture. I find this deeply concerning. When I serve in Asia, Africa, and Latin America, I see the opposite. People are passionate about Scripture. They devour, honor, and memorize it. They interpret it contextually while

---

33. Yong, *Spirit Poured Out on All Flesh*, 27.
34. Yong, *Spirit Poured Out on All Flesh*, 28.

maintaining a conservative bias. They apply it creatively and bravely. This is instructive for those of us in the West. We need a revival in our enthusiasm for Scripture. This isn't so that we "fall in love" with Scripture. Instead, we devour Scripture to know, adore, follow, and magnify our Lord Jesus Christ.

2. The Bible must be interpreted glocally.

The local is in the global, and the global is in the local. We can't confine biblical interpretation to local contexts, ignoring global trends. Nor can we do it so that it ignores the insights and applications of local interpretive communities. Instead, we must seek to interpret Scripture *glocally*. There is a beneficial mutual exchange between local and global interpretations.

Those of us in the West must learn from the passion for Jesus Christ and his Scriptures in other cultures. We must wrestle with the church's *multi-voiced* and *multi-peopled* nature and biblical interpretation. Western cultures no longer define how Christians understand, believe, and interpret the Bible. We must put Western interpretive approaches into *a glocal* conversation as the church. This broadens and enriches the way we believe the Bible. It heralds a transformation of the church, as Christians believe and interpret the Bible in fresh ways.

It's time we acknowledged that global ethnic diversity is de-Westernizing the global church. It is de-Westernizing *glocal* biblical interpretations. This is a good thing. It enhances our understanding of Scripture as we listen to Indigenous and Majority World interpretations. We must improve at hearing and heeding the Scriptural interpretations of other cultures and Christian theological traditions. The church needs to interpret Scripture *glocally*. Let's multiply forums that enable *glocal* interpretations of the Bible and *glocal* theological constructions.

3. The Bible is to be believed, obeyed, identified with, and applied.

The Spirit of Christ is calling us to deepen our belief in the authority of Scripture. Christians need a high concept of the Bible as Scripture and the word of God. We must sincerely regard Scripture "as a locus of unquestionable truth and liberation."[35]

While we must have a high regard for the authority of Scripture, we still need to deal with questions about how we know that Scripture is

---

35. Segovia, "Emerging Project of Asian Biblical Hermeneutics," 372.

authoritative and accurate. We must tackle questions about the relationship between objectivity and subjectivity in our biblical interpretations.

I tend toward *critical realism*. N. T. Wright says that we need critical awareness as we approach Scripture and history. There's no "gods eye view . . . available to human beings." We interpret everything from the world "through a grid of expectations, memories, stories, psychological states, and so on." This is "peculiar in terms of my worldview." The way we understand the world is shaped by our belonging "to a particular human community . . . Every human community shares and cherishes certain assumptions, traditions, expectations, anxieties, and so forth, encouraging its members to construe reality in particular ways." I agree with N. T. Wright's form of *critical realism*:

> This is a way of describing the process of 'knowing' that acknowledges the *reality of thing known, as something other than the knower* (hence realism), whilst also fully acknowledging that the only access we have to this reality lies along the spiraling path of appropriate *dialogue or conversation between the knower and thing known* (hence 'critical). This path leads to critical reflection on the products of our enquiry into 'reality', so that our assertions about 'reality' acknowledge their own provisionality. Knowledge, in other words, although in principle concerning realities independent of the mid of the knower, is never itself independent of the knower.[36]

We must complement this *critical realism*—which has a high view of the authority of Scripture—with risky, innovative, and radical applications. We need to deepen our application of the Bible to everyday life. I've outlined how Majority World and Indigenous Christians do this. They apply Scripture to familial, political, postcolonial, inter-faith, and other settings. What creative applications and interpretations can you construct for your location?

As they do in the Majority World, we must reactivate our identification with the biblical text and its stories. Our cultures are often different from biblical ones. But biblical stories, images, analogies, and instructions can still speak to us in fresh and transformative ways.

---

36. Wright, *New Testament and the People of God*, 35–36.

PART 3: REVITALIZING OUR CHURCHES

4. The Bible needs to be contextualized.

Worthwhile biblical interpretation is *both* contextual and committed to the authority of Scripture. C. René Padilla claims, "A xeroxed copy of a theology made in Europe or North America can never satisfy the theological needs of the Church in the Third World. Now that the Church has become a world community, the time has come for it to manifest the universality of the Gospel in terms of a theology that is not bound by a particular culture but shows the many-sided wisdom of God."[37] But contextualization isn't enough. C. René Padilla says that contextualized biblical theology must have a high view of the authority and relevance of Scripture. It is "based *on* Biblical revelation, *in* the life context, and *for* obedience to Christ today ... The *basis* of theology is the Word of God ... The *context* of theology is the concrete historical situation ... The *purpose* of theology is obedience to Christ."[38] Such readings are faithful to Jesus Christ. They have a high regard for Scripture. We construct and apply these readings locally. We engage with the processes of *critical contextualization*.[39]

We must cultivate contextual readings in our settings. This involves asking these kinds of questions. How do we identify and nurture diverse and contextual readings of the Bible in our culture? How do we do this with a high regard for the inspiration and authority of Scripture? How do we do this within our communities and life contexts? How can these contextual readings of Scripture lead to obedience to Christ? How can they enable mission, ministry, fellowship, worship, and discipleship?

5. The Bible can be interpreted by ordinary believers in communities.

In the West, we often act as though only pastors and theologians can interpret the Bible well. Then we wonder why people don't read their Bibles! But the Bible and its interpretation aren't for the ivory tower. Ordinary believers often come up with the most creative readings and courageous applications. Churches must encourage ordinary local believers to interpret Scripture together. This involves helping them make sense of its themes and message in their context. It's empowering people to move from interpretation to formation and application. People do this best in groups, including marriages, families, ministry teams, congregations, and communities.

37. Padilla, "Contextualization of the Gospel," 28.
38. Padilla, "Contextualization of the Gospel," 28 (italics added for emphasis).
39. See Hiebert, "Critical Contextualization."

6. The Bible confronts and transforms cultures, principalities, and powers.

Are we allowing Scripture to address the issues relevant to our culture? In the Majority World, this is poverty, injustice, reconciliation, spirits, sickness, deliverance, suffering, famine, war, sexual violence, colonialism, persecution, and corruption. What are the issues in your culture? Do you need to confront ethno-religious violence, gender discrimination, rampant consumerism, or strident individualism? Or are there other issues? Why have so many Western Christians lost confidence in the transforming power of the word of God for individuals and whole nations? How will you and I access Scripture to confront and address the issues of our culture and time?

Some friends have recently protested Australia's treatment of refugees and asylum seekers. International humanitarian organizations and the United Nations have condemned Australia's behavior. As my friends read Scripture, they concluded that the Bible calls for compassion, hospitality, welcome, and justice. So, they arranged peaceful "sit-ins" at the offices of high-profile politicians. This included the office of our Prime Minister. Together, they traveled to these politician's offices. They refused to leave until the police arrested them. They asked these politicians to change our national laws. Australia must meet its international humanitarian obligations and act with mercy, compassion, and justice. Police have arrested them many times. Politicians have taken them to court. But judges refuse to charge them. Australia hasn't yet changed its laws. It hasn't reversed its offshore processing and resettlement of asylum seekers. It continues to detain vulnerable and traumatized men, women, and children in appalling conditions. It continues to resettle people in dangerous third countries where their well-being and lives are at risk. But these friends continue to protest. They believe Christ's truth and love can transform cultures, politics, principalities, and powers. As Christians, we must read and apply the Bible in ways that lead to the transformation of social and political realities. This may cost us dearly. Change may not happen quickly. But we must be strong and do the courageous and right thing.

7. The oppressed, marginal, weak, and despised understand the Bible.

This shouldn't surprise us. Majority World and Indigenous writers regularly develop this theme. The foolish things of the world shame the wise. The weak things embarrass the strong. God chooses to reveal himself in the most unlikely places. He reveals his truth to the least "deserving," least qualified, and most marginalized people. So, we must listen to the biblical interpretations of marginalized, disregarded, and silenced groups. What is the Spirit saying to us through them? How do they help us understand the truths of Scripture, the gospel, and the kingdom of God?

8. The Bible is essential in pluralist settings.

Sometimes, we're timid about biblical truth in pluralist and multi-faith settings. But we don't need to be faint-hearted. We can be *confident* in the truth of Scripture, the power of the gospel, and Christ's uniqueness, even in pluralist settings. Such conviction doesn't preclude dialogue. Dialogue can enhance our assurance.

David Bosch, writing from the South African context, discusses three interfaith approaches. These are exclusivism, relativism, and Christianity as the fulfillment of other religions. He dismisses these three. Bosch calls for Christians to dialogue with other religions.

What commitments must we make to do this well? David Bosch maps these out for us.[40] We need to be confident in the gospel and the truth in Scripture. We need a willing acceptance of religious coexistence and pluralism. We must be open to dialogue, which we root in a confident and deep commitment to the gospel of Jesus Christ. We should desire to see where God is already working in other cultures, convictions, and religions. We need a commitment to conducting dialogue with humility and grace. We must recognize the diversity of religions and within religions. (The Christian gospel relates differently to Islam, Buddhism, Hinduism, and groups within those religions.)

We also need a passion for missions. "Dialogue is neither a substitute nor a subterfuge for mission . . . They are neither to be viewed as identical nor irrevocably opposed to each other." (The same is true of biblical interpretation. Such interpretation must always serve the mission of God.) But we must focus our dialogue on more than "eternal salvation." It must have a vision of lives and communities transformed with Jesus Christ as its center and Lord. It must lead to "cleansing, forgiveness, reconciliation, and renewal to participate in the mighty works of God."[41]

Finally, we must be willing to wrestle with the tension between mission and dialogue. There's a tension between the uniqueness of Jesus Christ and his presence in other religions and the world.

---

40. Bosch, *Transforming Mission*, 474–89.
41. Bosch, *Transforming Mission*, 483 and 489.

Bosch expresses the heart of an emerging Christian missional perspective. The debate over the relationship between Bible interpretation, mission, and dialogue will remain heated. But many Majority World thinkers are helping the global church navigate this critical relationship. We must elevate Scripture whenever we enter dialogue with other faiths. We must be confident in its truth and power. *Critical realism* helps us be humble and willing to learn. The Bible is fundamental to Christian faith and apologetics in pluralist cultures.

9. The Bible must be interpreted in communities.

Westerners tend to read and interpret the Bible individualistically. Individual devotion and spiritual discipline are good. But there's greater transforming power in communal reading and interpretation and application. Community magnifies the power of Scripture to change lives. Community amplifies our ability to understand, contextualize, and proclaim Scripture. As the analogy goes, taking coal out of the fire quickly makes the coal go cold. But if you leave it in with the other red-hot coals and continue throwing fuel on it, watch it blaze! Our discipleship is the same. To burn red hot for Christ, we need others and fuel. We must saturate our Bible reading and application in corporate prayer, worship, and mission.

10. The Bible needs to be read and applied with spiritual expectation.

When you and I read and apply the Bible, do we do so in a spirit of expectation? Majority World and Indigenous readers do. God reveals Godself, transforms lives, and overcomes evil with good and darkness with light. God heals, forgives, liberates, and transforms. We should read Scripture expecting to experience the Holy Spirit's power, presence, provision, and protection.

PART 3: REVITALIZING OUR CHURCHES

Study Questions

1. How are you developing your love for the Bible? Are you growing in your trust in its authority and relevance? Are you being obedient to its commands? Do you understand its content in and for your context?

2. How can you apply Bible reading to your life, relationships, service, and mission?

3. How can churches teach Christians to love and trust the Scriptures and the Christ they reveal? How can churches help people interpret Scripture for themselves?

4. What does it mean for your congregation to develop contextualized readings of Scripture? How can your congregation read Scripture in and for your context?

5. Is your congregation reading Scripture missionally, and are you? How are you perceiving and responding to the missional themes and narratives of Scripture?

6. How is Scripture shaping your understanding and practice of mission?

18.

Renewing Education

The Tenth Expression

SINCE 2004, THE ARAB Baptist Theological Seminary in Lebanon has been running Middle East Consultations "to equip the church to live Christ-like witness amid the complex realities of ministry in and beyond Middle Eastern contexts." The 2023 consultation is called "My Peace I Give You: Practicing Peacemaking in the Middle East." Many Christians keep their heads down when there is political conflict. But this seminary has decided to innovate in theological education that addresses politics, conflict, refugees, peacemaking, interreligious dialogue, reconciliation, and more. The Arab Baptist Theological Seminary makes a valuable contribution in the Middle East for Jesus and the gospel values of reconciliation, mercy, righteousness, peacemaking, justice, and hope.

In 2009, ABTS launched a new curriculum focusing on formation through multidimensional learning. The curriculum integrates four main areas during three years of study. The areas are biblical, historical-theological, sociological-cultural, and personal-ministerial. This culminates in an integrative project.[1]

The ABTS integrative model embraces critical values. They value authentic worship, missional church, Christ-like leadership, empowerment, reflective practice, community cohesion, and personal and spiritual

---

1. See details and diagrams on the Arab Baptist Theological Seminary website: http://www.abtslebanon.org.

development. This model has been so successful that ten other Majority World seminaries are now following suit. Once these ten seminaries have done this, the plan is to roll out this model to another two hundred seminaries in the Majority World (in a contextualized way).[2]

This is just one example of contextualized and creative theological education in the Majority World. Theological and ministry education has expanded in many parts of the Majority World. We see this all over Africa, Asia, Latin America, and the Pacific. However, theological education also faces challenges.

Southeast Asia is an example of the growth and challenges for theological education in the Majority World. The Association for Theological Education in Southeast Asia (ATESEA) was established in 1957. It began with sixteen Protestant schools. "ATESEA was the first formal regional association of theological schools in the non-Western world. Today, it is the largest theological education association outside North America."[3] Based in Manila, the Philippines, ATESEA has 102 member institutions and schools in sixteen countries. It has more than twenty thousand students and 1,500 faculty members. These institutions are evangelical, Pentecostal, and Adventist. Twenty-six institutions are in the Philippines, seventeen in Indonesia, and seventeen in Myanmar.[4]

But it is not all good news or smooth sailing. Dietrich Werner writes of the challenges and prospects facing theological education in Asia. These are many. There is an "unequal allocation of resources" and "unbalanced accessibility to theological education." There are discrepancies between standards in "different national contexts and regions within Asia." There's "the unfinished work of contextualizing theological education in Asia." Seminaries are still not good at relating theological education to today's multi-religious Asian setting. There's the need to overcome "the ecumenical/evangelical divide" and explore "possibilities for state recognition." Seminaries face increasing "public visibility" and scrutiny. There's the need to ensure quality in standards and delivery and to strengthen theological associations. The challenge is "deepening the movement to do theology with Asian resources."[5]

Similarly, Huang Po Ho writes of the rapid growth of theological education in Asia over the last fifty years. For Ho, the challenges reside in quality

---

2. Shaw, *Transforming Theological Education*, 95.

3. Anderson, "Developments in Theological Education in Southeast Asia," 96.

4. I discuss the *Critical Asian Principle* (CAP) and the *Guidelines for Doing Theology in Asia* later in this chapter.

5. Werner, "Memorandum on the Future of Theological Education in Asia," 209–22.

control and contextualization. There are also challenges for curriculum renewal and faculty development. Asian education must grapple with rapidly changing Asian cultures. It must deal with globalization and unpredictable political systems. It needs to cultivate association and networking. It needs to foster organizational health. Not least, Asian theological colleges grapple with churches' and denominations' expectations, needs, and demands.[6]

This chapter considers the nature of Majority World theological education. It is multidimensional: contextual, grassroots, postcolonial, liberating, engendered, missional, transformational, Spirit-empowered, and biblically focused. It equips people practically for ministry and mission. I explore these themes in Majority World theological education in that order.

Contextual and Intercontextual Education

Western churches can learn much from theological education in the Majority World. Contextualization is a clear example. Majority World institutions believe in the contextualization of curriculum and delivery and methods. This includes accountability and dialogue with students in contextualization processes. Students need tools for diagnosing their societal and contextual needs. They also need opportunities to plan the best integration of theory and practice to address those needs. This includes forums to check their progress in missional and ministry skills. Training bodies must show reciprocal, democratic, enabling, and participatory leadership styles. This way, graduates can reflect such a style in their future ministries.

Majority World theologians have long advocated for contextualized churches and missions. They've called for contextual approaches to theology and theological education.[7] Contextualization can carry many nuances of meaning. There is more than one model of contextualization. The meanings we assign depend on our theological tradition and cultural background.[8]

Tite Tiénou writes about the contextualization of theology. "Contextualization is the inner dynamic of the theologizing process. It is not a matter of borrowing existing forms or an established theology to fit them into various contexts. Rather, contextualization is capturing the meaning of the gospel in such a way that a given society communicates with God.

---

6. Ho, "Theological Education in the Changing Societies of Asia," 6–13.
7. Padilla, "Contextualization of the Gospel," 30.
8. Moreau, *Contextualization in World Missions*.

Therein theology is born."[9] Tite Tiénou and Shoki Coe argue that we must contextualize theology *and* theological education.[10]

How does contextualization express itself in the Majority World? An example from Asia illustrates this. ATESEA member seminaries developed the Critical Asian Principle (CAP). They also formed "Guidelines for Doing Theology in Asia." The CAP uses "the common spiritual and socio-economic context of Southeast Asian countries as the point of reference for biblical reflection and theologizing." These seminaries developed critical principles for doing Asian theology. These principles engaged Asian contexts, interpretations, missions, and education.

ATESEA seminaries then developed "Guidelines for Doing Theology in Asia." These Guidelines grew in response to the many challenges facing the region. These challenges include religious fundamentalism, gender issues, ecological problems, and natural disasters. The region is also coming to terms with globalization and colonization. One must not forget the Asian search for spirituality, meaning, and identity. The region deals with political upheavals, power struggles, and contextual issues. So, these Asians formed guidelines for doing theology in Asia, with its opportunities and challenges.

The guidelines call for Asians to contextualize Asian theological education so that it does the following. It promotes "responsive engagement with the diverse Asian contexts." It fosters "critical engagement with Indigenous cultures and wisdom for preserving and sustaining life." It encourages "reflective engagement with the sufferings of the Asian people to provide hope for the marginalized, women, Indigenous people, children, differently-abled people, and migrant workers." It challenges students to "restore the inter-connectedness of the whole creation." It nurtures "interfaith dialogue as well as intra-faith communion and communication for the fullness of life and the well-being of the society." It enhances "capacity building to serve people experiencing disaster, conflict, and disease as well as those suffering physical, emotional, and mental disabilities." It inspires "prophetic resistance against the powers of economic imperialism." It equips "Christians for witnessing and spreading the gospel of Jesus with loving care and service to fulfill the Christian mission of evangelism."[11]

---

9. Tienou, "Contextualization of Theology for Theological Education," 51.

10. Coe, "Contextualizing Theology," 22.

11. Association for Theological Education in Southeast Asia, "Guidelines for Doing Theology in Asia."

Grassroots Education

Evaluations of traditional, extractional forms of theological education are common in the Majority World. Ross Kinsler researches educational trends in those cultures. He has identified six reasons why many people in those cultures are reassessing traditional, residential models of ministry training.[12]

Theological

"What is the ministry?" Traditional theological education may create an unhealthy distinction between graduates and congregations.[13] The gifts and talents within congregations are then poorly developed and used. This is because people form a dependency on professional ministers. Missiology is often marginalized in the curriculum. Before long, there is little evidence "that mission is the mother of theology."[14]

Historical

"Can the people participate fully in theological study and ministry?" Viewed historically, traditional forms of theological education equip people poorly for mission. They don't often provide effective practical or theological training for missional contexts. Students become consumed with their studies and academic commitments. They often don't have the time to apply what they are learning. Residential seminaries often extract critical leaders from their local churches and missional contexts. This model reduces local discipleship, mission, ministry, and church planting.

Sociological

"Who are the leaders?" Traditional theological institutions often select young people who haven't proven themselves in society. They place them in artificial academic and spiritual surroundings. These settings are rarely missional or local. Residential seminaries exclude them from the normal

---

12. Kinsler, *The Extension Movement in Theological Education*. I'm summarizing Kinsler in these six points—I don't share all his opinions.

13. Kinsler, *Extension Movement*, 4.

14. Kähler, *Schriften Zu Christologie Und Mission*, 189; Bosch, *Transforming Mission*, 489.

Indigenous leadership development and selection processes. After graduation, denominations often place these young people in authority over their elders and contemporaries. Local apprenticeship training models are often more helpful for ministry and missional formation.

Educational

"How can leaders be trained?" Both secular and theological educational institutions often create elite groups within cultures. These institutions may not integrate theory and practice in leadership development. Such integration is critical in the formation of missional church leaders. Technical competencies are often taught instead of necessary ministry and missional skills. Seminaries and teachers need to redesign their curriculum. They must emphasize the integration of theory and practice. Curriculum and methods need a missional focus. They must develop missional leaders for congregations in pluralistic cultures.

Financial

"What kind of theological education can we afford?" The church needs to use its financial resources wisely. This is especially true in poorer cultures. When it comes to finances, do extractional residential colleges make sense? Do educational programs based in local churches make more financial sense? Professional graduates from seminaries often demand higher salaries. They expect full-time ministry positions that average congregations have difficulty affording. The movement from "pedagogue to professional" hasn't helped the church's mission. This professionalization of ministry is hurting the church in the West and the Majority World. We must return to grassroots, more affordable ministry training models.[15] Training for bivocational ministry will become more critical and valuable.

Missional

"What are the goals of our training programs?" Theological education must serve the mission of God. It must enable the church to meet its missional mandate. It must develop a passion for mission and ministry within students. Traditional theological institutions are often too introverted to pursue this goal. Denominational seminaries often foster competition,

---

15. Guder and Barrett, *Missional Church*, 194–95.

criticism, and rivalry between denominations. To help rectify this, theological education must partner with local churches. It must collaborate with grassroots missional initiatives. It must place the mission of God at the center of everything it does—curriculum, methods, and goals. Pastors, churches, and missional leaders should collaborate with seminaries in shaping and delivering training.

Ross Kinsler builds an argument for grassroots ministry education. He draws on case studies from Africa, Asia, Latin America, and the West. Kinsler advocates *Theological Education by Extension* (TEE). He champions *Diversified Theological Education* (DTE). TEE is a decentralized, church-based form of theological and ministry education. DTE seeks to bridge the gap between TEE and traditional, residential theological education. DTE emphasizes a diversity "of methods, models, and concepts of theological education." DTE doesn't just focus on one approach to training. It often combines "centralized and decentralized elements."[16] It acknowledges this global diversity in theological education. But it is especially interested in developments in the Majority World.

Some criticize TEE. They're critical of the quality of curriculum and educators. They question whether it is sufficiently contextualized, administered, and funded. Yet, forms of TEE now operate in Africa, Asia, and Latin America. TEE is also popular in the Pacific, Eastern Europe, and among Indigenous peoples. DTE is more flexible and difficult to define and is a global phenomenon. It will only expand as theological education becomes increasingly diverse and multidimensional.

Grassroots theological education is broader than TEE. Hence, Kangwa Mabuluki says TEE is a form of DTE. He says that grassroots theological education needs to maintain academic standards and foster deep contextualization. It needs accreditation and oversight. It must collaborate between diverse models. It needs to be aware of gender issues. It should use technologies cleverly. Grassroots theological education must shape the head, heart, and hands. It must be owned and sustained by local churches.[17]

The global church needs to be a learning community. It needs to be one characterized by grassroots participation and global dialogue. TEE and DTE offer clues about the shape of a local-global (glocal) learning community.

---

16. Kinsler, *Diversified Theological Education*, 2.
17. Mabuluki, "Diversified Theological Education," 251–62.

PART 3: REVITALIZING OUR CHURCHES

Postcolonial and Liberating Education

Postcolonial and liberationist concerns are growing in theological education in the Majority World. These are concerns for the liberation and education of people experiencing poverty. The powerless, oppressed, voiceless, marginalized, and colonized need freedom and education.

Postcolonialism is hard to define. It is an evolving field of research. It is the study of how humans dominate and control each other. It also studies how we experience and respond to this oppression. Colonizing forces oppress others because of their race, gender, class, age, poverty, religion, and sexuality. Postcolonialism is a conversation arising from the abusive behavior of colonialism. It is a conversation that now influences learning all over the globe.

Namsoon King notes that old binaries of "oppressor-oppressed," "victimizer-victimized," or "colonizer-colonized" are redundant. They're no longer accepted in postcolonial theory or theology. Postcolonial theology doesn't depose the "West-as-center" and set up the "Majority-World-as-center." Such binaries are expressions of the "politics of domination." They express colonialism's oppressive core. All cultures should be self-critical. King says there isn't just a "colonialism-out-there." There's also a "colonialism-in-here." One can be the oppressor and the oppressed at the same time.[18]

This means that postcolonial theology is a discourse of resistance and liberation. As a *discourse of resistance*, it resists oppressive and dominating structures and relationships. As a *discourse of liberation*, it seeks to liberate people from such experiences. It tries to free them from the mentalities, systems, and practices that support subjugation.[19]

Postcolonial theological education resists perspectives and practices that promote control and domination. How do power relations work in our institutions? How do our seminaries "colonize" people based on race, gender, knowledge, disability, education, medical condition, class, theology, language, and so on? Are we resisting such attitudes and actions? Are we practicing opposite, liberating behaviors?

---

18. Kang, "Envisioning Postcolonial Theological Education," 33.
19. Kang, "Envisioning Postcolonial Theological Education," 34.

Equal Education

Men tend to fill most pastoral ministries. This is true in Western, Indigenous, and Majority World settings. Given the cultural, historical, and theological influences, this shouldn't surprise us.

The Hartford Institute for Religion Research reports that a third of all seminary students in the US are women. The percentage of women entering seminary and ministry is increasing. But women tend to drop out of seminary in their last year. They do this when they realize how difficult it is to secure pastoral positions. Women also find it hard to get senior positions.[20] African-American, Asian, Hispanic, Latino, Indigenous, and First Nation women face even more significant hurdles.

Majority World contexts tend to be conservative. This conservatism extends to biblical interpretation, societal expectations, and gender roles. In the West, women face more significant challenges than men when entering seminary and ministry. This varies between Majority World cultures, depending on cultural, historical, and theological factors. Gender inequality is a significant issue in many parts of the Majority World.

Some seminaries and educators are seeking to address this inequality. Beverley Haddad writes from the South African context. She argues for the transformation of theological education to be relevant to women's lives. This can only happen when poor and marginalized women collaborate in that transformation.

Gender equality must be a value and an organizational goal. This is as true in the West as in Majority World and Indigenous settings. Discussions about gender are not discussions about "women's issues." They are about men and women. It's about both genders and how they relate to each other, the church, and the world. These discussions must move from the margins to the center. They need to move from the few to the mainstream. This is true regardless of our position on women in ministry.

Haddad notes the links between gender and poverty in Africa. She argues that theological education plays a role in delinking these realities. Theological education must become just and equal. "The role that gender plays in the transformation process should not be an afterthought to transformation but lies at the heart of the process."[21]

---

20. Hartford Institute for Religion Research, "Fast facts about American Religion."
21. Haddad, "Engendering Theological Education for Transformation," 65–66.

PART 3: REVITALIZING OUR CHURCHES

Missional and Transformational Education

Mission and transformation are significant themes in Majority World theology and practice. Theological education reflects this. Western theology and theological education can learn much from these emphases.

By *missional*, I mean education that prioritizes the missional nature of God and church and ministry. It equips leaders and churches to take part in the mission of God. Missional education teaches mission theory and practice. It forms people *in* and *for* and *through* mission. It shapes its curriculum around missional theology and practices. It teaches people to interpret and apply Scripture through a missional paradigm.

By *transformational*, I mean education that transforms individuals, churches, families, and cultures. Transformational education is about

> the change from the condition of human existence contrary to God's purpose to one in which people can enjoy fullness in harmony with God (John 10:10; Col. 3:8–15; Eph. 4:13). This transformation can only take place through the obedience of individuals and communities to the gospel of Jesus Christ, whose power changes the lives of men and women by releasing them from guilt, power, and consequences of sin, enabling them to respond with love toward God and towards others (Rom. 5:5), and making them 'new creatures in Christ' (2 Cor. 5:17).[22]

Theological education that is missional and transformational focuses on the mission of God. Such education pursues *transformational mission*. It seeks stewardship of creation, equality between human beings, and reconciliation of peoples. It pursues social justice and mercy. It equips people to lead socio-economic, political, and spiritual freedom. It values the mission and transformation at the heart of the gospel of Jesus Christ.

In 2010, the *Third Lausanne Congress on World Evangelization* brought together 4,200 leaders from 198 countries. They met in Cape Town, South Africa. The *Cape Town Commitment* was the fruit of that gathering. Here is what they declared about the missional nature of theological education:

> The mission of the church on earth is to serve the mission of God, and the mission of theological education is to strengthen and accompany the mission of the church...

Those of us who lead churches and mission agencies need to acknowledge that theological education is intrinsically missional. Those of us who provide theological education need to ensure that it is intentionally missional,

---

22. Samuel and Sugden, *Church in Response to Human Need*, xi.

since its place within the academy is not an end, but to serve the mission of the church in the world . . .

Theological education stands in partnership with all forms of missional engagement. We will encourage and support all who provide biblically faithful theological education, formal and non-formal, at local, national, regional and international levels . . .

> We urge that institutions and programs of theological education conduct a 'missional audit' of their curricula, structures, and ethos to ensure that they truly serve the needs and opportunities facing the church in their cultures.[23]

Writing from South Africa, Steve de Gruchy says theological education requires missional practice. Mission needs theological education. Missional practice orients theological education toward the world. It focuses education on the mission of God. It provides theological education with a direction and purpose. It aligns such education with God's redemptive purposes. It forces theological reflection into engaged practice. Such practices enrich theology, the church, and the world. Missional practice demands theology be interdisciplinary.

Conversely, theological education ensures that missional practice is reflective and self-critical. It emphasizes the importance of a robust theology of the mission of God. Theological education recognizes the role of various doctrines in the mission of God and the church. These include our theologies of the *missio Dei* and the *missiones ecclesia*. Trinitarian theology is another example. Theological education deconstructs colonial missionary legacies. Finally, when seminaries do theological education well, it's an example of missional vitality. Students take part in local missions and efforts to transform groups. Mission, ministry, societal engagement, and theological education go hand in hand. Theological education must "assist the missional practice of the church to stay on the cutting edge of what God is doing in the world."[24]

Tite Tiénou, Samuel Escobar, and Ken Gnanakan write about missional and transformational emphases in theological education. They're writing from African, Latin American, and Asian perspectives. They suggest that such education has specific characteristics.[25] I summarize their ideas here

---

23. Lausanne, "Cape Town Commitment."

24. De Gruchy, "Theological Education and Missional Practice," 50.

25. Tienou, "Training of Missiologists for an African Context"; Escobar, "Training of Missiologists for a Latin American Context"; Gnanakan, "Training of Missiologists for Asian Contexts."

and add a few of my own. In the final chapter, I explore holisticostal theological education further.

Biblical

It is faithful to Scripture. It values the missional themes running through the entire biblical narrative.

Contextual

It develops a language, curriculum, and method for mission and theology that is local, contextual, and Indigenous. It trains people for mission and ministry within their context.

Transformational

It prepares people for their contexts' moral, spiritual, political, and economic transformation. It promotes transformation through the liberation offered in the gospel. It values active participation in social, political, ecclesial, and economic arenas.

Holistic

It develops the whole person for a transformational mission. This includes the *head* (theological and theoretical knowledge). It incorporates the *heart* (character and spirituality). It skills the *hands* (competencies).

Spiritual

It cultivates a spirituality that sustains mission and transformational leadership.

Reflective-practice

It trains people for reflective practice. It uses an action-reflection model of training.

Theological

It ensures theological reflections are critical and systematic. This includes reflection on Scripture, history, context, culture, classics, and social sciences.

Integrative

It encourages an integrative learning environment. Students engage in interdisciplinary study and spiritual formation. They develop competencies through praxis and academic rigor. They learn through public engagement, serving in churches, and missional activities.

Mobilized

It mobilizes people for mission, ministry, and transformational leadership. It equips for service inside and outside the church. It mobilizes all the ministry gifts. It develops the apostolic, prophetic, evangelistic, teaching, and pastoral gifts. It shapes and releases many other types of gifts.

Multidimensional

It has a diverse set of characteristics that help missional reflection and formation. These include but aren't limited to (1) action reflection learning; (2) decentered and missionally focused training; (3) postcolonial and trinitarian theology; (4) conversational and dialogical approaches; (5) discernment in seminary and church and local community, and (6) high-trust, low-control models of leadership.

Engaging

It takes engagement seriously. This includes engagement with pluralism, globalization, other religions, and new religious movements. It involves wrestling with colonialism, post-colonialism, and secular humanism.

Purposeful

It shapes curriculum, methods, and goals around the gospel. It shapes its educational approaches and values around God's mission. It's purposeful in its role in social transformation.

Interpretative

It teaches a missional reading of Scripture.

Formational and Praxeological

It forms students with focused attention to missional and transformational practices.

Spirit-Empowered Education

The growth of Pentecostalism in the Majority World, and globally, has been astonishing. Some put the number of Pentecostals and charismatics between 500 and 600 million. A large percentage of these are in the Majority World.

Pentecostal-charismatic and neo-Pentecostal groups emphasize Spirit-empowered ministry education. The breadth of the terms *Pentecostal-charismatic* and *neo-Pentecostal* show the diversity of Pentecostal groups—David Barrett and Todd Johnson catalog twelve general forms of Pentecostalism.[26]

Wonsuk Ma has written a book chapter on "Theological Education in Pentecostal Churches in Asia." Ma studies the growth of Pentecostal and charismatic churches in Asia. He focuses on South Korea, the Philippines, Malaysia, Singapore, and India. He then describes how theological education has developed in those contexts. Expanding such education relates to the growth of Pentecostal and charismatic groups. Ma says that in Asia, "Pentecostals began training programs for church work from the start of their missionary operation, and these schools have been the main contribution to the growth of the Pentecostal church."[27]

The West has much to learn from such Pentecostal and charismatic learning communities. Wonsuk Ma claims that Pentecostal and charismatic

---

26. Barrett et al., *World Christian Encyclopedia*.
27. Ma, "Theological Education in Pentecostal Churches in Asia," 733.

theological education is missional, pneumatological, democratized, mobilized, educational, networked, and adaptational.

> *Missional.* It dedicates its training to the mission of God. It seeks the transformation of society. It values the missional health and expansion of the church.
>
> *Pneumatological.* It values the ways the Holy Spirit empowers men and women for ministry.
>
> *Democratized and mobilized.* It mobilizes the whole church for mission and ministry. This includes laity, church planters, pastors, and missionaries.
>
> *Educational.* It helps people access education and develop advanced critical and research competencies. It allows disadvantaged persons and communities to access education.
>
> *Networked.* It provides students, faculty, and Christian leaders with opportunities to build strong connections. It facilitates beneficial exchanges with other parts of the Majority World. Theological consortiums have an essential role.
>
> *Adaptational.* Wonsuk Ma says these Pentecostal and charismatic churches and seminaries face challenges. They must adapt. These challenges include relevance to modernizing cultures and globalization and its implications. They accept the potential distance between academic programs and societal needs. They deal with heresies and divisions. They teach future leaders to embrace biblical servant leadership (rejecting authoritarian leadership). They shape new missional models for contemporary cultural challenges. They cultivate a vital public witness.

Renewing Theological Education: Concluding Reflections

What's the future of theological education and ministry training in the West? What's its future in Indigenous cultures and the Majority World? How will this education adapt to rapidly changing cultures?

This chapter offered reflections on theological education in the Majority World. It considered what the West could learn from such education. The Majority World can help Western educational institutions become learning communities. It can show us how to shape education characterized

PART 3: REVITALIZING OUR CHURCHES

by contextualization, grassroots participation, missional vitality, ministry competency, and deep spirituality.

Here are seventeen things we learn from how Majority World Christians are renewing theological and ministry education.

1. Renewed education is Christ-centered, gospel-focused, biblically grounded.

It's easy for us to focus on secondary issues in theological education. Teaching methodologies and academic programs grab our attention. Staff shortages and limited finances weigh on our shoulders. We spend time designing the curriculum, allocating resources, and marking papers. We worry about government legislation and student numbers. We're concerned about keeping denominations and churches happy and about getting accredited. Many secondary issues demand attention in our classes. For instance, do I use a psychotherapeutic, managerial, pastoral, or other paradigm when I teach pastoral studies? Theological educators manage competing roles. They are teachers, administrators, pastors, researchers, writers, public speakers, and leaders in local churches.

All these things are essential. But they can distract us from our primary purpose. As theological educators, we often get bogged down in all this. But we must stay focused on the main thing—forming women and men as disciples of Jesus Christ and shaping them to love and serve Jesus, his church, and his world.

Our training must be Christ-centered, gospel-focused, and biblically grounded to do discipleship well. Everything we do must glorify Christ. We must ensure that we place Jesus Christ and his gospel at the center of our teaching, formation, research, writing, and everything else we do. We place Scripture at the heart of our theological education and ministry training. We evaluate our training and formation through the lens of Scripture. We teach students to be disciples of Jesus who read, interpret, and communicate Scripture accurately, contextually, skillfully, and clearly.

2. Renewed education equips the whole believer to take the whole gospel to the whole world.

The Lausanne Theology Working Group brought together sixty people from all continents to consider the three themes of the Lausanne slogan, "the whole church taking the whole gospel to the whole world." You can find an excellent outline of their conclusions at http://www.lausanne.org.

I served as the Vice-Principal of Morling Baptist Theological College in Sydney for many years. Listening closely to this global conversation, Morling aims to "equip the whole believer to take the whole gospel to the whole world."[28] Morling pursues this aim through eight strategic objectives. We mobilize people for mission and ministry. We cultivate discipleship and personal and spiritual formation. We pursue excellence and innovation in education and research. We foster community. We facilitate worldview engagement. We provide ongoing training to pastors, missionaries, and people serving outside ministry roles. We support and resource congregations, pastors, and Christian organizations. We collaborate with like-minded bodies.

I'm confident that "equipping the whole believer to take the whole gospel to the whole world" begins with our values. While I was at Morling, we spent much time pondering what these values must be. We concluded that they should be fivefold: transformational discipleship, unity in diversity, evangelical conviction, missional focus, and educational excellence.

Here's how we described these values at Morling College:

Believers who take the whole gospel to the whole world must pursue *transformational discipleship*. We long to be people who love God with all our heart and soul and mind and strength. So, we will balance academic study, practical training, and spiritual formation. We know that such integration transforms us as whole persons.

Believers who take the whole gospel to the whole world must foster *unity in diversity*. We welcome a diversity of theological opinions and ministry practice on secondary issues. We do this within a framework of shared evangelical conviction. We delight in our college community's diversity of cultures, backgrounds, and gifts. We seek to give practical expression to the unity we have in Christ.

Believers who take the whole gospel to the whole world must embrace *evangelical conviction*. We are committed to the centrality of the gospel of Jesus Christ in the life and mission of the church, in prayerful dependence on the power of the Spirit, to the glory of God. We gladly submit to the authority of Scripture as God's authoritative word. We seek to honor the trustworthiness of God's Word in our teaching. We aim to combine intellectual rigor and integrity with a humble and gracious orthodoxy.

Believers who take the whole gospel to the whole world must commit to *a missional focus*. We aim to equip men and women to take the whole gospel to the whole world with vision, courage, wisdom, and creativity. We

---

28. Morling College, "Mission, Values, and Statement of Beliefs."

recognize the crucial importance of both evangelistic proclamation and active social concern. We affirm the centrality of the church within the purposes of God for the world. We train pastors, teachers, and evangelists to serve the church and its mission worldwide.

Believers who take the whole gospel to the whole world must seek training in a context of *educational excellence*. We are committed to advancing knowledge and understanding through dedicated involvement in scholarly activities. We enable individuals to grow and learn through personal and character formation and the enhancement of life-long learning. We are committed to quality education and the professional formation of students. We value professional development, ministry training, missional equipping, and academic contribution.

"Equipping the whole believer to take the whole gospel to the whole world" requires us to develop clear values and strategies. I encourage you to develop those that are suitable for your setting.

3. Renewed education develops learning communities.

Students and educators pursue learning together. Lecturers may have more knowledge in a particular area. But it isn't that some are "experts" and others "novices." Instead, theological education happens best in learning communities. This kind of education is experiential, participatory, interactive, and communal. Together, we explore faith and theology and curriculum and mission and ministry. Together, we shape learning communities characterized by contextual theology, *glocal* conversations, and grassroots participation. This is a move from hierarchy to equality. It's a change from monological transmission of information to participatory learning. It's a shift from mere intellectual stimulation to the formation of whole persons in life and community. Learning communities focus on the formation of the whole person in the whole community. They do this to equip whole believers to take the gospel to the whole world. Learning communities build shared educational experiences. They invite contributions by educators, students, families, churches, and others. Learning communities consult with students, churches, educationalists, and pastors when shaping and evaluating curriculum and methods. They foster emotional authenticity, interpersonal connection, active teaming, spiritual depth, community vitality, and interaction between students and educators.

4. Renewed education grows through glocal conversations.

I've described *glocalization* and *glocal* theology in another chapter. The best kind of theological education introduces students to *glocal* conversations. It expands their worldview beyond Western theologies and personalities. It introduces students to theological themes, ministry models, and missional experiments in Majority World and Indigenous settings. It invites students to put their local, contextual experiences and theology into conversation with global voices. It teaches students the value of *glocal*. It trains them to hear and cultivate *glocal* conversations.

5. Renewed education shapes its vision ministry training around Scripture.

I've noted that Majority World contexts usually practice conservative biblical interpretation. They carry this into their expectations for ministerial education and practice. A conservative reading of Scripture informs their approaches and expectations.

Majority World churches expect their pastoral leaders to be above reproach. Theological institutions in the Majority World pay careful attention to Scripture in pastoral formation. Key texts include Matt 5:1–12, 6:33, and 10:26–33; Mark 10:35–45; Acts 20:17–35; Rom 12:1–13; 1 Cor 12–13; 2 Cor 4–5; Gal 5:16–26; Eph 4:1–16; Phil 3:7–17; Col 1:28–29; 1 Tim 3–4; Titus 1; 1 Pet 5:1–11; and Jude 20–23.

Here are some pastoral qualities sourced from these passages. They are exemplary rather than exhaustive. They surface repeatedly in Majority World writings. They are often the goals of Majority World ministry education. They inform their aims in ministry training, and they must inform ours, too. These may feel like a random group of exhortations. But they are biblical instructions for Christian leaders, and they must shape our ministry training and formation.

So, what does Scripture say to graduates and colleges that engage in their formation? Be poor in spirit and willing to mourn or be persecuted for righteousness sake. Be merciful, meek, and pure of heart. Be peacemakers who hunger and thirst after righteousness. Seek first the kingdom and God's righteousness. Boldly and fearlessly proclaim the gospel. Demonstrate the characteristics and qualities of a servant. Serve the Lord with humility. Faithfully proclaim the gospel. Obey God's leading. Consider one's life worth nothing save obedience to Christ. Keep watch over oneself and the flock as faithful shepherds. Offer one's body as a living sacrifice. Be transformed by the renewing of the mind. Use one's gifts enthusiastically. Never lack in zeal. Keep one's spiritual hunger. Serve the Lord. Honor all members of the Body of Christ and their unique spiritual gifts. Demonstrate the qualities of divine love. Set forth the truth plainly. Preach the Lord Jesus Christ. Persevere under trials. Fix one's eyes on what is unseen and eternal. Live by faith, not by sight. Make it one's goal to please the Lord because of his return. Commit to the ministry and the message of reconciliation through Christ Jesus. Live by the Spirit rather than gratifying the desires of the sinful nature. Demonstrate the fruit of the Spirit—love, joy, peace, patience, kindness, goodness, faithfulness, gentleness, and self-control.

Other biblical exhortations are essential as we design ministry training that emphasizes formation. Here are some examples. Crucify the sinful nature with its passions and desires. Live by the Spirit while keeping in step with him. Live a life worthy of God's call. Be humble, gentle, and patient. Maintain unity in the church. Humbly use one's gifts and ministry to prepare God's people for works of service. Build up the Body of Christ toward maturity and the whole measure of the fullness of Christ. Speak the truth in love, with a view to the whole body growing into Christ. Consider everything loss compared to the surpassing greatness of knowing Christ, for whose sake you have lost all things. Seek to be found in Christ. Have a righteousness that comes by faith. Strive to know Christ and the power of his resurrection, the fellowship of sharing in his sufferings, becoming like him in his death, attaining the resurrection from the dead. Press on to take hold of that for which Christ Jesus took hold of you. Forget what is behind. Strain toward what is ahead. Press on toward the goal to win the prize for which God has called you in Christ. Follow the example and pattern of those who have exemplified this life.

What other biblical qualities and competencies should our ministry graduates show? They should proclaim Christ. Admonish and teach with all wisdom to present everyone perfect in Christ. Struggle with all Christ's energy, which so powerfully works in you. Be above reproach, faithful in marriage, and exemplify an honorable family life. Be temperate, self-controlled, respectable, hospitable, able to teach, and not given to drunkenness. Don't be violent, but be gentle. Don't be quarrelsome. Don't be a lover of money. Have a good reputation in the world. Keep hold of the gospel with a clear conscience. Hold firmly to and teach consistently the truth of the gospel. Train oneself in godliness. Set an example in speech, life, love, faith, and purity. Faithfully serve through one's spiritual gifts. Watch your life and doctrine closely. Be blameless. Don't be quick-tempered, drunk, violent, or a pursuer of dishonest gain. Be hospitable. Love what is good. Be self-controlled, upright, holy, disciplined, and gospel-focused. Be a shepherd who is eager to serve and self-controlled. Resist the devil. Stand firm in the faith. Be an example to the flock, a servant leader, and clothed with humility. Build yourself up in your most holy faith. Pray in the Holy Spirit. Practice mercy. Be passionate about the gospel and salvation. Hate sin.

As we seek to form hearts, hands, and heads, these biblical instructions to Christian leaders must play a pivotal role.

6. Renewed education forms hearts, hands, and heads. Theological education must be student-focused, not student-led.

Student-focused education is a formative process. Theological educators must shape student-focused learning around the holistic formation of students' hearts, hands, and heads. They must invite the active participation of students in their education and formation. Student-led education is a consumeristic enterprise. It shapes education around the tastes and choices of students. It rarely asks whether these choices positively contribute to student formation. I prefer a student-focused approach over a student-led approach to theological education.

We need theological colleges that form the whole person in collaboration with students and churches. These colleges prioritize ministry competency, theological insight, missional enthusiasm, and spiritual passion.

We must develop specific outcomes for our pastoral and other graduates to do this well. By *outcomes*, I mean: "The qualities and skills and commitments we're hoping to see in our graduates." These outcomes should be biblically based. They should be appropriate to a student's study area and chosen ministry. Colleges might shape these outcomes around these areas: Bible and theology, communication and preaching, pastoral and ministry competencies, leadership, ethics, spirituality, character, church life, worship, interpersonal skills, mission, apologetics, and cultural analysis.[29]

Majority World theological colleges and churches expect specific outcomes from theological training. They expect graduates to grow in particular ways. Wilson Chow writes that ministry education must integrate many essential things. This includes the Bible, theology, pastoral competencies,

---

29. Hill et al., "Morling College Outcomes." Ministry education strives for these outcomes in other settings, too. But these characteristics are noticeable in Majority World theological education. While working through the literature on Majority World ministry and theological education, I was asked to form a task force to develop such *outcomes* at Morling College, Sydney, Australia. At Morling, we developed a document listing these objectives for pastoral and other graduates (called *Morling College Outcomes*). I draw on that document here.

spirituality, church life, ministry fieldwork, worship, and mission. Keith Ferdinando says that theological education must follow apprenticeship and whole-of-life patterns. Jesus modeled these in the way he trained his disciples.[30] Integrated theological education must be about the whole of a person's life. It needs an intentional and integrated approach. This "covers the academic, spiritual, and practical formation of leadership in one whole."[31]

Ministry education in the Majority World usually does all it can to see graduates develop in the ABCs (Affective and Behavioral and Cognitive domains). The first is the *heart* (maturation of attitudes, values, faith, and spirituality). The second is the *hands* (achievement of practical competencies). The third is the *head* (cognitive development, acquisition of knowledge, and intellectual progress). This is especially the case for pastoral and missionary graduates (but not only that group). Those of us in the West must also focus on student formation so that they evidence these ABCs.

Affective (Heart)

This is about our theological education and ministry training forming students and graduates who value and develop Christian character. It's about forming graduates who embrace personal and spiritual formation. In Majority World theological education, spiritual formation "is not simply a goal among others, but a permeation of all educational goals."[32] This includes forming Christ-like character qualities and integrity that reflect Scriptural standards.

What else should be sought in our formation of student's hearts? What personal and spiritual qualities are we seeking? There are many things. Here are some examples. We want them to shape priorities around the mind of Christ. Embrace ethical standards and personal integrity in obedience to the imperatives of Scripture. Conduct themselves in a way consistent with Christian teaching and values. Maintain sexual purity, especially, but not only, in relationships in ministry. Willingly observe ministerial ethics, including loyalty to peers and colleagues. Cultivate thinking reflective of a clear understanding of biblical values. Be above reproach, as reflected in the passages listed in the previous section of this chapter. Be emotionally mature, including healthy self-awareness and self-acceptance. Be emotionally stable over time and under difficult and various circumstances. Foster awareness of behavioral patterns, motivations, and growth areas. Respond

30. Ferdinando, "Jesus, the Theological Educator."
31. Chow, "Integrated Approach to Theological Education," 60.
32. Naidoo, "Spiritual Formation in Protestant Theological Institutions," 193.

well to difficulty, anxiety, and conflict. Develop self-discipline in ministry and life. Cultivate spiritual disciplines (including prayer, reflection, Bible reading, and other personal encounters with God). Apply biblical truth to self and life and ministry.

Take devotional time to bring their lives into line with God's Word. Align theology with personal application, ministry praxis, and spiritual growth. Demonstrate a vital personal faith in every area of life (private life and ministry). Live in a Spirit-filled way. Live according to the prompting, fruit, and guidance of the Spirit. Consistently make space to commune with God. Demonstrate a love for time with God and in the Scriptures. Cultivate a rich devotional life, including regular prayer and biblical study. Strengthen and deepen their relationship with God. Respond to the call of God revealed by the Spirit in the Word. Seek God's call on their lives through the church, Scripture, mission, reflection, and prayer. Cultivate an attitude toward ministry that reflects a sense of obedience to the leading of God. Be consistently and authentically immersed in a local church and ministry. Be committed to the local expression of the Body of Christ. Meet with Christians in a local church regularly. Submit to appropriate discipline. Be committed to corporate worship. Have an authentic spiritual enthusiasm and passion for God's kingdom and righteousness.

Behavioral (Hands)

This is about our theological education and ministry training, forming graduates with competent mission and ministry skills. We want to see them embrace an authentic commitment to the local church. Be an active participant in a local church community. Explore their ministry vocation in local churches and other opportunities. Encourage evangelism in organized missionary work and through personal encounters and relationships. Support mission through announcement (proclamation) and demonstration (social concern and action). Understand themselves as Christians called to world mission. This includes local, regional, national, and global missions. Be ready for appropriate Christian ministry, mission, and service. Show a commitment to ministerial and missional formation. Be competent interpreters, teachers, and proclaimers of Scripture. Demonstrate a solid understanding of hermeneutics, exegesis, and homiletics. Be able to exposit the Scriptures accurately. Apply Scripture to their own and other lives and communicate these truths effectively. Be able to preach and teach capably in the context of their ministries.

What other expressions of behavioral formation must we seek? We desire students and graduates to interpret the cultural context for ministry and mission. Apply principles that will promote church growth and mission by the whole congregation. Actively seek to lead others to a personal relationship with God. Know how to help various unbelievers move toward a commitment to Christ. Practice hospitality and welcoming the stranger. Demonstrate a capacity to relate to people from cultural backgrounds significantly different from the one they know best. Adapt well to changing and unpredictable and new ministry settings. Apply the insights of missiology to the whole life and outreach of the church. Articulate their Christian faith, especially concerning other belief systems and worldviews. Show and *publicly* communicate what it means to be a Christ-like Christian leader.

Effective pastoral, leadership, and interpersonal skills are also vital. We hope our formation will lead to students and graduates with competent interpersonal relationships. They'll know how to give and receive love and respect. Be able to form healthy relationships with the opposite sex. Identify, develop, equip, and release others to ministry and mission with integrity. Value the equipping role of Christian ministry. Disciple others. Develop a culture of discipleship in their ministries. Demonstrate competent empowerment of others for service. Understand how to lead change and transition in their ministries. Learn how to manage and resolve conflict. Understand and demonstrate the skills of servant leadership (*servantship*).[33] Pay attention to developing the next generation of leaders, who can likewise build up and develop others. Seek to equip others for ministry (Ephesians 4). Be able to lead through sound administrative and management capabilities. Embrace prayerful and compassionate care of others. Demonstrate skills in spiritual caregiving. Be competent in pastoral care and visitation. Develop and oversee systems and structures of pastoral care (appropriate to the context). Nurture persons, families, and congregations through crisis, change, and difficulty. This involves using pastoral competencies, personal integrity, and biblical wisdom.

Graduates also need skills in cultural engagement. They need to be able to put theological and ministry learning into conversation with cultures and contexts. Do this for the sake of salvation and liberation and mission. Applying this principle to the African context, James Amanze says that African spirituality has enriched the church, and the church has deepened Africa's spirituality. Future and current church leaders need to find creative

---

33. Hill, *Servantship*.

ways to put theology, faith, and spirituality into conversation with local cultures.[34]

Gnana Robinson calls for "reorientating theological education for a relevant ministry." Ministry education in Indigenous and Western and Majority World settings needs constant renewal. It needs a reorientation to the outcomes I've detailed. This is vital for a relevant ministry. "Changing socio-economic and political situations in countries like Asia, Africa, and Latin America call for relevant ministries which, in turn, demands a change in the traditional pattern of ministries . . . Reorientation of theological education thus demands reorientation to our culture, our understanding of God, the world, the people of God, the pattern of ministry we want, and spirituality."[35]

Cognitive (Head)

Our theological education and ministry training must form graduates with competent theological skills. We want to see them demonstrate critical competencies. Here are some examples. Develop in biblical passion and knowledge. Interpret the Bible accurately for themselves. Demonstrate an understanding of the word of God, including appreciating the big picture and plotline of Scripture. Understand the Christian gospel and be able to share it with others. Be able to convey and apply the truths of Scripture to their own and others' lives in effective ministry. Have a keen interest in the Bible and theology. Grow and feed themselves in understanding and skills beyond study at theological college. Hold to a trinitarian orthodoxy (one God exists in one substance and three Persons: Father, Son, and Holy Spirit). Uphold the historicity of the crucifixion and resurrection. Preserve the centrality of the person and work of Christ and his divine/human nature. Proclaim Jesus's saving work on the cross as the only means for salvation and the forgiveness of sins. Affirm the Bible as authoritative. Believe that it's God's revelation to humanity. Know that it's the supreme source of authority in matters of faith and practice. Understand their beliefs in the light of Christian history. Appreciate their Christian heritage and tradition. Develop a sound fundamental understanding of Christian history and the historic Christian faith. Evaluate current theology and practices in the light of that history. Pursue a robust understanding and theology of ministry, leadership, church, worship, mission, training, and discipleship.

34. Amanze, "Contextuality," 19.

35. Robinson, "Re-Orientation of Theological Education for a Relevant Ministry," 46.

This list of affective, behavioral, and cognitive graduate outcomes may give the impression we're reaching for the perfect graduate. That's not the case. Graduates come in all shapes and sizes. They have unique skills, passions, and callings. But having clear graduate outcomes for hearts and hands and heads keeps our theological education and ministry training focused. Our training is then student-focused, not student-led. It seeks to take graduates through a holistic formation process. It desires that they glorify God the Father, witness to Jesus Christ, and serve in the Holy Spirit's power in their lives and ministries.

7. Renewed education is contextual and inter-contextual.

We must contextualize our curriculum, delivery, theology, and methods. As we've seen already, Shoki Coe and others outline the significance of contextualization for education and theology. Paulo Freire says that skills in contextualized education include *problematization* and *conscientization*.[36] These have become core values in many educational institutions in the Majority World. They are also popular in Western education. They may be instructive for Western seminaries and churches.

Problemization

This encourages critical, analytical, wise, free, open, and uninhibited dialogue between teachers and students. Teachers encourage students to mirror this process in their ministries. Students teach congregations to embrace these practices. Problemization aims to develop students into critical, expressive thinkers, leaders, and change agents. It helps them wrestle with issues in their context. It encourages students to practice critical, imaginative thinking and problem-solving in ministry. It's a vital skill set for missions.

Conscientization

This is about enabling students to develop a "deepening awareness both of the socio-cultural reality which shapes their lives and of their capacity to transform that reality."[37] The message of the gospel relates to the whole of a person's life. This, of course, includes every aspect of their context. Theological education must reflect this truth. It must help leaders develop

---

36. Freire, *Pedagogy*.
37. Freire, *Cultural Action for Freedom*, 51.

missional congregations that engage their cultures. It must give students an awareness of the realities of their context. Most importantly, it must help them embrace their "capacity to transform that reality."[38]

Contextualization is not adequate in isolation from inter-contextual, global reflection. Huang Po Ho spells this out from an Asian perspective. Contextual theology is not subsumed into inter-contextuality but enriched by it. Inter-contextuality is about different groups sharing what they are learning in their contexts. This way, they enrich each other's contexts.

Ho writes, "To emphasize contextuality does not mean to isolate a single context or to neglect the inter-relations in which a context is involved with other contexts. Accordingly, a genuine contextual theology must be a theology that not only delves into the depth and nature of a given context but also explores its connectedness with other wider contexts." Ho still prioritizes context. A "particular context is not only the starting point of any contextual theological endeavor but also remains the subject of the project as well as the object of all the concerns of that theology."[39]

M. Thomas Thangaraj says that robust contextual theology follows the formula: *Local + Global = Contextual*. Contextual theology needs inter-contextual, global theology to flourish. So, contextual theological education is at its best when it engages both local and global issues.[40]

Paul Hiebert speaks of *critical contextualization*. The church is a global "hermeneutical community." It tests "the contextualization of cultural practices as well as theologies." Critical contextualization isn't monocultural. Nor is it "premised upon the pluralism of incommensurable cultures."[41] It takes global, cultural, and historical contexts seriously.

Theological colleges must contextualize their curriculum and methodologies. This contextualization should consider a range of questions. What are the educational and experiential entry levels of the students? What are the contexts of the local supporting churches and the local community? What are the national, denominational, and ecumenical contexts? What are the motivations of the students to undertake the program? (This includes their interests, values, and course expectations). How will this study relate to the conceptual and cognitive styles of the students? What's the best way to determine the objectives of the program? (Ideally, seminaries should develop these objectives in consultation with students and their

---

38. Freire, *Cultural Action for Freedom*, 51.
39. Ho, "Contextualization and Inter-Contextuality in Theological Education," 127.
40. Thangaraj, "Formula for Contextual Theology," 107.
41. Hiebert, "Critical Contextualization," 100.

local churches). How will we relate these objectives to developing the three key areas (head, heart, and hands)?

We need to ask even more questions to contextualize our curriculum and methodologies. What resources are available (space, time, books, human, materials, etc.)? What cultural restrictions, norms, and taboos exist? What are the external, physical, geographical, and organizational constraints? Are there any cost and administrative considerations? Are there pressing local and global realities that influence this culture? What are the relevant historical, cultural, and political factors influencing the status, function, and accessibility of education? What access is there to technologies? What are lecturers' preferences, abilities, experiences, training, attitudes, and styles? What are the requirements of accrediting agencies? How do we design and apply an appropriate grading system? (This needs to consider the local culture's view of competition, achievement, etc.)

Theological colleges and churches need to contextualize theological education—both content and methods. We do this to be faithful to the gospel in particular settings. We do this to form men and women for service.

Contextualization helps theological education influence cultures. It helps to uphold and preserve appropriate values in cultures. It challenges sin in cultures. It can reverse the colonizing forces within and beyond cultures. Contextualization honors what God is doing at the grassroots of cultures.

8. Renewed education places mission at the center of curriculum and methods.

Most theological education isn't missional. Sure, it may have a few mission subjects. It may even have a mission faculty or institute. But to be truly missional, theological education must shape its entire curriculum around missional theology and practices.

The doctrine of the *missio Dei* has revolutionized how we understand theology, mission, and church. It must reshape our theological education and ministry training. We need to teach all subjects from a missional perspective. This includes pastoral, systematics, preaching, biblical interpretation, etc. Colleges must form students *for* mission and *in* mission and *through* mission. Theological reflection is *for* mission and *in* mission. Since discipleship is participation in the *missio Dei*, theological education must also be participation in the *missio Dei*. It should prioritize the missional nature of God and church and ministry. Theological reflection and spiritual formation should happen in the mission context, not only in the academy or church.

Theological education must equip leaders and churches to participate in God's mission. It should be *outwardly oriented*. It equips people to engage fully in God's mission in the world. It should be *incarnational*. It's located in our world's lives, contexts, and cultures. It should be *discipleship-focused*. It enables people to follow Jesus Christ and his mission in the world. It should be thoroughly *missional*. It reshapes its curricula, structures, faculty, assessment, and ethos through missional paradigms, theologies, and experiences. It should be *formational*. It forms the whole person to serve the whole mission of Christ.

Our theological education must teach people to interpret and apply Scripture through a missional paradigm. To use technical terms, they need a *missional hermeneutic*.

Lastly, such missional education integrates the fourteen characteristics Tite Tiénou, Samuel Escobar, and Ken Gnanakan described. I outlined these earlier in this chapter.

Re-missionizing theological education takes courage. It takes time. It's risky to those leading the charge since it threatens existing educational models and curriculum design. But it's imperative if we take the *missio Dei* seriously.

9. Renewed education equips the whole Body of Christ.

It doesn't just train pastors and missionaries. These are significant gifts to the church. But they're not the only gifts. If theological education will train all the fivefold gifts and more, it must serve the whole church. It must develop and release apostles, pastors, teachers, evangelists, prophets, and other gifts. Theological education should equip mums and dads and entire families. It should train mechanics, lawyers, plumbers, doctors, hairdressers, teachers, counselors, carpenters, etc. Worthwhile theological education mustn't have an unnatural, Christendom-formed focus on one or two ministry gifts. Instead, worthwhile theological education and ministry training must equip the whole Body of Christ.

10. Renewed education models and cultivates servantship.

It's time we demonstrated a reciprocal, servanthood, enabling, and participatory leadership style as theological educators. This means modeling Christ-honoring spiritual leadership to our students. It means rejecting hierarchical and corporate models of leadership.

Servantship is following Jesus Christ, the servant Lord, and his mission. It's a life of discipleship to him. It follows his self-emptying, humility, sacrifice, love, values, and mission. Servantship is humbly valuing others more than yourself. It's looking out for the interests and well-being of others.

Servantship is the cultivation of the same attitude of mind as Christ Jesus. It's making yourself nothing. It's being a servant and humbling yourself. It's submitting yourself to the will and purposes of the triune God. Since servantship is the imitation of Christ, it involves an unreserved participation in his mission. Servantship recognizes in word, thought, and deed that Christian leaders are servants. "Whoever wants to become great among you must be your servant, and whoever wants to be first must be your slave—just as the Son of Man did not come to be served, but to serve, and to give his life as a ransom for many."[42]

11. Renewed education applies instruction-action-reflection models of learning.

We need *instruction–action–reflection* approaches to education. Students receive *instruction*, undertake specific *actions*, and *reflect* on their experiences and learnings. Here are the four stages. (1) Instruction leads to new experiences in ministry. (2) These lead to new observations and reflections. (3) Students then develop new skills, concepts, and characteristics. (4) Further experimentation is then integrated with more instruction. This four-stage cycle continues repeatedly. This approach helps form people for discipleship, ministry, and mission. This model integrates action, theory, and reflection. It combines theology, formation, and fieldwork. Educators must provide opportunities for reflection on new theologies, skills, and experiences.

This model integrates at least six things. The first is theological and biblical reflection. The second is theoretical perspectives on ministry practice. The third is spiritual formation. The fourth is personal, relational, and emotional growth. The fifth is ministry praxis and competency. The sixth is missional theology and development.

Instruction-action-reflection aims to develop students holistically as disciples and for mission and ministry. The goal is to do this in their contexts. It allows those trainees to develop within the context of their local churches and communities. It makes sure they have competent supervision and guidance. The *instruction-action-reflection* cycle requires students to integrate theory and practice and spiritual formation in concrete settings.

42. Mark 10:43–44.

It's an apprenticeship and whole-of-life pattern to theological and ministry education. It uses the way Jesus trained his disciples as a model.[43]

12. Renewed education offers diversified approaches to learning.

It offers *diversified theological education* (DTE) by combining modes of education. Examples include residential and online, part-time and full-time, and on-campus and in churches. Education is no longer a "one size fits all" affair. It needs to be flexible. During their studies, students will most likely combine a variety of modes of education. It's now difficult for many colleges to talk about discrete online, full-time, or part-time groups. They blend. When we're focused on formation, such diversification can enhance our education.

13. Renewed education resists colonizing people.

The best kind of theological education rejects "colonizing" people because of their race, gender, knowledge, disability, education, medical condition, class, theology, and language. It's not blind to these things. But it doesn't colonize. It refuses to use a "cookie cutter" approach to training. Instead, it practices the opposite, liberating behavior. Even though we must practice theological education in the community, we must still encourage unique and even "eccentric" contributions. These are a gift to education and the church. Some are revolutionary and prophetic. All are a grace from God.

14. Renewed education addresses issues of access and power.

Who can access our theological education? Are we addressing the gendered dimensions of power relations? Can both women and men fully participate in our theological and ministry education?

This is not just about women. It is about men *and* women. It's about their relations before Jesus Christ. Gender is often about power relations. Theological institutions have a responsibility to address these dynamics. Theological institutions must evaluate how "gender issues are incorporated into the transformation process. An engendered transformation process

---

43. Ferdinando, "Jesus, the Theological Educator."

occurs through organizational change, program development, and collaboration with poor and marginalized women."[44]

Isabel Apawo Phiri, Esther Mombo, Limatula Longkumer, and Ofelia Ortega call for engendered theological education. They do this from African, Asian, and Latin American perspectives. They speak prophetically into local and global ministry education. I'm indebted here to their perspectives.

The church must address some critical questions if women are to participate in theological education fully. Here are some examples. What are women's socio-economic status and roles in our society? How do we feel about this? How do we respond to women's long histories of subordinate roles in church and society? Do we want "separate" or "specialized" forms of women's ministry? What's our position on the ordination of women? What are the challenges facing women who want to attend residential colleges? What are the unique contributions of women to theology, church, and education? Have we developed a biblical theology of gender and addressed the associated interpretive challenges? Do we have inclusive language in liturgy, training, and theology? What do we do about shaping theological curricula and structures by (mostly) men? What access do women have to shaping theological methods, curriculum, and institutions? Do we value integrative approaches that incorporate theology, praxis, and formation?

Other vital questions emerge. Do we have interdisciplinary courses that empower people for life and service, enriching learning experiences? Have we offered special scholarships and opportunities for women? Do we encourage innovative forms and patterns of ministry led by women? Have we considered the importance of a needs-based curriculum? Does our curriculum address gender, race, environment, class, health, human trafficking, poverty, etc.? Are our faculties, seminaries, churches, and leaders willing to address the issues?

Engendering theological education takes courage and conviction. Beverley Haddad says:

> Engendering theological education is critical to transformation. Courage is needed, particularly by male educators, to get involved in this complex process that requires attention on several different levels. It requires long-term institutional change. It requires thoughtful and deliberate programme development. Perhaps, most difficult of all, it requires profound personal change so that we can better see, hear, and include our sisters who will

---

44. Haddad, "Engendering Theological Education for Transformation."

never grace the doors of the academy, and yet are key subjects in the engendering process.[45]

15. Renewed education is Spirit-empowered.

We must learn from Pentecostal and charismatic approaches to theological education in the Majority World. We can learn from their dependency on the Spirit to empower women and men for ministry. Too many theological institutions focus on academic learning and ministry competency but neglect discipleship, formation, and spirit empowerment. People go into ministry and discover they're in a spiritual battle for which they're unprepared. The Holy Spirit empowers us for ministry and the spiritual battle we're engaged in. He regenerates, sanctifies, guides, unifies, and empowers us. We dare not neglect Spirit-empowerment in ministry or our ministry training.

16. Renewed education seeks a global "renaissance" in theology and training.

Timothy Tennent describes global shifts in theology. He says that these arise from the stunning growth of Majority World Christianity. He then explores four ways the rise of the Majority World church might help theology. These four also have a positive influence on emerging forms of theological education. This rise of Majority World theology and education will lead to a "renaissance in Western theological scholarship."[46] The renaissance Timothy Tennent envisages won't stop in the West. It will be a global renewal of theological discourse and education.

First, this renaissance will mean the "reintegration of the theological disciplines." The disciplines of systematic theology, biblical theology, applied theology, missiology, apologetics, etc., are more integrated in the Majority World. They must become more integrated in the West.

Second, it will lead to a "renaissance in systematic theology." Systematic theology in the Majority World converses with contextual, spiritual, and missional themes. Those themes shape systematic theology. This is also necessary in the West. "This reconnection between theological scholarship

---

45. Haddad, "Engendering Theological Education for Transformation," 80.
46. Tennent, *Theology in the Context of World Christianity*, 250–72.

and the church's mission is vital to the future of a truly robust Christian movement."[47]

Third, it will result in the "particularization of theological discourse." Theological reflection and learning in the Majority World are often concerned with local needs. It addresses local concerns and challenges. Majority World, Indigenous, and Western theologies must engage in local and global conversations. In this chapter, I have sought to listen to educational themes in Africa, Asia, and Latin America. "If we engage in this sustained cross-cultural theological discourse with the church worldwide, the sheer diversity of global Christianity will help free the church from any particular cultural bias."[48]

Fourth, it inspires "theological engagement with ideologies of unbelief and non-Christian religions." Majority World theology and theological education tends to engage with its pluralistic context. It seeks to talk with other ideologies, worldviews, and religions. It pursues engagement with Islam, Hinduism, Atheism, Confucianism, Buddhism, religious sects, new spiritualities and religious movements, and so forth. The West is also becoming pluralistic. It needs theology and theological education to thrive in diverse, pluralistic settings.

17. Renewed education integrates the three "publics" of academy, church, and society.

Global conversations are essential. Majority World, Indigenous, and Western theologies and education can renew each other. But they will only do this through robust dialogue. These conversations can contribute to the renewal of the global church. They can enhance their participation in God's mission in the world.

David Bosch says that theology and theological education must renew themselves. They do this by integrating the three "publics" of the academy, church, and society. Theology (and theological education) mustn't only be relevant to these three "publics." It must engage with them critically. A critical conversation between theology, the academy, the church, and society is necessary. This critical conversation enables theology (and theological education) to contribute to the well-being and renewal of the academy, church, and society. It helps theology and theological education take part fully in the mission of God in the world.

---

47. Tennent, *Theology in the Context of World Christianity*, 261.
48. Tennent, *Theology in the Context of World Christianity*, 265.

Theology and theological education, then, involve a dynamic interplay and a creative tension between *theoria, poiesis* and *praxis*, between head, heart and hand, between faith, hope and love, between the cognitive, the constitutive and the critical, between the intellectual, the relational and the intentional. It combines knowing, being and doing and seeks to communicate what is true, what is of God, and what is just.

Unless theological education succeeds—however inadequately—to embody these dimensions, it will not be credible to any of its three publics. In the world of *academia*, it will be viewed as an atavistic enterprise, a throw-back to a bygone era. The *church* will regard it as peripheral to its life, as diffuse and cafeteria-like, lacking a unifying vision. *Society* will perceive it as pedantic, irrelevant and doctrinaire. In each of these instances our students will, in their search for an integrating world- and life-view, feel obliged to look elsewhere for help in respect of what really matters, even if they comply formally with our degree requirements.[49]

May theological educators and institutions have the courage to embody *theoria, poiesis,* and *praxis* in the three public spheres of the academy, church, and society. May theological and ministry education serve the mission of God. In the words of the *Lausanne Cape Town Commitment*, may it enable the mission of God and his church. May theological educators have the courage to "conduct a 'missional audit' of their curricula, structures, and ethos, to ensure that they truly serve the needs and opportunities facing the church in their cultures."

---

49. Bosch, "Nature of Theological Education," 23.

PART 3: REVITALIZING OUR CHURCHES

Study Questions

1. Is your church, ministry, or organization developing and using the gifts and talents in your organization and setting? How could you become more effective at this?

2. Is your church, ministry, or organization mobilizing people for mission, ministry, and transformational leadership? How can you equip them for service *inside* and *outside* the church?

3. How can your church, ministry, or organization mobilize all the ministry gifts (apostolic, prophetic, evangelistic, teaching, and pastoral gifts are only the start)?

4. How is your church training people's *heads* (knowledge), *hearts* (character), and *hands* (competencies)? Are you equipping them well for ministry and mission and church planting? What are the goals of your training programs?

5. Are you collaborating with theological institutions, denominations, secular organizations, churches, and missional initiatives to train people for ministry and mission?

6. How can your church, small group, or ministry prepare people for the moral, spiritual, political, and economic transformation of their contexts? Do you promote the transformation of lives and groups through the liberation of the gospel? Do you seek it through active participation in social, political, church, and economic arenas?

19.

Practicing Servantship

The Eleventh Expression

MANY EXAMPLES OF EXCELLENT, sound, and flawed leadership exist in the Majority World. There are as many examples of virtuous and flawed leadership in the Majority World as in the West.

Let's consider an example of outstanding Christian leadership. Samuel Lamb (Lin Xiangao) was a gospel preacher and a leader of the Chinese house church movement. Chinese authorities imprisoned him in these ministries for more than twenty years. He was tortured, starved, imprisoned, and repeatedly beaten for his ministry in China. While imprisoned, Lamb was forced to do hard labor in the dreaded Shanxi Talyuan Coal Mine. But Lamb continued to preach the gospel of Jesus Christ. He made disciples. He baptized believers.

Once released, Samuel Lamb refused to participate in the Chinese state-controlled "Three-Self Patriotic Movement" churches. He suffered relentless persecution by Chinese authorities for that stance. But the church he planted quickly grew to five thousand worshipers. To the dismay of authorities, each time they arrested and imprisoned Lamb, his church grew. Lamb published two hundred booklets called "The Voice of the Spirit." Lamb died in 2013, and thirty thousand mourners attended his funeral in Guangzhou, China.

Some estimate that there are now nearly 100 million house-church Christians in China. Samuel Lamb and a generation of Chinese Christian leaders like him made a remarkable contribution to the growth of the Chinese church. His spiritual leadership was exemplary.

What do we see when we consider excellent Christian leadership in Asia, Africa, Latin America, Eastern Europe, First Nations, and Indigenous cultures? This chapter unpacks the key leadership themes that emerge. These themes are *servantship* and culturally specific and cross-cultural leadership. Other themes include disciple-making, church-multiplying, missional, and spiritual leadership.

Servant Leadership (Servantship)

Imagine the impact of Christian leadership shaped around service. This servant leadership has no selfish ambition or vain conceit. It humbly esteems others above itself. It looks to the interests and needs of others. Servant leadership cultivates the same attitude of mind as that of Christ Jesus. It doesn't grasp after its own advantage. It humbles itself obediently to the will and mission of God in human history.

I am describing a leadership that seeks to witness to Christ Jesus. It depends on the power of the Holy Spirit. It brings glory to God the Father. Picture the eternal legacy of Christian leadership shaped around the service of God. Serving God means wholeheartedly serving his mission, church, and world.

It would be wrong to suggest that most Majority World leadership is servant leadership. In many places, it is the opposite. But there has been a move among Majority World thinkers to reconceive leadership as servantship. This shift involves allowing a theology of service to shape our understanding and practice of Christian leadership.[1]

Here is my definition of servantship:

Servantship is following Jesus Christ, the servant Lord, and his mission. It's a life of discipleship to him. It follows his self-emptying, humility, sacrifice, love, values, and mission. Servantship is humbly valuing others more than yourself. It's looking out for the interests and well-being of others. Servantship is the cultivation of the same attitude of mind as Christ Jesus. It's making yourself nothing. It's being a servant and humbling yourself. It's submitting yourself to the will and purposes of the triune God. Since servantship is the imitation of Christ, it involves an unreserved participation in his mission. (By this, I mean the *missio Dei*—the trinitarian mission of God). Servantship recognizes in word, thought, and deed that Christian leaders are servants. "Whoever wants to become great among you must be

1. Some of this material was first published in Hill, *Servantship*.

your servant, and whoever wants to be first must be your slave—just as the Son of Man did not come to be served, but to serve, and to give his life as a ransom for many" (Matt 20:26–28).

Elizabeth Petersen's perspectives on servantship among the "Broken Ones" serve as an example. She's led an extraordinary servant ministry as SAFFI's founder and executive director, which is short for the South African Faith and Family Institute. Petersen established SAFFI in 2008 to address violence against women and children in South Africa. Her ministry deals with sexual violence, domestic abuse, neglect, and the exploitation of children. She addresses the systemic structures and biblical misinterpretations that support such violence. SAFFI seeks to address faith issues and root causes of violence against women by being a resource to religious leaders, their faith communities, and secular domestic violence advocates to advance comprehensive, coordinated, culturally informed strategies and interventions.[2]

SAFFI's strategies include educational seminars and perpetrator intervention programs. They conduct gender reconciliation workshops and do research and advocacy. They offer technical support to community-based domestic violence initiatives. They run interfaith forums on preventing and dealing with violence against women.

SAFFI also challenges patriarchal theological traditions that condone or excuse such violence. SAFFI promotes "Scriptural and theological teachings that encourage intimate relationships that set people free to live their full potential in supportive unions."[3]

Petersen provides perspectives on the nature of Christian servantship "via the Broken Ones." This is a servantship shaped by humility, service, and sacrifice. This servantship collaborates with those society has "stripped of their human dignity." She shows us a servantship that "co-suffers and co-creates" with "the Broken Ones." Petersen says these broken people "keep me accountable for living my calling with integrity and authenticity." For Petersen, "the Broken Ones are Christ and the broken others in our society."[4]

Elizabeth Petersen shares how she realized Christian servantship is about serving broken people. She discovered Jesus present among them.

> I began to realize that these women and children were going to help me find my voice and that I needed them to help me find the expressions for my calling as a social worker. The Broken Ones became those who kept me accountable for living

---

2. From South African Faith and Family Institute website at http://www.saffi.org.za.
3. South African Faith and Family Institute website at http://www.saffi.org.za.
4. Petersen and Swart, "Via the Broken Ones," 12.

my calling with integrity and authenticity. I began to find God in and through the voices and stories of those who have been stripped of their human dignity through sexual, physically violent, and other forms of abuse. I began to discover the life-giving presence of God amid my engagement with these women ... co-suffering and co-creating with us all.[5]

Petersen helps us understand the nature of servantship. She does this through her reflections, writing, and ministry among abused and broken women and children in South Africa.

Servantship contrasts many leadership principles and practices of the global political and corporate age. Christians shape their servantship after the humility, sacrifice, and values of the suffering servant, Jesus Christ. We need a servantship formed by the imitation of Jesus Christ. We show this servantship through a lifestyle of service. We shape a life of servantship through love, hope, faith, and self-sacrifice. "Whoever would be great among you must be your servant" (Matt 20:26).

William F. Kumuyi founded Deeper Life Bible Church in Nigeria in 1982. Kumuyi's church has planted close to nine thousand churches throughout Africa. The main church (in Lagos, Nigeria) has 120,000 attendees every Sunday. Some estimate that in Nigeria alone, 800,000 people worship in the Deeper Life Bible Church family of churches every Sunday. In April 2013, Foreign Policy Magazine named Kumuyi one of the "500 most powerful people on the planet."[6]

William F. Kumuyi is deeply committed to servantship despite this success and acclaim. He writes, "What Africa needs for its redemption is servant leadership instead of the self-serving governance that the continent is famed for. Our leaders should add the servanthood attitude to their attributes and demonstrate that their primary motivation for seeking to lead the people is rooted in a deep desire to serve and help others."[7] Concerned about Africa's future, Kumuyi says servantship is the rejection of leadership that's "a money-spinning business venture or a rare opportunity to feather one's nest and bequeath material security to one's offspring."[8]

Kumuyi calls for African political, military, corporate, and church leadership reform. He calls for a systematic reform of African governance based on servant leadership. "Despite the extensive damage that colonialism

---

5. Petersen and Swart, "Via the Broken Ones," 9–10.
6. Foreign Policy Magazine, "FP Power Map."
7. Kumuyi, "Case for Servant Leadership," 18.
8. Kumuyi, "Case for Servant Leadership," 19.

has done to Africa's capacity for holistic development, the continent can reinvent itself by effective leadership shorn of graft."[9]

Africa is not the only continent crying out for servantship. Western Christianity obsesses over leadership. Domineering and hierarchical leadership personalities and forms plague Western churches. But Jesus called his disciples to service. He modeled servantship and called his disciples to be servants. Societies practice leadership in culturally specific ways. Even though this is the case, all Christian leadership has service, humility, and love at its heart. You cannot be a Christian leader without being a servant.

Culturally-Specific and Cross-Cultural Leadership

Recently, significant research has been conducted into how different cultures *conceptualize* and *practice* leadership. This research deals with how cultures affect leadership expectations, preferences, models, and styles. It also considers how leadership adapts to multicultural and cross-cultural settings.[10]

The GLOBE study of how sixty-two cultures conceptualize, value, and practice leadership is a fascinating example.[11] This major study involved 170 researchers from sixty-two cultures across the globe. Almost two-thirds of the researchers were from the Majority World. They designed the research instruments and collected and interpreted the data. The researchers asked how different cultures conceive and practice leadership. They also asked, "How is culture related to societal, organizational, and leadership effectiveness?"

The GLOBE researchers "tested twenty-seven hypotheses that linked culture to interesting outcomes, with data from 17,300 managers in 951 organizations" in sixty-two cultures worldwide.

> They measured the variables with cultural sensitivity, developing instruments in consultation with members of the relevant cultures. Using focus groups and heavy dependence on the previous literature, the investigators developed instruments that

---

9. Kumuyi, "Functions of a Servant-Leader," 30.

10. See, for instance, Lewis's text on managing and leading successfully across cultures: Lewis, *When Cultures Collide*.

11. The GLOBE study builds on the pioneering work of Geert Hofstede into the cultures and values of nations and people groups. Hofstede, *Culture's Consequences*; Hofstede, *Culture's Consequences*; Hofstede et al., *Cultures and Organizations*.

tapped local meanings that were appropriate for each level of the data and had equivalence across cultures.[12]

The research sought answers to these questions:

> Are leader behaviors, attributes, and organizational practices universally accepted and effective across cultures? Are leader behaviors, attributes, and organizational practices accepted and effective in only some cultures? How do attributes of societal and organizational cultures affect the kinds of leader behaviors and organizational practices that are accepted and effective? What is the effect of violating cultural norms relevant to leadership and organizational practices? What is the relative standing of each culture studied on each of the nine core dimensions of culture? Can the universal and culture-specific aspects of leader behaviors, attributes, and organizational practices be explained using an underlying theory that accounts for systematic differences across cultures?[13]

The research proposed nine cultural attributes. It related these to leadership styles and practices in the sixty-two cultures. In the words of the researchers, these nine are the following:

1. *Uncertainty Avoidance* is the extent to which members of an organization or society strive to avoid uncertainty by reliance on social norms, rituals, and bureaucratic practices to alleviate the unpredictability of future events.

2. *Power Distance* is the degree to which members of an organization or society expect and agree that power should be unequally shared.

3. *Collectivism I (institutional collectivism)* is the degree to which organizational and societal institutional practices encourage and reward collective distribution of resources and collective action.

4. *Collectivism II (in-group collectivism)* is the degree to which individuals express pride, loyalty, and cohesiveness in their organizations or families.

5. *Gender Egalitarianism* is the extent to which an organization or a society minimizes gender role differences.

---

12. House et al., *Culture, Leadership, and Organizations*, xv.
13. House et al., "Cultural Influences on Leadership and Organizations: Project Globe," 11–12; House et al., *Culture, Leadership, and Organizations*, 10.

6. *Assertiveness* is the degree to which individuals in organizations or societiesare assertive, confrontational, and aggressive in social relationships.

7. *Future Orientation* is the degree to which individuals in organizations or societies engage in future-oriented behaviors such as planning, investing in the future, and delaying gratification.

8. *Performance Orientation* is the extent to which an organization or society encourages and rewards group members for performance improvement and excellence.

9. *Humane Orientation* is the degree to which individuals in organizations or societies encourage and reward individuals for being fair, altruistic, friendly, generous, caring, and kind to others.[14]

Researchers identified ten cultural clusters. These are Anglo cultures, Arab cultures, Confucian Asia, Eastern Europe, Germanic Europe, Latin America, Latin Europe, Nordic Europe, Southern Asia, and Sub-Sahara Africa.[15] Researchers also identified six styles/theories of leadership. They correlated these with the nine cultural attributes and ten cultural clusters detailed above. They called these styles "culturally endorsed implicit theories of leadership":

1. *Charismatic/values-based leadership.* Such leadership is characterized by vision, inspiration, self-sacrifice, integrity, decisiveness, and performance-orientation. (Flip side: can be dictatorial and inattentive to relationships).

2. *Team-oriented leadership.* Such leadership is characterized by collaborative team orientation, team integration, diplomacy, and administrative competency. (Flip side: can use these traits malevolently to achieve own ends).

3. *Participative leadership.* Such leadership is characterized by participative behavior, gender egalitarianism, and attention to relationships. (Flip side: can be indecisive and unassertive).

4. *Human-oriented leadership.* Such leadership is characterized by humility, modesty, and altruistic compassion for others. (Flip side: can fail to develop high-performing organizations).

---

14. House et al., *Culture, Leadership, and Organizations*, 30; House et al., "Cultural Influences on Leadership and Organizations," 24–26.

15. House et al., *Culture, Leadership, and Organizations*, 32.

5. *Autonomous leadership.* Such leadership is characterized by individualism, independence, autonomous initiative, and unique contributions. (Flip side: can ignore the importance of institutional collectivism and humane behaviors).

6. *Self-protective leadership.* Such leadership is characterized by attention to procedures and, at times, positive forms of "saving face." (Flip side: can be self-centered, negatively "face-saving," status-conscious, conflict-inducing, poor performing, gender discriminating, and overly procedural).[16]

So, what did the research find? So much! The study concluded that there are correlations between the nine cultural attributes, the ten cultural clusters, and the six leadership styles/theories. The study also found that what cultures *value* is more closely aligned with their preferred *leadership style/theory* than what they practice.

In other words, *cultural values shape leadership preferences*. This is true even when other things shape leadership practices (e.g., other cultures or globalization). *Cultural values determine preferences for leadership styles.* This is true even when those cultures practice leadership styles that misalign with their values.

How do *cultural values* affect preferences for *leadership styles*?

Performance orientation in cultures positively correlates with all leadership styles except self-protective leadership.

Uncertainty avoidance in cultures positively predicts self-protective, team-oriented, and humane-oriented leadership. It's a negative predictor of participative leadership.

Future and *humane orientation* in cultures are positive predictors of humane-oriented, team-oriented, and charismatic/value-based leadership.

In-group collectivism in cultures positively predicts charismatic/values-based and team-oriented leadership. It's a negative predictor of self-protective leadership.

Gender egalitarianism in cultures positively predicts participative, charismatic, and values-based leadership. It's a negative predictor of self-protective leadership.

Institutional collectivism in cultures is a negative predictor of autonomous leadership.

---

16. House et al., *Culture, Leadership, and Organizations*, 45–48.

Power distance in cultures is a positive predictor of self-protective leadership. It's a negative predictor of charismatic, values-based, and participatory leadership.[17]

In terms of total support across *all* cultures, here's the progression from the *most* to the *least* supported leadership style/theory: (1) charismatic/values-based, (2) team-oriented, (3) participative, (4) humane-oriented, (5) autonomous, and (6) self-protective.

Charismatic/values-based leadership receives the most support in Anglo, Latin American, Latin European, Nordic European, Southern Asian, and Germanic European cultures. (It receives the least support in Middle Eastern cultures.) Nevertheless, this style of leadership is *enormously* valued across *all* cultural clusters. (It is valued more highly across all cultures than any other style.)

Team-oriented leadership receives the most support in Latin American, Confucian Asian, and Southern Asian cultures. (It receives the least support in Middle Eastern and Germanic European cultures.) But, again, this style of leadership is *highly* valued across *all* cultural clusters.

Participative leadership receives the most support in Germanic European, Nordic European, and Anglo cultures. (It receives the least support in Middle Eastern, Eastern European, Southern Asian, and Confucian Asian cultures.) Nevertheless, this style of leadership is *mostly* valued across *all* cultural clusters. (But it is less valued across all cultures than charismatic, values-based, and team leadership styles).

Humane-oriented leadership receives the most support in Southern Asian, Sub-Saharan African, Anglo, and Confucian Asian cultures. (It receives the least support in Nordic and Latin European cultures.) This style of leadership only receives *moderate* support across all cultures.

Autonomous leadership receives the most support in Eastern European and Germanic European cultures. (It receives the least support in Latin American, Latin European, and Sub-Saharan African cultures.) This style of leadership receives *minimal* support in most cultures.

Self-protective leadership receives the most support in Southern Asian, Confucian Asian, Middle Eastern, Latin American, and Eastern European cultures. (It receives the least support in Nordic European and Anglo and Germanic European cultures.) This style of leadership receives *hardly any support* in most cultures.[18]

The GLOBE research found that across all cultures, people are looking for the following things from leadership: integrity, inspiration, vision,

---

17. House et al., *Culture, Leadership, and Organizations*, 45.
18. House et al., *Culture, Leadership, and Organizations*, 42–45.

performance, collaborative team building, decisiveness, administrative competence, diplomacy, communication, self-sacrifice, humility, and modesty. All cultures value visionary, empowering, and transformational leadership. (This is also called charismatic/values-based leadership.) But culture determines how leadership is demonstrated—whether participative, autocratic, or between.[19] Individual leaders within those cultures determine whether transformational leadership is damaging or enriching, controlling or liberating, self-centered or serving, and autocratic or serving. Leaders best provide vision, transformation, and empowerment when they serve people—putting the organization and its people above their own ego.

There has also been a recent surge of publications in the West on multiethnic and cross-cultural leadership. Much of this is written by first, second, and third-generation Asian Americans, Hispanic Americans, and African Americans. (Those who minister within these communities are writing these books too.) Like the GLOBE research, these authors agree that today's leaders must be servant leaders. They must do this across cultures and ethnicities and people groups. We now live in multiethnic and multicultural cities. Culturally responsive servantship is more crucial than ever.

Disciple-Making and Church-Multiplying and Missional Leadership

A clear theme comes through in Majority World and Indigenous writings on Christian leadership. This is the need to develop Indigenous, mission-focused servant leaders through homegrown means. In most of the Majority World, this usually occurs through *disciple-making*. It also happens through *church-multiplying* and *missional movements*.

Disciple-making Movements and Leadership

Mitsuo Fukudo of Japan describes the indigenous disciple-making movements of Asia. These movements pass on the baton to future generations of Christians. Disciple-making movements focus on *compassion* for the lost. They seek *obedience* to the Great Commission and the Great Commandment. They pursue the *multiplication* of homegrown disciples who multiply homegrown disciples.

Mitsuo Fukudo says these disciples embrace distinct emphases that help them multiply more disciples. These include praying for "persons of

---

19. Dickson et al., "Conceptualizing Leadership across Cultures," 491.

peace" and connecting through food and hospitality. They also focus on healing the sick and proclaiming the coming of Jesus Christ. New converts learn "to listen to God, to reach the world, and to catalyze organic fellowships."[20]

This grassroots disciple-making and leadership development must be Indigenous to its culture. In Japan, for example, the training must be family-focused and group-oriented. Indigenous disciple-making movements do not just multiply disciples. They multiply Indigenous churches. These churches have Indigenous leaders. These leaders minister to the needs of local cultures and people groups. These disciple-making movements are also church multiplication movements.

Church-multiplying Movements and Leadership

David Lim is from the Philippines. He says that *church multiplication movements* have made Indigenous leadership training successful in Asia. These movements focus on transformational missions and Indigenous leadership development. The rapid multiplication of churches—usually through church planting—characterizes Asian Christianity. These church multiplication movements are sometimes called *insider movements*. This is because the multiplied churches are Indigenous to their setting. So are their leaders.

David Garrison provides a comprehensive account of these church-planting movements. Here is a snapshot of his findings (this is in his own words):[21]

> In Madhya Pradesh, a Church Planting Movement produces 4,000 new churches in less than seven years. In the 1990s, nearly 1,000 new churches are planted in Orissa with another 1,000 new outreach points. By 2001, a new church was being started every 24 hours . . .
>
> A Church Planting Movement in a northern Chinese province sees 20,000 new believers and 500 new churches started in less than five years. In Henan Province Christianity explodes from less than a million to more than five million in only eight years. Chinese Christians in Qing'an County of Heilongjiang Province plant 236 new churches in a single month. In southern China, a Church Planting Movement produces more than 90,000 baptized believers in 920 house churches in eight years

---

20. Fukuda, "Empowering Fourth Generation Disciples," 61–62.

21. The following is quoted directly from David Garrison's research, as presented in Garrison, *Church Planting Movements*, 35, 49, 65, 99, 123.

time. In 2001, a newly emerging Church Planting Movement yields 48,000 new believers and 1,700 new churches in one year . . .

During the decade of the nineties, Church Planting Movements in Outer Mongolia and Inner Mongolia produce more than 60,000 new believers. A Church Planting Movement transforms Cambodia's killing fields into fields of new life with more than 60,000 new Christians and hundreds of new churches planted over the past ten years. Despite government attempts to eliminate Christianity, a Church Planting Movement in one Southeast Asian country adds more than 50,000 new believers in five years . . .

More Muslims have come to Christ in the past two decades than at any other time in history. A Central Asian Church Planting Movement sees 13,000 Kazakhs come to faith in Christ over a decade and a half. Up to 12,000 Kashmiri Muslims turn from jihad to the Prince of Peace. In an Asian Muslim country, more than 150,000 Muslims embrace Jesus and gather in more than 3,000 locally led Isa Jamaats (Jesus Groups) . . .

Every Saturday night, 18,000 youth line up to enter a stadium for worship in Bogotá, Colombia. Each week another 500 youth commit their lives to Christ and the core values of prayer, fasting, and holiness. During the week, they gather in 8,000 youth cell groups. Among the Kekchi people in remote Guatemala, evangelical Christianity grows from 20,000 believers to more than 60,000 in three decades. During the decade of the 1990s, Christians in a Latin American country overcame relentless government persecution to grow from 235 churches to more than 4,000 churches with a further 40,000 converts awaiting baptism.

Increasingly, these church plants focus on transformational missions. This involves the proclamation of the gospel. But it also involves the transformation of local communities through the pursuit of justice. This justice is often sought amid oppression. It involves a distinct commitment to community development. It also involves strengthening families and building better societies. These church plants are also focused on multiplying Indigenous leaders. Such leaders dedicate themselves to multiplying churches and transforming local communities.

David Lim says that leadership development within church multiplication movements is transformational. This is because it expresses servant leadership in three ways—it is holistic, contextual, and empowering. By *holistic*, he means that this leadership development commits to transforming whole persons, families, and communities. By *contextual*, he means that these movements shape leadership development around cultural forms of faith and leadership. By *empowering*, he means it commits to equipping and releasing Indigenous leaders. These homegrown leaders are empowered to transform communities and multiply churches.

These indigenous leaders experience "simple, people-centered, practical, contextual, and participatory" training. Even though the training is simple, the goals are extraordinary. For example, "The Filipino mission movement seeks to mobilize a million tentmakers to do this type of mission and [transformational leadership development] by 2020."[22]

The West can learn much from this Indigenous disciple-making and church multiplication movements. We must learn from their simple and contextual approaches. Their whole-of-life approaches to *transformational leadership development* can guide us.

Missional movements and leadership. Recently, I spent time in Seoul, South Korea. I was ministering with All Nations Church. As I listened to how this church multiplies disciples and churches throughout Asia, I felt like I was listening to stories from the book of Acts. The stories of people who had given up everything for the sake of mission in China, India, Russia, Myanmar, Thailand, and Japan astonished me. I knew that I was witnessing a missional movement. I witnessed a movement developing the next generation of holisticostal leaders.

All Nations Church is pursuing a missional strategy soaked in prayer, discipleship, and sacrifice. It's moved by a dream to see Asia won for Jesus Christ. Every day of the year, even mid-winter when it is snowing and bitterly cold, teams of evangelists go out into the streets and from home to home. From a church that started ten years ago in a home with seventeen people, it now has over one thousand members. This is primarily because of its missional endeavors. All Nations Church believes that God desires to bring revival to the nations. This is because he is a missionary God. They believe that this means that they must be a missionary community. They must multiply missional disciples and churches and leaders.

After sending hundreds of full-time missionaries throughout Asia, they have decided to go further afield in their mission. They now send missionaries to nations that once sent missionaries to Korea. Instead of summer camps, young adults go on annual short-term mission trips. These youth pray about whether God is calling them into full-time missions. All Nations Church intends to send another thousand full-time missionaries

---

22. Lim, "Developing Transformational Leaders for Church Multiplication Movements in the Buddhist World," 101.

into these countries over the next decade. They want as many missionaries on the field as people attending their Sunday worship services.

All Nations Church in Seoul is an excellent example of a *missional church* that has become a *missional movement*. It releases thousands of *missional leaders* throughout the world.[23] It is only one story among countless others across Asia, Africa, Eastern Europe, and Latin America.

Roger D. Ibengi of the Democratic Republic of Congo calls pastors to missional leadership. He says it is time for the church to reexamine its missional passion and practice. The church must know if this line up "with God's mission of reconciling all of humankind to himself. God has raised leaders to equip and empower the church to engage in mission. We need to see the world as God sees it and help others embrace the same vision of reaching the whole world with the gospel of Jesus Christ."[24] Ibengi says leaders will never be missional until they become spiritual leaders with Christ-like character. Only servant leadership can be missional since our Messiah himself is a servant. We express spiritual leadership through integrity, prayer, mission, and service.

Spiritual Leadership

Ajith Fernando embodies spiritual leadership. *Christianity Today* recently ran a story on Fernando's life and ministry. Fernando serves as the national director of Youth for Christ in Sri Lanka. Amidst the poverty, drug abuse, violence, hatred, and hostility of war-torn Sri Lanka, Ajith Fernando is a spiritual giant. He speaks to thousands at conferences around the world. But Fernando lives a simple life of service and mission among the wounded, impoverished, and needy in Sri Lanka and other parts of Asia.

Tim Stafford of *Christianity Today* writes, "Everything Ajith Fernando writes and teaches is forged on the anvil of poverty, suffering, ethnic strife, and war—and tedious, patient administration . . . Though he speaks worldwide, he carefully limits that to twenty percent of his time, with half in Asia. Where he lives and breathes and theologizes is Sri Lanka, with all its pain."[25]

Fernando says we develop infectious passion and spiritual leadership as we travel down the road of frustration, suffering, and pain.[26] He asserts that Christian spiritual leadership has distinct qualities. He deals with these

23. Hill, *Salt, Light, and a City*, xv.

24. Ibengi and Starcher, "Missional Leadership for the African Church," no page numbers.

25. Stafford, "Choice," 44.

26. Fernando, *Jesus Driven Ministry*, 25–26.

themes often in his books, articles, seminars, and sermons. At its core, spiritual leadership is servant leadership. Spiritual leaders commit to the supremacy of Christ and his gospel. They identify with people (especially the broken, vulnerable, suffering, and poor). The Holy Spirit empowers their ministries (the Spirit gives power and fullness for service). They regularly retreat from activity (for times of solitude, prayer, study, and fasting). Spiritual leaders embrace servantship instead of drivenness, dominance, power, and control (servanthood is a regular theme in his writings). They saturate themselves in Scripture (the Scriptures are our authority, strength, security, qualification, and delight). They commit to bearing Good News. For Fernando, bearing Good News includes such things as (1) preaching the gospel, (2) relating to those of other faiths, (3) witnessing to Jesus Christ in our whole lives, (4) participating in God's mission in the world, (5) sharing the truth in love, and (6) engaging in social justice, compassionate service, and community development.

Spiritual leaders have other qualities. They grow in community and team and build deep spiritual friendships. They disciple the next generation of leaders. They launch disciples into ministry. They minister to the sick, demon-possessed, powerless, oppressed, and silenced. Spiritual leaders speak truth to secular and religious powers. They grow through suffering, frustration, pain, grief, and loss. They find spiritual and vocational fulfillment in service, sacrifice, and difficulty. They cultivate a life of prayer. Spiritual leaders understand that prayer is a source of power in ministry, a prevention of burnout, and a spring of spiritual vitality. They commune with the suffering servant. Jesus empowers spiritual leaders to serve him, his church, and his world.

Servantship: Concluding Reflections

We have seen that servant leadership (*servantship*) has many dimensions. It's culturally specific and cross-cultural. It's disciple-making and church-multiplying. It's missional. Its deep spirituality relies on the Holy Spirit's power, presence, and provision.

Here are six things we learn from how Majority World Christians practice servantship:

1. Servantship is biblical, and it glorifies Jesus Christ.

Hierarchical and authoritarian leadership is unbiblical. It pollutes, corrupts, and erodes the church. It points away from Christ. It degrades the church's worship, ministry, fellowship, and witness. Autocratic and ego-driven leadership never brings glory to God.

Servantship is the imitation of Jesus Christ. It is imitation through love and service. Servantship does not dismiss notions of leadership or servant leadership altogether. But it does evaluate and reshape these concepts. It examines and reconceives notions of power, authority, and influence.[27] Servantship cultivates a biblically informed and practical theology of leadership. This theology engages our understanding of church, servanthood, discipleship, Jesus, and mission.

Darrell Jackson is right when he says that Jesus re-conceived status in the kingdom of God as bonded service.[28] Such service is "accompanied by the forfeiture of social status and personal freedom, and characterized by utter reliance on the one to whom bonded service was being rendered."[29] Servantship reflects the Spirit of Jesus Christ. This is especially true when servantship evidences the characteristics of servanthood revealed in Phil 2:1–11 and other Scriptures. The metaphor of servanthood—and the servant mission and ministry of Jesus—must shape our practices of Christian servantship. Only then will it be Jesus-centered and outwardly focused Christian servantship.

In Phil 2:7, we read that Jesus "made himself nothing." He "emptied himself." Genuine Christian service is a movement away from selfish ambition, pride, and self-centeredness. Such service is a movement toward the same attitude as that of Jesus Christ. It's emptying oneself of pride, status, and control over others. It's being a servant. It's humbling oneself. Self-emptied discipleship is submission to God's love, will, and mission. "The ultimate characteristic of servantship is love leadership. I can serve people but not love them. However, I cannot love people and not serve them. The central point of the incarnation was love."[30]

We practice and reveal servantship through love. It must be the love demonstrated in the Incarnation and at the Cross. Servantship isn't an abstract or idealized love. It's concrete and embodied and tangible love. Elizabeth Petersen says we must practice our theology of the Cross. We serve the poor, broken, marginalized, silenced, and oppressed. Only then can we say that we love as Jesus loved. "God is present and active *amid*

---

27. See the excellent treatment of servant leadership by Puerto Rican American theologian Efrian Agosto in Agosto, *Servant Leadership*.

28. Jackson, "For the Son of Man Did Not Come to Lead, But to Be Led," 28.

29. Jackson, "For the Son of Man Did Not Come to Lead, But to Be Led."

30. Helland, "Nothing Leadership," 36. Helland coined the terms *downward missional leadership* and *nothing leadership* to describe Christian leadership.

the Broken Ones."[31] Such loving service is costly. You cannot practice loving service without heartbreak, suffering, and loss. But our eternal joy is more significant.

Why do Christian leaders embrace unbiblical, self-serving, or controlling leadership models? Sometimes, they do this because of pride. Sometimes, they do this because they've traded theology for pragmatics. Servantship demands biblically grounded and self-reflective theology. It demands ministry practices rooted in Trinitarian theology. It requires us to nourish our ministry practices with theologies of church and mission and ministry. *Servantship is only possible when it's rooted in the dynamic theological imagination of the people of God.* In other words, it thrives in an environment of theological thought and relational connection. It flourishes where God's people take Scripture seriously, including Christ's call to service, humility, and love. This theological imagination is not restricted to the academy. It finds its fullest expression in a living conversation. This conversation must include scholars, leaders, churches, the gospel narrative, traditions, theologies, and cultures. This theological imagination finds its fullest expression in conversation with the needs and challenges of specific contexts.

How do we move toward servantship? We embrace servantship by genuinely wanting to glorify Christ and not us, exalting him and making ourselves nothing, rejecting self-seeking and self-serving and domineering forms of leadership, embracing the servanthood exemplified by Jesus Christ, reflecting theologically on Scripture, meditating on passages like Philippians 2, and the four Gospels, and putting our biblical observations and convictions into practice.

Jesus described himself as a servant. So did the apostle Paul. Repeatedly, Scripture commands us to serve Jesus, his church, and his world. Jesus drives us from control to service, from competition to love, from a scarcity mindset to a generous spirit, from pride to humility, from ambition to self-denial, from drivenness to servanthood, from ego strength to interdependent vigor, and from identification with the powerful to servantship "via the Broken Ones." "Whoever wants to be great among you must be your servant, and whoever wants to be first must be a servant of all. For even the Son of Man did not come to be served, but to serve, and to give his life as a ransom for many" (Mark 10:43–45 and Matt 20:26–28).

Examining the biblical material, my friend Darrell Jackson forms a powerful conclusion:

---

31. Petersen and Swart, "Via the Broken Ones," 20. Italics added for emphases.

PART 3: REVITALIZING OUR CHURCHES

> By redefining the concepts of greatness and status within the kingdom of God with reference to the hallmarks of service and humility, Jesus initiates a revolution of ruling and leadership. This is a vital insight for those who lead churches and Christian organizations . . . Far from the throne-rooms and boardrooms, the "scum" of the earth (1 Corinthians 4:13) are exercising a ministry of service and humility that is frequently regarded with contempt, is typically accompanied by sacrificial suffering, yet which is capable of a revolution on a cosmic scale, for it is a call to royal service in a kingdom against which the gates of Hades will not prevail (Matthew 16:18).[32]

This biblical servantship is revolutionary. It redefines ruling, status, and leadership. It glorifies our Lord Jesus Christ. Through poverty, tears, humility, righteousness, mercy, purity, peacemaking, suffering, love for enemies, and the service of all, servantship witnesses to the "kingdom of God among you" (Matthew 5–7). It joins Jesus's mission to heal, transform, and redeem the world.

2. Servantship is sustained by a dynamic theology and lifestyle of service.

This flows from the previous point. We need to develop a biblical theology of servantship. We must shape this in a multifaceted and multi-voiced way. We do this in conversation with theology, Scripture, contexts, traditions, cultures, etc. We do this in dialogue and service with "the least of these." My book *Servantship* makes a start on this theology of service and servantship. But much more work needs to be done.

Those of us in Christian leadership are rarely comfortable with service. We want to be "leaders," not "servants." So, we try to soften the radical demands of servanthood with a hyphenated term like "servant-leadership." That way, we can still discuss servanthood but take on leaders' posture. We can wax lyrical about service but pride ourselves on being leaders. We can avoid the revolutionary outlook and demands of servantship. "Over the past forty years, the idea of servant leadership entered the church leadership discussion. But leaders could not bear the concept of "servant-ship" as a stand-alone term. "Leadership" had to be added to the equation. Being a servant is the form of leadership urged upon us by Jesus [and] the ethos of leadership is not a posture but a result."[33]

---

32. Jackson, "For the Son of Man Did Not Come to Lead, But to Be Led," 30–31.
33. Lance Ford, *Unleader*, 85–86.

We bolster our servantship through a vibrant theology *and* lifestyle of service. We need to be careful not to turn a theology of servantship into a rigid ideology. When we do this, we grasp after ideological control and power. Instead, we will integrate our theology of *servantship* with a lifestyle of sacrificial service, gratuitous love, Spirit-empowered grace, deep relationships, and genuine humility.[34] We will let our theology of servantship emerge from our lifestyle of service. We will enrich our service through a vigorous theology of servantship.

3. Servantship is "shaped via the Broken Ones."[35]

Remember that the Broken Ones "are not objects to be ignored, manipulated, and denigrated, but are the significant partners for an incipient understanding of leadership, shaped *via* an engagement with the Broken Ones amid their circumstances of brokenness."[36]

Our servantship must transcend "typical center/edge stereotypes in the power relations of engagement with broken people." This way, we learn what it means to serve as Christian leaders "via the Broken Ones." In other words, we will learn to serve via their courage, brokenness, resilience, voices, and stories.[37] The people whom the world scorns and despises and sidelines teach us to serve. Who are those people in your culture?

Servantship is *soul work*. It's a process of personal transformation we embrace as we serve with Jesus Christ and the Broken Ones in our society. Jesus transforms us as co-creators, co-sufferers, and co-servers with him and his Broken Ones. "It is leadership formation via the presence of the Broken One amid the Broken Ones."[38] It's time we saw the Broken Ones as gifts and graces to our communities and theologies and formation as servants.

4. Servantship is expressed in culturally-sensitive and culturally-contradicting ways.

The GLOBE study of sixty-two cultures helps us understand how different societies conceive and practice leadership. Cultural attributes affect leader

---

34. Petersen and Swart, "Via the Broken Ones," 26.
35. Petersen and Swart, "Via the Broken Ones," 18.
36. Petersen and Swart, "Via the Broken Ones," 19.
37. Petersen and Swart, "Via the Broken Ones," 12.
38. Petersen and Swart, "Via the Broken Ones," 22.

behaviors and organizational practices. Culture shapes people's values in their leader's traits, behaviors, and attitudes.

All cultures value certain things in leaders. These include integrity, vision, collaboration, diplomacy, communication, self-sacrifice, humility, and modesty. Servantship enhances these things. This is because it makes us less ego-driven, selfish, and authoritarian. Servantship involves joining with Jesus Christ as he empowers and transforms people and organizations. It involves inviting people to join Jesus in his vision for their lives, organizations, and the world. When we are servants of Christ and his church, we can provide Christ-honoring vision, transformation, and empowerment. We put people before programs, service before ego, love before demands, well-being before results, and human flourishing before productivity. We empower people and organizations to allow Christ's vision for their lives and the world to transform them.

The challenge is to express servantship in culturally sensitive ways. We need to respect the culture. We don't want to be unaware of cultural norms and expectations. Let me use an example. My Australian culture is individualistic and egalitarian. People treat leaders as friends. Australians have little regard for titles, honors, and formal positions. So, Australian Christian leaders must build credibility with Australians over a long period based on character and competency. But, when I minister in South Korea, for example, I don't want to offend people by my egalitarian ways. Korea is a collectivist, hierarchical, and harmony-oriented culture. I need to respect that when I minister and serve there. I tailor my service to the people and church of Korea according to their culture.

But we also need to show servantship qualities that contradict how leadership is usually done. Jesus told his disciples not to act like the rulers of the Gentiles. Instead, he expected them to be servants. So, what are the leadership behaviors and postures in your culture that the gospel calls you to contradict? Some things emerge in most cultures (e.g., ego, dominance, self-seeking, and self-serving behaviors). But there may be leadership expectations, behaviors, and postures in your culture that you will challenge through your life as much as your words. The good news is that in all cultures, people want their leaders to show qualities that servantship enhances.

5. Servantship multiplies missional leaders and congregations.

We see this repeatedly in the Majority World. I've provided examples in this chapter. These missional leaders and congregations have vital characteristics. They're homegrown and Indigenous to their cultures. They're committed to disciple-making and church multiplication and mission. What's the result? We see astonishing growth in Majority World churches. We see an extraordinary multiplication of churches. We see missional movements multiplying throughout Asia, Africa, Eastern Europe, and Latin America.

6. Servantship is at the heart of Christian spirituality, and Christian spirituality is essential to servantship.

Elizabeth Petersen, Ajith Fernando, Roger D. Ibengi, and other Majority World leaders clearly state that servantship is at the heart of Christian spirituality. Jesus makes this clear in the Gospels, too. Servantship enriches and enlarges Christian spirituality. Our spiritual lives expand as we serve Jesus and his church and his world. In John 13, Jesus washes his disciples' feet. He shows them what discipleship and Christian spirituality looks like. It's a life of service. "Now that I, your Lord and Teacher, have washed your feet, you also should wash one another's feet. I have set you an example that you should do as I have done for you" (John 13:14–15).

Servantship is crucial to Christian spirituality. Christian spirituality is vital to servantship. These are interdependent. One cannot exist without the other.

As we seek to be servants, we remember the example and words of Jesus:

> You call me 'Teacher' and 'Lord,' and rightly so, for that is what I am. Now that I, your Lord and Teacher, have washed your feet, you also should wash one another's feet. I have set you an example that you should do as I have done for you. Very truly I tell you, servants are not greater than their master, nor are messengers greater than the one who sent them. Now that you know these things, you will be blessed if you do them. (John 13:13–17)

PART 3: REVITALIZING OUR CHURCHES

Study Questions

1. Who are the *Broken Ones* in your community that you are serving? Are they leading you toward more authentic healing, transformation, and spiritual insight?

2. What does it mean for you to *practice servantship* in your setting? What does it mean for you to be a servant?

3. Is your form of leadership culturally relevant and not only for your church culture?

4. What practices are you forming that sustain your spiritual leadership?

5. How are you prioritizing these spiritual practices? Who will you ask to keep you accountable for these practices?

6. As a small group or ministry team, consider Ajith Fernando's list of the *distinct qualities of spiritual leadership*. These are detailed in this chapter. How will you develop these qualities individually and as a group? How will you cultivate them in your church, family, small group, ministry team, or personal discipleship?

20.

Recovering Community

The Twelfth Expression

CHRISTIAN CHURCHES NEED TO rediscover the power of community. We need to recover *relationships* as the heart of human fullness and well-being. "The person is a being with a heart, one who has the capacity to be open to attraction by another, to be in communication and interpersonal communion with another, others, and God. This is what distinguishes us as persons: The capacity to be toward others in a relation of one, mutual Love."[1]

In this chapter, I discuss the need to shape churches characterized by community. I show how Christian theology helps us grasp the relationship between human nature and community. I indicate how trinitarian theology helps us grasp the relationship between God's nature and the church's mission and community. From there, I consider lessons for Western churches.

Theology, Humanity, and Community

Communion is a theme that runs through Majority World and Indigenous writings on the church. The church is not made up of autonomous and independent individuals. God calls the church to communion. This communion is among humans. It's with the Father and Son and Holy Spirit. Gustavo Gutiérrez, for example, develops the theme of community in his

---

1. Downey, *Altogether Gift*, 70.

writings. He associates interpersonal and human-divine communion with key theological themes:

> Salvation—the communion of human beings with God and among themselves—is something which embraces all human reality.[2]
>
> In the final analysis, to set free is to give life—communion with God and with others—or, to use the language of Puebla, liberation for communion and participation.[3]
>
> Liberation . . . is a journey toward communion. Communion, however, is a gift of Christ who sets us free in order that we may be free, free to love; it is in this communion that full freedom resides.[4]

Christian theology emphasizes the communion of human beings with God and each other. It associates such communion with the nature of humans, God, and the church. In Christian theology, humans are created beings. God creates us in his image. We're sexual, physical, embodied, and relational beings. We're not self-sufficient. We're profoundly relational. We are wholly and essentially *persons-in-relationship*—from and for God and others.[5] In Christian anthropology, to be an integrated and authentic self is to be in relationships. The person doesn't simply have relationships. The person *is relationship*. God forms us from "dust"—not as a closed historical event, but as a relational process.[6] We're fashioned from "clay" by our Creator at our conception. Our entire lives testify to the relational renewal process and creative Divine genius. To be a creature is to be shaped by God from nothing. It's to be birthed into a process of being. God calls and creates us. He does this so that we might fulfill our God-ordained purpose. Our purpose is to glorify him through our relational beings and capacities.

God continually and lovingly creates human beings. We're firmly located within creation. The created order is relational. In *Believing Three Ways in One God*, Nicholas Lash writes, "What makes the doctrine of createdness good news is the discovery that God makes the world 'parentally.'"[7] We experience God's parental nurture, interpersonal communion, and love. We experience these in our createdness and our embodiment. (Here, I am

---

2. Gutiérrez, *Theology of Liberation*, 85.
3. Gutiérrez, *We Drink from Our Own Wells*, 92.
4. Gutiérrez, *Truth Shall Make You Free*, 103.
5. Gen 1:26–27.
6. Gen 2:7.
7. Lash, *Believing Three Ways in One God*, 43.

referring to our experience of these in our creation, through the person and work of Christ, and a myriad of other ways.) God continually forms and sustains creation parentally. As part of creation, human beings enjoy the parental care and concern of the Creator God.

Visions of grandeur, independence, control, and self-sufficiency often delude us. Western understandings of self often encourage us to view ourselves this way. But we aren't self-made. We're not independent. We're not in control. We're continually created out of the abundance of God's immeasurable love, grace, and power. We connect with God and others as relational, created, and interdependent beings.

The Incarnation affirms humans as created, relational beings—as persons-in-relationship. In the Incarnation, God elevates the created order by his grace. He comes into our context to redeem and heal. The Incarnation affirms the value of creation, humanity, and relationship. In the Incarnation, Jesus Christ reveals his ongoing relationship to creation and humanity. Christ willingly and lovingly immerses himself in creation. He engages time and space and flesh and matter. He takes on human form. He lovingly meets, touches, and values people. Each one created in his relational image to be essentially, utterly relational. Christ's Incarnation shows his passion for trinitarian relations. It shows his desire for a relationship with us. Human beings yearn for a relationship with each other and God. Christ has enabled this through Creation and Incarnation and death and resurrection.

God's ongoing creative activity and incarnational presence sustain a Christ-dependent world. This world is in an authentic and dependent relationship with the triune God. (This is the case even though the Creator is distinct from the world and though the world is in rebellion from him.) God is in an ongoing relationship with creation, which includes humanity. He reveals creation's future—a kingdom of glory, praise, and relationship with him. Humanity, as part of creation, glorifies God along with the rest of creation. Our glorification of the triune God is an interpersonal outpouring of love and communion. This is the movement toward self-transcendence to which personal development models refer. Communion with God and others draws us away from self-centeredness. It enables us to focus on the God who is beyond us. It liberates us to connect with other human beings and with creation.[8]

We open ourselves to God to live in his creative love, to put off self, and to make him the new center of our beings. We desire his life to flow through us. We want this Divine life to express itself in the newness and wholeness of our lives. We grow personally, then, when we let go of self. We

---

8. Clarke, "To Be Is to Be Self-Communicative," 450–53.

grow as we embrace God and others. We grow in love, compassion, humility, and interdependence through our relationship with God and others.

The doctrines of Creation and Incarnation, then, tell us much. They show us that human beings have relationships at the center of their beings. "Relationships are constitutive of who and all that we are. We are unthinkable outside of a relationship. Outside of the God relationship and relationships with others, we are nothing. We are no-thing. We would not exist."[9] In one sense, our divine purpose to glorify God and experience union with him is beyond the world. Yet, we're now entirely and relationally in the world. Being human means expressing our bodiliness, sexuality, and relationality in the world. That's why we're responsible for (and influenced by) families, relationships, ecologies, societies, and creation. Embodiment, personhood, world, and history are relational concepts. They're knit together in the interdependent web of all created things. They take shape after their relational Creator God. They're interconnected when they're beautiful, mundane, or horrifying.

This interpersonal and mutually responsible relatedness means we aren't only located in creation. We are responsible for nurturing, healing, and restoring it (after God's will and kingdom). We follow the mission of Christ. We seek the restoration of creation, persons, bodies, cultures, societies, and communities. We do this in dependent communion with God and interdependent relationship with others. We do this for the glory of the Father, Son, and Holy Spirit.

Humans can shape their lives and communities by participating in what God is doing around us. This is an essential and relational dimension of the hopeful expectation of human existence. We participate in God's loving and restoring activity in creation—in bodies, families, social systems, the world, and human history.

We participate in God's redemption and experience wholeness in our relationship with God and others. Our theologies of Creation, Incarnation, Trinity, humanity, mission, salvation, and the church tell us we are fundamentally *persons-in-relationship*.

Trinity, Mission, and Community

Trinitarian theology is popular in the East and other Majority World settings. For many Majority World theologians, it shapes their understanding of the church. Theologians who exemplify this include Jung Young Lee, James Henry Owino Kombo, Nozomu Miyahira, Miroslav Volf, John

9. Jackson, "TH568 Lecture Notes," 4.

Zizioulas, Ricardo Barbosa de Sousa, Simon Chan, Leonardo Boff, Damon So, Athanasius, Gregory of Nazianzus, and Basil the Great (see the Cappadocian Fathers).

What do we learn from these authors about the trinitarian and human community? Unity and oneness permeate the Trinity. The Triune God *is* relations.[10] The people of God are the beneficiaries of the relationship of love, intimacy, and communion between the persons of the Godhead. Jesus's redemptive mission springs from his love for the Father. It flows from his longing to fulfill his Father's will. In the Godhead, we see the highest example of self-sacrifice and mutual dedication. Three divine Persons exist in perfect harmony and unity. They share divine faculties, power, holiness, perfection, and love.[11]

To be human is to be in the grip of God's grace. God moves us toward union with him. He draws us to interpersonal communion with him. In the Trinity, we see a dynamic process of self-giving, self-communicating, and self-reciprocating love. This love penetrates the essence and relations of the Trinity. This trinitarian love draws us in as beneficiaries and participants. This love shapes our being and personhood. It makes us essentially relational and dependent on Divine and human relationships.[12] It's the reason for our yearning for the other. It's the source of our desire for God. It's the cause of our hopelessness (or struggle for meaning) outside of loving communion and community.

The intradivine communion within the person of God gives rich meaning and theological depth to the idea of *person-in-relationship*. God is a dialogical, communing being. He exists in an intradivine relationship. This understanding of the nature of God uncovers the true nature of humanity. We are relational and interdependent. The trinitarian relationships reveal human nature. They explain our profound yearning for others and our desire for the triune God.

Human beings do not consist of a closed self. We exist in relationship with others and God. Our interior lives reflect the nature of the Trinity—moreover, the whole human self corresponds to the divine substance. (There are, of course, limitations to the correspondence.) The whole of our being is relational. We reflect (imperfectly and in a creaturely way) the Trinity.[13] Where do we see human yearnings for divine-human communion and grace and relationship? We see it in the desire for deeper relationships and

---

10. Cunningham, *These Three Are One*, 71.
11. Hill, *Salt, Light, and a City*, 233–35.
12. Hill, *Salt, Light, and a City*, 257–60.
13. Ratzinger, "Retrieving the Tradition," 444.

community. We see it in the frustration about the inadequacy of everything acquired and achieved. We see it in modern and ancient spiritual quests. We see it in the radical protests of loneliness and death. These urges are relational urges. Much human suffering is the direct result of alienation and isolation.

At our core, we're interpersonal, relational, and intersubjective. The triune God creates us in his relational image. He enjoys perfect relationships, love, and communion. He invites us into this Divine communion and relationships with others. Communion with the Divine and with other persons is the means of salvation. There is no gospel, no saving truth, outside of a relationship with the Trinity and his people. Relationships are the means of fulfilled, authentic, and integrated living and selfhood. "The core of our integration as a person requires union with the God who is the ground of our being. Integration and spiritual wholeness involve living out of that union. Firstly, it's union with the Trinity. Then it's union with others."[14]

We shape missional churches and practices with attention to two things. Firstly, we allow the interior life of the Trinity—*the social or immanent Trinity*—to shape our imagination, aims, and relations. Secondly, the acts, roles, and purposes of the trinitarian Persons in history—*the economic Trinity*—define our theology, gospel, and mission. I focused on this in a chapter of my first volume on missional ecclesiology: *Salt, Light, and a City*. The social reality of the Trinity has the potential to help us appreciate the social community of the church. The correspondence is essential. But, as Croatian theologian Miroslav Volf reminds us, the analogy has both benefits and limitations.[15]

Likewise, the functions of each member of the Trinity in the mission of God help us understand the missional nature of the church. The Trinity allows us to participate in "creation, re-creation, and final consummation."[16] The sending activity and the missional nature of the triune God are the source of the church's mission. The Father sends the Son. The Father and Son send the Spirit. The Trinity sends the church into the world. "This perspective helps us understand the creation of a church considering God's being, God's social reality as a Trinity, and the work of all three persons. The church's ministry, in turn, must reflect all three aspects of the Godhead."[17]

Leonardo Boff has written extensively on this. He describes the relationship between the Trinity and the church's mission, community,

---

14. Jackson, "TH568 Lecture Notes," 5.
15. Volf, *After Our Likeness*, 198–200.
16. Van Gelder, *Essence of the Church*, 35 and 97.
17. Van Gelder, *Essence of the Church*, 130.

structures, and liberating actions. For Boff, the Trinity is the model of a perfect community and social liberation. Through the doctrine of the Trinity, Boff dismantles authoritarian notions. He deconstructs ideas that support centralized power. He attacks a-trinitarian monotheistic models of church. Instead, in trinitarian theology, Boff finds resources for diversity-in-communion. He also finds inspiration for liberating relationships and missional passion.

Firstly, trinitarian communing with others involves *the presence of one to another*. This is a communicative and relational openness. Secondly, it requires *reciprocity*. This is generous and self-sacrificial giving and receiving. Thirdly, it demands *immediacy*. This is "intimacy, transparency of intention, union of hearts, and convergence of interests." It's forming "bonds of communion." Fourthly, trinitarian communing with others needs *community*. By that, I mean the formation of a communing people. Fifthly, it involves *being-in-openness*. "Only a being open to others can communicate with, relate to, and build a community with other, con-natural beings." Sixthly, trinitarian communing with others includes *being-in-transcendence*. This is reaching beyond oneself for the sake of communion with others. It's doing this to establish "bonds of interdependence." Lastly, trinitarian communion with others enables *being-us*. This means allowing communion to create a real community. This isn't just a visible community—it's "a mode of being." Through this community, we choose to become differentiated but also "part of a single whole."[18]

This leads us to the trinitarian ground of mission. It takes us to the trinitarian foundations of the missional and liberating life of the church. The communion and mission of the Trinity are inextricably linked. We cannot consider them as separate dimensions of God. Nor can we consider communion and mission separate realities shaping disconnected dimensions of the church. This is because the mission of the Triune God is to bring humanity back into communion with the Father, Son, and Holy Spirit.

Communion within the triune God is the source or wellspring of his divine mission. The triune God directs his mission toward his divine communion. In other words, *the communion of the Triune God is the mission of the Triune God, and the mission of the Triune God is the communion of the Triune God*. Again, God's being-in-communion is God's being-on-mission. God's being-on-mission is God's being-in-communion. A missional understanding of the church claims that the church reflects this trinitarian dynamic. The church's being-in-communion is the church's being-on-mission, and vice versa.

18. Boff, "Trinitarian Community," 293–95.

For the church, there's no true communion without mission and no true mission without communion. Scripture doesn't allow for a mission that is separate from a community-on-mission. It doesn't allow for a community that is separate from a missional community.[19] The Spirit must vivify and empower a genuinely participative community modeled after the trinitarian relations. The Spirit shapes a communing and missional people in the image of the Trinity.[20]

This leaves us with an important question. "How can we cultivate a community of Trinity-imaging relationships?" I've discussed the importance of shaping churches characterized by meaningful relationships. I've talked about how crucial it is that our churches show Trinity-imaging mission and communion. I now turn to the concrete lessons Majority World thinkers teach us.

Community: Concluding Reflections

Building a community is not easy. Individualism is deeply entrenched in Western cultures. Our churches are often embroiled in conflict and division. Yet, we must *be* faith communities that enrich lives, nurture relationships, and show Jesus's love. We must witness to Jesus through our love, humility, and unity.

The church will experience community and engage in a compelling mission when it practices *koinonia*. *Koinonia* is the deep, intimate, participatory, and communing fellowship believers experience with each other and with God. The word appears nineteen times in the Greek New Testament. We can translate it as "fellowship," "sharing," "joint participation," "contribution," or "communion."

Here are eight things we learn from how Majority World Christians value community and relationship.

1. *Koinonia* churches emphasize relational discipleship and spirituality.

Western cultures are individualistic. Western Christians absorb this individualism. It permeates Western Christian spirituality. But humans are inherently social. Christian spirituality thrives in deep communion with God and others.

---

19. Hill, *Salt, Light, and a City*, 233–35.
20. Volf, "Community Formation as an Image of the Triune God," 235.

Jesus confronts unhelpful and destructive forms of spirituality. These are individualistic and independent. They're vain and privatized. They're disembodied and self-justifying. They're legalistic. They're immoral and idolatrous. They're hostile and given to bitter conflict. They're jealous, and they enjoy disunity. They're conceited and envious.

True discipleship builds relationships. It fosters community. It glorifies Christ. It enjoys faith, hope, and love. Christian spirituality shows love, joy, and peace alone or in relationships. It's patient, kind, and good. It's faithful, gentle, and self-controlled.[21] It values and nurtures relationships and communities.

Authentic spirituality desires communion with God and others. It's located and nurtured in an authentic and local community. Within a community, authentic Christian spirituality experiences personal growth and integration. In a community, it grows in Christlikeness, holiness, and love. Through community, it grows in compassion and faith and hope and conversion. The primary forum for these things is relationships. Relationships are the hubs of this spiritual expression of growth and development.

2. *Koinonia* churches embark on "a journey toward communion."

Gustavo Gutiérrez reminds us that communion with God and others is a divine gift. Such communion is "a gift of Christ who sets us free so that we may be free, free to love; it is in this communion that full freedom resides."[22] God frees us by his grace—in all areas of life—so that we can embark on a "journey of communion" with him and others.[23] Our communion with God and other human beings is often less than ideal. But we need to remember that communion is a grace. We are on a journey. We'll know complete and perfect communion with God and others at the end of the age. Our responsibility is to keep in step with the Spirit on this journey toward communion.

3. *Koinonia* churches emulate the trinitarian relations.

Many Majority World theologians assert that the church must imitate the trinitarian communion. We need to allow the Trinity's mission, love, intimacy, community, and unity to be a model for our mission and fellowship.

21. Gal 5:13–26.
22. Gutiérrez, *Truth Shall Make You Free*, 103.
23. Gutiérrez, *Truth Shall Make You Free*, 103.

Craig Van Gelder claims that "a trinitarian understanding is now the common starting point for thinking about God's people in the world, the church, and how the church participates in God's mission in the world."[24] I agree with Craig Van Gelder when he asserts that ecclesiology and missiology aren't only "interrelated and complementary." They're both grounded in the doctrine of the Trinity. They both find their source in "the Triune God in mission to all creation."[25]

The interior life of the Trinity can help us understand the nature and potential of communion among God's people. The love, intimacy, unity, and embrace of the members of the Trinity provide a model or analogy for the church. Here, I'm referring to the immanent (ontological) Trinity.

Volf reminds us that there are ways in which ecclesial communion corresponds to trinitarian communion. There are limitations to the analogy. Volf's trinitarian ecclesiology affects his understanding of communion within local churches. It shapes his understanding of human personhood. It defines his theology of ecclesial relationships. The Trinity is his determining analogy for the church's nature, structures, relations, ministries, and mission. Volf is right when he says the trinitarian analogy should shape the church. It can shape our church's self-understanding and life together. It can deepen our love. It can help us navigate the complexities and paradoxes of unity and diversity as we seek to *image the Trinity*.[26] The love and communion between Christians and churches should correspond, as far as possible, to the trinitarian relations.

4. *Koinonia* churches embrace distinctive qualities.

Leonardo Boff outlines the qualities of churches that imitate trinitarian relations. Individual Christians can cultivate these virtues, too. These churches nurture presence, reciprocity, immediacy, and community. What does this mean? Boff says that Trinity-imaging Christians (1) are present to one another. (They do this through communicative and relational openness.) (2) They embrace reciprocity. (They do this through generous and self-sacrificial giving and receiving.) (3) They pursue immediacy. (They do this through "intimacy, transparency of intention, union of hearts, convergence of interests," and "bonds of communion.") (4) They develop authentic community. They are single-focused in their formation of communing and missional people.

24. Van Gelder, *Essence of the Church*, 11.
25. Van Gelder, *Essence of the Church*, 31.
26. Volf, *After Our Likeness*, 194–97.

What other qualities do we observe? (5) Trinity-imaging churches cultivate *self-in-relationship*. There is no self without relationships. These churches recognize this. So, they prioritize and nurture deep relationships. (6) They nurture *being-in-openness*. This means being genuinely open to others. (7) They foster *being-in-transcendence*. This involves reaching beyond themselves for the sake of communion with others. They establish "bonds of interdependence." (8) They encourage *being-us*. This means being differentiated but also "part of a single whole."[27]

5. *Koinonia* churches practice extravagant welcome and hospitality.

Ruth Padilla DeBorst drives this point home. We must be churches, homes, and families "at which immigrants, people of diverse cultural backgrounds and different languages are welcome, not as oddities or welfare cases, but as fully-fledged members."[28] We replace exclusion with embrace, hostility with love, prejudice with respect, judgment with grace, greed with generosity, envy with contentment, fear with hope, rejection with welcome, frigidity with warmth, and isolation with community and hospitality. We do this *in response* to the extravagant grace and welcome Jesus Christ offers us. We do this *as witnesses* to Christ and the coming age. He is our peace. He reconciled us to God and each other.

> Consequently, you are no longer foreigners and strangers but fellow citizens with God's people and members of his household, built on the foundation of the apostles and prophets, with Christ Jesus himself as the chief cornerstone. The whole building is joined together in him and rises to become a holy temple in the Lord. In him, you, too, are being built together to become a dwelling in which God lives by his Spirit. (Eph 2:19–22)

On the final day, Jesus Christ will gather a great multitude from every nation, tribe, people, and language to worship him (Rev 7:9–17). The welcome and hospitality we practice now reflect what he has already done and what he will do in the coming age.

---

27. Boff, "Trinitarian Community," 293–95.
28. DeBorst, "'Unexpected' Guests," 75–76.

PART 3: REVITALIZING OUR CHURCHES

6. *Koinonia* churches generate *communitas*.

Communitas is a significant term for understanding the Christian community. It's an anthropological idea. It has implications for the church and its community and mission.

Victor and Edith Turner developed their understanding of *communitas* while studying groups and rites of passage in Indigenous and Majority World cultures.[29] Victor Turner was a cultural anthropologist studying Indigenous people groups. He described *communitas* as the profound community spirit, social solidarity, and togetherness felt by groups going through change and transition. This is a *liminal* experience. Groups experience *liminality* when they're going through transition. *Liminality* is the disorienting and ambiguous stage between *what a group is* and *what it is becoming*. Liminality alters their social relationships. Their sense of meaning and identity shifts. The experience enriches their spirituality, community, and shared identity. During transition phases, these groups experience uncertainty and fear, fresh courage, revived rites of passage, new meanings, shared mission, and deep interconnectedness. They experience community in fresh and profound ways. They experience a renewal of social cohesion, shared values, and fresh group identity.

In 2012, Edith Turner produced a complete treatment of *communitas*. She provided fascinating examples from all over the world.[30] Victor and Edith Turner suggest that Western cultures can learn much from *liminality* and *communitas* in Majority World and Indigenous cultures. This is especially true for the church during periods of change, upheaval, and transition. God draws his church into sacred covenant and intimate communion through periods of liminality. He leads his church into *communitas* and *koinonia*. God then sends the church into the world as a sign, foretaste, and witness to the gospel, the kingdom, and trinitarian communion.

7. *Koinonia* churches cultivate spiritual friendships.

Ajith Fernando believes that we must retrieve the Christian tradition of spiritual friendship. Such friendship builds an authentic community. We must develop spiritual friendships marked by love, prayer, vulnerability, commitment, forgiveness, mission, and respect.

---

29. Turner, *Communitas*; Turner, *Ritual Process*; Turner, *Dramas, Fields, and Metaphors*.

30. Turner, *Communitas*.

In *Reclaiming Friendship*, Fernando claims that real friendship is often alien to our culture and churches. We shape such friendship around trinitarian relations and the values of the kingdom of God. The presence and power of the Spirit enables true friendship. Genuine spiritual friendship is a rare gift. Even though it's rare, it's essential for the Christian community. Christian morality and virtue are crucial to successful friendships. Friendship is about relational and personal holism. This is because deep and genuine friendships demand much from us. They need commitment and love and honesty and loyalty and respect. We discover spiritual friendship through shared lives, dreams, worship, love, mission, and respect. Fernando says that we need to reclaim spiritual friendship. We need it for the sake of discipleship and community and mission and personal wholeness.

Aelred of Rievaulx's *Spiritual Friendship* portrays a friend as a guardian of love and the spirit. A friend is a companion of one's soul from whom we hide nothing. A friend is the medicine of life that we choose and test with care and caution, and one whom we can trust our affections and deepest secrets. For Aelred, the goal of friendship is Jesus Christ. Those "who abide in friendship abide in God and God in them."[31] Friendship can lead to union with Christ. It points the way to Christ. Aelred believed that the stages toward perfect spiritual friendship are selection, probation, admission, and harmony. Union with a spiritual friend can lead to union with Christ. The culmination of spiritual friendship is union with God in Christ.

Fernando says that deep spiritual friendship involves lingering with others. It involves telling them the truth in a spirit of grace and love. Spiritual friendships require the wise choice of friends. We nurture spiritual friendships through vulnerability, openness, redeemed egos, and unselfish commitment. We care for spiritual friends through gracious forgiveness, healthy communication, and covenant love. We encourage their spiritual life and discipline. They foster ours. We enrich spiritual friends through prayer, presence, healing wounds, and controlling our tongues. We provide spiritual friends with comfort during grief and loss and celebration during joy and success.[32] Our relationship with God enables us to pursue healthy spiritual friendships.

Our modern world tends to exalt individualism and autonomous human existence and rights. Radical individualism leads people into a life of personal and social fragmentation. But a healthy community can lead toward wholeness.

---

31. Aelred, *Spiritual Friendship*, 1:69–70.
32. Fernando, *Reclaiming Friendship*.

PART 3: REVITALIZING OUR CHURCHES

Much Majority World and Indigenous thought challenge deep-seated individualism. It challenges an individualism that sees humans as standing outside traditions or communities. Human beings are individuals-within-community. Social networks and communities are integral and indispensable to human existence. We form worldviews, spiritualities, and personal identities within communities. We find meaning, virtues, morals, identity, vocation, and personal formation within communities. These themes peak in a theology of the social Trinity and Christian *koinonia*.

8. *Koinonia* churches reactivate *koinonia*.

How can the church reactivate *koinonia*? I will answer this by engaging some of the thoughts of five Majority World theologians. These are S. Wesley Ariarajah, Ruth Padilla DeBorst, Samuel Escobar, Izunna Okonkwo, and M. M. Thomas. These five thinkers show us that we reactivate *koinonia* through eight practices:

First, we build *koinonia* on trinitarian and Christological foundations. As we have seen in this chapter, the true Christian community is trinitarian in theology and practice. It's participatory, reciprocal, decentralized, mutual, and so on. Such *koinonia* is Christ-centered. It shapes its being, ministries, structures, and mission around the person, gospel, and mission of Jesus Christ.

Second, we enhance *koinonia* as we release all believers to ministry. Contribution and participation are at the heart of *koinonia*. Liberating and non-manipulative pastoral ministry seeks to identify, develop, and release all God's people to ministry. It enables them to discover their God-given contribution to the community and mission. Karl Barth puts it well. "There can be no "ecclesiastics" and "lay people," there cannot be one church that simply "instructs," and another that is "under instruction," because no member of the church exists who is not all of that in their own right." Jürgen Moltmann says, "The power behind unity is love. The power behind diversity is freedom."[33]

Third, we foster *koinonia* by engaging pluralities. Diversities and pluralities bring richness, possibilities, conflicts, and difficulties. Today, diversity and plurality characterize the global and local church. The church is in pluralist, multicultural, and multi-religious societies. We foster *koinonia* amid such diversity. We nurture *koinonia* by cultivating a Christian "spirituality for plurality" and "communities of peace" for all peoples. S. Wesley

---

33. Escobar, "Church as Community," 142–51 (Barth and Moltmann are quoted by Alberto Fernando Roldan on page 151 of this book).

Ariarajah suggests we nurture a positive and enthusiastic attitude to plurality. He says we do this by affirming ethnic and cultural identities. We do it by embracing justice and peace as the bases for building community. We need mechanisms for reconciliation and communication. We need to reject violence.

I agree with much that Ariarajah proposes. But I'm committed to diversity and peace without diminishing the uniqueness of the Christian gospel.[34] God has a "multicultural kingdom table."[35]

Fourth, we unlock *koinonia* through liturgy, sacraments, and worship. The sacraments help reveal God to humanity. They make us receptive to him. They develop bonds of intimacy and communion. We aren't only bonded to God through the sacraments of baptism and Eucharist. We're also bonded to each other. "An individual receives a sacrament as an integral member of a believing community that awaits the second coming of her Lord and Master in glory. As such, though the sacraments are given to each member of the church one by one, they (sacraments) are "experiences" which go beyond a particular individual and involve the entire church."[36]

Fifth, we integrate *koinonia* with our theology and practice of mission. "In the apostolic teaching about the life and mission of the church, a correlation between the fullness of Christian living and the complexity of integral mission can be established."[37] Real community and mission happen when the *centrifugal* (moving outward and away from the center in mission) and *centripetal* (moving inward and toward the center in fellowship) dimensions of the church are in harmony. They enrich each other in profound ways. *Koinonia-in-Christ* has social, political, missional, and ecological effects. There is a "widespread search by churches, Christian social action groups, and Christian peace movements throughout the world for a corporate spirituality and political theology for their participation in the struggles for justice, peace, and the protection of creation." The Eucharist is "a Sacrament of Love that unites all the recipients with Christ; strengthens them and makes 'holy' their relationship with fellow Christians, and other human beings." The church needs to rediscover the *koinonia* present in the sacraments. The sacraments can inspire and nurture love, unity, sharing, and community.[38]

---

34. Ariarajah, "Challenge of Building Communities of Peace for All."
35. DeBorst, "'Unexpected' Guests," 65.
36. Okonkwo, "Sacrament of the Eucharist (as Koinonia) and African Sense of Communalism," 91–93.
37. Escobar, "Local Church, Agent of Transformation," 136.
38. Thomas, "Will Koinonia Emerge as a Vital Theological Theme?" 182.

PART 3: REVITALIZING OUR CHURCHES

Koinonia is the effective infrastructure of missions. Deep, authentic, and communing relationships provide the basis and infrastructure of missions. The New Testament, church history, and the contemporary growth of the Majority World church witness to this. "The story of the relationship between Paul, Epaphroditus, and the Philippians is a telling illustration of this Christian attitude. Such human integration in Christ makes mission possible."[39]

Sixth, we revolutionize *koinonia* through our apostolic practices of discipleship. Apostolic discipleship practices integrate community experiences with missional endeavors in the discipleship process. They always do this in the context of deep immersion in the communing life of the church. "Middle-class evangelicals generally have not experienced the full healing force of this sense of belonging. But the socially marginalized, especially those in the cities, experience this life in the church as a consolation, a refuge, and a place of integration. This experience has the power to transform and reorient their existence."[40]

Seventh, we broaden *koinonia* with an emphasis on creation-community. *Koinonia* and radical conversion are about restored relationships with God, creation, and others. Ruth Padilla DeBorst makes this point. "Caring, faithful, truthful relationships are at the core of any hope for a better world. These are gifts of grace, granted by the God-who-is-community."[41] We experience many conversions during life by the grace of God. He calls us to restore relationships through these conversations—restored communion with Godself, the earth, and people. We can't ignore creation in this mix. "Care of the earth is a spiritual matter and rampant destruction of it is blasphemy, an offense to our Creator."[42] The church is the *creation-community*. It is *relational-and-holistic-koinonia*. God calls his church to "converted covenantal relations." These are with all creation and with God himself—to the glory of the Creator God.[43]

Lastly, we enrich *koinonia* through *third-culture lifestyles and missions*. Ruth Padilla DeBorst challenges churches to develop disciples and fellowships that are *third-culture*. By this, she means that Christians must embrace the culture of the Christian faith. But they must also engage "meaningfully, and with a sense of belonging, with people from very diverse cultural

---

39. Escobar, "Local Church, Agent of Transformation," 142.

40. Escobar, "Local Church, Agent of Transformation," 139.

41. DeBorst, "Living Creation-Community," 61.

42. DeBorst, "Living Creation-Community," 65.

43. DeBorst, "God's Earth and God's People"; DeBorst, "New Heaven and a New Earth."

backgrounds." (She uses third-culture children as an example. These grow up with two cultures. They find meaningful and creative ways to put these cultures into dialogue.)[44] God calls us individually and communally to this task. It's vital to the reactivation of *koinonia* and the fulfillment of missions.

Ruth Padilla DeBorst puts it well:

> God's kingdom is not some amorphous, supra-cultural, other-world milieu. Rather, it is a space of vibrant, life-giving, God-honoring encounters of spice and color, smell and sound, here and now, in the complex entanglement of human relations. As third-culture people, followers of Jesus are called to live today in the light of the completion of God's story, with daily expectation of Christ's imminent return. They are called to express in their daily interactions the confident belief that one day, the triumphal choir before God's throne will be composed of a great multitude from every nation, tribe, and people, proclaiming, on bended knee, God's sovereignty in their own distinct languages ... As far as Christian communities the world over live together considering God's grace-full story, they become historically visible and culturally alternative out-workings of God's mission and localized expressions of the bountiful banquet of God's kingdom.[45]

---

44. DeBorst, "'Unexpected' Guests," 73.
45. DeBorst, "'Unexpected' Guests," 75–76.

PART 3: REVITALIZING OUR CHURCHES

Study Questions

1. Do you agree that in the church, *there is no true communion without mission and no true mission without communion*? Why or why not?
2. If the statement in the first question is true, what does it mean for the fellowship and mission of your church in the coming year?
3. How can you cultivate deep and spiritual friendships in your personal life and among your congregation?
4. How can your congregation practice and reactivate *koinonia*?
5. Take time over the next few months to read Lesslie Newbigin's *The Open Secret*.[46] Under three headings, list practical ways that your church can do the following trinitarian actions: (1) Proclaim the kingdom of the Father ("mission as faith in action"). (2) Share the life of the Son ("mission as love in action"). (3) Bear the witness of the Spirit ("mission as hope in action").
6. Consider the features of churches that practice *koinonia*. (I outline these in the latter part of this chapter.) Work through these as a church over the next six to twelve months. Ask how you will practically and concretely respond to the following questions.
7. How are we cultivating *koinonia* in our church that does the following?

- builds community upon trinitarian and Christological foundations?
- releases all believers to ministry, service, and contribution?
- cultivates a spirituality for diversity and plurality?
- unlocks the community-building power of the sacraments?
- integrates community life with mission?
- fosters *koinonia* as the affective infrastructure of mission?
- recovers the apostolic practices of discipleship?
- embraces creation community?
- develops *koinonia* as radical conversion to restored relationships?
- nurtures third-place lifestyles and community?

---

46. Newbigin, *Open Secret*.

21.

Developing Spirituality and Discipleship

The Thirteenth Expression

WITHOUT ATTENTION TO DISCIPLESHIP and spirituality, the church is fatally weakened. It is time to draw Indigenous and Majority World thinkers into this conversation. We must carefully consider discipleship and spiritual formation in these emerging global settings.[1] We can understand Majority World and Indigenous discipleship and spirituality through critical themes. These are theology, Jesus, Spirit, culture, tradition, community, disciplines, creation, suffering, and mission.

What Are Spirituality and Discipleship?

At its heart, *Christian spirituality is a life of communion with God in Jesus Christ*. It's expressed through a living and committed discipleship to Jesus. It's participation in the triune God's community, life, love, holiness, kingdom, and mission. By "communion with God," I mean "communion with the triune God" (i.e., the Spirit-enabled participation in the Sonship of Jesus, along the lines of Romans 8, Galatians 4, and so on).

How do *spirituality* and *discipleship* relate to each other? I suspect that we conflate and confuse these terms, even when we are unclear about

---

1. Galilea, *Way of Living Faith*, 20.

what they mean by them. Everyone (Christian or not) has a "spirituality." *Spirituality* is people's "way of relating to God" (which is one way I define spirituality in general, although my culture thinks "spiritual" is anything that's not material). So, spirituality differs highly from person to person. I would say the inner life and how people relate to God in many Western settings is governed by their Internet and media life. Whatever they plug into "forms" their inner life or perhaps a life with God. *Discipleship* is optional, however. It's an intentional choice to relate one's whole life to God through the life, death, and resurrection of Jesus Christ.

So, what are the characteristics of Christian spirituality and discipleship? How do they relate to each other? When we consider the minor differences between spirituality and discipleship, we see that the two overlap. They're integrated.

Spirituality seeks participation in God's being. Discipleship learns participation in God's doing.

Spirituality relates to our responses to meaning, persons, creation, sacred things, transcendence, and, most importantly, God. Discipleship is the whole gamut of disciplined life in response to the call of Jesus.

Spirituality is a relationship with God, others, self, and creation. It's about how those relationships manifest themselves in our Christian faith. Discipleship is about the practices of following Jesus Christ. It's about integrating the concrete practices of those spiritual relationships into the whole of our lives as we seek to be Jesus's disciples.

Spirituality isn't necessarily Christian. But when it is Christian, we manifest it as faith in, and relationship with, the triune God revealed in Jesus Christ. Discipleship is the outworking of that relationship in conformity to Christ Jesus.

When it is Christian, spirituality is defined by discipleship to Jesus Christ. Discipleship isn't simply doing what Jesus commanded or following his example. Discipleship is becoming like him. This involves engaging in the spiritual reality of the Kingdom of God and seeing that reality become manifest in the world.

Again, while there are some differences between spirituality and discipleship, there is substantial overlap. Jeffrey Greenman defines Christian spiritual formation as "our continuing response to the reality of God's grace shaping us into the likeness of Jesus Christ, through the work of the Holy Spirit, in the community of faith, for the sake of the world."[2] When this is the case, Christian spiritual formation and discipleship integrate. They have *trinitarian*, *relational*, and *missional* orientations.

---

2. Greenman, "Spiritual Formation in Theological Perspective," 24.

DEVELOPING SPIRITUALITY AND DISCIPLESHIP

Greenman's and my definitions of Christian spirituality focus on *the Trinity*, community, and *mission*. I value Greenman's focus on the *ongoing formation process* as we respond to God's gracious work. To these emphases, my definition adds a *kingdom* focus. Christian spirituality and discipleship reveal that God the Father inaugurated the kingdom in the Son's incarnation and the Spirit's eschatological outpouring. We must pursue spiritual formation and discipleship by focusing on (at least) these five things: Trinity, community, mission, process, and kingdom.

Unfortunately, post-Enlightenment dualism shapes most books on Christian spirituality. It separates the *phenomenal* from the *noumenal*. The phenomenal are things perceptible by the senses or through immediate experience. The noumenal are things, like ideas, that we know as true or real, without the need for perception, the senses, or experience. This dualistic separation is unhelpful. It leads to "spirituality" approaches that are not complementary to authentic Christian discipleship. It leads to concepts of devotional life and piety that have nothing to do with justice or mercy or subverting a fallen status quo. Spiritual dualism prevents people from living out the lifestyle of the inaugurated kingdom. It leads to concepts of truth where people can talk theology but never engage in praxis (especially beyond individual and family life). It leads to concepts of spirituality where pietism shapes the evangelical world. Then, evangelicals are tempted to be accusers of the world rather than motivated by God's love.

This post-Enlightenment dualism shapes much of contemporary Western Christian spirituality. It arises out of individualism. It leads to inadequate forms of discipleship where people's lives, desires, and how they spend their time and money are no different from their neighbors. It fails to understand that a wise view of walking in the Spirit arises from good trinitarian theology. (This is contra those who say trinitarian theology is just Greek.) Good trinitarian theology helps us understand what being a person and a disciple means. The last Adam shows what it means to be truly human. He was truly human in the power of the Spirit. So, as we follow in his way, we'll understand biblical and theological categories that won't allow us to think or act in the dualism that exists in post-Enlightenment spirituality.

Jesus's incarnation and the eschatological outpouring of the Spirit lead to a view of discipleship that is *spirituality shaped by the inbreaking of God's kingdom*. It's a discipleship that stands in contrast to post-Enlightenment dualism. It's a holistic and integrated spirituality. It transforms the whole life of the whole person with the whole gospel in the whole community.

Two astounding events occurred with the incarnation and the eschatological outpouring of the Spirit. One was that the Creator Covenant God of Israel unveiled God's being as Father, Son, and Spirit. He invites us into the fellowship life of the triune Creator. Second, the kingdom was inaugurated in the incarnation and the eschatological outpouring of the Spirit. Those two unique events have too little influence on how most Protestant Christians in the West live. But they must encounter and transform our faith and discipleship and spirituality and mission. Mortimer Arias says, "Discipleship is both an end and an instrument. It is for mission, it is for the kingdom, to give witness to the kingdom . . . discipleship includes formation and mission, formation for mission, formation in mission. So, discipleship was the model created by Jesus to make real and to announce the Kingdom of God."[3]

Spirituality and the Trinity

What does it mean to say that Christian spirituality and discipleship must be trinitarian? First, we must shape discipleship and spiritual formation around the truth that the Creator Covenant God of Israel unveiled God's being as Father, Son, and Spirit, and around the joy that this triune Creator invites us into his fellowship life. Second, our discipleship and spiritual formation must reveal that the kingdom was inaugurated in the incarnation of Jesus Christ and the eschatological outpouring of the Holy Spirit. These two astonishing events are our bedrock. They are the source of authentic Christian discipleship, spirituality, and spiritual formation.

How do Majority World thinkers articulate these truths? How are they the foundation for Majority World writing on spirituality?

Two Brazilians provide us with excellent examples. These are Leonardo Boff (*Holy Trinity, Perfect Community*) and Ricardo Barbosa de Sousa (*The Trinity and Spirituality*). Leonardo Boff constructs an elaborate theology of the Trinity. He then discusses the implications for churches, Christian faith, and spiritual formation.

> The trinitarian mystery is reflected in each human person, in the family, and in society. But it is in the church that this august mystery of communion and life finds its most visible expression in history. The church is inherently the community of faith, hope, and love seeking to live the ideal of union proposed by Jesus Christ himself: ". . . that they may all be one. As you, father, are in me and I am in you, may they also be in us" (Jn 17:21).[4]

---

3. Arias, "Announcing the Kingdom as Challenge," 4.
4. Boff, *Holy Trinity*, 43.

DEVELOPING SPIRITUALITY AND DISCIPLESHIP

The church is essentially a community. It images the trinitarian union. The church fosters spiritual formation through inclusion, participation, and interpersonal communion. We grow into discipleship within communities that image the love, fellowship, inclusion, embrace, and unity of the Trinity. We are welcomed into the trinitarian fellowship life of God and the church. In that community, we become disciples.

Ricardo Barbosa de Sousa writes that Christian spirituality is inconceivable without a trinitarian framework. Barbosa de Sousa says that trinitarian relations must shape the church's understanding of human nature, community, love, happiness, freedom, and creativity. Trinitarian thought isn't mere abstraction. It has concrete implications for our churches, spirituality, worship, and life in the world.

Ricardo Barbosa de Sousa says the doctrine of the Trinity has implications for Christian spirituality. Trinitarian theology helps us rediscover richer theologies of personhood, vocation, mission, spiritual friendship, relationship, discipleship, spirituality, and love.

Rediscovering personhood: "The Trinity establishes the meaning and significance of being a person. Based on this doctrine, people see themselves as beings in relationships, and precisely in this relationship with others [and with God], they discover their personhood."[5]

Rediscovering vocation: "Christian vocation is essentially relational. The invitation to discipleship is an invitation to personal communion with God and with the family of faith ... The only way to know myself is to open myself up to relationship of love with another person."[6]

Rediscovering mission: "Christian mission is, above all, an invitation to life in community."[7]

Rediscovering spiritual friendship: "Communion and friendship within the people of God becomes an external and visible sign of the life within the Trinity."[8]

Rediscovering relationship:

> Spirituality born from the trinitarian experience has a meaning that is absolutely revolutionary for our generation. This spirituality does not inspire us to seek power and control or anything else except personal and affective relationships with God and with our neighbors ... To rediscover the Trinity is to rediscover the way of personal and affective relationships, both with God

---

5. De Sousa, "Trinity and Spirituality," 31.
6. De Sousa, "Trinity and Spirituality," 35.
7. De Sousa, "Trinity and Spirituality," 39.
8. De Sousa, "Trinity and Spirituality," 43.

and with our neighbor. It is to rediscover the way of love and of genuine friendship as the greatest expression of our spirituality and devotion.[9]

Rediscovering discipleship and spirituality: The Trinity is central to our spirituality and mission. "Without an adequate understanding of God's [trinitarian] nature, we can have no significant comprehension or grasp of our faith. Modern consumerism and utilitarian individualism completely deny the Trinity and compromise the church's entire spirituality." We need to allow the triune God to transform our churches. They must be places where "countercultural experiences take place, where the Trinity provides meaning and freedom."[10]

Rediscovering love: "To rediscover the triune God is to rediscover the essential secret of Christian faith and devotion. God, before everything else, is love."[11]

We turn now to how Christian spirituality must reveal that the kingdom was inaugurated in the incarnation of Jesus Christ and the eschatological outpouring of the Holy Spirit.

Spirituality, Jesus, and the Spirit

Christian spirituality that witnesses to the inaugurated kingdom centers on Jesus. It focuses on his incarnation, life, death, and resurrection. These events have ushered in the inaugurated kingdom. Therefore, they are at the center of Christian spirituality.

I have said that *Christian spirituality is a life of communion with God in Jesus Christ. It is expressed through a living and committed discipleship to Jesus.* Following Jesus—discipleship to him—is at the heart and definition of all authentic Christian spirituality.

Gustavo Gutierrez writes much on how the person of Jesus Christ and his inaugurated kingdom shape Christian discipleship.[12] Jesus's teaching on the kingdom shapes our discipleship. This kingdom is counter-cultural. It stands in contrast to the oppressive and exploitative systems of this world. This kingdom demands that disciples renounce materialism, violence, competition, immorality, oppression, pride, and social evil.

---

9. De Sousa, "Trinity and Spirituality," 58–59.
10. De Sousa, "Trinity and Spirituality," 68.
11. De Sousa, "Trinity and Spirituality," 69.
12. Gutiérrez and Nickoloff, *Essential Writings*, 173–74.

DEVELOPING SPIRITUALITY AND DISCIPLESHIP

Disciples reject all that is not of the kingdom of God. They embrace all that is. Disciples pursue righteousness and peace. They do this even when it comes at a personal cost. The cost might be misunderstanding, persecution, marginalization, and suffering. Discipleship to Jesus, in the way of his kingdom, is counter-cultural. Disciples are willing to sacrifice ambition, reputation, relationships, and security. They'll even sacrifice life. They do this for the sake of Jesus and his kingdom.

The kingdom is a grace. But it demands the whole person. Sacrifice and suffering are characteristic of the kingdom. But so are love, joy, peace, hope, justice, and reconciliation. In the words of Jesus, "Whoever wants to be my disciple must deny themselves and take up their cross daily and follow me."[13]

Richard Shaull and Waldo Cesar consider the rise of Pentecostalism in Brazil. They arrive at a compelling conclusion: *spiritual formation is growth toward the reign of God.*[14]

Pedro Casaldaliga (Brazilian) and Jose-Maria Vigil (Nicaraguan) distinguish between two types of spirituality. The first is an essential *ethical-political spirituality*. All people, regardless of whether they follow Christ, can share it. "This level of spirituality, though it comes in the final analysis from the source of the Spirit of God, drinks from the sources of life: history, social conditions, praxis, reflection, wisdom, contemplation—all that feeds the heart and mind."[15] People express this first type of spirituality in many ways. This includes ethical indignation and spiritual contemplation. People show it through radical faithfulness to others. They express it through solidarity with the poor and oppressed. People reveal this spirituality in purposeful and positive action. They show it through hospitality, openness, and passion for life. There are many ways that humans show this essential ethical-political spirituality.

The second type of spirituality is a *religious, evangelical-ecclesial spirituality*. It's available to Christians through "the liberating Spirit of Jesus Christ."[16] It's a spirituality of discipleship to Jesus. This Christian spirituality witnesses to the kingdom of Christ. It testifies through word, action, and orientation. It announces the liberating reign of Christ. This is a spirituality patterned after Jesus. It reveals Jesus's kingdom. It's devoted to Jesus's reign. It subverts other kingdoms. This spirituality serves with people experiencing

---

13. Luke 9:23.
14. Shaull and Cesar, *Pentecostalism and the Future of the Christian Churches*, 219–26.
15. Casaldáliga and Vigil, *Political Holiness*, 14.
16. Casaldáliga and Vigil, *Political Holiness*, 14.

poverty and embraces persecution. It lives with integrity in prosperity and suffering. Its hallmark is discipleship to Jesus and in the way of Jesus.

True discipleship is not merely Jesus-centered. It's trinitarian. Therefore, Christian spirituality and discipleship witness to Christ and his kingdom in the power of the Holy Spirit, to the glory of the Father. Christian spirituality is possible because of God's empowering presence.

What does it mean to follow Jesus in the power of the Spirit? Some of my favorite writers on this subject are Pedro Casaldaliga, Jose-Maria Vigil, Kosuke Koyama, Anthony Bloom (Anthony of Sourozh), Frank Laubach, Simon Chan, and Jose Comblin.

These writers tell us that following Jesus in the power of the Spirit shapes our Christian spirituality. How do we express Christian spirituality when we are disciples of Jesus? We're prophetically indignant about injustice and oppression. We show solidarity and generosity with the poor, outcasts, marginalized, silenced, and exploited. We're in constant communion in prayer with Father, Son, and Holy Spirit. We're persons of prayer—patterning our prayers and prayer lives after Jesus. We leave aside "ties and interests, security and status, comfort and consumerism, good name, and prestige."[17] We have the "courage to take up our cross every day, without fearing conflict and without saving up even our own lives."[18] We're passionate about developing a discipling community, "always socializing our spiritual experience."[19] We show self-sacrificial action: putting love into costly, self-sacrificial practice. We embrace political holiness: being "salt, light, and a city on a hill" as an alternative culture. We're a people who witness to Jesus Christ through justice, peace, liberation, hope, equality, love, mercy, etc.

What are other ways in which discipleship to Jesus shapes Christian spirituality?

> *Liberation.* Discipleship to Jesus inspires us to cultivate a spirituality of liberation. This spirituality is characterized by a focus on Christ's reign and kingdom. We focus on discipleship to Jesus and pursuing his justice, peace, truth, love, freedom, etc. We root a spirituality of liberation in the real world, history, place, among people experiencing poverty, and in politics. We're critical of oppressive structures and systems and powers. We're committed to liberating action. We pursue wholeness without reductions or dichotomies. This means we eliminate the

---

17. Casaldáliga and Vigil, *Political Holiness*, 100. The first ten points are developed by Casaldaliga and Vigil.

18. Casaldáliga and Vigil, *Political Holiness*, 100.

19. Casaldáliga and Vigil, *Political Holiness*, 100.

DEVELOPING SPIRITUALITY AND DISCIPLESHIP

divisions between sacred and secular, material and spiritual, "us" and "others," etc.[20]

Movement. Disciples take part in the "movement" of the Trinity. They especially join in the movement of the Spirit of Christ. "All attributes of the Spirit denote movement: the Spirit is giving, loving, living. The Spirit comes at the end of the movement of God, but the beginning of God's going out to creation. It is the start of creation's road back to the Father."[21] Discipleship to Jesus means keeping in step with his Spirit and going where he wants us to go. It's about moving with him in mission, worship, fellowship, discipleship, and ministry.

Power and holiness. The Spirit of Jesus is his empowering and sanctifying presence with his disciples. Jesus fills us with his power and holiness when the Spirit fills us. "Pentecostal power and passion mean nothing if they do not issue from a life filled with the Spirit of holiness."[22]

Crucified minds. Disciples have minds captivated by "the foolishness and weakness of God." This means forming attitudes and hearts upon the mind of Jesus Christ. "The mind which has decided to live by the power of the crucified Lord is the crucified mind."[23]

Risen minds. Disciples of Jesus, enjoy and proclaim the risen Christ as victor and Lord! Anthony Bloom rejoices: "The resurrection is the only event of the Gospel which belongs to history not only past but also present. Only in the light of the resurrection did everything else make sense to me."[24] Discipleship to Jesus means embracing crucified and risen minds. The Spirit enables us to be dead to self but alive to the resurrected Lord and his power and regeneration.

Spirit-filled discipleship isn't divorced from history or culture. These always influence our Christian spirituality and discipleship.

---

20. Casaldaliga and Vigil devote a chapter to these themes: Casaldáliga and Vigil, *Political Holiness*, 203–7.

21. Comblin, *Holy Spirit and Liberation*, 186.

22. Chan, *Pentecostal Theology*, 70.

23. Koyama, *No Handle on the Cross*, 8–12; Laubach, *Prayer*, 98–102.

24. Koyama, *No Handle on the Cross*, 119; Barclay and Davies, *We Believe in God*, 26.

PART 3: REVITALIZING OUR CHURCHES

Spirituality and Culture

Culture affects the shape of spirituality and discipleship. No spirituality is meaningful (or possible) apart from its cultural background and context. Culture and spirituality are mutually forming. This is true whether they are in harmony or confrontation. Many forms of spirituality have evolved within and for their Western cultural context. This is also true of the many approaches to spirituality and discipleship that have developed within Asian, African, Latin American, Indigenous, and other contexts.

Our goal, then, is not to reproduce these forms. We don't want carbon copies of them in our setting. We need to adapt them to our culture and context. Successful application of these forms of spirituality and approaches to discipleship in our culture will mean reconceiving and transforming them for our setting.

The West can learn much from the spirituality of Christians in other cultures. In my own country, Australia, non-Indigenous Christians are finally beginning to learn from the spiritual contributions of our Indigenous sisters and brothers. In Australian Aboriginal spirituality, creation, holism, and relationship are essential.

Creation: "The land is the basis of all realities—human selfhood and identity. [Aboriginal culture] perceives all realities from creation perspectives" (rather than from human-centered thinking). God is beyond creation but also in creation. He is perceived in creation (more so than in human history). Religious activities focus on the earth and soil and our relationship to these things.

Holism: There are no sharp dualisms. "There is no clear-cut distinction between sacred and secular, religion and non-religion, etc." Aboriginal spirituality is "holistic in thinking." Australian Aboriginal spirituality values ritual and ceremony, earth and soil, land and sea, welcome and hospitality, family and community, generosity and contentment, art and music, storytelling and dancing, and balance and harmony with the whole cosmos. There's no dualism between the natural and the spiritual.

Relationship: Spirituality is person and community oriented. "Relationships between individuals in society are more important than the simple performance of tasks." Cooperation and community are valued. Generosity is more important than saving money or building riches. Aboriginal spirituality values an interdependent connection with God and others and all creation.[25]

---

25. NATSIEC, *Christ and Culture*, 36–41.

DEVELOPING SPIRITUALITY AND DISCIPLESHIP

Let's briefly examine some culturally formed approaches to Christian spirituality and discipleship in Africa and Asia. We need to reshape these, of course, for our own culture. Africa and Asia, of course, are enormous continents. They have a multitude of cultures and religions and Christian traditions. Euro-American Christianity has influenced African and Asian Christian spiritualities. However, local cultures and spiritual traditions have also resulted in the indigenization (or contextualization) of spirituality and discipleship in the many cultures of Africa and Asia.

An awareness of the spiritual world characterizes African Christian spiritualities. There's a focus on angels, demons, spirits, the Holy Spirit, and Satan. Africans often work this out in the context of hunger and plenty, illness and health, suffering and healing, poverty and wealth, and death and life.

Africans value a concrete and whole-of-life spirituality. John S. Mbiti provides a collection of African prayers offered within the concrete experiences of African life. These are prayers for health, healing, prosperity, protection, harvest, peace, fertility, rain, joy, and blessings.[26] Such prayers are a part of traditional African spirituality. Africans are as likely to develop Christian spirituality in a large urban metropolis as in a small, rural village (e.g., huge cities like Lagos, Kinshasa, Johannesburg-Ekurhuleni, Khartoum-Umm Durman, Mogadishu, or Nairobi). In the future, most Africans and Asians will live in cities—many in mega-cities.

Madge Karecki and Celia Kourie describe how Africans express their Christian spirituality. They are spiritually sensitive. They connect their faith to creation, the body, the land, and physicality. They desire deep human connection, especially in family, church, and local community. They develop a theology of ancestry and heritage, including Jesus Christ as the Proto-Ancestor. They embrace public demonstrations of faith (e.g., boisterous worship services and passionate evangelistic rallies). They pursue zealous missions and evangelism.[27]

Ghanaian theologian John S. Pobee says that African spirituality emphasizes joy and celebration. It focuses on the power and presence of the Spirit. It identifies with Old Testament "textures" and "orientations." African Christians feel connected to the values, themes, and motifs within Old Testament cultures. These include family, hospitality, corporate personality, imagery, symbolism, the exodus motif, priests, holy leaders, and sacred sites.

---

26. Mbiti, *Prayers of African Religion*.
27. Sheldrake, *New Westminster Dictionary of Christian Spirituality*, 92–93.

PART 3: REVITALIZING OUR CHURCHES

African Independent Churches emphasize community and engagement with the spirit world. They pursue dramatic encounters with the Holy Spirit.[28] They use symbolism to aid spiritual formation. Symbols include colors, water, garments, rings, oils, candles, crosses, etc. "They easily blend and integrate African culture and tradition with that of Christian doctrine ... The symbols help the leadership and membership of the [African Independent Churches] to be spiritual in all spheres of their Christian journey. They have, thus, used symbols to contribute immensely to the level of spirituality in African Christianity."[29]

Emefie Ikenga-Metuh says that African Christian spirituality has distinct features: (1) African Christians are passionate in prayer; (2) they pursue mystical experiences; (3) they have a deep sense of the holy; (4) they desire spiritual power (e.g., healings, miracles, prophecy, and tongues), (5) they love the land, and (6) they have a commitment to communities.[30]

The spiritual-religious traditions of Asia influence Asian Christian spiritualities. So do Western spiritualities imported and adapted for Asia. Christian spiritualties derived from (or influenced by) the spiritual-religious traditions of Asia often focus on three things. These are contemplation, inter-religious dialogue, and care for creation.

Sundar Singh of India is an example of an Asian spiritual leader who focused on these three things. Singh was the "wanderer for Christ." He embraced poverty, chastity, and homelessness for the sake of mission among the poorest of India. Singh "chose the disciplined life of a mendicant preacher, living in caves and jungles and devoting himself to the remote hill peoples." He entered conversations with the other religious traditions of India. Singh devoted himself to contemplation. He challenged Christians to care for the earth. He did all this while proclaiming the uniqueness of Christ and the gospel. Singh's eight devotional books are now considered spiritual classics.[31]

Homegrown Asian Christian spiritualities often focus on liberation from oppression (examples include Minjung theology in South Korea, Dalit theology in India, and "theologies of struggle" in the Philippines). These spiritualities develop an Indigenous shape with contextual concerns. Meanwhile, imported varieties struggle to do the same.[32]

---

28. Pobee, *Skenosis*.
29. Oduro, "Symbolisms in African Independent Churches," 82.
30. Ikenga-Metuh, "Revival of African Christian Spirituality."
31. Dobe, "Wanderer for Christ."
32. Sheldrake, *New Westminster Dictionary of Christian Spirituality*, 133–35.

Aruna Gnanadason says a "spirituality of struggle" is "not an ephemeral, otherworldly, private, esoteric reality. It is earthy, grounded in the grim realities of living and surviving in an inhumane, exploitative world." Gnanadason writes that this type of Asian spirituality forces people to dig deep into their spiritual heritage. It compels them to recover the heritage they've often lost to oppressive and colonial traditions. This kind of spirituality supplies people with the resources to challenge issues of "race, caste, gender, religion, and culture." It's a "spirituality of new life, of hope and of a future where justice and peace will reign—a spirituality wherein the Holy Spirit will empower those ground to the dust to rise and dance the dance of freedom and liberation—it is this spirituality that sustains us in our struggles."[33]

As in Africa, many Asian Christians are developing forms of spirituality and approaches to discipleship in huge and globally significant cities (e.g., Tokyo, Seoul, Shanghai, Karachi, Beijing, Mumbai, Jakarta, Delhi, Osaka-Kobe-Kyoto, Manila, Bangkok, Singapore, Hanoi, or Yangon). Like Westerners, Asians and Africans are learning what it means to be disciples in a global world where most people live in cities.

A massive shift is happening in our generation. It has significant implications for the shape and importance of urban mission and spirituality (especially among the poorest of the poor). The shift is toward cities. More than that, it's toward mega-cities of more than ten million people. The top ten mega-cities in 2030 will be Tokyo, Delhi, Shanghai, Dhaka, São Paulo, Mexico City, Cairo, Beijing, Mumbai, and Osaka. Of these, seven are in Asia, two in South America, and one in North Africa. Depending on who you read, there are probably thirty-three mega-cities in the world today, most of which are in Asia.

Even in these huge mega-cities, community and relationship are common themes in Majority World approaches to spirituality and discipleship.

Spirituality as Collective Adventure

Individualism distorts much of Western spirituality. We need a *spirituality of community*. Christian spirituality is *relational*. It cannot occur outside of communion with others and with God. The Trinity is a perfect community.[34] By grace, the Father, Son, and Spirit invite the church into that community. The church participates in the fellowship and mission of the Trinity. We become disciples as we engage in communion and mission with the Trinity and the church.

33. Gnanadason, "Spirituality That Sustains Us in Our Struggles," 37–41.
34. Boff, *Holy Trinity*.

Argentinian pastor Juan Carlos Ortiz places relationships at the center of discipleship. Ortiz says, "The oxygen of the kingdom is love . . . Darkness is individualism, selfishness. Light is love, communion, fellowship."[35] Love for God, our neighbor, and our sisters and brothers in Christ characterizes discipleship. Discipleship flourishes in divine love. "Jesus wants us to be one. Just as the Trinity is one—Father, Son, and Holy Spirit—he wants us to be one. He wants this in evangelistic efforts and fellowship meetings; he wants us to love one another."[36] Ortiz says that this love and unity is the center of authentic discipleship.

Gutierrez says that discipleship is *collective walking in the Spirit*. Discipleship is a *collective adventure*. "The following of Jesus is not, purely or primarily, an individual matter but a collective adventure. The journey of the people of God is set in motion by a direct encounter with the Lord but an encounter in a community: '*We* have found the Messiah.'"[37] Together, we develop as disciples and learn the spiritual disciplines of discipleship.

Spiritual Disciplines and Developing Disciples

Much has been made of the spirituality of the Argentinian Pope of the Catholic Church, Jorge Mario Bergoglio (Pope Francis). He chooses simpler papal attire. Instead of living in the official papal residence in the Apostolic Palace, he lives in the Vatican guesthouse. He ministers in the slums.

In November 2013, Francis made headlines. He embraced and kissed and prayed with Vinicio Riva. Riva is a Christian disfigured by neurofibromatosis, a skin disease. Francis is widely acclaimed for his humility, love for people experiencing poverty, desire to dialogue with other worldviews and practice of spiritual disciplines. He is compassionate, humble, open, prayerful, and Christ-like. *Time Magazine* named Francis 2013 Person of the Year for these qualities.

Elizabeth Tenety wrote an opinion piece for the Washington Post titled *Like Pope Francis? You'll Love Jesus*. In that piece, Tenety shows how Jesus is the source of Pope Francis's spirituality. She says that if people like the humility and compassion of Francis, they will love Jesus. Jesus inspires and amplifies these traits.[38]

This fresh Latin American servantship and spirituality is revitalizing the Catholic Church. Francis's spirituality focuses on spiritual disciplines,

---

35. Ortiz, *Disciple*, 40–41.
36. Ortiz and Buckingham, *Call to Discipleship*, 136.
37. Gutiérrez, *We Drink from Our Own Wells*, 42.
38. Tenety, "Like Pope Francis? You'll Love Jesus."

encounters with Christ, and witness in the world.[39] Francis nurtures his spirituality and communion with Jesus through spiritual disciplines and service. Spiritual disciplines are essential for our development as disciples. These spiritual practices enable spiritual formation. They nourish authentic discipleship.

Richard Foster and others have written valuable guides on spiritual disciplines.[40] Westerners write most of these guides. Francis shows the importance of learning about spiritual formation from outside the West.

Majority World and Indigenous thinkers emphasize the following spiritual disciplines. This is not an exhaustive list, just a few disciplines that stand out.

1. Disciplined, upside-down discipleship

The spiritual discipline of holding our values, beliefs, practices, and desires up to the scrutiny of the gospel and allowing Jesus to turn this upside-down. Anthony of Sourozh (Russian theologian) challenges the gospel he encounters in the West:

> The Gospel is a harsh document; the Gospel is ruthless and specific in what it says, the Gospel is not meant to be re-worded, watered down and brought to the level of either our understanding or our taste. The Gospel is proclaiming something which is beyond us, and which is there to stretch our mind, to widen our heart beyond the bearable at times, to recondition all our life, to give us a world view which is simply the world upside-down and this we are not keen to accept.[41]

2. Disciplined prayer (*ascesis*)

We need discipline in our prayer lives. We need a disciplined life of prayer. Such prayer isn't only practiced in the spontaneous, suffering, ecstatic, or enthusiastic moments. It's also practiced during the ordinary, drab, mundane, or routine times. We need resources to persevere in prayer, even when God seems absent or remote. Anthony of Sourozh says we nurture this kind of *ascesis*—a disciplined life of prayer—through various prayer

---

39. Bunson, *Pope Francis*, 189–90 (I have made the translation gender inclusive).
40. Foster, *Celebration of Discipline*.
41. Bloom, "Can Modern Man Believe?"

practices. These practices include meditation on Scripture, liturgical prayer, the prayer of silence, praying the Lord's Prayer, etc.[42]

Simon Chan talks about the need to develop a *rule of life*—regular prayer practices like those developed by Benedict. Chan says spiritual direction and Christian mentoring nurture this.[43] He offers spiritual disciplines focusing on God and self (e.g., self-examining and contemplative prayer practices). He suggests practices focusing on the Word (e.g., meditating on Scripture, spiritual reading, and biblical memorization). He outlines disciplines directed toward the world (e.g., spiritual friendship, meditation on creation, spiritual discernment, and a spirituality of social involvement and liberation).[44]

3. Disciplined acts of liberation, justice, and mercy

Majority World spiritual disciplines are not typically interior and mystical and otherworldly. Many write about the spiritual discipline of intentionally practicing justice, dissent, and liberation. This is fasting as loosing the chains of injustice, untying the cords of the yoke, setting the oppressed free, breaking every yoke, sharing food with those experiencing hunger, clothing and providing for people experiencing poverty, sheltering people experiencing homelessness and statelessness, spending ourselves on behalf of the hungry, and satisfying the needs of the oppressed (Isaiah 58). Writing about these spiritual disciplines is prolific in Asia, Africa, and Latin America.

4. Disciplined care for creation

Spiritual practices that are liberating must include justice for both humanity and the creation. I will not say much about this because I have dedicated a chapter to eco-spirituality in Majority World thinking. Leonard Boff writes extensively on eco-spirituality. Boff believes "a new spirituality, one adequate to the ecological revolution, is urgently needed."[45] The practices of this spirituality include simple living and celebrating ecological interdependency. It includes thankfulness for God's creation's wonder, beauty, and sacredness. Boff demonstrates how St. Francis of Assisi exemplifies "all the

---

42. Bloom, *Living Prayer*.

43. For treatment of spiritual direction in Africa, Asia, Latin America, and multicultural contexts, see Rakoczy, *Common Journey, Different Paths*.

44. Chan, *Spiritual Theology*, Part 2.

45. Boff, *Cry of the Earth, Cry of the Poor*, 189.

cardinal ecological virtues." He demonstrates the spiritual disciplines that exemplify creation care.[46] Amos Yong says that we need a Spirit-centered theology of the environment. "Life in the Spirit is ultimately about life in this world, our world, God's world."[47]

George E. Tinker is an Osage Christian theologian. Tinker reveals the extent to which Westerners can learn from Native American love for the land. We can learn from their sense of deep connection to and dependency on the land. Tinker says Westerners must learn spiritual practices that respect and nourish the land. They must learn these practices from First Nations—from "Indigenous prophets."

> The whites, too, shall pass—perhaps sooner than other tribes. Continue to contaminate your bed, and you will one night suffocate in your own waste. When the buffalo are all slaughtered, the wild horses all tamed, the secret corners of the forest heavy with the scent of men, and the view of the ripe hills blotted by talking wires, where is the thicket? Gone. Where is the eagle? Gone. What is it to say goodbye to the swift and the hunt, the end of living and the end of survival?[48]

Randy S. Woodley is a Keetoowah Cherokee teacher, poet, activist, pastor, missiologist, and historian. In *Shalom and the Community of Creation*, Woodley avoids romanticizing Native American relations with the land. Instead, Woodley shows how a Christian theology of creation resonates with native traditions. He also shows how Christian practices of creation-care—let's call them eco-spiritual disciplines—can complement and integrate with native earth-keeping traditions. Woodley invites the church to move away from imperial metaphors like *the kingdom of God*. Instead, he'd prefer we embrace a metaphor like *the community of creation*.[49]

I'm sympathetic to Woodley's concerns. I appreciate his concern about dealing with images that may be oppressive to some. But my problem with this replacement of metaphors is that the Lamb who was slain is victorious. He sits on the throne. He overthrows powers and principalities and rulers and kingdoms. So, is it right to do away with this metaphor? Can we afford to throw it away? To take the kingdom and rule out of the metaphor strips it of its ability to overthrow the enemy and the kingdoms of darkness and the world.

---

46. Boff, *Cry of the Earth, Cry of the Poor*, 203–20.
47. Yong, *Spirit Poured out on All Flesh*, 299.
48. Tinker, "Native Americans and the Land," 74.
49. Woodley, *Shalom and the Community of Creation*, 39. Italics added for emphasis.

Having said that, when Woodley refers to the community of creation, he has several things in mind—first, the replacement of the imperial side of Christendom. So, Woodley uses the term *Shalom Kingdom*, tying the kingdom metaphor into shalom. (This is a peaceable and reconciling and healing kingdom. It's a kingdom characterized by these other notions associated with the meta-construct of shalom). Secondly, Woodley wants to move into a less human-centered spirituality and worldview. Jesus Christ incarnates, lives, dies, and resurrects for all creation—not just humanity. We must reflect this in our spiritual practices and our disciplined care for creation.

Suffering is a common human experience. First Nations and poorer countries know it well. We turn now to Christian spirituality and discipleship in suffering.

Spirituality and Suffering

A recent Pew Research Forum report showed, "More than 2.2 billion people—nearly a third (32%) of the world's total population of 6.9 billion—live in countries where either government restrictions on religion or social hostilities involving religion rose substantially over the three years studied [mid-2006 to mid-2009]." Christians are persecuted in 131 countries. It is hard to get an exact figure, but nearly 100,000 Christians are martyred yearly.[50]

Andrew F. Walls provides a moving account of the life and martyrdom of the African Christian leader Gudina Tumsa. Derg soldiers murdered Tumsa in 1979. He's been called the Dietrich Bonhoeffer of Africa. Walls shows how Tumsa's murder follows a pattern of persecution, suffering, martyrdom, and witness in the African church. Walls describes earlier episodes of witness and martyrdom in Africa (these include the martyrs of Scilli, the life of Takla Haymanot of Ethiopia, the Ugandan martyrs, and the murder of Christians in the Sudan today). "The test of discipleship is suffering; and Africa, which has known so much suffering, has often been a furnace for the testing of Christian quality . . . The word *martyr* has come to mean one who dies for the sake of Christ, but the basic meaning is simply *witness*."[51]

Majority World literature reminds us that "to serve is to suffer." Discipleship comes at a cost. As Leonardo and Clodovis Boff remind us, Christians often suffer because of their solidarity with the suffering and oppressed and silenced. Christian spirituality and discipleship are forged in

---

50. Pew Research, "Rising Restrictions on Religion."
51. Walls, "Cost of Discipleship," 434.

suffering. Ajith Fernando says, "If the Apostle Paul knew fatigue, anger, and anxiety in his ministry, what makes us think we can avoid them in ours?"[52]

Rene Padilla links discipleship, mission, and suffering. "Christian mission and Christian discipleship are two sides of the same coin. Both derive their meaning from Jesus, the crucified Messiah, who even as Lord remains crucified. The Christian mission is the mission of those who have identified themselves with the Crucified and are willing to follow him to the cross. Mission is suffering."[53]

Spirituality and the Mission of God

Recently, there has been an upsurge of interest in missional spirituality in the West. Dwight J. Zscheile, for example, released a collection of essays on missional spiritual formation. Roger Helland and Leonard Hjalmarson have released a book called *Missional Spirituality*. In that book, they identify some of the practices of missional spirituality. These practices include reflection on missional theology and union with Christ and practicing humility. They include surrendering to God's will, love for God and neighbor, and reading Scripture missionally.[54]

Majority World thinking and practice link spirituality, discipleship, and mission. As Rene Padilla claims, discipleship and mission are two sides of one coin. Asian, African, and Latin American thinkers and churches challenge the West with a profound truth: *There's no true mission without discipleship and no authentic discipleship without mission.*

Latin American thinkers cast a compelling vision for missional spirituality. Samuel Escobar, for example, puts the interdependence between spirituality and mission like this: "Spirituality without involvement in social, economic, and political concerns is mere religiosity."[55] Mission and service form Christian spirituality and discipleship. Just as mission forges Christian theology, "the same is true for piety, prayer, and the spiritual disciplines."[56] Jose Miguez Bonino says, "Evangelism, prayer, worship, and private devotions do not have to be abandoned. They must be converted to Christ."[57]

Orlando Costas describes a spirituality of missional engagement.

52. Fernando, "To Serve Is to Suffer," 31.
53. Padilla, "Bible Studies," 338.
54. Helland and Hjalmarson, *Missional Spirituality*; Zscheile, *Cultivating Sent Communities*.
55. Bassham, *Mission Theology, 1948–1975*, 237.
56. Escobar, "Recruitment of Students for Mission," 543.
57. Bonino, "Present Crisis in Mission," 41.

PART 3: REVITALIZING OUR CHURCHES

To take head-on oppressive structures like consumerism, technology, militarism, multinational capitalism, international communism, racism, and sexism, we need a *spirituality of missional engagement*: a devotional attitude, a personal ethic, a continuous liturgical experience that flows out of and expresses itself in apostolic obedience. Prayer, Bible study, personal ethics, and worship will not mean withdrawal from the world but *immersion in its suffering and struggles*. Likewise, participation in the struggles of history will not mean an abandonment of piety and contemplation but an experience of God from the depths of human suffering.

Mission without spirituality cannot survive any more than combustion without oxygen. The nature of the world in which we live and the gospel that we have been committed to communicate therein demand *that it be a spirituality of engagement, not of withdrawal.* Such a spirituality can only be cultivated in obedience and discipleship and not in the isolated comfort of one's inner self. By the same token, it can only be verified in the liberating struggles against the principalities and powers that hold so many millions in bondage.[58]

Costas does not stop there. A spirituality of missional engagement means that worship and mission are inseparable. It is misleading to say that we grow spiritually through worship *and* mission—as though the two are separate. Costas says that we worship as we experience redemption through Christ's mission. We respond by participating in Christ's mission as an act of worship. Our spiritual formation testifies to mission, worship, and community inseparability.

There is no dichotomy between worship and mission. Worship is the gathering of the people sent into the world to celebrate what God has done in Christ and is doing through their participation in the Spirit's witnessing action. Mission is the culmination and anticipation of worship. In worship and mission, the redeemed community gives evidence to the fact that it is a praying and witnessing people.

Liturgy without mission is like a river without a spring. Mission without worship is like a river without a sea. Both are necessary. Without the one, the other loses its vitality and meaning. Put in other terms, the test of a vigorous worship experience will be a dynamic participation in mission. The test of a faithful missional involvement will be a profound worship experience.[59]

---

58. Costas, *Christ Outside the Gate*, 171–72. Italics added for emphasis.
59. Costas, *Integrity of Mission*, 91.

Leonardo Boff claims that the church needs a new spirituality. It needs one that makes prayer, politics, liberation, community, and mission inseparable. This spirituality is evidenced by "prayer materialized in action." This is especially action with and among the suffering and oppressed. We come together as a community to share our missional experiences, liberating actions, and prayers for the world. This is a movement from individual to corporate prayer and action. Boff says liturgy must be a "celebration of life." As we pray together, we celebrate our freedoms, hopes, cultures, and life. This prayer is also a "critical prayer." As we pray together, we challenge each other to fuller expression, integration, and integrity in discipleship and mission.

Such spirituality requires "political holiness." As we pray together, we *cultivate* a holiness characterized by justice, mercy, and righteousness. We *stand together against* poverty, oppression, exploitation, and the destruction of people, cultures, and creation.[60] This spirituality also demands "prophetic courage and historical patience." Our spirituality must give us courage in mission and justice- and peace-making. "This attitude springs from a contemplative vision of history, whose only sovereign is God."

Boff says that we need "an attitude of Easter." A missional spirituality will involve hardship, suffering, and martyrdom. We suffer with our Crucified Lord, triumph along with our Resurrected Christ, and anticipate the fullness of his final triumph.[61]

Christian Spirituality: Concluding Reflections

Being a disciple of Jesus is a thrilling and demanding adventure. *Communion with God in Jesus Christ* involves discipleship, intimacy with God and others, and participation in his mission. It's participation in his community, life, love, kingdom, and mission.

Here are eleven things we learn from how Majority World Christians practice Christian spirituality and discipleship.

---

60. Casaldaliga and Vigil provide a comprehensive treatment of *political holiness* in Casaldáliga and Vigil, *Political Holiness*.

61. See Thomas, "Holy Spirit and the Spirituality for Political Struggles"; Gnanadason, "Spirituality That Sustains Us in Our Struggles."

PART 3: REVITALIZING OUR CHURCHES

1. Christian spirituality cultivates a life of communion with God in Jesus Christ.

We express this life of communion with God through discipleship to Jesus. Communion with God brings love, joy, rest, and peace. But it also brings change, discomfort, and suffering. When we enjoy communion with God, we embrace his community, life, love, holiness, kingdom, and mission.

While it may be possible to entertain a spiritual life in various ways, Christian spirituality, as a specific pathway, develops through discipleship to Jesus Christ. It's living in and for the kingdom of God, with the people of God, in communion with God the Son, by the power of God the Spirit. It's living the resurrection life and its personal and community transformation and restoration. Christian spirituality is radical communion and union with the Father, Son, and Holy Spirit. The Holy Spirit empowers Christian spirituality. He enables us to be disciples of Jesus Christ for the glory of God the Father. Christian spirituality is a lived experience of faith in Jesus Christ. We develop it through relationships with others and union with the triune God.

2. Christian spirituality explores the concrete implications of trinitarian theology.

We've seen how Leonardo Boff and Ricardo de Sousa place trinitarian theology at the heart of Christian spirituality. Simon Chan also understands spiritual formation as participation in trinitarian and human fellowship. He demonstrates that deep spirituality doesn't just focus on the Trinity. It also focuses on the individual members of the Trinity.

Spirituality *focused on the Father* emphasizes creation, covenant, and life. It's a *sacramental spirituality*. It presupposes "an indirect working of grace through created things."

Spirituality *focused on the Son* stresses the kingdom's inauguration in the incarnation. It also underlines "the gospel events of Jesus's life, death, resurrection, ascension, and coming again." It's an *evangelical spirituality*. It's "marked by a warm and intimate relationship with Jesus Christ as Lord, Savior, friend, etc."

Spirituality *focused on the Spirit* emphasizes God's empowering presence. It focuses on the eschatological outpouring of the Spirit. It's a *charismatic spirituality*. It's "open to the direct workings of the Spirit coming

DEVELOPING SPIRITUALITY AND DISCIPLESHIP

from "beyond history" (Zizioulas) in surprising ways, such as prophecies and healings."[62]

We need each of these emphases—Father, Son, and Holy Spirit—to develop a whole spiritual life. We must explore the concrete implications of trinitarian theology for the church and our discipleship. For example, what does the doctrine of the Trinity mean for our prayer, worship, and community practices? How does it shape our practices of mission, friendship, and discipleship? How do we form churches that tap into the best sacramental, evangelical, and charismatic traditions?

3. Christian spirituality follows Jesus in the power of the Spirit.

In this chapter, we've seen that we follow Jesus in the power of the Spirit in various ways. Such Spirit-empowered discipleship pursues holy indignation, self-sacrificial action, and political holiness. It desires the gifts and fruit of the Spirit. Spirit-filled discipleship shows solidarity with the poor and powerless. It cultivates crucified and risen minds. It receives the power, presence, and provision of the Spirit. It's holy and loving and righteous. It joins in the *missio Dei*. It witnesses to the gospel in word, action, and presence.

4. Christian spirituality learns from First Nation and Indigenous faith.

As Christians, we need to learn from the expressions of Christian spirituality in other cultures. As I travel throughout Asia, Africa, and Latin America, I'm constantly challenged about what being a disciple of Jesus Christ means.

We must also be open and responsive to what Indigenous and First Nations peoples teach us about Christian discipleship and spirituality. This is especially true of the people who are Indigenous to our area. For me, this is the Eora people of the Sydney Basin. While non-Indigenous people have lived in Sydney for just over two hundred years, the Eora people have lived here for 60,000 years. We can learn so much from Indigenous and First Nations peoples. We can learn from their creation care and earth-keeping, their welcome and hospitality, their family and community, their generosity and contentment, and their denial of any distinctions between the natural

---

62. Scorgie et al., *Dictionary of Christian Spirituality*, 53; Chan, *Spiritual Theology*, chapter 2.

and the spiritual. We can learn from their courage, faith, forgiveness, and spirituality in the face of invasion, occupation, and colonialism. We do the same in response to other cultures that are different from our own.

5. Christian spirituality engages culture critically.

I've outlined some culturally formed approaches to Christian spirituality and discipleship in this chapter. I've primarily focused on Africa, Asia, Indigenous cultures, and First Nations. As Christians, we must examine how our culture has shaped our discipleship and vice versa. For example, when you consider Christian approaches to money, sex, work, and family, how much of your conclusions are formed by Scripture or your culture? Our spiritual life cannot flourish without a critical engagement with culture and its influence on us.

Part of that critical process is putting our expressions of faith into conversation with other forms of discipleship from other cultures. This shows us how culture influences our faith and how our faith can embrace fresh expressions.

6. Christian spirituality moves from individualism to community.

Christian spirituality is a collective adventure. We must relinquish spiritual individualism and pursue spirituality in communities.

Relationships are the hubs of authentic human personhood. Relationships are central to personal growth and integration—with God and others. Psychosocial theories back up this theological claim. Psychosocial theories say that we achieve fuller psychological and emotional wholeness when facing crises with others. These relationships don't just sustain and support us through crises. They help make us more mature and integrated persons. Psychosocial theories say that this is human nature. Relationships enrich us as we interact with a widening radius of significant individuals and institutions. We should put weight on the meaning people attach to significant relationships. These relationships are crucial for personal growth, well-being, and integration.

Psychosocial and socio-phenomenological theories emphasize the importance of relationships. Relationships are critical to our discipleship, wholeness, and personhood. Relationships are the key to the movement toward—or away from—authentic personhood and integration. Our interpersonal experiences and interpretations of them shape the assumptions we build from these experiences. They lead to authentic personhood, growth, and integration. (Or these interpersonal experiences lead away from these things. This is especially true when relationships are damaging, or we respond to them in unhealthy ways.)

The movement of faith development through various stages is an example (see the work of Robert Kegan and James Fowler). This is a movement from no faith to self-surrender and self-transcendence. It is the movement from intuitive faith to self-transcending and self-sacrificing faith. Relationships are the hubs of this growth. How do we manifest authentic selfhood? How do we grow as spiritual beings? Through loving relationship with God and others. This wholeness and spirituality are impossible apart from community.

The movement from self-centeredness to self-transcendence is essential to Christian spirituality. It's as important to Christian spirituality as it is to developmental psychology. It's about growth in personal integrity, wholeness, faith, hope, love, and Christlikeness. So, both traditions speak of this phenomenon. But they use different terms and reference points.

The whole psychological self is *the loving self-in-relationship*. But, in Christian terms, what is the whole spiritual self? It's *the trusting, interdependent, loving self-in-relationship (from and for God and others)*.

7. Christian spirituality is shaped through practices.

As Christians, we need to develop spiritual disciplines and practices that allow Jesus to turn upside-down our values, practices, priorities, and desires. This includes scrutinizing these things in the light of the words and example of Jesus Christ. He wants to turn our worldview, values, and lifestyle upside-down.

Jesus shapes our Christian spirituality through his grace. But he also uses our practices. So, we need prayer, meditation, fasting, spiritual reading, and biblical memorization. We need spiritual friendship and worship in communities. We nurture Christian spirituality through our engagement in social justice. We enlarge it through our involvement in missions. We earth Christian spirituality through our creation care. We enrich it through our earth-keeping practices. (Among other things, earth-keeping practices include planting gardens, tending trees, growing vegetables, recycling waste, conserving energy, producing and consuming locally, and campaigning for ecological well-being and justice.)

PART 3: REVITALIZING OUR CHURCHES

8. Christian spirituality welcomes pleasure and suffering.

This is hard. It's too easy for me to make such a statement from the safety and comfort of my Australian home. Just this week, the terrorist group Islamic State brutally murdered twenty-one Egyptian Christians for being "people of the cross." As Christians, we welcome liberation, joy, faith, love, peace, and hope as the fruit of discipleship and divine grace. But we will also welcome fatigue, persecution, hardship, martyrdom, and suffering as the fruit of discipleship and witness to Jesus Christ and his gospel and kingdom.

The book of Job reminds us that suffering isn't consistently cleansing, educational, testing, or edifying. Job's friends make the mistake of offering the sufferer theological clichés and complicated explanations. Job needed comfort, presence, and solidarity, not clichéd answers. Life is full of contradictions and pain. The righteous and innocent sufferer may find hope and peace in trusting God. This can be the case even if they can't find satisfactory answers to their painful questions.

The Bible shows us that God is not distanced from human suffering. He suffers greatly. Jesus experienced profound suffering: *physical* (from hunger, weariness, flogging, and crucifixion), *emotional* (he wept for Lazarus), and *mental* and *spiritual* (such as his agony in the garden and his torment on the cross). Jesus identifies with the innocent sufferer because he is an innocent sufferer. We are not alone in our pain. When we suffer, he suffers with us. Sadhu Sundar Singh tells us that Jesus says, "Since I bore the cross, I can deliver and keep all who are cross-bearers in perfect safety. Even when they walk through the fires of persecution, I am there."[63]

Since God enters our suffering, he can work through it for our good (even though suffering is never good in itself). God is with us when we suffer. He may use suffering to draw us to Christ and lead us to Christian maturity (he *uses* not *causes* suffering for his people). We grow spiritually as we hold on to the promise that God is with us in our suffering and cling to the hope of eternal healing. We show others compassion and solidarity in their suffering or persecution. We refuse simplistic or clichéd answers. We engage in prayer for healing and ministry among those who suffer. We stand in solidarity with those who suffer. We remember the Cross. The Cross and resurrection show us that God suffers and shares our pain, that resurrection life is ours, and that we have eternal hope. We are in radical union with a suffering and crucified and resurrected Lord.

God forges our discipleship amid suffering. This has been the way for millennia. As witnesses to the mission of God through Jesus Christ, we

---

63. Singh, *At the Feet of the Master*, 74; Singh and Moore, *Sadhu Sundar Singh*, 81–90.

endure suffering. The Spirit enables us to be suffering and vindicated witnesses to the gospel of Jesus Christ.

9. Christian spirituality rejects religiosity.

As disciples, we reject mere religiosity. We refuse the "form" of godliness that denies the power of God (2 Tim 3:5). Instead, we embrace a spirituality of personal transformation, immersion in a community, and conversion to the neighbor. We involve ourselves in our generation's political, economic, ecological, moral, and social struggles (and of our location). We seek authentic conversion to the gospel of Christ, the will of the Father, and the power of the Spirit. We love the Lord our God with all our heart, soul, mind, and strength. We love our neighbor as ourselves (Luke 10:27).

10. Christian spirituality is holistic and integrative.

Christian spirituality in the West is often dualistic. The sacred is separated from the secular. The body is separated from the spirit. The individual is separated from the communal. The event is separated from the process. Evangelism is separated from social action. The public is separated from the private. The objective is separated from the subjective. But, as Christians, we must seek integrative spiritual formation. We must break down these divisions. We do this by nurturing a discipleship that's holistic and integrative. What do we integrate? Mission and discipleship. Rejoicing and suffering. Body and spirit. Prayer and political holiness. Evangelism and social action. Bible and Spirit. Worship and liberating action. Contemplation and selfless service. That's just the start.

11. Christian spirituality is inseparable from mission.

Christian spirituality and discipleship grow in mission. They resource mission. They're inseparable from missions. They're the oxygen for missions. They need missions to flourish. The great South African missiologist, David Bosch, says we don't have to choose between spirituality and mission.

> Spirituality is not contemplation over against action. It is not a flight from the world over against involvement in the world... The involvement in this world should lead to a deepening of our relationship with and dependence on God, and the deepening of this relationship should lead to increasing involvement in the

world. Pouring out our love on people in selfless dedication is a form of prayer . . . Spirituality is all-pervading.[64]

We shape our Christian spirituality around the truth that God unveiled his being as Father, Son, and Spirit. This triune God invites us into his fellowship life. God calls us to witness to the astonishing inbreaking of the kingdom of God in this world. Our Christian spirituality and discipleship witness to the kingdom inaugurated in the Incarnation of Jesus and the outpouring of the Spirit. We offer this witness by the grace and will of God the Father. Christian spirituality is a life of communion with God in Jesus Christ.

Study Questions

1. What one or two things stood out to you as you read this chapter?

2. How are you enjoying a life of communion with God in Jesus Christ?

3. Are spiritual formation and discipleship prioritized in your church? Are they at the center of your life together? Are they connected to your mission together in the world? What needs to change?

4. Are you following Jesus in the power of the Spirit? This chapter shows that this includes indignation, solidarity, communion, relinquishment, courage, community, prayer, self-sacrificial action, political holiness, social action, holiness, and crucified and risen minds.

5. Is Christian spirituality a collective adventure for you? Or a privatized and individualized experience?

6. How is your prayer materialized in missional witness, gratuitous love, just actions, political holiness, and prophetic courage?

---

64. Bosch, *Spirituality of the Road*, 13–14.

22.

Conclusion: World Christianity
A Cause for Renewal, Celebration, and Joy

THE SPIRIT OF CHRIST is causing a fascinating and thrilling shift in global Christianity. Western Christians can no longer claim to be the center or heartbeat of the global church. The shift toward the Majority World is undeniable. Majority World churches are booming in numbers and growing at an exponential rate. Many scholars have documented this growth, and I've described it in this book. "By 2025, fully two-thirds of Christians will live in Africa, Latin America, and Asia."[1] In 2011, the Pew Research Center wrote, "A century ago, the Global North (commonly defined as North America, Europe, Australia, Japan, and New Zealand) contained more than four times as many Christians as the Global South (the rest of the world). Today . . . more than 1.3 billion Christians live in the Global South [61% of all Christians live in Asia, Africa, and Latin America], compared with about 860 million in the Global North (39%)."[2] In 2019, the Center for the Study of Global Christianity made the following observation: "By 2020 fully two-thirds of all Christians were in the Global South, with only one-third in the Global North. By 2050 we anticipate that 77 percent of all Christians will live in the Global South."[3] The Spirit enabled this astonishing shift to happen in only one hundred years.[4]

---

1. Bevans et al., "Missiology after Bosch," 69.
2. Pew Research Center, *Global Christianity*.
3. Zurlo et al., "World Christianity and Mission 2020."
4. See Barrett et al., *World Christian Encyclopedia*, 12–15.

PART 3: REVITALIZING OUR CHURCHES

At the same time, the churches of the West are declining. The West is in desperate need of re-missionalization. Patrick Johnstone observes that Europe's Christian growth rate "turned into absolute decline by 1980. This has rapidly accelerated and is likely to far exceed even the general population decline." Secularization and other forces have eroded North America's churches. They will likely experience "a reduction of the Christian growth rate to almost zero in 2050."[5]

Western societies have shifted away from Christendom. They have mostly become post-Christendom cultures. Christendom took many forms in the West. But it's now finished in these cultures. Christendom was that period in Western history when church and state were closely aligned. During the Western experience of Christendom, Christianity became the majority religion in many nations. Christianity forged close connections with those nations. It often aligned itself with their politics and political goals. It often supported their institutions and instruments of power. Philip Jenkins has demonstrated that some parts of Asia, Africa, and Latin America are experiencing new Christendoms.[6] But Western cultures and contexts are going in the opposite direction. They are moving away from Christendom settings and into post-Christendom dynamics.

What is post-Christendom? Stuart Murray defines it clearly. "Post-Christendom is the culture that emerges as the Christian faith loses coherence within a society that has been definitively shaped by the Christian story and as the institutions that have been developed to express Christian convictions decline in influence."[7] Many Western churches find themselves on the margins of post-Christendom cultures. A post-Christendom recalibration of the church and its mission is necessary. This includes a missional recalibration of mission, ministry, worship, discipleship, and community. Western churches need to be more missional. Mission is a defining characteristic of the booming churches of the Majority World. The Western church faces its cultural captivity. It must recalibrate itself in the light of the gospel and the *missio Dei* (the mission of God). This recalibration is necessary for the Western church to be missional in post-Christendom cultures. The church must pursue missional approaches to theology, ministry, service, and servantship. Missional recalibration is vital if the Western church is to stop its decline.

There's been a recent surge of books considering the church's mission. These examine how we might re-missionalize the church and re-evangelize

---

5. Johnstone, *Future of the Global Church*, 99.
6. Jenkins, *Next Christendom*.
7. Murray, *Post-Christendom*, 19.

CONCLUSION: WORLD CHRISTIANITY

the West. But North Americans have written most of these books. Australian, European, and British authors have also written many of these books. I recently heard a leading missional thinker make a claim. He said, "The future of Western cultures and churches rests with the North American church. North American Christian experiments and innovations hold the key for winning the West for Christ."[8]

I believe he's appealing to the dominant narrative in North America. But he's wrong. It's time that we embraced a new narrative. The future of the global church isn't found in the United States. How could we even think that when the church's exponential growth is in the Majority World? Western churches, theologies, and missions aren't the future. We're *a part* of the future, as important as any other part of the global church. But we're not *the* future. The future of the global church exists in dynamic and global conversations. We need to move from a Eurocentric and Americentric view of mission and the church to one that prioritizes, respects, includes, and hears the whole global church. These conversations must be multivocal, multicultural, multi-peopled, missional, and *glocal* (global and local). They must involve people from the Majority World, First Nations, Indigenous cultures, and the West. The global church needs a thrilling *glocal* exchange. We need one characterized by mutuality, respect, partnership, and interdependence. Such exchange helps Majority World, First Nation, Indigenous, and Western churches learn from each other. It enables them to pursue theologies and practice in their own contexts, with attention to global exchanges. As Christians, we must replace a Western-centric (including Eurocentric and Americentric) worldview with a holisticostal one. See Table 22.1.

Table 22.1. Western-centric Worldview versus a Holisticostal Worldview

Western-centric Worldview	Holisticostal Worldview
Eurocentric & Americentric Methodology	World Christianity Methodology
Monocentric	Polycentric
Monovocal	Polyvocal
Monocultural	Intercultural
Dualistic	Integral (holistic)
Human Ingenuity	Pentecostal presence & power
Western	Glocal (global–local)

---

8. I'm intentionally not naming this person.

Note: The Western-centric worldview is superior, colonizing, monocentric, monovocal, dualistic, parochial, dismissive, oppressive, exceptionalistic, nostalgic, and reliant on human ingenuity.	Note: The holisticostal worldview is humble, mutual, polycentric, polyvocal, integral (holistic), broad, attentive, liberating, universal, visionary, and reliant on the Spirit's power and presence to bring unity and in diversity and create the new humanity in Jesus Christ.

The holisticostal worldview aligns with Paul's vision of the new humanity in Jesus Christ. Paul's vision of a new humanity in Christ is one of the central themes of his letters in the New Testament. This vision is anchored in the belief that through Jesus Christ, God has initiated a new creation, breaking down barriers and redefining human relationships. Here are some critical aspects of this vision:

1. Unity in Christ: Paul famously declares in Gal 3:28, "There is neither Jew nor Greek, there is neither slave nor free, there is no male and female, for you are all one in Christ Jesus." This means that ethnic, social, and gender divisions that typically defined identities and relationships in the ancient world are transcended in Christ.

2. New Creation: In 2 Cor 5:17, Paul says, "Therefore, if anyone is in Christ, he is a new creation. The old has passed away; behold, the new has come." This speaks of personal transformation and points to God's broader work of renewing all things through Christ.

3. Reconciliation: A significant part of this new humanity is people's reconciliation with God and one another. Paul emphasizes in Eph 2:14–16 that Christ has broken down the dividing wall of hostility between Jews and Gentiles, making the two one and reconciling them to God.

4. Ethical Transformation: Paul believed that believers, being in Christ, are called to live out this new identity by walking in the Spirit and exhibiting the fruit of the Spirit (Gal 5:22–26). This involves setting aside old behavior patterns and adopting new ways of living characterized by love, joy, peace, patience, kindness, goodness, faithfulness, gentleness, and self-control.

5. Future Hope: While there is a present reality to this new humanity in Christ, there's also a future aspect. Paul looked forward to the resurrection when believers would fully conform to Christ's image, and creation itself would be liberated from its bondage to decay (Rom 8:18–25).

Paul's vision of a new humanity in Christ is about God's transformative work, where barriers are broken, relationships are healed, ethical lives are pursued, and a future hope in Christ is eagerly anticipated. This new humanity participates in the life and mission of Christ, reflecting God's intended design for humanity.

A Humble Reckoning: The Western-centric Worldview and the Seven Deadly Sins

In an era awash with information and influence, the pervasive influence of a Western-centric worldview cannot be understated. As we unpack the layers of this worldview, it becomes evident that many of its facets echo the seven deadly sins.

The Western-centric worldview is often seen as *superior*, casting other cultures, traditions, and knowledge bases as inferior or irrelevant. This form of superiority mirrors the sin of *pride*. As the sages have often mused, any worldview that sees itself as the measure of all things inevitably distorts the grand diversity and multiplicity of human existence.

The term *monocentric* captures the West's inclination to place itself at the center of every narrative. This mirrors *greed*, an insatiable desire to be the focal point, disregarding the myriad stories that have shaped the human experience outside the Western lens. There's a profound truth in the wisdom that warns against avarice and self-centeredness: the world is richer and more complex than any one culture's story.

Similarly, the *monocultural* lens, which pushes for assimilation over diversity, is akin to *gluttony*. Just as gluttony overindulges in one type of sustenance, a monocultural view starves us of the wide variety of experiences, insights, and wisdom the global community offers.

When a single voice or narrative monopolizes the discourse—being *monovocal*—it silences the diversity and multiplicity of voices that have equally valid perspectives. This can be seen as an outworking of *envy*, where only one voice is deemed worthy, and all others are pushed aside.

The *dualistic* nature of the Western worldview, which often simplifies issues into binaries (good vs. bad, us vs. them), harks to the sin of *wrath*. Wrath divides and creates enmity, just as dualism fails to appreciate the nuances and complexities of life.

The *parochial* nature of this worldview, its limited scope, and reluctance to engage with the broader world embodies *sloth*. It's a reluctance to venture beyond comfort zones, seeking more profound understanding and mutual enrichment.

Lastly, colonialism, oppression, and exceptionalism speak to *lust*—an unchecked desire for control, dominance, and singular exceptionalism, with nostalgia for days of old when such control was more manifest.

Yet, amidst the seven deadly sins and their echoes, there is hope. The challenges of our age beckon us to re-examine our perspectives to decentralize and diversify our stories. Many wise voices, both past and present, have challenged us to break free from these deadly echoes.

Some remind us that the God of the cosmos is a God of all peoples, and God's redemptive purposes unfold through stories from every corner of the earth. They call us to a radical re-imagining of community, urging us to see strength in diversity, richness in multiplicity, and beauty in every voice.

Others challenge the church to be a beacon of hope and a counter-cultural force against these sins. The gospel is for everyone and beckons us to a deeper understanding, mutual respect, and shared mission. We're called to a kingdom vision that transcends borders and shatters monocentric worldviews.

Still, others remind us of the God who hears the cries of the oppressed, aligning with those on the margins. This is a call to deconstruct oppressive systems and to champion justice, equity, and love.

This humbling reckoning reminds us of the need to shift away from human ingenuity and recognize our interdependence. True wisdom lies not in exceptionalism but the shared journey of faith, hope, and love. Only then can we hope to overcome the shadows of these seven deadly sins.

A Lamp of Renewal: The Holisticostal Antidote

In a time of global fragmentation, where divisions seem sharper, and understanding seems elusive, the emergence of a "holisticostal" worldview offers hope and a transformative paradigm shift. As we reflect on the profound challenges a Western-centric worldview presents, the holisticostal perspective rises as a redemptive force against those challenges.

The first antidote is to espouse a *world Christianity methodological* approach. We find ourselves in a global village, where dialogues are no longer confined to close quarters but stretch across continents. Such a methodology is inherently humble, emphasizing listening as much as speaking. It reminds us of the apostle Paul's timeless advice: in humility, consider others better than oneself. In this renewed narrative, theology is not a solitary pursuit, but a communal, global dialogue constantly refined by mutual exchanges.

Secondly, *polycentricity* emerges as a vibrant counter to monocentric dominance. This approach values multiple centers of influence, understanding, and insight. The world's wisdom isn't confined to one geography or tradition. In the vast expanse of human history, God has been at work everywhere, speaking truths into the hearts of those who would listen from every corner of the world.

The third pillar, *polyvocality*, underscores the importance of many voices. Like a symphony with numerous instruments, the truth is more richly understood when heard from diverse voices. It challenges the monovocal nature that has historically overshadowed others, urging us to recognize the Spirit's voice even in the whispers of the marginalized.

Embracing *interculturality* is to welcome the mingling of cultures, traditions, and insights. Rather than being threatened by difference, interculturality sees it as a source of strength. This interconnectedness tears down walls of pride and superiority, fostering a more profound sense of global community.

The call for an *integral (holistic)* theology, church, and mission is reminiscent of the biblical call for shalom—peace and wholeness encompassing every aspect of life. It's not merely about spiritual matters but also social, political, and ecological concerns, echoing the voices that have long proclaimed God's heart for justice, love, and holistic redemption.

The sixth aspect, recognizing our reliance on the *Spirit's pentecostal power and presence*, is crucial. The Spirit can truly forge unity in diversity, reminding us of our primary identity in Christ, transcending earthly divisions. As architects of peace and love have posited, the vision of a new humanity can be realized only through the Spirit.

Finally, *glocal dynamics* harmoniously blend the global with the local. It recognizes the significance of local stories within global narratives. By valuing both, we learn to discern the universal truths echoed in local tales, fostering mutual respect and understanding.

In this holisticostal worldview, we find a lamp of renewal, a counter-narrative to the seven deadly echoes of the Western-centric perspective. Grounded in humility, mutual respect, and the indomitable power of the Spirit, this worldview paves the way for a more united, compassionate, ethical, and just world that reflects Christ's vision of the kingdom of God.

In our journey towards this vision, let's remember the wisdom of those who have trodden similar paths before us, those who, across ages, ethnicities, and geographies, have championed love over pride, unity over division, and the transcendent truth that in our diversity, we find a richer, fuller understanding of the Divine.

PART 3: REVITALIZING OUR CHURCHES

World Christianity:
A Cause for Renewal, Celebration, and Joy

We need a contrary narrative to the one that dominates. I want the global church to embrace a new narrative. Here it is: Christ's holisticostal church needs a holisticostal worldview. Western Christians must carefully consider the church's future as it emerges from the Majority World and vice versa. The truth is that the future isn't emerging from any *one* context. It's emerging globally. It's especially emerging from the Majority World. (We see this in mission, worship, theology, spirituality, hermeneutics, the reading of church history, and more.) The future is emerging from the multi-voiced and multi-peopled conversations I've described.

Western Christians can learn much from their sisters and brothers in Majority World and Indigenous cultures. We can learn from their contextual mission, servantship, ethics, hospitality, creation care, education, and Spirit empowerment. We can learn from how they prioritize Scripture, discipleship, mission, beauty, and relationships.

I hope to encourage the new narrative I've described. I want to stimulate global conversations. Many themes in Majority World theology and practice are, of course, present in Western literature, too. But global voices and perspectives enrich them. This includes conversations between persons of different cultures, ages, genders, traditions, and theologies—both locally and globally.

In this book, I've explored how Christians can be the *salt* of the earth, the *light* of the world, and a *city* set on a hill. I've considered how we do this locally, globally, and as Jesus Christ's holisticostal church. We do this by listening to others. We do this by learning from each other. We do this through local, national, regional, and global collaborations. We do this through brave and contextual applications of our mutual, global, and missional discoveries. Majority World and Indigenous voices help Westerners grow in our understanding and practice of mission, church, and theology. They stir us to think in fresh ways about what it means to be salt, light, and a city. We've too often ignored these voices. But we can't do this anymore. We mustn't do this anymore. We need to embrace a new narrative—one that's global and missional. We must reshape our conversations, renew our mission, and revitalize our churches. Father, Son, and Holy Spirit have ushered in the age of world Christianity, and that's a cause for enormous renewal, celebration, and joy.

23.

A Closing Prayer

Eternal and Loving Creator God, *the great Artist of the universe, who has masterfully crafted creation and humanity in colors of diversity and culture, steer our spirits ever closer to the heartbeat of your love.*

In your divine wisdom, you crafted us in your image. Divisions have been bridged through the redemptive work of Christ—you unite us across ethnicities, races, genders, languages, Christian traditions, and nations. On the day of Pentecost, your Spirit empowered diverse tongues to declare your wonders. Today, we are reminded that all who call on your name will be saved, making us one body with many members, each essential and unique.

Embolden us to stand for justice, to reach out in genuine embrace, and to amplify the voices that have long been overshadowed.

Lord Jesus, you tore down walls of hostility and called us into unity. As you reconcile diverse peoples, may we recognize our shared identity in you. Bestow upon us a love that mirrors yours—a love that binds, heals, and identifies us as your disciples. May the world come to know your salvation and peace through this love.

As we reflect upon the magnificent vision of the multitude, each from every corner of the Earth, singing praises before your throne, instill within us enduring hope, coupled with a fiery passion to act justly and love mercifully.

May our daily steps be in tandem with your kingdom's rhythm, as we eagerly await the glorious day when every tribe, language, and nation unites in harmonious adoration under your boundless love and grace.

In the unity of the Spirit and trust in God's eternal grace, we offer these prayers through Jesus Christ, our Lord and Savior.

Amen.

Appendix 1

Who Are These Majority World and Indigenous Theologians and Practitioners?

Here's a link to a webpage with short biographies of the 100+ Majority World and Indigenous thinkers I engage in this book. Many live, serve, and write from Majority World, First Nations, and Indigenous contexts. (This is the bulk of the persons on this list). Others have moved to Western settings.

Those who live in Majority World and Indigenous societies bring invaluable perspectives from their cultural settings. Those who have moved to Western contexts bring the value of hybrid or bi-cultural perspectives. I do not engage each thinker equally. Instead, I deal with them according to their relevance to the particular themes of the chapters of this book.

I could have consulted the work of thousands of thinkers, writers, and practitioners in this book. However, I have limited myself to a sample of those who speak directly to the themes of this book.

These African, Asian, Caribbean, Eastern European, First Nations, Indigenous, Latin American, Middle Eastern, and Oceanian Christian practitioners and theologians inspire us to think in fresh ways about missions, church vitality, theology, and the kingdom of God. They challenge us to renew the worship, community, and mission of Jesus Christ's church.

Here's the link:
https://grahamjosephhill.com/shortbiographies/

Appendix 2

World Christianity Links at GrahamJosephHill.com

You'll find links to further reading on world Christianity on my website. Go here for these links:

https://grahamjosephhill.com/links/

The links include the following:

Celucian L. Joseph, "20 Haitian Theologians and Biblical Scholars You Should Know About"

Jocabed Solano and Drew Jennings-Grisham, "Some Indigenous Women Theologians You Should Know About"

Stephanie A. Lowery, "9 African Women Theologians You Should Know About"

Emmanuella Carter, "17 African American Women Theologians You Should Know About"

Juliany González Nieves, "23 Latin American Women and USA Latinas in Theology and Religion You Should Know About"

Grace Al-Zoughbi Arteen and Graham Joseph Hill, "18 Arab Female Theologians and Christian Leaders You Should Know About"

Jessie Giyou Kim and Graham Joseph Hill, "18 Asian Female Theologians You Should Know About (Plus Others For You To Explore)"

Graham Joseph Hill and Jen Barker, "20 Australian and New Zealander Female Theologians You Should Know About"

Graham Joseph Hill and Jen Barker, "160+ Australian and New Zealander Women in Theology You Should Know About"

WORLD CHRISTIANITY LINKS AT GRAHAMJOSEPHHILL.COM

Graham Joseph Hill and Jessie Giyou Kim, "12 Women on Changing the World: A 12-Session Film Series on Transforming Society and Neighborhoods"

Juliany González Nieves, "Caribbean Christian Theology: A Bibliography"

Juliany González Nieves offers "A Reading List on Latinx and Latin American Theologies"

APPENDIX 3

The Global Church Project Video Series

OVER THE PREVIOUS DECADE, I've done hundreds of filmed interviews with Majority World, Indigenous, First Nations, and Western theologians and practitioners. I've now uploaded these to Vimeo and YouTube, and here are the links:

https://youtube.com/@GrahamJosephHill_Author

https://grahamjosephhill.com/worldchristianity/

Interviewees include Miroslav Volf, Wonsuk Ma, Ruth Padilla DeBorst, Ash Barker, Melba Maggay, John M. Perkins, Randy Woodley, Tite Tienou, Tim Costello, Al Tizon, Alan Hirsch, Michael Frost, Amal Nassar, Amos Yong, Jo Saxton, Daniel Bourdanné, Emmanuel Katongole, Grace Ji-Sun Kim, Jack Sara, Kevin Doi, Lamin Sanneh, Lisa Rodriguez Watson, Noel Castellanos, René August, C. Rene Padilla, Rosalee Velloso Ewell, Samuel Chetti, Soong-Chan Rah, Gina Zurlo, Amy Williams, Jossy Chacko, Johannes Reimer, M.L. Daneel, Madezha Cepeda, Alexander Chow, Daniel Jeyaraj, Oscar García-Johnson, Peter Kuzmic, David L. Ro, Norberto Saracco, Sebastian Kim, Fernando Sevogia, Craig Stewart, Vitor Westelle, Munib Younan, Sam Marullo, Ajith Fernando, Frederick Douglas Powe Jr., Mitri Raheb, Sami B. Awad, Shaul David Judelman, Elias Chacour, Charles Ringma, Joel Edwards, Perry Shaw, Michael Goheen, Raymond Minniecon, Ken Kamau, Mandy Marshall, Omar Djoeandy, Jayakumar Christian, James Bryan Smith, Carol Kingston-Smith, Gary Nelson, Siufung Wu, Cory Ishida, Barbara M. Leung Lai, David Congdon, German Galvez, Frank Macchia, La Verne Tolbert,

THE GLOBAL CHURCH PROJECT VIDEO SERIES

Elisa Padilla, Greg Lake, Peter Seeberger, Liz Mark Galpin, Harvey Kwiyani, Frank Paul, Emil Jonathan L. Soriano, Quang Nguyen, Dave Bookless, and more.

Appendix 4

Other Books and Resources by Graham Joseph Hill

Author Website and YouTube Channel

Graham's author website: GrahamJosephHill.com
Graham's YouTube channel with filmed interviews with Christian leaders and scholars from across the world: youtube.com/@GrahamJosephHill_Author.

Books

Healing Our Broken Humanity: Practices for Revitalizing the Church and Renewing the World. Downers Grove, IL: InterVarsity, 2018 (with Grace Ji-Sun Kim).

Hide This in Your Heart: Memorizing Scripture for Kingdom Impact. Colorado Springs, CO: NavPress, 2020 (with Michael Frost).

Holding Up Half the Sky: A Biblical Case for Women Leading and Teaching in the Church. Eugene, OR: Cascade, 2020.

Salt, Light, and a City: Conformation—Ecclesiology for the Global Missional Community: Volume 2, Majority World Voices. Eugene, OR: Cascade, 2020.

Salt, Light, and a City: Ecclesiology for the Global Missional Community: Volume 1, Western Voices. Eugene, OR: Cascade, 2017.

OTHER BOOKS AND RESOURCES BY GRAHAM JOSEPH HILL

Sunburnt Country, Sweeping Pains: The Experiences of Asian Australian Women in Ministry and Mission. Eugene, OR: Wipf & Stock, 2022.

The Soul Online: Bereavement, Social Media, and Competent Care. Eugene, OR: Cascade, 2022 (with Desiree Geldenhuys).

World Christianity: An Introduction. Eugene, OR: Cascade, 2024.

Devotional Series

Genesis: Embracing Beginnings and Honoring Covenants: A 50-Day Devotional on Genesis.

Matthew: Seeking the Kingdom and Living Righteousness: A 50-Day Devotional on Matthew.

Stay tuned for more books in the devotional series, "Daily Devotions with Jesus." Devotional books in this series will cover every book of the Bible and a two-volume devotional book on Christian missions. See all the devotional books here: grahamjosephhill.com/devotional-books.

Bibliography

Adichie, Chimamanda Ngozi. *Half of a Yellow Sun*. London: Fourth Estate, 2006.
Adrahtas, Vassills. "Perceptions of Land in Indigenous Australian Christian Texts." *Studies in World Christianity* 11 (2005) 200–214.
Aelred of Rievaulx, et al. *Aelred of Rievaulx: Spiritual Friendship*. Cistercian Fathers Series. Collegeville, MN: Liturgical, 2010.
Agosto, Efrain. *Servant Leadership: Jesus and Paul*. St. Louis: Chalice, 2005.
Allport, Gordon. *The Nature of Prejudice*. Reading, MA: Addison-Wesley, 1954.
Amanze, James N. "Contextuality: African Spirituality as a Catalyst for Spiritual Formation in Theological Education in Africa." *Ogbomoso Journal of Theology* 16 (2011) 1–23.
Anderson, Allan. *An Introduction to Pentecostalism: Global Charismatic Christianity*. Cambridge: Cambridge University Press, 2004.
———. "Towards a Pentecostal Missiology for the Majority World." *Asian Journal of Pentecostal Studies* 8 (2005) 29–47.
———. "Types and Butterflies: African Initiated Churches and European Typologies." *International Bulletin of Missionary Research* 25 (2001) 107.
Anderson, Gerald H. "Developments in Theological Education in South East Asia." *International Bulletin of Missionary Research* 30 (2006) 96.
Andrews, Dale. *Practical Theology for Black Churches: Bridging Black Theology and African American Folk Religion*. Louisville: Westminster John Knox, 2022.
Angelici, Reuben. *Richard of Saint Victor, On the Trinity: English Translation and Commentary*. Eugene, OR: Cascade Books, 2011.
Aquini, Maria Pilar, and Maria Jose Rosado-Nunes, eds. *Feminist Intercultural Theology: Latina Explorations for a Just World*. Studies in Latino/a Catholicism. Maryknoll, NY: Orbis, 2007.
Ariarajah, S. Wesley. "The Challenge of Building Communities of Peace for All: The Richness and Dilemma of Diversities." *Ecumenical Review* 57 (2005) 124–35.
Arias, Mortimer. "Announcing the Kingdom as Challenge: Discipleship Evangelization." *Impact* 8 (1982) 1–14.
———. "Centripetal Mission or Evangelization by Hospitality." *Missiology* 10 (1982) 69–81.
Arrupe, Pedro. "Letter to the Whole Society on Inculturation." In *Other Apostolates Today: Selected Letters and Addresses of Pedro Arrupe*, edited by Jerome Aixala, 172–81. St Louis: Institute of Jesuit Sources, 1978.

BIBLIOGRAPHY

Assmann, Hugo. *Teología Desde la praxis de la liberación: Ensayo telógico desde la America dependiente*. Salamanca: Sigueme, 1976.

Azariah, Jayapaul. "Ethical Management of Natural Resources." In *Eco-Theology*, edited by Elaine Wainwright et al., 120–26. London: SCM, 2009.

Bakhtin, Mikhail. "Discourse in the Novel." In *The Dialogic Imagination: Four Essays by M. M. Bakhtin*. Translated by Caryl Emerson and Michael Holquist, 259–422. Austin: University of Texas Press, 1981.

Barclay, William, and Rupert E. Davies. *We Believe in God*. Unwin Forum. London: Allen & Unwin, 1968.

Barker, Ash. *Slum Life Rising: How to Enflesh Hope within a New Urban World*. Dandenong: Urban Neighbours of Hope, 2013.

Barrett, David B., et al. *World Christian Encyclopedia: A Comparative Survey of Churches and Religions in the Modern World*. 2nd ed. 2 vols. New York: Oxford University Press, 2001.

Bassham, Rodger C. *Mission Theology, 1948–1975: Years of Worldwide Creative Tension—Ecumenical, Evangelical, and Roman Catholic*. Pasadena, CA: William Carey, 1979.

Bebbington, David W. *Evangelicalism in Modern Britain: A History from the 1730s to the 1980s*. Milton Park, UK: Routledge, 2003.

Bediako, Kwame. *Jesus in Africa: The Christian Gospel in African History and Experience*. Theological Reflections from the South. Carlisle, UK: Paternoster, 2000.

———. "The Significance of Modern African Christianity—a Manifesto." *Studies in World Christianity* 1 (1995) 51–67.

Benedict XVI, Pope. "Retrieving the Tradition: Concerning the Notion of Person in Theology." *Communio* 17 (1990) 440–54.

Berg, Clayton L., and Paul E. Pretiz. *Spontaneous Combustion: Grass Roots Christianity, Latin American Style*. Pasadena, CA: William Carey, 1996.

Bergunder, Michael, et al. "The Pentecostal Movement and Basic Ecclesial Communities in Latin America: Sociological Theories and Theological Debates." *International Review of Mission* 91 (2002) 163–86.

Bernhardt, Reinhold. "Interkulturelle Theologie." *Theologische Rundschau* 77 (2012) 344–64.

Berryman, Phillip. *Religion in the Megacity: Catholic and Protestant Portraits from Latin America*. Maryknoll, NY: Orbis, 1996.

Bevans, Stephen B., ed. *Mission and Culture: The Louis J. Luzbetak Lectures*. American Society of Missiology Series 48. Maryknoll, NY: Orbis, 2012.

Bevans, Stephen B., and Roger Schroeder. *Constants in Context: A Theology of Mission for Today*. American Society of Missiology Series 30. Maryknoll, NY: Orbis, 2004.

Bevans, Stephen B., et al. "Missiology after Bosch: Reverencing a Classic by Moving Beyond." *International Bulletin of Missionary Research* 29 (2005) 69–72.

Bhabha, Homi K. *The Location of Culture*. London: Routledge, 1994.

Bloom, Anthony. *Living Prayer*. Springfield, IL: Templegate, 1966.

Boas, Franz. *Race, Language, and Culture*. New York: Macmillan, 1940.

Boff, Clodovis. "Methodology of the Theology of Liberation." In *Systematic Theology: Prespectives from Liberation Theology*, edited by Jon Sobrino and Ignacio Ellacuria, 1–21. Maryknoll, NY: Orbis, 1996.

Boff, Leonardo. *Cry of the Earth, Cry of the Poor*. Translated by Philip Berryman. Ecology and Justice Series. Maryknoll, NY: Orbis, 1997.

———. "Earth as Gaia: An Ethical and Spiritual Challenge." In *Eco-Theology*, edited by Elaine Wainwright et al., 24–32. London: SCM, 2009.

———. *Ecclesiogenesis: The Base Communities Reinvent the Church*. Translated by Robert R. Barr. Maryknoll, NY: Orbis, 1986.

———. *Ecology & Liberation: A New Paradigm*. Translated by John Cumming. Ecology and Justice Series. Maryknoll, NY: Orbis, 1995.

———. *Faith on the Edge: Religion and Marginalized Existence*. San Francisco: Harper & Row, 1989.

———. *Holy Trinity, Perfect Community*. Translated by Philip Berryman. Maryknoll, NY: Orbis, 2000.

———. "The Need for Political Saints: From a Spirituality of Libertion to the Practice of Liberation." *Cross Currents* 30 (1980) 369–76.

———. *Saint Francis: A Model for Human Liberation*. Translated by John W. Diercksmeier. New York: Crossroad, 1982.

———. "Trinitarian Community and Social Liberation." *Cross Currents* 38 (1988) 289–308.

———. *When Theology Listens to the Poor*. Translated by Robert R. Barr. San Francisco: Harper & Row, 1988.

Boff, Leonardo, and Clodovis Boff. *Introducing Liberation Theology*. Translated by Paul Burns. Maryknoll, NY: Orbis, 1987.

Boff, Leonardo, and Virgilio P. Elizondo, eds. *Ecology and Poverty: Cry of the Earth, Cry of the Poor*. Concilium 1995/5. Maryknoll, NY: Orbis, 1995.

Bokovay, W. Kelly. "The Relationship of Physical Healing to the Atonement." *Didaskalia* 3 (1991) 24–39.

Bonhoeffer, Dietrich. *Letters and Papers from Prison*. 1st American English ed. New York: Macmillan, 1972.

Bosch, David J. *Believing in the Future: Toward a Missiology of Western Culture*. New York: Trinity, 1995.

———. "The Nature of Theological Education." *Theologia Evangelica* 25 (1992) 8–23.

———. *A Spirituality of the Road*. Missionary Studies. Scottdale, PA: Herald, 1979.

———. *Transforming Mission: Paradigm Shifts in Theology of Mission*. American Society of Missiology Series 16. Maryknoll, NY: Orbis, 1991.

Brandner, Tobias. "Hosts and Guests: Hospitality as an Emerging Paradigm in Mission." *International Review of Mission* 102 (2013) 94–102.

Bronfenbrenner, Urie. *The Ecology of Human Development: Experiments by Nature and Design*. Cambridge: Harvard University Press, 1979.

Browning, Don S. *A Fundamental Practical Theology: Descriptive and Strategic Proposals*. Minneapolis: Fortress, 1991.

Browning, Don S., ed. *Practical Theology: The Emerging Field in Theology, Church, and World*. San Francisco: Harper & Row. 1983.

Browning, Don S., et al. *The Education of the Practical Theologian: Responses to Joseph Hough and John Cobb's Christian Identity and Theological Education*. Scholars Press Studies in Theological Education. Atlanta: Scholars, 1989.

Bujo, Bénézet. "Differentiations in African Ethics." In *The Blackwell Companion to Religious Ethics*, edited by William Schweiker, 423–37. Blackwell Companions to Religion. Malden, MA: Blackwell, 2005.

Bunson, Matthew. *Pope Francis*. 1st ed. Huntington, IN: Our Sunday Visitor, 2013.

Butler, Judith. *Gender Trouble: Feminism and the Subversion of Identity.* Thinking Gender. New York: Routledge, 1990.
Cameron, Helen, et al. *Talking about God in* Practice : *Theological Action Research and Practical Theology.* London: SCM, 2010.
Carroll R., M. Daniel. "The Relevance of Cultural Conditioning for Social Ethics." *Journal of the Evangelical Theological Society* 29 (1986) 307–15.
Carson, D. A. *Matthew.* The Expositor's Bible Commentary. Grand Rapids: Zondervan, 1995.
Cartledge, Mark J., and David Cheetham, eds. *Intercultural Theology: Approaches and Themes* London: SCM, 2011.
Carvalhaes, Cláudio. "Borders, Globalization and Eucharistic Hospitality." *Dialog* 49 (2010) 45–55.
Casaldáliga, Pedro, and Jose-Maria Vigil. *Political Holiness: A Spirituality of Liberation.* Theology and Justice Series. Maryknoll, NY: Orbis, 1994.
Catford, Cheryl, ed. *Following Fire: How the Spirit Leads Us to Fight Injustice.* Springvale, Vic., Australia: Urban Neighbours of Hope, 2008.
Chan, Simon. "Evidential Glossolalia and the Doctrine of Subsequence." *Asian Journal of Pentecostal Studies* 2 (1999) 195–211.

———. "Mother Church: Toward a Pentecostal Ecclesiology." *Pneuma: The Journal of the Society for Pentecostal Studies* 22 (2000) 177–208.

———. *Pentecostal Theology and the Christian Spiritual Tradition.* Journal of Pentecostal Theology Supplement Series 21. Sheffield: Sheffield Academic, 2000.

———. *Spiritual Theology: A Systematic Study of the Christian Life.* Downers Grove, IL: InterVarsity, 1998.

Chester, Tim, ed. *Justice, Mercy and Humility: Integral Mission and the Poor.* Carlisle, UK: Paternoster, 2002.
Cho, Paul Yonggi. *The Holy Spirit, My Senior Partner.* Milton Keynes, UK: Word, 1989.
Chow, Wilson W. "An Integrated Approach to Theological Education." In *Evangelical Theological Education Today: An International Perspective,* edited by Paul Bowers, 49–60. Nairobi: Evangel, 1982.
Christaller, Walter. *Central Places in Southern Germany.* Englewood Cliffs, NJ: Prentice-Hall, 1966.
Christian, Jayakumar. *God of the Empty-Handed: Poverty, Power, and the Kingdom of God.* Monrovia, CA: MARC, 1999.
Chrysostom, John. "Homily 21 on Romans." In *Homilies on Acts of the Apostles,* edited by J. Walker and J. Sheppard. Nicene and Post-Nicene Fathers of the Christian Church, 504–5. New York: Christian Literature, 1889.
Clarke, W Norris. "To Be Is to Be Self-Communicative: St. Thomas' View of Personal Being." *Theology Digest* 33 (1986) 441–54.
Clifford, James. *Writing Culture: The Poetics and Politics of Ethnography.* Los Angeles: University of California Press, 1986.
Coakley, Sarah. *God, Sexuality, and the Self: An Essay 'On the Trinity.'* Cambridge: Cambridge University Press, 2013.
Coe, Shoki. "Contextualizing Theology." In *Mission Trends No. 3 Third World Theologies,* edited by Gerald H. Anderson and Thomas F. Stransky, 22. New York: Paulist, 1976.
Comblin, José. *The Holy Spirit and Liberation.* Translated by Paul Burns. Theology and Justice Series. Maryknoll, NY: Orbis, 1989.

Cone, James H. *Black Theology of Liberation*. 2nd ed. Maryknoll, NY: Orbis, 1990.
Congdon, David W. "Emancipatory Intercultural Hermeneutics: Interpreting Theo Sundermeier's Differenzhermeneutik." *Mission Studies* 33 (2016) 127–46.
Coote, Robert T., and John Stott, eds. *Down to Earth: Studies in Christianity and Culture: The Papers of the Lausanne Consultation on Gospel and Culture*. Grand Rapids: Eerdmans, 1980.
Costas, Orlando E. *Christ Outside the Gate: Mission Beyond Christendom*. Maryknoll, NY: Orbis, 1982.
———. *The Church and Its Mission: A Shattering Critique from the Third World*. Wheaton, IL: Tyndale House, 1974.
———. "Contextualization and Incarnation." *Journal of Theology for Southern Africa* 29 (1979) 23–30.
———. *The Integrity of Mission: The Inner Life and Outreach of the Church*. San Francisco: Harper and Row, 1979.
———. *Liberating News: A Theology of Contextual Evangelization*. Grand Rapids: Eerdmans, 1989.
Crenshaw, Kimberlé. *On Intersectionality: Essential Writings*. New York: New Press, 2016.
Crouch, Andy. *Playing God: Redeeming the Gift of Power*. Downers Grove, IL: IVP Books, 2013.
Cunningham, David S. *These Three Are One: The Practice of Trinitarian Theology*. London: Blackwell, 1997.
Daneel, Marthinus L. "African Independent Church Pneumatology and the Salvation of All Creation." *International Review of Mission* 82 (1993) 143–66.
Darragh, Neil. "An Ascetic Theology, Spirituality, and Praxis." In *Eco-Theology*, edited by Elaine Wainwright et al., 76–85. London: SCM, 2009.
Davidson, Max, and Graham Joseph Hill. "Liberation Theology." Lecture notes. Macquarie Park, Morling College, 2015.
DeBorst, Ruth Padilla. "God's Earth and God's People: Relationships Restored." *Journal of Latin American Theology* 5 (2010) 6–17.
———. "Living Creation-Community in God's World Today." *Journal of Latin American Theology* 5 (2010) 56–72.
———. "'Unexpected' Guests at God's Banquet Table Gospel in Mission and Culture." *Evangelical Review of Theology* 33 (2009) 62–76.
De Gruchy, Steve. "Theological Education and Missional Practice: A Vital Dialogue." In *Handbook of Theological Education in World Christianity: Theological Perspectives, Regional Surveys, Ecumenical Trends*, edited by Dietrich Werner et al., 42–50. Oxford: Regnum, 2010.
Dickson, Marcus W., et al. "Conceptualizing Leadership across Cultures." *Journal of World Business* 47 (2012) 483–92.
Downey, Michael. *Altogether Gift: A Trinitarian Spirituality*. Maryknoll, NY: Orbis, 2000.
Driver, J. *Images of the Church in Mission*. Scottdale, PA: Herald, 1997.
Dube, Musa W. "Go Tla Siama. O Tla Fola: Doing Biblical Studies in an Hiv and Aids Context." *Black Theology: An International Journal* 8 (2010) 212–41.
———. "Reducing Women's Vulnerability and Combating Stigma." *Church and Society* 94 (2003) 64–72.

BIBLIOGRAPHY

Dunn, James D. G. *The Christ and the Spirit: Pneumatology.* Grand Rapids: Eerdmans, 1998.

Eilers, Franz-Josef, ed. *For All the Peoples of Asia: Federation of Asian Bishops' Conferences. Documents from 1997 to 2002.* Quezon City, Philippines: Claretian, 2002.

Ela, Jean-Marc. *African Cry.* Translated by Robert R. Barr. Reprint, Eugene, OR: Wipf & Stock, 2005.

Ellacuría, Ignacio. "Discernir el 'signo' de los tiempos." *Diakonia* 17 (1981) 57–59.

Escobar, Samuel. "The Church as Community." In *The Local Church, Agent of Transformation: An Ecclesiology for Integral Mission,* edited by C. René Padilla and Tetsunao Yamamori, 125–50. Buenos Aires: Kairos, 2004.

———. *The New Global Mission: The Gospel from Everywhere to Everyone.* Christian Doctrine in Global Perspective. Downers Grove, IL: InterVarsity, 2003.

———. "Recruitment of Students for Mission." *Missiology* 15 (1987) 529–45.

———. *A Time for Mission: The Challenge for Global Christianity.* Leicester, UK: InterVarsity, 2003.

———. "The Training of Missiologists for a Latin American Context." In *Missiological Education for the Twenty-First Century: The Book, the Circle, and the Sandals,* edited by Paul Everett Pierson et al., 101–11. Maryknoll, NY: Orbis, 1996.

Faulkner, William. *As I Lay Dying.* New York: Vintage, 1999.

Ferdinando, Keith. "Jesus, the Theological Educator." *Themelios* 38 (2013) 360–74.

Ferguson, Sinclair B., et al., eds. *New Dictionary of Theology.* The Master Reference Collection. Downers Grove, IL: InterVarsity, 1988.

Fernando, Ajith. *Jesus Driven Ministry.* Wheaton, IL: Crossway, 2002.

———. *Reclaiming Friendship: Relating to Each Other in a Frenzied World.* Scottdale, PA: Herald, 1993.

———. "To Serve Is to Suffer: If the Apostle Paul Knew Fatigue, Anger, and Anxiety in His Ministry, What Makes Us Think We Can Avoid Them in Ours?" *Christianity Today* 54 (2010) 30–33.

Flett, John G. "Method in Mission Studies: Comparing World Christianity and Intercultural Theology." *Theologische Literaturzeitung* 143 (2018) 717–31.

———. *The Witness of God: The Trinity, Christian Witness, and Mission.* Grand Rapids: Eerdmans, 2010.

Ford, Lance. *UnLeader: Reimagining Leadership . . . and Why We Must.* Kansas City, MO: Foundry, 2012.

Foster, Richard J. *Celebration of Discipline: The Path to Spiritual Growth.* 20th anniversary ed. San Francisco: HarperSanFrancisco, 1998.

Francis, Pope. *Evangelii Gaudium—the Joy of the Gospel.* Frederick, MD: Word Among Us, 2014.

Franklin, Kirk J. "A Case Study: A Journey of Leading in Polycentric Theory and Practice in Mission." *Transformation* 38 (2021) 254–75.

Franklin, Kirk J., and Nelus Niemandt. "Polycentrism in the Missio Dei." *Hts Teologiese Studies–Theological Studies* 72 (2016) 9.

Frederiks, Martha. "World Chrstianity: Contours of an Approach." In *World Christianity: Methodological Considerations,* edited by Martha Frederiks and Dorottya Nagy, 10–39. Theology and Mission in World Christianity 19. Leiden: Brill, 2021.

Freire, Paulo. *Cultural Action for Freedom.* Middlesex: Penguin, 1970.

BIBLIOGRAPHY

———. *Pedagogy of the Oppressed*. New York, NY: Herder and Herder, 1968.
Fuellenbach, J. *Church: Community for the Kingdom*. London: Orbis, 2002.
Fukuda, Mitsuo. *Developing a Contextualized Church as a Bridge to Christianity in Japan*. Gloucester: Wide Margin, 2012.
———. "Empowering Fourth Generation Disciples: Grassroots Leadership Training in Japan and Beyond." In *Developing Indigenous Leaders: Lessons in Mission from Buddhist Asia*, edited by Paul H. De Neui, 39–64. Pasadena, CA: William Carey, 2013.
Fuller, Lon L. and Kenneth I. Winston. "The Forms and Limits of Adjudication." *Harvard Law Review* 92 (1978) 353–409.
Galilea, Segundo. *The Way of Living Faith: A Spirituality of Liberation*. San Francisco, CA: Harper & Row, 1988.
Garrison, David. *Church Planting Movements: How God Is Redeeming a Lost World*. Richmond, VA: Wigtake, 2003.
Geertz, Clifford. *The Interpretation of Cultures: Selected Essays*. New York: Basic, 1973.
George, Sherron Kay. "From Liberation to Evangelization: New Latin American Hermeneutical Keys." *Interpretation* 55 (2001) 367–77.
Gnanadason, Aruna. *Listen to the Women! Listen to the Earth!* Geneva: World Council of Churches, 2005.
———. "A Spirituality That Sustains Us in Our Struggles." *International Review of Mission* 80 (1991) 29–41.
———. "Women, Economy and Ecology." In *Ecotheology: Voices from South and North*, edited by David G. Hallman, 179–85. Maryknoll, NY: Orbis, 1994.
Gnanakan, Ken. *God's World: A Theology of the Environment*. London: SPCK, 1999.
———. *Responsible Stewardship of Creation*. Bangalore: Theological Book Trust, 2004.
———. "The Training of Missiologists for Asian Contexts." In *Missiological Education for the Twenty-First Century: The Book, the Circle, and the Sandals*, edited by Paul Everett Pierson et al., 120–29. Maryknoll, NY: Orbis, 1996.
Goldsworthy, Graeme. *Gospel and Kingdom: A Christian Interpretation of the Old Testament*. Exeter: Paternoster, 1981.
Graham, Elaine L. *Transforming Practice: Pastoral Theology in an Age of Uncertainty*. London: Mowbray, 1996.
Greenman, Jeffrey P. "Spiritual Formation in Theological Perspective." In *Life in the Spirit: Spiritual Formation in Theological Perspective*, edited by Jeffrey P. Greenman and George Kalantzis, 24. Downers Grove, IL: IVP Academic, 2010.
Greenman, Jeffrey P., and Gene L. Green. *Global Theology in Evangelical Perspective: Exploring the Contextual Nature of Theology and Mission*. Downers Grove, IL: IVP Academic, 2012.
Grenz, Stanley James, and John R. Franke. *Beyond Foundationalism: Shaping Theology in a Postmodern Context*. Louisville: Westminster John Knox, 2001.
Groome, Thomas. *Sharing Faith: A Comprehensive Approach to Religious Education and Pastoral Ministry: The Way of Shared Praxis*. San Francisco: HarperSanFrancisco, 1991.
Gruber, Judith. *Intercultural Theology: Exploring World Christianity after the Cultural Turn*. Research in Contemporary Religion 25. Göttingen: Vandenhoeck & Ruprecht, 2017.

Guder, Darrell L., and Lois Barrett. *Missional Church: A Vision for the Sending of the Church in North America*. The Gospel and Our Culture Series. Grand Rapids: Eerdmans, 1998.

Gutiérrez, Gustavo. *The Density of the Present: Selected Writings*. Maryknoll, NY: Orbis, 1999.

———. *The Power of the Poor in History: Selected Writings*. Translated by Robert R. Barr. London: SCM, 1983.

———. *A Theology of Liberation: History, Politics, and Salvation*. Translated by Sister Caridad Inda and John Eagleson. Maryknoll, NY: Orbis, 1988.

———. *The Truth Shall Make You Free: Confrontations*. Maryknoll, NY: Orbis, 1990.

———. *We Drink from Our Own Wells: The Spiritual Journey of a People*. Maryknoll, NY: Orbis, 1984.

Gutiérrez, Gustavo, and James B. Nickoloff, eds. *Gustavo Gutiérrez: Essential Writings*. Maryknoll, NY: Orbis, 1996.

Haddad, Beverley. "Engendering Theological Education for Transformation." *Journal of Theology for Southern Africa* no. 116 (2003) 65–80.

Hall, Edward T. *The Silent Language: Intercultural Communication and Its Importance to Survival*. New York: Doubleday, 1959.

Hall, Stuart. *Representation: Cultural Representations and Signifying Practices*. London: Sage, 1997.

Hallman, David G., ed. *Ecotheology: Voices from South and North*. Maryknoll, NY: Orbis, 1994.

———. *Spiritual Values for Earth Community*. Geneva: WCC Publications, 2000.

Handley, Joseph. *Polycentric Mission Leadership: Toward A New Theoretical Model for Global Leadership*. Oxford: Regnum, 2022.

Harris, Paul G. *World Ethics and Climate Change: From International to Global Justice*. Edinburgh Studies in World Ethics. Edinburgh: Edinburgh University Press, 2010.

Harvey, Barry A. *Another City: An Ecclesiological Primer for a Post-Christian World*. New York: Trinity, 1999.

Harvey, Graham. "Sacred Places in the Construction of Indigenous Environmentalism." *Ecotheology: Journal of Religion, Nature and the Environment* 7 (2002) 60.

Hastings, Ross. *Missional God, Missional Church: Hope for Re-Evangelizing the West*. Downers Grove, IL: IVP Academic, 2012.

Heitink, Gerben. *Practical Theology: History, Theory, Action Domains: Manual for Practical Theology*. Grand Rapids: Eerdmans, 1999.

Helland, Roger. "Nothing Leadership: The Locus of Missional Servantship." In *Servantship: Sixteen Servants on the Four Movements of Radical Servantship*, edited by Graham Joseph Hill. Eugene, OR: Wipf & Stock, 2013.

Helland, Roger, and Len Hjalmarson. *Missional Spirituality: Embodying God's Love from the Inside Out*. Downers Grove, IL: InterVarsity, 2011.

Hermann, Adrian, and Ciprian Burlacioiu. "Introduction: Klaus Koschorke and the 'Munich School' Perspective on the History of World Christianity." *Journal of World Christianity* 6 (2016) 4–27.

Hiebert, Paul G. "Critical Contextualization." *International Bulletin of Missionary Research* 11 (1987) 104–11.

Hill, Graham Joseph. "A Conversation with Lamin Sanneh on World Christianity, Christian-Muslim Relations, and Translating the Christian Message." https://grahamjosephhill.com/lamin-sanneh/.

———, et al. *Morling College Outcomes*. Sydney: Morling College, 2015.
———, ed. *Servantship: Sixteen Servants on the Four Movements of Radical Servantship*. Eugene, OR: Wipf & Stock, 2013.
———. *Salt, Light, and a City: Introducing Missional Ecclesiology*. Eugene, OR: Wipf & Stock, 2012.
———. *Salt, Light, and a City: Conformation—Ecclesiology for the Global Missional Community*. Majority World Voices 2. 2nd ed. Eugene, OR: Cascade, 2020.
———. *Salt, Light, and a City: Ecclesiology for the Global Missional Community*. Western Voices 1. 2nd ed. Eugene, OR: Cascade, 2017.
Ho, Huang Po. "Contextualization and Inter-Contextuality in Theological Education: An Asian Perspective." In *Handbook of Theological Education in World Christianity: Theological Perspectives—Regional Surveys—Ecumenical Trends*, edited by Dietrich Werner et al., 123–37. Oxford: Regnum, 2010.
———. "Theological Education in the Changing Societies of Asia." *Ministerial Formation* 109 (2007) 6–13.
Hofstede, Geert H. *Cultures and Organizations: Software of the Mind*. 4th ed. New York: McGraw-Hill, 2011.
———. *Culture's Consequences: Comparing Values, Behaviors, Institutions, and Organizations across Nations*. 2nd ed. Thousand Oaks, CA: Sage, 2001.
———. *Culture's Consequences: International Differences in Work-Related Values*. Cross Cultural Research and Methodology Series. Beverly Hills, CA: Sage, 1980.
Hollenweger, Walter J. "Intercultural Theology." *Theology Today* 43 (1986) 28–35.
———. *Pentecostalism: Origins and Developments Worldwide*. Peabody, MA: Hendrickson, 1997.
Hollenweger, Walter J., and Jan A. B. Jongeneel, eds. *Pentecost, Mission, and Ecumenism: Essays on Intercultural Theology: Festschrift in Honour of Professor Walter J. Hollenweger*. Studies in the Intercultural History of Christianity 75. New York: Lang, 1992.
Holmes, Arthur Frank. *Ethics: Approaching Moral Decisions*. Contours of Christian Philosophy. Downers Grove, IL: InterVarsity, 1984.
Horton, Michael. "Evangelical Arminians." *Modern Reformation* 1 (1992) 15–19.
House, Robert J., et al., eds. *Culture, Leadership, and Organizations: The Globe Study of 62 Societies*. Thousand Oaks, CA: Sage, 2004.
Hull, J. M. *Mission-Shaped Church: A Theological Response*. London: SCM, 2006.
Hymes, Dell. *Foundations in Sociolinguistics: An Ethnographic Approach*. Philadelphia: University of Pennsylvania Press, 1974.
Ibengi, Roger, and Richard L. Starcher. "Missional Leadership for the African Church." *Global Missiology English* 1 (2011) n.d.
Ikenga-Metuh, Emefie. "The Revival of African Christian Spirituality: The Experience of African Independent Churches." *Mission Studies* 7 (1990) 151–71.
Isasi-Díaz, Ada María. "Mujeristas: A Name of Our Own." *Christian Century* (May 24–31, 1989) 560.
Jackson, Darrell. "For the Son of Man Did Not Come to Lead, but to Be Led: Matthew 20:20–28 and Royal Service." In *Servantship*, edited by Graham Joseph Hill, 15–31. Eugene, OR: Wipf & Stock, 2013.
Jackson, Michael. *TH568 Lecture Notes: The Christian Understanding of Person in the Light of the Doctrines of Creation and the Trinity*. 2002. The University of Notre Dame Australia, Fremantle.

BIBLIOGRAPHY

Jenkins, Philip. "Believing in the Global South." *First Things* 168 (2006) 12–18.

———. *The New Faces of Christianity: Believing the Bible in the Global South*. Oxford: Oxford University Press, 2006.

———. *The Next Christendom: The Coming of Global Christianity*. 3rd ed. Oxford: Oxford University Press, 2011.

John Paul II, Pope. "Redemptoris Missio: On the Permanent Validity of the Church's Missionary Mandate." Rome, December 7, 1990. https://www.catholicsociety.com/documents/john_paul_ii_encyclicals/Redemptoris_missio.pdf.

Johnstone, Patrick J. *The Future of the Global Church: History, Trends and Possibilities*. Colorado Springs: Biblica, 2011.

Junge, Daniel. "They Killed Sister Dorothy." Produced by Henry Ansbacher et al. London: Just Media Productions, 2008.

Kähler, Martin. *Schriften Zu Christologie Und Mission*. Munich: Kaiser, 1971.

Kang, Namsoon. "Envisioning Postcolonial Theological Education: Dilemmas and Possibilities." In *Handbook of Theological Education in World Christianity: Theological Perspectives—Regional Surveys—Ecumenical Trends*, edited by Dietrich Werner et al., 30–41. Oxford: Regnum, 2010.

Kanyoro, Musimbi. "Reading the Bible from an African Perspective." *Ecumenical Review* 51 (1999) 18–24.

Kärkkäinen, Veli-Matti. *The Spirit in the World: Emerging Pentecostal Theologies in Global Contexts*. Grand Rapids: Eerdmans, 2009.

Kato, Byang H. *Theological Pitfalls*. Kisumu: Evangel, 1975.

Katongole, Emmanuel M. *The Sacrifice of Africa: A Political Theology for Africa*. Grand Rapids: Eerdmans, 2011.

Katongole, Emmanuel M., and Chris Rice. *Reconciling All Things: A Christian Vision for Justice, Peace and Healing*. Downers Grove, IL: InterVarsity, 2008.

Keum, Jooseop, ed. *Together Towards Life: Mission and Evangelism in Changing Landscapes*. Le Grand-Saconnex: World Council of Churches, 2013.

Kim, Grace Ji-Sun. "A Global Understanding of the Spirit." *Dialogue and Alliance* 21 (2007) 17–31.

King, Fergus. "Across the Great Divide: Higher Criticism, the Writers of the New Testament, and African Biblical Interpretation." *Mission Studies* 15 (1998) 13–28.

Kinsler, F. Ross. *Diversified Theological Education: Equipping All God's People*. Pasadena, CA: William Carey, 2008.

———. *The Extension Movement in Theological Education*. Pasadena, CA: William Carey, 1977.

Kitamori, Kazoh. *Theology of the Pain of God*. 1966. Reprint, Eugene, OR: Wipf & Stock, 2005.

Knitter, Paul F. *The Myth of Religious Superiority: A Multi-Faith Exploration*. Faith Meets Faith. Maryknoll, NY: Orbis, 2016.

Kombo, James, ed. *African Theology*. Edited by Jeffrey P. Greenman and Gene L. Green. Global Theology in Evangelical Perspective: Exploring the Contextual Nature of Theology and Mission. Downers Grove, IL: IVP Academic, 2012.

Koschorke, Klaus, et al., eds. *A History of Christianity in Asia, Africa, and Latin America, 1450–1990: A Documentary Sourcebook*. Grand Rapids: Eerdmans, 2007.

Koyama, Kōsuke. "The Asian Approach to Christ." *Missiology* 12 (1984) 435–47.

———. *No Handle on the Cross: An Asian Meditation on the Crucified Mind*. Maryknoll, NY: Orbis, 1977.

———. "Reformation in the Global Context: The Disturbing Spaciousness of Jesus Christ." *Currents in Theology and Mission* 30 (2003) 119–28.
———. *Water Buffalo Theology*. Twenty-Fifth Anniversary ed. Maryknoll, NY: Orbis, 1999.
Kumuyi, William Folorunso. "The Case for Servant Leadership." *New African* 476 (2007) 18–19.
———. "The Functions of a Servant-Leader." *New African* no. 468 (2007) 30–31.
Küng, Hans. *The Church*. Translated by Ray and Rosaleen Ockenden. New York: Sheed & Ward, 1967.
———. *Global Responsibility: In Search of a New World Ethic*. Translated by John Bowden. New York: Crossroad, 1991.
Kunhiyop, Samuel Waje. *African Christian Ethics*. Nairobi: Hippo, 2008.
Küster, Volker. "Intercultural Theology is a Must." *International Bulletin of Missionary Research* 35 (2014) 171–76.
Kwok, Pui-Lan. *Introducing Asian Feminist Theology*. Introductions in Feminist Theology 4. Cleveland: Pilgrim, 2000.
———. *Postcolonial Imagination and Feminist Theology*. Louisville: Westminster John Knox, 2005.
Lartey, Emmanuel Y. *In Living Color: An Intercultural Approach to Pastoral Care and Counseling*. London: Kingsley, 2003.
Lash, Nicholas. *Believing Three Ways in One God: A Reading of the Apostles' Creed*. Notre Dame, IN: University of Notre Dame Press, 1993.
Laubach, Frank C. *Prayer: The Mightiest Force in the World*. Old Tappan, NJ: Spire, 1956.
Lausanne Movement. "The Cape Town Commitment: A Confession of Faith and a Call to Action." https://lausanne.org/content/ctc/ctcommitment.
———. "Integral Mission." https://lausanne.org/networks/issues/integral-mission.
———. "The Lausanne Covenant." https://lausanne.org/content/covenant/lausanne-covenant.
———. "The Manila Manifesto." https://lausanne.org/content/manifesto/the-manila-manifesto.
Lewis, Richard D. *When Cultures Collide: Leading across Cultures : A Major New Edition of the Global Guide*. 3rd ed. London: Brealey, 2005.
Lim, David S. "Developing Transformational Leaders for Church Multiplication Movements in the Buddhist World." In *Developing Indigenous Leaders: Lessons in Mission from Buddhist Asia*, edited by Paul H. De Neui, 83–110. Pasadena, CA: William Carey, 2013.
Lösch, August. *The Economics of Location*. New Haven, CO: Yale University, 1954.
Lumbala, F. Kabasele. *Celebrating Jesus Christ in Africa: Liturgy and Inculturation*. Faith and Cultures Series. Maryknoll, NY: Orbis, 1998.
Ma, Julie C. "Pentecostalism and Asian Mission." *Missiology* 35 (2007) 23–37.
Ma, Julie C., and Wonsuk Ma. *Mission in the Spirit: Towards a Pentecostal/Charismatic Missiology*. Eugene, OR: Wipf & Stock, 2010.
Ma, Wonsuk. "Theological Education in Pentecostal Churches in Asia." In *Handbook of Theological Education in World Christianity: Theological Perspectives—Regional Surveys—Ecumenical Trends*, edited by Dietrich Werner et al., 729–35. Oxford: Regnum, 2010.

BIBLIOGRAPHY

Ma, Wonsuk, and Brian Woolnough, eds. *Holistic Mission: God's Plan for God's People*. Oxford: Regnum, 2010.
Ma, Wonsuk, and Julie C. Ma. "Jesus Christ in Asia: Our Journey with Him as Pentecostal Believers." *International Review of Mission* 94 (2005) 493–506.
Mabuluki, Kangwa. "Diversified Theological Education: Genesis, Development, and Ecumenical Potential of Theological Education by Extension (Tee)." In *Handbook of Theological Education in World Christianity: Theological Perspectives—Regional Surveys—Ecumenical Trends*, edited by Dietrich Werner et al., 251–62. Oxford: Regnum, 2010.
Maggay, Melba Padilla. *Transforming Society*. Oxford: Regnum, 1994.
Mangalwadi, Vishal. *Truth and Social Reform*. 3rd ed. New Delhi: Nivedit, 1996.
Mastra, I. Wayan. "Christianity and Culture in Bali." *International Review of Mission* 63.251 (1974) 386–99.
Mbiti, John S. *African Religions and Philosophy*. London: Heinemann, 1969.
———. *New Testament Eschatology in an African Background: A Study of the Encounter between New Testament Theology and African Traditional Concepts*. Oxford: Oxford University Press, 1971.
———. *The Prayers of African Religion*. Maryknoll, NY: Orbis, 1975.
Mead, Margaret. *Coming of Age in Samoa*. New York: William Morrow, 1928.
Mellor, H., and T. Yates. *Mission and Spirituality: Creative Ways of Being Church*. Sheffield, UK: Cliff College, 2002.
Mendez, Angel F. "Divine Alimentation: Gastroeroticism and Eucharistic Desire." In *Hunger, Bread and Eucharist*, edited by Christophe Boureux et al., 14–20. London: SCM, 2005.
Micah Network. "Declaration on Creation Stewardship and Climate Change." *International Bulletin of Missionary Research* 33 (2009) 182–84.
———. "Micah Network Declaration on Integral Mission." https://d1c2gz5q23tkko.cloudfront.net/assets/uploads/3390139/asset/Micah_Network_Declaration_on_Integral_Mission.pdf?1662641257/.
Migliore, Daniel L. *Faith Seeking Understanding: An Introduction to Christian Theology*. 2nd ed. Grand Rapids: Eerdmans, 2004.
Míguez-Bonino, José. "The Present Crisis in Mission." *The Future of the Missionary Enterprise* 9 (1974) 74–78.
Míguez, Néstor O. "Latin American Reading of the Bible: Experiences, Challenges and Its Practice." *Expository Times* 118 (2006) 120–29.
Moltmann, Jürgen. *The Church in the Power of the Spirit: A Contribution to Messianic Ecclesiology*. 2nd ed. London: SCM, 1992.
———. *The Source of Life: The Holy Spirit and the Theology of Life*. Translated by Margaret Kohl. Minneapolis: Fortress, 1997.
Moore, Stephen D., and Fernando F. Segovia, eds. *Postcolonial Biblical Criticism: Interdisciplinary Intersections*. The Bible and Postcolonialism. London: T. & T. Clark, 2005.
Mor Coorilos, Geevarghese. "Toward a Missiology That Begins with Creation." *International Review of Mission* 100 (2011) 310–21.
Moreau, A. Scott. *Contextualization in World Missions: Mapping and Assessing Evangelical Models*. Grand Rapids: Kregel, 2012.
Murray, S. M. *Post-Christendom: Church and Mission in a Strange New World*. Carlisle, UK: Paternoster, 2004.

BIBLIOGRAPHY

Mwombeki, Fidon. "Reading the Bible in Contemporary Africa." *Word and World* 21 (2001) 121–28.
Nagy, Dorottya. "Recalling the Term 'World Christianity': Excursions into Worldings of Literature, Philosophy, and History." In *World Christianity: Methodological Considerations*, edited by Martha Frederiks and Dorottya Nagy, 40–64. Leiden: Brill, 2020.
Naidoo, Marilyn. "Spiritual Formation in Protestant Theological Institutions." In *Handbook of Theological Education in World Christianity: Theological Perspectives—Regional Surveys—Ecumenical Trends*, edited by Dietrich Werner et al., 185–95. Oxford: Regnum, 2010.
NATSIEC, ed. *Christ and Culture: Christ through Culture*. Ballina: National Council of Churches in Australia, 2010.
Newbigin, Lesslie. *The Gospel in a Pluralist Society*. London: SPCK, 2004.
———. *The Open Secret: An Introduction to the Theology of Mission*. Grand Rapids: Eerdmans, 1995.
Nicholls, Bruce. *Contextualization: A Theology of Gospel and Culture*. Downers Grove, IL: InterVarsity, 1979.
Nirmal, Arvind P., and V. Devasahayam, eds. *A Reader in Dalit Theology*. Madras: Research Institute for Dalit Theology, 1990.
Norman, William H. "Kanzo Uchimura—the Church." *Contemporary Religions in Japan* 5 (1964) 355–60.
Novak, Michael. "Liberation Theology—What's Left?" *First Things* 14 (1991) 10–12.
———. "Will It Liberate? Questions About Liberation Theology." *Christianity and Crisis* 47 (1987) 246–47.
Ntamburi, Zablon, and Daniel Waruta. "Biblical Hermeneutics in African Instituted Churches." In *The Bible in African Christianity: Essays in Biblical Theology*, edited by Hannah Kinoti and John Waliggo, 40–57. Nairobi: Acton, 1997.
Núñez, Emilio Antonio. *Crisis and Hope in Latin America: An Evangelical Perspective*. Rev. ed. Pasadena, CA: William Carey, 1996.
Nwaigbo, Ferdinand. "Cosmic Christology and Eco-Theology in Africa." *AFER* 53 (2011) 437–61.
Odozor, Paulinus Ikechukwu. "An African Moral Theology of Inculturation: Methodological Considerations." *Theological Studies* 69 (2008) 583–609.
Oduro, Thomas. "Symbolisms in African Independent Churches: Aides to Spirituality and Spiritual Formation." *Ogbomoso Journal of Theology* 16 (2011) 67–84.
Oduyoye, Mercy Amba. "Feminist Theology in an African Perspective." In *Paths of African Theology*, edited by Rosino Gibellini, 166–81. Maryknoll, NY: Orbis, 1994.
———. *Hearing and Knowing: Theological Reflections on Christianity in Africa*. Maryknoll, NY: Orbis, 1986.
———. *Introducing African Women's Theology*. Introductions in Feminist Theology. Cleveland: Pilgrim, 2001.
Okonkwo, Izunna. "The Sacrament of the Eucharist (as Koinonia) and African Sense of Communalism: Towards a Synthesis." *Journal of Theology for Southern Africa* 137 (2010) 88–103.
Olupona, Jacob Obafemi Kehinde. "The Spirituality of Matter: Religion and Environment in Yoruba Tradition, Nigeria." *Dialogue and Alliance* 9 (1995) 69–80.
Onyinah, Opoku. "Pneumatological Foundations for Mission: From a Pentecostal Perspective." *International Review of Mission* 101 (2012) 331–34.

Oommen, George. "The Emerging Dalit Theology: A Historical Appraisal." *Indian Church History Review* 34 (2000) 19–37.
Orevillo-Montenegro, Muriel. *The Jesus of Asian Women. Women from the Margins.* Maryknoll, NY: Orbis, 2006.
Ortiz, Juan Carlos. *Disciple.* Carol Stream, IL: Creation House, 1975.
Ortiz, Juan Carlos, and Jamie Buckingham. *Call to Discipleship.* Plainfield, NJ: Logos International, 1975.
Osmer, Richard R. *Practical Theology: An Introduction.* Grand Rapids: Eerdmans, 2008.
Ostrom, Elinor. "Polycentric Systems for Coping with Collective Action and Global Environmental Change." *Global Environmental Change* 20 (2010) 550–57.
Ostrom, Vincent. "Polycentricity (Part 1)." In *Polycentricity and Local Public Economies: Readings from the Workshop in Political Theory and Policy Analysis*, edited by Michael D. McGinnis, 52–74. Institutional Analysis. Ann Arbor: University of Michigan Press, 1990.
Ott, Craig, and Harold A. Netland. *Globalizing Theology: Belief and Practice in an Era of World Christianity.* Grand Rapids: Baker Academic, 2006.
———, eds. *Globalizing Theology: Belief and Practice in an Era of World Christianity.* Grand Rapids: Baker Academic, 2006.
Ott, Craig, et al. *Encountering Theology of Mission: Biblical Foundations, Historical Developments, and Contemporary Issues.* Encountering Mission. Grand Rapids: Baker Academic, 2010.
Padilla, C. René. "Bible Studies." *Missiology* 10 (1982) 319–38.
———. "The Contextualization of the Gospel." *Journal of Theology for Southern Africa*, no. 24 (1978) 12–30.
———. "Liberation Theology: An Appraisal." In *Freedom and Discipleship*, 34–50. Maryknoll, NY: Orbis, 1989.
———. "Liberation Theology: An Evaluation." *Reformed Journal* 33 (1983) 21–23.
———. *Mission between the Times: Essays on the Kingdom.* Grand Rapids: Eerdmans, 1985.
———. "A New Ecclesiology in Latin America." *International Bulletin of Missionary Research* 11 (1987) 156–64.
Padilla, C. René, and Tetsunao Yamamori, eds. *The Local Church, Agent of Transformation: An Ecclesiology for Integral Mission.* Buenos Aires: Kairos, 2004.
Padilla, C. René, et al. *What is Integral Mission?* Oxford: Regnum, 2021.
Parker, Evelyn L. "Karibu: A New Meaning for Hospitality." *Mid-Stream* 36 (1997) 15–19.
Parratt, John, ed. *An Introduction to Third World Theologies.* Cambridge: Cambridge University Press, 2004.
Petersen, Elizabeth, and Jannie Swart. "Via the Broken Ones: Towards a Phenomenological Theology of Ecclesial Leadership in Post–Apartheid South Africa." *Journal of Religious Leadership* 8 (2009) 7–34.
Petrella, Ivan. *The Future of Liberation Theology: An Argument and Manifesto.* Burlington, VT: Ashgate, 2004.
———. *Latin American Liberation Theology: The Next Generation.* Maryknoll, NY: Orbis, 2005.
Pew Research Center. "Global Christianity—A Report on the Size and Distribution of the World's Christian Population." https://www.pewresearch.org/religion/12/19/global-christianity-exec/.

BIBLIOGRAPHY

Phan, Peter C. *Christianities in Asia*. Blackwell Guides to Global Christianity. Malden, MA: Wiley-Blackwell, 2011.

———. *Christianity with an Asian Face: Asian American Theology in the Making.* Maryknoll, NY: Orbis, 2015.

———. "Doing Theology in World Christianity: Different Resources and New Methods." *Journal of World Christianity* 1 (2008) 27–53.

———. "Global Healing and Reconciliation: The Gift and Task of Religion, a Buddhist–Christian Perspective." *Buddhist-Christian Studies* 26 (2006) 89–108.

———. *In Our Own Tongues: Perspectives from Asia on Mission and Inculturation.* Maryknoll, NY: Orbis, 2015.

———. "World Christianity: Its Implications for History, Religious Studies, and Theology." *Horizons* 39 (2012) 175.

Pinnock, C. H. *Flame of Love: A Theology of the Holy Spirit*. Downers Grove, IL: InterVarsity, 1996.

Pobee, John S. *Skenosis: Christian Faith in an African Context*. Gweru: Mambo, 1992.

Pohl, Christine D. *Making Room: Recovering Hospitality as a Christian Tradition*. Grand Rapids: Eerdmans, 1999.

Rah, Soong-Chan *The Next Evangelicalism: Freeing the Church from Western Cultural Captivity*. Downers Grove, IL: InterVarsity, 2018.

Rakoczy, Susan. *Common Journey, Different Paths: Spiritual Direction in Cross–Cultural Perspective*. Maryknoll, NY: Orbis, 1992.

Ramachandra, Vinoth. "Integral Mission: Exploring a Concept." In *Integral Mission: The Way Forward*, edited by C.V. Mathew, 44–59. Kerala: Christava Sahitya Samithy, 2006.

———. *Subverting Global Myths : Theology and the Public Issues Shaping Our World*. Downers Grove, IL: IVP Academic, 2008.

Richardson, Don. *Peace Child*. 4th ed. Ventura, CA: Regal, 2005.

Ro, Bong Rin. "Theological Trends in Asia: Asian Theology." *Asian Theological News* 13 (1987) 2–3, 15–17.

Ro, Bong Rin, and Ruth Eshenaur, eds. *The Bible and Theology in Asian Contexts: An Evangelical Perspective on Asian Theology*. Taichung: Asia Theological Association, 1984.

Robinson, Gnana. "Re-Orientation of Theological Education for a Relevant Ministry." *East Asia Journal of Theology* 4 (1986) 46–51.

Romero, Oscar A., and James R. Brockman. *The Violence of Love*. Maryknoll, NY: Orbis, 2004.

Roxburgh, A. J. *What Is Missional Church? An Introduction to the Missional Church Conversation*. Eagle, ID: Allelon, 2007.

———. *The Missionary Congregation, Leadership, and Liminality*. New York, NY: Trinity, 1997.

Ruether, Rosemary Radford. "Religious Ecofeminism: Healing the Ecological Crisis." In *The Oxford Handbook of Religion and Ecology*, edited by Roger S. Gottlieb, 362–75. Oxford: Oxford University Press, 2006.

———. *Sexism and God-Talk: Toward a Feminist Theology*. Boston: Beacon, 1983.

———, ed. *Women Healing Earth: Third World Women on Ecology, Feminism, and Religion*. Ecology and Justice. Maryknoll, NY: Orbis, 1996.

Russell, L. M. *Church in the Round: Feminist Interpretation of the Church*. Louisville: Westminster, 1993.

Said, Edward W. *The World, the Text, and the Critic.* Cambridge: Harvard University Press, 1983.
Samuel, Vinay, and Albrecht Hauser, eds. *Proclaiming Christ in Christ's Way: Studies in Integral Evangelism.* Oxford: Regnum, 1989.
Samuel, Vinay, and Chris Sugden, eds. *The Church in Response to Human Need.* Grand Rapids: Eerdmans, 1987.
———, eds. *Mission as Transformation: A Theology of the Whole Gospel.* Oxford: Regnum, 1999.
Sanders, Douglas E. "Indigenous Peoples: Issues of Definition." *International Journal of Cultural Property* 8 (1999) 4–13.
Sanneh, Lamin. *Disciples of All Nations: Pillars of World Christianity.* Oxford: Oxford University Press, 2007.
———. *Translating the Message: The Missionary Impact on Culture.* Maryknoll, NY: Orbis, 2015.
———. *Whose Religion Is Christianity? The Gospel beyond the West.* Grand Rapids: Eerdmans, 2004.
Schreiter, Robert J. "The Changing Contexts of Intercultural Theology: A Global View." *Studia Missionalia* 45 (1996) 359–80.
Schwartz, Shalom. *Cultural Values: Sources, Domains, and Targets.* New York: Sage, 1992.
Scorgie, Glen G., et al., eds. *Dictionary of Christian Spirituality.* Grand Rapids: Zondervan, 2011.
Segovia, Fernando F. *Decolonizing Biblical Studies: A View from the Margins.* Maryknoll, NY: Orbis, 2000.
———. "The Emerging Project of Asian Biblical Hermeneutics: Reading Asian Readers." *Biblical Interpretation* 2 (1994) 371–73.
Segovia, Fernando F., and R. S. Sugirtharajah. *A Postcolonial Commentary on the New Testament Writings.* The Bible and Postcolonialism. London: T. & T. Clark, 2009.
Segundo, Juan Luis. *Liberation of Theology.* Translated by John Drury. Maryknoll, NY: Orbis, 1976.
Sen, Amartya. *Development as Freedom.* Oxford: Oxford University Press, 2001.
Shaull, Richard, and Waldo A. Cesar. *Pentecostalism and the Future of the Christian Churches: Promises, Limitations, Challenges.* Grand Rapids: Eerdmans, 2000.
Shaw, Perry. *Transforming Theological Education: A Practical Handbook for Integrative Learning.* Springwood: Langham Global Library, 2014.
Sheldrake, Philip. *The New Westminster Dictionary of Christian Spirituality.* 1st American ed. Louisville: Westminster John Knox, 2005.
Sherif, Muzafer. *The Robbers Cave Experiment: Intergroup Conflict and Cooperation.* Middletown, CT: Wesleyan University Press, 1961.
Singh, Sadhu Sundar. *At the Feet of the Master.* London: Hodder & Stoughton, 1985.
Singh, Sadhu Sundar, and Charles E. Moore. *Sadhu Sundar Singh: Essential Writings.* Modern Spiritual Masters. Maryknoll, NY: Orbis, 2005.
Sobrino, Jon. *Christ the Liberator: A View from the Victims.* Translated by Paul Burns. Maryknoll, NY: Orbis, 2001.
———. *Jesus the Liberator: A Historical-Theological Reading of Jesus of Nazareth.* Translated by Paul Burns and Francis McDonagh. Maryknoll, NY: Orbis, 1993.
———. "Redeeming Globalization through Its Victims." In *Globalization and Its Victims*, edited by Jon Sobrino and Felix Wilfred, 105–14. London: SCM, 2001.

BIBLIOGRAPHY

———. *The True Church and the Poor*. Translated by Mathew J. O'Connell. Maryknoll, NY: Orbis, 1984.

Sobrino, Jon, and Ignacio Ellacuría, eds. *Systematic Theology: Perpspectives from Liberation Theology: Readings from Mysterium Liberationis*. Maryknoll, NY: Orbis, 1996.

Solivan, Samuel. "Interreligious Dialogue: An Hispanic American Pentecostal Perspective." In *Grounds for Understanding: Ecumencial Responses to Religious Pluralism*, edited by S. Mark Heim, 37–45. Grand Rapids: Eerdmans, 1998.

Song, C. S. *Theology from the Womb of Asia*. 1986. Reprint, Eugene, OR: Wipf & Stock, 2005.

Spivak, Gayatri Chakravorty. *In Other Worlds: Essays in Cultural Politics*. New York: Methuen, 1988.

Ssettuuma, Benedict, and John Mary Waliggo. "The Rights of a Child." *AFER* 52 (2011) 47–67.

Stafford, Tim. "The Choice." *Christianity Today* 56 (2012) 40–44.

Stanley, Brian. *Christianity in the Twentieth Century: A World History*. Princeton: Princeton University Press, 2019.

Starling, David I. "Theology and the Future of the Church." *Case* 28 (2011) 10–15.

Stassen, Glen H., and David P. Gushee. *Kingdom Ethics: Following Jesus in Contemporary Context*. Downers Grove, IL: InterVarsity, 2003.

Stinton, Diane B. "Africa, East and West." In *An Introduction to Third World Theologies*, edited by John Parratt, 105–36. Cambridge: Cambridge University Press, 2004.

———. *Jesus of Africa: Voices of Contemporary African Christology*. Faith and Cultures Series. Maryknoll, NY: Orbis, 2004.

Sugirtharajah, R. S. *Asian Biblical Hermeneutics and Postcolonialism: Contesting the Interpretations*. The Bible and Justice Series. Maryknoll, NY: Orbis, 1998.

———. *The Bible and the Third World: Precolonial, Colonial, and Postcolonial Encounters*. Cambridge: Cambridge University Press, 2001.

———. *The Postcolonial Bible*. Bible and Postcolonialism 1. Sheffield: Sheffield Academic, 1998.

———. *Postcolonial Criticism and Biblical Interpretation*. Oxford: Oxford University Press, 2002.

———. "Textual Take-Aways: Third World Texts in Western Metropolitan Centers." *Black Theology in Britain* 2 (1999) 33.

———. *Voices from the Margin: Interpreting the Bible in the Third World*. Rev. and exp. 3rd ed. Maryknoll, NY: Orbis, 2006.

Sundermeier, Theo. *Den Fremden verstehen: Eine theologische Studie*. Sammlung Vandenhoeck. Göttingen: Vandenhoeck & Ruprecht, 1995.

———. *Was ist Religion?* Translated by John Bowden. London: SCM, 1997.

Susin, Luiz Carlos. "Sister Dorothy Stang: A Model of Holiness and Martyrdom." In *Eco-Theology*, edited by Elaine Wainwright et al., 109–13. London: SCM, 2009.

Swanson, Tod D. "A Civil Art: The Persuasive Moral Voice of Oscar Romero." *Journal of Religious Ethics* 29 (2001) 127–44.

Swinton, John, and Harriet Mowatt. *Practical Theology and Qualitative Research*. London: SCM, 2006.

Tan, Betty O. S. "The Contextualization of the Chinese New Year Festival." *Asia Journal of Theology* 15 (2001) 115.

Tannen, Deborah. *You Just Don't Understand: Women and Men in Conversation*. New York: Ballantine, 1990.

BIBLIOGRAPHY

Taylor, John V. *The Go-Between God: The Holy Spirit and the Christian Mission*. Eugene, OR: Wipf & Stock, 2015.

Ten Kortenaar, Neil. *Postcolonial Literature and the Impact of Literacy: Reading and Writing in African and Caribbean Fiction*. Cambridge: Cambridge University Press, 2011.

Tennent, Timothy C. *Theology in the Context of World Christianity: How the Global Church Is Influencing the Way We Think about and Discuss Theology*. Grand Rapids: Zondervan, 2007.

Thangaraj, M. Thomas. "A Formula for Contextual Theology: Local + Global = Contextual." In *Contextualizing Theological Education*, edited by Theodore Brelsford and P. Alice Rogers, xii. Cleveland: Pilgrim, 2008.

Thomas, M. M. "The Holy Spirit and the Spirituality for Political Struggles." *Ecumenical Review* 42 (1990) 216–24.

———. "Will Koinonia Emerge as a Vital Theological Theme?" *Ecumenical Review* 41 (1989) 177–83.

Tiénou, Tite. "The Church in African Theology." In *Biblical Interpretation and the Church: Text and Context*, edited by D. A. Carson, 151–65. Exeter, UK: Paternoster, 1984.

———. "Contextualization of Theology for Theological Education." In *Evangelical Theological Education Today: Agenda for Renewal*, edited by Paul Bowers, 42–52. Nairobi: Evangel, 1982.

———. "The Training of Missiologists for an African Context." In *Missiological Education for the Twenty-First Century: The Book, the Circle, and the Sandals*, edited by Paul Everett Pierson et al., 93–100. Maryknoll, NY: Orbis, 1996.

Tiénou, Tite, and Paul G. Hiebert. "Missional Theology." *Missiology* 34 (2006) 219–38.

Tinker, George E. "An American Indian Theological Response to Ecojustice." *Ecotheology: Journal of Religion, Nature and the Environment* 5 (1997) 85.

———. "Native Americans and the Land: "The End of Living, and the Beginning of Survival." *Word and World* 6 (1986) 66–75.

Tippett, Alan R. *Introduction to Missiology*. Pasadena, CA: William Carey Library, 1987.

Tizon, Al. *Transformation after Lausanne: Radical Evangelical Mission in Global-Local Perspective*. Eugene, OR: Wipf & Stock, 2008.

Triandis, Harry. *Culture and Social Behavior*. New York: McGraw-Hill, 1994.

Turner, Edith. *Communitas: The Anthropology of Collective Joy*. New York: Palgrave Macmillan, 2012.

Turner, Victor. *Dramas, Fields, and Metaphors*. Ithaca, NY: Cornell University Press, 1974.

———. *The Ritual Process*. Ithaca: Cornell University Press, 1969.

Tutu, Desmond. "A Passion for Justice." *Third Way* 17 (1994) 4.

Ukpong, Justin S. "Rereading the Bible with African Eyes : Inculturation and Hermeneutics." *Journal of Theology for Southern Africa* no. 91 (1995) 3–14.

UNHCR. "Global Trends Report 2022." https://www.unhcr.org/au/global-trends.

Vaage, Leif E. *Subversive Scriptures: Revolutionary Readings of the Christian Bible in Latin America*. Valley Forge, PA: Trinity, 1997.

Van Dyke, Joel, and Kris Rocke. "Asking the Beautiful Question: Reading the Bible through the Eyes of Outsiders Can Awaken the Church from Numbness." *Christianity Today* 54 (2010) 44–47.

Van Gelder, Craig. *The Essence of the Church: A Community Created by the Spirit.* Grand Rapids: Baker, 2000.
Villa-Vicencio, Charles, and John W. De Gruchy. *Doing Ethics in Context: South African Perspectives.* Theology and Praxis. Cape Town: Philip, 1994.
Volf, Miroslav. *After Our Likeness: The Church as the Image of the Trinity.* Grand Rapids: Eerdmans, 1998.
———. "Against a Pretentious Church: A Rejoinder to Bell's Response." *Modern Theology* 19 (2003) 281–85.
———. "The Church as a Prophetic Community and a Sign of Hope." *European Journal of Theology* no. 2 (1993) 9–30.
———. "Community Formation as an Image of the Triune God: A Congregational Model of Church Order and Life." In *Community Formation: In the Early Church and in the Church Today*, edited by Richard N. Longenecker, 213–37. Peabody, MA: Hendrickson, 2002.
Waliggo, John Mary. "The African Clan as the True Model of the African Church." In *The Church in African Christianity: Innovative Essays in Ecclesiology*, edited by J.N.K. Mugambi and Laurenti Magesa, 111–27. Nairobi: Initiatives, 1990.
———. "The Church and Hiv/Aids (a Ugandan Pastoral Experience)." *AFER* 46 (2004) 23–34.
———. "Inculturation and the Hiv/Aids Pandemic in the Amecea Region." *AFER* 47 (2006) 290–308.
———. "The Plight of Women and Children in Areas of Armed Conflicts in Uganda." *AFER* 45 (2003) 373–86.
Walls, Andrew F. "The Cost of Discipleship: The Witness of the African Church." *Word and World* 25 (2005) 433–43.
———. *The Cross-Cultural Process in Christian History: Studies in the Transmission and Appropriation of Faith.* Maryknoll, NY: Orbis, 2002.
———. *The Missionary Movement in Christian History: Studies in the Transmission of Faith.* Ossining, NY: Orbis, 1996.
Wasike, Anne Nasimiyu. "Vatican II: The Problem of Inculturation." PhD diss., Duquesne University, 1986.
Webster, J. B. "The Visible Attests the Invisible." In *The Community of the Word: Toward an Evangelical Ecclesiology*, edited by M. Husbands and D. J. Treier, 96–113. Leicester, UK: Apollos, 2005.
Werner, Dietrich. "Memorandum on the Future of Theological Education in Asia." *The Ecumenical Review* 26 (2012) 209–22.
West, Gerald. *Biblical Hermeneutics in Africa.* University of Kwa-Zulu Natal, Natal, 2008.
White, Erin. "Between Suspicion and Hope: Paul Ricoeur's Vital Hermeneutic." *Literature and Theology* 5 (1991) 311–21.
Wink, Walter. *Engaging the Powers: Discernment and Resistance in a World of Domination.* The Powers. Minneapolis: Fortress, 1992.
Wiseman, Richard. *Intercultural Communication: A Practical Guide.* 2nd ed. Oxford: Oneworld, 2018.
Woodley, Randy S. *Shalom and the Community of Creation: An Indigenous Vision.* Prophetic Christianity. Grand Rapids: Eerdmans, 2012.
Wright, Christopher J. H. *Old Testament Ethics for the People of God.* Downers Grove, IL: InterVarsity, 2004.

Wright, N. T. *The New Testament and the People of God. Christian Origins and the Question of God*. Minneapolis: Fortress, 1996.

Wrogemann, Henning. *Intercultural Theology*, Vol. 1: *Intercultural Hermeneutics*. Downers Grove, IL: IVP Academic, 2016.

———. *Intercultural Theology*, Vol. 3: *A Theology of Interreligious Relations*. Downers Grove, IL: IVP Academic, 2019.

———. *Intercultural Theology*, Vol. 2: *Theologies of Mission*. Downers Grove, IL: IVP Academic, 2018.

Yamamori, Tetsunao, et al., eds. *Serving with the Poor in Latin America*. Cases in Holistic Ministry. Monrovia, CA: MARC, 1997.

Yang, Fenggang. *Religion in China: Survival and Revival under Communist Rule*. Oxford: Oxford University Press, 2012.

Yang, Fenggang, and Graeme Lang. *Social Scientific Studies of Religion in China: Methodology, Theories, and Findings*. Religion in Chinese Societies. Leiden: Brill, 2011.

Yang, Fenggang, and Joseph B. Tamney. *Confucianism and Spiritual Traditions in Modern China and Beyond*. Religion in Chinese Societies. Leiden: Brill, 2012.

Yeh, Allen. *Polycentric Missiology: 21st-Century Mission from Everyone to Everywhere*. Downers Grove, IL: IVP Academic, 2016.

Yoder, John Howard. *The Royal Priesthood: Essays Ecclesiological and Ecumenical*. Grand Rapids: Eerdmans, 1994.

———. "Sacrament as Social Process: Christ the Transformer of Culture." *Theology Today* 48 (1991) 33–44.

Yong, Amos. "Beyond beyond the Impasse? Responding to Dale Irvin." *Journal of Pentecostal Theology* 12 (2004) 281–85.

———. *Discerning the Spirit(s) A Pentecostal-Charismatic Contribution to Christian Thelogy of Religions*. Journal of Pentecostal Theology Supplement Series 20. Sheffield: Sheffield Academic, 2000.

———. *Hospitality and the Other: Pentecost, Christian Practices, and the Neighbor*. Faith Meets Faith. Maryknoll, NY: Orbis, 2008.

———. "Many Tongues, Many Practices." In *Mission after Christendom: Emergent Themes in Contemporary Mission*, edited by Ogbu Kalu et al., 43–58. Louisville: Westminster, 2010.

———. "The Marks of the Church: A Pentecostal Re-Reading." *Evangelical Review of Theology* 26 (2002) 45–67.

———. "A P(new)matological Paradigm for Christian Mission in a Religiously Plural World." *Missiology* 33 (2005) 175–91.

———. "The Spirit of Hospitality: Pentecostal Perspectives toward a Performative Theology of Interreligious Encounter." *Missiology* 35 (2007) 55–73.

———. *The Spirit Poured out on All Flesh: Pentecostalism and the Possibility of Global Theology*. Grand Rapids: Baker Academic, 2005.

Yun, Koo Dong. *Baptism in the Holy Spirit: An Ecumenical Theology of Spirit Baptism*. Lanham, MD: University Press of America, 2003.

———. "Water Baptism and Spirit Baptism: Pentecostals and Lutherans in Dialogue." *Dialog: A Journal of Theology* 43 (2004) 344–51.

Yung, Hwa. "Recover the Supernatural." *Christianity Today* 54 (2010) 32–33.

Zscheile, Dwight J., ed. *Cultivating Sent Communities: Missional Spiritual Formation*. Missional Church Series. Grand Rapids: Eerdmans, 2012.

Zurlo, G. A., et al. "World Christianity and Mission 2020: Ongoing Shift to the Global South." *International Bulletin of Mission Research* 44 (2020) 8–19.

www.ingramcontent.com/pod-product-compliance
Lightning Source LLC
Chambersburg PA
CBHW031948290426
44108CB00011B/716